D0848126

HANDBOOK OF EVALUATION RESEARCH

THE SOCIETY FOR THE PSYCHOLOGICAL STUDY OF SOCIAL ISSUES (SPSSI)

As Division 9 of the American Psychological Association, SPSSI began as and continues to be a unique organization. From its very beginning in 1936 it established as the nexus of its concern the application of behavioral science research to the major social dilemmas of modern man; war, poverty, intergroup prejudice, urban stress, industrial strife, and other problems. Implicit in this concern was the compelling assumption that science could not be value free; that in its desire to ameliorate the ills of modern society its systematic research endeavors would have political and social consequences as well as scientific ones. Lewin was right when he stated that research should be socially useful as well as theoretically meaningful, but this could only occur if the researchers involved conceptualized, organized, and directed their investigations with this end in mind.

Excerpt from 1972 Presidential Message by Harold M. Proshansky

Volume 1

Handbook
of
Evaluation
Research

Edited by

ELMER L. STRUENING
Columbia University

and

MARCIA GUTTENTAG
Harvard University

Ⓢ SAGE Publications   Beverly Hills • London

For information address:

SAGE PUBLICATIONS, INC.
275 South Beverly Drive
Beverly Hills, California 90212

SAGE PUBLICATIONS LTD
St George's House / 44 Hatton Garden
London EC1N 8ER

Printed in the United States of America
International Standard Book Number 0-8039-0428-2
Library of Congress Catalog Card No. 74-15764

FOURTH PRINTING

CONTENTS

Dedicated to the memory of

STEVE PRATT
1917-1973

Good Friend and Esteemed Colleague

I

PREFACE

THE HANDBOOK: ITS PURPOSE AND ORGANIZATION

ELMER L. STRUENING
and
MARCIA GUTTENTAG

INTRODUCTION

The successful completion of an evaluation research study may be conceptualized as a sequence of events, a process through time, or a series of steps, each demanding a certain level of performance if the study is to meet standards of replication, to be accepted by the scientific community, and to be applied by planners and administrators.

Each of the steps involved in completing an evaluation study is a point of vulnerability which, if not sturdily constructed, will create an end result that is invalid and unusable. Among the crucial steps involved in completing evaluation studies are the following: conceptualizing the problem, reviewing relevant literature, developing a research strategy, determining a research design, selecting and maintaining a sample, choosing measures and assessing their psychometric properties, selecting appropriate personnel to conduct the study, maintaining data collection standards, analyzing the data, and communicating the results. Many options are open to evaluators as they develop each crucial step in their specific studies. To select options of the highest quality would require a team of experts each contributing as a specialist in the development of a particular step, while acquiring a general knowledge of the study as a whole. The luxury of quality advice for the many facets of evaluation studies is seldom available to evaluators or study directors, and they frequently make decisions without adequate information or sufficient grasp of how their decisions will influence the outcome of their studies.

One purpose of this Handbook is to provide evaluators with a sample of experts, a panel of consultants between hard covers, with whom they can communicate as

they develop the crucial steps of their studies. More specifically, the Handbook provides the type of information that should lead to the consideration of alternative approaches to evaluation and, by virtue of considering these alternatives, to the development of the most appropriate research plan.

The Handbook is also designed to serve as a textbook for courses in evaluation at the graduate level. The first volume emphasizes strategies and methods of evaluation while the second volume reviews the literature of selected content areas. In the writers' experience, the second year of graduate school, following basic courses in statistics and other research methods, would be an optimal time to complete a course in evaluation. Experience in an evaluation research setting is highly recommended while the student is taking the course or immediately thereafter.

ORGANIZATION OF VOLUME I

As indicated in the table of contents, this volume of the Handbook is divided into eight parts, each focused on some aspect of the evaluation process. In Chapter 2, Carol Weiss informs the reader of some of the realities and challenges facing evaluators as they attempt to understand and document the relative value of human service programs. She describes what experienced evaluators have learned the hard way, that evaluation studies take place in a social and organizational context where the goals and values of evaluators and administrators are sometimes in conflict, leading to a continuum of resolution ranging from mutually acceptable compromise to the exit of the least powerful. Chapters by Lee Gurel and Gideon Sjoberg, in Volume II of this Handbook, provide additional perspectives on the general topic of politics and values in evaluation research.

Chapter 3, by David Twain, proceeds on the assumption that the planning and administration of human service systems and programs of intervention should be based on information derived from carefully monitored evaluation research studies. He further asserts that the need to develop a process termed "rational program development" requires the active and close collaboration of administrators, service practitioners, and evaluators. His chapter describes how these goals might be accomplished by developing strategies designed to anticipate and overcome the obstacles that sometimes impede development of a workable evaluation contract involving administrators, service delivery personnel, and evaluators.

Drawing on his extensive experience in evaluation, W. Edwards Deming describes the role of the evaluator as one who asks carefully formulated questions within a scientific frame of reference and then somewhat skeptically reviews answers to these questions as he documents the pitfalls of statistical inference in the absence of controlled experimental studies. Dr. Deming describes and illustrates different types of evaluation studies, documents their limitations and sources of error, and informs us of the potential influence of human judgment on the outcome of the study. He dwells on the logical processes involved in various evaluation strategies; understanding of these processes is enhanced by his use of analogous examples drawn from the more familiar physical sciences.

Part III of this volume is concerned with the conceptualization and design of

evaluation studies. Chapter 5, by Donald T. Campbell, provides keen insight into characteristics of the social, political, and emotional climates surrounding the evaluation of reforms, especially those receiving extensive publicity such as the effectiveness of Head Start and the mortality due to car accidents. Dr. Campbell indicates the potential biases involved in interpreting reform evaluation results and then lucidly describes a series of research designs for establishing optimal validity in various types of evaluation studies. The reprinting of this slightly revised chapter, known particularly to psychologists but to members of other disciplines as well, is justified on the basis of its quality and the assumption that the Handbook will reach some who have not read it. Instructors using the Handbook as a text will have convenient access to an important paper; those who have read it will surely want to read it again.

Change is the key issue in experimental evaluation research. The measurement of change is a thorny issue in the applied social sciences; it is frequently a weak link in many evaluation studies, producing questionable results which, at best, are difficult to interpret. In Chapter 6, Jum C. Nunnally first conceptualizes a series of problems involved in the measurement of change, with special emphasis on properties of measures which detract from or enhance the accurate measurement of change. This section is followed by the description of a series of research designs focused on the assessment of change under various research conditions. Dr. Nunnally makes it clear that the measurement of change is a controversial subject among measurement experts, but one of profound importance to those conducting experimental evaluation studies.

Characteristic of any growing speciality is the exploration of relevant conceptual and methodological perspectives developed in associated disciplines. New approaches to study are welcome in the applied disciplines and are necessary to their continued growth and development. Chapter 7, by Ward Edwards, Marcia Guttentag, and Kurt Snapper, demonstrates the usefulness of such exploration, presenting perspectives drawn from current work in the area of decision analysis. Examples of specific applications of multi-attribute utility analysis are presented, and the value of this general framework for the dissemination and utilization of evaluative findings is discussed.

The writers of Chapter 8 are known for their interest in the most rigorous, experimental approach to the evaluation of social intervention programs. Having experienced the problems of achieving convincingly similar samples for experimental studies, Clarence C. Sherwood, John N. Morris, and Sylvia Sherwood have devised a set of procedures for selecting samples matched on a number of subject characteristics. Assurance that experimental and control groups have very similar characteristics on a profile of carefully selected variables is of obvious importance for experimental evaluation studies and should greatly facilitate interpretation of results.

As an applied science, evaluation research often relies on the operational definitions of constructs developed by related disciplines. Frequently these measures are not appropriate for the demands of the evaluation study. Measures may not be sufficiently reliable to assess change, they may not be relevant to the program or

intervention influence being evaluated, and their validity may not be adequately demonstrated. If they face the problem squarely, evaluators are frequently in a dilemma: either they must develop a new measure or scale, a time-consuming and expensive procedure, or they must use an instrument with questionable reliability, relevance, and validity.

For these reasons Part IV is focused on the development and evaluation of measures. In Chapter 9, Jum C. Nunnally and William H. Wilson present some of the problems of measurement and design in evaluation, followed by methods for developing and evaluating measures for evaluation studies. In Chapter 10, Jum C. Nunnally and Robert L. Durham discuss the different types of validity and how they are assessed in evaluation studies. The reliability of measures as a psychometric property is discussed, followed by methods of computing and interpreting reliability coefficients. In summary, both chapters are characterized by a lucid discussion of the logic of measurement in relatively nontechnical terms, followed by a clear presentation on how to construct evaluation measures and, subsequently, to assess and judge their psychometric properties.

Part V of this volume is concerned with two primary sources of data in evaluation studies: interviews and record systems. In Chapter 11, Carol Weiss presents a critical review of the research on sources of error, or biases in interviewing as they influence evaluation studies. Experienced evaluators are sensitive to the potential influence of interview biases and the uneven distribution of their effects over various segments of sampled populations. Such conditions, which create nightmares for interpreters of results, should obviously be avoided by consulting the literature and experienced interviewers in the early, pilot stages of the study.

In Chapter 12, Abbott Weinstein describes the uses of record systems in answering important evaluation questions, such as the characteristics of clients selectively seeking treatment in a large mental health system, the movement of clients through various components of the system, and, following termination of treatment, the length of time before clients again seek treatment. Record systems provide important descriptive information about the behavior of institutions and their effectiveness in working with clients. Data derived from records are frequently used to select samples of clients for experimental treatment programs and thus serve a useful role in the planning and development of experimental evaluation studies. In his chapter, Mr. Weinstein describes the methodology of developing a large record system and the problems involved in maintaining, monitoring, and mining the yield of such a system.

National concern with ecological issues has influenced social and medical scientists and program evaluators to consider more carefully characteristics of situations or environments as they influence the health, mental health, and behaviors of their inhabitants. Part VI includes four chapters on conceptual and methodological approaches to understanding the relationships of individuals and defined populations to attributes of their environmental contexts.

In Chapter 13 Stanley Lehmann notes the reluctance of social scientists, particularly psychologists, to conceptualize appropriately the role of situations, social

contexts, and communities in their studies of behavior, even though they readily acknowledge the influence of environment on behavior. Dr. Lehmann indicates that little systematic attention has been paid to the study of communities and, as one result, our knowledge of the relationships between living organisms and their environments is fragmented and incomplete. He then develops a theoretical frame of reference for the evaluator as innovator and change agent to consider as they attempt to change communities through social intervention or service delivery programs.

In Chapter 14, Mervyn Susser describes the work of epidemiologists as they attempt to understand, and subsequently to control, the distribution and determinants of states of health in human populations. By reviewing a number of classical epidemiological studies, Dr. Susser illustrates the logic and method of several types of epidemiological investigation, with particular emphasis on relationships between environments and their human populations. This chapter provides further evidence of the intimate relationships between the welfare of people and the quality of their environments.

In Chapter 15, Elmer L. Struening defines types of evaluation research, describes the role of the evaluator, and illustrates the method of social area analysis as applied to evaluation problems. Emphasis is placed on understanding the selective use of human service systems by residents of the catchment areas they serve. The use of social area analysis for understanding relationships of characteristics of environments to the health and behavior of their residents is illustrated; experimental evaluation studies of innovation or change in service delivery systems, using the methods of social areas analysis, are also described.

In Chapter 16, John Cassell, in a synthesis of the results of studies from several disciplines, develops a theoretical framework for explaining the influence of various aspects of environments on the health, mental health, and behavior of their inhabitants. Among the factors considered are the nature and change of important life events, the quality of support and affiliation systems, and the individual's perception or evaluation of his or her immediate social context. These factors would appear to be important to administrators and evaluators as they plan, design, and implement human service systems in communities which vary greatly in cultural values, affiliation patterns, family structures, and support systems.

Part VII is concerned with multivariate approach to evaluation studies. This approach argues for the consideration of a number of theoretically relevant variables in planning studies attempting to predict and explain variation in the complexities of human behavior.

In Chapter 17, Herbert E. Eber describes the logic of statistical reasoning within a scientific framework and develops a rationale for the application of multivariate statistical procedures to evaluation studies. He then presents a series of data analytic models, including for example, data reduction procedures, the detection of group differences, and the use of multiple regression. Strategic approaches to data analysis, valuable at both the planning and data analytic stages of evaluation, are described and illustrated. Practical advice on how to detect and reduce errors in research data should be especially valuable to the inexperienced evaluator.

In Chapter 18, Jacob Cohen describes and illustrates the remarkable flexibility of multiple regression as a general data-analytic system. He develops a series of perfect analogies existing between multiple regression and selected analysis of variance designs. Methods for expressing categorical or nominal scale data as independent variables in multiple regression analyses are described. Attention is also given to methods for handling interactions, curvilinearity, missing data, and co-variates in multiple regression analyses. A recently published book entitled *Applied Multiple Regression/Correlation Analysis for the Behavioral Sciences,* written by Jacob and Patricia Cohen, develops and illustrates many additional applications of multiple regression to a variety of data analytic problems.

In Chapter 19, Donald T. Campbell and Albert Erlebacher describe some of the pitfalls of evaluation research, including the precarious role of evaluators who make judgments about the effectiveness of controversial social intervention programs influencing large numbers of children. The authors elaborate on important issues in evaluation research, including matching procedures in experimental studies, the limitations of ex post facto designs, problems in the measurement, and when not to use analysis of covariance. Drs. Campbell and Erlebacher make the salient point that collecting masses of data does not assure the evaluator of accurate answers to important questions. In short, there is nothing like a planned research study designed to answer specific questions with appropriate consideration of sampling procedures and psychometric properties of measures. Within a cost-benefit frame-work, this more planful approach to evaluation may be much cheaper in the long run. This paper was reprinted because an important subject is lucidly presented and clearly relevant to a number of problems in evaluation research.

The final part of this volume is concerned with the communication and use of evaluation results and a selective bibliography on evaluation methodology.

Evaluators have not completed their work even when they clearly understand the implications of their findings. They must also communicate the results in a clear and understandable style, at times writing in both the language of the scientist and that of the informed administrator or layman. Presentations, workshops, con-ferences, and other media help to communicate evaluation results. The effective application of results in other settings is the subject of Chapter 20 by Howard Davis and Susan Salasin. Working from the premise that evaluation studies offer much for the beneficiaries of human service programs, the authors examine the array of forces impinging on the likelihood of effective utilization and propose a guideline for use by those who may wish to enhance the career of their results.

In the final chapter, Barry Milcarek and Elmer Struening have selected writings concerned with describing methodological resources, their limitations, and the modifications demanded by practical application. Though it is not comprehensive, it is hoped that this selective overview will prove useful for both instructional and research purposes.

ACKNOWLEDGMENTS

We appreciate the willingness of each of the following journals and publishers to provide permission to reproduce previously published articles or selected portions of previously published articles and books: *American Psychologist, Psychological Bulletin, Evaluation, International Journal of Health Services,* Baywood Publishing Company, McGraw-Hill Book Company, and Brunner/Mazel, Incorporated.

The support of the Mental Health Services Developmental Branches of the National Institute of Mental Health, as specified in contract HSM 426981, played an important role in the development of both volumes of *The Handbook of Evaluation Research.* We gratefully acknowledge this support. We thank Howard Davis for his continued interest and contributions to the Handbook.

We appreciate the contribution of the New York State Department of Mental Hygiene in supporting staff members involved in this project.

We are especially grateful to colleagues who have read, commented on, and, in some instances, revised or adapted portions of the chapters to follow. Among those especially helpful were Rheta Bank, Jerome Beker, Jacob Cohen, Patricia Cohen, Joanne Gersten, Barry Milcarek, Gregory Muhlin, and Judith Rabkin. We wish to thank Gerhard Raabe for contributing to the solution of data analytic problems of a chapter in Volume II.

We appreciate the contributions of Amy-Beth Snell and Muguette B. Martel in the editing and preparation of manuscripts. We especially thank Mattie L. Jones who, with quiet competence, enduring patience, and refulgent disposition, completed the many tasks associated with developing the Handbook.

To my (ELS) wife, Sue, and children, Karen and Aviva, I am grateful for the understanding and affection provided during the completion of this project.

Elmer L. Struening

New York State
Department of Mental Hygiene
and Columbia University

Marcia Guttentag

Harvard University

II

POLICY AND STRATEGY IN EVALUATION RESEARCH

2

EVALUATION RESEARCH IN THE POLITICAL CONTEXT

CAROL H. WEISS

Bureau of Applied Social Research
Columbia University

Evaluation research is a rational enterprise. It examines the effects of policies and programs on their targets (individuals, groups, institutions, communities) in terms of the goals they are meant to achieve. By objective and systematic methods, evaluation research assesses the extent to which goals are realized and looks at the factors associated with successful or unsuccessful outcomes. The assumption is that by providing "the facts," evaluation assists decision-makers to make wise choices among future courses of action. Careful and unbiased data on the consequences of programs should improve decision-making.

But evaluation is a rational enterprise that takes place in a political context. Political considerations intrude in three major ways, and the evaluator who fails to recognize their presence is in for a series of shocks and frustrations. First, the policies and programs with which evaluation deals are the creatures of political decisions. They were proposed, defined, debated, enacted, and funded through political processes; and in implementation they remain subject to pressures, both supportive and hostile, which arise out of the play of politics. Second, because evaluation is undertaken *in order to* feed into decision-making, its reports enter the political arena. There evaluative evidence of program outcomes has to compete for attention with other factors that carry weight in the political process. Third, and perhaps least recognized, evaluation itself has a political stance. By its very nature, it makes implicit political statements about such issues as the problematic nature of

AUTHOR'S NOTE: Paper presented at the annual meeting of the American Psychologic Association, Montreal, August 30, 1973.

some programs and the unassailableness of others, the legitimacy of program goals, the legitimacy of program strategies, the utility of strategies of incremental reform, and even the appropriate role of the social scientist in policy and program formation.

Knowing that there are political constraints and resistances is not a reason for abandoning evaluation research; rather it is a precondition for usable evaluation research. Only when the evaluator has insight into the interests and motivations of the other actors in the system, understands the roles that he himself is consciously or inadvertently playing, realizes the obstacles and opportunities that impinge upon the evaluative effort, and the limitations and possibilities for putting the results of evaluation to work—only with sensitivity to the politics of evaluation research can the evaluator be as creative and strategically useful as he should be.

PROGRAMS ARE POLITICAL CREATURES

Evaluation research assesses the effects of social programs, which in recent years have increasingly been governmental programs and larger in scale and scope than the programs studied in earlier decades. There have been important evaluations of job training programs, compensatory education, mental health centers, community health services, Head Start and Follow Through, community action, law enforcement, corrections, and other government interventions. Most evaluation efforts have been addressed to new programs; while there have been occasional studies of long-established traditional services, it is the program into which new money is being poured that tends to raise the most immediate questions about viability and continuation.

The programs with which the evaluator deals are not neutral, antiseptic, laboratory-type entities. They emerged from the rough-and-tumble of political support, opposition, and bargaining; and attached to them are the reputations of legislative sponsors, the careers of administrators, the jobs of program staff, and the expectations of clients (who may be more concerned with hanging on to the attention, services, and resources available than with long-run consequences). The support of these groups coalesces around the program. But the counterpressures that were activated during its development remain active, and it remains vulnerable to interference from legislatures, bureaucracies, interest groups, professional guilds, the media. It is affected by interagency and intra-agency jockeying for advantage and influence.

The politics of program survival is an ancient and important art. Much of the literature on bureaucracy stresses the investment that organizations have in maintaining their existence, their influence, and their empires. As Halperin (1971) succinctly notes:

> Organizational interests, then, are for many participants a dominant factor in determining the face of the issue which they see and the stand which they take. . . . Organizations with missions strive to maintain or to improve their (1) autonomy, (2) organizational morale, (3) organizational "essence," and (4) roles and missions. Organizations with high-cost capabilities are also concerned with maintaining or increasing (5) budgets.

It is not only around evaluation that social scientists bemoan the political factors that distort what they see as rational behavior. An economist recently noted:

> ... you may go through a scientific analysis to answer the question of where the airport should be located, but an altogether different decision may finally emerge from the bureaucracy. [Margolis, 1971]

Bureaucrats, or in our terms program administrators and operators, are not irrational; they have a different model of rationality in mind. They are concerned not just with today's progress in achieving program goals, but with building long-term support for the program. This may require attention to factors and to people who can be helpful in later events and future contests. Administrators also must build and maintain the organization—recruit staff with needed qualifications, train them to the appropriate functions, arrange effective interstaff relations and communications, keep people happy and working enthusiastically, expand the influence and mission of the agency. There are budgetary interests, too, the need to maintain, increase, or maximize appropriations for agency functioning. Clients have to be attracted, a favorable public image developed, and a complex system managed and operated. Accomplishing the goals for which the program was set up is not unimportant, but it is not the only, the largest, or usually the most immediate of the concerns on the administrator's docket.

Particularly when an organization is newly formed to run new programs, its viability may be uncertain. If the organization is dealing with marginal clienteles, it can fall heir to the marginal repute of its clients, and it is likely to have relatively low public acceptance. Organizational vulnerability can become the dominant factor in determining what actions to take, and the need to build and maintain support can overwhelm the imperatives to achieve program goals.

In sum, social programs are the creatures of legislative and bureaucratic politics. The model of the system that is most salient to program managers—and the components of the system with which they are concerned—are bound to be different from the model of the social scientist/evaluator. Their view is probably no less rational. In fact, evidence suggests that programs can and do survive evaluations showing dismal failure to achieve goals. They are less likely to survive a hostile congressional committee, newspaper exposes, or withdrawal of the support of professional groups.

There have been occasional references in the evaluation literature to the need to pay attention to the achievement of organizational "system" objectives as well as to the achievement of program goals (e.g., Schulberg and Baker, 1968; Weiss, 1970), but the notion has never caught on. So evaluators continue to regard these concerns of program staff as diversions from their true mission, and give them no points on the scorecard for effectiveness in the politics of organizational survival.

The disparity in viewpoint between evaluation researchers and program managers has consequences for the kind of study that is done, how well it is done, and the reception it gets when completed. Obviously the political sensitivities of program managers can dim their receptivity to any evaluation at all, and when a study *is* undertaken, can limit their cooperation on decisive issues of research design and data collection (Weiss, 1973). Again at the completion of the study, their political

perspectives will lessen the likelihood that they view the evaluative findings as conclusive or the need to act on them as imperative. Even rigorously documented evidence of outcomes may not outweigh all their other interests and concerns.

More subtly, some of the political fallout shapes the very definition of the evaluation study. As an example let us look at the specification of program goals which become the evaluator's criteria for effectiveness. Because of the political processes of persuasion and negotiation required to get a program enacted, inflated promises are made in the guise of program goals. Public housing will not only provide decent living space; it will also improve health, enhance marital stability, reduce crime, and lead to improved school performance. Because statements of goals are designed to secure support for programs, they set extravagant levels of expectation. Furthermore, the goals often lack the clarity and intellectual coherence that evaluation criteria should have. Rather than being clear, specific, and measurable, they are diffuse and sometimes inherently incompatible. Again, it is the need to develop coalition support that leaves its mark. Holders of diverse values and different interests have to be won over, and in the process a host of realistic and unrealistic goal commitments are made.

Given the consequent grandiosity and diffuseness of program goals, there tends to be little agreement, even within the program, on which goals are real, real in the sense that effort is actually going into attaining them, and which are window dressing. With this ambiguity, actors at different levels in the system perceive and interpret goals in different ways. What the Congress writes into legislation as program objectives are not necessarily what the secretary's office or the director of the program see as their mission, nor what the state or local project managers or the operating staff actually try to accomplish. The evaluator is faced with the task of sifting the real from the unreal, the important from the unimportant, perhaps even uncovering the covert goals that genuinely set the direction of the program but are unlikely to surface in open discussion, and discovering priorities among goals. Unless he is astute enough to direct his research toward authentic goals, he winds up evaluating the program against meaningless criteria. Unless he is skillful enough to devise measures that provide valid indicators of success in this complex web of expectations, he runs the risk of having his report disowned and disregarded. It is not uncommon for evaluation reports to meet the disclaimer: "But that's not what we were trying to do."

While the evaluation study is in progress, political pressures can alter or undermine it. Let us look at one final example of how organizational politics can affect the shape of evaluation research. Programs do not always keep to their original course; over time, often a short span of time, they can shift in activities and in overall strategy and even in the objectives they seek to attain. They are responding to a host of factors: budget cutting or budget expansion, changes in administration or in top officials, veering of the ideological winds, changes in congressional support, public appraisal, initiation of rival agencies and rival programs, pervasive client dissatisfaction, critical media coverage. Whereas the evaluator wants to study the effects of a stable and specifiable stimulus, program managers have much less interest in the integrity of the study than in assuring that the program makes the

best possible adaptation to conditions. Which leaves the evaluator in a predicament. He is measuring outcomes of a "program" that has little coherence: What are the inputs? To what are the outcomes attributable? If the program succeeds, what activities should be replicated? If the program fails, what features were at fault? Unless programs under study are sheltered from the extremes of political turbulence, evaluation research produces outcome data that are almost impossible to interpret. On the other hand, to expect programs to remain unchanging laboratory treatments is to ignore the political imperatives. In this regard, as in others, programs have a logic and a rationality of their own.

THE POLITICS OF HIGHER ECHELON DECISION-MAKING

Much evaluation research is sponsored not by individual projects or by managers of federal programs but by superordinate levels, such as the director of the agency or the secretary or assistant secretary of the federal department, and the reports often go to cognizant officials in the Office of Management and Budget (OMB) and the White House and to members of Congressional committees. If the organizations that run programs have a vested interest in their protection, these higher-level decision-makers can view the conclusions of evaluation research with a more open mind. They are likely to be less concerned with issues of organizational survival or expansion and more with ensuring that public policies are worth their money and produce the desired effects. Of course, some legislators and Cabinet or sub-Cabinet officials are members of the alliance that supports particular programs; but it is generally true that the further removed the decision-maker is from direct responsibility for running the program, the more dispassionately he considers the evidence.

This of course does not mean that policy-makers venerate outcome data or regard it as the decisive input for decision. They are members of a policy-making system that has its own values and its own rules. Their model of the system, its boundaries and pivotal components, goes far beyond concern with program effectiveness. Their decisions are rooted in all the complexities of the democratic decision-making process, the allocation of power and authority, the development of coalitions, the trade-offs with interest groups, professional guilds, and salient publics. How well a program is doing may be less important than the position of the congressional committee chairman, the political clout of its supporters, or the other demands on the budget. A considerable amount of ineffectiveness may be tolerated if a program fits well with the prevailing values, satisfies voters, or pays off political debts.

What evaluation research can do is clarify what the political trade-offs involve. It should show how much is being given up to satisfy political demands and what kinds of program effects decision-makers are settling for or foregoing when they adopt a position. It will not be the sole basis for a decision, and legitimately so: other information and other values inevitably enter a democratic policy process. But evidence of effectiveness should be introduced to indicate the consequences that various decisions entail.

As a matter of record, relatively few evaluation studies have had a noticeable effect on the making and remaking of public policy. There are some striking exceptions, and in any case, our time frame may be too short. Perhaps it takes five or ten years or more before decision makers respond to the accumulation of consistent evidence. There may need to be a sharp change in administration or a decisive shift in expectations. But to date, devastating evidence of program failure has left some policies and programs unscathed, and positive evidence has not shielded others from dissolution (Rossi, 1969). Clearly other factors weigh heavily in the politics of the decision process.

Perhaps one of the reasons that evaluations are so readily disregarded is that they address only official goals. If they also assessed programs on their effectiveness on political goals—such as showing that the Administration was "doing something," placating interest groups, enhancing the influence of a particular department—they might learn more about the measures of success valued by decision makers. They might show why some programs survive despite abysmal outcomes, why some that look fine on indicators of goal achievement go down the drain, and which factors have the most influence on the making and persistence of policy. Just as economic cost-benefit analysis added the vital dimension of cost to analysis of outcomes, *political-benefit* analysis might help to resolve questions about political benefits and foregone opportunities.

It is true that many public officials in the Congress and the Executive Branch sincerely believe that policy choices should consistently be based on what works and what does not. It is also true that, like all the other actors in the drama, policy-makers respond to the imperatives of their own institutions. One seemingly peripheral but consequential factor is the time horizon of the policy process. Presidents, governors, legislators have a relatively short time perspective. They want to make a record before the next election. Appointed officials in the top positions of government agencies tend to serve for even shorter periods. Their average tenure in federal departments is a little over two years (Stanley, Mann, and Doig, 1967). The emphasis therefore tends to be on takeoffs not on landings. It is often more important to a politically astute official to launch a program with great fanfare to show how much he is doing than to worry about how effectively the program serves people's needs. The annual cycle of the budget process also has the effect of foreshortening the time perspective. When decisions on funding level have to be made within twelve months, there is little time to gather evidence (at least competent evidence) on program outcomes or to consider it.

What does it take to get the results of evaluation research a hearing? In a discussion of policy analysis (of which evaluation research is one phase), Lindblom (1968) states that differences in values and value priorities constitute an inevitable limitation on the use of objective rational analysis. As we have already noted, maximizing program effectiveness is only one of many values that enter decisions. Therefore, Lindblom (1968: 34, 117) explains, the way that analysis is used is not as a substitute for politics but as a

tactic in the play of power. . . . It does not avoid fighting over policy; it is a method of fighting. . . . And it does not run afoul of disagreement on goals or

values . . . because it accepts as generally valid the values of the policy-maker to whom it is addressed.

It does appear that evaluation research is most likely to affect decisions when it accepts the values, assumptions, and objectives of the decision-maker. Research evidence is pressed into service to support the preexisting values and programmatic objectives of decision-makers. This means obviously that decision-makers heed and use results that come out the way they want them to. But it suggests more than the rationalization of predetermined positions. There is a further important implication that those who value the *criteria* that evaluation research uses, those who are concerned with the achievement of official program goals, will pay attention as well. The key factor is that they accept the assumptions built into the study. Whether or not the outcome results agree with their own wishes, they are likely to give the evidence a hearing. But evaluation results are not likely to be persuasive to those for whom other values have higher priority. If a decision maker thinks it is important for job trainees to get and hold on to skilled jobs, he will take negative evaluation findings seriously; but if he is satisfied that job training programs seem to keep the ghettos quiet, then job outcome data mean much less.

THE POLITICS IMPLICIT IN EVALUATION RESEARCH

The third element of politics in the evaluation context is the stance of evaluation itself. Social scientists tend to see evaluation research, like all research, as objective, unbiased, nonpolitical, a corrective for the special pleading and selfish interests of program operators and policy-makers alike. Evaluation produces hard evidence of actual outcomes, but it incorporates as well a series of assumptions; and many researchers are unaware of the political nature of the assumptions they make and the role they play.

First, evaluation research asks the question: How effective is the program in meeting its goals? Thus, it accepts the desirability of achieving those goals. By testing the effectiveness of the program against the goal criteria, it not only accepts the rightness of the goals, it also tends to accept the premises underlying the program. There is an implicit assumption that this type of program strategy is a reasonable way to deal with the problem, that there is justification for the social diagnosis and prescription that the program represents. Further, it assumes that the program has a realistic chance of reaching the goals, or else the study would be a frittering away of time, energy, and talent. These are political statements with a status quo cast.

For many programs, social science knowledge and theory would suggest that the goals are not well reasoned, that the problem diagnosis and the selection of the point and type of intervention are inappropriate, and that chances of success are slight. But when the social scientist agrees to evaluate a program, he gives it an aura of legitimacy.

Furthermore, as Warren (1973) has noted, by limiting his study to the effects of the experimental variables—those few factors that the program manipulates—the evaluator conveys the message that other elements in the situation are either

unimportant or are fixed and unchangeable. The intervention strategy is viewed as the key element, and all other conditions that may give rise to, sustain, or alter the problem are brushed aside. In particular, most evaluations—by accepting a program emphasis on services—tend to ignore the social and institutional structures within which the problems of the target groups are generated and sustained. The evaluation study generally focuses on identifying changes in those who receive program services compared to those who do not, and holds constant (by randomization or other techniques) critical structural variables in the lives of the people.

Warren suggests that there is an unhappy convergence between the preferred methodology of evaluation research—the controlled experiment—and the preferred method of operation of most single-focus agencies. Agencies tend to deal in piecemeal programs, addressing a single problem with a limited intervention, and

> . . . for various reasons of practice and practicality they confine themselves to a very limited, relatively identifiable type of intervention, while other things in the life situation of the target population are . . . left unaltered. . . . The more piecemeal, the fewer the experimental variables involved, the more applicable is the [experimental] research design. [Warren, 1973: 4, 9]

Methodologically, of course, experimental designs can be applied to highly complex programs (which is what factorial designs are about), but in practice there does seem to be an affinity between the experiment and the limited focus program. And if there is anything that we should have learned from the history of social reform, it is that fragmented program approaches make very little headway in solving serious social problems. An hour of counseling a week, or the introduction of paraprofessional aides, or citizen representation on the board of directors—efforts like these cannot possibly have significant consequences in alleviating major ills.

Another political statement is implicit in the selection of some programs to undergo evaluation, while others go unexamined. The unanalyzed program is safe and undisturbed, while the evaluated program is subjected to scrutiny. What criteria are used in selecting programs to evaluate? Obviously, newness is one criterion. The old established program is rarely a candidate for evaluation research. It is the new and (perhaps) innovative program that is put on trial while the hardy perennials go on, whether or not they are accomplishing their goals, through the sheer weight of tradition.

Other criteria for selecting programs for evaluations are even more overtly political. Thus in a discussion of program analysis, Schultze (1968) makes two recommendations: (1) program analysts should give more consideration to programs that do not directly affect the structure of institutional and political power than to programs that fundamentally affect income distribution or impinge on the power structure, and (2) analysts can be more useful by studying new and expanding programs than long-existing programs with well-organized constituencies (cf. Hatry, Winnie, and Fisk, 1973: 110-111). There are persuasive reasons for such prescriptions. Evaluators, like all other analysts, who ignore the political constraints of special interests, institutional power, and protective layers of alliances, may confront the decision maker with troublesome information. If time after time they

bring in news that calls for difficult political choices, if they too often put him in a position that is politically unviable, they may discredit evaluation research as a useful tool. Nevertheless, there are serious political implications in restricting evaluation to the unprotected program and the program marginal to the distribution of economic and political power.

The structure of the evaluation research enterprise also has political overtones. Evaluation is generally commissioned by the agency responsible for the program, not by the recipients of its efforts. This is so obvious and taken for granted that its implications are easily overlooked. Some of the consequences are that the officials' goal statements form the basis for study and if recipients have different needs or different ends in mind, these do not surface. Another probability is that the evaluator interprets his data in light of the contingencies open to the agency: the agency is the client, and he tries to gear his recommendations to accord with realistic practicalities. Furthermore, study findings are reported to decision-makers and managers, and usually not to program participants; if the findings are negative, officials may not completely bury the report (although sometimes they try), but they can at least release it with their own interpretations: "We need more money," "We need more time," "The evaluation was too crude to measure the important changes that took place." (For further common defenses, see Ward and Kassebaum in Weiss, 1972: 302.) To the extent that administrators' interpretations shape the understanding of the study's import, they constrain the decisions likely to be made about the program in the future and even to influence the demands of the target groups. An evaluation report showing that Program A is doing little good, if interpreted from the perspective of the participants in the program, might well lead to very different recommendations from those developed by an agency-oriented evaluator or a program official.

Most of these political implications of evaluation research have an "establishment" orientation. They accept the world as it is, as it is defined in agency structure, in official diagnoses of social problems, and in the types of ameliorative activities that are run. But the basic proclivity of evaluation research is reformist. Its whole thrust is to improve the way that society copes with social problems. While accepting program assumptions, evaluation research subjects them to scrutiny; its aim is to locate discrepancies between intent and actual outcome.

In fact, social science evaluators tend to be more liberal in orientation than many of the agencies they study (Orlans, 1973). Their perspectives inevitably affect their research. No study collects neutral "facts." All research entails value decisions and to some degree reflects the researcher's selections, assumptions, and interpretations. This liberal bias of much evaluation research can threaten its credibility to officialdom. Thus, a federal assistant secretary writes:

> The choices of conceptual frameworks, assumptions, output measures, variables, hypotheses, and data provide wide latitude for judgment, and values of the researcher often guide the decisions to at least some degree. Evaluation is much more of an art than a science, and the artist's soul may be as influential as his mind. To the extent that this is true, the evaluator becomes another special interest or advocate rather than a purveyor of objectively developed

evidence and insights, and *the credibility of his work can be challenged.* [Lynn, 1973: 57; italics added]

In this statement, there seems to be an assumption that such a thing as "objectively developed evidence" exists and that assumptions and values are foreign intrusions. But the message that comes through is that "objectively developed evidence" is that which develops only out of government-sanctioned assumptions and values. Certainly evaluators should be able to look at other variables and other outcomes, wanted and unwanted, in addition to those set by official policy.

The intrinsically reformist orientation of evaluation research is apparent in its product. Evaluation conclusions are the identification of some greater or lesser shortfall between goals and outcomes, and the usual recommendations will call for modifications in program operation. The assumptions here are (1) that reforms in current policies and programs will serve to improve government performance without drastic restructuring and (2) that decision-makers will heed the evidence and respond by improving programming. It is worthwhile examining both these assumptions, particularly when we take note of one major piece of intelligence: evaluation research discloses that most programs dealing with social problems fail to accomplish their goals. The finding of little impact is pervasive over a wide band of program fields and program strategies. True, much of the evaluation research has been methodologically deficient and needs upgrading (Mushkin, 1973; Campbell and Erlebacher, 1970), but there is little evidence that methodologically sounder studies find more positive outcomes. Numbers of excellent studies have been carried out, and they generally report findings at least as negative as do the poor ones. Moreover, the pattern of null results is dolefully consistent. So despite the conceptual and methodological shortcomings of many of the studies, the cumulative evidence has to be taken seriously.

What does the evaluation researcher recommend when he finds that the program is ineffective? For a time, it may be a reasonable response to call attention to possible variations that may increase success: higher levels of funding, more skilled management, better trained staff, better coordination with other services, more intensive treatment, and so on. If these recommendations are ignored, if the political response is to persist with the same low-cost low-trouble program, there is not much more that the social scientist can learn by evaluating participant outcomes. If program changes are made, then further evaluation research is in order. But there comes a time when scores or even hundreds of variants of a program have been run, for example, in compensatory education or rehabilitation of criminal offenders, and none of them has shown much success. If it was not evident before, it should be clear by then that tinkering with the same approaches in different combination is unlikely to pay off. There needs to be serious reexamination of the basic problem, how it is defined, what social phenomena nurture and sustain it, how it is related to other social conditions and social processes, and the total configuration of forces that have overwhelmed past program efforts. Fragmented, one-service-at-a-time programs, dissociated from people's total patterns of living, may have to be abandoned; and as Moynihan (1970) has suggested, integrated policies that reach deeper into the social fabric will have to be developed. What this

suggests is that in fields where the whole array of past program approaches has proved bankrupt, the assumption is no longer tenable that evaluation research of one program at a time can draw useful implications for action or that piecemeal modifications will improve effectiveness (Weiss, 1970).

As for the other major premise on which the utility of evaluation research is based, that policy-makers will heed research results and respond by improving programming, there is not much positive evidence either. We have noted how the politics of program survival and the politics of higher policy-making accord evaluative evidence relatively minor weight in the decisional calculus. It is when evaluation results confirm what decision-makers already believe or disclose what they are predisposed to accept that evaluation is most apt to get serious attention. Thus, for example, the Nixon Administration was willing to listen to the negative findings about the Johnson Great Society programs. As Schick (1971) has pointed out, evaluation research is comfortably compatible with a government perspective of disillusionment with major program initiatives, stock-taking, and retrenchment. The fiscal year 1973 budget submitted to Congress proposed to cut out or cut back programs that were not working. The evaluation researcher—now that somebody was paying attention to findings—was cast in the role of political hatchet man. Because evaluation researchers tend to be liberal, reformist, humanitarian, and advocates of the underdog, it is exceedingly uncomfortable to have evaluation findings used to justify an end to spending on domestic social programs. On the other hand, it is extremely difficult for evaluators to advocate continuation of programs they have found had no apparent results. The political dilemma is real and painful. It has led some social scientists to justify continued spending on avowedly ineffective programs to preserve the illusion that something is being done. Others have called for continued spending, whatever the outcome, so as not to lose the momentum of social progress. Others justify the programs in ways that they used to belittle in self-serving program staff: the programs serve other purposes, the evaluations are not very good, the programs need more money, they need more time. My own bent is to find some truth in each of these justifications, but they tend to be declarations based on social ideology and faith, rather than on evidence that these factors are responsible for the poor showing or that the programs are achieving other valued ends.

What would be a responsible position for evaluation research? It seems to me that there are a few steps that can be taken. One reform in evaluation research would be to put program goals in sensible perspective. Among the many reasons for the negative pall of evaluation results is that studies have accepted bloated promises and political rhetoric as authentic program goals. Whatever eager sponsors may say, day care centers will not end welfare dependency, and neighborhood government will not create widespread feelings of citizen efficacy. Programs should have more modest expectations (helping people to cope is not an unimportant contribution), and they should be evaluated against more reasonable goals.

Another course would be to evaluate a particularly strong version of the program before, or along with, the evaluation of the ordinary levels at which it functions.

This would tend to show whether the program at its best can achieve the desired results, whether accomplishments diminish as resource level or skills decline, and how intensive an effort it takes for a program to work. If the full-strength "model" program has little effect, then it is fruitless to tinker with modest, low-budget versions of it.

More fundamentally, however, it seems to me that now in some fields there is a limit to how much more evaluation research can accomplish. In areas where numbers of good studies have been done and have found negative results, there seems little point in devoting significant effort to evaluations of minor program variants. Evaluation research is not likely to tell much more. There is apparently something wrong with many of our social policies and much social programming. We do not know *how* to solve some of the major problems facing the society. We do not apply the knowledge that we have. We mount limited-focus programs to cope with broad-gauge problems. We devote limited resources to long-standing and stubborn problems. Above all, we concentrate attention on changing the attitudes and behavior of target groups without concomitant attention to the institutional structures and social arrangements that tend to keep them "target groups."

For the social scientist who wants to contribute to the improvement of social programming, there may be more effective routes at this point than through evaluation research. There may be greater potential in doing research on the processes that give rise to social problems, the institutional structures that contribute to their origin and persistence, the social arrangements that overwhelm efforts to eradicate them, and the points at which they are vulnerable to societal intervention. Pivotal contributions are needed in understanding the dynamics of such processes and in applying the knowledge, theory, and experience that exist to the formulation of policy. I suspect that in many areas, this effort will lead us to think in new categories and suggest different orders of intervention. As we gain deeper awareness of the complexities and interrelationships that maintain problem behavior, perhaps we can develop coherent, integrated, mutually supportive sets of activities, incentives, regulations, and rewards that represent a concerted attack and begin to deserve the title of "policy."

How receptive will established institutions be to new ways of looking at problems and to the new courses of action that derive from them? We suggested earlier that decision-makers tend to use research only when its results match their preconceptions and its assumptions accord with their values. There will certainly be resistance to analysis that suggests changes in power relations and in institutional policy and practice; but legislatures and agencies are not monoliths, and there may well be some supporters, too. As time goes on, if confirming evidence piles up year after year on the failures of old approaches, if mounting data suggest new modes of intervention, this will percolate through the concerned publics. When the political climate veers toward the search for new initiative, or if sudden crises arise and there is a scramble for effective policy mechanisms, some empirically grounded guidelines will be available.

Of course, there remains a vital role for evaluation research. It is important to focus attention on the consequences of programs, old and new, to keep uncovering

their shortcomings so that the message gets through, and to locate those programs that do have positive effects and can be extended and expanded. It is important to improve the craft of evaluation so that we have greater confidence in its results. To have immediate and direct influence on decisions, there is a vital place for "inside evaluation" that is consonant with decision-makers' goals and values—and perhaps stretches their sights a bit. There is also a place for independent evaluation based on different assumptions with wider perspectives, and for the structures to sustain it. One of the more interesting roles for evaluation is as "social experimentation" on proposed new program ventures, to test controlled small-scale prototypes before major programs are launched and gain good measures of their consequences.

Nevertheless, given the record of largely ineffective social programming, I think the time has come to put more of our research talents into even earlier phases of the policy process, into work that contributes to the development of schemes and prototypes. I believe that we need more research on the social processes and institutional structures that sustain the problems of the society. I have hope that this can contribute to understanding which factors have to be altered if change is to occur and, in time, to more effective program and policy formation.

REFERENCES

Campbell, Donald T. and Albert Erlebacher, "How Regression Artifacts in Quasi-Experimental Evaluations Can Mistakenly Make Compensatory Education Look Harmful," in J. Hellmuth (ed.) *Compensatory Education: A National Debate,* vol. 3. New York: Brunner/Mazel, 1970.

Caplan, Nathan and Stephen D. Nelson, "On Being Useful: The Nature and Consequences of Psychological Research on Social Problems." *American Psychologist,* 28, 3: (1973) 199-211.

Halperin, Morton H., "Why Bureaucrats Play Games." Reprint 199. Washington, D.C.: Brookings Institution, 1971.

Hatry, Harry P., Richard E. Winnie and Donald M. Fisk, *Practical Program Evaluation for State and Local Government Officials.* Washington: The Urban Institute, 1973.

Lindblom, Charles E., *The Policy-Making Process.* Englewood Cliffs, N.J.: Prentice-Hall, 1968.

Lynn, Laurence E., Jr., "A Federal Evaluation Office?" *Evaluation,* 1, 2: (1973) 56-59, 92, 96.

Margolis, Julius, "Evaluative Criteria in Social Policy," pp. 25-31 in T. R. Dye (ed.) *The Measurement of Policy Impact.* Florida State University, 1971.

Moynihan, Daniel P., "Policy vs. Program in the '70's." *The Public Interest,* no. 20: (1970) 90-100.

Mushkin, Selma J., "Evaluations: Use with Caution." *Evaluation* 1, 2: (1973) 30-35.

Orlans, Harold, *Contracting for Knowledge.* San Francisco: Jossey-Bass, 1973.

Rossi, Peter, "Practice, Method, and Theory in Evaluating Social-Action Programs," pp. 217-234 in J. L. Sundquist (ed.) *On Fighting Poverty: Perspectives from Experience.* New York: Basic Books, 1969.

Schick, Allen, "From Analysis to Evaluation." *Annals of the American Academy of Political and Social Science* 394: (1971) 57-71.

Schulberg, Herbert C. and Frank Baker, "Program Evaluation Models and the Implementation of Research Findings." *American Journal of Public Health* 58, 7: (1968) 1248-1255.

Schultze, Charles L., *The Politics and Economics of Public Spending.* Washington, D.C.: Brookings Institution, 1968.

Stanley, David T., Dean E. Mann and Jameson W. Doig, *Men Who Govern: A Biographical Profile of Federal Political Executives.* Washington, D.C.: Brookings Institution, 1967.

Ward, David A. and Gene G. Kassebaum, "On Biting the Hand that Feeds: Some Implications of Sociological Evaluations of Correctional Effectiveness," pp. 300-310 in Carol H. Weiss (ed.) *Evaluating Action Programs: Readings in Social Action and Education.* Boston: Allyn and Bacon, 1972.

Warren, Roland, "The Social Context of Program Evaluation Research." Paper presented at Ohio State University Symposium on Evaluation in Human Service Programs, June 1973.

Weiss, Carol H., "The Politics of Impact Measurement." *Policy Studies Journal* 1, 3: (1973) 179-183.

– – –, *Evaluation Research: Methods of Assessing Program Effectiveness.* Englewood Cliffs, N.J.: Prentice-Hall, 1972.

– – –, "The Politicization of Evaluation Research." *Journal of Social Issues* 26, 4: (1970) 57-68.

3

DEVELOPING AND IMPLEMENTING A RESEARCH STRATEGY

DAVID TWAIN

RESEARCH AND ACTION PROGRAMS—VALUES AND ORIENTATIONS

Intervention programs designed to have impact on human problems should be based on systematically researched models and should be carefully monitored and evaluated (Kahn and Mann, 1969). Furthermore, the utilization of subsequent research findings should be an integral aspect of decision-making in the development of those human service programs (Gross, 1966; Provus, 1969). To realize a process that can be termed "rational program development," the action-research enterprise will depend upon close collaboration among agency administrator, service practitioner, and researcher.

The Need for Rational Program Development

Research is aimed primarily at building knowledge and understanding while the human service agency is oriented toward coping with or alleviating social problems. Nonetheless, while research and human service may be viewed as distinct endeavors, each is essential to the other if the common goal is rational program development, the systematic evolution of intervention approaches that are responsive to explicitly defined needs and are capable of producing desired results.

Research can do much to reduce the uncertainty with which every human service agency must deal by providing the administrator with a clearer picture of the social problem he is expected to affect, by separating what is significant from what is merely prominent, by testing the accuracy of assumptions about clients to

AUTHOR'S NOTE: Revised and adapted from *Research and Human Services: A Guide to Collaboration for Program Development* by David Twain, Eleanor Harlow and Donald Merwin, 1970. A publication of the Research and Development Center Jewish Board of Guardians, New York City.

ensure that the agency is dealing with the population it believes it is serving, and by describing in detail the nature of services or treatment provided in an effort to determine and to assure that agency programs as formally defined are in fact being carried out. Research, however, is not always an available tool to a human service agency (Etzioni, 1968). Because of pressures from various publics or because of binding commitments to particular approaches, agency administrators may be unable to engage in serious assessment or to experiment with new designs. On the other hand, the agency with more freedom to modify present services or to set up new programs may find few functional superior models to emulate.

Frequent failure of research and human services to achieve a mutually beneficial relationship suggests that *there are problems unique to the design, initiation, and conduct of research in the human service agency* or "action" setting which not only differ from those in laboratory research, but may be more difficult to solve. Some of these problems may be generated by ideological differences between research and practice, by the difficulties inherent in applying social science techniques to social problems (Campbell, 1969), or by conflicts in perceived goals, priorities, or professional obligations. Still other obstacles may arise from agency structure which affects both the conduct of the research and the utilization of the product for program development (Fairweather, 1967).

Collaboration in Developing the "Strategy of Search"

Research begins with an idea, a question, a problem. In the human service setting, however, the task is not only to design a good study or experiment but to work out a total situation, a program context, in which a research design might be developed and implemented.

The ideology of the researcher tends to be incongruent with that of the practitioner or the administrator (Miller, 1969; Albee, 1970). The research ethic places its faith, not in any particular practice, but in the research findings regarding that practice. The researcher is a member of a profession in which status and advancement depend on productivity in ways which have less to do with the success or failure of a particular approach to a problem than with his ability to develop information about that approach. The social scientist often is inclined to challenge existing values and assumptions or program practice because his profession rewards such activity. The practitioner, in contrast, may feel reluctant to doubt his techniques. Without implicit faith that what he is doing is constructive, he may not be able to practice at all.

A second difference between researchers and practitioners is in career patterns. The conduct of research and experimentation in the human service agency may be, for the researcher, a significant stepping-stone in building a reputation and furthering his career. The relation of the research project to the career of the practitioner may be quite different: his career pattern normally requires the accumulation of professional training, experience, and credentials in the use of established techniques, not in the search for better ones.

A similar difference in orientation exists between the research enterprise and the agency as an organization. Traditional practices in any organization and the values

and assumptions on which they are based are not only the means by which the agency and its staff have attained status and recognition, but they are also the vehicles of action. Were these basic values and assumptions questioned, the agency itself would most likely be immobilized (Borgatta, 1966).

Recognizing the constraints implied by these very real differences, collaboration between research and the human service agency must be built up through negotiation and through interaction involving not only the researcher and the agency administrator but also each of the other members of the potential agency research team.

While the specific nature of the action-research effort will vary according to the particular constraints and available resources in each situation, essential to the success of any such undertaking are the adaptation of a *strategy of search* and a sound supporting institutional structure.

The strategy of search, one with which the researcher feels comfortable, differs in the action setting from the "academic" search in that it recognizes and incorporates the real concerns of the agency, the needs of the population served, and the values of society. By contrast, the agency administrator and practitioner are more at home with a "strategy of activity" with its acceptance of certain fundamental assumptions upon which programs of intervention are based. The use of a particular technique depends not upon rigorous evaluation of its effectiveness but upon a general impression of its workability. The problem with this strategy is not that it evokes erroneous conclusions—obviously some worthwhile programs have been developed in this way—but that it provides no reliable means of distinguishing success from failure.

Another essential element of an action-research effort is supportive *institutional structure* (Special Commission, 1969). Without institutional support, the agency and the researcher may work together periodically on a project of interest to one or to the other, but such research is likely to be isolated from program and to be lacking in continuity.

To recapitulate, orientation and value differences among social scientists and human service delivery professionals can be reconciled because the fundamental interests of each group include the development of knowledge for rational and effective action. Research and development efforts in the human services must be based on several tasks: (1) establishing structures for the support of ongoing research; and (2) maintaining the viability of research and program development by resolving professional attitudinal differences, by overcoming social and institutional inertia, and by negotiating workable arrangements within existing limitations and constraints.

NEGOTIATING THE RESEARCH

Initial Contacts-Roles and Attitudes Within the Agency

Moving from the idea for research to a situation in which that idea might be investigated is often a delicate process. If the agency administrator approaches the researcher for help in handling a problem of concern to him, it may be less difficult,

at least in the early stages, to find a basis for working together. The administrator, by asking the question, has indicated willingness to assess the problem, and by contracting a social scientist, he has shown an awareness of the need for specialized research methods. Additionally, his initiative has suggested that his agency and the environment in which it functions allow a certain amount of probing and examination.

If the researcher comes up with an issue he would like to study, he may have to "shop around" for an agency both willing and able to work with him. Whether a particular agency is an appropriate setting for a research program will be determined, in part, by practical considerations of its purpose, organization, and capacity (Struening and Peck, 1968). A small agency with a limited clientele, although financially able and temperamentally willing, may be too dependent upon a complex set of relationships with other agencies to provide what is needed. Also, some agencies are committed to a particular program or approach, either by legal mandate or by the demands of funding bodies, and are, therefore, unable to put into practice research findings. Neither a subunit entirely subject to dictation from above nor a central agency with little control over its field units is a particularly good research setting. Programs can develop most systematically and effectively in settings which possess flexibility with order, adequate authority located at the points where decisions must be made, and sufficient scope to engage a problem in a substantial manner.

Other indications of an agency's readiness for research are the extent to which efforts are being made to develop new approaches to new (or old) problems, the willingness to utilize contributions of a wide range of professions, and the recognition that there may be problems for which traditional methods do not provide solutions. A further index of "research readiness" is the agency's data use and data collection efforts. While methods of recording, reporting, and retaining information about clients and about interventions may be relatively unsophisticated, the fact that the agency actively seeks knowledge is in itself an indication that it may be ready to use additional research techniques.

The leadership style of the agency administrator—his flexibility, his attitude toward research, and his perception of its relevance to agency functioning—also affects the choice of a setting for a research program. Some administrators who recognize that systematic study is essential to planning and who recognize that even negative results are of value are quite ready to enter into a partnership with the researcher; others, without a real understanding of the nature of research, will at least give the social scientist a hearing. At the far extreme is the administrator who is completely against "wasting his time and the taxpayers' money on endless and irrelevant studies while people are waiting to be helped."

One of the first tasks of the administrator and the researcher during preliminary discussions is to determine just how their collaboration might be beneficial to each of them and to any others whose cooperation will be required. The experience of social scientists and program administrators in working out their mutual interests has shown that *there must be some "payoff" for each of the major participants* if collaboration is to be successful, and these benefits, both immediate and potential, must be recognized at the outset.

The preliminary contacts between the agency and the researcher thus may be crucial in that they must determine the agency's potential for research by honestly assessing the constraints which may derive from the ideological climate or political setting to determine how much and what kind of research the setting will permit, as well as the possible payoff for everyone involved. A basis for cooperation may be found in the process of clearly defining the interests of each party. Phrasing or rephrasing the original research idea to demonstrate its concurrence with agency concerns may be necessary so that the idea of change is presented in a positive light. Restating the purposes and nature of the inquiry often eliminates threatening overtones (e.g., the word "evaluation" may in and of itself be threatening unless clearly understood) while pinpointing areas of real benefit.

Frequently the idea for research is not merely rephrased, but it is significantly modified so that there is a proper match between the agency's concerns and resources and the type of research program it undertakes. So that neither party sacrifices a highly valued objective; the search for common interests should continue until each perceives a gain from the collaboration. The social scientist, for his part, should resist demands that endanger the quality of research. Negotiation, on the other hand, requires that the researcher demonstrate the values of his project in terms of its relevance to social and agency problems.

A second principle of successful collaboration is that *individual roles and functions must be respected.* Cooperation can hardly be expected if the proposed study or project is interpreted as a threat to professional careers (Wright and Hyman, 1964).

Negotiation with Other Relevant Agencies and Officials

Once a basic agreement between the agency and the researcher has been reached, it may be necessary to enlist the participation of other service agencies or gain the approval of other organizations, local officials, or community residents, for example, in financing or budgeting. Such negotiations are the joint concern of the researcher and the agency administrator. Sometimes the proposed research, perhaps an especially innovative program, does not fit into the ongoing agency program so that a separate action-research project may have to be instituted. Still, the client population probably will come from some existing agency, and negotiation will be necessary. To avoid confusion and to keep from working at cross purposes, the agency administrator and the researcher must have a secure basis for cooperation: a project in which the interests of both are served.

Community and official resistance is likely to vary with the nature of the proposed research. In some communities, there may be opposition to a particular type of systems analysis or to the development of a data base. In others, officials may be quite unwilling to expose present programs to any degree of inquiry: yet, they will give enthusiastic support to the establishment of an innovative service project. Despite a probably hostile reaction, the researcher must tactfully explore with community leaders the reasons for instituting a research project or a new program so that time and money may be wisely invested. It is necessary not only to obtain the initial nod of approval from the community but to take steps to ensure their continued cooperation throughout the life of the research program. This

becomes particularly important where personnel may change. One effective method of ensuring continued participation is to *institutionalize some mechanism for continued negotiation.* There are strong indications that, if the proposed research will affect a number of agencies, the group situation may facilitate agreement (Ellison et al., 1971).

Experience in both group setting and with individual officials suggests that ensuring that each participant will benefit from the proposed research may not be sufficient motivation for continued cooperation. An expression of willingness to let others invest in the program does not guarantee that such "support" will not be withdrawn at a later date. Each individual or group upon which the program will depend should make a commitment to it in terms of funds, time, facilities, or other valuable resources.

Developing the "Contract"

The collaboration among research and other program elements in the human service agency, like most relationships in an organizational context, is based on a "contract." Although much of this contract may be unwritten, the entire agreement needs to be quite explicit. Development of the contract begins in the early discussions between the researcher and the agency and proceeds throughout the succeeding stages of planning. Some adjustments may continue to be negotiated when the program is under way, but the original "contract" provides a basis from which to work. The purpose of the agreement is to protect all parties including other agencies, the community, and funding bodies, as well as to stand as a statement of their mutual relationship. The importance of developing such a contract cannot be overemphasized, because the future of the research program will depend on the extent to which potential sources of conflict or confusion are identified, differences are reconciled, and working relationships defined. Each contract differs in accordance with the specific nature of the research, the research setting, the attitudes of the participants, and the constraints imposed by the research design and by the agency or the community.

Constraints on research in the human service agency generally differ from those that exist in the laboratory and must be clearly defined in the "contract." The researcher must know in advance the limits on his investigation or experimentation; the administrator must have some assurance that research can be conducted within these limitations. While constraints must continually be dealt with throughout the life of the program, adjustments usually can be made if they are identified and planned for early in negotiation. For example, when proposed action-research will require significant departure from the usual agency routine, the administrator and researcher may negotiate among several alternatives: staff for the special project, train agency staff in new techniques, or modify project design to take advantage of existing skills; or for example, when the project design requires that clients to the project be chosen at random, rather than on any other basis, the researcher and the administrator should agree on implementing this procedure into normal agency operations.

Other constraints on agency operation may derive from the need to standardize

the experimental treatment. In this case, agency staff may resent the limitations on the full use of their capacities. Also, research projects often require more detailed reporting than the practitioner believes to be useful. Both researcher and administrator must agree on methods of informing staff, eliciting their support, and overcoming operational objections.

Constraints also may be exerted on research by the agency or by the publics with which the agency must deal. If the orientation of the agency or the attitudes of the community are likely to prevent or impede the operation of the project, the researcher and the administrator must decide whether the idea for research should be altered or whether a campaign of public education or staff training should precede the project. The administrator is in a unique position to influence both public opinion and staff attitudes on the need for special research procedures and on the potential benefits from the research design.

Expectations of the agency and of the researcher with regard to the time required to achieve results and to the potential value of the findings also must be specified in the contract. It must be clearly understood by all that *no solution to a problem can be promised in advance* and that the process of research may be long and difficult. Each participant must be prepared to accept results with which he may not be pleased and to recognize that the most dismal failure may be vital for planning new directions and avoiding costly mistakes.

The contract agreement also should include: (1) specific and detailed definitions of the proposed *division of labor* and the distribution of responsibilities for each aspect of the research project; (2) a guarantee of some degree of *financial security* for the research program and an understanding that essential funds will be provided until the project is completed; (3) a description of *termination plans* for the demonstration project and for each phase of the research, including plans for possible early termination if indicated by the findings; and (4) an explicit statement of *goals for utilization* of the results of research and plans for dissemination of the findings so that they will be available for application.

A contract not only binds all parties involved, but also represents, as fully as possible, their varying interests. The energy devoted to formulating the contract is well spent if it helps the participants appreciate what each expects from the others and what each is obligated to give in return.

PLANNING FOR RESEARCH

Organizational Issues

The various organizational arrangements for agency participation in research can be depicted as lying along two axes, the first dealing with the sponsorship of research and the second related to the locus and objects of study. At one end of the continuum of *sponsorship,* the agency is the sole support of the research, all researchers are regular members of agency staff, and all expenses are met out of regular agency funds. At the other end of the axis, the agency bears no responsibility for financing the research, and the researchers are on the staff of some outside organization. Intermediate points along this axis include: (1) agency sup-

port for the administrative and ongoing features of the research program with reliance on outside support for specific projects; (2) establishment of a separate, but related, organization to perform the research functions; (3) participation with a number of other agencies in a research consortium supported by member contributions and/or outside grants; and (4) contract arrangements with university or independent research units.

The choice of an appropriate organizational arrangement will depend partly on the capacity of the agency in terms of size, structure, ideological commitments, and finances, but it will also be determined by the nature and goals of the research program. If research is intended to guide long-range program development, experience suggests that the research function should be well integrated into the agency. The researcher who is a staff member of the agency may be in an excellent position to identify decision points, to distinguish the issues that are significant from those most often verbalized, and to spot concealed sources of strength or weakness in the organization. Most important, he is usually able to translate his findings into program modification and to use them as a basis for further research (Sellitz, 1965).

While the research program should be a continuing function within the agency, there may be special experimental/demonstration projects which might better be undertaken by an independent researcher with some support from outside funds. When the researcher is independent of the fiscal and administrative control of the agency with which he is working, there is less danger that organizational expedience or constraints will override critical research elements in the design of the project or that economic leverage can be used to bias results. To his disadvantage, however, the researcher who is external to the setting he is studying may be cut off from valuable sources of data, particularly those that grow out of informal channels of communication. To compensate, he may have to make a greater effort to interact with program staff and with clients. Also, some administrators feel that the independent researcher is less committed to the agency and more concerned with his particular project than with the agency research program.

The second axis of agency research depicts the range of possibilities for the *locus of research and the objects of study.* The human service agency is concerned not only with its own role in dealing with a particular social problem, but also with the nature and origins of the problem itself and with the ways in which related agencies or social institutions affect the client and have impact on its own efforts. For example, an agency charged with community mental health, thus, may concentrate on a study of patterns of interaction in the families of young children, while a community school system may study the relationship between child rearing practices and academic failure.

At one end of the continuum of study focus, the agency is concerned exclusively with its own internal functioning. At the other end, the focus is on outside events which are presumed to affect agency operations or the problem area in which the agency works. The focus of the research program may shift over time from the agency itself to forces impinging on the agency or to interactions between the two.

The choice of the organizational arrangement and the locus and objects of study rests primarily with the agency administrator. The researcher can help to identify

and assess constraints on agency participation, to suggest the kinds of research within agency capabilities, and to point out the areas in which questions might be asked.

Developing the Long-Range Strategy

Long-term objectives may be met through a "master plan" research program in which exploratory studies provide knowledge for later, experimental projects, where agency policy-makers review each step, and where researchers guide the inquiry along relevant lines.

Planning for research in the human service setting requires knowledge in the several areas of research method and design, in agency operations from both administrative and practice points of view, in the special problems of conducting research in the action setting, and in the nature of planning itself. Because a combination of these specialties is rare indeed, because knowledge about planning for research is relatively undeveloped, and because it is a complex, time-consuming process (Klein, 1968), this phase of research generally is given too little attention. To overcome these problems, it may be helpful to form a planning committee involving primarily those whose interests will be most vitally affected by the research but also drawing on the assistance of consultants, as needed. Although systematic planning may save much in the long run by avoiding costly mistakes (even eliminating the need for some projects), funding organizations generally have been reluctant to provide financial support for this phase of program development. (Much planning is done hastily on staff time "stolen" from ongoing agency activities.) Ideally, an operating agency would build research activities into its budget and thus provide funds needed for planning.

The long-range strategy, then, is developed through the joint efforts of the administrator and the researcher, often assisted at successive stages by consultants from the various social science disciplines, from management and business, from specialists in technology or planning (Hyman et al., 1962: 75), from community officials, and from practitioners with specialized knowledge. The use of consultants and part-time staff is maximized through the existence of a long-range plan in the hands of a core staff providing continuity.

Research is a *developmental process* in which each successive step is dictated largely by the knowledge gained in previous stages and related to the whole by theory and conceptualization. While every effort should be made to predict all contingencies so that projects can proceed along a scheduled plan, the long-range strategy must be flexible enough to permit modification should the unexpected occur.

Because of the tentative nature of the long-range plan, research objectives for the later stages are likely to be phrased in conditional terms. The long-range strategy must allow for an assessment at each stage, for consideration of what has been learned, and for integrating the findings and their implications into the next phase of research.

Assuming that only a general idea of the proposed action-research program exists at the time that planning begins, the tasks to be accomplished will include:

definition of the problem; determination of what is already known and what further information is needed; identification of the kinds of research needed to produce this information; location of resources; and development of the long-range plan which defines the place of each service and research component as well as their relationships to one another and to the long-range objectives.

Defining the Problem

Defining the problem to which research will be addressed is not a simple matter of selecting among the issues the administrator views as pertinent. An explicit statement of the problem and its logical relation to specific program objectives must be made in terms that permit systematic study. It is not enough to know that the problem is "delinquency" or "poverty" or "school failure." A more exacting description of the problem and of those aspects with which the agency is most concerned must be clearly drawn (Gruenberg, 1966). Thus, there are two tasks to be accomplished: delimiting and describing the problem area; and formulating researchable questions within the area as it is defined. These tasks may proceed together, each contributing to the other as assumptions about the problem, agency clients, and service methods are tested and new questions emerge.

Defining the problem area often is given little attention in the human services, and it is this failure that contributes to erratic reforms in procedure (Wilson, 1968). New programs or methods are instituted because they "make sense" or sound progressive, not because they proceed logically from the problem as it has been objectively assessed. Before programs are designed, the problems themselves must be thoroughly understood.

An excellent case in point is the moon explorations. When the current space program was initiated, no one expected scientists to begin by putting a man into a rocket and sending him to the moon. It was commonly understood that, even if by pure chance a man could be launched free of earth's gravity, his likelihood of reaching the moon would be small—to say nothing of his safe return. It was clear that a space program would be successful only through a long-range strategy of search involving a step-by-step accumulation of knowledge. This long-range, problem-oriented approach allowed an interdisciplinary team of theorists, engineers, scientists, and others to build a knowledge base upon which a successful launch and return eventually might be made.

Even though it is unlikely that a program of equivalent magnitude will soon be undertaken with respect to social problems, agency administrators still might devote much more time than they have in the past to the development of basic knowledge about the social problem and about their clients.

Selecting specific issues for study and formulating researchable questions within the problem area are the tasks of the researcher and the agency administrator together. The administrator may have a number of ideas for research in areas of particular interest to his agency. His close contact with other areas of human service and with sources of community influence also enables him to identify problems of importance to these groups. The social scientist is trained to view problems analytically, to spot untested generalizations, and to press for specific elaboration

of objectives and of program descriptions in order that impact may be accurately measured. In examining the working assumptions behind agency actions, in verbalizing explicit goals, and in relating program activities to these goals, the administrator is likely to identify additional areas in which more information would be useful. Working together, the administrator provides the agency viewpoint to ensure that research will focus on issues of real concern to practice, while the researcher concentrates on devising a sound basis for investigation of the problems identified.

There are several sources of possible misunderstanding in this joint effort. First, the administrator may not see that there is a "problem." If, for example, he has received funds to expand agency operations, he may view necessary action in terms of policy decision-making to select areas in which expansion is desirable. The researcher who suggests that they examine the issue of optimum resource allocation seems to be creating a problem and is unlikely to be met with immediate enthusiasm. If the administrator recognizes the contribution of research to the assessment and comparison of program components, he is more likely to see the value of systematic analysis in the development and expansion of program.

In a second situation, the administrator may already have in mind a question he would like to study, yet find that the research program would begin by investigating quite a different issue. The superintendent of a correctional institution may be concerned about runaways, while the researcher translates that interest into a study of the effects of increased supervision on disciplinary problems among inmates. The researcher has learned that intervening to affect one factor almost always has some impact on other elements (Buckley, 1968) and that initial studies should concentrate on a few of the most important variables.

In a third case, the administrator and the researcher may agree on the choice of the problem for study, yet when the research has been designed, its description sounds nothing like what the administrator had in mind. The administrator may feel that the researcher is off on his own track, heading in some incomprehensible direction. The administrator who thought the object was to set up and evaluate an experimental reading program may find the researcher engaged in a demonstration of "the differential effects of teacher orientation on school behavior as suggested by an impact model relating treatment environment to differential skill acquisition and motivational/attitudinal modification to response patterns." For the purposes of experimental research, the description of program may have to be translated into operational terms which indicate the nature of the study, the intermediate and long-range goals, and the ways in which inputs relate to process and outcome (Barton and Anderson, 1969).

Very often the administrator will present the problem in a form which is really a proposal. He wants to set up a residential treatment center, or undertake a "head-start" program, and he wants "proof" from research that the new program works. In this case, it will be necessary to work backward from the desired project to devise a plan that might lead up to such a result. Exploratory studies, however, may indicate that the program is not feasible, or that the idea should be modified. Depending on the level of data and conceptualization at the outset, the problem might better be phrased, "to determine the feasibility of alternatives to the present

program." This may require some study of current methods or of the population being served to clarify objectives and develop hypotheses related to their attainment. Only then may alternative ways of obtaining similar or better results be considered, preliminary tests of their feasibility be conducted, and the implementation of an experimental project be begun.

Specifying Goals and Objectives

An integral part of defining the long-range strategy for research is the specification of goals of the service program and of the research itself (Herzog, 1959). Often program objectives are far too generally stated to permit accurate assessment, conflicting goals exist, and different staff members have yet other ideas about the objectives of intervention. All these must be considered and integrated into the specifications.

In many agency research efforts, a major source of difficulty has been the program administrator's preoccupation with the components of programs without reference to the kinds of change (goals) the program is expected to produce.

For example, in a research program that involved the design and assessment of a community-based multiservice center, it was observed that, to the practitioner, the components of the program (employment, family casework, health, legal and other traditional services) fell together quite naturally. The specific goals of a multiservice center, however, emerged only with considerable probing. Initially, the practitioner pointed out that the center's aim was to "help" people. More discussion explored whether research could assess whether and how much a client had been "helped" through each of the program components.

The research responsibility in assessing outcome cannot be fulfilled unless outcomes are defined in terms that can be operationalized and measured. Where long-range goals are mediated by shorter-range goals, research also requires a statement of the assumptions about the relationships of service to immediate goals and to ultimate goals. If the practitioner or the administrator does not or cannot specify both the objectives and the underlying assumptions, it will remain for the researcher to infer these from the components of the program or insistently to help his program colleagues state the goals and their theoretical links (Freeman and Sherwood, 1965).

It also must be demonstrated that stated objectives are reasonable in terms of agency capacities and the nature of the program. Social or political pressures, frequently from funding sources, on the human service agency often impose unrealistic demands for effects on broad social problems that the agency is not equipped to produce (Weiss, 1970).

Wherever long-range objectives are as general as mental health or social welfare, the definition of objectives really is a community-consumer problem. The public tends to relegate the task of preventing social deviance or of reducing poverty to the human service agency without considering how this might be done or where in the hierarchy of social goals such objectives should be placed. Involving the community-consumer in defining objectives with the service agency might result in

a critical examination of assumptions leading to more realistic demands on the agency.

Planning the long-range strategy also requires the definition of objectives for the research component. The overall research objective is expressed by the "strategy of search," but a strategy of search for what? If utilization of research is a long-range goal, it will be important not only to ask *what* but to ask *why* (Weiss and Rein, 1969). Knowledge about the problem as it has been defined is a primary consideration, but whether the research is intended to produce empirical data about the problem, to monitor change in program, or to assess changes in outcome will have to be specified (Suchman, 1967), and the research strategy should be communicated to all personnel in as much detail as possible.

Defining Criteria for Goal Achievement

Most human service agencies (as agents of change in some area of social functioning) will at some time select as a research goal the assessment of service outcome, that is, evaluating the impact of an existing program or exploring ways in which positive impact can be increased, either absolutely in direction or degree, or relatively in terms of resource expenditure. Some of the more perplexing problems in designing studies of the effectiveness of intervention strategies are met in the selection of *outcome criteria* which will be both specific enough to permit accurate measurement and broad enough to be of practical use in program administration (Ballard and Mudd, 1957). First, outcome criteria must be specifically related to service goals. Where there is little agreement on goals, it will be more difficult to identify shared criteria of outcome by which goal achievement can be known. Program may be assessed in terms of client behavior modification or attitude change, reduction in resource expenditure, changes in social institutions, improved cost-effectiveness, and a range of other objectives. To avoid dilution of the research effort and confusion of results, the number of goals for any single study should be kept small and the outcome criteria should be understood and agreed upon by all.

Second, the criteria of outcome must be operationally defined to enable accurate measurement. For example, if the broad problem is "delinquency" and the goal of service is the reduction of offending, then it must be decided how delinquency will be measured, whether by adjudications of delinquency, contacts with police, or some other recognized indicator.

Third, measures of outcome must be related to the intervention in a demonstrable way. Because the goals of intervention may be long-range, intermediate, or short-range, criteria may differ according to the time scale chosen. If outcome criteria are related to long-range goals and long-range goals are achieved only indirectly by service methods (that is, if they are mediated by the achievement of subgoals), then the relationships among short-range and long-range goals must be established before the criteria can be viewed as valid measures of program effect or outcome (Suchman, 1969).

Fourth, criteria of outcome should enable the isolation of results from the interference of non-treatment variables. This may require that measurement of

results be made as close to the termination of the intervention as possible so that what is measured is *program impact* and not the outcome of program plus subsequent events. Among the many deficiencies of the often used criterion of recidivism is that between the intervention experience and the reappearance of the problem, the operation of many other contingencies may have adversely affected whatever impact a rehabilitation program might have had. To avoid the contaminating effect of these intervening experiences, some research has utilized the more immediate and measurable criteria of attitude and behavior change over the treatment period as judged by the client, his peers, or staff members just prior to release from the treatment.

Besides being measurable, operational, and related to goals and to service, outcome criteria should be matched to the level of knowledge available for all components of the study. Where the intervention strategy itself is not measurable in very precise terms, outcome measurement should not be attempted in excessive detail. Criteria that attempt to specify to the fourth decimal the impact of a program defined only in the most general terms (such as "psychotherapy") provide a pseudo precision which is misleading. On the other hand, very vague criteria, such as "delinquency" or "recidivism" or "mental health," unless they are much more specifically defined, are so gross as to provide no precision at all.

Impact assessment is a key researchable issue as well as a major methodological problem, and *the development and testing of reliable impact measures is a priority task for research in the human services* (Wallace, 1965). Until dependable measures of service impact have been developed, most outcome research should concentrate on a few specific goals and *utilize varied measures of achievement of those goals* (Miller, 1961). Until research can offer better guidelines about the best measures of goal achievement, it is far safer to use all the measures that are available, both "hard" and "soft," and to take measures at several different times during and after the intervention effort.

Use of Theory and Assumption

Construction of adequate theory is a profoundly difficult but essential task ensuring that each research project grows out of the previous one in logical, developmental progression. To the degree that theory is effectively utilized, both human service practice and the process of research are facilitated.

Scientific theory, of course, differs in logic, in construction, and in the extent to which it is testable and tested from the more casual theorizing on which action is based, but theory and conceptualization are not foreign to practice. In any human service program, both the administrator and the practitioner daily work on the basis of certain underlying assumptions about the nature and causes of the problem and about appropriate intervention methods. Decisions usually are based on a set of theoretical postulates, even though these are likely to be implicit and untested.

Theory and conceptualization may be used at every stage of research on a social problem and its prevention or control. A new program design may be constructed by operationalizing assumptions about the problem and about appropriate interventions, or controlled experiment may be designed to test the validity of the theory on which program is based. Research data may be made more compre-

hensible by the construction of new theory capable of explaining why a particular result occurred, and an experiment may be conducted to test this explanation. In the collection and analysis of data, theory suggests what to look for and what to ignore and suggests interpretations for the findings. Without an adequate conceptual framework, the gathering of more information may confuse rather than clarify (Simon, 1969).

One way in which theory is used in action research is in the construction of an *impact model* (Aronson and Sherwood, 1967), which suggests how service is related directly to intermediate goals and indirectly to long-range goals. The impact model is derived by making explicit the basic assumptions about means of goal attainment, or the "impact" of service methods on the problem to achieve the desired results.

Operationalizing the Research Program

Having defined a problem within the context of a long-range strategy, having specified program goals and criteria for goal attainment, and having identified as clearly as possible the theory or operating assumptions which are basic to the intervention program, what remains is to operationalize the research and action elements, a problem of matching design and method with agency capacity for and interest in research. The list in Table 3.1 suggests the kind of data which could be developed for a service program.

TABLE 3.1   ASPECTS OF AGENCY PROGRAM

I. Inputs
  A.   Human
       1.   Clients
       2.   Staff
       3.   Community
  B.   Material
       1.   Financial resources
       2.   Physical facilities
       3.   Equipment
  C.   Ideational
       1.   Goals and objectives of the organization
       2.   Theory and program methods
       3.   Attitudes and values of the staff
       4.   Attitudes and values of the clients

II. Process
  A.   The program of intervention as formally described and intended by the organization
  B.   The program as it actually functions
  C.   The impact of external systems and events

III. Outcomes
  A.   Behavior change in clients
  B.   Attitude change in clients
  C.   Changes in related systems
  D.   Relationship of intervention to observed change
  E.   Broadened informational base for continuing study

CONDUCTING THE RESEARCH PROGRAM

The problems associated with conducting research in the agency are: budgeting and funding the research program and projects, selecting and training staff, structuring and maintaining the relationship between research and service components, carrying out the design, and interpreting the findings.

Budgeting and Funding

For stability and continuity of a research program, the provision of long-term funding to maintain institutional support for a core of full-time research staff is essential. As projects are terminated, successive projects should be worked into the budget. (Whenever a project is expected to require a greater investment than the budget allows, outside financial support may be sought.)

There is much debate about the procedure of "phase funding," the financing of research projects in periodic grants contingent upon a demonstration of the value of each phase of the project. While this may be an effective means of monitoring the quality of research, the practice confuses the problems of funding a particular project with the financing of a long-term program of research. Long-term core funding of the overall research program or of the institutional structure for ongoing search of a problem area provides the framework within which projects can be well planned and thoroughly evaluated, and the results incorporated into practice.

Staff Selection and Training

In research study of a system of intervention, two different staffs—research and program—may have to be recruited and developed. Specifying exactly what skills will be needed and selecting staff on the basis of functionally defined job categories rather than by professional titles has proved successful. When manpower needs are described in terms of occupational titles, some essential tasks may be difficult to allocate because staff members do not view such work as their professional responsibility. If the nature of the job is not spelled out before recruitment, staff may attempt to modify the job to make it conform to their professional self-image and their special abilities (Lipton and Klein, 1970).

Second, tensions between research and service can be reduced if the practitioners selected have some understanding of the requirements of research and if the researchers selected have both empathy and knowledge about the problems of practice.

Third, every research project might well begin with a training session for all research and program staff, as well as for administrative personnel, to help practitioners understand what is to be studied, how the process of research may affect their work, what they may gain in the long run, and why it will be important to supply the research team with information. At the same time, the research staff may be given an overview of agency structure and functions and some insights into the needs of service. Where training for new tasks will be required, these orientation sessions in research strategy may precede training for specific functions.

If a new action-research program is to be instituted, selection and training of

staff presents rather different and often more serious problems. The first consideration here will be whether regular agency personnel will staff the new program or
whether practitioners will be specially developed for this purpose. If the program
design requires the use of new or unusual techniques or if the research demands
rigorous conformity to plan, it may become necessary to recruit and train personnel
specifically for experimental work.

Despite the difficulties in obtaining adherence to program design, there are
several good reasons regular staff should be utilized even in an experimental study.
First, the development of agency program is facilitated if the experimental project
is not viewed as a special case with limited application. While a crucial test of
program impact may be more easily conducted with specially trained staff and with
special facilities and materials, the results of such a study may not be viewed as
applicable to the normal agency situation. To demonstrate the utility of the
program for agency operation, it may be necessary to conduct the experiment with
the same resources, including staff, as those available to the ongoing agency
program. If a line administrator can accept an innovative program as his own, the
possibilities for incorporation and expansion are enhanced. (Unfortunately, the
possibilities of institutionalizing an unsuccessful program also are enhanced.)

Recruitment and training issues may arise during the assessment of program
results. Because practitioners are responsible for implementing the program, the
quality of workers may influence success or failure. If the quality or variable use of
staff is not experimentally assessed, then how staff are selected, how they are
trained, what they do, and how they feel about the program should be closely
observed and recorded. If the applicability of findings to other settings must be
determined in the absence of control over staff characteristics, at least the facts
should be reported to others who may consider utilizing the research.

Structuring Research and Service Relationships

A basic problem of research in the action setting is the achievement and
maintenance of the proper relationship between the research and program components (Scott, 1969). If an experimental design is used, the researcher must
somehow *control* implementation without allowing the research component to
unduly *affect* implementation and outcome. This requires a stance which is both
communicative and controlling as well as somewhat withdrawn. The extreme
difficulty of structuring such a relationship and then of maintaining it throughout
the research is evident from the accounts of many experimental projects. If the
design is such that service methods are developed during research, communication
between research and program must be facilitated and development must be
monitored through analysis of data recording all aspects of the intervention process.
This may require close involvement of research with program (Warren, 1970).

In structuring research and program interaction, there are several related considerations: structural arrangements for "quality control" (control over program
implementation to ensure adherence to the experimental design); maintenance of
research integrity (obtaining the cooperation of all personnel to prevent violations
of the research design which would threaten the validity of the findings); and the

use and control of "feedback" (control of the amount and kinds of research data which are returned to program).

Quality Control and Research Integrity

When a new program is set up, consideration must be given to lines of responsibility. The division of labor and of authority may depend on the need for strict adherence to design and the extent to which staff cooperation can be assured. In an action-research project, especially where unusual demands will be made on program staff, it may be best if the research director has full responsibility for both research and program staff and if lines of supervisory authority lead clearly and directly to him.

In many experimental projects, control over implementation may be difficult. Experience suggests that in projects where workers are relatively unsupervised, adequate control may be virtually impossible. However, even here, control in the hands of *research or research-oriented personnel* seems the best way to maximize clarity and avoid gross inefficiency in the use of resources. One director for both research and program tends to provide more consistency in research and service strategies and to facilitate rational, data-based social planning.

Many research projects have been hampered in assessing outcome by the fact that workers have changed their approach in midstream. Tight supervision and the active cooperation of a well informed staff in a controlled experiment will help ensure that the design is followed.

One of the more common threats to research design is the attempt by management to use project staff for other agency purposes. The difficulties that may be experienced in maintaining the balance between involvement and distance are illustrated by the process that one social scientist has called—only partly in jest—the "seduction of the researcher." The researcher begins with an orientation toward research "purity" reinforced by his training, his reference groups, academic rewards, and scientific dogmas concerning objectivity and replicability of the data gathering processes. At the same time, he is propelled toward involvement in action by the need to establish rapport with program personnel and to maintain access to sources of information.

Soon after the researcher begins to get involved, the practitioner may make requests for help, advice, special considerations, or information. To the extent that the researcher accommodates such requests, he moves even further toward the action pole. At the same time, however, friction may develop between researcher and practitioner because of different points of view. If the researcher views the practitioner's lack of interest in his concerns as an indication of apathy or unprofessional attitude, he may pull back toward a position of greater distance. In time, the researcher realizes not only that he must get into the action in order to learn what is happening, but that he must be certain that something is happening to provide the data he needs. Consequently, he tends to act as a program catalyst, encouraging action for the purposes of evaluation. By this time, the researcher realizes that he has invested himself in the action program, if only to guarantee that his research will have some theoretical relevance.

Use and Control of Feedback

Feedback is information about action which is returned to the source of action (Lewin, 1968). In research in the human service agency, there are three major kinds of within-program feedback: (1) the return of data collected about program to program staff in the form of information about how they are doing, preliminary findings about program impact, or new insights about any of the variables under study; (2) the reporting of the findings of research to agency administrators, along with the implications for use in program development; and (3) the communication of agency responses to or feelings about a new program or about the direction of the research to the research team or to program designers. The use and control of feedback differs for different kinds of research.

In control group research, where research interference with program implementation must be minimized, every effort is made to reduce and control feedback to practitioners about progress until the experiment, or each phase of it, is completed. If program staff were to have ready access to preliminary findings, they might be tempted to change their approach prematurely, thus making experimental assessment difficult. Wherever new action occurs as a result of such feedback, then feedback becomes part of the design. In a controlled experiment, this means that new baseline data must be obtained. Unless programmatic change in the middle of an experiment is clearly necessary, this adjustment to new conditions is wasteful and inadvisable.

By contrast, where research is involved with the development of program through the study of variable client-service interactions, feedback to practitioners is an intentional part of the design (Rosenthal and Weiss, 1966). As data is collected and knowledge is built, information about program, new theory, or new possibilities for action is provided to practitioners for incorporation into current service techniques. While the kinds of information returned to program may be carefully controlled, feedback itself is not reduced or eliminated, but is utilized purposefully as an essential tool for program development.

The second kind of feedback, the report to administrators and other policy-makers, may be similarly restricted in the experimental design whenever it is felt that communication of early findings would lead to inappropriate utilization. Where the administrator is closely involved in the research project, he may control the source of feedback himself by not returning information to program until the experiment is terminated. In developmental/interaction research, feedback to administrators may be utilized to generate some modification of program design where change appears to be advisable. In regard to both experimental and developmental research, feedback to policy-makers becomes vital once control is no longer required. If research is to be utilized for further study or for program modification, *the administrator must receive complete and thorough reports on each phase of the research program,* including all the latest findings and their implications for action.

The third kind of feedback is the communication to researchers and program designers of agency and community reactions to a new project. If research is to be incorporated into service development, it must consider the needs of service and the

concerns of influential public (Brooks, 1965). When the research program is under way, some arrangements for continuing dialogue with agency administrators, practitioners, community officials, and other interested parties will help to ensure that the research program is consistent with the broader interests of practice and of society, and thus that results may be utilized in future efforts in social planning and change.

Maintaining Ongoing Collaboration

Neither research nor human service activities are static; as a result, their relationship may be doubly dynamic. In addition, community attitudes change over time and political realities cannot be counted on to stay the same. The agency research effort must include some means of maintaining ongoing collaboration, of dealing with new constraints, of working out new differences, and of devising new strategies for collaborative action (Sanford, 1970).

Some developments may so change the context of agency research that continuing collaboration becomes impossible. Replacement of the agency director by a new administrator who sees little use for research, community demands for termination of project services, or a serious and unanticipated cutback in funds for research may simply end the relationship. Most new problems, however, are negotiable if a solid basis for communication and mutual agreement exists.

The same mechanisms used in the planning stages to obtain support might be used throughout the project as channels for feedback, as means of quality control and measurement of service variables, and after the project is terminated, as a method to facilitate utilization and further research. The adequacy of the "contract" agreement, the training of program staff in the research strategy, and the structural arrangements between research and program are fully tested at this time. The degree to which the project is able to overcome obstacles will determine the *level of implementation* of the project design and thus the ability to assess accurately the intervention itself.

Aside from the unique qualities of the participants and a certain amount of good fortune, what seems most to determine the success of the agency-research relationship over time is the existence of a *variety of formal and informal means to develop and maintain an effective communication network*. Regular staff meetings, "gripe" sessions, established channels of communication (a "hot line") with top decision-makers, informal contacts between the research team and program staff, and periodic meetings with representatives of the community and other agencies are all likely to contribute to a more productive relationship and to the solution of new problems.

Data Collection

For any research effort, the obtaining of useful data requires a clear understanding of the research goals and the present needs for information, as well as an ability to anticipate the kind and quality of data which may be needed at a later date for outcome assessment or for further research. When questions arise after the

termination of a project, it is extremely difficult to try to extract information from research logs and reports if such data have not been purposefully gathered and organized during the project.

The conceptual framework and underlying theory will largely determine what variables are considered important, and the level of conceptualization will suggest how much data should be collected. Excessive data may be "noise," yet in the absence of a high level of conceptualization, perhaps few kinds of data can be viewed as excessive. In most areas of human behavior and social intervention, so little is known that to oversimplify by excluding factors of possible relevance may be a mistake.

That research in the human services so far has provided few reliable guidelines for action can be attributed not only to weaknesses in theory but to inadequacies in the collection of empirical data (Morris and Rein, 1969). Problems have been oversimplified, and some important dimensions such as (1) the extent and nature of service (level of implementation) and (2) the differential impact of service components on different clients have received insufficient attention. *It cannot be known whether a service program is effective until its variable impacts on different clients are tested* (McCord and McCord, 1959). Analyses of research data show the serious distortions introduced when a target population is viewed as though it were a homogeneous collection of individuals and when type of worker, type of environment, and type of treatment are not distinguished. The beneficial effects of treatment on some clients, together with the detrimental effects of the same treatment on other clients, tend to mask each other, providing little or no evidence of "effectiveness" and few guidelines for practice. Further, when treatment goals are not individualized to fit the needs of different clients, a change in scores on any measure may not be indicative of improvement for a given client.

It also cannot be said that a service is effective until its nature and intensity are known. *A major deficiency in many research projects has been the insufficient attention to the dimension of service exposure:* the number and duration of contacts between practitioner and client and the intensity of the relationship which develops during these contacts.

Data from those few research projects which have reported on service in rigorous detail clearly suggest that *where service has been judged ineffective, it may have been that the service was not actually provided.* Because it cannot be assumed that intensive service is better, program design should allow for controlled variation in intensity and the testing of different amounts of service with different individuals. Data on what services were provided, in terms both of quality and quantity, plus a description of critical incidents and their effects should be included in any reports disseminated to others for purposes of utilization.

In justice to the many research projects that have failed to provide this kind of data, it must be admitted that the task of describing intervention techniques in terms that will permit both assessment and future application is far from simple. It requires the ability to make sophisticated discriminations between the universal and the idiosyncratic elements of a situation, as well as to measure aspects of service

which cannot be easily operationalized. An equally serious impediment is the lack of a generally understood language for the description of social and behavioral phenomena.

Data collection is further complicated by the fact that agency records are not easily utilized in research. The service agency traditionally records practitioner observations in a discursive and inconsistent prose style which does not discriminate clearly between fact and opinion. Evaluative research requires quantifiable data consistently recorded along well-defined dimensions. While they may capture the unique quality of daily activities, agency records do not usually permit the categorization and measurement essential to evaluative research.

In addition, data collection and the process of research often are hindered by differences in practitioner and researcher perspectives on the proper use of information. Often the research unit must know by name and other identifying information those people who were given service so that individuals may be followed up throughout the treatment period and beyond. The practitioner, however, is likely to feel that some types of information should not be recorded or that some types should not be open to scrutiny. Research does not, however, focus on individuals so much as it does on individual and social characteristics; the personal identity of individual clients is irrelevant.

Analysis of Data and Interpretation of Findings

Sometimes the data that have been obtained from a study appear to bear little relationship to the goals of the project; the measures used have produced an incomprehensible array of isolated facts; or results are so unexpected that it is difficult to explain how outcomes are related to what was done. Problems associated with the analysis and interpretation of data arise from the previous stages: planning and designing both research and program, implementing program and gathering information. Weaknesses in any of these areas—whether a failure to obtain cooperation from staff, to specify goals, to test assumptions, to control for extraneous influences, to adhere to design, to obtain good measures of service, or to collect data on all important variables—are likely to show up in the analysis of data.

Because the specifics of data analysis are difficult to discuss out of the context of a particular project, only a few of the more common problems of interpreting the results of research can be mentioned. One of these is the conflict which may arise from differences in the interpretation of positive and negative findings as they relate to program "success" or "failure." Many agency administrators are uneasy about the possibility of negative findings, especially about program impact, and some have suppressed research results that appear to threaten the agency's public image. For these reasons, data should be analyzed in sufficient complexity to determine whether negative results really are negative, and if they are, that both the researcher and the administrator share an understanding of what they mean for future action.

If preliminary analyses of the data suggest that program had little impact or negative impact and that goals of service were not achieved, an assessment of program as ineffective may be premature. Review of the entire design and imple-

mentation of a program is necessary to determine whether the program was adequately tested; whether the service objectives were realistic and attainable; whether measures accurately reflected goal achievement; whether enough was known about program components to be certain that research was dealing with the realities of service; whether, how much, and at what level of implementation service was actually provided; whether obstacles to program were overcome; whether program staff changed their approach unexpectedly; whether non-treatment factors were taken into account, and whether the data reflected program and not staff quality or the use of particular facilities or resources.

In addition to the specifics of design and implementation, the way in which data were organized for analysis will have to be examined. Did oversimplification mask the effectiveness of program on certain types of client? Had clients or program components been classified before application, would differential impact (some positive and some negative) have been evident? Were negative outcomes assessed in terms of the time factor, for example, the treatment may have increased the length of time before failure—a positive result? Was the existence of the program better than no program at all? Was the study population composed of very poor risks? Was, in this case, relative success or partial failure a good result?

Even if negative findings are found to be valid, they rarely represent a final evaluation of the total program. Such findings should be used to suggest directions for modification or for new inquiries. If findings are suppressed in the mistaken belief that they are a serious indictment of the whole program, an opportunity for refinement and further interpretation is lost.

Termination of Research

At the present level of knowledge, it is difficult to imagine an action-research project that would not raise as many questions as it answered. While the researcher should be responsible for answering the questions originally raised in the period of time proposed, many new leads are likely to have appeared from the data. New hypotheses may be built around those aspects of the program which look most hopeful or which offer a crucial test of some program component. Particularly if the program operates from a unifying theoretical base, new program directions will be based on systematic hypothesis development, moving toward increasing specificity in sorting out the differential effects of various treatment elements, alone or in combination. Analysis of data from a single project may produce only a basis for refinement and elaboration through further research.

If research does move on to new studies and results of the first project are still being refined, *when can findings be utilized in program development?* How much data is needed and how conclusive does evidence have to be to institute major changes in agency program?

There are many areas in which application of findings is possible, short of that last final report (Lippitt, 1965). If utilization is carefully planned for and users are well informed, selected aspects of the research project (e.g., a classification scheme, a well-tested method with one type of client) can be applied, even while the research program continues.

On the other hand, research projects do end while service programs may go on. Sometimes, unfortunately, the program is continued even after research has shown it to be ineffective or even detrimental (Ward and Kassebaum, 1966). In other instances, the program is found to be worth expanding or continuing after the research is terminated.

What happens when the research team pulls out? If phasing out and termination are well planned for in advance and if staff have been fully trained to take over administration and service functions, the transition may be fairly smooth. Often, however, the research team has been providing the theory, the conceptualizations, the organizing procedures, the motivation and enthusiasm that help make the program work. Sometimes, the primary motivation for staff meetings has come from the researcher's need to obtain data, so that when the research is terminated, these meetings—which also are important in providing treatment direction and assessing progress—are discontinued. When research pulls out, the program may drift away from the tested design without the staff's being aware of changes in impact or of the reasons for such changes.

Perhaps the best means of preparing for program operation after termination of research is to develop an information system and to train staff not only to run the program but to monitor program development and to evaluate ongoing operations themselves. If the agency maintains a check on program by continuing to collect data and to use it for planning and evaluating, then the research project has been of value far beyond itself and its final report.

SUMMARY

Action research and program evaluation can make a major contribution to the development of human services. Organizational resistance to the incorporation of research and development methods into social policy-making and practice, however, requires concerted effort of researchers drawn from many disciplines and of professional personnel from many occupational specialties. Successful action research also requires a social and political climate favorable to honest evaluation and experimentation, as well as both public and private financial support over a long period of time. Traditional pressures to "get out and do something"—be they political, professional, or idealistic—must be replaced by frames of reference which are more rational in terms of the time, money, and talent that will be needed for the systematic development of knowledge.

Means of supporting *long-term* research in a problem area must be found. Research must be *built into* the human service agency and into the decision-making process as an ongoing function. All participants should be *trained* in the operations of research in the social setting: the social scientist in the workings of the service agency; the practitioner and administrator in research procedures; and each in planning and implementing the research project.

Alterations in structure always produce some kind of strain. Tensions and difficulties should be expected, planned for, and dealt with openly, rather than disguised or ignored. Perhaps the best way in which to approach agency research is

to admit frankly that it is and must be a collaborative venture, that no one has all the answers, but that if the participants can develop and maintain sufficient means of *communicating* and sharing their specialized knowledge and skills, a beginning at least can be made.

REFERENCES

Albee, G. W. The short unhappy life of clinical psychology. *Psychology Today,* 1970, 4.

Aronson, S. H. and C. Sherwood. Researcher versus practitioner; Problems in social action research. *Social Work,* 12, (4): 1967, 89-96.

Ballard, R. G. and E. H. Mudd. Some theoretical and practical problems in evaluating effectiveness of counseling. *Social Casework,* 1957, 38: 534.

Barton, A. H. and B. Anderson. Change in an organizational system: Formalization of a qualitative study. Pp. 540-558 in A. Etzioni (ed.) *A sociological reader on complex organizations.* New York: Holt, Rinehart and Winston, 1969.

Borgatta, E. F. Research problems in evaluation of health service demonstrations. *Milbank Memorial Fund Quarterly,* 1966, 44 (2).

Brooks, M. P. The community action program as a setting for applied research. *Journal of Social Issues,* 21 (1), 1965.

Buckley, W. Society as a complex adaptive system. Pp. 511 in W. Buckley (ed.) *Modern systems research for the behavioral scientist.* Chicago: Aldine, 1968.

Campbell, D. T. Reforms as experiments. *American Psychologist,* 1969, 24: 409-429.

Ellison, D. L., R. M. Hessler, J. Hitchcock and J. Wolford. Problems in developing a community-based research component for a mental health center. *Mental Hygiene,* 1971, 55 (3): 312-318.

Etzioni, A. "Shortcuts" to social change? *The Public Interest,* 1968, 12: 40-51.

Fairweather, G. W. *Methods for experimental social innovation.* New York: John Wiley, 1967.

Freeman, H. and C. Sherwood. Research in large scale intervention programs. *Journal of Social Issues,* 1965, 21 (2): 11-28.

Gross, B. M. *The state of the nation: Social system accounting.* London: Tavistock, 1966.

Gruenberg, E. M. (ed.) Evaluating the effectiveness of mental health services. *Milbank Memorial Fund Quarterly,* 44 (2): 1966, 353.

Herzog, E. *Some guidelines for evaluative research.* Washington, D.C.: U.S. Department of Health, Education and Welfare, Childrens Bureau, 1959.

Hyman, H. H., C. R. Wright and T. K. Hopkins. *Applications of methods of evaluation: Four studies of the encampment for citizenship.* Berkeley: University of California Press, 1962.

Kahn, R. and F. Mann. Developing research partnerships. Pp. 45-52 in G. J. McCall and J. L. Simmons (eds.) *Issues in participant observation: A text and reader.* Reading, Mass.: Addison-Wesley, 1969.

Katz, D. and R. L. Kahn. *The social psychology of organizations.* New York: John Wiley, 1966, 154.

Klein, D. C. *Community dynamics and mental health.* New York: John Wiley, 1968. Pp. 174-179.

Lewin, K. Feedback problems of social diagnosis and action. Pp. 441-445 in W. Buckley (ed.) *Modern systems research for the behavioral scientist.* Chicago: Aldine, 1968.

Lippitt, R. The use of social research to improve social practice. *American Journal of Orthopsychiatry,* 35, 4: 1965, 663-669.

Lipton, H. and D. C. Klein. Training psychologists for practice and research in problems of change in the community. In D. Adelson and B. Kalis (eds.) *Community psychology and mental health.* Scranton, Pa.: Chandler, 1970.

McCord, J. and W. McCord. A follow-up report on the Cambridge-Somrerville youth study. *Annals of the American Academy of Political and Social Science,* 1959, 322: 89-97.

Miller, G. Psychology as a means of promoting human welfare. *American Psychologist,* 1969, 24: 1063-1075.

Miller, N. W. Analytical studies of drive and reward. *American Psychologist,* 1961, 16: 739-754.

Morris, P. and M. Rein. *Dilemmas of social reform: Poverty and community action in the United States.* New York: Atherton, 1969. Pp. 191-208.

Provus, M. Evaluation of ongoing programs in the public school system. Pp. 269-283 in R. W. Tyler (ed.) *Educational evaluation: New roles, new means.* Chicago: University of Chicago Press, 1969.

Rosenthal, R. A. and R. S. Weiss. Problems of organizational feedback processes. Pp. 302-341 in R. A. Bauer (ed.) *Social indicators.* Cambridge: M.I.T. Press, 1966.

Sanford, N. Whatever happened to action research? *Journal of Social Issues,* 1970, 26 (4): 3-23.

Scott, W. R. Field methods in the study of organizations. Pp. 558-576 in A. Etzioni (ed.) *A sociological reader on complex organizations.* New York: Holt, Rinehart and Winston, 1969.

Sellitz, Claire et al. *Research methods in social relations.* New York: Holt, Rinehart and Winston, 1965. Pp. 455-477.

Simon, J. L. *Basic research methods in social science: The art of empirical investigation.* New York: Random House, 1969. Pp. 35-37.

Special Commission on the Social Sciences. *Knowledge into Action: Improving the nation's use of the social sciences.* Washington, D.C.: National Science Foundation, 1969.

Struening, E. L. and H. B. Peck. The role of research in evaluation. Pp. 167-197 in R. H. Williams and L. D. Ozarin (eds.) *Community mental health.* San Francisco: Jossey-Bass, 1968.

Suchman, E. A. Evaluating educational programs. *The Urban Review,* 1969, 3 (4): 15-17.

———. *Evaluative research: Principles and practice in public service and social action programs.* New York: Russell Sage Foundation, 1967. Pp. 91-111.

Wallace, S. R. Criteria for what? *American Psychologist,* 1965, 20: 416-417.

Ward, D. A. and G. G. Kassebaum. Biting the hand that feeds. Paper presented at the meeting of the American Sociological Associations, 1966.

Warren, M. Q. Correctional treatment in community settings: A report of current research. Paper presented at the III International Congress on Criminology, Madrid, Spain, September, 1970.

Weiss, C. The politicalization of evaluation research. *Journal of Social Issues,* 1970, 26 (4): 57-68.

Weiss, R. S. and M. Rein. The evaluation of broad-aim programs: A cautionary case and a moral. *Annals of the American Academy of Political and Social Sciences,* 1969, 385: 133-142.

Wilson, J. Q. The urban unease. *The Public Interest,* 12: 1968, 26.

Wright, C. R. and H. H. Hyman. The evaluators, in P. E. Hammond (ed.) *Sociologists at work.* New York: Basic Books, 1964.

4

THE LOGIC OF EVALUATION

W. EDWARDS DEMING

WHAT IS EVALUATION?

The point of view here will be that evaluation is a pronouncement concerning the effectiveness of some treatment or plan that has been tried or put into effect. The purpose of this chapter will be to explain some of the problems in the design and interpretation of a study whose aim is to evaluate the effectiveness of some treatment or plan; also to point out some of the difficulties of studying by retrospect the cause of success or failure, or the cause of a disease or of a specific alleged cure therefor. Emphasis will be placed on ways to improve the reliability of evaluation by understanding and avoiding possible misuses of statistical techniques in evaluation.

It is fascinating to look around us and to observe how often people apply some treatment in the hope of producing a desired effect, then claim success if events turn in their favor, but suppress the whole affair if they do not.

A governor put 200 additional policemen on the highways to decrease the rate of accidents (he hoped). Serious accidents dropped from 74 to 63 the month following his action. Was this decrease attributable to the policemen, as he claimed? The answer seems at first to be so obvious: yes, of course. But wait. If every accident be independent of every other accident, then the student of statistical theory would recognize the number of accidents in a given period of time as a Poisson variate. He would then accept the square root of the number of accidents as a random variable distributed normally with variance ¼. The difference between the square roots of the number of accidents in two months would be distributed normally about O with variance ¼ + ¼. On this basis, one would calculate

$$t = \frac{\sqrt{74} - \sqrt{63}}{\sqrt{¼ + ¼}} = .94$$

for the t-value of the observed difference.

Without any calculation at all, one could only say that (1) any two months will be different; and (2) the decrease in accidents was consistent with the hypothesis that the governor's efforts had some effect. What does the above calculation add to our knowledge? It tells us that it would be rash to conclude that the data establish the hypothesis, for the small value of t admits a competing hypothesis, namely, that the observed difference was simply a random fluctuation, the kind of difference that would turn up in scoop after scoop of black and white beans drawn from a bushel of black and white beans mixed and remixed between scoops. Lack of independence between accidents, such as icy roads that persist over several days, would only decrease t, and would weaken further any argument that the governor's efforts were successful. We therefore see no statistical evidence from the figures given that the governor's efforts had any effect. Maybe they did. We shall never know.

Examples that show results that went in the wrong direction are hard to find: they get buried, not published. No one is around to take the negative credit for a failure.

A mother tries to persuade a child, by precept, example, or punishment, to cease and desist from some practice or habit. How effective is she? A young man saves money and gives up his job for a year in order that he may go to school. He applies education to himself, in the hope of improving in the future his economic and social status in life. He may eventually evaluate his decision: he may be satisfied that he did the right thing, or he may decide otherwise. By what criteria should he evaluate his decision?

Do fluorides in the drinking water retard greatly the decay of teeth? Does smoking cause cancer? Is marijuana really harmful? How effective is Head Start? In what way? Do seat belts save lives? How effective are loss leaders in a grocery store? What can go wrong in a test market?

Did the Federal Reserve Board make some right moves in the depression of 1969-1972? Will Variety A of wheat, sown in some specified area next year, show a yield at least 5 more bushels per acre than Variety B? Is EXTHRX effective as an antidepressant? For what kind of patients? What are some of the side effects, and how long before they appear? Does a certain plan of parole and education achieve the goals claimed in advance?

How effective are incentives for reenlistment in the Navy? What is the loss to a grocer who runs out of stock Saturday noon of a popular item? What is the cost of a defective item that goes out from a manufacturer to a consumer?

A prototype of some assembly or machine (e.g., an airplane) is put together for test. Will tests of the prototype predict the performance of machines that will later come out of regular production? Why not?

May one estimate from the results of an accelerated test establish the length of life of a lamp, or of a vacuum tube, or of a vacuum cleaner, or the mean time to failure of a complex apparatus? Why not? Or if so, how?

A flash of lightning brightens the landscape. A clap of thunder hits our ears a few seconds later. We never raise a question about the cause of the thunder; we agree that the lightning caused it, and we do not try to convince anyone that the

thunder caused the lightning. Innoculation for smallpox is effective. Cholera in London came from drinking water that came from wells. Certain treatments and drugs for tuberculosis are effective. Most of these statements, well accepted now, were learned without benefit of statistical design.

Social programs and wide-scale tests of treatments are unfortunately laid out almost always so that statistical evaluation of their effectiveness cannot be evaluated. Government regulations on safety of mechanical and electrical devices are meaningless. And what about the side effects from noxious by-products of catalytic converters?

No one can calculate by statistical theory in advance, or even afterward, the effect of changes in interest rates, the impact of a merger, or of a step taken by the Federal Reserve Board. A statistically designed test is impossible, though accidental comparisons may of course turn up.

A firm advertises in magazines and newspapers and other media, or by direct mail, to increase sales. Adequate design of the experiment is usually difficult, and not even attempted. As a result, the effectiveness of the campaign is still in doubt after the experiment, just as it was before. An increase in sales could be the result of the campaign, but there are usually half a dozen competing hypotheses such as the effects of nonresponse or of other failures in cooperation of respondents, errors in response, changes in economic conditions, impact of competition, new products, new models, any one of which could explain what was observed.

The advantages of evaluation with the help of a statistical designed experiment, when such a thing is possible, are better grounds for understanding the results, speed, and economy. But we have to learn to use statistical inferences that are conditional, relating only to special conditions.

When men arrive at a consensus on cause and effect, they have solved, temporarily at least, a problem in evaluation. Textbooks in statistics and in the social sciences are replete with methods and examples of evaluation (not necessarily called by this name), without warning of pitfalls. The most important lesson we can learn about statistical methods in evaluation is that circumstances where one may depend wholly on statistical inference are rare.

NEED FOR CARE IN DEFINITIONS OF TERMS

There has never in man's history been an era of greater effort toward safe drugs, safe automobiles, safe apparatus, safety on the job, decrease in pollution, war on poverty, aids to underprivileged children, and all sorts of well-meant social programs. The problems of evaluation of these efforts are compounded by failure to define terms operationally, as well as by failure to lay down criteria by which to weigh gains and advantages against losses and disadvantages. A drug that helps thousands may be harmful to a few people. Is it safe?

Any adjective that is to be used in evaluation requires an operational definition, which can be stated only in statistical terms. Unemployed, improved, good, acceptable, safe, round, reliable, accurate, dangerous, polluted, flammable, on-time performance (as of an airline or train) have no meaning except in terms of a stated statistical degree of uniformity and reproducibility of a test method or criterion.

There is no such thing as the true value of anything.

The label on a blanket reads "50% wool." What does this mean? Half wool, on the average, over a month's production? Or does it relate somehow to this blanket that we purchased? By weight? If so, at what humidity? The bottom half of the blanket is wool and the top half is something else? Is the blanket 50% wool? Does 50% wool mean that there must be some wool in any random cross-section the size of a half dollar? If so, how many cuts shall be tested? How must they be selected? What criterion must the average satisfy? And how much variation between cuts is permissible? Obviously, the meaning of 50% wool requires statistical criteria. Words will not suffice.

FOUR REQUIREMENTS FOR AN EFFECTIVE SYSTEM OF EVALUATION

The four requirements for an effective system of evaluation are:

1. A meaningful operational measure of success or of failure, satisfactory to experts in the subject matter, of some proposed treatment applied to specified material,[1] under specified conditions. (Examples: a medical criterion of recovery or improvement in some affliction: a criterion for recognition of a definite and notable increase in production of wheat or of rice; a criterion for recognition of a definite and notable improvement of quality of a textile or of a carburetor; a criterion for improvement in quality of transmission of signals; a criterion for recognition of a definite and notable increase in the speed of learning a language.)

2. Some satisfactory design of experiments, tests, surveys, or examination of data already recorded. The design of a new study will include selection of samples of the specified material; a record, for the duration of each phase of the study, of certain specified environmental conditions that appear to be important; procedures for carrying out the investigation; and statistical controls to aid supervision of the investigation.

3. Methods for presentation and interpretation of the results of the experiments, tests, survey, or other investigation, that will not lead to action different from the action that would be taken on the basis of the original data.[2] The data must include a record of the environmental conditions, including test method, questionnaire, perhaps the names of the observers. They must include a description of the frame.

4. Some official or some group of people authorized to take action (with or without evidence).

LIMITATIONS OF STATISTICAL INFERENCE

A statistical study, prospective or retrospective, proceeds by investigation of some or all of the material in a frame.[3] A complete investigation is called a census. The frame is an aggregate of tangible units of material of some kind, any or all of which may be selected and investigated. The frame may be lists of people, dwelling units, schoolchildren, areas, blocks and plots in agricultural trials, business establishments, materials, manufactured parts, or other units that would supposedly yield useful results if the whole frame were investigated.

A point often forgotten is that the results of statistical inference refer only to

the material in the frame that was studied, the instrument of test, and the method of using it, and to the ranges of economic and physical conditions and stresses within which there was randomization. Statistical inference ends with the frame and the environmental conditions under which the frame was studied. The theory of probability cannot help us outside these limits.

All probabilities are conditional and all statistical inference likewise, being conditional on the frame and the environmental conditions of the experiment. Any probability calculated from an experiment, if it has any use at all, is a prediction that future experiments on samples of material drawn by random numbers from the same frame, tested in the same way, and under the same environmental conditions, would show about the same results within calculable limits. Unfortunately, in an analytic study (next section), where the aim is to provide a basis for action on a process (if we get any good at all out of the experiment), the environmental conditions will be different from those that governed the experiment. It follows that any estimate or other evaluation based on an experiment can be used in an analytic study only on the authority of an expert in the subject matter who is willing to offer a judgment on whether the results are applicable to other conditions.

A good question to ask in the early stages of preparation of a study is this: What will the results refer to? How do you propose to use them?

ENUMERATIVE STUDIES CONTRASTED WITH ANALYTIC STUDIES

Effective use of statistical methods requires careful distinction between enumerative studies and analytic studies, with continual recognition of the limitations of statistical inference. The aim of any statistical study is to provide a basis for action. There are two broad types of action:

Enumerative—Action on the frame.
Analytic—Action on the cause-system (process) that produced the frame and will produce more frames in the future.

The methods of statistical design and of statistical inference are different for the two types of action. Failure to make the distinction between them has led to uninspired teaching of statistical methods and to misguided inferences.[4]

In an enumerative study, action will be taken on the frame and will depend purely on the estimate of the number or proportion of the people or materials in the frame that have certain characteristics (sometimes on the maximum or minimum). The action does not depend on how or why man or nature produced the frame. Examples:

1. We may need to know how many children by age there are in a certain region whose diet is below a minimum tolerable level (perhaps in calories, perhaps in vitamin or protein content). The reason to make the count is to know how much food to supply and what kind.
2. A quick count of the number of people left without homes and without food by a flood or earthquake. A vital question is how many people, adults, infants, and infirm are in need of the necessities of life.

3. The census of the U.S. for congressional apportionment, district by district.
4. A census of a city taken as a basis for an increase in financial support from the state.
5. We may need to know the total debits and credits in dollars on the books of some railway for services that they performed jointly with other railways during the past year. The frame could be, for example, 3 million interline abstracts in the files of this railway.
6. An inventory of certain materials is to be taken to assess the total value of an inventory. This inventory may determine the selling price of the material, or it may find its way into the auditor's annual report, or it may be used for tax purposes.
7. Cores bored from bales of wool selected by random numbers from a shipload of wool as it is unloaded, and analyzed by a chemist for clean content, determine the price and the duty to be paid on the whole shipload.
8. A telephone company may make a field inspection of the equipment it owns to determine the present worth of this equipment as a basis for rates for service.

In an analytic study, the aim is to try to learn something about the cause-system (process) to be in a position to change it or to leave it alone, whichever appears to be better for the future benefit of man or of his pocketbook. The frame studied (material or people) in an analytic problem is not of interest in itself. A complete census or study of the entire frame (all the people in an area, or all of last week's product) is still only a sample of what the cause system can produce, and did.

There is no finite multiplier of the form $1/n - 1/N$ in an estimate of variance in an analytic study. This same multiplier is of course very important in an enumerative study, as it reduces the sampling variation to zero for a complete census, that is, when $n = N$.

Some studies serve both enumerative and analytic uses. The census of any country, aside from enumerative uses (number of representatives or number of councilmen for an area, allocation of water, electricity, teachers) furnishes information by which economists, sociologists, and agricultural experts construct and test theories of migration, fertility, growth of the population, aging of the population, consumption of food, the aim being to understand better the changes in fertility and longevity that take place in the distribution of the population by sex, age, education, income, employment, occupation, industry, and urbanization. One aim among other aims might be to alter the causes of poverty and malnutrition.

A study of accounts receivable, primarily for an enumerative purpose, namely, this year's financial statement, may also yield information that is helpful in reducing errors of certain types in the future.

TWO POSSIBLE MISTAKES IN AN ENUMERATIVE STUDY

One may make either one of two types of error in taking action on the basis of an enumerative study. To take a concrete example, we are about to purchase a load of ore. The price to pay will depend on the results of assay of samples of the ore. We may, as a result of the sampling and assay:

1. Pay more by an amount D than the ore is worth;

or

2. Sell it for less by an amount D′ than it is worth.

We must pause at these words. We talk as if it were possible to find out what the load of ore is worth. We can proceed only if we are willing to accept some method as a master standard. Thus, we might agree that the master standard shall be the result of assays that follow a specified procedure on a large number of samples of the ore, more than we think are necessary for our purchase to be made presently. In practice, we take enough samples to provide a useful estimate of the master standard.

Statistical theory enables us to minimize the net economic loss in such problems from too much testing and from not enough testing.[5]

Techniques that are useful in enumerative studies are theory of sampling, including, of course, theory for optimum allocation of effort, losses in precision in estimates for the whole of a frame when differential sampling fractions are specified in order to get separate estimates for a particular stratum. Confidence intervals and fiducial intervals are useful in inference. Controls by appropriate statistical techniques of the instruments and of the methods of using them, and control of field-work, are essential for reliability and economy, and to understand the results. Calculation of the risk of being wrong in an inference from a statistically designed study in an enumerative problem is in the nature of a mathematical consequence.[6]

Unfortunately, as we shall see, no such beauty of theory exists in an analytic study.

TWO POSSIBLE MISTAKES IN AN ANALYTIC STUDY

There are also two types of mistake in taking action in an analytic study. These mistakes are totally different in nature from the mistakes of using an enumerative study. In an analytic problem:

1. We may adopt Treatment B in preference to A based partly or wholly on a statistical study, only to regret later our action to adopt it;

or

2. We may fail to adopt B, retain A, only to regret later our failure to adopt B.

One may make either mistake, with or without the help of an experiment, and it requires no high degree of education to make them. It is easy to bet on the wrong horse, to use an ineffective method of advertising, to purchase and install a machine that turns out later on to be a mistake, to plant the variety of wheat with the lesser outturn, misjudge a drug, approve social legislation that turns out to backfire, and so on.

The aim in the use of statistical theory should be to develop rules that will minimize in the long run the net loss from both mistakes. How to use statistical inference in analytic problems has received, so far, scant treatment in the statistical literature.

We shall not pause here for an example, as one will appear later. Suffice it to say here that, in contrast with the possible errors of using an enumerative study, we cannot, in an analytic study, calculate or govern by statistical methods the risks of making either error. The reason is that our action will be tested on future material, not yet produced, and we know not in advance what these future conditions may be. Even if we knew, we do not know except by substantive knowledge how they would affect the cause-system (treatment) of the future.

The watchmaker works on your watch and claims after a few weeks that it keeps perfect time. You wear it under other conditions—other temperatures, movements, irregular winding—and it loses time or becomes erratic. The watchmaker evaluates himself on the performance of your watch on the job, not by the record in his shop. This is why he tells you to bring the watch back after a few weeks so that he may adjust it if necessary.

The season, date, climate, rainfall, levels, dosage, length of treatment, age, ranges of concentration, pressure, temperature, speed, or voltage, or other stresses that may affect the performance of the process will be different in the future. Two varieties of wheat tested at Rothamsted may show that Variety B delivers under certain conditions much greater yield than Variety A. But does this result tell you which variety would do better on your farm in Illinois? Can you evaluate from the experiment at Rothamsted the probability of going wrong in adopting Variety B in Illinois? No. Tests of varieties of wheat lead to valid statistical inference only for the climate, rainfall, and soil that the study was conducted on. We shall never meet these conditions again. Yet the results, carefully presented, may be useful in the hands of the expert in the subject matter.

We must face the fact that it is impossible to calculate from the data of an experiment the risk of making the wrong choice. The difficulty is that there is no statistical theory that will predict from data of the past what will happen under economic or physical conditions outside the range of the study. We can only be sure that conditions outside this range will be encountered. There is thus no such thing as the power of a statistical test. (These assertions conflict sharply with books and teaching on tests of hypotheses, to which I will return later with a comment.)

Generalization to people from results of medical tests on rats is a perennial problem. Statistical theory can only tell us about rats. Generalization to people is the responsibility of the expert in the subject matter (chemistry, or various specialisms in medical science).

The aim of evaluation is to provide a basis for action in the future, with the aim to improve the product, or to help people to live better, whatever be the definition of better. Evaluation is a study of causes. Evaluation is thus analytic, not enumerative.

USE OF JUDGMENT-SAMPLES

It is hazardous to try to estimate or generalize from a judgment-sample to a portion or all of the frame whence the sample was selected. Use of a judgment-sample instead of a percentage or total of the frame for this purpose is worth no

more than the reputation of the man that signs it. The reason is that there is no way except by judgment to set limits on the margin of uncertainty of the estimate.

Nevertheless, judgment-samples serve at times a very useful purpose by throwing light on a comparison of treatments. In spite of the fact that we are permitted to carry out a comparison of treatments only on patients who are highly abnormal (usually patients who do not need either treatment, or which neither treatment can help), or at a selected location such as Rothamsted, it is comforting to note that if the two treatments appropriately randomized and tested under these special conditions turn out to show results different by as much as D, then we have learned something: we may assert that the two treatments are materially different in some way—chemically, socially, psychologically, genetically, or otherwise. This we may assert even though we may never again use the treatments with patients like the ones tested, nor raise wheat under the same environmental conditions. The establishment of a difference of economic or scientific importance under any conditions may constitute important new knowledge.

Such a result, however, does not permit generalization: we cannot assert by statistical inference that other patients, nor other pupils, nor two varieties of wheat raised in some other location would show similar differences. Further experimentation would be required.

Randomization within a judgment-sample of plots within blocks (for trials of wheat), or of patients (for comparison of treatments) removes an important area of doubt and justifies the use of probability for conditional inferences. To understand the power of randomization within a judgment-sample of plots, one need only reflect on the contributions to our knowledge and economy that have emanated from the Rothamsted Experimental Station.

One could even go so far as to say that all analytic studies are carried out on judgment-samples of materials and environmental conditions, because application of the results will be to conditions beyond the boundaries of the experiment. This is why substantive judgment is so important in an analytic study.

We may often minimize the doubts about a series of experiments by choosing conditions for the study that will approximate (in the judgment of substantive experts) the conditions to be met in the future. Or, there may be a chance to run tests over a wide range of conditions. Thus, for tests of a variety of wheat, we might be able to run comparative experiments under different conditions of rainfall, irrigation, soil, climate, and length of growing season. One might, by substantive judgment, not by statistical theory, feel safe in planting or in not planting one of the varieties under test. In other words, one might, by substantive judgment, in fortunate circumstances, claim that the risk of the error of type 1 in a given analytic study is very small.

Thus, the law in physics that F = ma requires no qualification. A student in physics learns it once for all time. Originated by Sir Isaac Newton in London, it appears to hold in Liverpool, Tokyo, Chicago.

The advantage brought into a state of statistical control—stable in the Shewhart sense[7]—is that we may use statistical theory to predict the characteristics of tomorrow's product.

EFFECTIVE STATISTICAL INFERENCE

The aim of statistical inference in an analytic problem should be to give the expert in the subject matter the best possible chance to take the right action, that is, to reduce to a minimum the losses from the two types of mistake. A careful description of the conditions of the experiment are, as Shewhart emphasized,[8] an important part of the data of the experiment: the expert in the subject matter requires this kind of information (unfortunately too often omitted by statisticians).

There is no knowledge without temporal spread, which implies prediction.[9] In most analytic problems, the substantive expert must contribute heavily to the conclusions, the knowledge, that can be drawn out of a study.

Statistical inference in an analytic problem is most effective when it is presented as conclusions valid for the frame studied and for the range of environmental conditions specified for the tests. It is important to make clear that conclusions drawn by statistical theory may not hold under other conditions, and that other conditions may well be encountered.

Tests of a medical treatment, to be useful to future patients, would specify ranges of dosage, length of treatment, severities and other characteristics of the illness treated, and observation of side effects; otherwise, there would be serious difficulties in evaluating of the test results. "The comparison was carried out over a period of three weeks. No side effects were observed." Consumer research on some products can be nigh meaningless without reference to the season, climate, and economic conditions, for example, studies on consumption of soft drinks, or of analgesics, or of intentions to travel.

The theory of sampling and design of experiment are important in analytic studies. Optimum allocation of effort in analytic studies often differs from optimum allocation of effort in enumerative studies, though there is no literature to cite. Analysis of variance is useful as a rough tool of inference, to be followed up with more careful analysis. The trouble with analysis of variance is that it obscures trends and differences between small segments. The same caution holds for factor analysis and for cluster analysis. Any technique can be useful if its limitations are understood and observed.

Techniques of analysis that are most efficient in analytic problems include run charts to detect trends and differences between small classes. A run chart is simply a plot of results in order of age, time, duration of test, stress, or geographic location. A scatter diagram is often helpful. A distribution, simple though it be, is a powerful tool. Extreme skewness and wiggles detect sources of variation and lead to improved understanding of the process. The Mosteller-Tukey double square-root paper is useful, even when results are moderately correlated and do not follow strictly the binomial distribution.[10]

STATISTICAL TESTS OF HYPOTHESES

Unfortunately, as already stated, no statistical technique will evaluate the risks in an analytic problem. A brief note in the negative about testing hypotheses belongs here. The sad truth is that so-called tests of hypotheses, tutored well but not wisely in books and in teaching, are not helpful in practical problems, and as a

system of logic, are misleading.[11] Two different treatments or two different varieties are never equal under any set of conditions: this we know without spending a nickel on an experiment. A difference between two treatments, though far too small to be of any economic or scientific consequence, will show up as "significantly different" if the experiment be conducted through a sufficient number of trials. A difference may be highly significant, yet be of no economic nor scientific importance. Obviously, such a test conveys no knowledge.

Likewise, tests of whether the data of a survey or an experiment fit some particular curve is of no scientific or economic importance. $P(\chi^2)$ for any curve, for any system, approaches zero as the number of observations increases. With enough data, no curve will fit.

The question that one faces in using some curve or relationship is whether it leads to a useful conclusion for experience in the future, or whether some other curve would do better? How robust are the conclusions?

Examples in the books on tests of hypotheses and in teaching are usually analytic in nature, but are treated as if they were enumerative, with inferences applicable to neither type.

Likewise, the teaching of regression estimates usually makes no distinction between (a) estimates of a total count in a frame, or the average per unit (enumerative uses), and (b) estimates of parameters (analytic). The techniques are different, the theory of optimum allocation of effort is different, and the uses even more so.

To state usefully the analytic problem in symbols, we first require from the substantive expert the number D, the difference that he requires between the two treatments (processes) to warrant action, which might of course be to continue the experiment. He needs an answer to the question

$$\text{Is } B \geq A + D\,?$$

What we really need to know is whether the difference D will persist under conditions other than those that govern the experiment. As the manager of a large firm put it to his statistician, in consideration of two possible sizes of product, how much would it cost to carry out experiments that would tell him with fair certainty whether size B of the product would bring in 15% more dollars in sales than size A would bring. Here, D = .15. If the difference is less than 15%, it would not be worthwhile (in the judgment of the manager) to change the size: above 15%, it would be.

The appropriate statistical design will depend on the value of D.

For an example, one need only open any book on mathematical statistics, or any journal in psychology or biometrics. To avoid innuendo, in Table 4.1 I give an example close to hand.[12] The characteristic is somnambulism in children.

There is no mention of what difference D might be important. Moreover, the results must surely be obscured by difficulties in observation: "The behavioral findings presented in this report were obtained from a parent or guardian, usually the child's mother" (p. 2). The questionnaire was left at the home, picked up later. There is no mention of any test on the reliability of such observations.

TABLE 4.1   UNPLEASANT DREAMS

Sex	Frequently	Not often	Never	Unknown
Both	1.8	41.8	52.1	4.3
Boys	2.0	41.2	52.0	4.8
Girls	1.6	42.4	52.1	3.9

While 10% of children in the national study were reported to have done some sleepwalking, only about 1% did so frequently. The data in the table, however, are sufficient to clearly establish the statistical significance of the relationship (X_4^2 = 35.3 for boys and 24.4 for girls, P < .001 for both boys and girls).

In my own experience, correlation between two informers or observers on such characteristics can only be described as disappointing, even at the extreme ends of the scale, where theory tells us that agreement should be good if both observers are independent and equal.[13] One could conclude that the differences between boys and girls in this study are measures of differences between observers, mostly mothers, instead of differences between boys and girls.

AN EXAMPLE OF AN ANALYTIC STUDY

Suppose that the problem is to decide whether the cause-system has the value p or p', or how much it has changed over a period of time, and why. As an example, p might be the birthrate per schizophrenic female in the state of New York in one 3-year period (e.g., 1934-1936) and p' the rate 20 years later (1954-1956), after drugs for schizophrenia had come into general use by most psychiatrists. The substantive problem is to find why the rate changed, if it changed. The plan is to study the records of patients that entered the hospitals in the state of New York over the two periods. The first step would be to screen the case notes of a sample of patients admitted in the specified periods, to decide which female patients within the prescribed range of age (i.e., 20 to 39) were schizophrenic. The results of the study are highly dependent on just who is classified in this screening as schizophrenic; hence the screening must be carried out by psychiatrists who are willing to abide by an accepted glossary. There must be controls in the form of independent judgments of a subsample of cases to measure the variance between psychiatrists and to develop an identifiable system of diagnosis. The statistical problem is more than to estimate p - p'.

The next step would be further examination of the case notes of the females classified as schizophrenic to discover whether they were on drugs in or out of the hospital, how many children had been born to them before admission, and to trace these females over a period of years to discover how many more children they had over a span of years, and how much time they spent in the hospital. It would be a simple matter, when the results are in, to calculate the overall change p - p'. But how would one use the standard error so calculated? Clearly, it would have little meaning and less use. The problem of interpreting the results would be difficult, even with the most skillful statistical design and interviewing of patients and

informants. The problem is not one in statistical significance. It is for this reason that extreme accuracy in an analytic study is wasted effort.

A change in rate from p to p′ by an amount D would be established or refuted only by examination in detail by age, size of community, orientation of the hospital. Useful statistical tools would be scatter diagrams aided by the sign test, and comparison of cumulative distributions.

We could go wrong in our conclusion, but unfortunately there is no statistical test we can apply to the data of the study that can tell us the risk of ascribing the change in birthrate to the use of drugs which decrease the time spent in the hospital, increase the time spent at home, when the experts decide in later years that drugs were not the cause of the change in birthrate. Neither is there a statistical test to tell us the contrary risk of eliminating drugs as a cause, when the experts decide in later years that drugs were definitely a contributing factor.

ANOTHER EXAMPLE

There are two methods of packing coffee into tins. Method A is the machinery already on the floor and the customary way of using it. Method B is new machinery that its manufacturer claims will turn out the work more rapidly and hit closer to any prescribed weight, so that with his machinery it is not necessary to put as many additional grains of coffee into a can to meet requirements of minimum weight as it is with the machinery in use. One machine of the new type is to be set up along a production line next week, and it is proposed to test it against the standard method of the past. It is hoped to reach a decision within a few weeks on whether the new machinery would be sufficiently advantageous to warrant the cost of replacement.

Would it be good management to try to be guided entirely on the results? One could run the two methods side by side and get figures, but what could he infer from these figures? Would the figures predict unforeseeable events such as time out for repairs, ability of the manufacturer of B to supply parts and service? The new machinery may not require repairs for six months, at the end of which time it may start to deteriorate.

Another possible difficulty is that the test to be run during the next few weeks could be unfair to the new machinery because the men that will operate it will be either operators of the regular machinery; or if sent in from the outside, they will hardly have a chance to accustom themselves to the new environment before the test will be running. As a further point, in spite of the manufacturer's efforts, Machine B may not be installed properly: it may require adjustments over a period of weeks.

Certain decisive results are of course possible. The new machinery may break down continually, or it may distinctly outclass the standard machinery and methods, with little danger (on engineering judgment, not statistical) of running into heavy costs of maintenance.

If forced, anybody could, at the end of a test, or with no test, make one decision or the other: (1) adopt the new machinery; (2) stay with the old machinery. Management would perhaps decide later that they had made a wise decision, or an

unwise one. More likely, they would never raise a question about their decision, nor be able to provide any information about it.

THE RETROSPECTIVE METHOD

This is a method of evaluation that is much used, even though the hazards of wrong conclusions are great unless the observations are interpreted with care. It may therefore be useful to explain the method in simple terms and to offer a few words of caution. In the retrospective method, one divides into groups (diseased, not diseased) a population as it exists today, and inquires into the past histories of the individuals in these groups. The aim is of course to discover whether the past histories are different in any meaningful way and thus to discover the causes of the differences observed today between the two groups. The method is tempting, by reasons of economy, speed, and simplicity: we do not need to follow over a long period of time the people or animals or plants that we wish to study, with all the problems of tracing people as they move about. Still more tempting, the retrospective method does not require us to try to divide a sample of people into two groups, A and B, and say to Group A, you people are not to smoke during the next 20 years, and to Group B, you people are to smoke 2 packs a day for the next 20 years (all of which is of course fantastic).

The following example explains the retrospective method (oversimplified, as every term requires a lengthy operational definition):

Cause 1 (C1): he was a smoker 20 years ago.
Cause 2 (C2): he was not a smoker 20 years ago.
Effect 1 (E1): alive now, diseased.
Effect 2 (E2): alive now, not diseased.

By examination of a proper sample of people living today, we may divide those that have attained a certain age, say 50, into four groups, shown in Table 4.2, into which we have entered the observed frequencies, x_{ij}. Now suppose that the frequencies off the diagonal were zero ($x_{12} = x_{21} = 0$). Every person diseased today was a smoker 20 years ago. Every person not diseased today was not a smoker 20 years ago. Could we conclude that smoking 20 years ago caused disease

TABLE 4.2

Cause (from history)	Result (observed today)		
	E 1 (diseased)	E 2 (not diseased)	Total
C 1 (smoked)	x_{11}	x_{12}	$x_{1.}$
C 2 (did not smoke)	x_{21}	x_{22}	$x_{2.}$
Total	$x_{.1}$	$x_{.2}$	$x_{..}$

today? No, but the retrospective method can raise question marks for further study.

The trouble with the retrospective method is that it studies only the survivors. We can study today only the survivors of 20 years ago. One must admit the possibility, and investigate it, that all the deaths that occurred over the interval of 20 years were nonsmokers; that smoking toughens one's resistance to diseases other than the specified disease, and that a smoker thus has a better chance to live 20 years, even though, at the end of that period, he will already have contracted the specified disease.

It is easy to make a wrong inference by a computation of chi-square for the 2 x 2 table under discussion. The survivors we study today are not a sample of the people who were alive 20 years ago. The survivors alive today do not tell us all that we need to know about the effects of the suspected causes that operated 20 years ago. We need to know what happened to the nonsurvivors. Where are the rest of the people, not alive today, who were alive 20 years ago? What happened to them? We cannot calculate limits of uncertainty on conclusions concerning suspected causes of disease drawn purely from observations on today's survivors. This is the great failing of the retrospective method, and it is serious.

Must we throw away the information acquired in a retrospective study? No, do not throw it away; supplement it. The retrospective method raises questions, hypotheses to study. The next step is to fill in the gaps, perhaps by making use of small prospective studies, pointed directly at the target. Unfortunately, one must wait for results.

NOTES

1. Following Frank Yates, I use the word *material* to denote people, patients, business establishments, accounts, cases, animals, agricultural products, industrial products, or anything else.

2. Shewhart's Rule 2, from Walter A. Shewhart, *Statistical Method from the Viewpoint of Quality Control* (Graduate School, Department of Agriculture, Washington, 1938), p. 92.

3. The concept of the frame was first defined but without use of any specific term by F. F. Stephan, American Sociological Review 1 (1936): 569-580.

4. The contrast between enumerative and analytic studies is set forth in chapter 7 of Deming, *Some Theory of Sampling* (Wiley, 1950; Dover, 1966). See also chapter 31 in *New Developments in Survey Sampling* by Norman L. Johnson and Harry Smith (Wiley-Interscience, 1969).

5. Richard H. Blythe, "The Economics of Sample-Size Applied to the Scaling of Sawlogs," The Biometrics Bulletin [Washington] 1 (1945): 67-70. Leo Törnqvist, "An Attempt to Analyze the Problem of an Economical Production of Statistical Data." Nordisk Tidsskrift for Teknisk Økonomi 37 (1948): 263-274.

6. Some pitfalls in estimation are described in chapter 31 in *New Developments in Survey Sampling* by Norman L. Johnson and Harry Smith cited earlier.

7. Walter A. Shewhart, *Statistical Method from the Viewpoint of Quality Control* (Graduate School, Department of Agriculture, 1939), chap. 3.

8. Ibid.

9. C. I. Lewis, *Mind and the World-Order* (Scribners, 1929), chaps. 6 and 7.

10. Frederick Mosteller and John W. Tukey, "The Uses and Usefulness of Probability Paper," Journal of the American Statistical Association 44 (1949): 174-212. The double square-root paper is manufactured by the Codex Book Company of Norwood, Mass.

11. Joseph Berkson, "Tests of Significance Considered as Evidence," Journal of the American Statistical Association 37 (1942): 325-335; Carl Earhardt, "Statistics, a Trap for the Unwary," Obstetrics and Gynecology 14 (Oct. 1959): 549-554; J. Wolfowitz, "Remarks on the Theory of Testing Hypotheses," The New York Statistician 18 (March 1967); W. Edwards Deming, "Boundaries of Statistical Inference," being chapter 31 in New Developments in Survey Sampling by Norman L. Johnson and Harry Smith (Wiley, 1969); Denton E. Morrison and Ramon E. Henkel, The Significance Test Controversy (Aldine, 1970).

12. Relationships among (sic) parent ratings of behavioral characteristics of children, National Center for Health Statistics, series 11, no. 121, Oct. 1972.

13. John Mandel, "Flammability of Children's Sleep-Wear," Standardization News [Philadelphia], May 1973, p. 11.

III

CONCEPTUALIZATION AND DESIGN OF EVALUATION STUDIES

5

REFORMS AS EXPERIMENTS

DONALD T. CAMPBELL

Northwestern University

The United States and other modern nations should be ready for an experimental approach to social reform, an approach in which we try out new programs designed to cure specific social problems, in which we learn whether or not these programs are effective, and in which we retain, imitate, modify, or discard them on the basis of apparent effectiveness on the multiple imperfect criteria available. Our readiness for this stage is indicated by the inclusion of specific provisions for program evaluation in the first wave of the "Great Society" legislation, and by the current congressional proposals for establishing "social indicators" and socially relevant "data banks." So long have we had good intentions in this regard that many may feel we are already at this stage, that we already are continuing or discontinuing programs on the basis of assessed effectiveness. It is a theme of this article that this is not at all so, that most ameliorative programs end up with *no* interpretable evaluation (Etzioni, 1968; Hyman and Wright, 1967; Schwartz, 1961). We must look hard at the sources of this condition, and design ways of overcoming the difficulties. This article is a preliminary effort in this regard.

AUTHOR'S NOTE: The preparation of this paper has been supported by National Science Foundation Grant GS1309X. Versions of this paper have been presented as the Northwestern University Alumni Fund Lecture, January 24, 1968; to the Social Psychology Section of the British Psychological Society at Oxford, September 20, 1968; to the International Conference on Social Psychology at Prague, October 7, 1968 (under a different title); and to several other groups. Requests for reprints should be sent to Donald T. Campbell, Department of Psychology, Northwestern University, Evanston, Illinois 60201.

EDITORS' NOTE: Reprinted, with some revisions by the author, from the *American Psychologist,* vol. 24, no. 4 (April 1969), by permission of the publisher.

Many of the difficulties lie in the intransigencies of the research setting and in the presence of recurrent seductive pitfalls of interpretation. The bulk of this article will be devoted to these problems. But the few available solutions turn out to depend upon correct administrative decisions in the initiation and execution of the program. These decisions are made in a political arena, and involve political jeopardies that are often sufficient to explain the lack of hard-headed evaluation of effects. Removing reform administrators from the political spotlight seems both highly unlikely, and undesirable even if it were possible. What is instead essential is that the social scientist research advisor understand the political realities of the situation, and that he aid by helping create a public demand for hard-headed evaluation, by contributing to those political inventions that reduce the liability of honest evaluation, and by educating future administrators to the problems and possibilities.

For this reason, there is also an attempt in this article to consider the political setting of program evaluation, and to offer suggestions as to political postures that might further a truly experimental approach to social reform. Although such considerations will be distributed as a minor theme throughout this article, it seems convenient to begin with some general points of this political nature.

POLITICAL VULNERABILITY FROM KNOWING OUTCOMES

It is one of the most characteristic aspects of the present situation that *specific reforms are advocated as though they were certain to be successful.* For this reason, knowing outcomes has immediate political implications. Given the inherent difficulty of making significant improvements by the means usually provided and given the discrepancy between promise and possibility, most administrators wisely prefer to limit the evaluations to those the outcomes of which they can control, particularly insofar as published outcomes or press releases are concerned. Ambiguity, lack of truly comparable comparison bases, and lack of concrete evidence all work to increase the administrator's control over what gets said, or at least to reduce the bite of criticism in the case of actual failure. There is safety under the cloak of ignorance. Over and above this tie-in of advocacy and administration, there is another source of vulnerability in that the facts relevant to experimental program evaluation are also available to argue the general efficiency and honesty of administrators. The public availability of such facts reduces the privacy and security of at least some administrators.

Even where there are ideological commitments to a hard-headed evaluation of organizational efficiency, or to a scientific organization of society, these two jeopardies lead to the failure to evaluate organizational experiments realistically. If the political and administrative system has committed itself in advance to the correctness and efficacy of its reforms, it cannot tolerate learning of failure. To be truly scientific we must be able to experiment. We must be able to advocate without that excess of commitment that blinds us to reality testing.

This predicament, abetted by public apathy and by deliberate corruption, may prove in the long run to permanently preclude a truly experimental approach to social amelioration. But our needs and our hopes for a better society demand we

make the effort. There are a few signs of hope. In the United States we have been able to achieve cost-of-living and unemployment indices that, however imperfect, have embarrassed the administrations that published them. We are able to conduct censuses that reduce the number of representatives a state has in Congress. These are grounds for optimism, although the corrupt tardiness of state governments in following their own constitutions in revising legislative districts illustrates the problem.

One simple shift in political posture which would reduce the problem is the shift from the advocacy of a specific reform to the advocacy of the seriousness of the problem, and hence to the advocacy of persistence in alternative reform efforts should the first one fail. The political stance would become: "This is a serious problem. We propose to initiate Policy A on an experimental basis. If after five years there has been no significant improvement, we will shift to Policy B." By making explicit that a given problem solution was only one of several that the administrator or party could in good conscience advocate, and by having ready a plausible alternative, the administrator could afford honest evaluation of outcomes. Negative results, a failure of the first program, would not jeopardize his job, for his job would be to keep after the problem until something was found that worked.

Coupled with this should be a general moratorium on ad hominem evaluative research, that is, on research designed to evaluate specific administrators rather than alternative policies. If we worry about the invasion-of-privacy problem in the data banks and social indicators of the future (e.g., Sawyer and Schechter, 1968), the touchiest point is the privacy of administrators. If we threaten this, the measurement system will surely be sabotaged in the innumerable ways possible. While this may sound unduly pessimistic, the recurrent anecdotes of administrators attempting to squelch unwanted research findings convince me of its accuracy. But we should be able to evaluate those alternative policies that a given administrator has the option of implementing.

FIELD EXPERIMENTS AND QUASI-EXPERIMENTAL DESIGNS

In efforts to extend the logic of laboratory experimentation into the "field," and into settings not fully experimental, an inventory of threats to experimental validity has been assembled, in terms of which some 15 or 20 experimental and quasi-experimental designs have been evaluated (Campbell, 1957, 1963; Campbell and Stanley, 1963). In the present article only three or four designs will be examined, and therefore not all of the validity threats will be relevant, but it will provide useful background to look briefly at them all. Following are nine threats to internal validity.[1]

1. *History:* events, other than the experimental treatment, occurring between pretest and posttest and thus providing alternate explanations of effects.
2. *Maturation:* processes within the respondents or observed social units producing changes as a function of the passage of time per se, such as growth, fatigue, secular trends, etc.
3. *Instability:* unreliability of measures, fluctuations in sampling persons or

components, autonomous instability of repeated or "equivalent" measures. (This is the only threat to which statistical tests of significance are relevant.)

4. *Testing:* the effect of taking a test upon the scores of a second testing. The effect of publication of a social indicator upon subsequent readings of that indicator.

5. *Instrumentation:* in which changes in the calibration of a measuring instrument or changes in the observers or scores used may produce changes in the obtained measurements.

6. *Regression artifacts:* pseudo-shifts occurring when persons or treatment units have been selected upon the basis of their extreme scores.

7. *Selection:* biases resulting from differential recruitment of comparison groups, producing different mean levels on the measure of effects.

8. *Experimental mortality:* the differential loss of respondents from comparison groups.

9. *Selection-maturation interaction:* selection biases resulting in differential rates of "maturation" or autonomous change.

If a change or difference occurs, these are rival explanations that could be used to explain away an effect and thus to deny that in this specific experiment any genuine effect of the experimental treatment had been demonstrated. These are faults that true experiments avoid, primarily through the use of randomization and control groups. In the approach here advocated, this checklist is used to evaluate specific quasi-experimental designs. This is evaluation, not rejection, for it often turns out that for a specific design in a specific setting the threat is implausible, or that there are supplementary data that can help rule it out even where randomization is impossible. The general ethic, here advocated for public administrators as well as social scientists, is to use the very best method possible, aiming at "true experiments" with random control groups. But where randomized treatments are not possible, a self-critical use of quasi-experimental designs is advocated. We must do the best we can with what is available to us.

Our posture vis-à-vis perfectionist critics from laboratory experimentation is more militant than this: the only threats to validity that we will allow to invalidate an experiment are those that admit of the status of empirical laws more dependable and more plausible than the law involving the treatment. The mere possibility of some alternative explanation is not enough—it is only the *plausible* rival hypotheses that are invalidating. Vis-à-vis correlational studies and common-sense descriptive studies, on the other hand, our stance is one of greater conservatism. For example, because of the specific methodological trap of regression artifacts, the sociological tradition of "ex post facto" designs (Chapin, 1947; Greenwood, 1945) is totally rejected (Campbell and Stanley, 1963: 240-241; 1966: 70-71).

Threats to external validity, which follow, cover the validity problems involved in interpreting experimental results, the threats to valid generalization of the results to other settings, to other versions of the treatment, or to other measures of the effect:[2]

1. *Interaction effects of testing:* the effect of a pretest in increasing or decreasing the respondent's sensitivity or responsiveness to the experimental

variable, thus making the results obtained for a pretested population unrepresentative of the effects of the experimental variable for the unpretested universe from which the experimental respondents were selected.

2. *Interaction of selection and experimental treatment:* unrepresentative responsiveness of the treated population.

3. *Reactive effects of experimental arrangements:* "artificiality"; conditions making the experimental setting atypical of conditions of regular application of the treatment: "Hawthorne effects."

4. *Multiple-treatment interference:* where multiple treatments are jointly applied, effects atypical of the separate application of the treatments.

5. *Irrelevant responsiveness of measures:* all measures are complex, and all include irrelevant components that may produce apparent effects.

6. *Irrelevant replicability of treatments:* treatments are complex, and replications of them may fail to include those components actually responsible for the effects.

These threats apply equally to true experiments and quasi-experiments. They are particularly relevant to applied experimentation. In the cumulative history of our methodology, this class of threats was first noted as a critique of true experiments involving pretests (Schanck and Goodman, 1939; Solomon, 1949). Such experiments provided a sound basis for generalizing to other *pretested* populations, but the reactions of unpretested populations to the treatment might well be quite different. As a result, there has been an advocacy of true experimental designs obviating the pretest (Campbell, 1957; Schanck and Goodman, 1939; Solomon, 1949) and a search for nonreactive measures (Webb, Campbell, Schwartz, and Sechrest, 1966).

These threats to validity will serve as a background against which we will discuss several research designs particularly appropriate for evaluating specific programs of social amelioration. These are the "interrupted time-series design," the "control series design," "regression discontinuity design," and various "true experiments." The order is from a weak but generally available design to stronger ones that require more administrative foresight and determination.

INTERRUPTED TIME-SERIES DESIGN

By and large, when a political unit initiates a reform it is put into effect across the board, with the total unit being affected. In this setting the only comparison base is the record of previous years. The usual mode of utilization is a casual version of a very weak quasi-experimental design, the one-group pretest-posttest design.

A convenient illustration comes from the 1955 Connecticut crackdown on speeding, which Sociologist H. Laurence Ross and I have been analyzing as a methodological illustration (Campbell and Ross, 1968; Glass, 1968; Ross and Campbell, 1968). After a record high of traffic fatalities in 1955, Governor Abraham Ribicoff instituted an unprecedentedly severe crackdown on speeding. At the end of a year of such enforcement there had been but 284 traffic deaths as compared with 324 the year before. In announcing this the Governor stated, "With the saving of 40 lives in 1956, a reduction of *12.3%* from the 1955 motor vehicle

death toll, we can say that the program is definitely worthwhile." These results are graphed in Figure 5.1, with a deliberate effort to make them look impressive.

In what follows, while we in the end decide that the crackdown had some beneficial effects, we criticize Ribicoff's interpretation of his results, from the point of view of the social scientist's proper standards of evidence. Were the now Senator Ribicoff not the man of stature that he is, this would be most unpolitic, because we could be alienating one of the strongest proponents of social experimentation in our nation. Given his character, however, we may feel sure that he shares our interests both in a progressive program of experimental social amelioration, and in making the most hard-headed evaluation possible of these experiments. Indeed, it was his integrity in using every available means at his disposal as Governor to make sure that the unpopular speeding crackdown was indeed enforced that make these data worth examining at all. But the potentials of this one illustration and our political temptation to substitute for it a less touchy one, point to the political problems that must be faced in experimenting with social reform.

Keeping Figure 5.1 and Ribicoff's statement in mind, let us look at the same data presented as a part of an extended time series in Figure 5.2 and go over the relevant threats to internal validity. First, *History*. Both presentations fail to control for the effects of other potential change agents. For instance, 1956 might have been a particularly dry year, with fewer accidents due to rain or snow. Or

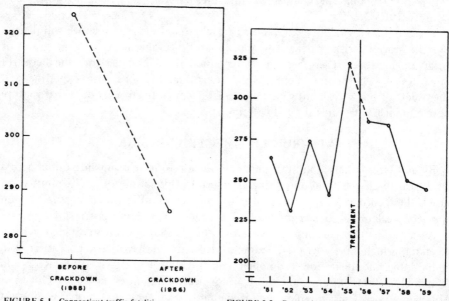

FIGURE 5.1 Connecticut traffic fatalities

FIGURE 5.2 Connecticut traffic fatalities. (Same data as in Figure 1 presented as part of an extended time series.)

there might have been a dramatic increase in use of seat belts, or other safety features. The advocated strategy in quasi-experimentation is not to throw up one's hands and refuse to use the evidence because of this lack of control, but rather to generate by informed criticism appropriate to this specific setting as many *plausible* rival hypotheses as possible, and then to do the supplementary research, as into weather records and safety-belt sales, for example, which would reflect on these rival hypotheses.

Maturation. This is a term coming from criticisms of training studies of children. Applied here to the simple pretest-posttest data of Figure 5.1, it could be the plausible rival hypothesis that death rates were steadily going down year after year (as indeed they are, relative to miles driven or population of automobiles). Here the extended time series has a strong methodological advantage, and rules out this threat to validity. The general trend is inconsistently up prior to the crackdown, and steadily down thereafter.

Instability. Seemingly implicit in the public pronouncement was the assumption that all of the change from 1955 to 1956 was due to the crackdown. There was no recognition of the fact that all time series are unstable even when no treatments are being applied. The degree of this normal instability is the crucial issue, and one of the main advantages of the extended time series is that it samples this instability. The great pretreatment instability now makes the treatment effect look relatively trivial. The 1955-56 shift is less than the gains of both 1954-55 and 1952-53. It is the largest drop in the series, but it exceeds the drops of 1951-52, 1953-54, and 1957-58 by trivial amounts. Thus the unexplained instabilities of the series are such as to make the 1955-56 drop understandable as more of the same. On the other hand, it is noteworthy that after the crackdown there are no year-to-year gains, and in this respect the character of the time series seems definitely to have changed.

The threat of instability is the only threat to which tests of significance are relevant. Box and Tiao (1965) have an elegant Bayesian model for the interrupted time series. Applied by Glass (1968) to our monthly data, with seasonal trends removed, it shows a statistically significant downward shift in the series after the crackdown. But as we shall see, an alternative explanation of at least part of this significant effect exists.

Regression. In true experiments the treatment is applied independently of the prior state of the units. In natural experiments exposure to treatment is often a cosymptom of the treated group's condition. The treatment is apt to be an *effect* rather than, or in addition to being, a cause. Psychotherapy is such a cosymptom treatment, as is any other in which the treated group is self-selected or assigned on the basis of need. These all present special problems of interpretation, of which the present illustration provides one type.

The selection-regression plausible rival hypothesis works this way: Given that the fatality rate has some degree of unreliability, then a subsample selected for its extremity in 1955 would on the average, merely as a reflection of that unreliability, be less extreme in 1956. Has there been selection for extremity in applying this treatment? Probably yes. Of all Connecticut fatality years, the most likely time for a crackdown would be after an exceptionally high year. If the time series showed instability, the subsequent year would on the average be less, *purely as a function*

of that instability. Regression artifacts are probably the most recurrent form of self-deception in the experimental social reform literature. It is hard to make them intuitively obvious. Let us try again. Take any time series with variability, including one generated of pure error. Move along it as in a time dimension. Pick a point that is the "highest so far." Look then at the next point. On the average this next point will be lower, or nearer the general trend.

In our present setting the most striking shift in the whole series is the upward shift just prior to the crackdown. It is highly probable that this caused the crackdown, rather than, or in addition to, the crackdown causing the 1956 drop. At least part of the 1956 drop is an artifact of the 1955 extremity. While in principle the degree of expected regression can be computed from the autocorrelation of the series, we lack here an extended-enough body of data to do this with any confidence.

Advice to administrators who want to do genuine reality-testing must include attention to this problem, and it will be a very hard problem to surmount. The most general advice would be to work on chronic problems of a persistent urgency or extremity, rather than reacting to momentary extremes. The administrator should look at the pretreatment time series to judge whether or not instability plus momentary extremity will explain away his program gains. If it will, he should schedule the treatment for a year or two later, so that his decision is more independent of the one year's extremity. (The selection biases remaining under such a procedure need further examination.)

In giving advice to the *experimental* administrator, one is also inevitably giving advice to those *trapped* administrators whose political predicament requires a favorable outcome whether valid or not. To such trapped administrators the advice is pick the very worst year, and the very worst social unit. If there is inherent instability, there is no where to go but up, for the average case at least.

Two other threats to internal validity need discussion in regard to this design. By *testing* we typically have in mind the condition under which a test of attitude, ability, or personality is itself a change agent, persuading, informing, practicing, or otherwise setting processes of change in action. No artificially introduced testing procedures are involved here. However, for the simple before-and-after design of Figure 1, if the pretest were the first data collection of its kind ever publicized, this publicity in itself might produce a reduction in traffic deaths which would have taken place even without a speeding crackdown. Many traffic safety programs assume this. The longer time-series evidence reassures us on this only to the extent that we can assume that the figures had been published each year with equivalent emphasis.[3]

Instrumentation changes are not a likely flaw in this instance, but would be if recording practices and institutional responsibility had shifted simultaneously with the crackdown. Probably in a case like this it is better to use raw frequencies rather than indices whose correction parameters are subject to periodic revision. Thus per capita rates are subject to periodic jumps as new census figures become available correcting old extrapolations. Analogously, a change in the miles per gallon assumed in estimating traffic mileage for mileage-based mortality rates might explain a shift. Such biases can of course work to disguise a true effect. Almost

certainly, Ribicoff's crackdown reduced traffic speed (Campbell and Ross, 1968). Such a decrease in speed increases the miles per gallon actually obtained, producing a concomitant drop in the estimate of miles driven, which would appear as an inflation of the estimate of mileage-based traffic fatalities if the same fixed approximation to actual miles per gallon were used, as it undoubtedly would be.

The "new broom" that introduces abrupt changes of policy is apt to reform the record keeping too, and thus confound reform treatments with instrumentation change. The ideal experimental administrator will, if possible, avoid doing this. He will prefer to keep comparable a partially imperfect measuring system rather than lose comparability altogether. The politics of the situation do not always make this possible, however. Consider, as an experimental reform, Orlando Wilson's reorganization of the police system in Chicago. Figure 5.3 shows his impact on petty larceny in Chicago—a striking *increase!* Wilson, of course, called this shot in advance, one aspect of his reform being a reform in the bookkeeping. (Note in the pre-Wilson records the suspicious absence of the expected upward secular trend.) In this situation Wilson had no choice. Had he left the record keeping as it was, for the purposes of better experimental design, his resentful patrolmen would have clobbered him with a crime wave by deliberately starting to record the many complaints that had not been getting into the books.[4]

Those who advocate the use of archival measures as social indicators (Bauer, 1966; Gross, 1966, 1967; Kaysen, 1967; Webb et al., 1966) must face up not only to their high degree of chaotic error and systematic bias, but also to the politically motivated changes in record keeping that will follow upon their public use as social indicators (Etzioni and Lehman, 1967). Not all measures are equally susceptible. In Figure 5.4, Orlando Wilson's effect on homicides seems negligible one way or the other.

Of the threats to external validity, the one most relevant to social experimentation is *Irrelevant Responsiveness of Measures.* This seems best discussed in terms of

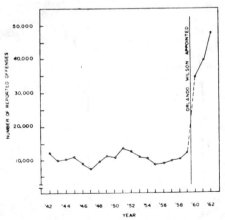

FIGURE 5.3   Number of reported larcenies under $50 in Chicago. Illinois, from 1942 to 1962 (data from *Uniform Crime Reports for the United States*, 1942-62).

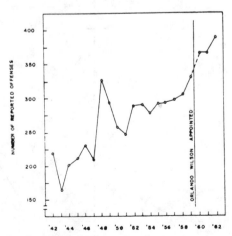

FIGURE 5.4   Number of reported murders and nonnegligent manslaughters in Chicago, Illinois, from 1942 to 1962 (data from *Uniform Crime Reports for the United States*, 1942-62).

the problem of generalizing from indicator to indicator or in terms of the imperfect validity of all measures that is only to be overcome by the use of multiple measures of independent imperfection (Campbell and Fiske, 1959; Webb et al., 1966).

For treatments on any given problem within any given governmental or business subunit, there will usually be something of a governmental monopoly on reform. Even though different divisions may optimally be trying different reforms, within each division there will usually be only one reform on a given problem going on at a time. But for measures of effect this need not and should not be the case. The administrative machinery should itself make multiple measures of potential benefits and of unwanted side effects. In addition, the loyal opposition should be allowed to add still other indicators, with the political process and adversary argument challenging both validity and relative importance, with social science methodologists testifying for both parties, and with the basic records kept public and under bipartisan audit (as are voting records under optimal conditions). This competitive scrutiny is indeed the main source of objectivity in sciences (Polanyi, 1966, 1967; Popper, 1963) and epitomizes an ideal of democratic practice in both judicial and legislative procedures.

The next few figures return again to the Connecticut crackdown on speeding and look to some other measures of effect. They are relevant to the confirming that there was indeed a crackdown, and to the issue of side effects. They also provide the methodological comfort of assuring us that in some cases the interrupted time-series design can provide clear-cut evidence of effect. Figure 5.5 shows the

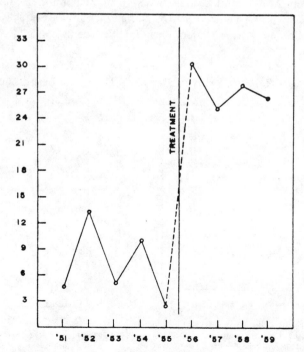

FIGURE 5.5   Suspensions of licenses for speeding, as a percentage of all suspensions.

jump in suspensions of licenses for speeding—evidence that severe punishment was abruptly instituted. Again a note to experimental administrators: with this weak design, *it is only abrupt and decisive changes that we have any chance of evaluating.* A gradually introduced reform will be indistinguishable from the background of secular change, from the net effect of the innumerable change agents continually impinging.

We would want intermediate evidence that traffic speed was modified. A sampling each year of a few hundred five-minute highway movies (random as to location and time) could have provided this at a moderate cost, but they were not collected. Of the public records available, perhaps the data of Figure 5.6, showing a reduction in speeding violations, indicate a reduction in traffic speed. But the effects on the legal system were complex, and in part undesirable. Driving with a suspended license markedly increased (Figure 5.7), at least in the biased sample of those arrested. Presumably because of the harshness of the punishment if guilty, judges may have become more lenient (Figure 5.8) although this effect is of marginal significance.

The relevance of indicators for the social problems we wish to cure must be kept continually in focus. The social indicators approach will tend to make the indicators themselves the goal of social action, rather than the social problems they but imperfectly indicate. There are apt to be tendencies to legislate changes in the indicators per se rather than changes in the social problems.

To illustrate the problem of the irrelevant responsiveness of measures, Figure 5.9 shows a result of the 1900 change in divorce law in Germany. In a recent reanalysis of the data with the Box and Tiao (1965) statistic, Glass (Glass, Tiao, and Maguire, 1971) has found the change highly significant, in contrast to earlier statistical analyses (Rheinstein, 1959; Wolf, Lüke, and Hax, 1959). But Rheinstein's emphasis would still be relevant: This indicator change indicates no likely improvement in marital harmony, or even in marital stability. Rather than reducing them, the legal change has made the divorce rate a less valid indicator of marital discord and separation than it had been earlier (see also Etzioni and Lehman, 1967).

CONTROL SERIES DESIGN

The interrupted time-series design as discussed so far is available for those settings in which no control group is possible, in which the total governmental unit has received the experimental treatment, the social reform measure. In the general program of quasi-experimental design, we argue the great advantage of untreated comparison groups even where these cannot be assigned at random. The most common of such designs is the nonequivalent control-group pretest-posttest design, in which for each of two natural groups, one of which receives the treatment, a pretest and posttest measure is taken. If the traditional mistaken practice is avoided of matching on pretest scores (with resultant regression artifacts), this design provides a useful control over those aspects of history, maturation, and test-retest effects shared by both groups. But it does not control for the plausible rival hypothesis of *selection-maturation interaction*—that is, the hypothesis that the selection differences in the natural aggregations involve not only differences in mean level, but differences in maturation rate.

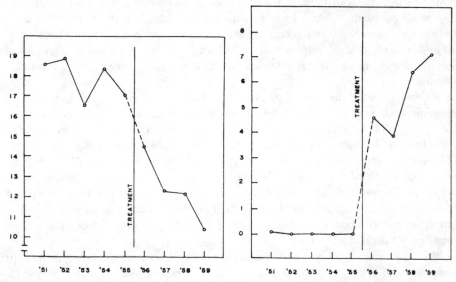

FIGURE 5.6   Speeding violations, as a percentage of all traffic violations.

FIGURE 5.7   Arrested while driving with a suspended license. as a percentage of suspensions.

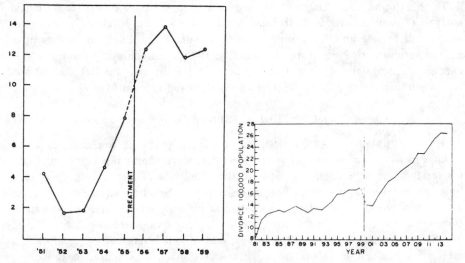

FIGURE 5.8   Percentage of speeding violations judged not
guilty.

FIGURE 5.9   Divorce rate for German Empire, 1881-1914

This point can be illustrated in terms of the traditional quasi-experimental design problem of the effects of Latin on English vocabulary (Campbell, 1963). In the hypothetical data of Figure 5.10B, two alternative interpretations remain open. Latin may have had effect, for those taking Latin gained more than those not. But, on the other hand, those students taking Latin may have a greater annual rate of vocabulary growth that would manifest itself whether or not they took Latin. Extending this common design into two time series provides relevant evidence, as comparison of the two alternative outcomes of Figure 5.10C and 5.10D shows. Thus approaching quasi-experimental design from either improving the nonequivalent control-group design or from improving the interrupted time-series design, we arrive at the control series design. Figure 5.11 shows this for the Connecticut speeding crackdown, adding evidence from the fatality rates of neighboring states. Here the data are presented as population-based fatality rates so as to make the two series of comparable magnitude.

The control series design of Figure 5.11 shows that downward trends were available in the other states for 1955-56 as due to history and maturation, that is, due to shared secular trends, weather, automotive safety features, etc. But the data also show a general trend for Connecticut to rise relatively closer to the other states

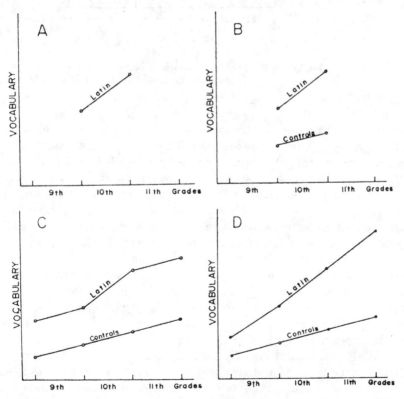

FIGURE 5.10   Forms of quasi-experimental analysis for the effect of specific course work, including control series design.

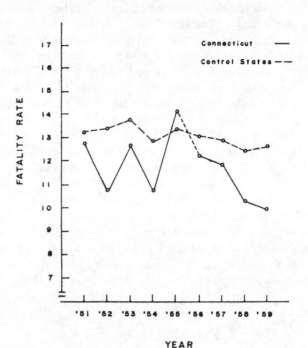

FIGURE 5.11 Control series design comparing Connecticut fatalities with those of four comparable states.

prior to 1955, and to steadily drop more rapidly than other states from 1956 on. Glass (1968) has used our monthly data for Connecticut and the control states to generate a monthly difference score, and this too shows a significant shift in trend in the Box and Tiao (1965) statistic. Impressed particularly by the 1957, 1958, and 1959 trend, we are willing to conclude that the crackdown had some effect, over and above the undeniable pseudo-effects of regression (Campbell and Ross, 1968).

The advantages of the control series design point to the advantages for social experimentation of a social system allowing subunit diversity. Our ability to estimate the effects of the speeding crackdown, Rose's (1952) and Stieber (1949) ability to estimate the effects on strikes of compulsory arbitration laws, and Simon's (1966) ability to estimate the price elasticity of liquor were made possible because the changes were not being put into effect in all states simultaneously, because they were matters of state legislation rather than national. I do not want to appear to justify on these grounds the wasteful and unjust diversity of laws and enforcement practices from state to state. But I would strongly advocate that social engineers make use of this diversity while it remains available, and plan cooperatively their changes in administrative policy and in record keeping so as to provide optimal experimental inference. More important is the recommendation that, for those aspects of social reform handled by the central government, a purposeful diversity of implementation be envisaged so that experimental and control groups

be available for analysis. Properly planned, these can approach true experiments, better than the casual and ad hoc comparison groups now available. But without such fundamental planning, uniform central control can reduce the present possibilities of reality testing, that is, of true social experimentation. In the same spirit, decentralization of decision making, both within large government and within private monopolies, can provide a useful competition for both efficiency and innovation, reflected in a multiplicity of indicators.

THE BRITISH BREATHALYSER CRACKDOWN

One further illustration of The Interrupted Time Series and the Control Series will be provided. The variety of illustrations so far have each illustrated some methodological point, and have thus ended up as "bad examples." To provide a "good example," an instance which survives methodological critique as a valid illustration of a successful reform, data from the British Road Safety Act of 1967 are provided in Figure 5.12 (Ross, Campbell, and Glass, 1970).

The data on a weekly-hours basis are only available for a composite category of fatalities plus serious injuries, and Figure 11A therefore uses this composite for all three bodies of data. "Weekend nights" comprises Friday and Saturday nights from 10:00 p.m. to 4:00 a.m. Here, as expected, the crackdown is most dramatically effective, producing initially more than a 40% drop, leveling off at perhaps 30%, although this involves dubious extrapolations in the absence of some control comparison to indicate what the trend over the years might have been without the crackdown. In this British case, no comparison state with comparable traffic conditions or drinking laws was available. But controls need not always be separate groups of persons, they may also be separate samples of times or stimulus materials (Campbell and Stanley, 1966: 43-47). A cigarette company may use the sales of its main competitor as a control comparison to evaluate a new advertising campaign. One should search around for the most nearly appropriate control comparison. For the Breathalyser crackdown, commuting hours when pubs had been long closed seemed ideal. (The "commuting hours" figures come from 7:00 a.m. to 10:00 a.m. and 4:00 p.m. to 5:00 p.m. Pubs are open for lunch from 12:00 to 2:00 or 2:30, and open again at 5:00 p.m.)

These commuting hours data convincingly show no effect, but are too unstable to help much with estimating the long term effects. They show a different annual cycle than do the weekend nights or the overall figures, and do not go back far enough to provide an adequate base for estimating this annual cycle with precision.

The use of a highly judgmental category such as "serious injuries" provides an opportunity for pseudo effects due to a shift in the classifiers' standards. The overall figures are available separately for fatalities, and these show a highly significant effect as strong as that found for the serious injury category or the composite shown in Figure 5.12.

More details and the methodological problems are considered in our fuller presentation (Ross, Campbell, and Glass, 1970). One rule for the use of this design needs emphasizing. The interrupted Time Series can only provide clear evidence of effect where the reform is introduced with a vigorous abruptness. A

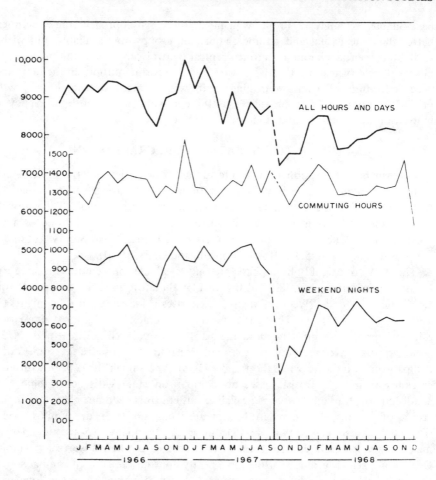

FIGURE 5.12 British traffic fatalities plus serious injuries,
before and after the Breathalyser crackdown
of October 1967 (seasonally adjusted.)

gradually introduced reform has little chance of being distinguished from shifts in secular trends or from the cumulative effect of the many other influences imping- ing during a prolonged period of introduction. In the Breathalyser crackdown, an intense publicity campaign naming the specific starting date preceded the actual crackdown. Although the impact seems primarily due to publicity and fear rather than an actual increase of arrests, an abrupt initiation date was achieved. Had the enforcement effort changed at the moment the act had passed, with public awareness being built up by subsequent publicity, the resulting data series would have been essentially uninterpretable.

REGRESSION DISCONTINUITY DESIGN

We shift now to social ameliorations that are in short supply, and that therefore cannot be given to all individuals. Such scarcity is inevitable under many circum-

stances, and can make possible an evaluation of effects that would otherwise be impossible. Consider the heroic Salk poliomyelitis vaccine trials in which some children were given the vaccine while others were given an inert saline placebo injection—and in which many more of these placebo controls would die than would have if they had been given the vaccine. Creation of these placebo controls would have been morally, psychologically, and socially impossible had there been enough vaccine for all. As it was, due to the scarcity, most children that year had to go without the vaccine anyway. The creation of experimental and control groups was the highly moral allocation of that scarcity so as to enable us to learn the true efficacy of the supposed good. The usual medical practice of introducing new cures on a so-called trial basis in general medical practice makes evaluation impossible by confounding prior status with treatment, that is, giving the drug to the most needy or most hopeless. It has the further social bias of giving the supposed benefit to those most assiduous in keeping their medical needs in the attention of the medical profession, that is, the upper and upper-middle classes. The political stance further-ing social experimentation here is the recognition of randomization as the most democratic and moral means of allocating scarce resources (and scarce hazardous duties), plus the moral imperative to further utilize the randomization so that society may indeed learn true value of the supposed boon. This is the ideology that makes possible "true experiments" in a large class of social reforms.

But if randomization is not politically feasible or morally justifiable in a given setting, there is a powerful quasi-experimental design available that allows the scarce good to be given to the most needy or the most deserving. This is the regression discontinuity design. All it requires is strict and orderly attention to the priority dimension. The design originated through an advocacy of a tie-breaking experiment to measure the effects of receiving a fellowship (Thistlethwaite and Campbell, 1960), and it seems easiest to explain it in that light. Consider as in Figure 5.13, pre-award ability-and-merit dimension, which would have some rela-tion to later success in life (finishing college, earnings 10 years later, etc.). Those higher on the premeasure are most deserving and receive the award. They do better in later life, but does the award have an effect? It is normally impossible to say

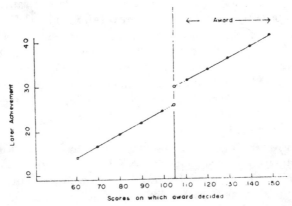

FIGURE 5.13   Tie-breaking experiment and regression discontinuity analysis.

because they would have done better in later life anyway. Full randomization of the award was impossible given the stated intention to reward merit and ability. But it might be possible to take a narrow band of ability at the cutting point, to regard all of these persons as tied, and to assign half of them to awards, half to no awards, by means of a tie-breaking randomization.

The tie-breaking rationale is still worth doing. but in considering that design it became obvious that, if the regression of premeasure on later effects were reasonably orderly, one should be able to extrapolate to the results of the tie-breaking experiment by plotting the regression of posttest on pretest separately for those in the award and nonaward regions. If there is no significant difference for these at the decision-point intercept, then the tie-breaking experiment should show no difference. In cases where the tie breakers would show an effect, there should be an abrupt discontinuity in the regression line. Such a discontinuity cannot be explained away by the normal regression of the posttest on pretest, for this normal regression, as extensively sampled within the nonaward area and within the award area, provides no such expectation.

Figure 5.13 presents, in terms of column means, an instance in which higher pretest scores would have led to higher posttest scores even without the treatment, and in which there is in addition a substantial treatment effect. Figure 5.14 shows a series of paired outcomes, those on the left to be interpreted as no effect, those in the center and on the right as effect. Note some particular cases. In instances of granting opportunity on the basis of merit, like 5.14a and 5.14b (and Figure 5.13), neglect of the background regression of pretest on posttest leads to optimistic pseudo-effects: in Figure 5.14a, those receiving the award do do better in later life, though not really because of the award. But in social ameliorative efforts, the setting is more apt to be like Figure 5.14d and e, where neglect of the background regression is apt to make the program look deleterious if no effect, or ineffective if there is a real effect.

The design will of course work just as well or better if the award dimension and the decision base, the pretest measure, are unrelated to the posttest dimension, if it is irrelevant or unfair, as instanced in Figure 5.14a, h, and i. In such cases the decision base is the functional equivalent of randomization. Negative background relationships are obviously possible, as in Figure 5.14j, k, and l. In Figure 5.14m, n, and o are included to emphasize that it is a jump in intercept at the cutting point that shows effect, and that differences in slope without differences at the cutting point are not acceptable as evidences of effect. This becomes more obvious if we remember that in cases like m, a tie-breaking randomization experiment would have shown no difference. Curvilinear background relationships, as in Figure 5.14p, q, and r, will provide added obstacles to clear inference in many instances, where sampling error could make Figure 5.14p look like 5.14b.

As further illustration, Figure 5.15 provides computer-simulated data, showing individual observations and fitted regression lines, in a fuller version of the no-effect outcome of Figure 5.14a. Figure 5.16 shows an outcome with effect. These have been generated[5] by assigning to each individual a weighted normal random number as a "true score," to which is added a weighted independent "error" to generate the

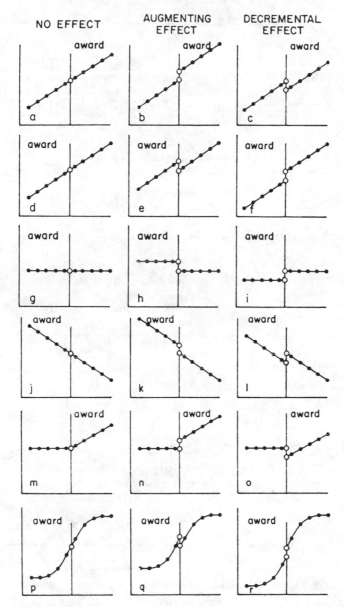

FIGURE 5.14   Illustrative outcomes of regression discontinuity analyses.

"pretest." The "true score" plus another independent "error" produces the "post-test" in no-effect cases such as Figure 5.15. In treatment-effect simulations, as in Figure 5.16, there are added into the posttest "effects points" for all "treated" cases, that is, those above the cutting point on the pretest score.

This design could be used in a number of settings. Consider Job Training Corps applicants, in larger number than the program can accommodate, with eligibility

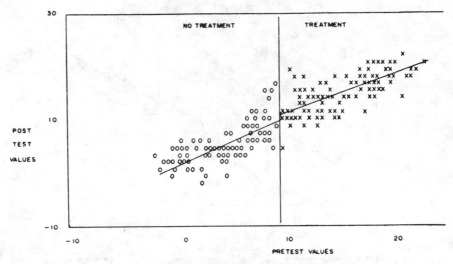

FIGURE 5.15   Regression discontinuity design: No effect.

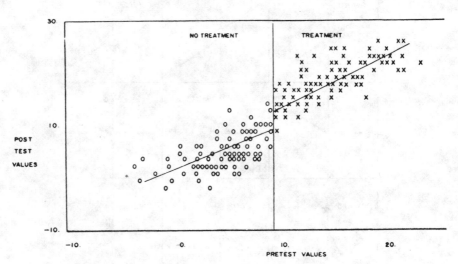

FIGURE 5.16   Regression discontinuity design: Genuine effect.

determined by need. The setting would be as in Figure 5.15d and e. The base-line decision dimension could be per capita family income, with those at below the cutoff getting training. The outcome dimension could be the amount of withholding tax withheld two years later, or the percentage drawing unemployment insurance, these follow-up figures being provided from the National Data Bank in response to categorized social security numbers fed in, without individual anonymity being breached, without any real invasion of privacy—by the technique of Mutually Insulated Data Banks. While the plotted points could be named, there is

no need that they be named. In a classic field experiment on tax compliance, Richard Schwartz and the Bureau of Internal Revenue have managed to put together sets of personally identified interviews and tax-return data so that statistical analyses such as these could be done, without the separate custodians of either interview or tax returns learning the corresponding data for specific persons (Schwartz and Orleans, 1967; see also Schwartz and Skolnick, 1963).

Applied to the Job Corps illustration, it would work as follows: Separate lists of Job Corps applicants (with social security numbers) would be prepared for every class interval on per capita family income. To each of these lists an alphabetical designation would be assigned at random. (Thus the $10.00 per week list might be labeled M; $11.00, C; $12.00, Z; $13.00, Q; $14.00, N, etc.) These lists would be sent to Internal Revenue, without the Internal Revenue personnel being able to learn anything interpretable about their traineeship status or family income. The Internal Revenue statisticians would locate the withholding tax collected for each person on each list, but would not return the data in that form. Instead, for each list, only the withholding tax amounts would be listed, and these in a newly randomized order. These would be returned to Job Corps research, who could use them to plot a graph like Figures 5.10 & 5.11, and do the appropriate statistical analyses by retranslating the alphabetical symbols into meaningful, base-line values. But within any list, they would be unable to learn which value belonged to which person. (To ensure this effective anonymity, it could be specified that no lists shorter than 100 persons be used, the base-line intervals being expanded if necessary to achieve this.) Manniche and Hayes (1957) have spelled out how a broker can be used in a two-staged matching of doubly coded data. Kaysen (1967) and Sawyer and Schechter (1968) have wise discussions of the more general problem.

What is required of the administrator of a scarce ameliorative commodity to use this design? Most essential is a sharp cutoff point on a decision-criterion dimension, on which several other qualitatively similar analytic cutoffs can be made both above and below the award cut. Let me explain this better by explaining why National Merit scholarships were unable to use the design for their actual fellowship decision (although it has been used for their Certificate of Merit). In their operation, diverse committees make small numbers of award decisions by considering a group of candidates and then picking from them the N best to which to award the N fellowships allocated them. This provides one cutting point on an unspecified pooled decision base, but fails to provide analogous potential cutting points above and below. What could be done is for each committee to collectively rank its group of 20 or so candidates. The top N would then receive the award. Pooling cases across committees, cases could be classified according to number of ranks above and below the cutting point, these other ranks being analogous to the award-nonaward cutting point as far as regression onto posttreatment measures was concerned. Such group ranking would be costly of committee time. An equally good procedure, if committees agreed, would be to have each member, after full discussion and freedom to revise, give each candidate a grade, A+, A, A-, B+, B, etc., and to award the fellowships to the N candidates averaging best on these ratings, with no revisions allowed after the averaging process. These ranking or rating units, even if not comparable from committee to committee in range of talent, in number

of persons ranked, or in cutting point, could be pooled without bias as far as a regression discontinuity is concerned, for that range of units above and below the cutting point in which all committees were represented.

It is the dimensionality and sharpness of the decision criterion that is at issue, not its components or validity. The ratings could be based upon nepotism, whimsey, and superstition and still serve. As has been stated, if the decision criterion is utterly invalid we approach the pure randomness of a true experiment. Thus the weakness of subjective committee decisions is not their subjectivity, but the fact that they provide only the one cutting point on their net subjective dimension. Even in the form of average ratings the recommended procedures probably represent some slight increase in committee work load. But this could be justified to the decision committees by the fact that through refusals, etc., it cannot be known at the time of the committee meeting the exact number to whom the fellowship can be offered. Other costs at the planning time are likewise minimal. The primary additional burden is in keeping as good records on the nonawardees as on the awardees. Thus at a low cost, an experimental administrator can lay the groundwork for later scientific follow-ups, the budgets for which need not yet be in sight.

Our present situation is more apt to be one where our pretreatment measures, aptitude measures, reference ratings, etc., can be combined via multiple correlation into an index that correlates highly but not perfectly with the award decision. For this dimension there is a fuzzy cutoff point. Can the design be used in this case? Probably not. Figure 5.17 shows the pseudo-effect possible if the award decision contributes any valid variance to the quantified pretest evidence, as it usually will. The award regression rides above the nonaward regression just because of that valid variance in this simulated case, there being no true award effect at all. (In simulating this case, the award decision has been based upon a composite of true score plus an independent award error.) Figure 5.18 shows a fuzzy cutting point plus a genuine award effect.[6] The recommendation to the administrator is clear:

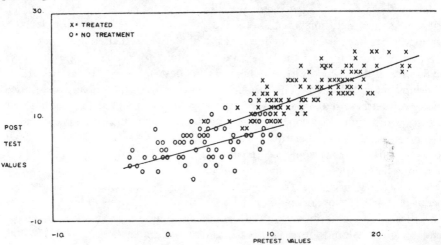

FIGURE 5.17 Regression discontinuity design: Fuzzy cutting point, pseudo treatment effect only.

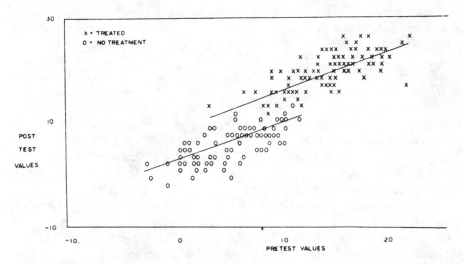

FIGURE 5.18   Regression discontinuity design: Fuzzy cutting point, with real treatment plus pseudo treatment effects.

aim for a sharp cutting point on a quantified decision criterion. If there are complex rules for eligibility, only one of which is quantified, seek out for follow-up that subset of persons for whom the quantitative dimension was determinate. If political patronage necessitates some decisions inconsistent with a sharp cutoff, record these cases under the heading "qualitative decision rule" and keep them out of your experimental analysis.

Almost all of our ameliorative programs designed for the disadvantaged could be studied via this design, and so too some major governmental actions affecting the lives of citizens in ways we do not think of as experimental. For example, for a considerable period, quantitative test scores have been used to call up for military service or reject as unfit at the lower ability range. If these cutting points, test scores, names, and social security numbers have been recorded for a number of steps both above and below the cutting point, we could make elegant studies of the effect of military service on later withholding taxes, mortality, number of dependents, etc.

This illustration points to one of the threats to external validity of this design, or of the tie-breaking experiment. The effect of the treatment has only been studied for that narrow range of talent near the cutting point, and generalization of the effects of military service, for example, from this low ability level to the careers of the most able would be hazardous in the extreme. But in the draft laws and the requirements of the military services there may be other sharp cutting points on a quantitative criterion that could also be used. For example, those over 6 feet 6 inches are excluded from service. Imagine a five-year-later follow-up of draftees grouped by inch in the 6 feet 1 inch to 6 feet 5 inches range, and a group of their counterparts who would have been drafted except for their heights, 6 feet 6 inches

to 6 feet 10 inches. (The fact that the other grounds of deferment might not have been examined by the draft board would be a problem here, but probably not insurmountable.) That we should not expect height in this range to have any relation to later-life variables is not at all a weakness of this design, and if we have indeed a subpopulation for which there is a sharp numerical cutting point, an internally valid measure of effects would result. Deferment under the present system is an unquantified committee decision. But just as the sense of justice of United States soldiers was quantified through paired comparisons of cases into an acceptable Demobilization Points system at the end of World War II (Guttman, 1946; Stouffer, 1949), so a quantified composite index of deferment priority could be achieved and applied as uniform justice across the nation, providing another numerical cutting point.

In addition to the National Data Bank type of indicators, there will be occasions in which new data collections as by interview or questionnaire are needed. For these there is the special problem of uneven cooperation that would be classified as instrumentation error. In our traditional mode of thinking, completeness of description is valued more highly than comparability. Thus if, in a fellowship study, a follow-up mailed out from the fellowship office would bring a higher return from past winners, this might seem desirable even if the nonawardees' rate of response was much lower. From the point of view of quasi-experimentation, however, it would be better to use an independent survey agency and a disguised purpose, achieving equally low response rates from both awardees and nonawardees, and avoiding a regression discontinuity in cooperation rate that might be misinterpreted as a discontinuity in more important effects.

RANDOMIZED CONTROL GROUP EXPERIMENTS

Experiments with randomization tend to be limited to the laboratory and agricultural experiment station. But this certainly need not be so. The randomization unit may be persons, families, precincts, or larger administrative units. For statistical purposes the randomization units should be numerous, and hence ideally small. But for reasons of external validity, including reactive arrangements, the randomization units should be selected on the basis of the units of administrative access. Where policies are administered through individual client contacts, randomization at the person level may be often inconspicuously achieved, with the clients unaware that different ones of them are getting different treatments. But for most social reforms, larger administrative units will be involved, such as classrooms, schools, cities, counties, or states. We need to develop the political postures and ideologies that make randomization at these levels possible.

"Pilot project" is a useful term already in our political vocabulary. It designates a trial program that, if it works, will be spread to other areas. By modifying actual practice in this regard, without going outside of the popular understanding of the term, a valuable experimental ideology could be developed. How are areas selected for pilot projects? If the public worries about this, it probably assumes a lobbying process in which the greater needs of some areas are only one consideration, political power and expediency being others. Without violating the public tolerance

or intent, one could probably devise a system in which the usual lobbying decided upon the areas eligible for a formal public lottery that would make final choices between matched pairs. Such decision procedures as the drawing of lots have had a justly esteemed position since time immemorial (e.g., Aubert, 1959). At the present time, record keeping for pilot projects tends to be limited to the experimental group only. In the experimental ideology, comparable data would be collected on designated controls. (There are of course exceptions, as in the heroic Public Health Service fluoridation experiments, in which the teeth of Oak Park children were examined year after year as controls for the Evanston experimentals [Blayney and Hill, 1967].)

Another general political stance making possible experimental social ameliora-tion is that of *staged innovation.* Even though by intent a new reform is to be put into effect in all units, the logistics of the situation usually dictate that simul-taneous introduction is not possible. What results is a haphazard sequence of convenience. Under the program of staged innovation, the introduction of the program would be deliberately spread out, and those units selected to be first and last would be randomly assigned (perhaps randomization from matched pairs), so that during the transition period the first recipients could be analyzed as experi-mental units, the last recipients as controls. A third ideology making possible true experiments has already been discussed: randomization as the democratic means of allocating scarce resources.

This article will not give true experimentation equal space with quasi-experimentation only because excellent discussions of, and statistical consultation on, true experimentation are readily available. True experiments should almost always be preferred to quasi-experiments where both are available. Only occa-sionally are the threats to external validity so much greater for the true experiment that one would prefer a quasi-experiment. The uneven allocation of space here should not be read as indicating otherwise.

MORE ADVICE FOR TRAPPED ADMINISTRATORS

But the competition is not really between the fairly interpretable quasi-experiments here reviewed and "true" experiments. Both stand together as rare excellencies in contrast with a morass of obfuscation and self-deception. Both to emphasize this contrast, and again as guidelines for the benefit of those trapped administrators whose political predicament will not allow the risk of failure, some of these alternatives should be mentioned.

Grateful Testimonials

Human courtesy and gratitude being what it is, the most dependable means of assuring a favorable evaluation is to use voluntary testimonials from those who have had the treatment. If the spontaneously produced testimonials are in short supply, these should be solicited from the recipients with whom the program is still in contact. The rosy glow resulting is analogous to the professor's impression of his teaching success when it is based solely upon the comments of those students who come up and talk with him after class. In many programs, as in psychotherapy, the

recipient, as well as the agency, has devoted much time and effort to the program and it is dissonance reducing for himself, as well as common courtesy to his therapist, to report improvement. These grateful testimonials can come in the language of letters and conversation, or be framed as answers to multiple-item "tests" in which a recurrent theme of "I am sick," "I am well," "I am happy," "I am sad" recurs. Probably the testimonials will be more favorable as: (a) the more the evaluative meaning of the response measure is clear to the recipient—it is completely clear in most personality, adjustment, morale, and attitude tests; (b) the more directly the recipient is identified by name with his answer; (c) the more the recipient gives the answer directly to the therapist or agent of reform; (d) the more the agent will continue to be influential in the recipient's life in the future; (e) the more the answers deal with feelings and evaluations rather than with verifiable facts; and (f) the more the recipients participating in the evaluation are a small and self-selected or agent-selected subset of all recipients. Properly designed, the grateful testimonial method can involve pretests as well as posttests, and randomized control groups as well as experimentals, for there are usually no placebo treatments, and the recipients know when they have had the boon.

Confounding Selection and Treatment

Another dependable tactic bound to give favorable outcomes is to confound selection and treatment, so that in the published comparison those receiving the treatment are also the more able and well placed. The often-cited evidence of the dollar value of a college education is of this nature—all careful studies show that most of the effect, and of the superior effect of superior colleges, is explainable in terms of superior talents and family connections, rather than in terms of what is learned or even the prestige of the degree. Matching techniques and statistical partialings generally undermatch and do not fully control for the selection differences—they introduce regression artifacts confusable as treatment effects.

There are two types of situations that must be distinguished. First, there are those treatments that are given to the most promising, treatments like a college education which are regularly given to those who need it least. For these, the later concomitants of the grounds of selection operate in the same direction as the treatment: those most likely to achieve anyway get into the college most likely to produce later achievement. For these settings, the trapped administrator should use the pooled mean of all those treated, comparing it with the mean of all untreated, although in this setting almost any comparison an administrator might hit upon would be biased in his favor.

At the other end of the talent continuum are those remedial treatments given to those who need it most. Here the later concomitants of the grounds of selection are poorer success. In the Job Training Corps example, casual comparisons of the later unemployment rate of those who received the training with those who did not are in general biased against showing an advantage to the training. This seems to have been the case in the major Head Start evaluation (Campbell and Erlebacher, 1970). Here the trapped administrator must be careful to seek out those few special comparisons biasing selection in his favor. For training programs such as Operation Head Start and tutoring programs, a useful solution is to compare the later success

of those who completed the training program with those who were invited but never showed plus those who came a few times and dropped out. By regarding only those who complete the program as "trained" and using the others as controls, one is selecting for conscientiousness, stable and supporting family backgrounds, enjoyment of the training activity, ability, determination to get ahead in the world—all factors promising well for future achievement even if the remedial program is valueless. To apply this tactic effectively in the Job Training Corps, one might have to eliminate from the so-called control group all those who quit the training program because they had found a job—but this would seem a reasonable practice and would not blemish the reception of a glowing progress report.

These are but two more samples of well-tried modes of analysis for the trapped administrator who cannot afford an honest evaluation of the social reform he directs. They remind us again that we must help create a political climate that demands more rigorous and less self-deceptive reality testing. We must provide political stances that permit true experiments, or good quasi-experiments. Of the several suggestions toward this end that are contained in this article, the most important is probably the initial theme: Administrators and parties must advocate the importance of the problem rather than the importance of the answer. They must advocate experimental sequences of reforms, rather than one certain cure-all, advocating Reform A with Alternative B available to try next should an honest evaluation of A prove it worthless or harmful.

MULTIPLE REPLICATION IN ENACTMENT

Too many social scientists expect single experiments to settle issues once and for all. This may be a mistaken generalization from the history of great crucial experiments in physics and chemistry. In actuality the significant experiments in the physical sciences are replicated thousands of times, not only in deliberate replication efforts, but.also as inevitable incidentals in successive experimentation and in utilizations of those many measurement devices (such as the galvanometer) that in their own operation embody the principles of classic experiments. Because we social scientists have less ability to achieve "experimental isolation," because we have good reason to expect our treatment effects to interact significantly with a wide variety of social factors many of which we have not yet mapped, we have much greater needs for replication experiments than do the physical sciences.

The implications are clear. We should not only do hard-headed reality testing in the initial pilot testing and choosing of which reform to make general law; but once it has been decided that the reform is to be adopted as standard practice in all administrative units, we should experimentally evaluate it in each of its implementations (Campbell, 1967).

CONCLUSIONS

Trapped administrators have so committed themselves in advance to the efficacy of the reform that they cannot afford honest evaluation. For them, favorably biased analyses are recommended, including capitalizing on regression, grateful testimonials, and confounding selection and treatment. *Experimental*˙*administra-*

tors have justified the reform on the basis of the importance of the problem, not the certainty of their answer, and are committed to going on to other potential solutions if the one first tried fails. They are therefore not threatened by a hard-headed analysis of the reform. For such, proper administrative decisions can lay the base for useful experimental or quasi-experimental analyses. Through the ideology of allocating scarce resources by lottery, through the use of staged innovation, and through the pilot project, true experiments with randomly assigned control groups can be achieved. If the reform must be introduced across the board, the interrupted time-series design is available. If there are similar units under independent administration, a control series design adds strength. If a scarce boon must be given to the most needy or to the most deserving, quantifying this need or merit makes possible the regression discontinuity analysis.

NOTES

1. This list has been expanded from the major previous presentations by the addition of *Instability* (but see Campbell, 1968; Campbell and Ross, 1968). This has been done in reaction to the sociological discussion of the use of tests of significance in nonexperimental or quasi-experimental research (e.g., Selvin, 1957; and as reviewed by Galtung, 1967, pp. 358-389). On the one hand, I join with the critics in criticizing the exaggerated status of "statistically significant differences" in establishing convictions of validity. Statistical tests are relevant to at best 1 out of 15 or so threats to validity. On the other hand, I join with those who defend their use in situations where randomization has not been employed. Even in those situations, it is relevant to say or to deny, "This is a trivial difference. It is of the order that would have occurred frequently *had* these measures been assigned to these classes solely by chance." Tests of significance, making use of random reassignments of the actual scores, are particularly useful in communicating this point.

2. This list has been lengthened from previous presentations to make more salient Threats 5 and 6 which are particularly relevant to social experimentation. Discussion in previous presentations (Campbell, 1957: 309-310; Campbell and Stanley, 1963: 203-204) had covered these points, but they had not been included in the checklist.

3. No doubt the public and press shared the Governor's special alarm over the 1955 death toll. This differential reaction could be seen as a negative feedback servosystem in which the dampening effect was proportional to the degree of upward deviation from the prior trend. Insofar as such alarm reduces traffic fatalities, it adds a negative component to the autocorrelation, increasing the regression effect. This component should probably be regarded as a rival cause or treatment rather than as artifact. (The regression effect is less as the positive autocorrelation is higher, and will be present to some degree insofar as this correlation is less than positive unity. Negative correlation in a time series would represent regression beyond the mean, in a way not quite analogous to negative correlation across persons. For an autocorrelation of Lag 1, high negative correlation would be represented by a series that oscillated maximally from one extreme to the other.)

4. Wilson's inconsistency in utilization of records and the political problem of relevant records are ably documented in Kamisar (1964). Etzioni (1968) reports that in New York City in 1965 a crime wave was proclaimed that turned out to be due to an unpublicized improvement in record keeping.

5. J. Sween and D. T. Campbell, "Computer programs for simulating and analyzing sharp and fuzzy regression-discontinuity experiments." In preparation.

6. There are some subtle statistical clues that might distinguish these two instances if one had enough cases. There should be increased pooled column variance in the mixed columns for a true effects case. If the data are arbitrarily treated as though there had been a sharp cutting point located in the middle of the overlap area, then there should be no discontinuity in the

no-effect case, and some discontinuity in the case of a real effect, albeit an underestimated discontinuity, since there are untreated cases above the cutting point and treated ones below, dampening the apparent effect. The degree of such dampening should be estimable, and correctable, perhaps by iterative procedures. But these are hopes for the future.

REFERENCES

Aubert, V. Chance in social affairs. *Inquiry,* 1959, 2: 1-24.

Bauer, R. M. *Social indicators.* Cambridge, Mass.: M.I.T. Press, 1966.

Blayney, M. R., and I. N. Hill. Fluorine and dental cares. *The Journal of the American Dental Association* (Special Issue), 1967, 74: 233-302.

Box, G. E. P., and G. C. Tiao. A change in level of nonstationary time series. *Biometrika,* 1965, 52: 181-192.

Campbell, D. T. Factors relevant to the validity of experiments in social settings. *Psychological Bulletin,* 1957, 54: 297-312.

———. From description to experimentation: Interpreting trends as quasi-experiments. In C. W. Harris (ed.) *Problems in measuring change.* Madison: University of Wisconsin Press, 1963.

———. Administrative experimentation, institutional records, and nonreactive measures. In J. C. Stanley (ed.) *Improving experimental design and statistical analysis.* Chicago: Rand McNally, 1967.

———. Quasi-experimental design. In D. L. Sills (ed.) *International Encyclopedia of the Social Sciences.* New York: MacMillan and Free Press, 1968. Vol. 5, pp. 259-263.

Campbell, D. T., and A. Erlebacher. How regression artifacts in quasi-experimental evaluations can mistakenly make compensatory education look harmful. Pp. 455-463 in J. Hellmuth (ed.) *Compensatory education: A national debate.* Vol. III of *The disadvantaged child.* New York: Brunner/Mazel, 1970.

———, and D. W. Fiske. Convergent and discriminant validation by the multitrait-multimethod matrix. *Psychological Bulletin,* 1959, 56: 81-105.

———, and H. L. Ross. The Connecticut crackdown on speeding; Time-series data in quasi-experimental analysis. *Law and Society Review,* 1968, 3 (1): 33-53.

———, and J. C. Stanley. Experimental and quasi-experimental designs for research on teaching. In N. L. Gage (ed.) *Handbook of research on teaching.* Chicago: Rand McNally, 1963. Reprinted as *Experimental and quasi-experimental design for research.* Chicago: Rand McNally, 1966.

Chapin, F. S. *Experimental design in sociological research.* New York: Harper, 1947.

Etzioni, A. "Shortcuts" to social change? *The Public Interest,* 1968, 12: 40-51.

———, and E. W. Lehman. Some dangers in "valid" social measurement. *Annals of the American Academy of Political and Social Science,* 1967, 373: 1-15.

Galtung, J. *Theory and methods of social research.* Oslo: Universitetsforloget; London: Allen & Unwin; New York: Columbia University Press, 1967.

Glass, G. V. Analysis of data on the Connecticut speeding crackdown as a time-series quasi-experiment. *Law and Society Review,* 1968, 3 (1): 55-76.

———, G. C. Tiao, and T. O. Maguire. Analysis of data on the 1900 revision of the German divorce laws as a quasi-experiment. *Law and Society Review,* 1971.

Greenwood, E. *Experimental sociology: A study in method.* New York: King's Crown Press, 1945.

Gross, B. M. *The state of the nation: Social system accounting.* London: Tavistock Publications, 1966. Also in R. M. Bauer, *Social indicators.* Cambridge, Mass.: M.I.T. Press, 1966.

——— (ed.) Social goals and indicators. *Annals of the American Academy of Political and Social Science,* 1967, 371: Part 1, May, pp. i-iii and 1-177; Part 2, September, pp. i-iii and 1-218.

Guttman, L. An approach for quantifying paired comparisons and rank order. *Annals of Mathematical Statistics,* 1946, 17: 144-163.

Hyman, H. H., and C. R. Wright. Evaluating social action programs. In P. F. Lazarfeld, W. H. Sewell, and H. L. Wilensky (eds.) *The uses of sociology.* New York: Basic Books, 1967.

Kamisar, Y. The tactics of police-persecution oriented critics of the courts. *Cornell Law Quarterly,* 1964, 49: 458-471.

Kaysen, C. Data banks and dossiers. *The Public Interest,* 1967, 7: 52-60.

Manniche, E., and D. P. Hayes. Respondent anonymity and data matching. *Public Opinion Quarterly,* 1957, 21 (3): 384-388.

Polanyi, M. A society of explorers. In *The tacit dimension* (chap. 3). New York: Doubleday, 1966.

–––. The growth of science in society. *Minerva,* 1967, 5: 533-545.

Popper, K. R. *Conjectures and refutations.* London: Routledge and Kegan Paul; New York: Basic Books, 1963.

Rheinstein, M. Divorce and the law in Germany: A review. *American Journal of Sociology,* 1959, 65: 489-498.

Rose, A. M. Needed research on the mediation of labor disputes. *Personnel Psychology,* 1952, 5: 187-200.

Ross, H. L., and D. T. Campbell. The Connecticut speed crackdown: A study of the effects of legal change. In H. L. Ross (ed.) *Perspectives on the social order: Readings in sociology.* New York: McGraw-Hill, 1968.

Ross, H. L., D. T. Campbell, and G. V. Glass. Determining the social effect of a legal reform: The British "Breathalyser" crackdown of 1967. *American Behavioral Scientist,* 1970, 13 (4): 493-509.

Sawyer, J., and H. Schechter. Computers, privacy, and the National Data Center: The responsibility of social scientists. *American Psychologist,* 1968, 23: 810-818.

Schanck, R. L., and C. Goodman. Reactions to propaganda on both sides of a controversial issue. *Public Opinion Quarterly,* 1939, 3: 107-112.

Schwartz, R. D. Field experimentation in sociological research. *Journal of Legal Education,* 1961, 13: 401-410.

–––, and S. Orleans. On Legal sanctions. *University of Chicago Law Review,* 1967, 34: 274-300.

Schwartz, R. D., and J. H. Skolnick. Televised communication and income tax compliance. In L. Arons and M. May (eds.) *Television and human behavior.* New York: Appleton-Century-Crofts, 1963.

Selvin, H. A critique of tests of significance in survey research. *American Sociological Review,* 1957, 22: 519-527.

Simon, J. L. The price elasticity of liquor in the U.S. and a simple method of determination. *Econometrica,* 1966, 34: 193-205.

Solomon, R. W. An extension of control group design. *Psychological Bulletin,* 1949, 46: 137-150.

Stieber, J. W. *Ten years of the Minnesota Labor Relations Act.* Minneapolis: Industrial Relations Center, University of Minnesota, 1949.

Stouffer, S. A. The point system for redeployment and discharge. In S. A. Stouffer et al., *The American soldier. Vol. 2, Combat and its aftermath.* Princeton: Princeton University Press, 1949.

Suchman, E. A. *Evaluative research: Principles and practice in public service and social action programs.* New York: Russell Sage, 1967.

Sween, J., and D. T. Campbell. A study of the effect of proximally auto-correlated error on tests of significance for the interrupted time-series quasi-experimental design. Available from the author, 1965. (Multilith)

Thistlethwaite, D. L., and D. T. Campbell. Regression-discontinuity analysis: An alternative to the ex post facto experiment. *Journal of Educational Psychology,* 1960, 51: 309-317.

Walker, H. M., and J. Lev. *Statistical inference.* New York: Holt, 1953.

Webb, E. J., D. T. Campbell, R. D. Schwartz, and L. B. Sechrest. *Unobtrusive measures: Nonreactive research in the social sciences.* Chicago: Rand McNally, 1966.

Wolf, E., G. Lüke, and H. Hax. *Scheidung und Scheidungsrecht: Grundfrägen der Ehescheidung in Deutschland.* Tübigen: J. C. B. Mohr, 1959.

6

THE STUDY OF CHANGE IN EVALUATION RESEARCH: PRINCIPLES CONCERNING MEASUREMENT, EXPERIMENTAL DESIGN, AND ANALYSIS

JUM C. NUNNALLY

If one inspects examples of evaluation research discussed in these volumes and in other places, it is apparent that the term evaluation research is generally concerned with the effectiveness of programs of social improvement. Thus, social improvement is involved in the introduction of the Peace Corps into a new country, the institution of community mental health programs, development of family planning programs, and the introduction of "new math" in a school system. In all cases the effort of the program is to improve some existing state of affairs among people; in all cases the effort of evaluation research is to document the amounts and kinds of improvements that actually occur, if any.

Of course, if a new program of social improvement actually is effective, people who participate in the program should improve during the course of their participation. This is another way of saying that they change over the time of participation. Thus it may be said that evaluation research is intimately related to the study of change.

As will be discussed more fully later, the introduction of a new program of social improvement is analogous to a "treatment" like that in the typical controlled experiment. Not only are experiments relating to programs of social improvement concerned with change, but all experiments of any kind with people are concerned with change. Thus, in the course of investigating the effectiveness of different drugs

AUTHOR'S NOTE: Appreciation is expressed to McGraw-Hill Book Co. for permission to borrow extensively from the following book for material adapted for this chapter: J. C. Nunnally, *Psychometric Theory* (New York: McGraw-Hill, 1967). Appreciation is also expressed to Robert L. Durham and William H. Wilson for their assistance.

on moods of depressed patients, the essence of the experiment is to document any changes that occur as a function of the drug administrations. Similarly, in comparing the effectiveness of three methods of instruction in foreign languages, in essence the experiment is concerned with changes in proficiency as a function of the different treatments.

Although it can be said that all experimentation is in essence concerned with change, there are some special problems of logic and technique in the study of change in evaluation research that either do not occur at all or occur to a lesser degree in the typical experiment with people. Consequently, this chapter is devoted to a discussion of problems that frequently arise in the study of change in evaluation research. The issues will be discussed in the logical order that they should occur to the scientist: measurement, then research design, and finally statistical analysis.

ILLUSTRATIVE PROBLEMS OF MEASUREMENT IN THE STUDY OF CHANGE

Throughout the previous two chapters, the theory and methodology of psychological measurement were discussed in terms of their relevance to evaluation research. Some special issues arise in evaluation research concerning the degree or type of measurement employed. Such issues will be discussed in this section.

Constructing Measures Ex Post Facto

It should go without saying that measures employed to evaluate a program concerning social improvement should be constructed before rather than after the program is under way. However, there still are many examples of programs that are completed before any effort is made to develop adequate measuring instruments. Surely no professional researcher would commit such a faux pas; but where adequate professional researchers have not been involved, examples are legion of this blunder occurring. An example was mentioned previously where the author was once asked for advice on evaluating a program of "new math" in a public school system after the program had been in effect for a year. It is surprising to find that even some administrative officials involved in various programs of social improvement apparently think that professional researchers can, by some form of legerdemain, pull adequate measuring instruments out of a hat at any time for any circumstance.

An exception to the principle that measures should be selected or constructed before new programs are undertaken is that in which the measuring instruments naturally grow out of the program while it is under way. An example would be in performing content analyses of changes during group psychotherapy. Whereas experimenters probably could formulate many of the content coding categories before the inception of the program, some of the important categories would make themselves known only after the therapy sessions had been going on for some time. It might, for example, become apparent after a number of sessions had occurred that special issues arose in those groups that were conducted by female rather than male therapists. Consequently, in midstream of performing content analyses of therapy sessions, experimenters would need to add some additional coding cate-

gories relating to this unforeseen issue. The new coding categories not only could be used henceforth in analyzing the program, but also could be applied retrospectively to the transcripts of earlier sessions.

Reactivity of Measurements

A problem that is encountered frequently in evaluation research is that pretest measures interact with treatment conditions in a program being evaluated. An example would be in the evaluation of neighborhood discussion groups as a way of reducing race prejudice. Before the group sessions are started, a pretest is given which consists of questions relating to race prejudice such as the following:

	Yes	No
1. When Negroes move into a neighborhood that was formerly all white, property values usually decrease.	_____	_____
2. Negroes are rapidly moving into professional positions in medicine, law, etc.	_____	_____
3. It is doubtful that the average intelligence of Negroes is as high as that of whites.	_____	_____

Rather obviously such a pretest measure would alert group members regarding issues and differentially sensitize them to various topics that arose in the discussion. After a series of group sessions extending over several months, the same inventory is given to all subjects. Large differences are found between pretest and posttest scores, but the differences may be due entirely to reactivity from participating in the pretest. The results would generalize only to those situations in which pretests were administered before group sessions were started, but this might not be the plan of the individuals who are developing the program. To prevent such reactivity, a better research design is one in which tests are given only at the end of a training program and in which the group that receives the training program is compared with a control group.

The only major exception to the foregoing principle is in a situation where the number of subjects necessarily is quite small, and thus every ounce of statistical muscle is needed. The major advantage of using a repeated measures design in which the same subjects are administered a pretest and a posttest is that the statistical power of comparisons frequently are substantially higher than in employing a between-groups design in which a treatment group is compared with a control group. For example, this circumstance might arise in an extensive program to train high-level personnel, such as airline pilots. Pilots who participate in the usual training program are compared with pilots who are given a radically new type of training in instrument flying. Unless there is strong suspicion that pretest measures would interact with treatment conditions, statistical power probably could be increased by employing both a pretest and a posttest. Campbell and Stanley (1968) have discussed numerous issues concerning appropriate designs when reactivity of measurement is a potential problem.

There are a number of steps one can take to ensure that pretest measures are not

interacting with treatment conditions in evaluation research. First, as was mentioned above, there are research designs in which this is not a problem. Second, in some instances one can employ measures that logically are nonreactive. Numerous such measures are discussed by Webb, Campbell, Schwartz, and Sechrest (1966). Two examples (not from Webb et al.) are as follows. A series of TV films is used in schools to increase interest in a wide variety of reading topics. Over the months following the films, the success of the program can be measured in part by the numbers and kinds of books checked out of the school library as compared to the situation before the films were shown. Another example is that of evaluating the success of a series of spot announcements on radio regarding the availability of free advice on birth planning. The success of the announcement can be measured in part by the relative increase in numbers of phone calls seeking appointments at the end of each broadcast and the overall increases from before until after the series is presented. However, the problem in so much evaluation research is that the purposes and content of measures are rather obvious, and consequently the measures potentially will interact with treatments.

Another approach to handling problems of reactivity is to learn at an early stage of the game whether pretest measures actually are interacting with treatments. The logic of employing research designs for this purpose is discussed by Campbell and Stanley (1968). If the reactivity is found to be very slight in the special research, one can employ simpler research designs for subsequent research on evaluating a program of action without worrying about reactivity of measurement.

A fourth potential approach to handling reactivity of measurement is to disguise the items in traditional tests of abilities and sentiments. For reasons which will be discussed later in this chapter, this approach usually fails.

Faking of Responses

A problem related to reactivity of measurement is that of faking. In many programs of evaluation research (even good ones), the people who operate the program are highly committed to their evaluations even before the research evidence is in. Sometimes they are convinced that a program is working poorly and want to prove that such is the case. This might occur when an agency of a local government investigates the effectiveness of a youth correction program. The people who conduct the research, or who engage others to do so, may strongly feel that the program is generally bad. If the people who hold this point of view actually conduct or otherwise influence the research activity, there are many ways in which data could be faked to support that point of view. (Here the word "faked" is being used in a very general sense concerning any methods that unfairly sample, analyze, or interpret research results. The faking may be of a patent, dishonest form in which the individual purposely distorts information; or the individual may be so committed to the outcome that, by one defense mechanism or another, he fools himself.)

The more frequently occurring situation is that in which the people who conduct evaluation research are highly committed to the positiveness of the program being evaluated. Most new social programs (e.g., a new type of school

instruction or the Peace Corps) originate because of the messianic zeal of the progenitors. Obviously it is very difficult for such persons to face up to the possibility that evaluation research will prove the program to be ineffective.

Faking can enter into evaluation research in many different ways. Psychotherapy patients usually want to please their therapist by indicating they have improved even if they have not. In rating the improvement of youth in a program of training for delinquent boys, the manager of the program might pick raters who sympathize with his points of view rather than other equally competent people in the institution who have different points of view. In comparisons of two groups that were subjected to different types of training programs, the test constructor might deliberately favor one group by selecting items specifically because they were considered more extensively in one method of training than the other.

Of course, one of the primary ways to prevent faking from markedly influencing results is to have the research conducted mainly by individuals who have very little personal stake in the outcome. In addition, there are other ways to lower the influence of faking. Another way, where it is feasible, is to employ the types of unobtrusive measures discussed and illustrated previously (Webb et al., 1966). Relatedly, a second principle is to ensure that as much as possible of the data generating and gathering process is out of the hands of individuals who are invested in the outcomes of evaluation research. For example, rather than have ratings made by people who function in a program of social action, it would be advisable to have such ratings made by trained persons who are not involved in the program being evaluated.

If the measuring instruments are easily faked (as most measures of sentiments, as opposed to abilities, are), a fourth principle is to try to reduce faking by specifically warning subjects of the need for strict objectivity, even if the real truth is unkind. Of course, such admonitions do not constitute a cure-all against faking, but it is surprising how frequently subjects are not carefully instructed in that way. Depending on the situation, various assurances can be given to subjects which promote objectivity. In many cases subjects can be told by research workers that the personnel of a program of social action (e.g., a job training program) will not see individual responses on questionnaires. In some cases, one can even go to the extent of specifically telling subjects not to place their names on questionnaires.

A fifth method is one that almost always fails, but it has absorbed so much energy from research workers, that it should be mentioned. When working with sentiments, behavioral scientists have spent a great deal of time and money in the effort to develop highly deceptive but valid measures of attitudes, values, and personality characteristics. One approach is with "sneaky" items. An example is a multiple-choice test with items like "If you were reincarnated, what type of person would you like to be?" Many other Machiavellian attempts have been made with projective tests, pupillary response, and numerous supposed physiological correlates of emotions. Valid indicators of sentiments have *not* yet come from work with such variables. (See discussions of these issues in Guilford, 1959, and in Nunnally, 1967.)

It is necessary to make a careful distinction between measures that are deceptive in the sneaky sense illustrated above and the previously mentioned and illustrated

types of unobtrusive measures. The latter also are deceptive in the sense of trying to get the individual to give away his own private feelings based on test items or other types of stimuli whose relationship to the traits in question are quite elliptical and remote. Thus, if in an unobtrusive measure one estimates the amount of alcoholic consumption in a household by counting the number of bottles found in the garbage each week, the measure is hidden from the view of the subject but rather obviously related to the trait in question. In contrast if one knocks on a man's door and asks him which one of ten magazines he thought would be more appropriate for an orphanage, the measure certainly is deceptive but not likely to be very predictive of alcoholic consumption in the household. Many years of trying to develop such measures have resulted mainly in disappointment.

Extent of Measurement Problem

The difficulty of constructing adequate measures for evaluation research varies considerably with the questions that those measures are intended to answer. If the program being evaluated largely concerns training in human capabilities, the measurement problems usually are rather straightforward. Examples are (1) the measurement of changes in knowledge about forestry brought about by a government financed training program, (2) the measurement of progress in swimming classes by objective indicators of performance and instructor's ratings, and (3) the use of commercially distributed achievement tests to measure the effects of special schooling on the culturally disadvantaged. However, sometimes the capability being investigated is much more illusive, such as capability with respect to public speaking, creativity, or effectiveness in job situations. Such characteristics present real challenges to measurement. They may be approached through ratings, various types of documentary evidence, and specially constructed achievement tests.

Rather than being concerned with improvement in capabilities (in the usual sense of the term), many programs that are evaluated concern habits and dispositions in daily life. Examples are (1) consumption of alcoholic beverages, (2) reckless driving, and (3) acts of courtesy. Problems of measuring such dispositions range from the absolutely trivial to the nearly insurmountable. At one extreme, there is no problem at all to "weigh the evidence" in a program to reduce obesity. In contrast, it would be much more difficult to obtain objective measures of improvements in highway safety of individuals (unless one monitored each person in his daily driving). However, even with some of the more illusive dispositions, it is possible to obtain measurements of changes in group performance even if one cannot finely measure such performance in individuals.

The most controversy concerning measurement in evaluation research has not been concerned with capabilities, as discussed above, but with what has been referred to as sentiments—attitudes, values, and preferences. In this realm the opaque instruments tend to be invalid, and the transparent instruments leave lingering doubts about faking. If the cautions that were mentioned previously with respect to faking are followed, then there is no major reason straightforward inventories and rating scales cannot be used as valid measuring instruments in nearly all evaluation research. Long ago the author came to the conclusion that generally

the most valid, economical, sometimes the only, way to learn about a person's sentiments is simply to ask him.

Subjective Assessments

Some of the most important human traits involved in evaluation research presently can be measured only in terms of subjective assessments rather than in terms of more objective means. For example, an individual's satisfaction with a series of training sessions in first aid necessarily would require a measurement of the participant's feelings about the course of instruction. Thus, in one sense or another, they would be required to rate their feelings about the program. In other instances, it would be necessary to obtain subjective assessments from persons in supervisory roles in a training program. This would be true, for example, in evaluating the progress of students in flight training programs of the Armed Forces. Because much anguish has been expressed concerning the need to employ such subjective assessments in evaluation research (and indeed, quite widely in research throughout the behavioral sciences), it would be worthwhile to consider the matter in some detail here.

The word "subjective" frequently is tossed about uncritically in a way that refers to at least four major issues concerning psychological measurement. First, objective measures have been distinguished from subjective measures in terms of the presence or absence of ostensive indicators of the trait in question. If a student correctly solves 26 of 32 problems on a test, then evidence regarding capability in that topic is present for everyone to see. If a program of evaluation research concerns training programs in underdeveloped countries regarding the production of rice, then the piles of rice coming from the fields can be witnessed and weighed in such a way that all present can witness the product. The effectiveness of spot announcements on TV regarding the availability of free birth planning assistance programs could be indexed partly in terms of the number of individuals applying. These examples concern the ostensiveness of data used to obtain dependent measures in evaluation research.

In many of the measures employed in the behavioral sciences, the data underlying measurements methods are not evidenced directly in palpable, sensory experience; but rather they are evidenced in the personal reactions of individuals. Thus, when an individual says that he prefers chocolate ice cream over vanilla ice cream, there are no ostensive data to back up the assertion. Of course, one could always investigate whether the individual purchased chocolate rather than vanilla ice cream when given the option, but that is not the same matter as measuring stated preferences. More germane to the issue of evaluation research, if supervisors rate trainees in a job-training program on a 7-point scale concerning motivation for employment, then the data underlying the measurement are literally in the head of the person making the ratings. In this sense, such ratings have been referred to as subjective. It is not necessarily bad that measures are subjective regarding the ostensiveness or lack of it in the measurement process; rather, the bad features that sometimes are present come because of some correlated problems, which will be discussed next.

Human impressions used to develop measures of psychological traits are referred to as subjective for another reason, namely because it is difficult to explicitly instruct subjects as to how to perform their rating tasks. An example was mentioned previously of that concerning supervisors' ratings of the motivation of students for employment. The 7-step scale used for that purpose might be indexed by "average, slightly above average, much above average," and so on. As any investigator knows, it becomes somewhat embarrassing if the respondent wants to know exactly what is meant by the terms and how he should distinguish between, for example, slightly above average and much above average. Although some general suggestions can be given in the printed instructions, admittedly the respondent is left largely to use the rating scale in a way that seems appropriate. Thus, the data themselves not only are subjective, but the method for making appraisals is subjective, in the sense that it relies on the intuitions of the respondent.

A third way in which many measures are said to be subjective concerns the sheer variability in results from rater to rater and from occasion to occasion. Because such sources of variability act as measurement error in most circumstances, it can be said that ratings tend to have only a modest reliability at best. For example, whereas one would expect two forms of an intelligence test to correlate at least .90, one would be very happy indeed to find that two supervisors made ratings of 40 trainees that correlated at least .60. The term subjective frequently is used where people differ markedly among themselves about events, and for this reason the word subjective frequently is used with respect to rating methods.

The word subjective is employed in a fourth important way with respect to rating methods used in evaluation research, namely that the results are influenced by numerous artifacts concerning the way people make ratings and in the rating tasks themselves. As one example, the rating given any person on any trait is markedly influenced by the group with which the individual is compared. An example would be in a training program for lifeguards. At the end of the program, supervisors make ratings on a number of traits concerning future job performance. One of the trainees, Fred Wilkerson, finds himself in an unusually capable, highly motivated, class of trainees. Fred would have looked good in a typical group of trainees; but in comparison to this premium group, he is given rather poor ratings by supervisors. Another artifact that occurs in ratings is that of the "halo effect." This is the tendency to rate people as all good or all bad on different traits rather than be more selective in making individual ratings. These and other artifacts in ratings are discussed in detail by Guilford (1954).

That rating methods are subjective in the first way mentioned above (lack of ostensiveness in the data) should pose no major problem for evaluation research. Many things are inherently subjective in that regard, and indeed a search for so-called objective indicators might be illogical. An example would be in having ladies rate their men friends in terms of overall desirability. The myriad underlying traits would be illusive and perhaps intractable to measurement. If one really is interested in the lady's evaluations rather than why she makes the choices that she does, the simplest approach is to have the individual rate the men by one psychometric device or another. The second way in which ratings are said to be subjective

causes some problems in the construction of measurement methods, but these are by no means insurmountable. There are better ways to construct rating scales and better ways to instruct subjects in their use (e.g., see discussion in Nunnally, 1967, chap. 14).

The third and fourth ways in which ratings are said to be subjective do constitute workaday problems in evaluation research. Ratings typically are not highly reliable; and although methods are available for increasing the reliability, a good dose of measurement error usually remains. A cardinal way to increase reliability is to employ multiple raters and average their responses, for example, three supervisors rating the participants in a training program. Artifacts of measurement also can be reduced markedly by the way in which rating scales are constructed and administered. Although there is not enough space here to go into the many special issues concerning the construction and use of rating scales, the reader who is not already familiar with these matters should avail himself of summaries of the available literature. These are presented in Guilford (1954) and Nunnally (1967). Up to the present time, much evaluation research has relied in large part on self-ratings and ratings by others; and although such measurement methods have their problems, they probably will be relied on heavily in the future.

THE SELECTION AND DEVELOPMENT OF MEASURES
FOR THE STUDY OF CHANGE

Of course, before it is possible to investigate changes that occur in people with respect to programs of sound improvement, it is necessary to have measures that document such changes. General principles for the selection and development of measurement methods were discussed in the previous two chapters. Some special issues that arise with respect to the study of change are discussed as follows.

Construction of Measures on the Basis of Change

Because evaluation research is concerned with the study of change, it is easy to fall into the semantic trap of assuming that measurement methods should be constructed on the basis of empirical evidence concerning the amount of change found in research. An approach that has been attempted in that regard is as follows. The program of social improvement concerns a new type of group psychotherapy. For constructing a test of the effectiveness of changes in psychotherapy, a large item pool is assembled, populated with items concerning a wide variety of values, opinions, and personality characteristics. Each item is rated as either "Agree" or "Disagree." The pool of items is administered to a sample of subjects before they undertake the group therapy and after the sessions of group therapy are completed. Then, so the reasoning goes, the items that show the most change from before to after are the ones most sensitive to the changes that occurred during the therapy sessions. A comparison is made of the percentages of agreements (in decimal form, p values). Items are rank-ordered in terms of the absolute magnitude of such differences, and the items that differ most in this regard are selected to form a test for the measurement of change over the period of psychotherapy. This approach has something to say for itself, in that it is grounded in the raw empiricism of what

actually changes over the period of psychotherapy; however, the liabilities of this approach far outweigh the apparent advantages.

The major problem with the above approach is that, at best, it would lead to a test which simultaneously measured a hodgepodge of possibly unrelated attributes. Thus, the collection of items used to form a test might concern introversion-extroversion, aggressiveness, tendency to accept opposing opinions, freedom from anxiety, and a host of other separable traits. Also, since the number of items relating to each trait would depend fortuitously upon the number of items originally tossed into the pool, the factorial composition of the conglomerate measure would be rather arbitrary. Consequently, even if in a statistical sense the measure served to index the amount of change that occurred during the therapy sessions, it would be all but impossible to understand the changes that occurred in underlying personality traits.

Even if it were logically defensible to select items for the measurement of change in terms of differences in p values from before to after, the approach might take great advantage of chance. Even if all subjects flipped coins to decide their answers on the before measure and the after measure, there would be differences in p values which could be used for the selection of items.

A third problem with this approach is that not all items which change markedly in p value from before to after any program necessarily are valid indicators of what occurred in the program. An example would be a multiple-choice item in which subjects were asked the name of the course instructor. Before the course was undertaken, many persons would not know; after the course was completed, almost everyone would know the instructor's name. The sheer logic of this approach would indicate this to be a highly valid item, which is nonsense, of course. Changes in p values from before to after a program provide only raw circumstantial evidence rather than direct evidence of validity.

Another approach that has been advocated for constructing measures based on actual changes during a program of social improvement concerns the percentages of individuals who change their scores from before to afterward. It should be obvious that this index is not necessarily related to that of changes in p values discussed above. Thus, before the program is undertaken, 50% of the people could agree with the item, and afterward 50% of the people could agree with the item; but the 50% of the people who agreed before could be the 50% of the people who disagreed afterward.

An example of constructing tests on the basis of before-after changes would be with respect to the item, "I look forward to getting up each morning and facing a new day." From before to after the sessions of group therapy, it might be found that 40% of the participants changed their answers—from agree to disagree or vice versa. So the argument goes, this means that the particular item is relatively sensitive to changes that occur in the particular type of group therapy.

The selection of items in terms of percentages of changes over a program of social improvement has the major faults of selecting items in terms of changes in p values plus an even more insidious fault of its own. At best, the method would lead to a conglomerate of items for which a total score would be largely uninterpretable.

This method also would tend to take advantage of chance and in many cases would not produce replicable results. This method also provides only rough circumstantial rather than direct evidence regarding validity of individual items. An important additional problem with this method is that it would lead to the selection of highly unreliable items for the eventual test. Obviously, according to the standard for selecting items, a good item would be one in which subjects actually flip coins to determine their answers before and afterward. In this case, the expectation is that 50% of the people would change their responses from before to afterward—either from agreement to disagreement or vice versa. Although in some cases one might find larger percentage reversals (e.g., from 70% agreeing to 80% disagreeing), in the analysis of such shifts it would be unusual to find items that changed as much as 50%.

Neither of the two approaches discussed above has proven successful in evaluation research, and both are condemned as general approaches for the measurement of change. The approaches discussed in the following section are far more appropriate.

Selection of Measures for the Study of Change

Far better than to construct measures ad hoc for particular investigations of change is to select existing measures that have proven themselves with respect to criteria discussed in chapter 3 of Psychometric Theory. Such measures should have the characteristics of being (1) constructed in such a way as to be homogeneous in content, (2) highly reliable with respect to various sources of measurement error, and (3) of known factorial composition as determined by factor analysis of various domains of content. As mentioned in chapter 3, tests with these characteristics lead to the development of a storehouse of standard yardsticks for investigating various types of capabilities and sentiments. Even in very large-scale programs of research, it takes years to develop standard measures of psychological characteristics that meet these standards. In particular, gathering evidence for construct validity is a matter that takes numerous years, at best. Consequently, it is usually foolhardy for those who are entering a program of evaluation research (which usually is limited both in terms of time and funds) to undertake the development and standardization of most of the measures that will be employed. The far better part of valor and the far better part of common sense is to seek suitable measures from those that have been ripening over the years.

Although the particular program of evaluation research may require tests of attributes not previously investigated in detail, this more frequently is the exception rather than the rule. More frequently, when investigators dive into a heavy program of developing their own measurement methods for evaluation research, they are either unaware of the psychometric standards that must be applied or unaware of much research that has been done to develop the measurement methods needed. In some cases the individual who is responsible for performing evaluation research is pardonably unacquainted with existing measures of human traits which can be found in the literature concerning the behavioral sciences. In that case, he probably would be helped considerably by inspecting (1) *The Seventh Mental*

Measurements Yearbook (Buros, 1972), (2) *Tests in Print* (Buros, 1961), (3) catalogues from commercial testing firms, (4) textbooks on educational and psychological measurement (e.g., Nunnally, 1970, 1972), and (5) some of the professional journals in the behavioral sciences. Through these sources and consultation with individuals who specialize in behavioral measurement, the investigator who is new to the field probably will find that measures of most psychological traits have been investigated by numerous people in the past; even if in many cases those investigations have not been highly successful in producing the necessary yardsticks.

CHANGE SCORES

Because evaluation research is in essence concerned with change from before to after people have undergone a program of social improvement, it is tempting to assume that the basic psychometric datum with which one works is the change score. Thus, if one is making comparisons of intelligence test scores at two points in time (symbolized by X_1 and X_2), it is assumed that the interest is in $X_2 - X_1$ and that such scores should be computed as one of the first steps in performing analyses. Actually, both the history of the problem and the logic of investigation indicate that the last thing one wants to do is to think in terms of or to compute such change scores unless the problem makes it absolutely necessary. As is generally known, the major problem in working directly with change scores is that they are ridden with a *regression effect*. The problem is illustrated in Figure 6.1. The variables X_1 and X_2 can be thought of as the raw scores obtained on the same test at two points in time, or the raw scores obtained on alternative forms of a test administered at two points in time. As necessarily must be the case, there is a regression line; and if the correlation is less than unity, the phenomena of regression toward the mean is present. If one computes change scores, he finds that the people who scored above the mean on the first occasion tend to have negative change scores, and that the people who scored below the mean on the first occasion tend to have positive change scores—all of this being purely an artifact of the way such scores are computed and the phenomena of regression toward the mean.

A horrible example is often cited (surely apocryphal) where a whole experiment was misinterpreted because of regression toward the mean. In this case a school teacher wanted to try out three different methods of instruction in reading speed in her class corresponding respectively to three groups in terms of scores at the beginning of the semester on a test of reading speed. The top third of the class was given one method of training; the middle third was given another method; and the bottom third was given still a third method. At the end of the semester, the test was readministered, and the statistical analyses were made of the change scores. The teacher found that the training given to the top third of the students actually hurt their reading speed, because the mean score was somewhat lower than it was at the beginning of the semester. The method of instruction provided for the bottom third of the students apparently worked very well, because their mean went up substantially. Apparently the instruction given to the middle third of the students had very little effect, because their mean was essentially the same as it was at the beginning

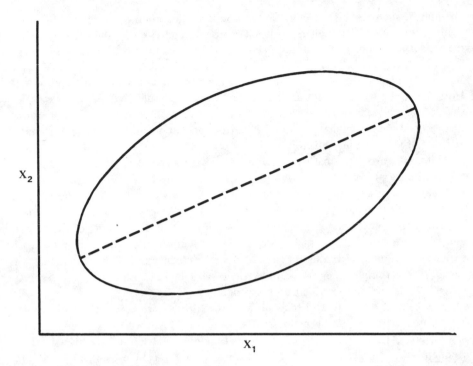

FIGURE 6.1 Regression line and correlation contour for scores on a test administered at two points in time.

of the semester. Of course, in these days to accuse anyone of performing such an experiment or being unaware of the serious limitations of change scores would be to attack a straw man; but the example does serve to illustrate the need either not to work with change scores at all or to work with some modification of them.

The modification of change scores that has been advocated most frequently is that of *residual change scores.* Quite simply, residual change scores consist of deviations of scores on a second occasion from those predicted by regression analysis from a knowledge of scores on a first occasion. Thus, in Figure 6.1 all scores above the regression line would have positive residual change scores, and all those below the regression line would have negative residual change scores. The advantage of working with residual change scores is that they circumvent the regression effect inherent in absolute change scores $(X_2 - X_1)$. However, this is not the end of a happy story, because a great deal of ink has been spilled over exactly how to compute such residual change scores. (An extensive review of the arguments is given in Cronbach and Furby, 1970.) Such residual change scores encounter both conceptual and psychometric problems.

The major psychometric problem with residual change scores is that they fail to take account of the measurement error inherent in both measurements. Thus, if X_2 were administered on the day following X_1 rather than an appreciable time later, scores would not be exactly the same, the correlation would probably be appreciably less than unity, and residual change scores could be computed and inspected.

Of course, such residual change scores would be due almost entirely to measurement error (unless the trait actually changed overnight) rather than to any systematic change in people. To take account of the measurement error inherent in residual change scores, it has been advocated that the correlation between X_1 and X_2 be corrected for attenuation before residual change scores are computed. However, there are questions as to exactly how that should be done. For example, should one correct the correlation only for measurement error in the first measurement, or should one make a double correction for measurement error to take account of the reliability inherent in the second measurement as well?

Numerous complex mathematical models have been developed for obtaining so-called pure measures of change (e.g., as discussed by Lord, 1963). However, the mathematical models involved are based on arguable assumptions about the logic of measuring change and presume that, in practice, one has much better evidence regarding reliabilities of scores and other psychometric characteristics of the before and after measures than usually is true in evaluation research. Also, individual experts concerned with the statistical issues involved express their own lack of certainty regarding proper procedures to be used in general, and various experts disagree with one another about proper procedures.

As a general rule it is wise to avoid working with change scores if at all possible. To summarize some of the major faults, they are (1) based on somewhat shaky assumptions, (2) derived by mathematical models which are controversial and frequently unfeasible in practice, (3) difficult for some people to understand, and are open to misinterpretation, and (4) as can be seen above, computationally rather complex. As Cronbach and Furby (1970) show, most problems regarding the measurement of change can be handled without thinking in terms of, or actually working with, residual change scores.

The major exception to the above statements regarding the avoidance of change scores is in the circumstance where evaluation research specifically concerns individual differences in the tendency to change in some way. An example would be that of individual differences in changes in reading comprehension test scores as a function of a particular type of training. A major concern for the investigator might be that of who changes more and who changes less. It might be desired to measure the amount of change, compute change scores, and then correlate such change scores with various measures of personality, ability, and characteristics of home environment. If it is feasible to employ it, a research design is available that allows one to estimate change scores in a sensible manner. The design circumvents most of the major problems that have plagued models for determining change scores. The design will be illustrated in the simple situation where a control group is compared with a treatment group on a single dependent measure. The logic can be extended to complex designs and multiple dependent measures. The design is as follows. An available group of subjects is randomly sorted into a treatment group and a control group. Both groups are tested at the same time before the treatment is applied. After the treatment is applied, subjects in both groups are retested with the same measure. (To take account of practice effects, alternate forms of the test could be employed, with counterbalancing within each group as to which form is used as

pretest and which form is used as posttest.) The data obtained in this way would permit a separate correlational analysis for the control group and for the treatment group. The regression lines and scatter plots could be depicted in the same figure. Hypothetical results in that regard are shown in Figure 6.2.

The bivariate statistical properties of the results for the control group are precisely what one would expect to find from the treatment group *if the treatment had no effect.* Because the two groups are randomly sorted originally, it is to be expected that the means, standard deviations, and other parameters of the pretest distributions will be the same. The posttest results for the treatment group could differ in these ways from the control group. In Figure 6.2, the two groups are shown as having the same pretest mean but different posttest means, which is what the experimenter hoped for when he designed the experiment. Although they are depicted in Figure 6.2 as being essentially the same, the standard deviation on the pretest for the treatment group could be different from that on the control group, and also the slopes of the two regression lines could be different. Of course, differences between means, variances, and regression slopes all provide interesting evidence regarding the treatment effect. What is important to realize in this circumstance is that change scores in the treatment group can be computed directly from the regression line in the control group. If a person in the treatment group is above the regression line for the control group, then he has a positive change score

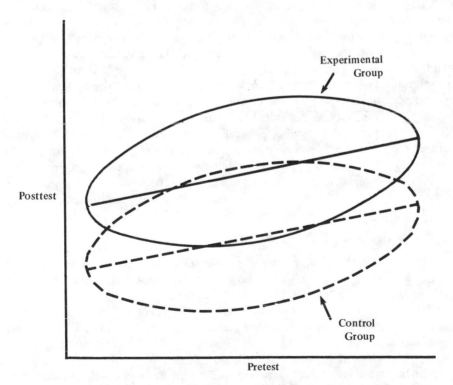

FIGURE 6.2 Regression lines and correlation contours for an experimental group and a control group on a pretest and a posttest measure.

equal to the indicated amount. Similarly, if a person in the treatment group is below the regression line for the control group, then he has actually lost ground by the amount indicated. One would compute residual change scores in the usual way for the treatment group, except that he would use the regression line obtained from the control group. This is a very sensible approach to the measurement of change scores.

The assumption that evaluation research requires the computation of some type of change scores is forced on the investigator by the same type of semantic innuendo that leads to the assumption that tests should be constructed in such a way as to capitalize on such change scores (as discussed in the previous section of this chapter). Actually, one could specialize in evaluation research for numerous years and never find an instance in which it was necessary actually to compute, inspect, analyze, or otherwise take direct action with respect to the change scores of *individuals*. As will be seen in subsequent sections of this chapter, nearly all of the problems concerning the changes that occur in evaluation research can be handled more simply and defensibly with respect to *group trends* without having to think in terms of or actually compute any type of change score for each individual in the investigation.

RESEARCH DESIGNS IN THE STUDY OF CHANGE

An ideal experiment has three essential features. First, experimental manipulations should concern only the treatment variable(s) and not some other, unsuspected (confounding) variable(s). Second, the dependent variables should be indexed by good measures—good in the sense of being reliable, otherwise well-standardized, valid, practicable, and having the other desirable features discussed in the previous two chapters of *Psychometric Theory*. Third, there should be an explicit plan for applying the treatments (independent variables) to subjects and measuring their effects on dependent variables. This section is concerned with the plan, or experimental design, as it is called. Of course, whole books have been written on general issues concerning experimental design and analysis; consequently, the discussion in this section will necessarily be limited to some issues that are particularly important for evaluation research. The opinions expressed in this section were influenced heavily by the writings of Campbell and his associates (e.g., Campbell and Stanley, 1968; and Campbell, 1969).

Types of Design

Following will be a discussion of some basic distinctions among types of experimental designs. Subsequently, designs that represent particular issues relating to these distinctions will be discussed in more detail.

Experimental versus quasi-experimental designs. Campbell and his associates make a distinction between true experimental designs and so-called quasi-experimental designs (e.g., Campbell and Stanley, 1968). True experimental designs are those in which it is possible to rule out all or most of the obvious, possible confounding variables in the experiment. A simplified example is that of evaluating the effect of a drug on the moods of hospitalized, depressed patients. All of the

depressed patients in a hospital are randomly divided into two groups, with equal numbers of subjects in each group. The patients in the other group are given a sugar pill which closely resembles in appearance the actual drug. The patients do not know which pill they are receiving, and the persons administering the pill do not know which pill they are administering. Dependent measures concern psycho-physiological processes, self-ratings of moods, and ratings by attendants concerning adjustment status of patients. One can see that in this simple example all of the major, possible confounding variables are controlled. For example, since the subjects are randomly assigned to groups, there is no reason to believe that they would differ on the average with respect to the dependent measures any more than could be expected by chance alone.

If it were necessary to sacrifice any of the three types of controls mentioned above in the study of a drug, then one would no longer be working with a true experimental design but rather with a quasi-experimental design. For example, for one reason or another, it might have been necessary to give the drug to all patients in one ward and compare them with patients in another ward who received the placebo, rather than randomly divide the total pool of subjects into an experimental and a control group. Measures are taken on all subjects at only one point in time—after the course of treatment has been completed for subjects in the experimental group. The reader can easily think of numerous, potential confounding variables in this experiment. As one example, the two groups of patients might have differed on the average initially in terms of the dependent measures. This would be so if there had been a tendency of the hospital staff to place more severely disturbed patients in one part of the hospital rather than another, which is quite likely the case. Another confounding variable would be differences in the general atmosphere of the two wards, related to differences of personnel, physical surroundings, social structure among patients, and myriad other things. When it is unethical or unfeasable to employ a true experimental design, either the phenomena must go uninvestigated or a quasi-experimental design must be employed instead. In essence, a good quasi-experimental design is one in which additional information is obtained which provides considerable circumstantial evidence regarding what the outcome would be if a true experimental design actually could be employed.

Temporal components. In evaluation research it is important to consider the amount of time over which measures of dependent variables will be applied. In most evaluation research, the time span itself is not so long as to be an important consideration. Typically, such evaluation research concerns a program of human improvement that lasts no more than six months or a year. This would be true of programs concerning (1) "new math" introduced into the fourth grade, (2) structured personal interviews intended to bring high school dropouts back to school, and (3) treatment for alcoholics. In these and other examples of evaluation research, typically most of the data on dependent measures would be obtained by the end of one year. Follow-up studies might be conducted over the next several years, but rarely does a program of evaluation research cover more than three years. When projects do cover more than three years, serious problems occur in terms of

research design, measurement, and analysis. For example, if the research program concerned periodic application of dependent measures at yearly intervals from age five to age ten, it probably would not be possible to apply the same measure to all those age groups. If a test contained written material at all, it obviously could not be employed with preschoolers. Regardless of the type of test, a test that would be of the right difficulty level for five-year-olds would be trivially easy for ten-year-olds. Many other severe problems occur in studies that span more than about three years. Such studies are developmental, in that they concern significant portions of the lives of the subjects. Extensive discussions concerning many aspects of the methodology of developmental research are presented in Nesselroade and Reese (1972).

Numbers of observations. A related issue to that of the amount of time over which observations are made is that of the number of observations in an experiment. One could have an experiment that lasted for 10 years but in which only two periods of observation occurred, in a pretest and in a posttest. In contrast, one could have an experiment that lasted only 30 days but in which testing occurred on each day. The reason that it is important to consider the number of observations is that it relates to problems of measurement and research design. Regarding the former, if the same measure is used over and over, there are quite likely to be "practice effects" of various kinds. Regarding experimental design, some of the quasi-experimental designs to be discussed later require numerous observations (applications of dependent measures) to help rule out potentially confounding variables. Also, as will be discussed later, in some types of research there are advantages to having only one observation period, after experimental treatments have been applied.

Experimental Designs

As mentioned above, true experimental designs form the backbone of science. Some important issues concerning experimental designs in evaluation research are discussed as follows.

Assignment of subjects. In the behavioral sciences, the bedrock essential for any true experimental design is the random assignment of subjects to treatment conditions. The design may entail only one independent variable, such as (1) presence or absence of a particular type of instruction in mathematics, (2) different levels of a particular drug administered to depressive patients, or (3) four levels of practice on a learning task. In practice, the number of levels on an independent variable range from two (usually a comparison of a treatment condition with a control condition) up to eight or more. The design may entail a number of independent variables rather than only one, such as a factorial design with (1) three levels of amount of practice, (2) four levels of amount of problem difficulty, and (3) five amounts of delay before testing for retention.

However simple or complex the design, the essence of the true experimental design is that the available pool of subjects is randomly sorted into the various cells. The only restriction usually employed in this regard is that an equal number of people be placed into each cell. By the process of randomly assigning people to cells

of the design (as with a table of random numbers), some of the cells will be filled before others, which necessitates ignoring these cells and allocating the remaining subjects in a random manner to cells not yet filled. This process of randomization requires first, a statement of the experimental design, and second, a designation of the total group of subjects available. The designation of the group available is not so much a matter of sampling, in the statistical sense, as it is of defining the population over which the results can be generalized. A typical group defined in this way is that of the first 100 students in Introductory Psychology who sign up for an experiment as part of a course requirement to participate in research. If the experiment concerned a simple 2 x 2 factorial design, then 25 students would be randomly placed in each of the four cells of the design. Then, the implicit intention is to obtain results that are generalizable to college students of the same *kind,* although one might not be able to say specifically what that meant.

A possibility that has been mentioned by various authors is that of improving on sheer randomization by matching the subjects in various cells of an experimental design in terms of some variable that is likely to be important for the outcome, for example, matching subjects on level of intelligence before comparing them on two methods of learning arithmetic. Such matching might reduce the amount of experimental error; however, it would be feasible only in very simple experimental designs, for example, comparing an experimental group with a control group. Even in that case, it would hardly be worth the trouble unless the number of subjects available was quite limited, for example, less than 20 subjects for each cell of the design. The possibility of matching subjects in this way is mentioned only in passing with respect to true experimental designs because it is mentioned both seriously and actually used in practice with some of the quasi-experimental designs discussed later.

Of course, the beauty of randomly assigning subjects to cells of an experimental design is that the procedure *absolutely guarantees* that subjects will not differ on the average with respect to any characteristic more than could be expected by chance alone prior to participation in experimental treatments. By "chance alone" is meant the probability distributions associated with the random sorting of subjects into treatment cells. Thus, the subjects in an investigation of methods of training in arithmetic would vary in terms of height, intelligence, social class, personality characteristics, and many other human traits before being introduced to experimental treatments. After being randomly allocated to cells of the design, subjects would still vary within cells with respect to all such human traits; and the sheer act of randomly allocating subjects would lead to a predictable amount of variation in average values of these traits over the cells of experimental designs. However, the randomization process would ensure that there were no systematic influences tending to make the average value of any extraneous variable higher in one cell than in another. Also, the random fluctuations that occur because of the process of sorting people into cells are taken account of in methods of statistics used to analyze results of the experiment.

Comparison groups. The most important consideration with respect to experimental designs is the groups that are compared. The simplest of all possible true

experimental designs is that in which the available pool of subjects is randomly sorted into two groups; one group is given the treatment and the other is not, and dependent measures are applied after the treatment to both groups. Following the lead of Campbell (e.g., Campbell and Stanley, 1968), a capital O will be used to stand for an observation or period of testing, and an X will be used to represent some type of treatment. This design can be symbolized as follows:

$$X \quad O_a$$
$$O_b$$

The two randomly selected groups are referred to as a and b, respectively. With this type of symbolism, each row represents a different group (or cell) in the experimental design. Although this is a very simple design, it has many virtues. It is probably used more widely than any other for evaluation research. An example would be that of taking a group of 100 mentally retarded preschool children and randomly dividing them into a treatment group and a control group. The treatment group would be given a variety of forms of stimulus enrichment, for example, numerous toys that lead to the discovery of simple principles concerning physical reality. These special experiences would be withheld from the control group. The observation (posttest) would consist of achievement test scores, quantitative skills, and other topics at the end of the first grade. The goal of the treatment would be to enhance learning rates during the first grade.

The posttest-only design can easily be extended to any number (k) of treatments:

$$X_a \quad O_a$$
$$X_b \quad O_b$$
$$X_c \quad O_c$$
$$\cdot \qquad \cdot$$
$$\cdot \qquad \cdot$$
$$\cdot \qquad \cdot$$
$$X_k \quad O_k$$
$$O_l$$

An example of a posttest-only design having multiple treatments would be that in which different types of stimulus enrichment were given to different, randomly determined groups of mental retardates (e.g., passive stimulus enrichment versus active opportunity to manipulate objects), and these in turn were compared with a control group. In some cases the term "control group" is a misnomer because it implies that no experiences relative to the dependent variable (observation) occur at all during the time that the experimental groups are receiving their respective treatments. The logic of the posttest-only design is the same regardless of the number of treatment conditions or independent variables.

The posttest-only design can easily be extended to accommodate more than one independent variable. For example, a factorial design could manipulate the effects of different kinds of practice and amounts of practice on the development of motor coordination in young children.

Rather than a posttest only, a method that has been advocated and frequently

used in evaluation research is that with a pretest as well as a posttest. An example would be evaluating the effectiveness of a series of films on health care with a questionnaire. Typical questions would be: "How frequently do you brush your teeth each day?" and "Approximately how many carbonated drinks do you consume each week?" All of the types of designs that can be employed with the posttest-only design also can be employed in a situation where both a pretest and a posttest are obtained. In a true experimental design, the available group of subjects would be randomly allocated to the various treatment conditions.

Potentially, the major advantage of the pretest-posttest design is that it allows one to obtain more information (statistical power) than would be true for a posttest-only design. The potential advantages could be important when (1) the number of subjects in each cell necessarily is small, (2) subjects vary widely with respect to the dependent measure in comparison to anticipated effects of the independent variables, and (3) the correlation within cells of before and after measures of dependent variables are expected to be high. All of these conditions would hold in the following circumstances. Methods are investigated for increasing the IQs of children in highly impoverished city areas. Three methods of training are to be compared with one another and with a control group. Because of the amount of time and funds required to undertake each of the three special training programs (treatments), it is feasible to have no more than about 50 children for each group. A total group of 200 children then is randomly divided into three treatment groups and a control group. It is important to determine not only the statistical significance of differences among the groups but also to precisely document the exact amounts of such differences. Consequently, it is necessary for experimental error to be reduced to the very minimum possible. The pretest shows that the average measured IQ is 85; more important, it is found that the standard deviation of the scores is large (about that of the normative population as a whole). Although it is hypothesized that the treatments will produce improvements over the control group and perhaps have different average effects from one another, it is anticipated that there will be a rather high correlation between pretest and posttest measures *within* each of the groups (e.g., on the order of .70 or higher). Because the research problem has all of the characteristics mentioned above, indicating the need for a pretest-posttest design, such a design definitely should be employed in this case.

In contrast to the above example, it usually is *unwise* to employ a pretest-posttest design rather than employ a posttest-design only. In most evaluation research, all three of the above circumstances that encourage one to use a pretest-posttest design are not present. Frequently the standard deviation of pretest measures is not large in comparison to the expected effects of treatments and/or the correlation between pretest and posttest measures is not high. These conditions probably would hold in comparing the effects of different drugs on the moods of depressed patients in mental hospitals. Most patients would rate themselves as rather glum, and there would not be a large standard deviation in that regard. Pretest and posttest measures probably would not correlate highly, both because of the small standard deviation on each occasion, and because moods tend to fluctuate in all people from day to day.

Most important, in the above and most other types of evaluation research, the

available group of subjects is not so limited in number as to require the time and expense of applying a pretest and of encountering a very real hazard. The hazard mentioned above is that of employing an experimental arrangement in which the pretest *sensitizes* subjects to some aspects of the forthcoming treatment condition. An example would be that previously mentioned of studying the effectiveness of a series of films on health care. If the pretests were administered soon before subjects viewed the films, the questionnaire itself would alert subjects to look for and retain information relative to the questions. An example would be the case in which part of a film stressed the importance of brushing teeth at least three times a day, including after lunch. One can imagine the impact this would have on an individual who indicated in the pretest that he only brushed his teeth twice a day, or less. On receiving the advice that it was very important to brush teeth after lunch, the respondent is likely to have taken special note of this in the light of his previous responses to the questionnaire.

An even more blatant example of the sensitization (interaction) of the pretest with the treatment condition would be where the films concerned racial prejudice. In the context of a love story, the film might entail a subtle presentation of the difficulties of Mexican-Americans in this country. Members of the audience might not fully grasp all of the subtle effects of ethnic prejudice shown in the film. However, if only the day before they were required to respond to questionnaires concerning their own feelings and beliefs about Mexican-Americans, they probably would be much more alert to issues regarding prejudice in the films. Whereas such effects are referred to as sensitization, more generally they should be spoken of as interaction of pretest and treatment. Although in some types of research this interaction has predictable effects, in others the effect might be quite surprising. In any case where the treatment concerns an increase in knowledge, the interaction should result in more improvement from the treatment then would occur if a posttest only were administered. In other cases, however, the effect might be very difficult to predict. An example would be that of a series of films intended to improve attitudes toward life in the armed forces. A pretest might not only sensitize people to the content of the films, but also have a boomerang effect. The pretest might have alerted subjects to the effort to manipulate their attitudes by use of the films, thus causing them to resist any changes in that regard, or even move toward more negative positions.

Potentially another problem with the pretest-posttest design is that the two testings will interact, which is usually referred to as a "practice effect." However, in most instances this is not a serious problem. In many cases the degree of such practice effects is known from previous studies, and known to be slight. This is true in the illustrative experiment concerning the measurement of intelligence before and after treatments. If a no-treatment control group is employed, interactions of measures (and also natural changes over time) can be separated out from the treatment effects. Also, in some types of research it is possible to employ alternate forms of a measuring instrument which at least partly rule out practice effects. This would be true in the study concerning intelligence if there were two forms available for the test. In the pretest, half of the subjects in each treatment group could

receive one test and the other half would receive the other test. In the posttest, subjects would receive the alternate form. This would supply all of the information necessary to separate the major component of practice effects from the treatment effects.

Research designs have been developed which further provide information about interaction of pretests with treatments and interactions of pretests with posttests. One such design is as follows:

$$O_{a1} \quad X_a \quad O_{a2}$$
$$X_b \quad O_{b2}$$
$$O_{c1} \quad \quad O_{c2}$$
$$O_{d2}$$

In the first row of the design, we have a complete pretest-posttest treatment in which measures are administered before and after. In the second row the same treatment is applied, but there is a posttest only. The third row represents a control group in which both pretests and posttests are given, but there is no intervening treatment. The fourth row symbolizes a condition in which only a posttest is given. The subscripts on observations indicate the time at which the observations (dependent measures) are taken. A comparison of the group in row 1 with that in row 2 would indicate the size of the interaction of pretest with treatment. A comparison of results from groups depicted in rows 3 and 4 would indicate the degree of interaction between pretests and posttests. If the mean posttest scores are not very different for the two groups, it indicates that the interaction was slight. If the mean difference on posttest measures for the two treatment conditions was slight, the data could be pooled. If mean differences on the posttest measure were small for the two control groups, the data could be combined. A simple comparison then could be made of the pooled treatment data with the pooled control data. This would lead to a very simple test of the difference between the treatment condition and the control condition. However, if differences within treatment groups and/or within control groups are relatively large, then the situation becomes rather messy. In particular, if the differences within the two types of groups are not very similar, the results become largely uninterpretable.

Rather than waste more time on the topic, it is better to say that such elaborate designs as those depicted above for testing artifacts in pretest-posttest designs are definitely not worth the trouble. If the experimenter has enough subjects available and resources that are required by elaborate designs like the four-group design above, then it would be utterly foolish to use the pretest-posttest design rather than the posttest-only design. In that case there would be no interaction of pretests with treatments or interactions of pretests with posttests. Not to employ the posttest-only design would be as foolish as the individual with a chronic ailment who bought only half of the medicine prescribed for his illness so that he could pay for many visits to the doctor's office in order to learn in precise detail about his deteriorating condition.

In summary, the posttest-only design is the workhorse of evaluation research, and with certain exceptions, should remain so. Pretest-posttest designs should be

used only when the three conditions discussed above prevail and there is reason to believe that pretest treatment interactions and pretest-posttest interactions are slight. Pretest-posttest interactions can be reduced considerably in some instances by employing alternative forms of measuring instruments, but it is very difficult to reduce appreciably pretest-treatment interactions.

Methods of analysis. There are no major problems in analyzing the results of true experiments in evaluation research. Whether the pretest-posttest design or the posttest-only design is employed, an abundance of statistical methods are available (e.g., those discussed by Kirk, 1968, and by Winer, 1971). Indeed, it is easy to get the feeling that the statistical machinery is overly elegant for the data we frequently feed into it. Generally speaking, heavy reliance is placed on the linear model in statistics, which considers variance manifested in an independent variable as being decomposable into uncorrelated additive components respectively concerning (1) treatment effects, (2) their interactions, (3) interaction of subjects and observations in a repeated measurements design, and (4) a residual component attributable to experimental error.

The first step in analyzing data from true experimental designs usually is to perform an overall analysis of variance to test for significance of main effects and interactions. This is no problem at all in the posttest-only design. In the pretest-posttest design, a problem (usually slight) occurs because of possible correlated errors from pretest to posttest. For example, people might tend to repeat some test-taking strategies from the first to the second testing, such as the tendency to guess when in doubt rather than be conservative in that regard. Such correlated errors would tend to increase the correlation between pretests and posttests, and thus reduce the error term below what it would be if such practice effects were not present. This is not a major problem because (1) there is little reason to believe that such correlated errors occur on most measures and (2) the research results should be taken seriously only if they are significant at a level which leaves little room to worry about such small artifacts.

As so many people have said over the last decade, tests of statistical significance alone provide only the most meager form of evidence regarding the results of experiments. To issue this warning again here should be on the order of attacking a straw man, but unfortunately there are still many research workers who overly glorify the importance of "hypothesis testing" with inferential statistics. Tests of statistical significance alone are best regarded as "wastebasket tests"; that is, if the data do not measure up in this regard, it probably would be better to toss the data sheets into the wastebasket than to try to make sense of them in any other way. Beyond providing comfort that *something* happened as a function of the treatments, such significant tests provide very little information indeed.

If data survive the wastebasket test, then three additional types of information should be obtained. First, if the independent variable(s) are on an ordered metric, then tests for various trends should be made. By an ordered metric is meant an independent variable measurable on a rank-order scale, an interval scale, or a ratio scale. Examples on an interval scale would be intelligence test scores and ratings of attitudes toward the United Nations. Of course, analysis of variance designs fre-

quently entail dependent variables that are not in terms of an ordered metric, such as comparisons of people from different occupations and comparisons of the effects of different types of drugs. If the independent and dependent variables are expressed in terms of an ordered metric, it is important to learn to what extent the trend is linear, quadratic, or otherwise. Also, the percentages of variance explained by the different trends provide very important information. Thus, if the linear trend explains 90% of the variation of the means of treatment groups and higher order components explain only the remaining 10%, this means that the trend can be spoken of as essentially linear.

The second type of analysis which should be performed in many cases is that of asserting statistical confidence bands about mean effects. This procedure might indicate, for example, that the odds are 99 out of 100 that the learning rate produced by one method of instruction is at least 50% better than that produced by another method of instruction. The logic and technique of developing such confidence bands are discussed in most advanced books on statistics (e.g., Kirk, 1968, and Winer, 1971).

The third thing one should do in addition to running tests of statistical significance is to compute various indices showing the strength of relationship between independent and dependent variables. A simple example would be that of comparing a treatment group with a control group, in which a t test shows that the two are significantly different. Although the test of significance would provide some assurance regarding the genuineness of the apparent difference, it would not necessarily provide any information at all about the amount of difference between the treatment group and the control group. The amount of difference could be obtained by the point-biserial correlation. It would mean a great deal of difference whether this correlation were, say, .60 rather than .20. The major measures employed to document the degree of relationship between independent and dependent variables are all variants of the product-moment correlation coefficient. These methods can be applied not only to the simple situation of comparing a control group with a treatment group, but also to any number of levels of a treatment group and to any number of combinations of such independent variables in a factorial design. These methods are discussed by Kirk (1968) and by Winer (1971).

Quasi-experimental Designs

As mentioned previously, essentially a quasi-experimental design is one in which some potentially important confounding variables are not controlled. It was said that essentially what one does in this situation is to obtain extra information (over that which would be obtained from a true experimental design) in order to weave a net of circumstantial evidence regarding the "reality" of observed findings. Evaluation research usually takes place in the crucible of ongoing important life activities of individuals, and consequently it frequently is either unethical or unfeasible to randomly divide subjects up for treatments or to do other things that would be needed to obtain precise experimental control. Here an effort will be made to summarize some of the most important considerations from the writings of Campbell and his associates; also, the author will state some opinions of his own

regarding the nature of quasi-experimental designs and their place in evaluation research.

Pre-experimental designs. To place in focus principles underlying quasi-experimental designs, Campbell and Stanley (1968) present three pre-experimental designs. The lack of experimental control in these designs is so obvious that it points up the need to provide additional information before any conclusions can be reached from research. A very crude form of pre-experimental design is as follows:

$$X \quad O$$

In the design, some type of treatment is applied and subsequently observations are made. An example would be that of introducing a new food supplement program in elementary schools for children in impoverished areas. At the end of the school year, children are given brief medical examinations to index general health and freedom from various symptoms of disorder. On the basis of such statistics and ratings, it is concluded that the children are in reasonably good health (a conclusion, of course, which cries out for a normative comparison with children in general of the same age group). On the basis of this impressionistic information, the researchers conclude (incorrectly, of course) that the food supplement program has actually benefited the children's health. The possible rival hypotheses relating to confounding variables are quite obvious. First, as mentioned, measurements taken at the observation period would have no meaningful basis of comparison in this case. However, in some uses of this pre-experimental design, comparison bases are available either in terms of norms or at least in terms of the impressions of the experimenters. Regarding the former possibility, norms for general health might have been available from a national survey or at least a sample throughout a geographic region. Similarly, in other uses of this pre-experimental design, there may be considerable normative data available, for example, in the form of standardized tests of achievement in various topics. When such standardized bases of comparison are not available, the "experimenters" frequently have some impressionistic standards in their heads. This probably would have been the case with the study of changes in general health as a function of nutritional supplements. The physicians performing the physical examinations probably were comparing the children in the study with children from the same socioeconomic environments who had not participated in the experimental program of food supplements. However, such comparisons are shaky at best, for reasons too obvious to merit detailed discussion.

A second fault of the above pre-experimental design is that it provides no evidence regarding the crucial issue of whether or not the treatment had any effect on the dependent variable(s). To reach any safe conclusions at all in that regard, the necessary starting point would be at least to add a pretest. This leads to the second pre-experimental design:

$$O_1 \quad X \quad O_2$$

The major uncontrolled variable in the second pre-experimental design is that of natural changes as a function of time and events, rather than by the experimental

treatment per se. There are numerous ways in which this can occur. For example, in a study of the effectiveness of communication programs concerning birth planning, any evaluation research that ranged over several years might be confounded by changes in attitudes of young people that had nothing at all to do with the communication programs. Psychological dispositions in that regard have been so cyclic over the last 40 years that natural changes over periods of several years would constitute potentially important confounding influences. Even over shorter periods of time, rapid changes frequently occur in the social milieu, which could induce large changes from pretest to posttest measures regardless of intervening experimental treatments. An example would be that of studying the effectiveness of group discussions on attitudes toward various aspects of an ongoing war. The pretest is given while the war is still on, treatments concerning group discussions go on over a period of two months, but a cease-fire is signed the day before posttest measures are to be given. The possible confound would be painfully obvious to the experimenter.

A second rival hypothesis concerning the one group, pretest-posttest design, concerns possible regression toward the mean. This condition would exist if the group of subjects being investigated had been preselected either on the pretest independent variable or on some variable that correlated substantially with the pretest variable. The former would be the case if children for a training program in remedial reading were selected initially in terms of their low scores on a reading achievement test and the same test was used for the posttest measure. The second possibility is illustrated in the situation where the children are selected not on the basis of the reading achievement test but on the basis of low scores on an IQ test. Because the two types of tests would correlate substantially, the experimental group would be well below average on reading comprehension as well as IQ. In either case, it is expected that there will be a regression toward the mean when subjects are selected because they are above or below average with respect to the pretest and posttest measures. This matter was discussed in detail earlier in this chapter and in *Psychometric Theory*. In addition to the two faults discussed above of this type of design, it also suffers from all of the problems concerning pretest-posttest designs mentioned with respect to true experiments. To reiterate, the major confounding variables are interaction of pretest with treatment and interaction of the two testings with each other.

A third type of experimental design employs a control group at the posttest period only, but the two groups involved are not formed randomly from some larger group. Instead, the groups were intact before the experiment was undertaken. This design can be symbolized as follows, with a dashed line between the rows representing the two groups signifying intact groups rather than randomly sampled groups.

$$\underline{X} \; \_ \; \_ \; \frac{O_a}{O_b}$$

Examples of this type of pre-experimental design are legion in evaluation research. An example is that of trying out a new program of dormitory counseling for

students at a college. There are two large men's dormitories available for the study. The counseling program is undertaken throughout one semester in one dormitory, and no changes are made in the other dormitory. Afterward dependent measures are administered concerning progress in school, self-ratings, and peer-ratings of various kinds.

An obvious rival hypothesis with this type of design is that men in the two dormitories differed initially with respect to the traits involved in the dependent measures. There are many ways in which this could happen. For example, it might be that the entire football team was housed in one of the dormitories. Campbell and Stanley (1968) mentioned a number of other confounding variables in this type of design, for example, possible differences between the two groups because of more willingness of the members of one group to participate in the research.

It is necessary to carefully distinguish between experiments comparing *intact* groups and ones that will be discussed later concerning *contrasted* groups. In studying intact groups, at least the intention is to compare groups that are approximately comparable with respect to traits involved in the dependent measures. Thus, in the previous example, by applying the treatment to one section of a course rather than another, it is hoped that the students in the two groups do not differ markedly on the average in terms of traits relating to the dependent variable. In many instances, this is a reasonable assumption; consequently, one should not rule out altogether evidence coming from this pre-experimental design. As will be discussed more fully later, contrasted groups are selected *because* it is thought that they differ markedly with respect to some important psychological traits.

From pre-experimental to quasi-experimental designs. Of course, if there were no practical or ethical problems involved, the wise experimenter always would change or extend the previously mentioned and other pre-experimental designs into true experimental designs. Illustrative of the fact that this is not always practicable is the situation in which it would be necessary to isolate schoolchildren from one another in their training in different methods of teaching foreign languages. To make comparisons among intact groups in the usual classroom situation might result in "group effects" where the feelings of children were communicated to one another, and this in turn influenced dependent measures. However, the alternative of giving separate instruction to each student in isolation from the others probably would be completely out of the question in terms of manpower and other resources.

That the employment of a true experimental design is not always ethical is evidenced in a study of two types of memorization tasks in deaf and normal children. It goes without saying that the experimenter would not take a large group of normal children and randomly deafen half of them in order to ensure that the niceties of true experimental designs were obtained. In these instances, and other instances that are far less obvious, it is necessary to employ quasi-experimental designs. Campbell and his associates have discussed numerous principles regarding a wide variety of such designs (e.g., Campbell and Stanley, 1968). Here only several major issues will be discussed.

One of the major problems incurred in research is the inability to achieve a true experimental design by the random assignment of subjects to groups. Previously, it was mentioned that some pre-experimental designs require the use of intact groups. As mentioned there, these problems frequently are not serious unless subjects are preselected on the dependent variable or on measures that correlate substantially with the dependent variable. Real problems arise, however, when the groups being compared are known to differ markedly in at least some traits. Examples of that would be comparing deaf with normals, males with females, mental hospital patients with persons outside, and groups from different countries. If a posttest-only design is used with such contrasted groups, differences on the posttest quite likely are because of initial differences among the groups rather than anything having to do with experimental treatments. A statistician could argue that it is absolutely hopeless to perform impeccable research by making comparisons among such groups. However, the problems will not go away simply because they pose problems for research. If the person actually is interested in differences among such contrasted groups, he must make comparisons among them and apply as many safeguards as possible against the intrusion of confounding variables.

The simplest type of design for contrasted groups is that in which the only "treatment" consists of group membership, and the members of each group are tested with respect to some attribute of interest. An example would be that of comparing political attitudes of people in different occupations, which would be symbolized as follows:

$$O_a$$
$$O_b$$
$$O_c$$
$$.$$
$$.$$
$$.$$
$$O_k$$

Differences in scores obtained for the above k groups could be submitted to analysis of variance and other types of statistical comparisons. If one is interested in differences in psychological traits of occupational groups or any other groups, then such comparisons are straightforward. However, because the groups differ from one another in so many ways, it might be very difficult to determine *why* the groups differ on the trait-being investigated. Also, the groups may differ from one another because of artifacts in the measurement procedures rather than because of any real differences among them. For example, if white interviewers interview both black and white adults regarding political attitudes, the presence of the white interviewer might make the black respondents give answers that are not representative of their true feelings. As another example, mental patients may show differences from normal persons in terms of various types of perceptual tasks, not because they really are deficient in their perceptual abilities, but because they are anxious and are distracted by their own personal problems. There are many other artifacts of measurement that could produce illusory differences among contrasted groups.

If the evaluation research concerns differences among contrasted groups when no treatment condition is applied, the major safeguard is to weave a network of circumstantial evidence over time regarding hypothesized differences. One should be quite chary of differences obtained in one setting with only one type of measure of an attribute. Thus, one should place very little faith in the comparison of one group of schizophrenic patients with one group of normal subjects on only one measure relating to perceptual accuracy. If essentially the same finding is obtained in other locales, and comparisons are made on a wide variety of measures concerning perceptual accuracy, then the circumstantial evidence accumulates to the point where considerable confidence can be placed in the tenability of the hypothesis at issue. In essence, when contrasted groups differ so markedly as deaf from normal and schizophrenic from normal, it is necessary to establish a type of construct validity, not unlike that discussed in the previous chapter with respect to the development of measures of psychological traits.

A research method that has been employed frequently in comparing the effects of treatments on contrasted groups is to match subjects from the two groups on one or more variables. An example would be that of a new method of teaching reading skills in the first grade in which a comparison is made of the amount of progress shown by children from a highly impoverished city area with children from a much more affluent area of the same city. A pretest shows that the average level of reading skill is very different for the two groups before the special method of instruction is applied. The experimenter puts children from the two groups in pairs such that their scores on the test of reading comprehension are very similar. In this way, the experimenter obtains two groups that have very similar average scores on the pretest and very similar standard deviations. This could be a disastrous approach to studying the issue. By matching subjects in this way, the experimenter would be selecting children with comparatively high reading scores in the lower socioeconomic group and children with comparatively low reading scores in the higher socioeconomic group. Then, purely because of measurement error in the test, there would be a regression toward the mean on the posttest. This would make it appear that the children from the lower socioeconomic group actually lost ground in terms of reading skills, and that the children from the higher socioeconomic group gained considerably. These would be the expected results regardless of any intervening treatment, and such regression effects could either produce artifactually significant findings from the experiment or at least muddy the waters considerably. There are many other problems that arise from attempts to match subjects in different treatment groups, or in treatment and control groups, for example, the unanswerable question as to whether subjects have been matched on *all* of the major possible confounding variables. When the experiment does not concern contrasted groups, matching usually is not worth the effort. When the experiment concerns contrasted groups, matching is a very hazardous practice that is definitely not recommended. Far better is to try to take account of initial differences between contrasted groups by research designs and methods of analysis discussed subsequently.

In some situations where either intact or contrasted groups are compared, observations are available on a number of occasions before the treatment and after

the treatment. Essentially, the advantage of having multiple observations before and/or after the treatment is that it provides an indication of the amount of normal variation in the phenomenon from time to time, irrespective of a treatment condition. An example would be that of comparing the achievement test scores in mathematics in the third through seventh grade for children in two schools in the same community. The study is performed retroactively for students who currently are in the seventh grade and have remained in schools from the third grade up to that time. In one of the schools (A), a new approach to teaching mathematics was introduced throughout the fifth grade, but this was not done in the other school (B). Because the achievement test is given routinely each year, there is no problem in having comparable measurements available for each of the five years. Some possible types of results are shown in Figures 6.3 through 6.5. Evidence for a treatment effect when there are multiple observations before and after the treatment over time consists of a sharp interaction from before to after the treatment for the two or more groups being compared, as seen in Figure 6.3. In Figure 6.4, the apparent change in school A is illusory because it is matched by a proportional change in school B. Rather than the treatment having any particular effect, the steepening curve probably is because of other (unknown) changes in instruction and general social milieu of the two schools. Another possibility is that the national norms for the test in question were obtained somewhat differently than in previous years, in such a way as to increase the apparent competence of students in these two schools in comparison to the national norms.

The results in Figure 6.4 suggest that the treatment had no effect at all on the students in school A beyond what would be expected from the usual instruction, as evidenced in school B. In Figure 6.5 such a sharp interaction is witnessed at the end of the fifth grade, but the increase in average performance shown for school A at the end of the fifth grade dwindles back to approximately the same level as before the treatment by the time testing is performed at the end of the seventh grade. This strongly suggests that the special training had only a temporary effect, and in the long-run the students in school A would have been as well off to have received the same training as students in school B. Of course, in a situation where there are multiple observations before and after testing, there are many other such results that would not have been nearly as clear as those depicted in Figures 6.3 through 6.5. Unless striking results are obtained like those depicted in the figures, usually it is quite hazardous to make any firm interpretations at all of studies concerning intact or contrasted groups.

In some evaluation research, no control condition at all is available for comparing effects of the treatment. This would be the case in the previous example if data were available only for school A. Studies where pre- and post-measures are available on a number of occasions before and after the experiment are referred to as *time-series experiments*. Usually when the name is employed, one has available at least three or more sets of observations before and after the experimental treatment. A typical design would be as follows:

$$O_1 \quad O_2 \quad O_3 \quad O_4 \quad X \quad O_5 \quad O_6 \quad O_7 \quad O_8$$

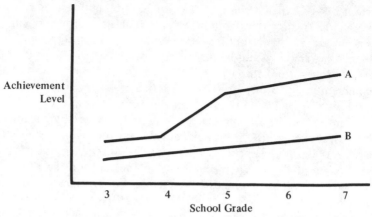

FIGURE 6.3   Comparison of an experimental group (A) with a control group (B) which
             indicates that the treatment had a definite effect.

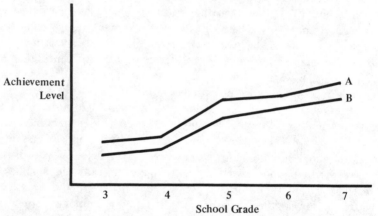

FIGURE 6.4   Comparison of an experimental group (A) with a control group (B) in which the
             apparent effect of the treatment is illusory.

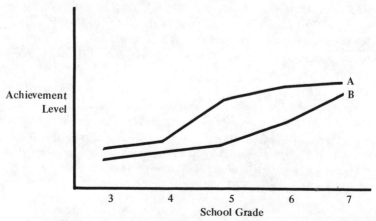

FIGURE 6.5   Comparison of an experimental group (A) with a control group (B) in which the
             treatment effect was only temporary.

Some of the many possible results from examining this time-series are depicted in Figure 6.6. In condition a, the curve goes up from before to after the treatment; but it was going up at the same rate before the treatment and continues up at the same rate after the treatment. Consequently, there is no reason to believe that the treatment had any effect. Curve b also goes up from before to after the treatment, but the variations both before and after treatment provide no confidence that the apparent treatment effect is real. In condition c, there is circumstantial evidence that the apparent increase from before to after the treatment is "real." However, since the curve goes back down to the same level as before the treatment, any effects of the treatment apparently were quite temporary. Strong circumstantial evidence for the occurrence of a treatment effect is presented in condition d.

For reasons which were discussed previously, the time-series experiments, without any form of comparison group (intact group or contrasted group), provide at best only very rough circumstantial evidence for a treatment effect. With any one-group experiment, many rival hypotheses are available to explain results. If there is only a pretest or a pretest and posttest, so many rival hypotheses are available that such designs are referred to as pre-experimental. When only a treatment group is available and no comparisons can be made either with an intact group or even a contrasted group, then no amount of observation before and after will permit the experimenter to reach strong conclusions about the results.

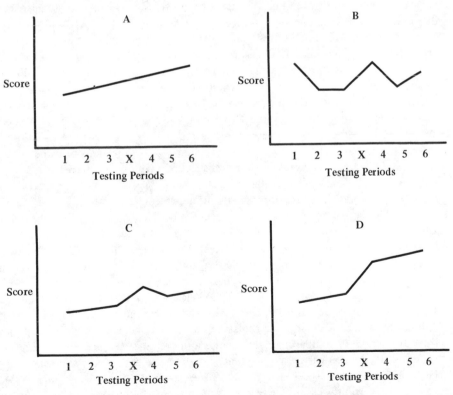

FIGURE 6.6   Four different types of results that could be obtained from a time-series study.

Methods of analysis. Whereas statistical methods for the analysis of true experiments generally are straightforward, methods of analysis for quasi-experimental designs are controversial in many cases. Methods for analyzing quasi-experimental designs are discussed in detail by Campbell and Stanley (1968); only some of the major principles will be discussed here. The better quasi-experimental designs have two features, which we will assume to be the case in discussing methods of analysis. First, there is a control group, which, however, usually consists of an intact similar group or a purposefully drawn contrasted group rather than a random sample of available subjects. Second, observations are made before and after the treatment on both the treatment group(s) and the control group. In some cases there may be more than one observation before and after the treatment is applied.

When either an intact group or a contrasted group is employed as a control group (or as one of two or more treatment groups), there is always the possibility that groups differ from one another on the pretest measure before treatments are applied. Examples were given previously of how this could be so. It has been recommended that covariance analysis (COVARAN) be used as a general tool for partialing out the effects of pretest differences on posttest differences. Covariance analysis actually has been employed for that purpose in many quasi-experimental designs.

At the present state of knowledge about the use of COVARAN, it is a *distinct mistake* to employ this method of analysis with quasi-experimental designs. First, there are some serious questions regarding the meaning of COVARAN in any type of statistical analysis. For example, even if the pretest measure can be partialed out of the results of the posttest measure, how does one control for variables which correlate with both the pretest and posttest variable but are not included in the analysis? An illustration would be where the pretest and posttest measure concerned an experiment on improvement of reading comprehension. Two classrooms are used as intact groups for the experiment, one classroom receiving a special treatment, the other acting as a control group. COVARAN is used to adjust for initial differences in the pretest measure for analysis of differences on the posttest measures. However, if the groups differ substantially with regard to reading comprehension initially, they also probably differ with respect to general intelligence. Then, if the pretest measure of reading comprehension is statistically held constant by COVARAN from the posttest measure, the two groups still could differ substantially in terms of average IQ. The sheer difference in IQ could affect differences between groups on the posttest measure even if the effect due to the pretest measure were held constant. Several questions of this kind arise about the logic of COVARAN and its use in all types of experimentation.

The second problem with the use of COVARAN with quasi-experimental designs is that the assumptions are frequently violated. A cardinal assumption is that the within-groups regression slope is the same for all groups. This assumption is quite likely to be false in comparing intact groups and even more so in contrasted groups, for example, in comparing pretest and posttest scores for normal persons and schizophrenic mental patients after both have participated in a treatment concerning training of motor skills. There are many reasons the regression slope might be

different in the two groups, for example, there could be an "end effect" in normals because the task is so easy that many subjects make the highest score possible, which in turn would tend to produce a nonlinear scatter plot and thus a reduced linear regression slope.

A third reason COVARAN should not be used in quasi-experimental designs is that there is quite a hassle about how to take account of measurement error (test reliability) in employing this class of statistical methods. This matter is discussed and illustrated by Werts and Linn (1971). The problem is that, if some correction due to measurement error is not made, then COVARAN undercorrects the posttest measure for differences in the pretest measure. If the reliabilities are far from unity (e.g., less than .90), either some type of correction for measurement error must be made or the statistical results obviously will be fallacious. Also, as Werts and Linn demonstrate (1971), the distortion may either result in an overly liberal or overly conservative statistical test of the differences between comparison groups.

Unfortunately, the experts are still arguing about how to adjust statistical parameters of COVARAN to take account of measurement error. Even if a logically acceptable solution were found, it apparently would entail the gathering of considerable data regarding the measurement error inherent in the pretest and posttest. Data of this kind usually are not available in most evaluation research, which means that the research time and effort would be increased considerably to gather this new information. Even if data concerning measurement of reliability were available from previous investigations, it would be hazardous to use such data because reliability coefficients might be different in previous research from those in the study at hand. Also, unless the data obtained from a previous study or from the study being conducted were based on a large number of subjects (e.g., at least 300), the reliability coefficients would be ridden with sampling error, and consequently any corrections based upon the reliability coefficients would provide rather poor estimates.

There is a much better general approach to analyzing quasi-experimental designs than COVARAN. The approach consists of considering differences between pretest and posttest measures as constituting a within-subjects factor in repeated measurements analysis of variance designs. Comparisons of treatments with one another and/or with a control group could also be a within-subjects factor, but usually this is a between-groups factor instead. Thus, the usual quasi-experimental design entails a within-subjects, repeated measurements factor, and a between-groups factor or factors. The major result of interest is the *interaction of treatment conditions with comparison groups.* A very simple example is presented in Figure 6.7. Here we have an imperfect control group, in the sense that an intact group happens to differ substantially on the pretest from the treatment group, or a contrasted group purposefully is chosen. In this case, imagine that standard deviations within groups on the pretest measure are small relative to the mean difference, hence the difference is statistically significant and large in terms of amount of variance explained. Rather than try to covary these differences, it is better to examine the interaction of the two groups with pretest and posttest measures. Although the two groups differed substantially on the pretest, they differ much more on the posttest.

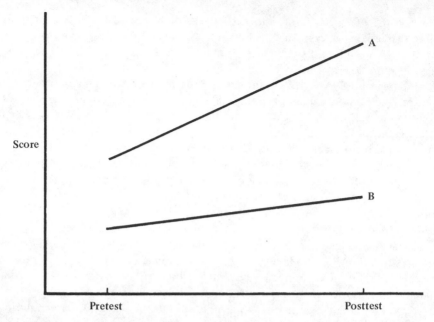

FIGURE 6.7   Comparison of an experimental group (A) with a control group (B) before and
after the experimental treatment.

The interaction variance can be examined straighforwardly for statistical significance (e.g., as discussed in Kirk, 1968; Winer, 1971).

Analyses of more complex experimental designs also usually involve interactions
of observations with treatment conditions. A complex example would be that of
multiple pretests and posttests in comparing a number of different treatments with
a control group. In this case all groups are nonrandomly sampled; rather they are
either intact groups or contrasted groups. Differences in average scores over time on
the multiple pretests would be evidence of differences in general standings of the
groups before the treatment is applied. Interactions of groups and pretest measures
would be evidence of different growth functions (differences in maturation or
effects of social events on the groups). Similar analysis could be performed on
posttest scores. Of most interest, however, would be various interaction terms
concerning pretest and posttest scores for the different treatments. Of interest
would be interactions of groups with immediate pretest and posttest scores, mean
scores over all pretest and posttest occasions, and selective other interaction terms.
Tests of significance can be performed on these. However, since a number of such
tests might be performed in a post hoc manner depending on the obtained results, it
would be wise to be conservative in interpretation of statistical tests, that is, to
place faith in only a high level of statistical significance, such as the .01 level or
lower probability. Measures of strength of association can be obtained for all main
effects and interactions in analysis of variance designs (cf. Winer, 1971: 428-430).
Such measures of association will provide suggestions regarding the size of differences among treatment conditions and their implications for the workaday world in
which evaluation research is conducted.

REFERENCES

Buros, O. K. *Tests in print.* Highland Park, N.J.: Gryphon Press, 1961.

———. *Seventh Mental Measurements Yearbook.* Highland Park, N.J.: Gryphon Press, 1972.

Campbell, D. T. Reforms as experiments. *American Psychologist,* 1969, 24: 409-429.

Campbell, D. T. and J. C. Stanley. *Experimental and quasi-experimental designs for research.* Chicago: Rand-McNally, fourth printing, 1968.

Cronbach, L. J. and L. Furby. How we should measure "change"—or should we? *Psychological Bulletin,* 1970, 74: 68-80.

Guilford, J. P. *Psychometric methods.* 2nd ed.; New York: McGraw-Hill, 1954.

———. *Personality.* New York: McGraw-Hill, 1959.

Kirk, R. E. *Experimental design: Procedures for the behavioral sciences.* Belmont, Cal.: Wadsworth, 1968.

Lord, F. M. Elementary models for measuring change. In C. W. Harris (ed.) *Problems in measuring change.* Madison: University of Wisconsin Press, 1963.

Nesselroade, J. R. and H. W. Reese (eds.) *Life-span developmental psychology.* New York: Academic Press, 1972.

Nunnally, J. C. *Psychometric theory.* New York: McGraw-Hill, 1967.

———. *Introduction to psychological measurement.* New York: McGraw-Hill, 1970.

———. *Educational measurement and evaluation.* 2nd ed.; New York: McGraw-Hill, 1972.

Webb, E. J., D. T. Campbell, R. D. Schwartz, and L. Sechrest. *Unobtrusive measures: Nonreactive research in the social sciences.* Chicago: Rand-McNally, 1966.

Werts, C. E. and R. L. Linn. Analyzing school effects ANOVA with a fallible covariate. *Educational and Psychological Measurement,* 1971, 31: 95-104.

Winer, B. J. *Statistical principles in experimental design.* 2nd ed.; New York: McGraw-Hill, 1971.

7

A DECISION-THEORETIC APPROACH
TO EVALUATION RESEARCH

WARD EDWARDS

University of Southern California

MARCIA GUTTENTAG

and

KURT SNAPPER

George Washington University

Two themes dominate the current literature on evaluation. One major theme is "Clean it up," meaning that programs should be as similar as possible to experiments, so that classical experimental designs and statistics can be used to evaluate them (Suchman, 1967; Campbell, 1974; Riecken et al., 1975). Researchers who adopt this view, a position not commonly held by program people, are fond of citing the few score examples of programs that have been designed, at least initially, as experiments, for example, the negative income tax (Boruch, 1973; Watts, 1969). Their efforts are primarily devoted to illustrating the usefulness and power of experimental designs when used for evaluation (Campbell, 1974; Gilbert, Light, and

AUTHORS' NOTE: We are grateful to John Busa and Saul Rosoff of the Office of Child Development for their help in the development of the decision-theoretic process within that agency.

Mosteller, 1974), in the belief that the central task of evaluation is to reach stronger casual inferences.

A more muted refrain, in a minor key, is chanted by a diverse group of skeptics. Their theme is, "Evaluation will not make a difference." Given the muddiness and complexity of organizational and bureaucratic practices, the separation between researchers and political decision makers, and the potent political context of many programs, they emphasize how rarely evaluation data are used in final program decisions. These critics locate the core problem of evaluation in the large, perhaps unbridgeable, gap between evaluation data and the decisions of policy makers (Weiss, 1972; Weiss and Rein, 1970; Williams and Evans, 1969). They are pessimistic about the likelihood of ever linking the two.

Both themes are valid. Much that is useful to doing and understanding evaluation has been produced by each group.

Yet the viewpoint of this article is that neither one addresses the central issue of evaluation research, which is the requirement for a usable conceptual framework and methodology that links *inferences about states of the world, the values of decision makers, and decisions.*

To understand why such a linkage is crucial to evaluation research methodologies, we will first discuss the distinctive characteristics of of evaluation research questions and contexts, and the ways in which evaluation research problems can be distinguished from other research problems. Then we will present a conceptual and methodological framework for evaluation research, essentially the ideas of decision analysis specialized to evaluation research interests. Within this framework the three elements—inferences, values, and decision—though distinct, combine in what we consider a logically compelling way. The role of casual inferences and experimentation will be discussed, including the dangers of the pseudo-experiment. The topic of handling political and bureaucratic complexities within the approach will be examined. The concrete steps of proposed methodology will then be presented, with an example of its use.

EVALUATION FOR DECISION

Evaluations, we believe, exist (or perhaps only should exist) to facilitate intelligent decision-making. The scientist who conducts evaluation research, and even his sponsor, may be interested in various hypotheses about the program (or whatever it is) being evaluated out of sheer intellectual curiosity. And an evaluation research program will often satisfy curiosities. But if it does no more, if it does not improve the basis for decisions about the program and its competitors, then it loses its distinctive character as *evaluation* research and becomes simply research. Most significant programs, we believe, are evaluated because some decision maker wants help in figuring out what to do. Sometimes there are clear-cut alternatives; occasionally they can even be meaningfully compared with one another. More often, programs of rather different characters with rather different purposes are competing for money. Perhaps the most common decision question of all is "Should we go on doing this or should we try something else, including doing nothing?"

STAKES, AS WELL AS ODDS, CONTROL DECISIONS

Decision makers, not researchers, make decisions. While the decision maker always should be, and sometimes is, willing to consider the evidence bearing on his options and his choice among them, virtually never is he willing to delegate to that evidence, or its finder, the task of being decisive. Nor, we believe, should he. Every human decision does, and should, depend on the answers to two questions: what are the odds, and what's at stake. Most research evidence bears directly on the first of these two questions, and at best indirectly on the second. But the second is the most important. Moreover, for every real-world decision the stakes are complicated, multidimensional, and high. For example, an educational program which, on the evidence, in fact educates no one may nevertheless be desirable. Perhaps it is addressed to a disadvantaged group and contributes to the feeling of members or leaders that the group's needs are being felt and responded to. Or perhaps some officeholder needs to be able to point to the program's existence to prove that he kept his campaign promises. Or both. As citizens, we may question whether these are proper reasons for continuing an educationally useless program. As evaluation researchers, however, we clearly fail in understanding the decision problem unless we recognize that these value dimensions are relevant to it. If we want to help the decision maker, our task is to provide him with techniques appropriate to assess the strength and relevance of each of these reasons for continuing or not continuing the program, to aggregate these values appropriately, and then to reach a decision that takes them all into account, each to the extent that its importance justifies.

INCONSISTENT VALUES HELD BY DISAGREEING GROUPS CONTROL MOST DECISIONS

So far we have written as though decisions were made by a single decision maker, with a single, though multidimensional, set of values. For any significant decision, that is absurd. Most organizations have identifiable decision makers. Their role in significant decisions was well summarized by Harry Truman's famous desk sign "The buck stops here." Our point about that sign, different from Truman's, is that the buck seldom started on Truman's desk. It started elsewhere—typically, in dozens of places. Options were formulated, values and costs were assessed. Most commonly, "the buck," by which we mean the decision, never reached Truman's desk; a choice was made by some decision-making group subordinate to him and presented to him, if at all, only for ratification. If it did reach him as a genuine decision problem, it was accompanied by extensive staff studies spelling out the relevant stakes and odds, and typically recommending one option over the others.

Whose values, then, are to be maximized? Occasionally, those of the decision maker, as understood by those who serve and advise him. More often, some amalgam of the values of many different groups all with stakes in the decision. A technology for explicating, comparing, and when possible, reconciling, and ultimately aggregating such inconsistent values of groups in conflict is clearly needed for social decision making. The germs of it exist, though much remains to be done.

Evaluation researchers can ignore this problem of group values in conflict only if they choose, as they often do, to ignore the problem of values altogether, typically by assuming some simple value as the only relevant one. Sometimes, this works well. Doctors, for example, can avoid many value problems by assuming that life is preferable to death and health to sickness. On those assumptions, value questions can be bypassed in favor of more researchable questions such as whether a given procedure does in fact contribute to preservation of life or restoration of health. But we need only to mention recent public discussions of euthanasia, abortion, and preservation of the lives of fetuses with severe genetic defects to illustrate that the values that should bear on medical decisions are often more complicated than that, and to suggest the danger of simplistic, ill-thought-through, unexplicated value systems. (For a careful study of the costs of such casual values, combined with other ingredients of seat-of-the-pants decision-making, in a medical context, see Fryback, 1974. That study also illustrates how decision-theoretical procedures, in this case Bayesian probabilistic inference, can reduce these costs—in Fryback's example, by almost 50%.)

FIVE COMPLAINTS ABOUT FOLKWAYS OF EVALUATION RESEARCHERS

Folkway 1: Reification of Programs

We have frequently encountered the idea that a program is a fixed, unchanging object, observable at various times and places. A common administrative fiction, especially in Washington, is that because some money associated with an administrative label (e.g., Head Start) has been spent at several places and over a period of time, that the entities spending the money are comparable from time to time and from place to place. Such assumptions can easily lead to evaluation-research disasters. Programs differ from place to place because places differ.

This topic is tricky. All entities subject to multiple observation vary, as every experimenting psychologist plagued by within-group individual differences and test-retest unreliability sorrowfully knows. Even batches of vaccine, or even individual doses within a batch, may vary in potency. The question is whether the variations from one observation to another associated with planned action (e.g., different levels of an independent variable) are large or small relative to those associated with spontaneous intra- or interentity variability. That, of course, is typically the question that an experiment sets out to answer, and often an experiment is needed to answer it. But, especially in the domain of social programs, it may be obvious by casual observation that program variability from time to time or from place to place is so large that no reasonable independent variable can be expected to have comparable variance-producing potency. In such cases, experimentation will be at best irrelevant; at worst, severely misleading.

That is no excuse for the evaluation researcher to throw up his hands in despair! The decision maker or decision-making organization *must* do something; the evaluation researcher should help as best he can. And, even in such situations, he can help a great deal.

Folkway 2: Insistence on Casual Inferences

We have often heard research-trained individuals in funding agencies say "If you cannot answer 'why,' don't bother to ask 'what.' " This sort of statement is philosophically dubious, and can lead both to bad science and bad decision-making. The definition of casual inference lies outside the scope of this paper (see, for example, Harre and Secord, 1972). Radical behaviorists typically assert that questions beginning "Why . . ." are really questions beginning "What . . ." ill phrased. Model-builders might disagree, asserting that "What . . ." refers to data while "Why . . ." refers to models. We think this is what those who insist on "Why . . ." questions in evaluation contexts really have in mind. But, as we have already suggested, evaluation-research contexts seldom permit enough precision for the construction of useful models. And a bad model often is worse than none, because its plausibility may turn off fruitful lines of study or action.

Whether or not a model is useful to a decision maker depends on the decision. Imagine, for example, that it were found that Head Start programs work, and that the reason they work is not because of anything that happens to children within the programs but rather because participants are selected, or select themselves, from among those more likely to succeed in school later. From a scientist's point of view this might be considered as a "What . . ." and its accompanying "Why. . . ." From a decision maker's point of view, it is simply two "Whats": his decision about whether or not to continue Head Start programs would presumably depend on the relative importance to him of selecting early those who later will succeed in school and of modifying the chances of success of Head Start participants. It is easy to imagine goal structures in which either value, or both, might be important.

Folkway 3: Pseudo-experiments

Our graduate school teachers of research design, statistical methods, and the like clearly are doing an extraordinarily effective job of selling experimental research as the high road to knowledge. (We have already commented on the frequently inappropriate assumption that knowledge of the kind obtainable from experiments is the crucial antecedent to appropriate decision.) Researchers who have been trained to believe that they must make inferences, that inferences are statistical, and that good statistical inferences grow from experiments therefore find themselves in dilemmas resulting from the intractable, insistently flexible diversity of the real world and programs embedded in it. Experimental and quasi-experimental designs are treated as Procrustean beds, into which programs must fit in order to be evaluated. The result is what we call pseudo-experiments.

One familiar phenomenon in pseudo-experiments is the insistence that the program being studied remain invariant while the data about it are being collected. Programs normally do not remain invariant (though sometimes they do), and a program in need of change is unlikely to remain unchanged to suit the needs of the evaluator. A much more likely outcome is disguised, unadvertised change.

Almost equally familiar is the control group that does not control. Often it is unclear what it is a control for. Defining a suitable control group in a real setting

that depends on voluntary participation is difficult. Medical researchers, for example, must resort to double-blind procedures in which neither patient nor doctor knows whether the drug being administered is one under test or a placebo. How can a social experiment be comparably controlled? Usually, it cannot. Sometimes there are obvious absurdities like matching an experimental city to a "comparable" control city. Less dramatic examples of the same difficulty include control schools, control teachers, control classes, control neighborhoods, and so on. Campbell (1974) argues that only random assignment of subject to treatments can provide really appropriate control groups. He chooses his examples from a field (remedial education) in which suitable control groups may be possible, though even in that field a set of control classes to be compared with a set of experimental classes may be easier to ask for than to obtain. But how can a set of control observations be made to help in evaluating a city-wide program? The necessary condition is a large enough set of entities that can in some sense be considered comparable, and that can be randomly assigned to experimental and control treatments. How often is that condition fulfilled?

The most common solution to this sort of problem is the pre-post design, in which each entity being observed serves as its own control. While this approach is considerably better than no control group at all, it leaves much to be desired, especially when the number of entities that can be observed is small (e.g., one). It confounds spontaneous variation and time-related variation with variation due to treatment, even when ideally done. More important, it is often difficult to do. Certain Alcohol Safety Action Programs, for example, attempted to use this kind of control by setting up roadside surveys in which drivers were stopped by a policeman and asked to take a voluntary breath test. These roadside surveys were conducted before and after community action programs designed to reduce the number of drunk drivers. Among the numerous difficulties of this procedure, one obvious one is that, since the test was voluntary, the drunks could and often did refuse to take it. If that refusal rate among drunks were constant, it would make little difference to the effectiveness of the control. But there is every reason to suppose that the word about being able to refuse with impunity got around, so that more drunks refused before than after the community program, thus providing spurious evidence of program effectiveness.

Don't get us wrong. We are against sin, and believe in both motherhood and control groups. It is almost always nice to have one set of numbers to compare with another set. However, in many evaluation research contexts, such comparisons, even (or perhaps especially) when made with highly sophisticated statistical tools, are more often than not misleading.

The convergent validity approach, where possible, is one way to avoid being misled.

A roadside survey finding of fewer drunk drivers after community action than before, by itself, merits little more than a "Hmm. Interesting." If accompanied by a decrease in drunk-driving arrests (along with some reason to believe that police effort was constant before and after), the interest increases. And a finding of fewer personal-injury accidents than before would raise the interest to fever pitch,

especially if other cities not participating in the program should not show such decrease. Each of these comparisons, by itself, is dubious; in none of them is the control an adequate protection against various kinds of error. Indeed, the conjunction of all of these comparisons would by no means be conclusive, given the degree to which motives other than devotion to pure science can influence the collection of social statistics at the source, and their subsequent processing. Yet the more different lines of evidence point in the same direction, the more persuaded we are likely to become.

To summarize: pseudo-experiments should be avoided if possible, but often it will not be possible. In some cases they may well be worth doing. But in such cases, convergent validity is essential to establish confidence in a conclusion, and the more different lines of evidence converge, the better.

How can a sufficient number of measures be assured so that convergent validity is possible? The use of a conceptual framework which forces the evaluation researcher into multiple measurement is needed. The approach that will be described creates just such a multiple measurement requirement of the evaluation researcher.

Because the conditions for internal validity are not met and error variance abounds in the usual pseudo-experiment in evaluation, the program is considered a failure, since significant effects are not found. But the failure to find such effects is the result of faults in the study, rather than faults in the program. In recent years, the federal government has bet with the null hypothesis, rather than against it, in the social experiments it has sponsored (e.g., negative income tax) in what may be an unconscious awareness of the problems in those evaluations which try to find positive effects of programs using classical procedures.

Folkway 4: Planning vs. Formative Evaluation vs. Summative Evaluation

Social programs often need continuous feedback to permit wise program management and adaptation, either to correct errors or to adapt to changing circumstances. The phrase *formative evaluation* was invented to describe this kind of feedback. It is often distinguished from *summative evaluation,* which is supposed to be the final verdict on the program. And both are distinguished from the planning that occurred before the program ever started.

Why? Obviously the decision problems faced at all three stages are essentially the same. Is this program a good idea? If so, what can we do to make it work as well as possible? If not, how can we devise something better, given our constraints?

As a program progresses, at least four kinds of changes occur. First, the values of both those served by the program and the program people change, both in response to experience with the program and in response to other, external causes. Second, the program evolves, changes shape and character. Third, the external societal circumstances to which the program is a response change. And fourth, knowledge of program events and consequences accumulates. All four of these kinds of changes affect the answer to the decision problem, and all four are continuous.

In our view, the ideal evaluation technique would be equally continuous. It

would assess program merit continuously, taking into account all four kinds of changes, and would permit exploration of the merits of alternative programs that could be had by changing this one, whether the changes were great or small. We believe that decision technology can do this.

Especially important, we think, is the possibility of direct comparison between the extent to which the values the program was intended to serve were expected to be served, and the extent to which they were actually served. Obviously this cannot be done unless those values, almost always multidimensional, can be quantified and aggregated.

In short, we cannot see any hard-and-fast lines to distinguish program evaluation at different stages in its life span. We therefore squirm about language or methods that imply such distinctions, or suggest that different techniques are appropriate for different states of program evaluation.

Folkway 5: The Baseball Statistician's Approach

Our phrase "the baseball statistician's approach" characterizes a very common, and in many ways very sensible approach to evaluation research, one rather unlike the experimentalist's approach we have discussed. The experimentalist wants to test a hypothesis; the baseball statistician wants to describe a phenomenon as thoroughly as possible. So he gathers information, usually as detailed as possible, about the program he is evaluating. He then reports it—again, usually in as detailed a way as possible. We call this the baseball statistician's approach because it is in fact used for evaluative purpose in baseball. Box scores and similar essentially narrative descriptions of what happened are the raw materials; relatively simple statistics like batting averages, earned run averages, and the like are about as sophisticated as the data processing typically gets.

When this approach is applied to anything as complicated as a large social program, it is likely to be costly and voluminous. It is also quite likely to be useful, as it is in baseball. It provides a program manager with detailed feedback, which can be very timely, about what is going on in his program. It provides decision makers with a set of numbers at least some of which must be relevant to their interests and the program's purposes. And it provides sponsors with evaluation reports that are thick and heavy enough to be thorough, and detailed enough to be thoroughly unread. As owners of the Kinsey reports will agree, a massive and unreadable book with an indexing system that permits retrieval of an occasional stimulating statistic can be a useful and appealing product of a research project.

Consider a program that sets out to reduce the incidence of drunk driving by providing severe punishments for drunks and remitting them if the culprit "volunteers" to participate in a supervised Antabuse program. (Antabuse is a drug which, if present in the body, makes you violently ill if you take even one drink.) The program may require that the participant seek therapy from community agencies, but supply no funds for that therapy. In these circumstances, the baseball statistician will certainly be able to document the number of participants, the length of their participation, the number of dropouts, and the number of drunk-driving arrests and accidents. He may also be able to document the increase of social

agency work load. If roadside surveys have been used, he may be able to provide whatever pre-post information they offer about the incidence of drunk driving. He will almost certainly be unable to examine what happens to participants and to others using community therapy services because of the increased load without increased funds. He will almost certainly be unable to examine the emotional consequences of depriving drinkers of their drug. He may or may not be able to provide statistics bearing on increased case loads for police and courts which are likely to accompany such a program; it is unlikely that he can assess the effect of these case loads on the quality of justice in that community. He can calculate the direct dollar costs of the program itself, to the extent that they are paid from program funds, but he almost certainly cannot calculate the total direct dollar costs to the community, since many of those costs are paid by community agencies and are not easily separable from non-program-related costs.

The decision maker wants to know "Was this program a good idea? Should it be continued? If so, at what level of funding and with what funding expectations from other agencies? Should it be taken as a model for programs in other communities? If so, how can leaders in those other communities be persuaded to accept its costs?" The baseball statistician cannot tell him the answers to any of these questions, though he can offer literally thousands or hundreds of thousands of numbers that bear on them in one way or another. Because the decision maker cannot understand or assimilate thousands of numbers, all only indirectly related to the question at hand, he has no choice but to select out a few, combine them with a large dose of intuition and political savvy, and make a seat-of-the-pants decision.

If forced to choose between the experimentalist's and the baseball statistician's approaches to program evaluation, we will choose the latter almost every time. Fact-gathering, however dull it may be, is indispensable to everything that comes after. And a reasonably exhaustive compendium of relevant facts about a program can, in principle and sometimes in practice, be interrogated by a decision maker about whatever he really wants to know.

But we feel that fact-gathering in itself has two severe deficiences as an evaluation method. The first, already indicated, is that too many facts are almost as difficult to use for decision making as too few. Indexing, summarizing, and information retrieval techniques tend to be the weakness of every baseball statistician's evaluation. And the more remote the decision maker is from the scientists who designed the program and/or ran the evaluation study, the more severe the difficulty becomes. This, we feel, explains one of the paradoxes of our time: in a government in which practically everything is studied, restudied, and evaluated to death, most decision makers feel simultaneously inundated with information they cannot effectively use and unable to obtain the rather small set of simple answers they need in order to make wise decisions. The complaint comes from Presidents, members of Congress, heads of government departments, and their counterparts in business; and we think the complaint is thoroughly justified. Too much information is almost as useless as too little. No one (not even the librarians or the computer-memory designers) feels other than queasy about the information explosion.

The other difficulty of the baseball statistician's approach to evaluation is that it

has virtually nothing to say about values. Almost inevitably these will escape the baseball statistician's number dredge, because they reside in the decision maker's head (or, more often, in the collective and disagreeing heads of the various organizations with a say in the decision), not in the detailed facts of the program itself.

AN OVERVIEW OF DECISION ANALYSIS AS IT APPLIES TO EVALUATION

Figure 7.1 is a block diagram of flow chart indicating the processes that lead up to a decision. In this and following block diagrams, rectangles enclose operations, and circles enclose the informational inputs to or outputs from operations. Arrows of course indicate direction of information flow. Only one instance exists within Figure 7.1 (and none in the other flow charts) in which informational outputs combine without intervening operations to produce other informational outputs. The list of available acts combines with the list of states relevant to outcomes of acts to generate the table of outcomes without any intervening processing because an outcome is, by definition, the intersection of an act and a state; for, in less mathematical language, an outcome is what happens if a given act is chosen and a particular state of the world turns out to obtain.

The main conclusion to which an initial look at Figure 7.1 must inevitably lead is that decision making fully analyzed is complicated. It divides into four phases. The first consists of recognition of a decision problem and definition of its nature and dimensions, the raw materials of a decision process. The second is called probability evaluation in Figure 7.1; other names used for the same process in other contexts are diagnosis, intelligence evaluation, data gathering and interpretation, and the like. It is itself a complicated process. Figure 7.1 indicates, in typical Bayesian fashion, that the output is a set of posterior probabilities of states, but less formal judgments of probability, like those contained in such intuitive processes as conventional medical diagnosis, and such formal ones as the acceptance or rejection of statistical hypotheses also fit here and might be substituted for the Bayesian version of the process by those less convinced of the Bayesian point of view.

A more detailed Bayesian version of what goes on in probability evaluation is given in Figure 7.2, which translates into flow diagram form some of the basic ideas of an information processing system called PIP (see Edwards, 1971), but applies just about equally well to any formal application of Bayesian ideas that distinguished between priors and likelihoods.

We believe that Bayesian techniques have much to offer evaluation research—unfortunately, too much to go into here. For expositions of the Bayesian position in statistics itself, see Edwards, Lindman, and Savage (1963) or Phillips (1973). For illustrations of how to use Bayesian inference in decision-making, see Raiffa (1968), Schlaifer (1969), or any of a dozen recent texts on the subject, mostly addressed to business school audiences. For an exciting example of application of Bayesian tools for evaluation alternative options in medical diagnosis, see Fryback (1974).

The essence of what these procedures have to offer evaluation researchers, we think, is flexibility. They do not make use of artificial devices such as null

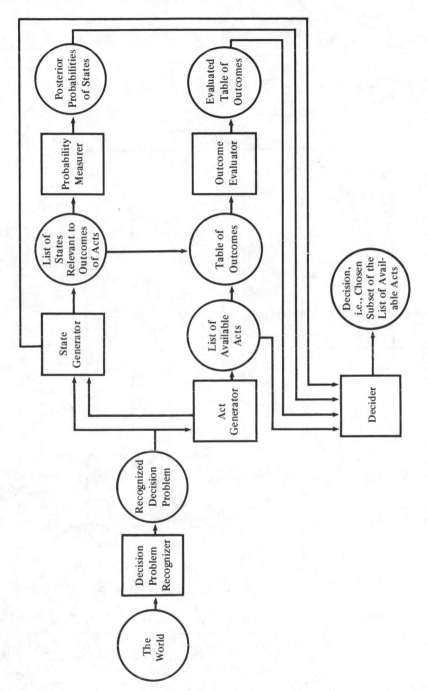

FIGURE 7.1   A block diagram or flow chart of the processes that lead up to a decision.

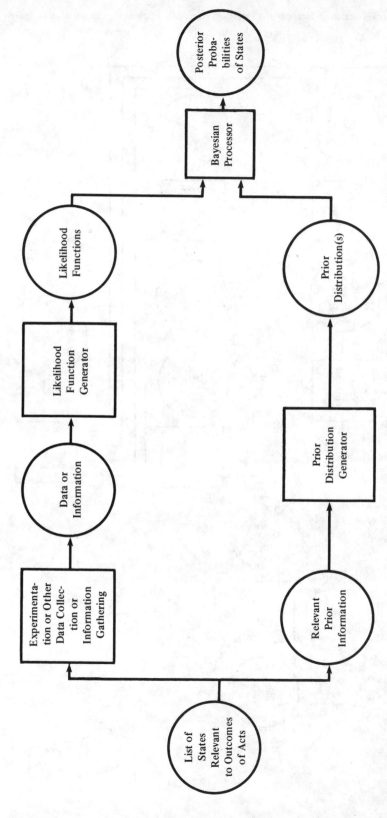

FIGURE 7.2   A flow chart of processes involved in probability evaluation. This is an elaboration of the "Probability Evaluation" block of Figure 1.

hypotheses. They permit, in fact, encourage, quantitative combination of evidence from different sources, different lines of inquiry, and different techniques of investigation. In particular, they make it easy to combine, in a formally appropriate numerical way, judgments with experimental or other empirical data. And they combine very naturally with the value judgments that are the main topic of this paper to produce wise decisions.

The third phase of decision making, as outlined in Figure 7.1, is outcome evaluation. "Evaluation" here means literally that: the attachment of values, preferably in numerical form, to outcomes. And those values are not probabilities; in our preferred version of the evaluation process, values are explicit, numerical answers to the question, "Is that particular outcome good or bad, and how good or how bad?" Another way of putting the question to be answered in outcome evaluation is: "Suppose I could know for certain that this particular act would lead to this particular outcome, and suppose I then chose this act. How attractive would its outcome be to me, or to someone, or to some collection of people?"

Note that outcomes, not acts, are evaluated. We often think of values as being attached to acts. That is in a sense appropriate, since the whole purpose of obtaining values of outcomes and probabilities of states is to permit the simple computation that associates an expected value with an act. In the special case of no uncertainty (i.e., some state has probability 1, or, more often, you treat it as though it had probability 1 even though you know that unlikely alternative states exist), each act has only one outcome, and so the value of the outcome is also the value of the act.

The fourth phase of decision making, as outlined in Figure 7.1, is actual choice among acts. It is based on the values of outcomes and the probabilities of states (or the intuitive substitutes for these numbers). In general, it is a rather trivial process. In a pick-one-act situation, one simply picks the act with the highest value, or expected value. In a pick-several-acts situation, more complex decision rules may be used, but they are still logically simple, and have essentially the character either that the acts that have the highest values, or the acts that return most value per unit of cost, are selected. Special situations, such as competitive games, gambler's-ruin problems, and sequential decision problems lead to still other, computationally more complex decision rules, but the input numbers are still the same.

Of these various processes, probability evaluation and outcome evaluation come closest to the heart of what evaluation research is typically supposed to be about. One contention of this chapter is that these two distinct operations have been lumped together under the label "evaluation research"; that they are different; that they require quite different kinds of procedures to provide answers; and that answers to both are typically necessary for wise decision making.

OUTCOME EVALUATION USING MULTI-ATTRIBUTE UTILITY ANALYSIS

Outcomes could be evaluated in many direct ways. Perhaps the most commonly used direct way is to equate outcome with price. The phrase "that's so cheap it can't be any good" is true enough, often enough, to illustrate the phenomenon, and its frequent falsity illustrates how unsatisfactory the procedure is. Price depends

more on the relation between supply and demand than on value. Air is free, but if some predatory corporation or country had a monopoly on it, would you not be willing to pay any amount within your means for a year's supply?

A more reasonable procedure, often used, is simply to consider the outcome and make a direct intuitive value judgment. We all do this every day; experts, such as diamond appraisers, make good livings by doing it exceptionally well with a limited field of expertise. While such judgments are most often phrased in language that is vague, categorical, or both, they can be expressed directly in numbers. Miller, Kaplan, and Edwards (1969) showed that a resource allocation system designed around such numbers far outperformed a system based on intuitive judgments. Yet this, too, is an extremely primitive way of making value judgments.

Most outcomes have value for a number of different reasons, that is, on a number of different dimensions. A remedial education program may contribute to the education of those receiving it. If so, the number of those people and the extent of the contribution made to each may be relevant to the value of the program. The cost of the program, in money, in teaching talent, in student time, and perhaps in educational materials and facilities, is also relevant. The durability of the educational gain is relevant. The program's target population may be relevant. The generalizability of the remedial education techniques used over students, over teachers, over settings, over cultures, and so on may be considered relevant. All of these considerations will, and should, enter into a decision about whether to continue, expand, or terminate the program. Other considerations may enter as well. The city in which the program is located may be on politically harmonious terms with the funding organization, or may not. The program may have no educative value whatever, and may nevertheless provide employment for otherwise unemployed teachers and administrators.

The program may offer opportunities for private profit, ranging from sale of textbooks to graft. It may keep off the street youths who otherwise would be smoking pot, shoplifting, committing assaults, and the like. At the other extreme, a superlatively successful program may disrupt the schools to which its graduates go by presenting its teachers with demands they cannot meet. And so on.

All these considerations—along with many others—may enter into a decision about whether to continue, expand, or terminate a program. Clearly this multiplicity of value dimensions presents a multiplicity of problems. Who determines what dimensions are relevant, and how relevant each is? How is that set of judgments made and used? How is the location of each possible outcome of each act being considered on each relevant dimension of value measured, judged, or otherwise discovered? Finally, what combination of judgmental transformation and arithmetical aggregation is used to translate all this input information into outcome evaluations?

An explicit technology, or, more precisely, several competing versions of an explicit technology, exists to answer some of these questions. Its name is multi-attribute utility measurement, and expositions of various versions of it have been presented by Raiffa (1968), Keeney (1972a), Edwards (1971), and others.

The version we present here, adapted from Edwards (1971), is oriented toward

easy communication and use in environments in which time is short and decision makers are numerous and busy. Further, it is a method that is psychologically meaningful to decision makers, who are required to give judgments that are intuitively reasonable. Still, unpublished studies strongly argue that the simple rating-scale procedures described below produce results essentially the same as much more complicated procedures involving imaginary lotteries.

The essence of multi-attribute utility measurements, in any of its versions, is that each outcome to be evaluated is located on each dimension of value by a procedure that may consist of experimentation, naturalistic observation, judgment, or some combination of these. These location measures are combined by means of an aggregation rule, most often simply a weighted linear combination. The weights are numbers describing the importance of each dimension of value relative to the others. In every application of multi-attribute utilities we know of, such numbers are judgmentally obtained. A flow diagram of this process is contained in Figure 7.3, which is an expansion of the block called "Outcome evaluation" in Figure 7.1.

Our implementation of Figure 7.3 consists of ten steps:

Step 1: Identify the person or organization whose utilities are to be maximized. If, as is often the case, several organizations have stakes and voices in the decision, they must all be identified. People who can speak for them must be identified and induced to cooperate.

Step 2: Identify the issue or issues (i.e., decisions) to which the utilities needed are relevant. The same objects or acts may have many different values, depending on context and purpose. In general, utility is a function of the evaluator, the entity being evaluated, and the purpose for which the evaluation is being made. The third argument of that function is sometimes neglected.

Step 3: Identify the entities to be evaluated. Previously, we have indicated that they are outcomes of possible actions. For example, the value of a dollar is the value of whatever you choose to buy with it; the value of an education is the value of the things that can be done with—but not without—it. Since it is always necessary to cut the decision tree somewhere—to stop considering outcomes as opportunities for further decisions and instead simply to treat them as outcomes with intrinsic values—the choice of what to call an outcome becomes largely one of convenience. Often, in practice, it is sufficient to treat an action itself as an outcome. This amounts to treating the action as having an inevitable outcome, that is, of assuming that uncertainty about outcomes is not involved in the evaluation of that action.

Step 4: Identify the relevant dimensions of value. The first three steps were more or less philosophical. The first answered the question: Whose utility? The second answered the question: Utility for what purpose? The third answered the question: Utility of what entities? With step 4 we come to the first technical task: Discover what dimensions of value are important to the evaluation of the entities we are interested in.

As Raiffa (1969) has noted, goals ordinarily come in hierarchies. But it is often practical and useful to ignore their hierarchical structure, and instead to specify a simple list of goals that seem important for the purpose at hand. Goals, for this

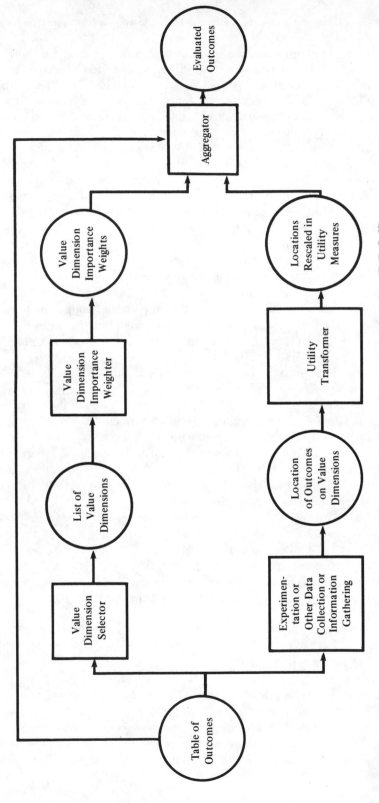

FIGURE 7.3   Illustration of the average scale values of all recommendations on four representative values (E, F, G, H).

purpose, should not be stated as target numbers (e.g., reduction of drinking-driver accidents by 50%), but rather as dimensions (reduction of drinking-driver accidents).

It is important not to be too expansive at this stage. The number of relevant dimensions of value should be kept down, for reasons that will be apparent shortly. This can often be done by restating and combining goals, or by moving upward in a goal hierarchy, thereby using fewer, more general values. Even more important, it can be done by simply omitting the less important goals. There is no requirement that the list evolved in this step be complete, and much reason to hope that it will not be.

Step 5: Rank the dimensions in order of importance. This ranking job, like Step 4, can be performed either by an individual, or by representatives of conflicting values acting separately, or by those representatives acting as a group. Our preferred technique is to try group processes first, mostly to get the arguments on the table and to make it more likely that the participants start from a common information base, and then to get separate judgments from each individual. The separate judgments will differ, of course, both here and in the following step.

Step 6: Rate dimensions in importance, preserving ratios. To do this, start by assigning the least important dimension an importance of 10. (We use 10 rather than 1 to permit subsequent judgments to be finely graded and nevertheless made in integers.) Now consider the next-least-important dimension. How many times more important (if any) is it than the least important? Assign it a number that reflects that ratio. Continue on up the list, checking each set of implied ratios as each new judgment is made. Thus, if a dimension is assigned a weight of 20, while another is assigned a weight of 80, it means that the 20 dimension is ¼ as important as the 80 dimension. And so on. By the time you get to the most important dimensions, there will be many checks to perform; typically, respondents will want to revise previous judgments to make them consistent with present ones. That's fine; they can do so. Once again, individual differences are likely to arise.

Step 7: Sum the importance weights, divide each by the sum, and multiply by 100. This is a purely computational step which converts importance weights into numbers that, mathematically, are rather like probabilities. The choice of a 0-to-100 scale is, of course, purely arbitrary.

At this step, the folly of including too many dimensions at Step 4 becomes glaringly apparent. If 100 points are to be distributed over a set of dimensions, and some dimensions are very much more important than others, then the less important dimensions will have non-trivial weights only if there are not too many of them. As a rule of thumb, 8 dimensions is plenty, and 15 is too many. Knowing this, you will want at Step 4 to discourage respondents from being too finely analytical: rather gross dimensions will be just right. Moreover, it may occur that the list of dimensions will be revised later, and that revision, if it occurs, will typically consist of including more rather than fewer.

Step 8: Measure the location of each entity being evaluated on each dimension. The word "measure" is used rather loosely here. There are three classes of dimensions: purely subjective, partly subjective, and purely objective. The purely

subjective dimensions are perhaps the easiest; you simply get an appropriate expert to estimate the position of that entity on that dimension on a 0-to-100 scale, where 0 is defined as the minimum plausible value on that dimension and 100 is defined as the maximum plausible value.

A partly subjective dimension is one in which the units of measurement are objective, but the locations of the entities must be subjectively estimated.

A wholly objective dimension is one that can be measured rather objectively, in objective units, before the decision. For partly or wholly objective dimensions, it is necessary to have the estimators provide not only values for each entity to be evaluated, but also minimum and maximum plausible values, in the natural units of each dimension.

The final task in Step 8 is to convert measures to the partly subjective and wholly objective dimensions into the 0-to-100 scale in which 0 is minimum plausible and 100 is maximum plausible.

A linear transformation is almost always adequate for this purpose; errors produced by linear approximations to monotonic nonlinear functions are likely to be unimportant relative to test-retest unreliability, interrespondent differences, and the like.

Now all entities have been located on the relevant value dimensions, and the location measures have been rescaled. In what sense, if any, are the scales comparable? The question cannot be considered separately from the question of what "importance," as it was judged at Step 6, means. Formally, judgments at Step 6 should be designed so that when the output of Step 7 (or of Step 6, which differs only by a linear transformation) is multiplied by the output of Step 8, equal numerical distances between these products on different dimensions correspond to equal changes in desirability. For example, suppose entity A has a location of 50 and entity B a location of 10 on value dimension X, while A has a location of 70 and B a location of 90 on value dimension Y (only X and Y are relevant). Suppose further that dimension Y is twice as important as dimension X. Then A and B should be equivalent in value. (The relevant arithmetic is: for A, $50 + 2(70) = 190$; for B, $10 + 2(90) = 190$. Another way of writing the same arithmetic, which makes clearer what is meant by saying that equal numerical differences between these products on different dimensions correspond to equal changes in desirability, is $(50 - 10) + 2(70 - 90) = 0$.) It is important that judges understand this concept as they perform both Steps 6 and 8.[1]

Step 9: Calculate utilities for entities. The equation is $U_i = \sum_i w_j u_{ij}$, remembering that $\sum_j w_j = 100$. U_i is the aggregate utility for the ith entity. w_j is the normalized importance weight of the jth dimension of value, and u_{ij} is the rescaled position of the ith entity on the jth dimension. Thus w_j is the output of Step 7 and u_{ij} is the output of Step 8. The equation, of course, is nothing more than the formula for a weighted average.

Step 10: Decide. If a single act is to be chosen, the rule is simple: maximize U_i. If a subset of i is to be chosen, then the subset for which $_iU_i$ is maximum is best.

A special case arises when one of the dimensions, such as cost, is subject to an upper bound, that is, there is a budget constraint. In that case, Steps 4 through 10 should be done ignoring the constrained dimension. Then the ratios U_i/C_i should be

calculated; these are the famous benefit-to-cost ratios. Actions should be chosen in decreasing order of that ratio until the budget constraint is used up. (More complicated arithmetic is needed if programs are interdependent or if this rule does not come very close to exactly exhausting the budget constraint.) This is the only case in which the benefit-to-cost ratio is the appropriate figure on which to base a decision. In the absence of budget constraints, cost is just another dimension of value, to be treated on the same footing as all other dimensions of value, entering into U_i with a minus sign, like other unattractive dimensions. In effect, in the general case it is the benefit-minus-cost difference, not the benefit-over-cost ratio, that should usually control action.

An important caveat needs to be added concerning benefit-to-cost ratios. Such ratios assume that both benefits and costs are measured on a ratio scale, that is, a scale with a true zero point and ratio properties. The concepts both of zero benefit and zero cost are somewhat slippery on close analysis. A not-too-bad solution to the problem is to assume that you know what zero cost means, and then attempt to find the zero point on the aggregate benefit scale. If that scale is reasonably densely populated with candidate programs, an approach to locating that zero point is to ask the decision maker "Would you undertake this program if it had the same benefits it has now, but had zero cost?" If the answer is yes, the program is above the zero point on the benefit scale; if the answer is no, it is below the zero point. In the Office of Child Development example discussed below, this procedure was tried, and seemed to work quite well. It permitted quite precise location of a zero point on the benefit scale. Ratio judgments of benefits to see if they were consistent with this zero point could have been tried, but were not.

The multi-attribute utility approach can easily be adapted to cases in which there are minimum or maximum acceptable values on a given dimension of value by simply excluding alternatives that lead to outcomes that transgress these limits.

Flexibilities of the Method

Practically every technical step in the preceding list has alternatives. For example Keeney (1972b) has proposed use of a multiplicative rather than an additive aggregation rule. Certain applications have combined multiplication and addition. The methods suggested above for obtaining location measures and importance weights have alternatives; the most common is the direct assignment of importance weights on a 0-to-100 scale. (We consider this procedure inferior to the one described above, but doubt that it makes much practical difference in most cases.)

Independence Properties

Either the additive or the multiplicative version of the aggregation rule assumes value independence. Roughly, that means that the extent of your preference for location a_2 over location a_1 of dimension A is unaffected by the position of the entity being evaluated on dimensions B, C, D. . . . Value independence is a strong assumption, not easily satisfied. Fortunately, in the presence of even modest amounts of measurement error, quite substantial amounts of deviation from value independence will make little difference to the ultimate number U_i, and even less to the rank ordering of the U_i values. (For recent discussions of the robustness of

linear models, on which this assertion depends, see Dawes and Corrigan [1974].) A frequently satisfied condition that makes the assumption of value independence very unlikely to cause trouble is monotonicity; that is, the additive approximation will almost always work well if, for each dimension, either more is preferable to less or less is preferable to more throughout the range of the dimension that is involved in the evaluation, for all available values of the other dimensions. When the assumption of value independence is unacceptable even as an approximation, much more complicated models and elicitation procedures that take value dependence into account are available.[2]

A trickier issue than value independence is what might be called environmental independence. The number of administrators, secretaries, and others involved in a program is extremely likely to be positively correlated with the number of people served by the program. Yet these two dimensions may be value-independent; the correlation simply means that programs involving few workers and many people served are unlikely to present themselves for evaluation.

Interpersonal and Intergroup Disagreements[3]

Nothing in the preceding discussion ensures that different respondents will come up with similar numbers, and such agreements are indeed rare.

We might expect that the magnitude of interpersonal disagreement produced by this procedure would be less than that produced by simply arguing about what to do. Gardiner (1974), in an application of the method described above, found just that. His stimuli were hypothetical applications for building permits in the California town of Venice. His subjects were members of the California Southern Coastal Commission, and others interested in the development of the California coastline, from both developer and conservationist points of view. (California law requires that all permits for building within 1,000 yards of the high-tide line be approved by the relevant regional Coastal Commission before building can commence.) His subjects both rated these permit requests on a wholistic numerical scale and applied an 8-dimensional multi-attribute utility technique. When one of the more extreme conservationists was compared with one of the more development-oriented subjects, the wholistic ratings correlated -.50. But the U_i's for the same permit requests and subjects correlated +.59. In addition, two groups of subjects were formed reflecting differing viewpoints with respect to the permits, and group evaluations were collected for each of the 14 permits using group wholistic ratings and group U_i's. These group ratings were then compared using an ANOVA (permit by group for mean permit worth). The results showed that the two groups differed significantly when wholistic ratings were compared (reflected by a significant interaction effect accounting for 12% of the variance) but that when compared using group U_i's this interaction virtually disappeared (no significant interaction effect and only 2% of the variance accounted for). In other words, use of the multi-attribute utility technique had turned substantial disagreement into modest agreement.

Why? A plausible answer is suggested by Gardiner's data. When making wholistic evaluations, those with strong points of view tend to concentrate on those aspects of the entities being evaluated that most strongly engage their biases. But the

multi-attribute procedure does not permit this; it separates judgment of the importance of a dimension from judgment of where a particular entity falls on that dimension. These applications, though they varied on various dimensions that are relevant to the environmentalist-versus-builder arguments, also varied on other dimensions not involved in that sort of issue. Agreement about those other dimensions tends to water down disagreement on controversial dimensions in a multi-attribute utility procedure.

Although multi-attribute utility measurement procedures can be expected to reduce the magnitude of disagreements, they cannot and should not eliminate them. What then?

We distinguish between two kinds of disagreements. Disagreements at Step 8 seem to us to be essentially like disagreements among different thermometers measuring the same temperature. If they are not too large, we have little compunction about taking an average. If they are, then we are likely to suspect that some of the thermometers are not working properly and to discard their readings. In general, we think that judgmentally determined location measures should reflect expertise, and typically we would expect different value dimensions to require different kinds of expertise and therefore different experts. In some practical contexts, we can avoid the problem of disagreement at Step 8 entirely by the simple expedient of asking only the best available expert for each dimension to make judgments about that dimension.

Disagreement at Steps 5 and 6 are another matter. These seem to us to be the essence of conflicting values, and we wish to respect them as much as possible. For that reason, we feel that the judges who perform Steps 5 and 6 should be either the decision maker(s) or well-chosen representatives. Considerable discussion, persuasion, and information exchange should be used in an attempt to reduce the disagreements as much as possible.

This will seldom reduce them to zero. For some organizations, we can at this point invoke once more Truman's desk sign "The buck stops here," this time with Truman's intended meaning. One function of an executive, boss, or decision maker is to resolve disagreements among subordinates. He can do this in various ways: by substituting his judgment for theirs, by picking one of them as "right" and rejecting the others, or, in the weighted-averaging spirit of multi-attribute utility measurement, by assigning a weight to each of the disagreeing subordinates and then calculating weighted-average importance weights.

If there is no decision maker to resolve disagreement, we can only carry through the evaluation separately for each of the disagreeing individuals or groups, hoping that the disagreements are small enough to have little or no action implications. And if that hope is not fulfilled, we have no suggestions to offer beyond the familiar political processes by means of which society functions in spite of conflicting interests. We offer technology, not miracles.

AN EXAMPLE FROM THE OFFICE OF CHILD DEVELOPMENT (OCD)

The multi-attribute utilities method was used in the planning process of OCD. Following the steps of the multi-attribute utilities method, the organization whose utilities were to be maximized (Step 1) was OCD. The issues to which the utilities

needed were relevant (Step 2) were plans for fiscal years 1974 and 1975-1979. The entities to be evaluated (Step 3) were of two kinds: recommendations for broad strategies that could be pursued by OCD and recommendations for specific program initiatives that fell within each broad strategy. Step 3 was conducted concurrently with Step 4, the identification of relevant dimensions of value. Both of these processes are described below.

We set out initially to measure three kinds of values separately: benefits to children and families (which might be considered "external" utilities), benefits to OCD as an agency in HEW (or "internal" benefits), and cost.

A small work group was assembled at OCD to develop the value dimensions. This group consisted of the Acting Director, Saul Rosoff, other members of the OCD staff, some of the Associate Regional Directors, and some child development consultants. In two days of discussion, the value dimensions work group decided on the following dimensions of benefits to children and families:

- Promote service continuity/eliminate fragmentation (includes idea of coordination).
- Invest in prototype/high-leverage programs.
- Enhance families' sense of efficacy and ability to obtain and use resources necessary for the healthy development of children.
- Promote child health.
- Maximize the number of children affected.
- Increase developmentally appropriate opportunities for choice and self-direction among older children.
- Increase probability that children will acquire skills necessary for successful performance of adult roles.
- Develop leadership capacity in communities served.
- Make the public and institutions more sensitive to the developmental needs of children.
- Contribute to knowledge expansion and/or use of knowledge for program planning.
- Individualize services and programs.
- Stimulate pluralistic child care delivery systems that provide for parental choice.
- Promote self-respect and mutual regard among children of diverse racial, cultural, class, and ethnic backgrounds.
- Enhance parental involvement in program planning and management.

This list of 14, presented here unordered, was refined from a much longer list that had been freely generated by group members. Overlapping values, duplications, and subsets of values already listed were refined and combined during the course of group discussion.

The group also developed a separate list of value dimensions that were oriented toward OCD and its internal role in HEW. These were:

- Use money for leverage, not services.
- Interagency coordination at federal, state, and local levels.

- Administrative feasibility.
- Make political leadership more sensitive to the needs of children.
- Promote understanding by and support from groups OCD works with and/or relates to.
- Influence national child care policy.
- Course of action capable of rational explication.
- Produce tangible short-term results.
- Maximize support by OCD staff.
- Make best use of OCD resources and personnel.
- Improve OCD's information base.
- Improve stewardship and accountability.

The above list resulted from a similar process of refinement accomplished during group discussion.

Next, each member of the value dimensions work group was asked to rank order the dimensions and to assign importance weights individually (Step 5).

At the same time that the value dimensions work was in progress, recommendations for broad strategies and for individual programs were being assembled. These came from a large number of sources. Major reports to OCD and to HEW, which contained a number of recommendations, were summarized. Recommendations were solicited from members of the OCD staff and from the Office of the Assistant Secretary for Planning and Evaluation in HEW. In addition, the Secretary's National Advisory Committee on Children, the National Academy of Science's Child Development Group, the Associate Regional Directors of OCD, and representatives of minority organizations, as well as child development experts throughout the country, were asked to submit recommendations for broad strategies and specific programs. The current strategies and programs also formed a part of this group of recommendations. Several hundred recommendations were assembled as the result of this process. At present, these recommendations are being refined and combined where redundant (Guttentag, 1973).

The following are a random sample of some of the concrete recommendations which were the result of the first phase:[4]

OCD should undertake a *feasibility study* to explore the whole area of providing training to child care givers, using modern technology—video, through both PBS and/or closed circuit (cable) outlets, films, cassettes, etc.

Cost: $50,000   Time: 1 year

*   *   *   *   *   *   *   *   *   *

Presently there are no official national standards for the administration of foster care licensing . . . in terms of personnel requirements, workload, or what is expected of a licensing service. CB should design a strategy for upgrading the quality of child foster care licensing in State welfare and health departments, including specification of the education and experience needed to qualify licensing personnel at operating, supervisory, and administrative levels; in-service training guidelines for licensing authorities; and its own plan for providing consultation and monitoring through self-study guides and other forms of evaluation. This should be developed cooperatively with CSA.

Cost: $1,500,000   Time: 3 years

*   *   *   *   *   *   *   *   *   *

OCD should support research on the effects of social climate, physical settings, crowding, and other environmental, non-program variables on the social and cognitive development of children in school settings. Initially, OCD should fund 4 or 5 independent *feasibility* studies, at $20,000–$25,000 each, to determine a research strategy.

Cost: $100,000   Time: 1 year

*   *   *   *   *   *   *   *   *   *

OCD should determine the feasibility of training and utilizing community residents as homemakers, or high school students as parent apprentices, in order to visit and assist families in which parents are overburdened with caring for old or sick relatives, meeting the needs of large families, housekeeping under difficult circumstances, etc. Many disadvantaged parents are unable to spend time in activities with their young children because of other demands in the home. Homemakers or parent apprentices could take over some of these responsibilities so that parents could be free to engage in activities with their younger children.

Cost: $100,000   Time: 1 year

*   *   *   *   *   *   *   *   *   *

OCD should develop and periodically disseminate a "State of the Child Report" describing the status of children and youth in the Nation within a given time frame.

As part of this effort, OCD should cooperate with the National Child Center for Social Statistics and others in developing the Report's statistical and narrative requirements.

Cost: $150,000   Time: 1 year

*   *   *   *   *   *   *   *   *   *

OCD should conduct longitudinal studies of the effects on children of transracial adoptions.

Cost: $500,000   Time: 3 years
(longitudinal research)

As a result of the importance weighting, only 13 value dimensions survived from the original list, that is, received any significant importance weights. These dimensions came from both the list of values to children and families and values to OCD. To facilitate translation from decision-theoretical jargon into government jargon, the words "value dimension" were replaced by the word "criterion."

The 13 surviving criteria were:

Criterion A (Importance weight = .007)

The extent to which a recommended activity is likely to foster service continuity/coordination and elimination of fragmentation, or is likely to contribute to this goal.

Criterion B (Importance weight = .145)

The extent to which a recommended activity represents an investment in a

prototypical and/or high-leverage activity, or is likely to contribute to the development of prototypical/high-leverage programs.

Criterion C (Importance weight = .061)

The extent to which a recommended activity increases or is likely to contribute to an increase in families' sense of efficacy and their ability to obtain and use resources necessary for the healthy development of children.

Criterion D (Importance weight = .052)

The extent to which a recommended activity is likely to increase the probability that children will acquire the skills necessary for successful performance of adult roles, or is likely to contribute to that goal.

Criterion E (Importance weight = .036)

The extent to which a recommended activity is likely to contribute to making the public and institutions more sensitive to the developmental needs of children.

Criterion F (Importance weight = .048)

The extent to which a recommended activity is likely to promote the individualization of services or programs, or is likely to contribute to this goal.

Criterion G (Importance weight = .043)

The extent to which a recommended activity is likely to stimulate the development of pluralistic child care delivery systems that provide for parental choice, or is likely to contribute to the expansion of such systems.

Criterion H (Importance weight = .014)

The extent to which a recommended activity is likely to promote self-respect and mutual regard among children from diverse racial, cultural, class, and ethnic backgrounds, or is likely to contribute to this goal.

Criterion I (Importance weight = .009)

The extent to which a recommended activity is likely to result in effective interagency coordination at federal, state, and local levels, or is likely to contribute to this goal.

Criterion J (Importance weight = .160)

The extent to which a recommended activity is consonant with administration and departmental policies and philosophy, or reflects prevailing public and social thinking.

Criterion K (Importance weight = .120)

The extent to which a recommended activity is likely to make public leadership more sensitive to the needs of children.

Criterion L (Importance weight = .145)

The extent to which a recommended activity is likely to influence national child care policy in a positive way.

Criterion M (Importance weight = .032)

The extent to which a recommended activity is capable of rational explication, that is, the extent to which it represents a logical extention of past results and conclusions, is indicated on theoretical grounds, or fulfills prior commitments.

Criterion N (Importance weight = .129)

   The extent to which a recommended activity is likely to produce tangible, short-term results, that is, the extent to which it is likely to produce or contribute to the production of solid conclusions, benefits, or results within a relatively short period of time.

There was some interpersonal disagreement about what the precise weights should be, although analysis showed that the disagreement was not systematically related to the race, sex, or organizational locus of the respondent. However, there was excellent agreement about what the most important dimensions were, in terms of rank order across individuals. The method proved to be useful for identifying the most important dimensions, although it did not produce, nor was it intended to produce, uniformity of weights across individuals. Figure 7.4 illustrates that there may be differences between the importance weights of individual participants, but that medians, or some other measure of central tendency, can more or less reflect the group consensus. Scatter plots of the type shown in Figure 7.4 were used as inputs about the group's values to the Acting Director of the Office of Child Development when later in the process he decided on the final importance weights.

   Following the next step of the process, each of the research recommendations had to be scaled for each value dimension. Individuals who did the scaling were told to think of an imaginary scale of 0 to 1,000. Their task was to estimate the extent to which a research recommendation contributed to a particular value or criterion. Since this task required some knowledge of the past work in each area of research, staff members of the Office of Child Development, with considerable familiarity with the research programs, were asked to make these judgments. Typically, three individuals judged each value dimension and each individual was assigned three value dimensions. In this way, three different scores were generated for each recommendation on each value. Figure 7.5 shows, for values E, F, G, and H, the location of each specific research recommendation. Note that all the recommendations fall below 500 on Criterion G, but some recommendations are above 750 on Criterion H, making a substantial contribution. Such differences also hold for individual judge data, and are not artifacts either of averaging or of assignments of different judges to different criteria.

   Following Step 9 in the process, utilities were then calculated for each research recommendation for all of the values taken together (A through N).

   Figure 7.6 shows rescaled utilities for the recommendations thus far. These rescaled utilities run from precisely 0 to precisely 1,000, because that is how they were calculated. The actual range of outputs of Step 9 was something like 200 to 550; a linear transformation was used to produce the rescaled numbers in Figure 7.6.

   Figure 7.7 gives the benefit-to-cost ratios for the recommendations developed in this phase of the process. The numbers indicate specific recommendations; the "/" simply indicated that two recommendations were approximately tied.

   This approach to planning and evaluation is an iterative one. At every step it is possible, indeed desirable, that the usefulness of the outcome be reconsidered.

(text continues on p. 168)

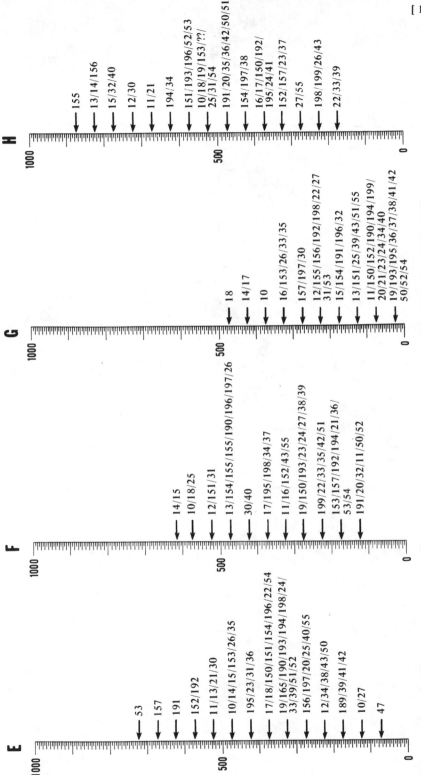

FIGURE 7.4   Illustration of the average scale values of all recommendations on four representative values (E, F, G, H).

1000 — −13

900 —

— −30/53

800 —
— −10

— −13
— −153

700 —

— −22

— −17/26
— −12/14
— −31
— −151/199
600 —
— −193/23
— −18/156/194
— −20/35
— −11
— −15/152/197
— −154/195/21
— −157
— −51
500 —

— −155
— −191/192
— −190
— −196
— −150

400 —

— −19

— −198/27/40
— −25
— −43
— −33/37/39

300 — — −32
— −24
— −42
— −38
— −54/55

200 —

— −50
— −36
— −52

100 —

— −41

0 — — −34

FIGURE 7.5   Standardized utilties for recommendations (First phase).

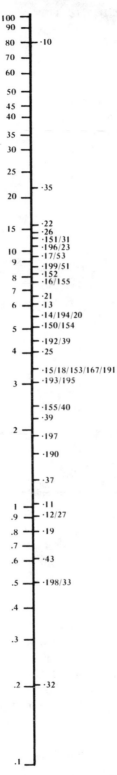

FIGURE 7.6   Benefit-to-cost ratios for the recommendations (First phase).

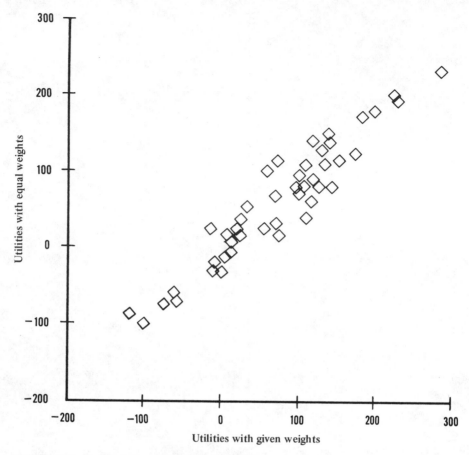

FIGURE 7.7   Recalculation of utilities with equal weights.

It became clear after the first phase, in which 13 value criteria had been applied to several hundred research recommendations, that both the values and recommendations could be clarified and made more general. In the following section, we will deal with the second phase and the changes made in value criteria in the research recommendations.

Phase Two—Values

The discussion of value dimensions in the first phase reflects a first cut at determining the structure of the agency's values. While refining the value dimensions, it became apparent that the agency's values were *hierarchically* structured (Raiffa, 1969), so that most of the values were subordinate to a relatively small number of superordinate values. Instead of depicting the agency's values as two sets of values, it was appropriate to identify the superordinate value dimensions. The process was facilitated by the fact that, in analyzing the weights attached by participants, there was excellent agreement about which values should be ranked highest, although there was disagreement about their precise weights.

After a discussion of the analysis with the Director and key participants, the Director decided that five value dimensions adequately reflected the agency's value structure. The decision was made, therefore, to utilize only these five superordinate values in the evaluation of substantive areas.

These five values, roughly equal in importance, were all considerably more important than any of the others. (See the earlier list of 13, which include these 5.) These value dimensions, which were then used in the second phase, were B, J, K, L, and N from the initial list. Their renormalized importance weights were:

Value Dimensions	Weight
(J) Consistent with departmental policy	.23
(L) Influences national child care policy positively	.21
(B) Prototype/high-leverage activity	.21
(N) Produces tangible short-term results	.18
(K) Makes public leadership more sensitive to children's needs	.17

The total of the non-renormalized weights is .699 or .70. The other eight value criteria, which are really subordinate hierarchical values, have a combined importance weight of only .30. While it is important to agree precisely upon what set of values will be used, Figure 7.8 shows that it is less important to agree upon what their weights are. Figure 7.8 indicates that a recalculation of utilities with equal weights assigned to the five values produces scores that correlate highly with the utilities calculated using the individual weights generated by the Office of Child Development Acting Director. This illustrates that, although people may believe that they are in disagreement, sharing common values should help to lead them to make the same decision, the same phenomenon Gardiner (1974) found.

Phase Two—Recommendations

As was described earlier, in the initial phase research recommendations were solicited from a wide variety of outside groups, for example, child development specialists, Office of Child Development staff, and current as well as previously considered research and programs of the Office of Child Development. Several hundred recommendations were solicited and refined. During the first phase, the values were applied to each of the several hundred recommendations and utilities were derived.

It became apparent, however, that there were some problems with recommendations (entities) defined as specifically as these were. First, because the recommendations had been solicited in an inductive manner, some important substantive areas were not covered. Second, a particular recommendation might well be one way, perhaps not the best way, of attacking its topic. Relatively minor improvements might lead to substantially higher utilities.

This became clear early in the process. In the second phase, therefore, a deductive approach to the research recommendations was used. This was done by mapping out a comprehensive taxonomy of all the possible competing major research options. The substantive areas in which OCD had previously done research

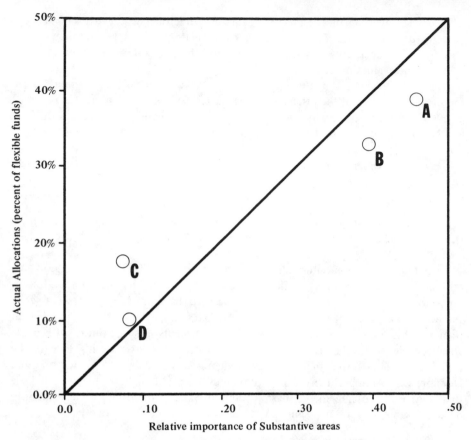

(Substantive areas: A—Children at risk and the child welfare system; B—Child development and the family; C—Child advocacy; D—Television and children.)

FIGURE 7.8   Final decisions: the relative importance of the substantive areas.

or had programs were reviewed. Extensive panel meetings with outside experts also
identified other salient issues which were considered in the overall plan. Position
papers were solicited on a number of these issues. What emerged during the second
phase was an identification of broad research topics and themes. These general
research foci subsumed most of the previously generated concrete, specific
recommendations.

The broad substantive research and program areas included the following: (a)
children at risk and the child welfare system; (b) child development and the family;
(c) child advocacy; (d) television and children.

Finally, using the five final value dimensions, each of the broad research and
program areas was evaluated (Step 8). In Step 9, utilities were established for each
of the general recommendations. The utility analysis indicated how the OCD
research and development budget could be allocated across different categories of
projects. The analysis also indicated how much money each substantive area could
receive given the results of the utility analysis.[5]

The rule used was that the amount of money each area would receive was directly proportional to the utility of that area. Under certain assumptions, this allocation rule maximizes the overall utility of the specific projects that would be funded. However, because the analysis did not involve the specific assessment of discrete research and development projects, this rule was used only as a rough rule-of-thumb, and was provided to the OCD Director as overall guidance.

At Step 10, the step of decision, the Director of the Office of Child Development, with the value dimensions in hand, but at first without the utilities which were the result of the judgments of the staff and a number of outside groups, intuitively allocated the flexible funds across the broad substantive areas. The Director's intuitive allocation and the guidance from the utility analysis were then compared. Although the agreement was good, it was by no means perfect.

As a result of the discrepancies between his own judgments and the utility analysis, the Director decided that, if possible, funds previously allocated for child advocacy would be reduced. He also decided that, since additional funds were expected from the termination of cutbacks in ongoing projects, that these monies would be distributed between the two areas that appeared to be funded at too low a level, given the utility analysis. In this case, the conformity between the Director's intuitive decisions and the utility analysis guidance was quite close, so that the analysis did not induce major changes in emphasis. However, it did affect the Director's decisions about how additional flexible funds would be allocated. When comparisons were made between fiscal year 1973 and fiscal year 1974, the differences and changes in budget emphases follow the 1974 utility analysis.

How does one go back from the broad substantive areas to specific research projects? Once the allocations across the broad substantive areas had been made, highly detailed and specific project specifications were worked out by the OCD staff. It is possible to use either the same or a separately generated set of specific research values to apply to the research recommendations within each substantive area.

The Office of Child Development research plan was then sent to the Office of Human Development and to the Assistant Secretary for Planning and Development in HEW. Each of these agencies makes decisions about the final research plan. Under ideal circumstances, each of these agencies should have made its values explicit and used the same utilities analysis system as had the Office of Child Development. If this had been done, it would have been possible for each of these agencies to know precisely where the differences and similarities in values between them lay. But the simultaneous conversion of several government agencies to a new methodology is too much to ask!

Social Psychology of the Process

Until this point, only the content of the decision-theoretic planning and evaluation process has been described. A large part of the actual process, however, is social in nature. This section deals with the ways in which group processes were used in the development of the OCD plan.

At Step 2, the identification of the issue or issues to which the utilities needed

are relevant, a group may or may not be involved. The definition of the issue or issues can, in the case of an agency or program where goals are multiple, be a target for debate.

Generally, however, groups become involved only at Step 4, the identification of the relevant dimensions of value. The multi-attribute utility technique does not specify whether or not face-to-face groups should be used. The agency can decide how it wants these relevant dimensions of value to be generated.

In past work, we have found that having the dimensions of value generated in a face-to-face group is quite useful for the agency. Individuals frequently agree more about values than they would predict. Since no values are excluded and no arguments occur, the value dimension generation process is often useful in providing information to members of a group about their own values.

When there are groups that clearly have different values inside and outside the program to be evaluated, it is often useful to have each group generate its own values independently. Then information about these values can be provided to every other group. Again, it is important to emphasize that, because at this stage there is no judgment of relative importances, the information generated is useful and unthreatening to each group.

Steps 5 and 6 can also be done either by face-to-face groups or by individuals whose rankings are later combined. Generally, the face-to-face group process is better if it is possible. It is better because the process tends to build a group consensus on the ordering of the values. When, however, there are clearly diverse groups, both within and outside a program or agency, it is most useful to permit each of these groups (or representatives of them) to perform their own rank ordering and importance weighting as a face-to-face group.

This is useful for three reasons. First, each group builds a consensus about its own values vis-a-vis the programs. This makes it possible to exchange information about the relative ordering of values between groups, so that discussions between groups about value differences can be quite explicit and quantified. This pleasantly cuts down the noise of rhetoric. Second, the same evaluation data can be fed back to each group. The same data, in a matrix in which values, rank order, and/or importance weights differ considerably, will yield very different final conclusions and decisions. Thus, a number of groups can, using the same data, come to very different conclusions about whether a program or programs are meeting their goals. This then provides them with a substantive basis for discussions with one another. Third, consensus is not a sine qua non of the evaluation process. If a number of different groups generate very different values, then data must be gathered which indicate how contemplated actions bear on every one of the values. This forces the evaluation researcher into multiple measurement. In addition, it means that decision makers receive research data on issues that may be foreign to their own values, but quite germane to the values of other groups, for example, persons affected by a program. The result of this value diversity is a much greater richness of evaluation information. All concerned groups benefit.

At Step 8, the measurement of the entity being evaluated on each dimension, the best choice is to use experts. At the planning stage, one presumes that whatever research or other evaluation data are available must be combined in some way to

generate a location measure. Therefore, it is best to use individuals who are able to make such judgments expertly.

The Integration of Planning and Evaluation

Only the OCD research plan has so far been described. Earlier, we asserted that the planning and evaluation process could and should be integrated. How, then, does one proceed from a research plan of this kind to the evaluation process?

As has been earlier noted, a matrix has been generated as part of the multi-attribute utility planning process. All of the values that have been rank ordered and importance weighted are in the matrix. The rows of the matrix consist of the programs, subprograms, and so on, that is, the entities being evaluated. The columns are the value dimensions. In each cell of the matrix, there is a location judgment of the extent to which program 1 is likely to contribute to value A, and the like. In the planning stage, this judgment has been made using all the available data on the program. Where programs do not exist, and are potential new options, these judgments are no more than educated guesses.

As the program proceeds, data are gathered. In cases in which the educated guess used in planning was specific enough to be modified by an observed number (e.g., number of participants in a voluntary program), the standard techniques of Bayesian statistics can be used to update initial guesses as data accumulate. In the OCD case, most of the value dimensions used were so abstract that numbers observable during a program are unlikely to represent them, though they obviously bear on them. In such cases, the entries in the matrix should still be updated, either by the direct use of expert judgment or by some more formal process, such as further decomposition of each value via the value hierarchy concept.

Thus the original evaluation structure used in planning the program can also be used to evaluate it as it proceeds, and to assess its merits when it is over.

However, values (here interpreted as importance weights) change as programs proceed, as circumstances change, as time passes. The weights appropriate this year may not be appropriate next year. This suggests that two different evaluative questions, both based on the same updated location measures, can and should be asked. One is "How does the present program measure up to the expectations we had for it when we planned it?" The other is "Given this year's values, how does the present program look? Should it be changed? If so, how?"

It is fairly often reasonable to define a value dimension as a goal. A very abstract dimension can often be operationalized by specifying some measure or set of measures such that attainment of them constitutes success, and failure to attain them constitutes failure. Then the probability of success can be treated as the location measure, and can be updated as data accumulate by standard Bayesian procedures. We will illustrate this technique in two examples, one hypothetical and one real.

A SIMPLE EXAMPLE INTEGRATING PLANNING AND EVALUATION

Suppose that a large city has a program for identifying and treating health problems, and that different "models" are being evaluated. Accordingly, 400

children are randomly assigned as "clients." Staffing patterns vary among the first three models. Model 1 is staffed by one full-time medical doctor and one full-time paraprofessional; Model 2 is staffed by one half-time medical doctor and five full-time paraprofessionals; and Model 3 is staffed by one one-fourth-time medical doctor and seven full-time paraprofessionals. Model 4 is a control, or no-treatment group, and indicates how well children do outside the program models. Staff members are randomly assigned to the different models (except Model 4), and the models are comparable in terms of total funding level, total salaries, equipment, medicine, access to ancillary services, and the like. All 400 children are tested on the first day of the program and retested after one year. Steps in a decision-theoretic approach to evaluation would proceed as follows. (The numbering does not correspond to that in the list of ten steps to evaluation via multi-attribute utility given earlier.)

Step 1: Identify Program Goals

Typically, program goals are consistent with the decision maker's values, and it is possible to make explicit the program's goals and their relative importance to the decision maker. Suppose that the program has three separate goals: to improve physical health, to improve mental health, and to improve social competency. In many instances, such broad goals must be subdivided and partitioned into subgoals that can be assessed separately. But this example is simplified by the assumption that these goals can be used without further elaboration. (This corresponds to Step 5 of our original list.)

Step 2: Determine the Relative Importance of Goals

Since the hypothetical program is targeted on health problems. It is plausible to assume that improving physical health is the most important and that improving social competency is the least important goal. Following our procedure, we assign an arbitrary importance weight of 10 to the least important goal (social competency), and the remaining two goals are weighed relative to the least important goal. Assume that the relative importance of these goals is expressed by weights of 10 (social competency), 20 (mental health), and 80 (physical health). (This corresponds to Step 6 of our original list.)

Step 3: Identify Probabilistic Measures of Goal Attainment

In this step operational definitions of the program's goals are specified. The appropriate measures may be very complex and difficult to measure, or they may be simply defined and amenable to measurement. For this example we will use simple, dichotomous goals, and the criterion for success will be whether a client exceeds predefined standards. For each goal, the location measure will be the probability that a (randomly chosen) client will exceed the standard.

Step 4: Estimate Prior Probabilities of Goal Attainment

Prior to implementation of programs there are typically few or no data about program maximization of goals. Nevertheless, decision makers have subjective prior

probabilities which should guide the planning process and govern the selection of activities. Recall that Guttentag (1973) refers to a planning process built upon wholly subjective, prior information. For the present example, suppose that the subjective prior probabilities for each goal are given in Table 7.1. These prior probabilities suggest that we initially expect Model 1 to be the best according to all goals, except that it is equal in value to Model 2 in terms of achieving the physical health goal. (This corresponds to Step 8 of our original list.)

Step 5: Calculate Prior Utilities

In this example, the worth of a model will be determined by the expected number of clients who achieve each goal, and the importance of each goal. Since the expected number is proportional to the prior probability, the prior utility for each model is

$$U_i = \sum_j (W_j \cdot P_{ij})$$

where W_j is the weight for the jth goal, and P_{ij} is the prior probability that a client in the ith model will achieve the jth goal. In words, the prior utility for a given model is proportional to the sum of the prior probabilities, each multiplied by the appropriate importance weight.

Step 6: Measure Goal Attainment

In this example there is an operational definition of goals, and pertinent data are frequency counts of goal achievement on retest. For the hypothetical example, we might assume that the proportions are given in Table 7.2. Clearly, these data run counter to prior expectations—on goals 2 and 3, Models 2 and 3 do better than Model 1. The computation, in Step 8, of posterior utilities will indicate how these data should change prior opinion about the value of these models.

Step 7: Calculate Posterior Probabilities

Before posterior utilities can be calculated, it is appropriate to revise the probabilities associated with goal attainment. Bayes's theorem (e.g., see Edwards, Lindman, and Savage, 1963) is the algorithm used to revise probabilities; the beta

TABLE 7.1

Model	Prior Probability of Client's Achieving Goal			Prior Utility
	Goal 1	Goal 2	Goal 3	
1	.40	.80	.60	54.00
2	.40	.75	.50	52.00
3	.30	.60	.45	40.50
4	.10	.30	.35	17.50

TABLE 7.2

Model	Proportion of Clients Achieving Goal		
	Goal 1	Goal 2	Goal 3
1	62/100	40/100	40/100
2	55/100	85/100	50/100
3	35/100	90/100	65/100
4	10/100	35/100	40/100

distribution is used as a prior in this example. Because the assessment of prior distributions can be controversial, we arbitrarily assume that the parameters of the prior beta distribution sum to 1.0. (This amounts to assuming that all prior opinions were very weakly held.) Using the prior distribution and the probabilities of the data for each model (described by the binomial distribution), the posterior probabilities (means of the posterior distributions) shown in Table 7.3 are derived.

(Note that the posterior probabilities in Table 7.4 are very nearly equal to the sample proportions in Table 7.3. This is an example of "stable estimation," since data exert a much larger effect on the posteriors that the priors do. If, however, there is little or no sample information, the posterior probabilities will be close to the prior probabilities. Thus, this method reflects the diagnosticity of data from program evaluation and provides a mathematically appropriate rule for modifying opinion about programs.)

TABLE 7.3

Model	Posterior Probabilities of Client's Achieving Goal			Posterior Utility
	Goal 1	Goal 2	Goal 3	
1	.62	.47	.41	61.90
2	.55	.86	.51	66.30
3	.35	.91	.66	52.80
4	.10	.35	.40	19.00

TABLE 7.4

Comparison Group	Prior Probability of Cient's Achieving Goal					Prior Utility
	Goal 1	Goal 2	Goal 3	Goal 4	Goal 5	
Graduates	.23	.30	.10	.07	.30	45.75
Nongraduates	.15	.22	.06	.12	.45	34.80

Step 8: Calculate Posterior Utilities

The computational formula for posterior utilities is (except for minor notational changes) identical to the equation in Step 5: to calculate posterior utilities, simply replace the prior probabilities in Step 5 with the posterior probabilities from Step 7. The posterior utilities are shown in Table 7.3.

This hypothetical example illustrates how evaluation data can be directly related to the decision maker's values, and how these data can be used to revise prior assessments of the worth of programs. By assessing the worth of each model across all dimensions at once, the utility score incorporates tradeoffs between goals or values. Note, for example, that Model 2 has a higher overall posterior utility than Model 1, although Model 1 has a somewhat higher posterior probability on Goal 1 than Model 2 does. These data indicate that the data from evaluation should induce the decision maker to rate Model 2 as a better investment than Model 1, and reverse his prior rank ordering.

An Example from the Career Education Project

Currently, a decision-theoretic approach is being used by the Career Education Project (CEP), Educational Development Center, Inc. A goal of this project is to reach potential members of the labor force, especially "homebased" women, and counsel them about career education or training opportunities. One way of evaluating this project is to specify goals in terms of status in education or training activities. The general approach can be illustrated using data from a formative stage of the project; these are follow-up for clients who terminated the service with the stated intention of enrolling in an education or training activity. (The tentative plans are for the latest evaluation to include a control group and a more complete set of goals.) For the follow-up study, the goals and importance weights (in parentheses) are: Goal 1, Client Enrolled and Completed ETR (90); Goal 2, Client Enrolled and Participating in ETR (60); Goal 3, Client Enrolled and Waiting for ETR to Begin (30); Goal 4, Client Tried to Enroll but Failed to Resolve Constraints (15); and Goal 5, Client Enrolled but Dropped ETR (10).

To evaluate the differential impact of the counseling service on different subgroups of clients, many comparative analyses were made. Utility is calculated for each separate subgroup. For example, high school graduates were compared to nongraduates. After appropriate instructions, subjective prior probability estimates were made by a project member; these, along with the prior utilities (calculated from Step 5) are shown in Table 7.4.

These prior probabilities were subjective estimates about what goal attainment would be six months after clients left the service. Data for these clients were obtained by talking with them after the six-month delay. Actual results are indicated in Table 7.5, which shows the posterior probabilities and utilities.

Murphy (1974) has suggested that comparing prior and posterior probabilities may highlight ways in which the program is not performing as expected. Disparity between the wholly subjective priors and the data-based posteriors could indicate that the program should be modified, or that additional research efforts might be

TABLE 7.5

Comparison Group	Posterior Probability of Client's Achieving Goal					Posterior Utility
	Goal 1	Goal 2	Goal 3	Goal 4	Goal 5	
Graduates	.21	.45	.05	.11	.18	50.85
Nongraduates	.29	.30	.01	.19	.21	49.35

required. In particular, such analyses may show that a program should be modified to better meet the needs of specific subgroups of clients.

In these analyses of the follow-up studies, no control group or randomization was used. Thus, self-selection among clients is a distinct possibility. Nevertheless, utility measures such as these indicate how classes of clients are interacting with the program and—regardless of their personal or demographic characteristics—indicate differences in outcomes for client groups. Thus, the utility scores are useful, even under nonexperimental conditions.

These illustrations show how the method discussed in this paper can be used in both nonexperimental conditions (e.g., the CEP follow-up study) and experimental conditions (the hypothetical example and the CEP evaluation plan). This flexibility is a major advantage over more conventional approaches, which are generally unrelated to planning or resource allocation decisions.

NOTES

1. This section on independence is more technical than the remainder of the paper. It can be skipped by those who are comfortable with simply making independence assumptions as a way of getting on with the job of evaluation, but should be read and pondered by those interested in the technical properties of multi-attribute utility measurement.

2. We are grateful to David Seaver, who first called the issue discussed in the following paragraphs to our attention.

3. Much of this material was originally presented in Guttentag (1973).

4. Much of this material will appear in a forthcoming issue of *Evaluation* (see Guttentag and Snapper, in press).

5. Snapper (1973) has described the hierarchical version of the multi-attribute utility model that was actually used in calculations. His notation is different from that used in this paper, so his argument is here paraphrased and the equations are given a form consistent with the notation used throughout.

When OCD attempted to use the nonhierarchical version of multi-attribute utility measurement, it became clear that the values to be served were at a very different level of abstraction from the specific projects; the logical and conceptual linkages between projects and values were therefore unclear. For that reason, a four-level hierarchical model was adopted. At the top level were the five value dimensions already chosen; the index j runs over them. Next below them came substantive areas (e.g., child advocacy, children at risk and the child welfare system); it was assumed that each substantive area had value within each of the value dimensions. The index k runs over them. Next below substantive areas came issues. Since different issues may arise within each substantive area, the index h_k runs over the issues within the kth substantive area. Finally, the index i runs over specific projects. If u_{ijkh_k} is the location measure of the ith

research project with respect to value dimension J, substantive area k, and issue within that substantive area h_k, the w's are the importances, and U_j is the aggregate value of the ith research project, then in this notation

$$U_i = \sum_j \left[w_j \left\{ \sum_k w_k \left(\sum_{h_k} w_{h_k} u_{ijkh_k} \right) \right\} \right]$$

subject to the following sum constraints:

$$\sum_j w_j = 1$$
$$\sum_k w_k = 1$$

For each value of k, $\sum_k w_{h_k} = 1$.

This hierarchical formulation of the multi-attribute utility model established logical and conceptual linkages between the value dimensions and specific projects, thereby meeting the first criticism. But how can a budget be allocated without the need for dubious cost estimates? As Snapper noted: "In many forward-planning contexts, the actual set of projects (or options) is unknown at the time budget allocation is required. This occurs, for example, when "directive" research involves project recommendations solicited from the field. When the set of projects is not complete . . . it is impossible . . . to apply the benefit-to-cost algorithm. . . . However, there are several bureaucratic techniques for allocating funds prior to the receipt of specific projects. The most plausible is to allocate funds to substantive areas in proportion to the importance weights."

Snapper went on to point out that benefit-to-cost rules will select projects with modest benefits only if their costs are correspondingly modest, and will select projects with large costs only if they also produce large benefits; that is, the rule produces a high positive correlation between benefit and costs for selected projects. Thus allocation of funds in proportion to importance weight approximates the result of a full benefit-to-cost analysis, since those weights are crucial to calculation of benefits.

The goal, then, is to allocate funds proportionally to w_k. Rather than directly estimating w_k, this was done by using the equation

$$w = w_j w_{kj}$$

The term w_{kj} is a judgment of the extent to which substantive area k satisfies, or fulfills, value dimension j. Of course

$$\sum_{kj} w_{kj} = 1.$$

Using this equation and the Director's estimates, the calculated importance weights w_k for the four substantive areas were:

Substantive Area	Importance Weight
Children at risk and the child welfare system	.46
Child development and the family	.39
Child advocacy	.08
Television and children	.07

6. Unlike the hypothetical example, the CEP application involves a multinomial distribution, and the prior distribution is Dirichlet rather than beta; however, the computation of posterior probabilities and utilities is analogous to that used in the binomial example.

REFERENCES

Boruch, Robert F. "Problems in research utilization: Use of social experiments, experimental results and auxiliary data in experiments." *Annals of the New York Academy of Sciences: Critical Human Behavioral Research Issues in Social Intervention Programs,* June 22, 1973, 218: 56-77.

Campbell, Donald T. "Assessing the impact of planned social change." Lecture given at Conference on Social Psychology, Budapest, Hungary, May 1974.

———. "Making the case for randomized assignment to treatments by considering the alternatives: six ways in which quasi-experimental evaluations in compensatory education tend to underestimate effects." Reconstruction and extension of lecture presented to the conference on Central Issues in Social Program Evaluation. In C. A. Bennet and A. Lumsdaine, *Central Issues in Social Program Evaluation,* in press.

Dawes, R. M. and B. Corrigan. "Linear Models in decision making." *Psychological Bulletin,* 1974, 81: 97-106.

Edwards, Ward. "Social utilities." *The Engineering Economist,* Summer Symposium Series, VI, 1971.

Edwards, W., H. Lindman and L. J. Savage. "Bayesian statistical inference for psychological research." *Psychological Review,* 1963, 70: 193-242.

Edwards, W., L. D. Phillips, W. L. Hays, and B. C. Goodman. "Probabilistic information processing systems: Design and evaluation." *IEEE Transaction on Systems Science and Cybernetics,* 1968, SSC-4: 248-265.

Fryback, Dennis Gene. "Subjective Probability Estimates in a medical decision making problem." Ph.D. thesis, University of Michigan, 1974.

Gardiner, Peter C., "The Application of decision technology and Monte Carlo simulation to multiple objective public policy decision making: A case study in California coastal zone management." Ph.D. dissertation, University of Southern California, 1974.

Gilbert, John P., Richard J. Light and Frederick Mosteller. "Assessing social innovations: An empirical base for policy." In C. A. Bennett and A. Lumsdaine (eds.) *Central Issues in Social Program Evaluation,* in press.

Guttentag, M. "Subjectivity and its use in evaluation research." *Evaluation,* 1973, 1 (2).

Guttentag, M. and K. J. Snapper. "Plans, evaluations, and decisions." *Evaluation,* in press.

Harre, Ron and Paul Secord. *The Explanation of Social Behavior.* Oxford: Blackwell and Mott, 1972.

Keeney, R. L. "Utility functions for multi-attributed consequences." *Management Science,* 1972a, 18, 276-287.

———. "Multiplicative utility functions." Technical Report #70, Operations Research Center. Boston: M.I.T., 1972b.

Miller, L. W., R. J. Kaplan, and W. Edwards. "JUDGE: A laboratory evaluation." *Organizational Behavior and Human Performance,* 1969, 4: 97-111.

Murphy, J. F. "Multi-attribute utility analysis: an application in social utilities." Career Education Project Technical Report (74-1, July 1974).

Phillips, L. D. *Bayesian Statistics for Social Scientists.* New York: Crowell, 1973.

Raiffa, H. *Decision Analysis: Introductory Lectures on Choices Under Certainty.* Reading, Mass.: Addison-Wesley, 1968.

———. Preferences for multi-attribute alternatives. The RAND Corp., Memorandum RM-5968-DOT/RC, April 1969.

Riecken, H. W., R. F. Boruch, D. T. Campbell, N. Caplan, T. K. Glennan, J. Pratt, A. Rees, and W. Williams. *Experimentation as a Method for Planning and Evaluating Social Innovations.* New York: Seminar Press, 1975.

Schlaifer, R. *Analysis of Decisions Under Uncertainty.* New York: McGraw-Hill, 1969.

Snapper, K. J. and C. Peterson. "Information seeking and data diagnosticity." *Journal of Cognitive Psychology,* 1971, 87: 429-433.

Suchman, E. *Evaluation Research.* New York: Russell Sage, 1967.

Watts, H. W. "Graduated work incentives: An experiment in negative taxation." *American Economic Review,* 1969, 59: 463-472.

Weiss, C. H. *Evaluation Research.* Englewood Cliffs, N.J.: Prentice-Hall, 1972.

Weiss, R. S. and M. Rein. "The evaluation of broad-aim programs: Experimental design, its difficulties, and an alternative." *Administrative Science Quarterly,* 1970, 15: 97-109.

Williams, W., and J. W. Evans. "The politics of evaluation: The case of Head Start." *The Annals,* 1969, 385: 118-132.

A MULTIVARIATE, NONRANDOMIZED MATCHING TECHNIQUE FOR STUDYING THE IMPACT OF SOCIAL INTERVENTIONS

CLARENCE C. SHERWOOD

*John Jay College of Criminal Justice,
City University of New York and
Project Consultant to
Fall River Housing Authority (FRHA),
Fall River, Massachusetts*

JOHN N. MORRIS

*Hebrew Rehabilitation Center for Aged (HRCA),
Boston, Massachusetts*

SYLVIA SHERWOOD

*Hebrew Rehabilitation Center for Aged (HRCA),
Boston, Massachusetts*

Social research frequently encounters the task of evaluating change produced in nonrandomly selected groups by events which are beyond the researcher's control. The social scientist must verify that there has in fact been a change, and that the indicated event is its cause. . . . Because in these situations the investigator has no control over the assignment of individuals or groups to "experimental" and "control" situations, the logic of the classical experiment must be reexamined in a search for optimal interpretative procedures. [Campbell and Ross, 1970: 110]

This was precisely the situation which stimulated the development of the multivariate matching technique described in this paper. In designing a study of the

AUTHORS' NOTE: This grant supported in part by DHEW/BHSR Grant #HS00903.

impact of an innovative social intervention into the lives of low income physically impaired and elderly persons, the investigators wished, but were unable, to allocate subjects to treatment on a random basis; that is, they "matched" because they were unable to randomize. This paper addresses the issues involved in formulating and implementing the procedure: (1) by examining the logical basis on which an acceptable nonrandomized matched experimental-control group design might be built; (2) by presenting a theoretically reasonable procedure which integrates multivariate statistical analysis, clinical verification, and individual-to-individual matching of experimentals and controls and by describing in detail the actual implementation of this design in the study for which the procedure was developed; and (3) by describing and analyzing the results of the implementation of the matching protocol in terms of whether or not the method produced an acceptable study sample, free from "threats to internal validity" (Campbell and Stanley, 1963) normally considered neutralized when randomization is the basis for selecting experimental and control groups.

ISSUES IN EXPERIMENTAL DESIGN

In the evaluation of the impact of a social intervention, the objective is to isolate the cause-and-effect relationships within a system of variables. A basic assumption is that the causality is unidirectional in the time dimension; that is, the causes precede the effects. At one point in time, the subjects (persons, organizations, etc.) are in a particular *state* or *condition* with respect to the relevant set of independent and dependent variables. At subsequent points in time, the same subjects are also in particular *states* or *conditions* with respect to these same variables. These *states* or *conditions* are presumably measurable, either directly or indirectly, and interrelated over the time dimension. It is an ongoing system *producing* sequences of *conditions* concerning which an observer may obtain *measurements* from time to time. The magnitudes of any sequential set of measurements (for a particular variable) may be the same or different. How large the observed differences have to be to warrant a conclusion of real difference depends upon the observer's position with respect to the fallibility of his measuring instrument. It is clearly the avowed and logical purpose of a social intervention to produce different sequences of conditions, sequences different from those that would have prevailed had the system been left alone. Assuming that for a particular variable higher magnitudes are more desirable than lower magnitudes, changes in sequence which may hopefully result from social intervention include: increases in magnitude over time where they would have been the same; greater increases in magnitude over time than would have prevailed; no change over time where there would have been decreases in magnitude; smaller decreases in magnitude over time than would have prevailed; and increases where there would have been decreases. The central issue is: on what evidential and logical grounds can the inference be made that the intervention has produced a different sequence of conditions than would have existed without the intervention? A major problem, particularly when the experimental material is heterogeneous and gen-

erally changing, is that there may be many possible sources of variability, both across subjects at any one point 'in time and within subjects over time. Kish (1959: 329-330) has examined these problems in some detail and analyzed them in terms of four types of variables.

I. The *explanatory* variables, sometimes called the "experimental" variables, are the objects of the research. They are the variables among which the researcher wishes to find and to measure some specified relationships. They include both the "dependent" and the "independent" variables, that is, the "predictand" and "predictor" variables. With respect to the aims of the research all other variables, of which there are three classes, are extraneous.

II. There are extraneous variables which *are controlled*. The control may be exercised in either or both the selection and the estimation procedures.

III. There may exist extraneous uncontrolled variables which are *confounded* with the Class I variables.

IV. There are extraneous uncontrolled variables which are treated as *randomized* errors. In "ideal" experiments . . . they are actually randomized. . . .

The aim of efficient design . . . is to place as many of the extraneous variables as is feasible into the second class. The aim of randomization in experiments is to place all of the third class into the fourth class.

Randomization thus provides a means for controlling extraneous influences that cannot be directly controlled and is generally agreed to be the soundest basis for making inferences concerning the effects of an intervention with respect to specified outcomes. As Hays (1963: 450) points out:

. . . given some sample it will always be true that factors other than the ones manipulated by the experimenter will contribute to the observed differences between subjects in the particular situation. If it should happen that some extraneous factor operates unevenly over several treatment groups or over different subjects, this can create spurious differences, or mask true effects in the data. Such a factor is a "nuisance-factor," playing a role analogous to "noise" in communication. Randomization over treatments is one device for "scattering" the effects of these nuisance factors through the data. . . . By randomization, the possibility of "pile-ups" of nuisance effects in particular treatment groups is identified with random error, and the experimenter can rest assured that [with] overall repetitions of his experiment under the same conditions, true effects will eventually emerge if they exist.

But there are circumstances under which the researcher is not in a position to implement a randomized design. Social interventions, particularly large-scale interventions, are generally not carried out in a closed laboratory situation in which the investigator can manipulate features of the intervention or the members of a potential study sample. Intake policies of the agencies providing service, governmental regulations, political, community, and financial pressures, as well as other practical considerations, are likely to affect decisions concerning sample selections with which the researcher must deal. When the list of applicants or the number of needy persons for a *new* service program is known and is much larger than the

number of openings, the researcher can argue on democratic as well as research grounds for the use of a lottery system, thus allowing a randomized design for the selection of program participants. But if there are just enough applicants at the start of a program, or if it has already been initiated with established intake policies and has been ongoing for some time, the researcher will have a much more difficult time overcoming community, agency policy, and financial pressures; and very often under such circumstances a randomized design will not be feasible.

Under such circumstances, what are the choices? They appear to be either: (a) make no attempt at a hard-nosed empirical evaluation, or (b) find a method that, without randomization, provides a reasonably sound basis for inferences about effects. The authors believe, along with Campbell and Ross (1970), that it is important to seek methods other than random allocation that provide a basis for sound causal inference.

The remainder of this paper is devoted to the rationale for, and description and analysis of, a multivariate matching technique which may hold such promise.

The Rationale

Matching as an alternative to randomization is generally viewed as inferior and, by some, as totally unacceptable. But opposition appears to be directed toward particular matching procedures—the use of ex post facto designs, matching on pre-measures of outcome variables, etc.—and not necessarily to the idea of matching per se. In fact, there is a sense in which randomization—with respect to the problem of subject differences, at least—may be viewed as an alternative to matching, since one of the goals of the procedure of randomly allocating treatments to subjects is to produce comparable or matched treatment groups. Keppel (1973: 24), for example, states:

> We have not mentioned yet a major source of uncontrolled variability present in any experiment, namely, the differences in performance among subjects. One obvious way to hold subject differences constant is to use the *same* subject in each treatment condition—a sort of biological analogue of absolute physical control. Unfortunately, even the same subject is not the same person each time he is tested. Moreover, there are potentially serious carry-over effects from one treatment to another, owing to the successive administration of the different treatments to the same subjects. To avoid this problem, we could try to *match* sets of subjects on important characteristics and then assign one member of each matched set to a different treatment, but matching would never be exact. Thus, neither attempt to control for individual differences among subjects guarantees that the treatment groups will contain subjects of the same average ability.
>
> This leads us to a third method, one which represents control of a different sort. Specifically, it consists of an elimination of *systematic* differences among the treatment conditions by means of *randomization*.

Crano and Brewer (1973: 30-31) take a similar position when they say:

> The success of the two-group experimental design depends primarily on the assumption that experimental and control groups are equivalent on all factors

except the independent variable. For a long time . . . the achieving of initial equivalence of groups was a serious problem in research design. . . . However, with the development and refinement of statistical theory the problem became resolvable through the technique of randomized assignment to groups.

It is generally recognized, however, that randomization is one of those "long-run" phenomena, and that the desired equivalence of groups will not necessarily occur in any one or even several applications. Keppel (1973: 25), in discussing the problem of biases because of subject differences in the comparison groups, states:

> The subjects who are chosen to participate in an experiment will differ widely on a whole host of characteristics. Some of these will affect the behavior being studied and, hence, must be controlled . . . random assignment of subjects to treatments will ensure in the long run that there will be an equivalence of subjects across the different treatments.

Cox (1958: 84) has expressed the same idea from a different point of view:

> The estimated treatment effects are *unbiased,* in the sense that the average of the estimates over a large number of independent repetitions of the experiment would be equal to the true treatment effects.

The desire for equivalent comparison groups is further reflected in the views of those who not only recognize the long-run requisite of randomization but express concern about its implications for use in the short-run, and particularly in the unrepeated experiment. Since in any one trial randomization may fail to control adequately for extraneous influences, that is, significant differences between the groups may occur by chance (Anderson and Bancroft, 1952: 221; Snedecor and Cochran, 1967: 110), some have suggested that when this occurs, randomly biased experimental and control comparisons should not be initiated. According to L. J. Savage (1962: 33):

> It is not enough to say something like this: "If you randomize here, you are very unlikely to make a mistake." It can happen that when the randomization is done, the experimenter sees that he has made a mistake, that is, sees that the experiment called for by the randomization is inappropriate. . . . In particular, randomization could accidentally closely correlate any variable that has not been controlled by stratification or some such device, with one of the treatments. For example, we might accidentally choose at random a latin square with the treatments running in regular slanting lines across the field. It would usually be most ill-advised to carry out such an experiment in which treatment is highly correlated with a possible gradient in fertility merely because this bad design had arisen at random.

A similar position has been taken by Cox (1958: 84, 87) in a discussion of the problem of error in the estimation of treatment effects:

> . . . in single small experiments the estimate of error is very inaccurate anyway. More importantly we have here a mathematical interpretation of randomization: that it leads to desirable properties in the long run, or on the

average, and on the other hand a practical problem—namely, the designing and drawing of useful conclusions from a particular single experiment. . . . Usually the concept that our procedures will work out well in the long run is a very helpful one, both quantitatively and in giving a vivid physical picture of the meaning of probabilities calculated in connection with a particular experiment. However, to adopt arrangements that we suspect are bad, simply because things will be all right in the long run, is to force our behavior into the Procrustean bed of a mathematical theory. Our object is the design of individual experiments that will work well: good long run properties are concepts that help us in doing this, but the exact fulfillment of long-run mathematical conditions is not the ultimate aim.

The desire for equivalent comparison groups in experimentation in the short run arises in part at least from the fact that experimental error and treatment effects are merged together in the difference between the outcome variable means. As Keppel (1973: 32) states:

> . . . differences among treatment means may reflect two *different quantities*: When the population means are equal, the differences among the group means will reflect the operation of experimental error alone; but when the population means are not equal, the differences among the group means will reflect the operation of an unsystematic component and a systematic component, i.e., experimental error and treatment effects, respectively.

The statistical model makes the decision about the significance of the postintervention differences on the basis of the postintervention within-group variability. The latter provides an estimate of the variability in the population from which the samples were drawn and thus the basis for computing the probability of drawing pairs of samples with mean differences of a specified size. Differences with probabilities less than a previously specified size (e.g., .05, .01, .001, etc.) are regarded as statistically significant; that is, the difference is judged to be too large to be attributed to experimental error, the chance of the draw. All of the difference, however, may be due to experimental error. The risk that this is in fact the case is the risk of Type I inference error. If, in fact, an experimental effect has occurred, it is totally confounded with the experimental error effect; in the long run, half of the time the observed differences will be less than the experimental effect and half of the time larger than the experimental effect, assuming no measurement error and no interaction between experimental effect and experimental error. The observed difference is therefore an algebraic combination of experimental effect and experimental error. Although statistically significant chance discrepancies between randomly allocated experimental and control groups are, of course, equally likely with samples of any size, the absolute magnitude of the difference necessary for significance decreases with increased sample size. Therefore, with respect to observed differences of any specified magnitude, the probable relative contribution of experimental error to that difference decreases with increased sample size. This emphasizes the importance of considering the probability of Type II inference error in the design of experiments, including the specification of the minimum magnitude of experimental effect it is desired the experiment be able to detect, estimates of

sample variability with respect to the criterion variable, estimates of the sample size required, etc. As Cohen (1969: 7) has stated:

> . . . the greater the precision of the sample results, other things being equal, the greater the probability of detecting a nonnull state of affairs, i.e., the more clearly the phenomenon under test can manifest itself against the background of (experimentally irrelevant) variability . . . increases in sample size increase statistical power, the probability of detecting the phenomenon under test.

Presumably, given initially truly equivalent groups and all subsequent influences controlled, including post-measure measurement error, all the postintervention postmeasure difference would be attributable to the effect of the intervention; and the more nearly initially equivalent the groups, the larger the proportion of the postintervention difference which would be attributable to the intervention. The assumption is that initial equivalence predicts later equivalence under the same conditions and that, when two initially equivalent groups are treated differently, each provides an estimate of the response of the other under opposite treatment.

To the extent that it is possible to construct subgroups of individuals who are alike on key variables that have been shown to or can be assumed to lead to similarities in the behavior of interest, then it is reasonable to believe that the matching of experimentals with controls within these subgroups should lead to the construction of equivalent experimental and control groups. This is the basic assumption underlying the multivariate matching procedure presented in this paper. Drawing upon the basic premises of the social sciences, the fundamental task is to identify the series of subgroups within the larger group that are distinguished in that they consist of similar types of individuals in terms of their predictable responses to similar sets of stimuli. Following from this social learning and experiential interpretation of human behavior, the experimental and control groups are equivalent if they contain the same proportions of members across the series of subcategories. The predicted similarity in response for members of the same subcategory is an outcome of prior similarities in experience. Individuals are occupants of a variety of social "categories" which lead to common experiences and expectations of self and from others. Some of these social categories are of a relatively fixed nature, for example, sex, race, and the like. With respect to others, there tends to be movement over time, for example, age, education, occupation, and so on. The assumption is that an individual—his ideas, attitudes, behavior, and the like—is in large part a product of the experiences and social expectations which impinge upon him because he occupies these socially defined "positions." Human beings respond to incumbency in identifiable groups by limiting their options in line with the expectations for members of such groups. Social background variables (age, sex, ethnic affiliation, etc.) are therefore indices of the presumed probability of similar experiences and socialization in the past and indices of the probability of similar patterns of responses in the future.

If group boundary separation is to be maintained, rules, rewards, and sanctions must exist. On this basis it is possible to assert that a large segment of the variability

in the individual's response to and functioning within real life situations is explainable on the basis of social positioning. This general position is further substantiated, within the general degrees of freedom idea, by reference to the linear model of relationships often reported for any body of data and the failure of successive variables to add to the predictability of a dependent variable following the consideration of other independent variables. What this means is that, in the long run, everything is connected to everything else. Therefore it appears that, when a large number of variables have already been controlled, all other variables functionally related to these known variables are also controlled.

It follows, from this social learning and experience perspective, then, that *the more "positions" and experiences an individual has in common with another individual, the greater the probability that they will be like one another with respect to other variables.*

If groups matched on variables of this type are in fact equivalent, they should manifest similarity in response to the premeasures of the outcome variables to be used in the assessment of the impact of the intervention. This might seem to suggest that the matching be made on the basis of the premeasures in the first place. Campbell and Erlebacher (1970: 205-206), however, have advanced very sound arguments against the use of matching on the basis of similarity of premeasures of outcome variables in an attempt to correct for initial differences between experimental and control pools:

> The compensatory program is made available to the most needy, and the "control" group then sought from among the untreated children of the same community. Often this untreated population is on the average more able than the "experimental" group. In such a situation the usual procedures of selection, adjustment, and analysis produce systematic biases in the direction of making the compensatory program look deleterious. [Campbell and Erlebacher, 1970: 185]

The interference to sound inference concerning the effects of the intervention stems from the regression to the mean phenomenon. Regression to the mean can be defined in terms of premeasure and postmeasure standard scores (z scores). For any given subject, the probability that his postmeasure z score will be nearer to zero increases with the size of his premeasure z score (plus or minus distance from zero). Therefore, to the extent that the members of a matched pair are from different segments of their premeasure distributions (in z score distances), they will have different probabilities of regressing to the mean. In the extreme case, as in Campbell and Erlebacher's example (1970: 180-190, Figs. 2-4), where most of the matches will pair members of the lower half of one distribution with members of the upper half of the other, the regression probabilities will not only be different but the regression tendencies will be in opposite directions. Campbell and Erlebacher (1970) point out that differential regression with respect to different population means is a probable outcome, and this negates any equating of the groups at premeasure by the time of the postmeasure. More specifically, they indicate that, "where scores have been selected because of their manifest values, they become biased estimates of true scores in the direction indicated by regression

to the mean. Matching . . . by obtained scores [is] just such [a] biasing process" (1970: 194). And further, "It is selection on the basis of extreme individual scores that creates most strongly the conditions under which obtained scores become biased estimates of true scores" (1970: 196).

The regression to the mean critique, therefore, forbids the use of matching on the basis of premeasures of outcome variables; however, it does not necessarily forbid matching on the basis of other variables.

The Campbell and Erlebacher position appears to be based on the issue of the extent to which the two population distributions are incongruent. There are several issues worthy of consideration here, however. The Campbell and Erlebacher example is essentially univariate in nature, which may be adequate in those instances where the search for effects is with respect to one outcome variable only, but in the case of multiple outcome variables, the issue of the congruence of population distributions is obviously more complicated. But what is more relevant to the position taken in this paper, Campbell and Erlebacher seem to have assumed that it is the mean of the group from which an individual is selected—for matching purposes, for example—that is pertinent to the issue of the probability and direction of regression in his posttest score(s). But the issue of what group an individual is a member of, in this sense, is by no means quite so simple. For example, whether two "accidental" pools of subjects are the distinct and unique population entities of concern is highly problematical. Lord's (1963: 31-32) views concerning the estimation of true gain scores using group performance in the estimation procedures seem particularly pertinent here:

> If the same individual were considered as a member of some other group, the estimated value for his change would probably be different even though his test scores remain unchanged. How can one justify basing the estimate for a given individual on the totally irrelevant performance of other individuals with whom he happens to be considered?
>
> The answer to this query comes in two parts. In the first place [the recommended estimation procedure] is applicable only if the given individual actually is a member of some natural group under consideration. . . .
>
> The second point is that knowledge that an individual belongs to a certain group constitutes genuine information about that individual. An efficient method of estimation can and should make use of this information. Furthermore, it is not to be expected or desired that an estimating procedure should yield the same estimate when the information available is altered, as is the case when we first consider an individual as a member of one group and then consider him as a member of another group.
>
> If the individual belongs to several different groups, the group statistics for [the estimating equation] should be derived from the subgroup consisting of those individuals who belong to all of these same groups. If the necessary group statistics are not available, then the information about group membership cannot be used efficiently.

To the extent that regression to the mean is a function of measurement error (the use of fallible measures[1]), the differential probabilities for regression for individuals with the same raw premeasure score, but from two populations, must be a function

of their premeasure error terms. An examination of any score sector of the scatter diagram of any two incongruent distributions of premeasure-postmeasure relations (e.g., Campbell and Erlebacher, 1970: 188-190, Figs. 2-4) shows the differential probabilities of regression to the mean for members of the same score segments in the two distributions. Assuming no premeasure-to-postmeasure change for both groups, the probability that a postmeasure will be nearer the premeasure mean is an inverse function of premeasure distance from the premeasure mean. That is, premeasure error terms are correlated positively with premeasure observed scores; postmeasure error terms are correlated positively with postmeasure observed scores; and the premeasure error terms and the postmeasure error terms are uncorrelated with each other. Therefore, the probabilities of regression to the mean in the same observed score sector of two incongruent distributions are different; the greater the incongruence, the greater the difference in probabilities. The exception to this occurs in the observed score sector bounded by the means of the two incongruent distributions; here, the probabilities are likely to be very similar, but the regression will be in the opposite direction. When pairs are selected from incongruent distributions by matching on premeasure score, they will have different probabilities of regression in the same direction or similar probabilities of regression in the opposite direction. They are in effect random selections from the same score segment of two distributions which have differential regression probabilities for the score segment.

However, when the matching is based on a configuration of a large number of other variables (other than premeasures of outcome variables) and the pairs turn out to be matched on the premeasures, there is reason to believe they are *not random* selections from the same score sector of two incongruent distributions. In this situation, the pair members not only have similar premeasure observed scores, but there is reason to believe they have similar premeasure true scores. Since the individuals were matched on the basis of a large number of *non*-premeasure variables, to the extent that those variables are related to the premeasure scores on the outcome variables, they could only be related to that part which is predictable, that is, to the true score component. If the members of a pair have the same observed score and the same true score, they must have the same error term and therefore the same directional regression probability: "The expected error score, for sampling over people in the subpopulation of people having any fixed true score, is zero" (Lord and Novick, 1968: 38).

And even if, for any given pair and any given outcome variable premeasure, some degree of dissimilarity exists in premeasure observed score and they have, therefore, different error terms, there appears to be no reason to assume that those error terms are correlated with treatment group membership and therefore no reason to believe that any systematic regression bias is involved that may interfere with sound inference concerning the effects of the intervention.

The above arguments at least suggest a logical justification for initiating pair-wise matching from within a series of homogeneous subpopulations and establish a basis for interpreting the preintervention experimental-control comparisons, both for the subpopulations and for the matched sample resulting from the matching procedures. The logic of this approach requires that homogeneous subpopulations first be identified.

A MULTIVARIATE MATCHING TECHNIQUE

Any experimental-control matched group design, in order to control for threats to internal validity, must be capable of producing samples that are as much alike as possible. The procedure to be described in this paper utilizes a somewhat unique methodology for matching pairs of individuals. The technique includes both multivariate statistical handling of theoretically important variables along with detailed case-by-case clinical judgments as to the appropriateness of individual matches.

Basic Principles and Procedures

The following are the assumptions on which the matching procedures are based:

1. The sample of study subjects does not consist of a pool of homogeneous subjects, that is, there is no one mold into which everyone in the sample will be placed.
2. A set of variables can be defined that is theoretically related to the need for, and potential impact of, the service intervention.
3. The number of distinct classes or subpools definable by the theoretically relevant variables will be less than the number of people in the study pool.
4. The definition of uniqueness for the subpools is derived from purely mathematical analysis of the information pertaining to the sample classified.
5. The matched subpools of controls and experimentals from which the individual-to-individual matches are to be made will be *more like themselves* on the theoretical variables than they are like people in other subpools. Thus, in a multidimensional space model, each subpool will have its own niche.

The matching procedure encompasses the following: Comparable data on a large number of variables (among which are the theoretically relevant independent variables, as well as the dependent variables of interest) are gathered for each member of the pools of potential experimentals and potential controls. This information is gathered prior to the exposure of the potential experimentals to the intervention. The theoretically relevant independent variables are factor analyzed to reduce the data to nonredundant information. (It is to be noted that the dependent variables, the premeasures of the outcome variables, are not to be included in this operation.) The factor analytic procedure permits the collapsing of the pool of variables into a smaller number of variables without losing key information. The assumption is that information not used is measurement error or is not related to the concept the items are designed to measure. Separate factor structures are then computed for the potential control pool and the potential experimental pool. If the structures for the two pools are sufficiently similar (Harman, 1967: 271-272), the experimental and control pools are combined and the data for this total pool are factor analyzed.

The several interpretable factors resulting from the factor analysis are then used in putting either the total pool or one or the other of the experimental or control pools through a numeric taxonomy classification program,[2] a program that classifies the sample members into a series of homogeneous groups on the basis of similar patterns of scores on the independent variables used. This is the basic statistical

procedure that identifies the niche in multidimensional space in which each cluster is located.

One widely used numeric taxonomy classification program, which is recommended by the authors of this paper, proceeds through a series of steps beginning with as many one-person clusters as there are persons and at each successive step combines the two clusters whose centroids (the intersection in multidimensional space of the means of all the independent variables) are closest together until, in the final step, all cases are in one cluster (Jones, 1968; Bartko, Strauss, and Carpenter, 1971). Figure 8.1 presents a hypothetical situation involving two independent variables and four persons. In this example, the cases would be clustered in the following order: Step 1 = A + B; Step 2 = C + D; and Step 3 = (A + B) + (C + D).

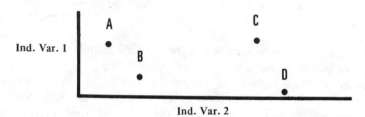

FIGURE 8.1   Hypothetical Two-Dimensional Distribution of cases to be clustered

The problem is to decide at which point to stop the clustering procedure. The objective is to divide the cases into the smallest number of clusters possible while still maintaining meaningful distinctions among clusters and a reasonable degree of homogeneity within clusters. One approach is for the investigator to make a provisional heuristic decision concerning the cluster step at which to initiate team judgment procedures. It is suggested that, when the total sample size is greater than 100, the provisional number of clusters be established at 20. At this point a team of judges (where appropriate, an interdisciplinary team of trained clinicians) reviews the persons in each cluster and judges whether or not the persons appear to be similar to one another.[3] On the one hand, if they indicate that the individuals in any cluster are not similar, the next higher number of clusters (in this example, 21) would be reviewed in the same way. This procedure is continued until the judgment is made that the individuals in each cluster are similar. On the other hand, if the judges indicate that the individuals within each of the first provisional sets of clusters are similar, the next lower number of clusters (in this example, 19) would be reviewed in the same way. This procedure is continued until the judgment of dissimilarity is made.

The total sample as clustered is then processed through a discriminant function analysis procedure (Rulon, Tiedeman, Tatsuoka and Langmuir, 1967: chap. 8) in order to measure the dissimilarity among the independent groups (in this instance, the several clusters) on the basis of the independent variables utilized in the clustering. Perfect or nearly perfect prediction of cluster membership provides an indication that each of the several clusters contains similar individuals. A basic assumption of this procedure is that the members of a cluster are not only similar

with respect to the variables utilized in the clustering procedures but that they are also similar in other ways as well.

If the clustering has been accomplished on the basis of only the controls or the experimentals rather than the total pool, the next step would consist of merging the remaining potential study sample into the cluster structure. This is accomplished by scoring the factors (used as the basis of clustering) for each member of the remaining sample according to the discriminant function weights found for the clustered pool. The members of the nonclustered pool would then be assigned to that cluster whose members have scores on the clustering factors most like their own.

Next, the controls and experimentals are hand-matched on a pair-wise basis within each of the clusters.[4] Specifically, the interdisciplinary team of clinicians evaluates all possible matches within the clusters and selects suitably matched pairs.[5]

Once the matched pairs are selected, a variety of tests are applied to determine the success or failure of the matching: for example, t-tests of the significance of the mean differences and interclass correlations across the array of premeasures of the outcome variables to be used in the assessment of the impact of the intervention.[6] The matched samples (experimental and control) are required to have highly similar scores on the premeasures of the outcome variables prior to the exposure of the experimentals to the intervention.

At this point, the sample selection procedure is completed, and from then on the assumption is that it has produced equivalent experimental and control groups; and the testing for impact of an intervention proceeds along the same lines as it would in studies in which the sample members had been randomly assigned to the experimental and control groups.[7]

The remainder of this paper will be devoted to a description of a particular implementation of this multivariate matching technique and, further, to a description and analysis of the results of the sample selection procedure in terms of whether or not it produced an acceptable study sample. Evidence will be examined concerning the extent to which the experimental and control groups are "equivalent," that is, reasonably capable of neutralizing the potentially causative claims for variables other than the experimental intervention itself.

An Implementation: The Highland Heights Study

The implementation of the multivariate matching design described above concerns the evaluation of the impact of Highland Heights, a low income, federally financed, medically oriented housing project for the physically impaired and elderly. A product of the joint efforts of the Fall River Housing Authority and Hussey Hospital, a municipal hospital for the treatment of chronic diseases in Fall River, Massachusetts, the building was constructed to house adults who live alone or with one other person and consists of 108 studio and 100 two-room apartments. The outpatient clinic of the hospital is located in the basement of the apartment house and includes physical therapy, occupational therapy, and outpatient treatments. Rooms and office space are also provided for ancillary services, meeting

halls, social and other activities. (See Slate, 1973, for a description of the service-support programs developed for Highland Heights residents within the first two years after it opened for occupancy in the fall of 1970.) It was envisioned that its basic features—the specialized architecture, the building's proximity to the hospital, special community services housed at the facility, and efforts to promote physical and social functioning—would result in a therapeutic environment for the residents.

Several months before Highland Heights was opened for residency, a HUD-DHEW/NCHSRD (now BHSR) jointly funded contract (H-1275) for a demonstration project was signed between HUD and the Fall River Housing Authority with a subcontract to the Department of Social Gerontological Research, Hebrew Rehabilitation Center for Aged in Boston. Since then the research efforts have been supported by NCHSRD (now BHSR) Grant HS00903.

The major research aims of the initial contract were: (1) to develop a research plan to evaluate the effectiveness of this type of sheltered housing on the health and well-being of the physically impaired; and (2) to initiate the implementation of this design (a) by collecting pretest baseline data for all applicants to the housing project as part of the application process and (b) by conducting a short-term impact study as a first step, using a sample of approximately 100 experimentals and 100 controls.

In line with the research mandate, as part of the application process data were collected concerning health, social isolation, cognitive and emotional state, living conditions, financial status, education, and other background variables. Each applicant was interviewed by a member of the research medical-social clinical team (usually a research social worker or research public health nurse). Items incorporated within this interview included questions to be used as premeasures of the outcome variables. The "health and well-being" outcome variables were broadly defined to include housing conditions, as well as physical, psychological, and social functioning. (See Sherwood, Greer, Morris and Sherwood, 1973, Appendix E, for the operational definitions and the scoring system for each of the outcome variables included in the premeasure interviews.)

In addition to the largely precoded interview form, case history notes by the clinician conducting the interview are also recorded. Using the data collected as part of the application process, each applicant considered eligible in terms of housing authority criteria (financial status and size of household) was screened in terms of degree of "need" for residency.[8]

The original design developed to study short-term (as well as long-term) impact called for random allocation of the applicant population into experimental and control groups, residency in Highland Heights constituting the "experimental" status. It had been assumed that there would be a large pool of applicants by the time of the opening of the building; and the Fall River Housing Authority had agreed that the apartments would be offered on a lottery basis to eligible applicants. This would have constituted both a democratically equitable system for allocating apartments and, at the same time, would have provided a sound method for studying impact. However, substantially less than the required number of eligible applicants came forth soon enough to allow for even the consideration of actually implementing a randomized design.

The alternative developed to select the experimental and control samples for the study of short-term impact has been described above. The major objective of the procedure is to match pairs of individuals, each pair to consist of one experimental and one control from one of the identified subpopulations through a combination of mathematical clustering and clinical verification.

Features present in the Highland Heights situation prior to the application of this matching design included:

1. The potential study members had applied for Highland Heights through the same application process during a period of about nine calendar months (from three months prior to opening to six months after the housing project was opened for occupancy).
2. The total sample pool from which pairs could be matched consisted of the first 420 persons to apply to Highland Heights.
3. A large array of identical self-reported and clinical judgment measures existed as a result of the application process for *all* potential study members. These measures included general background, as well as preintervention outcome items gathered by experienced research clinicians using a standardized structured instrument.
4. Highland Heights was a new facility, and the pool of 235 potential experimentals included all early applicants who were willing to accept occupancy. There was no exclusion, systematic or otherwise, of applicants from residency.
5. The potential control pool of 185 nonresidents consisted in large part of the next wave of applicants after the facility had been initially filled.

The following is a description of the implementation of the multivariate matching procedures applied to the population of 420 physically impaired and elderly adults who were either residents of Highland Heights or nonresident potential controls.

Step A. While several theoretically relevant variables were reserved for final stratification purposes (see Step E below), the following variables defined as theoretically relevant were selected for factor analysis:

1. Years of schooling
2. Primary language usually spoken (English only; Portuguese and/or English; French and/or English)
3. Literacy (ability to read English newspaper)
4. U.S. citizenship status
5. Religious affiliation
6. Employment status
7. Usual occupation
8. Number of persons in household at time of application
9. Length of residence in community at time of application
10. Whether or not applicant was Fall River resident
11. Whether or not moved in past year
12. Number of moves in past five years
13. Quality of intra-household relations

14. Permanent or transient residence
15. Whether or not applicant was head of household at time of application
16. Handicap status of companion applicant applying with
17. Number of children in the area
18. Sources of financial assistance (OAA, welfare/other; OAA, welfare, MAA/other)
19. Housing arrangement at time of application (nursing home, hospital, own home, or apartment)
20. Number of rooms for exclusive use of self (or self and spouse) at time of application
21. Housing conditions (substandard or not) at time of application
22. Private bath for self (or self and spouse) or not at time of application
23. Proximity to medical services

Data for the factor analysis were from the application (premeasure) interview. In preparation for factor analysis, all nominal variables were dichotomized into one or more dummy variables. The combined list consisted of 33 variables. Four were dropped, however, because the distribution of responses was too highly skewed in the total study pool of 420 cases.[9] The criterion for dropping these variables was as follows: more than 95% of the individuals in the total pool had the same response. One additional variable, proximity to medical services, was dropped from the analysis because of insufficient information.

Separate principal component factor analyses followed by varimax rotation were initiated for the pools of 185 potential controls and 235 potential experimentals. Since the resulting four-factor varimax solutions for each of these samples were similar, a pooled factor analysis based on the 420 cases was completed. A variable was considered to contribute importantly to a factor if its factor loading was equal to, or greater than, plus or minus .30 (see Table 8.1).[10]

The four factors used as clustering variables, then, consisted of the following significant items:

Variables	High Factor Score
Factor 1	
Number of persons in household at time of application	High
Whether applicant head of household at time of application	No
Handicap status of companion applicant applying with	Handicapped
Whether applicant living alone at time of application	No
Whether applicant living with spouse at time of application	Yes
Source of income (OAA, welfare, MAA)	No
Factor II	
Length of residence in community at time of application	Low
Number of moves in past five years	High
Whether moved in past year	Yes
Housing arrangement at time of application	Not own home or apartment
Housing arrangement at time of application	Nursing home or hospital
Number of rooms for exclusive use	Fewer
Private bath for self (or self and spouse)	No
Like to work	Yes
Fall River resident	No

(text continues on p. 202)

TABLE 8.1   VARIMAX ROTATION OF PRINCIPAL COMPONENT FACTORS
FOR THEORETICALLY RELEVANT CLUSTERING VARIABLES

	Factor 1		
Variable Description	Total Sample (N=420)	Potential Experimentals (N=235)	Potential Controls (N=185)
Years of schooling	-0.120	-0.182	-0.063
Primary language usually spoken not "English only"	0.099	0.073	0.104
Primary language usually spoken not "Portuguese and/or English and Portuguese"	-0.078	-0.073	-0.100
Primary language usually spoken not "French and/or English and French"	0.007	0.015	0.050
Religion not Catholic	0.011	-0.014	0.130
Religion not Protestant	0.071	0.077	-0.021
Employment status	-0.014	-0.076	0.064
Would not like to work	-0.060	-0.119	0.028
Usual occupation not professional/managerial	0.105	0.236	0.016
Usual occupation not sales or clerical	-0.073	-0.134	0.028
Usual occupation not blue collar	-0.033	-0.077	-0.030
Not Fall River resident	0.223	0.153	0.311
Length of residence	-0.016	0.014	-0.071
Number of moves in past five years	0.007	0.083	-0.089
Moved in past year	0.090	0.024	0.194
Number of persons in household (1/2/3 +)	0.848	0.808	0.884
Composition of household—not alone	0.918	0.900	0.928
Composition of household—not living with spouse	-0.844	-0.853	-0.834
Head of household is other than applicant	0.661	0.683	0.648
Applicant not applying with a handicapped companion	-0.780	-0.804	-0.743
Children in the area (none/1/2/3 +)	0.198	0.114	0.302
Financial assistance (OAA, welfare/other)	0.248	0.285	0.126
Financial assistance (OAA, welfare, MAA/other)	0.313	0.353	0.165
Housing—not own home or apartment	0.042	-0.030	0.111
Housing—not in nursing home or hospital	0.119	0.112	0.132
Number of rooms for exclusive use	0.206	0.248	0.167
Bathroom facilities not private	-0.026	-0.044	0.003
Housing conditions not substandard	0.220	0.212	0.218
	Factor 2		
Years of schooling	0.022	0.055	0.016
Primary language usually spoken not "English only"	-0.038	-0.022	-0.119
Primary language usually spoken not "Portuguese and/or English and Portuguese"	-0.102	-0.071	-0.075
Primary language usually spoken not "French and/or English and French"	-0.005	-0.045	0.050
Religion not Catholic	-0.003	0.042	-0.108
Religion not Protestant	-0.022	-0.064	0.039
Employment status	-0.169	-0.203	-0.241
Would not like to work	-0.308	-0.394	-0.253
Usual occupation not professional/managerial	0.122	0.089	0.193
Usual occupation not sales or clerical	0.004	-0.039	0.027

TABLE 8.1 (continued)

	Factor 2		
Variable Description	Total Sample (N=420)	Potential Experimentals (N=235)	Potential Controls (N=185)
Usual occupation not blue collar	-0.102	-0.055	-0.165
Not Fall River resident	0.326	0.435	0.177
Length of residence	-0.412	-0.362	-0.455
Number of moves in past five years	0.606	0.546	0.671
Moved in past year	0.576	0.585	0.525
Number of persons in household (1/2/3 +)	0.119	0.121	0.156
Composition of household—not alone	-0.015	0.035	-0.041
Composition of household—not living with spouse	0.116	0.065	0.162
Head of household is other than applicant	0.020	0.027	0.021
Applicant not applying with a handicapped companion	0.151	0.119	0.170
Children in the area (none/1/2/3 +)	0.008	-0.004	-0.042
Financial assistance (OAA, welfare/other)	0.152	0.096	0.210
Financial assistance (OAA, welfare, MAA/other)	0.175	0.119	0.231
Housing—not own home or apartment	0.852	0.829	0.857
Housing—not in nursing home or hospital	-0.663	-0.642	-0.623
Number of rooms for exclusive use	-0.792	-0.760	-0.810
Bathroom facilities not private	0.762	0.785	0.718
Housing conditions not substandard	0.086	0.055	0.100
	Factor 3		
Years of schooling	0.225	0.256	0.189
Primary language usually spoken not "English only"	-0.689	-0.704	-0.707
Primary language usually spoken not "Portuguese and/or English and Portuguese"	0.265	0.239	0.318
Primary language usually spoken not "French and/or English and French"	0.606	0.619	0.586
Religion not Catholic	0.798	0.781	0.781
Religion not Protestant	-0.849	-0.832	-0.838
Employment status	0.008	-0.043	-0.017
Would not like to work	0.132	0.112	0.152
Usual occupation not professional/managerial	0.058	0.144	0.013
Usual occupation not sales or clerical	-0.028	-0.083	0.002
Usual occupation not blue collar	-0.019	-0.017	-0.025
Not Fall River resident	0.258	0.238	0.233
Length of residence	-0.114	-0.149	-0.066
Number of moves in past five years	0.088	0.073	0.092
Moved in past year	0.004	-0.124	0.146
Number of persons in household (1/2/3 +)	-0.049	-0.094	-0.055
Composition of household—not alone	-0.074	-0.120	-0.082
Composition of household—not living with spouse	0.051	0.089	0.073
Head of household is other than applicant	0.049	0.006	0.038
Applicant not applying with a handicapped companion	-0.015	0.048	-0.023

TABLE 8.1 (continued)

Variable Description	Factor 3		
	Total Sample (N=420)	Potential Experimentals (N=235)	Potential Controls (N=185)
Children in area (none/1/2/3 +)	-0.045	-0.182	0.057
Financial assistance (OAA, welfare/other)	0.186	0.074	0.233
Financial assistance (OAA, welfare, MAA/other)	0.156	-0.022	0.280
Housing–not own home or apartment	-0.047	-0.081	-0.066
Housing–not in nursing home or hospital	0.036	0.046	0.066
Number of rooms for exclusive use	-0.029	-0.037	0.005
Bathroom facilities not private	-0.055	-0.049	-0.101
Housing conditions not substandard	-0.069	-0.070	-0.091

Variable Description	Factor 4		
	Total Sample (N=420)	Potential Experimentals (N=235)	Potential Controls (N=185)
Years of schooling	0.537	0.534	0.521
Primary language usually spoken not "English only"	-0.085	-0.090	-0.118
Primary language usually spoken not "Portuguese and/or English and Portuguese"	0.192	0.242	0.132
Primary language usually spoken not "French and/or English and French"	0.081	0.043	0.166
Religion not Catholic	0.064	0.119	0.026
Religion not Protestant	0.097	0.034	0.150
Employment status	0.029	0.011	0.121
Would not like to work	0.007	0.031	-0.013
Usual occupation not professional/managerial	-0.654	-0.624	-0.632
Usual occupation not sales or clerical	-0.532	-0.546	-0.524
Usual occupation not blue collar	0.885	0.868	0.870
Not Fall River resident	0.207	0.194	0.228
Length of residence	-0.024	-0.084	0.070
Number of moves in past five years	-0.063	-0.104	0.009
Moved in past year	-0.046	-0.073	-0.017
Number of persons in household (1/2/3 +)	-0.033	0.018	-0.029
Composition of household–not alone	-0.052	-0.012	-0.030
Composition of household–not living with spouse	0.099	0.078	0.069
Head of household is other than applicant	-0.019	-0.020	0.033
Applicant not applying with a handicapped companion	0.032	0.039	-0.041
Children in the area (none/1/2/3 +)	0.057	0.086	-0.005
Financial assistance (OAA, welfare/other)	0.397	0.382	0.495
Financial assistance (OAA, welfare, MAA/other)	0.409	0.440	0.452
Housing–not own home or apartment	0.061	0.082	0.049
Housing–not in nursing home or hospital	-0.084	-0.086	-0.117
Number of rooms for exclusive use	-0.022	-0.002	-0.037
Bathroom facilities not private	0.022	0.032	0.008
Housing conditions not substandard	0.162	0.183	0.186

Factor III

Primary Language—English/other	English
Primary Language—French/other	Other
Religion—Catholic/other	Other
Religion—Protestant/other	Protestant

Factor IV

Number of years of schooling	Low
Usual occupation—professional or managerial/other	Other
Usual occupation—sales and clerical/other	Other
Usual occupation—blue collar/other	Blue collar
Source of income—OAA, welfare/other	OAA or welfare
Source of income—OAA, welfare, MAA/other	OAA, MAA, or welfare

Four of the 28 variables factor analyzed were not considered pertinent to a descriptive interpretation of any of these factors. Furthermore, 3 of these were marginal items on the basis of their relatively skewed distributions: over 90% of the cases were distributed within a single category. They were, therefore, excluded at this point from further consideration, except for their negligible contribution to the computation of the factor scores. These excluded variables were: primary language—not "some Portuguese"; employment status; and whether or not their housing at time of application was substandard. The remaining item, number of children in area, is statistically independent of the 4 previously identified factors, and on this basis was included by itself as an additional independent clustering variable. Thus, the clustering analysis was based on 5 measures: 4 factors and an independent raw score variable.

Step B. The members of the nonresident pool were then clustered through the use of the numeric taxonomy classification program referred to above (Jones, 1968: 125-128), using the 5 variables described in Step A. This procedure is a preliminary step in identifying the niche in multidimensional space in which each subpopulation is located. The preferred procedure is to cluster the entire study pool. However, the clustering computer program available permitted a maximum of 200 cases, and limited time and funds ruled out the possibility of reprogramming. With these constraints in mind, the factor structures of the two pools, potential experimentals and potential controls, were compared and judged to be sufficiently similar to permit the clustering of one of the pools to form the basis for clustering the members of the other pool. Since there were fewer nonresidents than residents, the control pool was selected to minimize the likelihood of losing nonresidents from the short-term evaluation study group.

The numeric taxonomy classification (cluster) program proceeded through a series of 184 steps, beginning with 185 one-person clusters and at each successive step combining the 2 clusters whose centroids were closest together. The interdisciplinary team (consisting of 3 social workers and a nurse) examined the clusters beginning at the step at which there were 20 clusters. Intra-cluster similarity was found for each of the 20 clusters. It should be noted that the clinical team's review was unstructured. Having access to all available raw material, including their own case history notes, they alone decided, on a case-specific basis, which were the salient factors. The clinical team also provided written descriptions of what they saw as the distinguishing features of each cluster.

Working independently from the clinical team, members of the research staff reviewed the pattern of factor scores, not only for each of the 20 clusters, but also for the clusters resulting from each of the succeeding steps to the step in which the sample was combined into one cluster. Based on a review of the pattern of scores being combined at each step and on the weighted sum of the within-group distances at each step, a tentative decision was made to stop the clustering program at 14 clusters. An examination of the pattern of factor scores in each of the 14 clusters led to a further reduction to 11 clusters by hand-combining clusters with similar patterns of scores which the cluster program had not combined until further along in the clustering sequence. To help establish the validity of stopping the program at 14 clusters, as well as the validity of the hand-matching of clusters, the written descriptions of the clusters were consulted. The decision to stop the clustering at 14 was supported by the clinical team's cluster descriptions. However, one of the hand-matched clusters could not be used because the clinical team's descriptions of the 2 clusters to be combined were markedly different. Thus, the potential control group of 185 cases was subdivided into 12 clusters.

Step C. Data concerning the 185 members of the potential control pool, including the cluster category as the dependent variable, were run through a discriminant function analysis program. The purpose was to measure the dissimilarity of the independent groups on the basis of the information provided, using the five measures described in Step A. The differences among the cluster discriminant function means were highly significant. More important, the functions were not only significant discriminators among the clusters but predicted category membership almost perfectly; of the 185 people in the 12 clusters, only 1 was misclassified.

Step D. The next step toward the construction of cluster-matched subpools of residents and nonresidents was the assignment of each resident as a potential match within 1, and only 1, cluster. This was accomplished by computing a set of discriminant function scores for each resident, using his factor scores and the weights resulting from the discriminant function analysis of the nonresidents data described in Step C. These discriminant function scores were then compared with the nonresident centroids (the intercepts of the 5 means) for each of the 12 clusters, and each resident was assigned to the cluster to which his scores were closest. (See Cooley and Lohnes, 1962: 134-150, for a detailed statement of the actual mathematics, logic, and computer program involved.)

Step E. The final step in the subpool identification procedure was to stratify the clusters on the basis of those important sociologically relevant variables purposely reserved for final subpopulation identification and therefore not included in the previous clustering stages. These variables were:

1. Age: whether 65 and over or under 65 years of age
2. Applicant status: whether applying alone or applying with someone else
3. Sex: whether male or female
4. Clinical team rating: low priority (ratings of 1 or 2) or high priority (ratings of 3 or 4)

This resulted in final homogeneous subpopulations within the mathematically defined clusters.

Step F. Members of the clinical team, working in pairs, then evaluated the possible matches of nonresidents with residents within each subpopulation pool. Specifically, they

1. Paired nonresidents and residents within each subpopulation;
2. Evaluated each of these pairs in terms of how good a match it was;
3. Whenever possible, identified alternative choices for matched pairs in case, for some reason, the "best" matched cases could not be used.

Step F marked the completion of the integrated multivariate statistical and clinical verification process for selecting paired experimentals and controls for the study sample. These procedures resulted in 91 pairs of residents and nonresidents (applicants).

AN ANALYSIS OF THE EQUIVALENCE OF THE HIGHLAND HEIGHTS EXPERIMENTAL AND CONTROL GROUPS

It is the thesis of this paper that the concept of group equivalence is central to a discussion of the extent to which a particular experimental-control group strategy provides a basis for drawing inferences concerning the impact of a social intervention. In this view, the achievement of equivalent groups eliminates the confounding effects of systematic biases resulting from the differential distributions of relevant variables across the experimental and control groups. Experimental methodologies have recommended the handling of the possible confounding influence of extraneous variables in two basic ways: (1) the direct control of such variables, the transference of Class III "uncontrolled" variables into Class II "controlled" variables (Kish, 1959: 329-330); and (2) randomization, the transference of Class III "uncontrolled" variables into Class IV "controlled by randomization" variables (Kish, 1959: 329-330). Both procedures appear to have equivalence as their goal, the function of which is to increase the probability of ruling out reasonably applicable and identifiable rival hypotheses to that of the experimental intervention as explanations for observed "effects." The position taken in this paper is that, for a set of procedures to constitute a reasonable alternative to randomization, those procedures should function like randomization in producing as equivalent groups as possible. The nonrandom matching procedure described in this paper attempts to attain this goal by equating groups through the selection of a series of homogeneous pairs of matched experimentals and controls. The equivalence of the groups produced by one application of this procedure will be analyzed in terms of the following questions:

1. How similar are the matched groups of experimentals and controls on measured variables that were not directly used in the clustering, subpopulation stratification, or paired-matching procedures?
2. How do the matched groups compare with a sample of 100 pairs of randomly drawn samples of the same size drawn from the same population?
3. What reason is there to believe that the matched groups are similar on other unmeasured variables that might be regarded as threats to the internal validity of the impact evaluation?

Similarity of Experimental and Control Groups

The first analysis to be presented is based upon a major assumption: namely, that social groups will, except in rare, hardly imaginable instances, exhibit wide diversity in response which in turn is a function of numerous combinations of factors, physical, experiential, and so on. It is this diversity of independent factors and dependent variable response which puts such pressure on designs of experiments dealing with human subjects and causes problems even for randomization in the short run. Homogeneity of experimental material, which often seems easily obtained in the physical science laboratory, is but a fond dream of the human behavior investigator. Given this virtually universal social fact, the congruence of comparison groups may be examined in terms of the relative proportions of homogeneous subpopulations in the two groups: the more similar the proportions, the more congruent the groups. In the implementation of this matching procedure, these proportions were made equal by pair-matching within the "identified" subpopulations. The basic question then is the extent to which the "identified" subpopulations are truly distinct. Assuming initial diversity, distinct subpopulations should exhibit dissimilarity (relative to total variablity) in their means or interclass variability; and the greater the dissimilarity among the subpopulation means, the more reason to believe that the members of the subpopulations across the experimental and control groups are truly similar. This position is an outgrowth of the sociological explanation for the relevancy of these subpopulations in which each such group is seen as representing a convergence of a series of forces that are specific to itself, forces that both capture the past and, most important, forecast (on the average) the future.

In the Highland Heights application of the matching procedure, the postulated subpopulation heterogeneity across noncontrolled variables is measured by the among-pairs dissimilarity for the outcome variable premeasures. In this instance, the 91 matched pairs are representative of a large number of subpopulations; and, by comparing the pairs (or really the pair averages for each variable), a minimal estimate of subpopulation dissimilarity is possible. It is a minimal estimate because of the multiple representation of some subpopulations by two or more pairs and the resultant similarity in such pair averages. For this analysis, dissimilarity was measured through a sum of squares computation in which the among-matched-groups sums of squares is compared with the "total" sums of squares. The statistics used are the Eta^2 (Diamond, 1959: 54-55) and partial Eta^2 (Cohen, 1973). In the case of Eta^2, the among-pairs sums of squares is divided by the total sums of squares, while in the case of the partial Eta^2, the denominator term is first reduced by the subtraction of all other "known" sums of squares, which in this instance is the between experimental and control sums of squares (a measure of experimental-control incongruence). In either case, the larger the resultant ratio, the greater the dissimilarity among the pairs.

The set of variables analyzed includes 39 outcome variable premeasures employed in the study of Highland Heights (but not used in matching). As can be seen from the data in Table 8.2, the Eta^2 and partial Eta^2 values are almost identical, reflecting the extremely low experimental-control sums of squares extracted. The Eta^2 coefficients are consistently high, with a range from .3833 to .7698; and 25 of

TABLE 8.2   MATCHED EXPERIMENTAL AND CONTROL GROUP COMPARISONS: PREMEASURES OF 39 OUTCOME VARIABLES

Variable[a]	Means		Mean Differences	Probability Levels	Experimental Control Eta^2	Interclass r^2 (Eta^2)[b]	Partial Interclass[c] r^2 (Partial Eta^2)	Number of Pairs[d]
	Experimentals	Controls						
Social intactness	20.209	19.802	.407	>.500	.0017	.4976	.4984	91
Trouble falling asleep	1.747	1.648	.099	.162	.0116	.4659	.4713	91
Hard to sleep through the night	1.637	1.681	-.044	>.500	.0022	.4129	.4138	91
Awakening time	1.744	1.856	-.112	.077	.0193	.4445	.4532	90
Judgment of emotional state	2.685	2.618	.067	>.500	.0013	.5761	.5768	89
Health compared to others	3.524	3.464	.060	>.500	.0008	.6028	.6033	84
Physical functioning scale	6.921	6.730	.191	.452	.0016	.7562	.7574	89
Katz-ADL scale	1.506	1.519	-.013	>.500	.0000	.7698	.7698	81
Rosow functional health scale	3.443	3.580	-.137	.292	.0049	.6144	.6174	88
Life pattern scale	6.477	6.250	.227	.191	.0055	.7216	.7256	88
Orientation	21.305	20.049	1.256	.018*	.0374	.4466	.4639	82
Vigor–vitality during interview	5.744	5.488	.256	.141	.0095	.6233	.6293	86
Frequency of attendance at religious services	2.275	2.286	-.011	>.500	.0000	.6295	.6295	91
Participation in church activities	2.411	2.456	-.045	>.500	.0005	.6559	.6563	91
Frequency of participation in activity—rides or walks	2.409	2.261	.148	.202	.0090	.5197	.5244	88
Employed	1.901	1.868	.033	.470	.0027	.5425	.5439	91
Satisfaction with social contacts	1.460	1.552	-.092	.241	.0085	.4712	.4752	87
See enough of friends and relatives	1.267	1.360	-.093	.208	.0100	.4601	.4648	86
Relationship with interviewer	18.242	17.659	.583	.438	.0036	.4594	.4610	91
PGC—Surgency	3.024	2.941	.083	>.500	.0014	.5852	.5860	85
PGC—Attitude toward own aging	1.797	1.797	.000	>.500	.0000	.5624	.5624	74

PGC—Accepts status quo	.690	.845	-.155	.132	.0149	.5378	.5459	71
PGC—Degree of agitation	2.800	2.813	-.013	>.500	.0000	.5479	.5479	80
PGC—Degree of optimism	1.519	1.543	-.024	>.500	.0002	.5644	.5645	81
PGC—Loneliness-dissatisfaction component	2.222	2.099	.123	.418	.0038	.5365	.5386	81
PGC—Moral scale (summation)	11.895	11.977	-.082	>.500	.0001	.5565	.5566	86
Judgment of respondent's attitude toward self	4.466	4.239	.227	.108	.0137	.5366	.5440	88
Judgment of respondent's self-assurance	4.091	4.227	-.136	.390	.0039	.5375	.5396	88
Degree of loneliness	1.306	1.376	-.070	.321	.0055	.5289	.5319	85
8-item despair scale	2.791	2.977	-.186	>.500	.0015	.5783	.5792	86
Degree of satisfaction with living situation	2.382	2.236	.146	.198	.0097	.4847	.4895	89
Preference for living situation	1.144	1.189	-.045	>.500	.0021	.5814	.5826	90
Has troublesome neighbors	1.901	1.890	.011	>.500	.0003	.4418	.4419	91
Dwelling physically poor	1.692	1.791	-.099	.172	.0128	.3833	.3882	91
Dwelling structure incompatible with illness	1.560	1.560	.000	>.500	.0000	.6208	.6208	91
Upkeep of services in present housing poor	1.791	1.835	-.044	.453	.0032	.4937	.4952	91
Lack of privacy	1.956	1.967	-.011	>.500	.0008	.4801	.4804	91
Dwelling too expensive	1.659	1.824	-.165	.016*	.0355	.4407	.4569	91

a. For operational definition and scoring (coding) of these variables, see Sherwood, Greer, Morris and Sherwood (1973: 93-104).

b. The Interclass r^2 is the term selected for the Eta^2 (Kennedy, 1970) coefficient in the present application where each of the classes (the 91 matched pairs) contain only two members. This Eta^2 coefficient records the ratio of among "pairs'" sums of squares to total sums of squares. Note that in The Highland Heights Experiment (Sherwood, Greer, Morris, and Sherwood, 1973), this statistical measure was labeled intra rather than interclass r^2.

c. The partial Interclass r^2 is identical to the partial Eta^2 (Cohen, 1973), and differs from the interclass Eta^2 coefficient in the denominator used in its calculation. In this instance the between groups sums of squares was subtracted from the total sums of squares prior to the calculation of the Eta^2. In this analysis, the Experimental-Control sums of squares, of course, represent part of the mismatching sums of squares.

d. Although the total number of pairs = 91, during the early months of the study there were several revisions of the pretest in which a number of the pre-measures of the outcome variables were added. Thus there are missing data for a number of variables for a number of persons in the impact sample. If there were missing data for one member of the pair, the data for the other member of the pair were excluded from these analyses.

the 39 variables have values greater than .5, indicating that over half of the total variance in these variables can be attributed to the interclass (or subpopulations) factor. On this basis, it is concluded that there is, in fact, a high degree of interclass (subpopulation) dissimilarity.

The direct measure of experimental-control group equivalence is provided by a comparison of the group means and the associated Eta^2 coefficients. The means for the experimental and control groups and the significance level for the mean differences are presented in Table 8.2. As can be seen from these findings, only 2 of the 39 variables had significant mean differences at the .05 level or lower, and the vast majority of such probability values were considerably higher.

One way of looking at this finding would be to assert that the occurrence of such differences, no matter how few in number, represents a sufficient justification for questioning, or even invalidating, the matched study sample. However, this would seem to be a most unrealistic position; and in point of fact one could assert that, given a set of 39 measures and an a priori probability level of .05, two such differences (or 5% of the 39 measures) are to be expected even for "good" random samples.

The Eta^2 coefficients for the experimental-control factor are an equally potent tool in any such analysis.

> . . . statistical significance is not the only, or even the best, evidence for a strong statistical association. A significant result implies that it is safe to say some association exists, but the estimate of $w^2 [\eta^2]$ tells how strong that association appears to be. It seems far more reasonable to decide to follow up a finding that is *both* significant *and* indicates a strong degree of association than to tie this course of action to significance level alone. [Hays, 1963: 328]

Of the 37 variables in Table 8.2 with probability values greater than .05, only 1 had an Eta^2 value as high as .02, and 24 had rounded values of .00 (or no variance explained by experimental group incumbency). The 2 remaining variables, with probability levels less than .05, had rounded Eta^2 values of only .04, and partial Eta^2 values of .07 and .08.

On the basis of these two sets of findings, the mean difference and Eta^2 computations, the experimentals and controls are considered to be satisfactorily similar on these 39 outcome variable premeasures.

The Matched Groups Compared with Pairs of Randomly Drawn Samples

Another approach to judging the matched pairs involves comparisons of the matched groups in the Highland Heights study with a sample of pairs of randomly drawn groups of the same size drawn from the same population. Scarcity of funds limited the number of pairs of randomly drawn samples to 100. Specifically, the 100 samples consisted of 182 persons, each drawn randomly, from the total pool of 420 potential study members, of which 91 were randomly allocated to one group (which can be regarded as experimentals) and the remaining 91 persons to the second group of the pair (regarded as controls). Scarcity of funds also limited the number of variables to be used for these comparisons to 15 randomly drawn from the total array of 39 premeasures of outcome variables which were presented in Table 8.2. (See Table 8.4 for a list of these 15 variables.) It should be noted that

the two variables, from the 39-variable array, previously identified as having significant experimental-control group mean differences at the .05 or less probability level (see Table 8.2) in the Highland Heights matched sample were not among the 15 variables drawn for this analysis.

The matched groups were compared with the 100 pairs of random samples in a number of ways:

1. *Statistically significant mean difference comparison.* Table 8.3 presents the distribution of samples according to the number of statistically-significant mean differences found for the array of 15 variables across the 100 pairs of random samples. Fifty-two of the pairs of randomly drawn samples were found to exhibit significant mean differences at the .05 or lower level for one or more variables, whereas no such difference exists between the experimental and control groups for the matched sample. These data indicate that the matched sample is behaving with respect to these variables as what may be classified as a *good* random sample.

TABLE 8.3   NUMBER OF STATISTICALLY SIGNIFICANT MEAN DIFFERENCES
FOR THE ARRAY OF 15 VARIABLES: THE MATCHED SAMPLE AND THE
DISTRIBUTION FOR THE 100 PAIRS OF RANDOM SAMPLES

Number of Variables per Sample with Probability Values ≤ .05 in the 15 Variable Array	Distribution Across the 100 Pairs of Random Samples	Matched Sample Value
Zero	48	1
One	33 ⎫	
Two	17 ⎬ = 52	
Three	2 ⎭	

2. *Tilton's Overlap.* These data were next used to provide a measure of the extent of experimental-control equivalence through an application of Tilton's measure of overlap.

> . . . greater use [should be made] of measures expressing the practical importance of differences instead of relying entirely on the hypothesis testing models. One such statistic . . . expresses the degree of overlap between two distributions. The overlap (O) between score distributions obtained by two groups is defined as the percentage of persons in one of the groups whose score may be matched by persons in the second group. . . . Two groups which overlap completely will have identical scores and an O of 100 percent. . . . Tilton's statistic is based on the ratio of the difference between the means of the two groups to the average of the two standard deviations. [Elster and Dunnette, 1971: 686]

Table 8.4 presents the Tilton overlap statistic for the 15 randomly drawn outcome variable premeasures. The lowest percentage value for the matched sample (across these 15 variables) was 91%; and in 11 instances the value was at the 95% overlap level or higher. Within the 100 pairs of random samples, the median overlap value was either 95% or 96%; and these levels can be interpreted as an estimate of the "long run" experimental-control sample overlap across these variables. Randomiza-

TABLE 8.4 DISTRIBUTION OF PERCENT OVERLAP OF EXPERIMENTAL AND CONTROL GROUPS USING TILTON'S 0: MATCHED SAMPLE AND 100 PAIRS OF RANDOM SAMPLES

Tilton's 0 % of Overlap	Dwelling Physically Poor	Dwelling Structure Incompatible with Illness of Applicant	Lack of Privacy	Frequency of Attendance at Religious Services	Trouble Falling Asleep	Satisfaction with Living Situation	Preference for Living Situation	Physical Functioning Scale	Satisfaction with Participation in Activity	Rosow Functional Health Scale	Social Intactness	Relationship with Interviewer	Employed	PGC—Degree of Optimism	PGC—Moral (Summation)
100	11	3*	10	2	4	1	1		2	1	1	2	9	1	
99	9	10	1	12*	6	9	12	9	11	13	18	11		10*	6*
98	10	15	21	15	10	12	11	9	18*	8	14	11	16	10	18
97	11	3	9*	10	14	11	9	15	7	17	14	17	21	11	14
96	12	14	9	13	10	14	11*	11*	15	7	11*	7	6	12	14
95	16	8	10	8	13	11	6	12	11	15	6	8*	12*	11	8
94	7	8	8	7	9	7	8	8	13	5*	3	9	8	8	11
93	3	11	4	5	8	7	13	5	6	13	8	10	2	9	8
92	6	9	12	10	7	2*	6	7	3	3	6	8	8	12	5
91	5*	10	2	4	4*	8	10	6	5	5	5	5	6	2	7
90	3	1	6	5	4	1	1	6	3	4	3	4	2	2	2
89	3	5	1	2	2	3	5	5	2	3	5	3	1	1	3
<89	4	3	7	7	9	14	7	7	4	6	6	5	9	11	4
Total Random Samples	100	100	100	100	100	100	100	100	100	100	100	100	100	100	100

* Indicates cell in which the matched sample falls (not included in the cell total).

tion succeeds, in part, within the multiple replication model because of the increased likelihood, over time, of achieving higher rather than lower sample overlap. From this perspective, any control and experimental sample would be a powerful tool for measuring impact were it able to achieve these median (or better) positions for a large percentage of the variables. In the case of the Highland Heights matched sample, this median position was surpassed in 10 out of the possible 15 instances (or 67% of the time). This finding further enhances the likelihood that the matched experimental and control groups will be at least as equivalent as would be produced by a good random draw.

3. *Mean Difference z Score Comparisons.* Comparisons were also made of the magnitude of the differences between the experimental group and control group means for the 15 variables. To permit comparisons of pooled differences, the scale metrics for the 15 variables were converted into comparable units by dividing each of the 100 paired groups' mean difference for each variable (as well as the mean difference for the matched sample) by the standard deviation of all mean differences for that variable within the 100 pairs of random samples. (These values are referred to as z scores in the analyses below.) Thus, for each variable, each of the experimental-control difference scores across the 100 pairs of random samples has a mean of 0 and a standard deviation of 1.

TABLE 8.5   AVERAGED STANDARDIZED DIFFERENCE (z) SCORES[a] FOR
15 VARIABLES: MATCHED SAMPLE AND DISTRIBUTION FOR
100 PAIRS OF RANDOM SAMPLES

100 Pairs of Random Samples		Matched Sample
Value	Frequency	
.300 - .399	1	Value = .634
.400 - .499	2	
.500 - .599	14	Number of pairs of random samples
.600 - .699	13	with lower value = 19
.700 - .799	18	
.800 - .899	21	Number of pairs of random samples
.900 - .999	20	with higher value = 81
1.000 - 1.999	9	
1.200 - 1.299	2	
	100	

$\bar{X}$ = .805
Median = .819
SD = .179

a. Formula for individual variable standardized difference (z) score:

$z_i = $ Experimental-control mean difference / Standard deviation of mean differences across the 100 pairs of random samples

In the first comparison, the 15 z scores (ignoring signs) were averaged within each of the 100 randomly drawn pairs of samples and within the matched sample. Table 8.5 presents the distribution of these average z scores for the 100 pairs of samples as compared with the average z score for the matched sample. These data,

as in the previous analyses, indicate that the matched sample is behaving like a "good" random sample. Indeed, as compared with the average for the matched sample, only 19 of the 100 pairs of random samples had values as low or lower, that is, as close or closer to the minimal possible averaged z score of 0.

Next, the lowest and highest of the mean difference z scores (ignoring sign) for the 100 pairs of samples and the matched sample were compared. Table 8.6 presents the distribution of lowest z scores across the 15 variable array for the 100 pairs of random samples and the matched sample. The lowest z score for the matched sample was 0; less than half of the pairs of random samples behaved as well, that is, had no experimental-control group differences for even one of the 15 variables.

TABLE 8.6   LOWEST STANDARDIZED DIFFERENCE (z) SCORES[a] FOR
15 VARIABLES: MATCHED SAMPLE AND DISTRIBUTION FOR
100 PAIRS OF RANDOM SAMPLES

100 Pairs of Random Samples		
Value	Frequency	Matched Sample
.000	41	Value = .000
.001 - .049	17	
.050 - .099	12	Number of pairs of random samples
.100 - .149	6	with lower value = 0
.150 - .199	15	
.200 - .249	3	Number of pairs of random samples
.250 - .299	6	with higher value = 59
	100	

$\overline{X}$ = .071
Median = .026
SD = .086

a. Formula for individual variable standardized difference (z) score:

$$z_i = \frac{\text{Experimental-control mean difference}}{\text{Standard deviation of mean differences across the 100 pairs of random samples}}$$

Table 8.7 presents the distribution of values with respect to the largest experimental-control group difference observed for each of the pairs of samples. Once again, the matched sample does very well in comparison with the 100 pairs of random samples. The highest z score for the matched sample was closer to the ideal (the standardized mean difference of 0) than the highest z score in 80 of the 100 pairs of randomly drawn samples.

The object of this final comparison was to determine the extent of z score variance of the total array of 15 variables within samples. If an experimental group is truly equivalent with a control group selected for studying the impact of an intervention, then, barring measurement error, there will be no observed mean differences on any premeasures of interest between the two groups; therefore, in the ideal experiment with truly equivalent groups, the grand mean in standardized scores for the mean differences for the total array of premeasures will be 0, the

TABLE 8.7 HIGHEST STANDARDIZED DIFFERENCE (z) SCORE[a] FOR
15 VARIABLES: MATCHED SAMPLE AND DISTRIBUTION FOR
100 PAIRS OF RANDOM SAMPLES

| 100 Pairs of Random Samples | | Matched Sample |
Value	Frequency	
.900 - 1.299	6	Value = 1.678
1.300 - 1.699	20	
1.700 - 2.099	32	Number of pairs of random samples
2.100 - 2.499	24	with lower value = 20
2.500 - 2.899	13	
2.900 - 3.299	5	Number of pairs of random samples
	100	with higher value = 80

$\overline{X}$ = 2.034
Median = 1.969
SD = .468

a. Formula for individual variable standardized difference (z) score:

$$z_i = \frac{\text{Experimental-control mean difference}}{\text{Standard deviation of mean differences across the 100 pairs of random samples}}$$

TABLE 8.8 SUMS OF SQUARES OF STANDARDIZED DIFFERENCE (z) SCORES[a]
FOR 15 VARIABLES: MATCHED SAMPLE AND DISTRIBUTION FOR
100 PAIRS OF RANDOM SAMPLES

| 100 Pairs of Random Samples | | Matched Sample |
Value	Frequency	
5 - 8	18	Value = 9.542
9 - 12	16	
13 - 16	35	Number of pairs of random samples
17 - 20	14	with lower value = 21
21 - 24	11	
25 - 28	4	Number of pairs of random samples
29 - 32	2	with higher value = 79
	100	

$\overline{X}$ = 15.153
Median = 14.856
SD = 5.927

a. Formula for individual variable standardized difference (z) score:

$$z_i = \frac{\text{Experimental-control mean difference}}{\text{Standard deviation of mean differences across the 100 pairs of random samples}}$$

$$\text{Sums of squares} = \sum_{i=1}^{15} (z_i - 0)^2$$

mean difference between the groups for any one premeasure will be 0, and the total sums of squares of the standardized mean differences from the grand mean will also be 0. From this point of view, then, the smaller the total sums of squares of the mean differences for the set of variables within a pair of samples, the more equivalent the groups. Using the "ideal" grand z mean of 0 between the experimental and control groups as the criterion, Table 8.8 presents the distributions of the sums of squares calculated in this manner for each of the 100 pairs of randomly drawn samples and for the matched sample. Here again, the matched samples compares very favorably, seeming to behave like a "good" random draw. Seventy-nine of the random samples had sums of squares greater than that of the matched sample. In fact, 24 of the pairs of random sample values were almost twice as great as that for the matched sample, and the mean sums of squares for the 100 random samples is over one and one-half times the sums of squares for the matched sample.

Similarity on Unmeasured Variables

One of the presumed major strengths of randomization pertains to its ability to handle sources of variation which have not been directly controlled in the design and conduct of an experiment. This power applies to not only unmeasured, but even unimagined, variables which might differentially influence the responses of the experimental and control group members. Arguments presented previously in this paper suggest rather convincingly that this power emerges primarily in the long run, or with large samples. In any particular randomization instance, the "other" variables are not distributed randomly across the groups but are a part of a set of interrelated variables. If the samples were drawn randomly from a population, they represent two estimates of the correlation matrix in the population. If they are random halves of a selected "sample" with no designatable population, they represent two versions or estimates of the correlation matrix of the total group of which they represent two halves. To the extent that one is a bad estimator of the larger matrix, the other must be similarly bad in a compensating sense. In any event, the means across variables within samples are interrelated. As pointed out by Lord (1963: 38),

> The reason is that under the null hypothesis the means of randomly chosen groups fall around the same regression line as do the individual cases.

Thus, given a sample of samples—for example, the 100 pairs of random samples drawn from the Highland Heights study population previously referred to—the relationships among the means for the samples should reflect the relationships among the scores in the population. But it may not be quite so obvious that the relationship among mean differences between pairs of samples across the set of variables should follow the same pattern.

As a check on this assumption, the 15 variables analyzed previously were designated as "independent" variables, and an additional 5 variables were randomly selected from the 39 study outcome variables and designated as "dependent" variables. Using the Highland Heights raw score data, for the 420 person population pool, each of the 5 designated dependent variables was regressed (using step-up multiple regression) on the 15 designated independent variables. The relevant findings for each of these analyses appear in Tables 8.9 through 8.13.

TABLE 8.9　EQUATION FOR PREDICTION OF DEPENDENT VARIABLE:　HARD TO SLEEP THROUGH THE NIGHT FOR INDIVIDUALS IN TOTAL STUDY POPULATION (N=420) AND FOR MEAN DIFFERENCES FOR 100 PAIRS OF RANDOM SAMPLES

Independent Variables with Beta's Significance ≤ .10 in 420 Person Sample	420 Person Population Raw Score Predictions			100 Random Samples Mean Differences		
		Regression			Regression	
	Zero Order Correlation	Beta Weight	Significance of Beta	Zero Order Correlation	Beta Weight	Significance of Beta
Trouble falling asleep	-.376	-.304	< .001	-.312	-.235	.022
PGC—morale	.305	.275	< .001	.189	.259	.062
Preference for living situation	-.082	-.093	.038	-.100	-.058	> .500
Dwelling physically poor	.112	.091	.043	.160	.160	.099
PGC—optimism	.096	-.098	.083	-.047	-.256	.049
		$R^2 = .207$ < .001			$R^2 = .166$ .004	

Zero Order Correlation Matrix of the Five Independent Predictor Variables for 420 Persons (Raw Score)

	1	2	3	4	5
Trouble falling asleep	1.000	-.268	.023	-.023	-.054
PGC—morale	-.268	1.000	.018	.132	.624
Preference for living situation	.023	.018	1.000	.153	.012
Dwelling physically poor	-.023	.132	.153	1.000	.079
PGC—optimism	-.054	.624	.012	.079	1.000

Zero Order Correlation Matrix of the Five Independent Predictor Variables for 100 Random Sample Mean Differences

	1	2	3	4	5
Trouble falling asleep	1.000	-.305	.089	-.068	-.068
PGC—morale	-.305	1.000	-.236	.078	.657
Preference for living situation	.089	-.236	1.000	.119	-.079
Dwelling physically poor	-.068	.078	.119	1.000	.113
PGC—optimism	-.068	.657	-.079	.113	1.000

TABLE 8.10   EQUATION FOR PREDICTION OF DEPENDENT VARIABLE: PGC–SURGENCY FOR INDIVIDUALS IN TOTAL STUDY POPULATION (N=420) AND FOR MEAN DIFFERENCES FOR 100 PAIRS OF RANDOM SAMPLES

Independent Variables with Beta's Significance ≤ .10 in 420 Person Sample	420 Person Population Raw Score Predictions			100 Random Samples Mean Differences		
		Regression			Regression	
	Zero Order Correlation	Beta Weight	Significance of Beta	Zero Order Correlation	Beta Weight	Significance of Beta
PGC–morale	.750	.756	<.001	.690	.708	<.001
Physical functioning scale	.152	.092	.006	.104	.017	>.500
Trouble falling asleep	-.133	.065	.053	-.117	.098	.226
Social intactness	.137	.056	.087	.190	.049	>.500
		$R^2 = .580$ <.001			$R^2 = .489$ <.001	

Zero Order Correlation Matrix of the Four Independent Predictor Variables for 420 Persons (Raw Scores)

	1	2	3	4
PGC–morale	1.000	.067	-.265	.086
Physical functioning scale	.067	1.000	.008	.148
Trouble falling asleep	-.265	.008	1.000	.024
Social intactness	.086	.148	.024	1.000

Zero Order Correlation Matrix of the Four Independent Predictor Variables for 100 Random Sample Mean Differences

	1	2	3	4
PGC–morale	1.000	.158	-.305	.185
Physical functioning scale	.158	1.000	-.247	-.013
Trouble falling asleep	-.305	-.247	1.000	.110
Social intactness	.185	-.013	.110	1.000

TABLE 8.11 EQUATION FOR PREDICTION OF DEPENDENT VARIABLE: SEE ENOUGH OF FRIENDS AND RELATIVES FOR INDIVIDUALS IN TOTAL STUDY POPULATION (N=420) AND FOR MEAN DIFFERENCES FOR 100 PAIRS OF RANDOM SAMPLES

Independent Variables with Beta's Significance ≤.10 in 420 Person Sample	420 Person Population Raw Score Predictions			100 Random Samples Mean Differences		
		Regression			Regression	
	Zero Order Correlation	Beta Weight	Significance of Beta	Zero Order Correlation	Beta Weight	Significance of Beta
PGC—morale	-.469	-.540		-.587	-.496	<.001
Social intactness	-.140	-.241	.008	-.114	.035	>.500
PGC—optimism	-.217	.118	.035	-.471	-.146	.190
Relationship with interviewer	-.100	.157	.082	-.085	-.069	.433
		$R^2 = .246$ <.001			$R^2 = .361$ <.001	

Zero Order Correlation Matrix of the Four Independent Predictor Variables for 420 Persons (Raw Scores)

	1	2	3	4
PGC—morale	1.000	.086	.624	.115
Social intactness	.086	1.000	.079	.876
PGC—optimism	.624	.079	1.000	.132
Relationship with interviewer	.115	.876	.132	1.000

Zero Order Correlation Matrix of the Four Independent Predictor Variables for 100 Random Sample Mean Differences

	1	2	3	4
PGC—morale	1.000	.185	.657	.025
Social intactness	.185	1.000	.234	.331
PGC—optimism	.657	.234	1.000	.104
Relationship with interviewer	.025	.331	.104	1.000

TABLE 8.12 EQUATION FOR PREDICTION OF DEPENDENT VARIABLE: JUDGMENT OF RESPONDENT'S ATTITUDE TOWARD SELF FOR INDIVIDUALS IN TOTAL STUDY POPULATION (N=420) AND FOR MEAN DIFFERENCES FOR 100 PAIRS OF RANDOM SAMPLES

Independent Variables with Beta's Significance ≤ .10 in 420 Person Sample	420 Person Population Raw Score Predictions			100 Random Samples Mean Differences		
	Zero Order Correlation	Regression Beta Weight	Regression Significance of Beta	Zero Order Correlation	Regression Beta Weight	Regression Significance of Beta
PGC–morale	.406	.360	<.001	.408	.280	.004
Physical functioning scale	.316	.325	<.001	.306	.327	.005
Relationship with interviewer	.183	.117	.006	-.101	-.137	.115
Satisfaction with participation in activity	.203	.142	.001	.226	.175	.056
Preference for living situation	-.130	-.097	.023	-.252	-.113	.222
Rosow functional health scale	-.155	-.110	.037	-.060	.144	.208
Employed	.111	.074	.078	.261	.191	.043
		$R^2 = .303$ <.001			$R^2 = .337$ <.001	

Zero Order Correlation Matrix of the Seven Independent Predictor Variables for 420 Persons (Raw Score)

	1	2	3	4	5	6	7
PGC–morale	1.000	.065	.112	.187	.018	-.164	.078
Physical functioning scale	.065	1.000	.081	.072	-.155	-.591	-.035
Relationship with interviewer	.112	.081	1.000	-.038	-.042	-.044	.076
Satisfaction with participation in activity	.187	.072	-.038	1.000	.113	-.093	-.051
Preference for living situation	.018	-.155	-.042	.113	1.000	.037	-.056
Rosow functional health scale	-.164	-.591	-.044	-.093	.037	1.000	.116
Employed	.078	-.035	.076	-.051	-.056	.116	1.000

Zero Order Correlation Matrix of the Seven Independent Predictor Variables for 100 Random Sample Mean Differences

	1	2	3	4	5	6	7
PGC–morale	1.000	.158	.025	.256	-.236	-.079	.105
Physical functioning scale	.158	1.000	-.031	-.069	-.125	.631	.104
Relationship with interviewer	.025	-.031	1.000	-.046	-.053	.076	.162
Satisfaction with participation in activity	.256	-.069	-.046	1.000	.032	.138	-.106
Preference for living situation	-.236	-.125	-.053	.032	1.000	.077	-.297
Rosow functional health scale	-.079	.631	.076	.138	.077	1.000	.099
Employed	.105	.104	.162	-.106	-.297	.099	1.000

TABLE 8.13 EQUATION FOR PREDICTION OF DEPENDENT VARIABLE: HEALTH COMPARED TO OTHERS FOR INDIVIDUALS IN TOTAL STUDY POPULATION (N=420) AND FOR MEAN DIFFERENCES FOR 100 PAIRS OF RANDOM SAMPLES

Independent Variables with Beta's Significance ≤.10 in 420 Person Sample	420 Person Population Raw Score Predictions			100 Random Samples Mean Differences		
	Zero Order Correlation	Regression		Zero Order Correlation	Regression	
		Beta Weight	Significance of Beta		Beta Weight	Significance of Beta
PGC—morale	.354	.350	<.001	.352	.301	.002
Physical functioning scale	.332	.295	<.001	.440	.384	<.001
Satisfaction with living situation	.049	.093	.042	.063	.061	>.500
Dwelling structure incompatible with illness	.129	.075	.094	.027	.013	>.500
		$R^2 = .236$ <.001			$R^2 = .279$ <.001	

Zero Order Correlation Matrix of the Four Independent Predictor Variables for 420 Persons (Raw Scores)

	1	2	3	4
PGC—morale	1.000	.055	-.205	.087
Physical functioning scale	.055	1.000	.108	.097
Satisfaction with living situation	-.205	.108	1.000	-.051
Dwelling structure incompatible with illness	.087	.097	-.051	1.000

Zero Order Correlation Matrix of the Four Independent Predictor Variables for 100 Random Sample Mean Differences

	1	2	3	4
PGC—morale	1.000	.158	-.185	.141
Physical functioning scale	.158	1.000	.157	-.043
Satisfaction with living situation	-.185	.157	1.000	-.185
Dwelling structure incompatible with illness	.141	-.043	-.185	1.000

Next, the experimental-control mean difference scores were analyzed for the 100 random samples. Each of the 5 dependent variables was regressed on the set of significant independent variables which appeared in the regression of the population raw scores, and the results of these analyses also appear in Tables 8.9 through 8.13. These data are in direct support of the anticipated relationships. Considerable similarity exists in both sets of betas and squared multiple correlations. In almost every instance the magnitude and sign for the betas in the two sets of equations are similar; and where there are differences, they are for the more unimportant contributors to each of the equations.

Two important points are suggested by these findings. There is a sense in which randomization does not control for other influences, except in the long run. This is particularly so with respect to the intra-individual relationships among variables in the case of randomization of subjects to groups. Discrepancies between the samples on measured variables predict related discrepancies on unmeasured variables and thus the further confounding of effects on the dependent variable subsequent to the intervention. Conversely, similarity between the samples on measured variables predicts related similarities on unmeasured variables, thus further controlling for potential confounding influences. Second, the same argument would appear to be applicable to the matched sample procedure; shifting to this latter focus, similarity between the groups on measured variables predicts similarity on other possible confounding unmeasured variables. Thus, in the Highland Heights example, where the experimental-control differences on known variables are very small, it is reasonable to assume that "other" unmeasured and unimagined variables will be similarly distributed across the experimental groups. On this basis, the threat to internal validity of the experiment due to unmeasured potentially confounding variables can be considered to be neutralized.

The critic of matched samples is prone to point out that there are probably other variables that explain observed differences. In the view presented here, there probably are not.

CONCLUSIONS

It has not been the purpose of the preceding discussion and analyses to try to dissuade the reader from randomizing treatments to subjects wherever feasible or from implementing more complex and sophisticated randomized designs, for that matter. To avoid any possible misunderstanding, the authors wish to restate their position at this point. Randomization is clearly generally accepted as the soundest research strategy for making inferences concerning whether observed differences among groups after a social intervention are due to chance or to the intervention. There is no excuse for not including randomization where it is feasible to do so.

The purpose has been to emphasize that randomization is not infallible, that fallibility increases to the extent that the probability of repeated experiments is low, and that this low probability of repeated experiments is particularly likely in the case of large-scale social interventions. The latter, in terms of social significance and costs, are the types of social programs concerning which society should be most

reluctant to forego empirical evaluation. They also seem to occur in situations in which randomization is likely to encounter formidable practical and social obstacles. In addition, there are situations in which it would be impossible to depend on randomization, even when randomization might have been used initially as the sampling procedure. For example, in the study by S. Sherwood (1973) of the effects of a program of "case specific" services to applicants to the Hebrew Rehabilitation Center for Aged in Boston, the services had an effect on who entered the facility. In this instance, more of the experimentals were able to stay in the community than were the controls, and the magnitude of the effect was considerable. This type of event, even within a randomized experiment, results in noncomparability of the samples when the problem of interest focuses on the effects of the original experimental intervention on the adjustment of those who eventually became residents.

In this paper the authors have suggested and described a technique which may, under suitable circumstances, provide a reasonable alternative to "true" experimentation. Careful scrutiny of others, its continued trial use in additional studies, and, if possible, a series of comparative studies utilizing both randomized designs and nonrandom multivariate matching for the impact evaluations of the same interventions would contribute toward a more soundly based judgment of its worth.[11] In the meantime until the jury returns its verdict, the following seems to represent a very reasonable stance:

> A final note on the treatment of uncontrolled variables is in order. On the one extreme there is that attitude often unwittingly inculcated in courses on experimental design, which looks askance at all efforts to make inferences where some variables have been left uncontrolled or where randomization has not taken place. In contrast, the quasi-experimental approach takes a radically different posture: any experiment is valid until proven invalid. The only invalidation comes from plausible rival explanations of the specific outcome. Regression effects and test-retest effects are such in many settings. An absence of randomization may in some specific way plausibly explain the obtained results. But unless one can specify such a hypothesis and the direction of its effects, it should not be regarded as invalidating. Subsequent consideration may uncover plausible rival hypotheses which have been overlooked, but such transitory validity is often the fate of laboratory experiments too. [Campbell and Ross, 1970: 123]

NOTES

1. Of course, if the measurement of a variable is devoid of error, and the potential study groups are equivalent except for their distribution with respect to this variable, there would appear to be no reason, other than the impact of an experimental intervention, to expect matched experimental and control pairs from these groups who are equivalent on this as well as the other variables of interest to regress differentially with respect to the measure in question.

2. Should there be reason to question the potential for initial homogeneity in experimental versus control group cluster structure, the total pool is to be used since the use of only one or the other of the experimental or control pools could lead to some level of "error" in

estimate. However, when there is no reason to question homogeneity in cluster structure and there are large numbers of potential experimentals and controls, the use of one or the other of these pools presents a more economical approach to the problem, particularly in terms of the clinical assessment costs incurred in validating the resulting clusters.

3. Another approach consists of an independent assessment of the factor scores for the members of each of the provisionally established clusters. Criteria for an assessment of this type have not been developed at this time, however.

4. If the investigator finds that he has one or more subpopulations with large numbers of matchable subjects, pair-wise matching may require a degree of discrimination within those subgroups that is difficult to attain and may lead to unnecessary within-pair error. In such a situation, matching may perhaps be better done on a subpopulation block basis.

5. Another possible procedure at this point is the simple random assignment of individuals to pairs within clusters.

6. Campbell and Erlebacher (1970) apply an additional standard centering on the actual pretest-posttest correlation or homogeneity of slopes in regressions over time. Unfortunately such criteria cannot be applied in impact studies because of the potential interaction effect on these coefficients from exposure to the intervention. For example, should there be inhomogeneity of slope, it could be attributed to either one or both of two explanations: (1) the samples were matched inappropriately, i.e., regression to the mean has taken place; or (2) the intervention had an interactive effect with premeasure score. It is also possible that, even when the slopes are homogeneous, the samples were matched inappropriately but a treatment effect has compensated and made homogeneous slopes of what would have otherwise been inhomogeneous slopes.

7. The application of probability-based statistical tests to nonrandomly drawn samples is, of course, controversial. Possible justification would seem to rest on an argument such as the following: preintervention equivalence requires that the samples be no more dissimilar initially than "good" random samples, and a decision in this regard requires the application of a statistical test on an "as if they were random" basis; and if the degree of preintervention equivalence is regarded as acceptable, the judgment of postintervention nonequivalence—the search for intervention effect—would seem to allow and require the same logic and tests on the same "as if" basis. In the first instance the question that is asked is: Is it reasonable to conclude that these two samples are from the same population? In the second instance, the question asked is: Is it reasonable to conclude that they are no longer from the same population?

8. Scored from 0 (no need) to 5 (too sick, needs institutionalization) by a medical-social assessment team, usually consisting of a research social worker and a research nurse, holding consultations with a physician for questionable cases. Persons rated 1 (a little) to 4 (extreme need, residency judged to be a viable alternative to institutionalization) were considered eligible according to medical-social criteria, with ratings of 1 and 2 considered low priority and ratings of 3 and 4 considered high priority. If there had been a sufficiently large number of applicants with high need, priority status would have been taken into consideration in the initial renting of apartments to eligible applicants. This, however, was not the case. (See Sherwood, Greer, Morris and Sherwood, 1973, Appendix A, for details concerning the screening techniques used in the tenant selection process and a statistical analysis of differences between the high priority and low priority groups.)

9. The variables dropped from analysis because of distribution of responses were: (1) literacy (almost all were literate in English); (2) citizenship (almost all were U.S. citizens); (3) intra-household relations (almost all reported getting along well with those in household at time of application); (4) permanent or transient residence (almost all were permanent residence).

10. Because of the concern with identifying the most theoretically relevant descriptive variables for each of the factors, a more conservative cutting point of .40 was employed when these data were described in *The Highland Heights Experiment* (Sherwood, Greer, Morris, and Sherwood, 1973), the report of the results of the short-term impact of the facility on its residents. For purposes of this analysis, the more commonly accepted .30 cutting point (Harman, 1960: 177) is being used.

11. The focus in this paper has been on the technique's potential for achieving internal validity (Campbell and Stanley, 1963: 5). Although the external validity of study findings is, of course, an additional vital issue, the acceptance of a design with respect to the criterion of internal validity would appear to be a logical prerequisite to such concern. The comment may be made, however, that the concept of subpopulations provides a possible basis for an analysis of the potential external validity of the technique in that expectations of impact might be made with reference to "types" of subjects rather than "samples" of subjects.

REFERENCES

Anderson, R. L. and T. A. Bancroft. *Statistical theory in research.* New York: McGraw-Hill, 1952.

Bartko, J., J. Strauss, and W. Carpenter. An evaluation of taxometric techniques for psychiatric data. *Classification Society Bulletin,* 1971, 2: 2-28.

Campbell, D. T. and A. Erlebacher. How regression artifacts in quasi-experimental evaluations can mistakenly make compensatory education look harmful. In J. Hellmuth (ed.) *Compensatory education: A national debate.* Vol. 3. New York: Brunner/Mazel, 1970.

Campbell, D. T. and H. L. Ross. The Connecticut crackdown on speeding: Time-series data in quasi-experimental analysis. In E. R. Tufte (ed.) *The quantitative analysis of social problems.* Reading, Mass.: Addison-Wesley, 1970.

Campbell, D. T. and J. C. Stanley. *Experimental and quasi-experimental designs for research.* Chicago: Rand McNally, 1963.

Cohen, J. Eta-squared and partial Eta-squared in fixed factor ANOVA designs. *Educational and Psychological Measurement,* 1973, 33: 107-112.

———. *Statistical power analysis for the behavioral sciences.* New York: Academic Press, 1969.

Cooley, W. W. and P. R. Lohnes. *Multivariate procedures for the behavioral sciences.* New York: John Wiley, 1962.

Cox, D. R. *Planning of experiments.* New York: John Wiley, 1958.

Crano, W. D. and M. B. Brewer. *Principles of research in social psychology.* New York: McGraw-Hill, 1973.

Diamond, S. *Information and error.* New York: Basic Books, 1959.

Elster, R. S. and M. D. Dunnette. The robustness of Tilton's measure of overlap. *Educational and Psychological Measurement,* 1971, 31: 685-698.

Harman, H. *Modern factor analysis.* Chicago: The University of Chicago Press, 1967.

Hays, L. W. *Statistics for psychologists.* New York: Holt, Rinehart and Winston, 1963.

Jones, K. J. Problems of grouping individuals and the method of modality. *Behavioral Science,* 1968, 13: 496-511.

Kennedy, J. J. The eta coefficient in complex anova designs. *Educational and Psychological Measurement,* 1970, 30: 885-889.

Keppel, G. *Design and analysis: A researcher's handbook.* Englewood Cliffs, N.J.: Prentice Hall, 1973.

Kish, L. Some statistical problems in research design. *American Sociological Review,* 1959, 24: 328-338.

Lord, F. M. Elementary models for measuring change. In C. W. Harris (ed.) *Problems of measuring change.* Madison: University of Wisconsin Press, 1963.

——— and M. R. Novick. *Statistical theories of mental test scores.* Reading, Mass.: Addison-Wesley, 1968.

Rulon, P. J., D. V. Tiedeman, M. M. Tatsuoka, and C. Langmuir. *Multivariate statistics for personnel classification.* New York: John Wiley, 1967.

Savage, L. J. Subjective probability and statistical practice. In M. S. Bartlett (ed.) *The foundation of statistical inference.* London: Methuen, 1962.

Sherwood, S. The impact of home care service programs. In T. O. Bjerts (ed.) *Housing and environment for the elderly.* Washington, D.C.: Gerontological Society, 1973.

Sherwood, S., D. S. Greer, J. N. Morris, and C. C. Sherwood. *The Highland Heights experiment: A final report.* Washington, D.C.: U.S. Government Printing Office, 1973.

Slate, S. Service support programs developed for Highland Heights residents since its development to fall 1972. In S. Sherwood, D. S. Greer, J. N. Morris, and C. C. Sherwood, *The Highland Heights experiment: A final report,* Washington, D.C.: U.S. Government Printing Office, 1973.

Snedecor, G. W. and W. G. Cochran. *Statistical methods.* Ames, Iowa: Iowa State University Press, 1967.

IV

DEVELOPMENT AND EVALUATION OF MEASURES

9

METHOD AND THEORY FOR DEVELOPING MEASURES
IN EVALUATION RESEARCH

JUM C. NUNNALLY
and
WILLIAM H. WILSON

In his monotonous way, an inchworm meters out the length of his leafy domain. Toes are dipped into the swimming pool in a crude, but highly relevant, assessment of the temperature. With the use of Herculean methods of data collection and analysis, astronomers estimate the rate at which the whole universe is expanding. All of these relate to the topic of measurement, an omnipresent concern in science and daily life. This and the following chapter will be concerned with psychological measurement in a highly important but sometimes difficult arena, namely that of evaluation research.

The overall theory and methodology of psychological measurement will be discussed in terms of the particular issues and problems encountered in evaluation research. As the term is being used here, evaluation research has two essential features. First, it concerns a rather broad program of social action intended to improve some states of affairs. Second, the overall problem in research is to determine the effectiveness of the program, both in general and in terms of specific effects.

SOME MAJOR PROBLEMS IN EVALUATION RESEARCH

Obviously, if there were no major problems in evaluation research, there also would be no need to write thick volumes such as this. As the reader knows, there

AUTHORS' NOTE: Appreciation is expressed to McGraw-Hill Book Company for permission to borrow extensively from the following book for material adapted for this chapter: J. C. Nunnally *Psychometric Theory* (New York: McGraw-Hill, 1967).

are many, many difficult problems in performing clean research on programs of social action. To set the tone for subsequent discussions, some of the major problems will be mentioned here.

Problems in Research Design

In years past (one would hope less so in the future), psychologists and other behavioral scientists have been brought into the picture only after a program of social action of some kind was under way or even completed. This was true, for example, when the senior author was asked to analyze the results of instituting a program of "new math" into a school system. The program had been under way for a school year, and retrospectively, efforts were made to determine the effectiveness of the program. Of course, as one learns in Introductory Statistics, research programs should be planned in advance rather than ex post facto.

Even when one is allowed to plan in advance, evaluation research often meets many difficulties in terms of effective experimental designs. The queen of research designs is one in which (1) a control group is compared with one or more treatment groups, and (2) initially, subjects are randomly assigned to groups. (Sometimes it is necessary to have more than one control group to rule out rival hypotheses in interpreting the treatment effects.) This is the ideal design for nearly all psychological research, but it has been employed very infrequently in evaluation research. The randomized groups design (with appropriate control groups) allows one to rule out such bugaboos in research as (1) initial differences between groups on dependent measures, (2) differential sensitivity of the groups to the various treatments, (3) practice effects from the first to the second application of the dependent measures, (4) maturational changes in subjects as a function of the interval between testings, (5) changes in the social milieu from the first to the second testing, and (6) numerous other artifacts.

Many of the research designs employed in evaluating programs of social action are, at best, halfway adequate. Worst of all is the design in which (1) there is only one treatment group and no control group, and (2) testing is done only after the treatment. An example would be that of employing a new method of instruction in mathematics for fourth-grade students and applying an achievement test at the end of the semester. If the students perform very well in comparison to national norms, this would provide some vaguely circumstantial evidence for the effectiveness of the treatment; but the test results could be explained by so many other factors, for example, the students would have scored as well if the old method of instruction had been applied. Slightly more information would have been obtained by testing students before, as well as after, the treatment, but again there would have been many rival hypotheses for explaining the results, for example, the gain was typical of that of any students during the first half of the fourth grade regardless of the type of training they received in mathematics.

In the aforementioned example, additional information would have been obtained by using one of two sections of the fourth grade as a control group, testing before and after, but employing the usual method of instruction rather than the innovation. (Note that the use of a priori groups is quite different from randomly assigning individuals to treatment groups.) Building up from these humble begin-

nings, one can depict a hierarchy of research designs that provide increasing amounts of information about experimental results. (Campbell and Stanley have discussed in detail the features of experimental designs required to rule out rival hypotheses, e.g., Campbell and Stanley, 1968.)

Problems of Measurement

Many programs of social action are concerned with changing psychological attributes that are very difficult to measure at the present time. This is true, for example, with some of the criteria of accomplishment of the Peace Corps. In addition to measuring its progress in terms of numbers of children taught to read and numbers of miles of roads built, people in the Peace Corps also must strive to change subtle aspects of attitudes as regards pride in personal development, desire for knowledge, national cohesiveness, and others. The measurement of such subtle psychological attributes is not all together hopeless, but difficult, to say the least. Even where the problem of measurement is not inherently difficult, frequently satisfactory measures do not exist for a particular program of evaluation research. This might be so, for example, for changes in values that occur in a rehabilitation program for drug addicts. Probably no existing measure of values would contain items relating to the particular types of values that would be changed by the program. Another example would be in a program of vocational training for jobless youth. To measure the effectiveness of the various subprograms, it probably would be necessary to construct special achievement tests.

Whereas in some cases an excellent method of measurement may be apparent, it might be prohibitively expensive or unfeasible for some other reason. For example, it might be apparent that the best way of testing the effectiveness of a program for treating disturbed children would be to have parents and others gather detailed records each day about the behavior of each child; but after considering how much time and expense would be involved in these operations, investigators are required to settle for a less thorough method of measuring the effectiveness of the program.

In some instances, the measures required in evaluation research are beyond present psychometric theory and methodology. A cardinal example is in any program of social action that goes on for numerous years, for example, as frequently occurs in experimental programs of schooling. Numerous difficulties arise in developing measures for this situation, ones that are not easily handled by current measurement methodologies. For example, there are severe questions as to whether the measures employed at different ages really concern the same attributes. (See Nunnally, 1972, for a detailed discussion of this matter.)

Problems in Obtaining Valid Results

Even if one has on paper an excellent research design and valid measures are available, there still are many problems in obtaining interpretible results in evaluation research. One problem is the old "Hawthorne effect," where what appear to be treatment effects are really the result of incidental aspects of the experimental setting rather than of the intended treatments per se. This tends to occur rather prominently in almost any new program of social action, say one related to some type of schooling. Typically teachers would be excited and enthusiastic about

employing the new methods and would directly or indirectly communicate these feelings to students. This attitude of excitement and well-being has much more effect on the students' learning than the new method of instruction. Consequently, one obtains a very illusory finding at the end of the experiment which indicates that the new method of instruction is much more effective than usual methods of instruction. As time goes on, either the same teachers or new teachers loose their enthusiasm, the newness wears off of the method, and students perform only slightly or no better than students who are given the customary treatment.

Another problem in obtaining valid results concerns playacting on the part of subjects in a way that is not representative of actual effects of the program of action. This very frequently occurs in measuring the effectiveness of programs of psychotherapy. Even if patients really are no better, they are under considerable pressure to rate themselves as being considerably improved. They usually like and respect their therapists, and they want to indicate these good feelings by rating themselves as having improved considerably. Frequently the investigations are undertaken in situations where the patients pay little or nothing for their treatment, which further disposes them to indicate that they have improved whether or not they have. Also, in this instance, sheer "cognitive dissonance" would induce people to indicate that they have improved. There are many, many other instances in which subjects are induced by various aspects of the research setting to provide nonvalid information about themselves.

Another difficulty is the interaction of "before" measurements with treatment conditions. Such interaction might occur, for example, in employing a film series concerning health care. After taking the initial tests, subjects who subsequently viewed the film series might be primed to look for and remember certain types of information in the films. Thus, the research results would not validly reflect the gain in information or changes in attitudes that would occur subsequently in employing the films in situations where "before" measures were not taken. (See Campbell and Stanley, 1968, for a detailed discussion of sources of invalidity in designs for evaluation research.)

Practical Problems

In addition to the aforementioned scientific problems in evaluation research, one frequently encounters various practical problems. Persons who direct and conduct programs of social action usually are committed to the effectiveness of the programs before they are undertaken, and consequently, they frequently are quite chary of objective programs of evaluation. As a dear friend of mine said recently, "Nobody wants to be evaluated." New programs of social action usually have large political and professional consequences for the people involved. If the new program is sponsored by the government, many persons in and out of the government probably have committed themselves heavily to the predicted worth of the program. Obviously, many persons stand to lose if the program proves to be ineffective. The pressure in this regard frequently is so strong that it becomes difficult for research workers to conduct impartial investigations. Either they are swept up in the whirlwind of fervor for proving (not testing) the worth of the program, or they are hindered in many ways from obtaining all of the information needed for a

thorough evaluation. Frequently, to ward off the negative effects of an adverse research report, people in the organization will find many reasons for belittling the thoroughness and objectivity of the research program.

Another practical problem in research concerns administrative procedures that disrupt experimental arrangements, for example, in research on "token economies" in a mental hospital. Patients on several wards are being compared in terms of different methods of structuring the token economies. In the middle of the experiment, the superintendent of the mental hospital decides that one ward must be moved to a new building while the present building is being refurbished. One cannot blame the administrator too much for his action, but the action could have an immense effect on the research program. Very large effects might be found for moving to new living quarters with many new types of physical facilities and arrangements. At least minor intrusions because of administrative decisions are more the rule than the exception.

Another practical problem that frequently occurs in obtaining cooperation of program personnel is that, at base, many people do not comprehend the nature and need for empirical research. Regretably, this tends to occur to a large extent among medical practitioners and other people concerned with various types of treatment (e.g., as so frequently occurs in social work). So many people in treatment-oriented activities are consumed by the idea that each case is a law unto himself and requires individual methods of diagnosis and individual methods of treatment. Consequently, it is repugnant to their nature to find in a research program that all persons in a treatment group are treated alike, at least with respect to the agent of change. Thus, if the investigation concerned various types of group psychotherapy, the experimenter would be conscience-stricken if he withheld the use of drugs for the patients even if his intuition told him that the drugs would add (however, in an unknown way) to the various treatments.

Other practical problems in evaluation research occur because of the sheer cost in time, effort, and money that is involved in some experimental designs and methods of measurement. To measure the effectiveness of day care centers on the intellectual and social development of children, it might be required to interview and give tests to the parents of all children. To test the effectiveness of new legislation and an information program on maintenance of automobile safety equipment, it might be necessary to give thorough inspections of a large sample of automobiles in a state. To test the effectiveness of new types of college education on opinions, attitudes, and values, it might be necessary to perform detailed measurements over a period of ten or more years. Of course, in all three of these instances, there would be huge practical problems in carrying out the research.

Perspectives on Evaluation Research

The foregoing sections have mentioned only some of the outstanding problems in evaluation research. Additional problems are considered in Chapter 10 and throughout this Handbook. Mentioning these problems, however, should not imply a derogation of evaluation research or even hint that such research should be discontinued. It is far too easy for the "pure" methodologist to point up the stringent requirements for pristine research and to induce guilt feelings in the poor

souls who have to do the best they can in evaluating programs of social action. The social problems involved will not go away simply because they pose problems for research. New programs for dealing with the problems are forthcoming and will be given their day in court even if clean experimental designs are difficult to employ, dependent measures are yet undeveloped, and there are many practical problems in carrying out the research. It would be foolish of research methodologists to imply that there is no value at all in simply trying out a program of social action and evaluating the results intuitively. However, the methodologist who is socially sensitive and wise in his profession will suggest that there are feasible ways of obtaining more information about the interworkings and overall effectiveness of social-action programs. Administrative officials and other participants in programs of social action can and should be convinced of the necessity of structuring programs in such a way as to provide meaningful answers from research. Good researchers can and should be aware that a great deal of important circumstantial evidence can be obtained from research strategies and measurement methods that fall short of the ideal.

THE NATURE OF PSYCHOLOGICAL MEASUREMENT

As was mentioned in previous sections, one of the most pressing problems in evaluation research is that of validly measuring important dependent variables such as changes in knowledge, skill, interests, values, personality characteristics, and other human attributes. Because measurement in evaluation research is a natural outgrowth of measurement in psychology as a whole, some general principles of measurement will be discussed as a prelude to discussing the particular problems that occur in evaluation research.

MEASUREMENT IN SCIENCE

Although tomes have been written on the nature of measurement, in the end it boils down to something rather simple: *measurement* consists of *rules for assigning numbers to objects to represent quantities of attributes.* The term "rules" indicates that the procedures for assigning numbers must be explicitly formulated. In some instances the rules are so obvious that detailed formulations are not required. This situation prevails when a yardstick is employed to measure lengths of lumber. What should be done is intuitively obvious, and consequently it is not necessary to study a thick manual of rules before undertaking the measurement. Such examples are, however, the exception rather than the rule in science. Certainly the rules for measuring most psychological attributes in evaluation research are not intuitively obvious. Examples are (1) measurement of changes in reading achievement during a special course of training, (2) measurement of changes in attitudes in relation to a special set of films on drug abuse employed with high school students, and (3) measurement of skills developed in training for the Peace Corps.

In the definition of measurement given above, the term "attribute" indicates that measurement always concerns some particular feature of objects. Strictly speaking, one does not measure objects: one measures their attributes. Thus one measures not the child, but rather the intelligence of the child. Although the

distinction may sound like mere hairsplitting, it is important. First, it demonstrates that measurement requires a process of abstraction. An attribute concerns relations among objects on a particular dimension, for example, weight and intelligence. A red rock and a white rock may weigh the same, and two white rocks may have different weights. Thus the attribute of weight is an abstraction which must not be confounded with all the particular features of objects.

A second reason for emphasizing that measurement always concerns a particular attribute is that it forces us to consider carefully the nature of the attribute before attempting to measure it. One possibility is that the attribute does not exist: For example, the many negative results obtained in the efforts to measure an attribute of "rigidity" in people make it doubtful that there is such an attribute. It is not necessarily true that all the terms used to describe people are matched by measurable attributes, for example, ego strength, extrasensory perception, and dogmatism. Another possibility is that a measure may concern a mixture of attributes rather than only one attribute. This frequently occurs in questionnaire measures of "adjustment," which tend to contain items relating to a number of separable attributes. Although such conglomerate measures sometimes are partly justifiable on practical grounds, the use of such conglomerate measures offers a poor foundation for psychological science. As this chapter will show in detail, each measure should concern some one *thing*, some unitary attribute. To the extent to which unitary attributes should be combined to form an overall appraisal, for example, of adjustment, they should be rationally combined from different measures rather than haphazardly combined within one measure.

Although the definition emphasizes that *rules* for quantification are at the heart of measurement, it does not specify the nature of such rules or place any limit on the "allowable" kinds of rules. This is because a clear distinction should be made between the standards of measurement, qua the measurement process, and standards for validating measures, or determining their usefulness, once they are in existence. Initially, any particular set or rules, or any class of rules, is only a hypothesis. The hypothesis must be tested with respect to standards that are external to the measurement process per se. In other words, the proof of the usefulness of any measure is determined by the extent to which it enhances scientific explanation.

In establishing rules for the employment of a particular measure, the crucial consideration is that there must be a set of rules that is unambiguous. The rules may be developed from an elaborate deductive model, they may be based on much previous experience, they may flow from common sense, or they may spring from only hunches, but the proof of the pudding is in how well the measure serves to explain important phenomena. Consequently *any* set of rules that unambiguously quantifies properties of objects constitutes a *legitimate* measure and has a right to compete with other measures for scientific usefulness. (How scientific usefulness is determined will be discussed in Chapter 10.) The importance of this point is that it indicates a way of settling disputes about the correctness of different methods of *scaling* psychological attributes (different classes of rules for their measurement).

Frequently reference is made to the standardization of measures of psychological attributes. Essentially a measure is said to be "well standardized" if different

people who employ the measure obtain very similar results. For instance one would say that an intelligence test is well standardized if different examiners give approximately the same scores to the same children. Formulating explicit rules for the assignment of numbers is a major aspect of the standardization of measures.

Advantages of Standardized Measures

Although the reader probably has a healthy respect for the importance of measurement in science, it might be useful to look at some of the particular advantages measurement provides. Perhaps the major advantage of employing a standarized measuring instrument is that it takes the guesswork out of scientific observation, that is, it provides objectivity. Thus, scientific theories are testable to the extent that there are unambiguous procedures for documenting empirical events. Standardized measures provide such procedures.

The quantification provided by standardized measures has two advantages. First, numerical indices make it possible to report results in finer detail than would be the case with personal judgments. Thus teachers may be able to reliably assign children to broad categories of intelligence such as "bright," "average," and "below normal." Intelligence tests, however, provide finer differentiations.

Second, numerical results permit the use of powerful methods of mathematical analysis. Without powerful methods of analysis, such as factor analysis and analysis of variance, it would be all but impossible to assess the results of research.

Science is a highly public enterprise in which efficient communication among scientists is essential. Each scientist builds on what has been learned in the past, and day by day he must compare his findings with those of other scientists working on the same types of problems. This essential communication is greatly facilitated when standardized measures are available.

Although frequently a great deal of work is required to develop standardized measures, once developed they usually are much more economical in terms of time and money than are subjective evaluations. In addition, standardized measures often free highly trained professionals for more important work. Consequently, a great saving is obtained in many instances when time-consuming observations by professionals are replaced by standardized measures.

Measurement Scales

There has been much talk in psychology about the different possible types of measurement scales, and there has been much soul-searching about the types of scales characterized by different types of psychological measures. Although these discussions represent a healthy self-consciousness about scientific methods, they have, the authors think, led to some unfortunate confusions. Essentially the issues concern what sorts of "interpretations" can be made of the numbers obtained from psychological measures. More precisely, the issues concern the legitimacy of employing particular classes of mathematical procedures with measures of psychological attributes. Does a measure of intelligence have the same mathematical status as does a yardstick? Does a measure of adjustment have the same mathematical status as a measure of electrical resistance? In this section will be presented a brief review of the conventional classification of measurement scales. The next section

will contain a more probing discussion about the nature of psychological measurement.

Labels and categories. Numbers are frequently used as a way of keeping track of things, without any suggestion that the numbers can be subjected to mathematical analyses. For example, a geologist working in the field might choose to number his specimens of rocks 1, 2, 3, and so on, in which case the numbers would be used purely as labels and would have no implications for mathematical analyses.

It must be emphasized that any measurement scale concerns an *intended use* of numbers. One intended use of numbers is for labeling or categorizing. In this instance there is no intention of performing mathematical analyses of the numbers, and the numbers are not considered to represent quantities of attributes.

Ordinal scales. An ordinal scale is one in which (1) a set of objects or people is ordered from "most" to "least" with respect to an attribute, (2) there is no indication of "how much" in an absolute sense any of the objects possess the attribute, and (3) there is no indication of how far apart the objects are with respect to the attribute. An ordinal scale is obtained, for example, when a group of boys is ordered from tallest to shortest.

Some have claimed that most psychological scales, for example, intelligence tests, should be considered as providing only a rank ordering of people rather than any higher form of measurement. In a later section issue will be taken with that point of view.

Interval scales. An interval scale is one in which (1) the rank ordering of objects is known with respect to an attribute and (2) it is known how far apart the objects are from one another with respect to the attribute, but (3) no information is available about the absolute magnitude of the attribute for any object, that is, no reference is made to an absolute or rational zero point. An interval scale would be obtained for the heights of a group of boys if, instead of being measured directly, the height of each boy was measured with respect to the shortest boy in the group. Thus the shortest boy would obtain a score of 0, a boy 2 inches taller than the shortest boy would obtain a score of 2, and a boy 3 inches taller would obtain a score of 3, and so on.

Ratio scales. A ratio scale is obtained when (1) the rank order of persons with respect to an attribute is known, (2) the intervals between persons are known, and (3) in addition, the distance from a rational zero is known for at least one of the persons. In other words, a ratio scale is a particular type of interval scale in which distances are stated with respect to a rational zero rather than with respect to, for example, the height of the tallest boy or the shortest boy or the mean height. Obviously, if an interval scale of height is available and in addition the absolute height (distance from zero) of any boy in the group is known, the absolute heights of all the other boys can be calculated.

Permissible operations. The relative importance of discussing different measurement scales is that some types of scales are open to many more forms of mathematical treatments than are others. For example, the ratio scale is susceptible to the fundamental operations of mathematics: addition, subtraction, division, and multiplication. With these operations come all the power of mathematics, including algebra, analytic geometry, calculus, and all the more powerful statistical methods.

Without such mathematical tools the scientist is almost out of business. (For a discussion of the permissible operations on the various scales, see Nunnally, 1967.)

Decisions about Measurement Scales

The previous section presented the "fundamentalist" point of view about measurement scales, which, to summarize, holds that (1) there are distinct types of measurement scales into which all possible measures of attributes can be classified, (2) each measure has some "real" characteristics that permit its proper classification, and (3) once a measure is classified, the classification specifies the types of mathematical analyses that can be employed with the measure. It will be argued that this is a narrow point of view which needs to be severely modified before it can meet the actualities of scientific inquiry.

Those who accept the fundamentalist point of view hold that (1) measurement scales have empirical reality in addition to being theoretical constructions, and (2) the investigator must show evidence of the scale properties of particular measures before employing certain methods of analysis. The first point will be severely questioned in a later section. Even if one accepts the first point, no one has made it clear what types of evidence would justify the assumption of a particular type of scale. The following sections will attempt an answer.

Ostensive characteristics. One way to judge the scale characteristics of a particular measure is in terms of the physical characteristics of the measurement operations. The best example of this, and perhaps the only pure one, is the measurement of length with a yardstick. To prove that the attribute in question is measured on a ratio scale requires (1) a proof of equal intervals and (2) the demonstration of an axiomatically unquestionable zero point. Anyone can see the zero point: it is where the yardstick starts. Back of that point is open space; in front of it is the wooden beginning of the measuring instrument. Who could argue that a more meaningful zero point could be located elsewhere on the yardstick? The equality of intervals is also easy to demonstrate. One way would be to saw the yardstick inch by inch and then compare the pieces two at a time to ensure that they are all equal.

The yardstick exemplifies the two ostensive characteristics supposedly required for a ratio scale: visually (or palpably otherwise) discernible zero and fractionation into visually equal intervals. No other measure so obviously passes the tests. The closest is the measurement of weight, and even here one does not really observe weight but rather the effects of weight on a balance. When measures of length and weight are set aside, it becomes obvious that almost all attributes are measured indirectly, and consequently one cannot look to the ostensive characteristics of the *correlate* to determine the scale characteristics by which the attribute itself is manifested in the correlate. Thus to observe the height of the column of mercury in a thermometer is to observe not temperature itself, but a correlate of temperature. In all sciences, and certainly in psychology, the observations required in the operations of measurement usually are not the same as observations of the attributes themselves. Thus in a measure of intelligence, one is observing not intelligence directly, but rather its supposed by-products.

Although perhaps none have said it directly, those who take the fundamentalist

point of view imply that scale properties can be judged only by ostensive characteristics. Since, for example, there are no ostensive properties to guarantee the equality of intervals in the measurement of intelligence, it has been argued that tests of intelligence constitute at best ordinal scales. It is hoped the previous paragraphs have shown that by the same standards there would be few measures in all science that could be considered more than ordinal scales; it is hoped the following sections will show that proper standards for judging the scale properties of a measure are not dependent on observing the ostensive characteristics of the attribute to be measured.

Scaling models. Another approach to the discussion of scale characteristics concerns the use of various models for the construction of measures. Each such model constitutes a set of axioms concerning how the data should appear when the measure is put to use. For example, a sensible axiom in any model for the development of interval scales is that of *transitivity*. If a model leads to independent scorings of intervals among persons on a scale of measurement and it is found that the score for person A is 5 points above that for person B and the score for person B is 5 points above that for person C, it should also be found that the score for person A is 10 points above that for person C. This extremely simple and commonsense assumption is mentioned only to illustrate the axioms that appear in different measurement models.

If the data obtained from applying a measurement scale fit the axioms of the particular model under consideration and the axioms (assumptions) of the model are correct, the measure has scale properties specified by the model. An example may help to clarify this important point. In a following section will be described a model proposed by Louis Guttman for the construction of ordinal scales. It makes a set of assumptions about patterns of responses of people to test items. After the items are administered to samples of persons, mathematical analyses can be made to determine how well the actual patterns of scores fit the patterns of scores predicted by the model. If the fit is good, the model stipulates that an ordinal scale of measurement has been obtained; if the fit is poor, the hypothesis of an ordinal scale is rejected.

There are two important points to be made about the place of scaling models in discussions of scale properties. First, this type of standard is based on empirical data, in contrast to standards concerning ostensive characteristics. In the former, one studies the results from applying a measure to objects in the real world; in the latter, one "studies" the observable characteristics of the measurement tool itself. For example, instead of determining the scale properties of yardsticks merely by looking at them, one could establish a model concerning the properties of ratio scales and then see if the data obtained from employing the yardstick to measure many objects fit the model. One could derive the scale properties of the yardstick from the model even if one had never seen a yardstick. This is what psychological scaling is about: it is an attempt to work backward from empirical data to test the fit to a model. In this way an attempt is made to develop ratio, interval, and ordinal scales for psychological attributes, many of which cannot be seen directly.

A second important point to make about the place of scaling models in

discussing the properties of measurement scales is that a model is no better and no worse than its assumptions (axioms). There is ample room for disagreement, and there is plenty of it, about the *fruitfulness* of different models. If psychologists are "allowed" to disagree about the correctness of different scaling models, how then are the scale characteristics of measures ever determined? If, for example, models for the development of interval scales are being tried on a particular type of data, for example, responses to statements concerning attitudes toward Negroes, the failure of the data to fit one model does not automatically prevent the measure from being considered as an interval scale; and if the data fit all the models under consideration, this does not automatically indicate that the measure should be considered as an interval scale. The final decision in this matter should be made with respect to standards discussed in the following sections.

Consequences of assumptions. Even if one believes that there is a "real" scale for each attribute, which is either mirrored directly in a particular measure or mirrored as some monotonic transformation, an important question is, "What difference does it make if the measure does not have the same zero point or proportionally equal intervals as the 'real' scale?" All that could go wrong would be that the scientist would make misstatements about the specific form of the relationship between the attribute and other variables. For example, using an "imperfect" interval scale, the scientist might report a linear relationship between the attribute and some other variable, whereas if he had employed the "real" interval scale, he would have found a power function instead.

How seriously are such misassumptions about scale properties likely to influence the reported results of scientific experiments? In psychology at the present time, the answer in most cases is "very little." The results of most studies are reported in the form of either (1) correlations between scores of individuals on different measures or (2) mean differences between differently treated groups. Regarding the former, correlations are affected very little by monotonic transformations of variables. Suppose that (1) a product-moment correlation is computed between a measure and another variable, (2) the measure is only an "imperfect" representation of the "real" scale, the intervals on the "real" scale being obtainable by a square-root transformation of the measure, and (3) the correlation is found to be .50. Would the correlation have been very different if the "real" scale rather than the "imperfect" scale had been correlated with the other variable? The correlation would change very little. It might, for example, go down to .48 or up to .52.

In analyzing differences between means in differently treated groups, of major concern are ratios of variances among different sources of variation. For example, an important ratio is the variance among treatment means divided by the pooled variance within treatment groups. This and other important ratios among sources of variation are affected very little by monotonic transformations of the dependent measure. Then if it is granted that the measure used in the experiment is at least monotonically related to the "real" scale, it usually will make little difference which is used in the analysis.

Convention. So far in this section it has been necessary to take seriously the fundamentalist point of view that it is meaningful to think in terms of "real" scales

and to think of actual measures as approximations of such "real" scales. These assumptions were tolerated up to this point to show that (1) they lead to unanswerable questions and (2) even if they were good assumptions, violations of them usually would not be harmful. As must be clear by this point, the authors oppose the concept of "real" scales and deplore the confusion this conception has wrought. It is much more appropriate to think of any measurement scale as a convention, an agreement among scientists that a particular scaling of an attribute is a "good" scaling.

A convention establishes the scale properties of a measure. If it is established as a ratio scale, then the zero point can be taken seriously and the intervals may be treated as equal in any forms of analysis. If it is established as an interval scale, the intervals may be treated as equal in all forms of analysis. This is not meant to imply that such conventions are, or should be, established quickly or until much evidence is in, but in the end they are conventions, not discoveries of "real" scales.

In saying that scales are established by convention (rather than God-given), it is not meant to imply that such conventions should be arbitrary. Before measures of particular attributes are constructed, all manner of wisdom should be brought to bear on the nature of the attribute. With some types of measures, the nature of a "good" scaling is so readily agreed on by all that a convention is easily established. Thus it is with length and weight: no one opposes the ways of setting the zero point and the establishment of intervals. In exasperation about the confusion in theories of measurement, it is tempting to wish that there were no yardsticks and no balances for the measurement of weight. Then all scientists might more readily see that measurement is a matter of convention rather than of discovering the "real" measure. (This issue is discussed in more detail in Nunnally, 1967, chap. 1.)

There are two major problems with considering scaling as a matter of convention. First, it is disquieting to those who think in terms of "real" scales and who wish for, but cannot find, some infallible test for the relationship between a particular measure and the "real" scale. Also, looking at measurement scaling as a matter of convention seems to make the problem "messy." How well a particular scaling of an attribute "fits in" with other variables is an open-ended question. Which variables? How good is a particular "fit"? To avoid such questions, however, is to blind one's self to the realities of scientific enterprise. To seek shelter in the apparent neatness of conceptions regarding "real" scales is not to provide answers about the properties of measurement scales but to ask logically unanswerable questions.

A second, and more serious, problem with considering scaling as a matter of convention is that there often are two or more conventions strongly competing with one another. For example, there has been much dispute about which of two methods of scaling certain dimensions of sensation—Thurstone's law of comparative judgment or the magnitude-estimation methods—is *the* correct method. When these methods are used to scale judgments about the loudness of tones, different scales are obtained: one is logarithmically related to the other. More appropriate than asking which is "correct" would be asking which in the long run will "fit" in better in a system of natural laws. For example, there already is evidence that scalings

based on methods of magnitude estimation have a broad generality over different modalities of sensation, which is the kind of evidence required to establish a convention for the employment of one method rather than others.

Generalizability

Much of what has been said and will be said about psychological measurement in evaluation research concerns the concept of *generalizability*. Of course, the major purpose of science is to develop very general propositions about nature. The apex of such general statements is the Einsteinian equation $E = MC^2$. At a less grandiose level, all empirical scientists try to develop and test general statements about people and things. Generalizability also is at the heart of psychological measurement. Thus, in developing an interval scale for the measurement of a simple skill such as spelling proficiency, the hope is to provide a measuring instrument that correlates very highly with the instruments developed by other people and in which the intervals of measurement are very much the same. In that case, it would not matter a great deal whether spelling proficiency were measured with one instrument rather than another. To the extent to which that is true of spelling tests in general, the result from any spelling test can be generalized to a host of measuring instruments.

A particular experimental design in evaluation research is valid to the extent to which it permits one to generalize from the circumstances of an experiment to the circumstances in real life. Previously, various artifacts were mentioned which make it difficult to formulate such generalizations.

The major criterion by which all research strategies and measurement methods inevitability must be judged is that of the extent to which generalization is promoted or hindered. For example, in this chapter it was said that the assumption of interval scales for most psychological measures leads to more powerful forms of mathematical generalization without attendant danger to generalizing. The concept of generalizability will appear at numerous other points in this chapter and in Chapter 10. In Chapter 10, for example, it will be shown that issues regarding reliability and validity really boil down to issues regarding generalizability of findings and relationships.

MODELS FOR SCALING PSYCHOLOGICAL ATTRIBUTES

Previously it was said that measurement concerns the assignment of numbers to objects to represent quantities of attributes. Although any system of operations that will so assign numbers can be spoken of as measurement, it helps to have some internally consistent plan for the development of a new measure. The plan is spoken of as a *scaling model*, and the measure that results from exercising the plan is spoken of as a *scale* ("scale" being another word for "measure"). The simplest example is that of the ruler as a scale of length. The methods for constructing and applying rulers constitute the scaling model in that case. The purpose of any scaling model is to generate a continuum on which persons or objects are located. In the following example, persons P_1, P_2, P_3, and P_4 are located on such a continuum:

The attribute could be thought of as anxiety or as spelling ability. Because it is an interval scale, the distances between persons are taken seriously. Thus P_1 is considerably higher in the attribute than the other persons, P_2 and P_3 are close together, and P_4 is far below the others.

In any particular measurement problem, scaling concerns a data matrix (table) such as that in Figure 9.1. On the front face of the cube, rows represent stimuli and columns represent responses to the stimuli. The "slices" of the cube going from front to back represent the responses of each person to each of the stimuli. The words "stimuli" and "responses" represent anything that the experimenter does to the subject and anything the subject does in return. Typical things (stimuli) the experimenter does to the subject are to have him lift weights, to present him with spelling words, or to show him a list of foods. Typical responses required for these types of stimuli would be judging which of two weights is heavier, indicating whether or not each word is correctly spelled, and rating how much each food is liked.

The data matrix illustrated in Figure 9.1 presents a very complex problem for scaling. The problem is much simpler when there is only a two-dimensional table, as when only one person is studied at a time. This also would be the case if only one type of response were made to each stimulus, for example, agreeing or

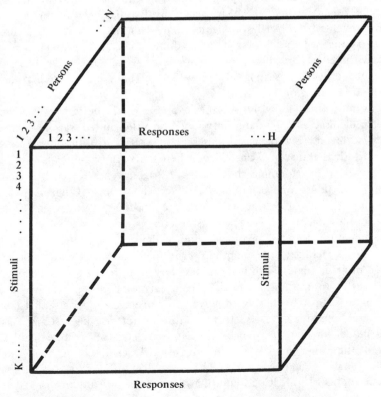

FIGURE 9.1　A data matrix for H responses of N persons to K stimuli.

disagreeing with each of a list of statements (stimuli). Also, there would be a two-dimensional table of data if each person made a number of different types of responses to the same stimulus, for example, rating the United Nations on different rating scales anchored by pairs of adjectives such as "effective-ineffective," "valuable-worthless," and "strong-weak." If in the problem there are more than one person, more than one stimulus, and more than one type of response required for each stimulus, there are many, many ways in which one of the three could be scaled. Usually an effort is made to simplify the problem by making the elements in one dimension "replicates" of one another, or at least assuming them to be so.

Some methods of scaling assume that persons are replicates of one another. For example, the percentage of persons in a *group* that says one weight is heavier than another is assumed to be the same as the percentage of times an ideal *modal individual* would say that one weight is heavier than another on different occasions. The assumption that individuals are replicates is frequently made in scaling stimuli. In scaling persons, it frequently is assumed that responses are replicates of one another. Thus in the previous example of rating stimuli on scales anchored by bipolar adjectives, an overall "favorableness" rating can be obtained by adding responses over the separate rating scales.

Starting with a two-dimensional table of data, the usual strategy in the development of a measurement method is to test for the presence of a unidimensional scale. Essentially this consists of trying to do away with one of the two dimensions. An example would be that in which each individual has been required to rank a number of weights from heaviest to lightest. The data matrix would then consist of the ranks of weights for each person, a two-dimensional table of data. One way to do away with the person dimension would be to average the ranks over persons, which would provide a scaling of the weights. The average ranking could be considered an ordering of the weights, and one might also want to take the intervals between average ranks seriously. Another example would be in having individuals either agree or disagree with statements concerning the United Nations. Agreement with each statement is thought to represent a positive attitude; disagreement, a negative attitude. Because only one object is being rated, a two-dimensional table of data is obtained. By summing the number of agreements for each person, one collapses the response dimension of the table. Then sums of agreements would constitute an ordering of the persons with respect to their attitudes, and one might want to take the intervals between persons seriously.

Before one turns a two-dimensional table of data into a one-dimensional scale, he should first state a set of assumptions regarding how the attribute in question is manifested in actual data. Then he must test how well the assumptions hold in the data. Each set of assumptions is a model. The discussion here is primarily concerned with the models most frequently employed for turning two-dimensional tables of data into unidimensional scales. If the data do not fit the assumptions of a particular model for unidimensional scaling, the investigator has three choices: (1) try one of the other models for unidimensional scaling, (2) try methods of multivariate analysis, or (3) try some other problem. If methods of multivariate analysis are applied, it might be found that more than one unidimensional scale is

required to account for the data. For example, with statements concerning attitudes toward the United Nations, factor analysis might indicate that the statements relate to two different dimensions of attitude. It might be found that some statements relate to a factor concerning the effectiveness of the United Nations in settling diplomatic disputes among nations and other statements relate to a factor concerning activities of the United Nations in economic matters. Then two scales of attitudes rather than only one would be developed.

Evaluation of models. These often are different models that can be used for the development of particular scales, and sometimes the models lead to different conclusions about the scale properties of the data. One model might lead to a scale that failed to have a linear relationship with a scale derived from another model applied to the same data. One model might reject the data as conforming to an ordinal scale, whereas another model would accept the data as conforming to an interval scale. How then does one know which model is appropriate for a particular problem? As was said previously, there is no sure way to know this in advance. The ultimate test is how well the scales which are derived fit in a nexus of lawful relations with other variables. Before time and effort are spent on such investigations, however, there are some criteria of "good sense" that can be applied.

Part of "good sense" concerns the intuitive appeal of a scaling model. Although the data of science must be objective, the scientist must rely on his intuition for research ideas. Looked at in one way, a measurement model is nothing more than an explicitly defined hunch, a hunch that particular operations on data will lead to an important measure. If the author's observations are correct, psychologists tend to find intuitively appealing those measurement models that relate to the measurement of simple physical attributes such as length and weight.

Another aspect of "good sense" in selecting scaling models concerns the evaluation of assumptions in the models in terms of what is already known about the type of data involved. For example, one of the models discussed below assumes that responses to individual test items are highly reliable, yet there is a wealth of evidence to show that such items usually are not highly reliable.

After a model is used to derive a scale and before strenuous efforts are made to find lawful relations with other variables, there are some preliminary forms of evidence regarding the usefulness of the scale. If the scale values for objects or persons are markedly affected by slightly different ways of gathering data, the scale probably will not work well in practice. There are, for example, numerous ways in which one can have subjects make judgments of weight. If two approaches that seem much the same lead to very different intervals of judged weight, one would be quite suspicious of the interval scales obtained by both approaches. An even more important type of preliminary evidence concerns the amount of measurement error involved in using a particular type of scale. A scale that occasions a great deal of measurement error cannot possibly be useful for any purpose. Beyond the standards of "good sense," however, the ultimate test of any model is the extent to which it produces scales with a high degree of explanatory power for natural phenomena.

Stimuli and people. Previously it was stated that scaling problems concern a

three-dimensional matrix of persons, stimuli, and types of responses. In unidimensional scaling, usually each person makes only one type of response to each stimulus; or if he makes more than one type of response, it is sensible to combine responses in some manner. (If there is doubt about the sensibility of combining responses, methods of multivariate analysis can be employed.) In either situation, a scaling model is applied to a two-dimensional matrix of data. What has not been made explicit so far is that usually methods of scaling employed for scaling stimuli are different from those for scaling people. Also, which of the two is to be scaled has a strong influence on the way responses are obtained.

It is probably easier to think of measurement problems in terms of the scaling of people. In a simple example, the data matrix is bordered by spelling words on the side and by people on the top. The required response is to indicate whether or not each word is correctly spelled (a single response to each stimulus). With the use of a 1 for correct spellings and a 0 for incorrect spellings, the data matrix would be filled with 1s and 0s. The dimension concerning stimuli (spelling words) would be collapsed by summing the number of 1s for each person. If it were not thought necessary to apply a more elaborate model to the data, the simple sums of correct responses would serve to scale people on the attribute of spelling ability.

Something more subtle is at issue when the object is to scale stimuli rather than people. For example, when subjects are asked to judge the loudness of tones by one method or another, the object is to generate a continuum of perceived loudness. In this instance the tones are quantified with respect to the attribute, and people are part of the measurement process. In another example of scaling stimuli, preferences for foods can be scaled by having a group of people rate each food on a like-dislike rating scale. One method of scaling in this instance would be to let the average rating of each food be its scale value.

It is important to make a distinction between the scaling of stimuli and the scaling of persons, because there are more severe problems with the former. In the scaling of stimuli, research issues frequently concern the exact nature of functional relations between scalings of the stimuli in different circumstances. Thus in the scaling of tones under different conditions, a careful study would be made of the exact "curves" between different scalings. Then it would make quite a difference if a particular relation was linear rather than logarithmic. In most studies concerning the scaling of people, exact forms of relationship between different scalings are not important—at least, not at the present stage of development of psychological science. The major requirement is that different scalings of people be monotonically related to one another, that is, that they rank-order people in the same way. Thus if there are two different methods for scaling people for the attribute of anxiety and the two are monotonically related, research results will be much the same regardless of which scale is employed.

Evaluation research usually is concerned much more with the scaling of people than with the scaling of stimuli; consequently, the remainder of the discussion here will concern the scaling of people. (A discussion of the scaling of stimuli appears in Nunnally, 1967, chap. 2.) Thus, in evaluation research, one is concerned with the scaling of individuals with respect to amounts of information, levels of skill,

interests, personality characteristics, and other such traits concerning differences among people.

Capabilities and sentiments. Although there are no two words that perfectly symbolize the distinction, one of the most important distinctions in measurement theory is that between responses concerning *capabilities* and those concerning *sentiments.* The word "capability" is used to cover all those types of responses where there is a *correct* response. This would be the case, for example, when a child is asked, "How much is two plus two?" This would also be the case when subjects are required to judge which of two tones is louder or which of two weights is heavier. In all these instances there is some *veridical comparison* for the subject's response, and it is possible to determine whether each response is correct or incorrect. With some types of capabilities, it also is possible to determine the degree of correctness and thus the relative accuracy. This would be true, for example, in measuring the accuracy with which motor skills were manifested in tasks that required sensory-motor coordination.

The word "sentiment" is used to cover all responses concerning personal reactions, preferences, interests, attitudes, and likes and dislikes. An individual makes responses concerning sentiments when he (1) rates boiled cabbage on a seven-step, like-dislike rating scale, (2) answers the question, "Which would you rather do, organize a club or work on a stamp collection?" and (3) rank-orders 10 actors in terms of his sentiments. The important difference between capability and sentiments is that with sentiments there is no veridical comparison. Thus if an individual says, "I like chocolate ice cream better than vanilla ice cream," it makes no sense to tell him, "You are incorrect." We may abhor another person's tastes for food or sentiments in any other sphere, but sentiments do not require veridical justification. Of course, it may be that the subject is incorrect in the sense that he lies or that he actually behaves in daily life in a manner different from that implied by his stated sentiments. The important point, however, concerns *what the subject is asked to do* in the experimental setting. When expressing a sentiment, the subject is asked to give a personal reaction to a stimulus, and there is no external standard of "accuracy" that makes sense.

Tests of capability usually require subjects to make judgments of one type or another. This is true in tests of mathematics, vocabulary, and reasoning ability. Either the subject exercises his judgment in supplying a correct answer for each item or he judges which of a number of alternative responses is most correct. Tests of interests concern sentiments: the subject indicates the activities that he likes and those that he dislikes. Measures of attitudes and personality can require either judgments or expressions of sentiment, and it is with these types of measures that the distinction frequently is obscure. On a personality inventory, when responding to the item, "Do you like to be the center of attention at parties?" the subject is asked to express a sentiment. When responding to the item, "Do you usually lead the discussion in group situations?" the subject is asked to make a judgment about his actual behavior in group situations. When responding to the item, "Do most people like you?" he is asked to make a judgment about other peoples' sentiments. Of course, with such items, subjects frequently get sentiments mixed up with

judgments, whether by intention or out of sheer confusion, and this is one reason it is difficult to develop valid inventories for measuring personality.

Models for Scaling People

Early in the chapter it was stated that problems of scaling potentially concern a three-dimensional table of data, with the dimensions representing persons, stimuli, and responses. (This was illustrated in Figure 9.1.) In the development of unidimensional scales for either persons or stimuli, it is usually possible to "collapse" the dimension concerning different types of responses. Either it is known from previous studies that all the types of responses concern the same attribute, for example, by a factor analysis of rating scales bounded by different pairs of adjectives, or only one type of response is required to each stimulus. The latter would be true, for example, if the subject were required only to agree or disagree with each statement in a list or to indicate whether each statement in a list is correct or incorrect. After the three-dimensional table is reduced to a two-dimensional table, models for developing unidimensional scales concern ways for collapsing one of the two remaining dimensions.

Multi-item measures. Prior to a discussion of models for collapsing the stimulus dimension of a two-dimensional table of data, it might be wise to reflect on the need for more than one stimulus in psychological measures. The word "items" will be used in a broad sense to stand for any stimuli used in measurement methods. Thus items may be words on a spelling test, comparisons between weights, statements concerning attitudes toward the United Nations, and reactions in a study of reaction time. What is presented the subject is the item (stimulus), and in each of the examples above, the subject is required to make only one type of response to each item.

There are a number of important reasons for requiring more than one item in nearly all measures for evaluation research. First, individual items usually have considerable *specificity*. That is, each item tends to have only a low correlation with the attribute being measured. On a spelling test, for example, whether or not a child could correctly spell "umpire" would depend in part on his interest in baseball. A boy who spent much time reading baseball stories might correctly spell the word even though he was a poor speller in general. Another example of the specificity of individual items is in rating the following statement on a seven-step scale of agreement-disagreement: "We give more to the United Nations than we get in return." Supposedly that is a negative statement about the United Nations, and people who agree with the statement *tend* to have negative attitudes. Even though a person might have an overall positive attitude, however, he might agree with the statement because he is not happy with the share of financing borne by our country.

In both examples above, it can be seen that each item relates only in a statistical sense with the attribute being measured. Each item tends to correlate with the attribute in question, but also correlates with attributes other than the one being measured.

Even if individual items had no specificity, there are other reasons measures

require more than one item. One reason is that most items attempt to categorize people into either two groups or only a relatively small number of groups. Thus an item requiring dichotomous responses (e.g., pass or fail) can at most distinguish between two levels of the attribute. A seven-step rating scale can at most distinguish between seven levels of an attribute. In most measurement problems it is desirable to make fine differentiations among people, and this can seldom be done with a one-item measure.

Even if there were no specificity in items and items were capable of making very fine distinctions among people, there still would be an important reason one-item measures would not suffice. Individual items have considerable measurement error; in other words, they are unreliable. Each item, in addition to its specificity, occasions a considerable amount of random error. This is seen when people are required to repeat a set of ratings after a period of time. The person who gave a rating of 3 on one occasion is likely to give a rating of 5 on another, and many other changes of this kind are expected. Another example would be in the solving of arithmetic problems on two occasions. The child who got the correct answer on one occasion might not get the correct answer to the same problem on another occasion, and vice versa. Thus there is some randomness related to any item, and consequently the individual item cannot be trusted to give reliable measurement of an attribute.

All three difficulties that have been discussed can be diminished by the use of multi-item measures. The specificity of items can be averaged out when they are combined. By combining items, one can make relatively fine distinctions among people. For reasons discussed in Chapter 10, the reliability tends to increase (measurement error is reduced) as the number of items in a combination increases. Thus nearly all measures of psychological attributes are multi-item measures. This is true both for measures used in studies of individual differences and for measures used in controlled experiments. The problem of scaling people with respect to attributes is then one of collapsing responses to a number of items so as to obtain one score (measurement) for each person.

The trace line. Nearly all models for scaling people can be depicted by different types of curves relating an attribute to the probability of responding in one way rather than another to items. Four different types of trace lines are depicted in Figures 9.2 to 9.5. Dichotomous items are depicted in these figures. For each item, it will be said that there are two types of responses, alpha and beta. Alpha would variously consist of passing rather than failing an item, agreeing rather than disagreeing with a statement.

In Figures 9.2 to 9.5, the attribute is the particular thing being measured. In this connection, it is important to make a distinction between the particular attribute being measured and some more general attribute of interest. Thus on vocabulary tests, identifying correct synonyms for words is a particular attribute, and it is hoped that this particular attribute relates to the general attribute of intelligence. A particular attribute will be referred to as an "attribute." More general attributes will be referred to as "constructs." The measurement problem itself concerns the relations between particular attributes and the probability of responding in one

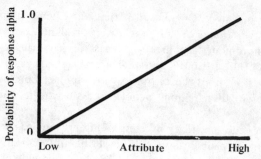

FIGURE 9.2   An ascending linear trace line for an item.

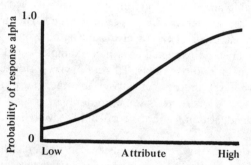

FIGURE 9.3   An ascending monotonic trace line for an item.

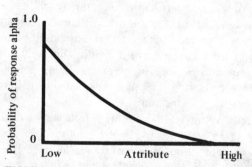

FIGURE 9.4   A descending monotonic trace line for an item.

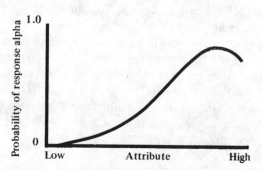

FIGURE 9.5   A nonmonotonic trace line for an item.

way rather than another. It is only after measures of particular attributes are constructed that they can be combined to measure more general attributes (constructs).

In the remainder of this chapter, the abscissa for models concerning trace lines will concern particular attributes. Attributes are defined in a circular sense in terms of whatever a number of items tends to measure in common. Thus a list of spelling words would tend to measure spelling ability. The word "tend" is used because it must be recognized that no attribute is perfectly mirrored in any set of items. Perfect measurement would be available, for example, if children were administered a spelling test containing all words in the English language. When there is a limited number of items, as there always is, there is some unreliability of measuring the particular attribute. Completely reliable measures of the attribute are called *true scores,* and the approximations to true scores obtained from any collection of items are called *fallible scores.* In all the figures showing item trace lines, the abscissa concerns true scores on the particular attribute. Of course, one does not know exactly what the true scores are, but they can be approximated by scores obtained from some combination of the available items. For this reason, after some way has been formulated for combining items, an approximate test can be made for the actual trace line of any particular item; for example, the trace line for a spelling item can be computed as a function of the number of words correctly spelled on the test.

The concept of trace lines also applies to multipoint items (items that are scorable on more than two points), an example of which is shown in Figure 9.6. Instead of depicting the probability of response alpha, the ordinate depicts the average score on the item. In Figure 9.6 are shown the average scores on a seven-step rating scale for persons at different levels of an attribute. Other multipoint items whose trace lines could be depicted in that way are scores on essay questions in a classroom examination, number of words correctly recalled in a study of memory, and amount of time in responding to a signal in studies of

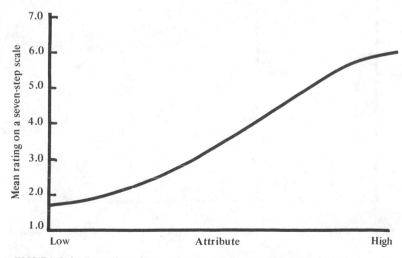

FIGURE 9.6 Trace line of average scores on a seven-step rating scale.

reaction time. It should be recalled that an average score is an *expected score,* and consequently Figure 9.6 depicts the expected score as a function of levels of an attribute.

In discussing trace lines, it is useful to think of the attribute as being completely continuous. Also, it is useful to think of there being a large number of persons at each of the infinite number of points on the attribute. In this hypothetical circumstance, the trace line shows the expected response for people at each level of the attribute, the expectation being expressed either as a probability of response alpha for dichotomous items or as an average score for multipoint items. By their nature, expectations are accompanied by some error. On dichotomous items, there is a probability of response alpha at each point, but there is no certainty as to *which* persons at a point will make response alpha and which persons will make response beta. On multipoint items, there is a band of error surrounding the expected average score. Thus although the expected score for a particular point on an attribute might be 3.0, the actual scores of people at that point might range from 1.5 to 4.5.

Deterministic Models for Scaling People

Deterministic models are so called because they assume that there is *no error* in item trace lines. For dichotomous items, at each point of the attribute it is assumed that the probability of response alpha is either 1.0 or zero. The particular deterministic model employed most frequently is one which assumes that up to a point on the attribute the probability of response alpha is zero (probability of responses beta is 1.0) and beyond that point the probability of response alpha is 1.0. An item of this type is shown in Figure 9.7, and a family of such items is shown in Figure 9.8. Each item has a biserial correlation of 1.0 with the attribute, and consequently

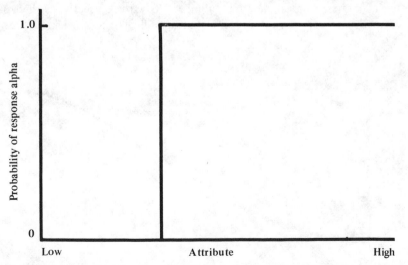

FIGURE 9.7   Trace line of an item that discriminates perfectly at one point on an attribute.

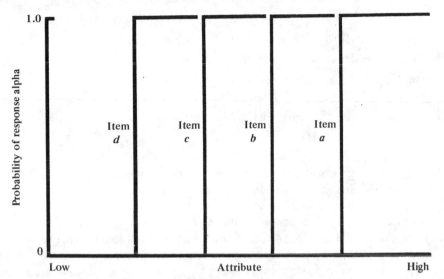

FIGURE 9.8　Family of trace lines for four items that meet the requirements of a monotone deterministic model.

each item perfectly discriminates at a particular point of the attribute. Intuitively, this is a very appealing model, because it is exactly what one expects to obtain in measurements of length. Thus one would expect to obtain a family of trace lines like that in Figure 9.8 for the following items.

	Yes	No
a. Are you above 6 feet 6 inches in height?	_____	_____
b. Are you above 6 feet 3 inches in height?	_____	_____
c. Are you above 6 feet in height?	_____	_____
d. Are you above 5 feet 9 inches in height?	_____	_____
e. Are you above 5 feet 6 inches in height?	_____	_____

Answering "yes" can be considered response alpha. Any person who answered yes to question (item) a would answer yes to the others. Any person who did not answer yes to a but did answer yes to b would also answer yes to questions c through e. For five people with different patterns of responses, a triangular pattern of data would be found like that in Table 9.10. An X symbolizes an answer of yes (response alpha).

Guttman scale. Although one never knows the exact nature of trace lines, one can look at data and see if they evolve into a triangular pattern like that in Table 9.1. (In so doing, however, one is making a subtle logical assumption, a point discussed later.) Some types of items tend to produce a pattern of data like that in Table 9.1. The following is an example.

	Yes	No
a. The United Nations is the savior of mankind.	_____	_____
b. The United Nations is our best hope for peace.	_____	_____
c. The United Nations is a constructive force in the world.	_____	_____
d. We should continue to participate in the United Nations.	_____	_____

For any person who answers yes to a, there is a high probability that he will answer yes to the other items. Any person who does not answer yes to a but does answer yes to b has a high probability of answering yes to the other items.

Any set of items that produces a pattern of responses approximately like that in Table 9.1 is called a "Guttman scale." In developing such a scale, what one does is administer a collection of items to a group of people and then attempt to arrange the responses so as to produce the required triangular pattern. (Since in actual data there would be more than one person at each level of the attribute, the data would appear in the form of a solid staircase, with the width of each step being proportional to the number of persons at each level.) There are numerous cut-and-dry methods for doing this (see Torgerson, 1958). Of course, obtaining the triangular pattern exactly is very unlikely, and therefore it is necessary (1) to discard some items and (2) to find the best possible ordering of items and people. Regarding the latter consideration, of primary concern is the *reproducibility* of score patterns. If the triangular pattern is perfectly obtained, a knowledge of the *number* of responses of yes allows one to reproduce all the person's responses. When the triangular pattern is approximately obtained, a knowledge of the number of *yeses* by a person allows one to approximately reproduce all that person's responses. For all people and all items, one can investigate the percentage of reproducibility, and it is this percentage which is all important in the development of Guttman scales.

Conceivably, Guttman scales could be developed for all types of items requiring dichotomous responses. This can be illustrated with a spelling test where there are 40 items. For each item, the subject indicates whether or not the word is correctly spelled. If the items had trace lines like those in Figure 9.8, a triangular pattern of data would be obtained. In this instance an x would stand for a correct response to the spelling of the word. If one person has a score of 35 and another a score of 34, this would necessarily mean that the former person got the *same* 34 items correct as

TABLE 9.1

Item	Person				
	1	2	3	4	5
a	X				
b	X	X			
c	X	X	X		
d	X	X	X	X	
e	X	X	X	X	X

the latter person, plus one additional item. If one knew how many words an individual passed, he would know exactly which items that person passed.

Evaluation of the Guttman scale. In spite of the intuitive appeal of the Guttman scale, it is highly impractical. First, it is highly unrealistic to think that items could have trace lines like those in Figure 9.8. No item correlates perfectly with any attribute. Although there is no way to obtain the trace lines directly, some good approximations are available. For example, with items concerning spelling, the number of words correctly spelled can be used as an approximation of the attribute (true scores in spelling). When the trace line is obtained in such instances, not only is it not perpendicular at a point, but it typically tends to have a relatively flat, approximately linear form. Typically, individual items correlate no higher than .40 with total scores. Consequently it is very unreasonable to work with a model that assumes perfect biserial correlations between items and an attribute.

Second, having the triangular pattern of data is no guarantee that items have trace lines like those in Figure 9.8. If items are spaced far enough apart in difficulty (popularity on nonability items), the triangular pattern can be obtained even if the trace lines are very flat rather than vertical. This is illustrated with the following four items.

a. Solve for x: $x^2 + 2x + 9 = 16$.
b. What is the meaning of the word "severe"?
c. How much is 10 X 38?
d. When do you use an umbrella? (given orally)

Although the author has not performed the experiment, the above four items administered to persons ranging in age from six to sixteen probably would form an excellent Guttman scale. Any person who got the first item correct probably could get the others correct. Any person who failed the first item but got the second correct would probably get the other two correct. Those four items would produce the required triangular pattern of data even though there is good evidence that they do not all belong to the same attribute ("factor," in the language of factor analysis). The reason they apparently fit the model for a unidimensional scale is that they are administered to an extremely diverse population. They would not fit the model if they were investigated within one age group only. Consequently, as was suggested earlier, it is not entirely logical to assume that having a triangular pattern of data like that in Table 9.1 is *sufficient* evidence for the presence of a unidimensional scale.

Because the triangular pattern of data can be approximated in any study where items vary greatly in difficulty, in practice this results in scales with very few items (seldom more than eight). To take an extreme case, if there are three items that respectively are passed by 10%, 50%, and 90% of the people, the triangular pattern will be obtained almost perfectly regardless of what the items concern. The difficulties of items can be dispersed in this way only if the final scale contains a small number of items. This usually is done by starting with a relatively large number of items (say, 20) and discarding all items but a few that vary widely in difficulty. This is only a way of fooling one's self into believing that a unidimensional scale has been obtained when it really has not. Also, since such scales seldom

have more than eight items, they can make only rather gross distinctions among people.

A third criticism of the Guttman scale is that it seeks to obtain only an ordinal measurement of human attributes. There are good reasons for believing that it is possible to measure human attributes on interval scales, if not usually on ratio scales. If psychology were to settle only for ordinal measurement, it would so limit the usable methods of mathematics that the science would be nearly crippled.

In summary, the deterministic model underlying the Guttman scale is thoroughly illogical for most psychological measurement because (1) almost no items exist that fit the model, (2) the presence of a triangular pattern is a necessary but not sufficient condition for the fit of the model in particular instances, (3) the triangular pattern can be (and usually is) artificially forced by dealing with a small number of items that vary greatly in difficulty, and (4) the model aspires only to develop ordinal scales. Considering this heavy weight of criticism, it is surprising that some people still consider this deterministic model a good basis for developing measures of psychological attributes.

Nonmonotone deterministic models. There are other deterministic models in addition to the Guttman scale (Torgerson, 1958). One of these makes the following assumptions. Each item is responded to in manner alpha by all the people at one level, and each person responds in manner alpha to only one item. Trace lines for three such items are shown in Figure 9.9. The pattern of data produced by such a model is shown in Table 9.2. In constrast to the Guttman scale, in this deterministic model each item has a nonmonotone trace line; that is, the line goes up and then comes down. The following four items would fit this model.

	Yes	No
a. Are you between 6 feet 3 inches tall and 6 feet 6?	_____	_____
b. Are you between 6 feet tall and 6 feet 3 inches?	_____	_____
c. Are you between 5 feet 9 inches tall and 6 feet?	_____	_____
d. Are you between 5 feet 6 inches tall and 5 feet 9?	_____	_____

Using the word "items" in the broadest sense, it would be very rare to find any items on psychological measures that would fit this model. All the criticisms that apply to the Guttman scale apply with added force to this nonmonotone deterministic model.

Deterministic models are of use mainly to specialists in the theory of psychological measurement. Such models frequently represent "limiting cases" of models

TABLE 9.2

Item	Person			
	1	2	3	4
a	X			
b		X		
c			X	
d				X

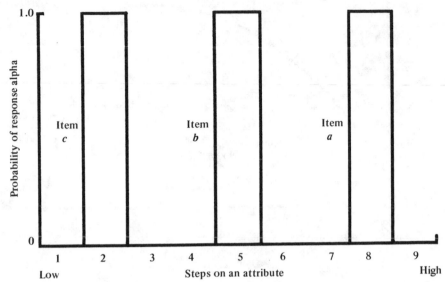

FIGURE 9.9   Trace lines for three items that meet the requirements of a nonmonotone, deterministic scaling model.

that are actually used to develop measures of psychological attributes. Other than this use, they are only interesting museum pieces. Only by working with some type of nondeterministic probability model can one develop the measures needed in research.

Probability Models for Scaling People

If trace lines are not assumed to have perpendicular ascents and descents, one is working with some type of probability model. There are numerous types of probability models, depending on the type of curve assumed for the trace lines. The most prominent models are discussed in the following sections.

Nonmonotone models. Analogous to nonmonotone deterministic models such as the one discussed above, there are nonmonotone probability models. Any type of curve that changes slope at some point from positive to negative or vice versa is nonmonotone. Some examples are shown in Figure 9.10. The only nonmonotone model that has been used frequently assumes that (1) the attribute is continuous and (2) each item has a trace line that approximates the normal distribution. The probability of responding in manner alpha is highest at a particular point on the attribute, and from that point the probability of responding in manner alpha falls off in both directions in general resemblance to the normal curve. Three such items are shown in Figure 9.11.

Trace lines need not be exactly normal, and standard deviations of trace lines need not be identical. This model has been used for only one purpose: the development of certain types of attitude scales. Because the scaling procedure was developed by Thurstone, the type of scale is referred to as a "Thurstone scale of attitudes." Items at three points on such a scale are as follows.

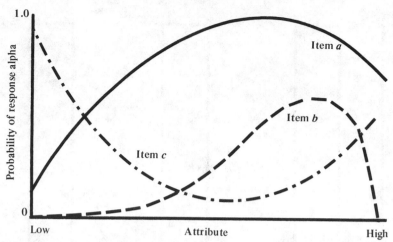

FIGURE 9.10   Three items with nonmonotone trace lines.

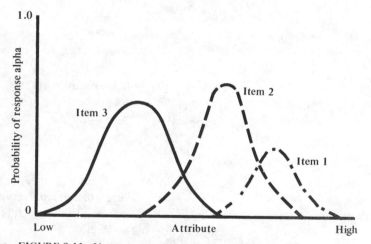

FIGURE 9.11   Nonmonotone, normal trace lines for three items.

	Agree	Disagree
1. I believe that the church is the greatest institution in America today.	_____	_____
2. When I go to church I enjoy a fine ritual service with good music.	_____	_____
3. The paternal and benevolent attitude of the church is quite distasteful to me.	_____	_____

The first step in obtaining a Thurstone scale is to have a large number of attitude statements rated by about 100 judges (see Edwards, 1957, for a complete discussion of procedures). Each statement is usually rated on an 11-step scale ranging from "strongly favorable statement" to "strongly unfavorable statement." Ten to twenty items are selected from the larger collection of items according to the

following two standards: (1) items that have small standard deviations of ratings over judges, that is, agreement is good among judges about where the items belong on the scale, and (2) items that range evenly from one extreme to the other.

The essence of the Thurstone nonmonotone model is that each item should tend to receive agreement (response alpha) at only one zone of the attribute. To assume an approximately normal distribution for the trace line is to admit that each item occasions some error.

The major fault of the Thurstone scale and of other nonmonotone probability models is that it is very difficult to find any items that fit. The model obviously would not fit most types of items. For example, how could one find spelling words such that each would be correctly spelled only by persons in a narrow band of the attribute of spelling ability? An item that "peaked" at the lower end of the scale would be one that is spelled correctly only by rather poor spellers. For an item that peaked in the middle of the scale, very few people with superior ability in spelling would give a correct response. This type of scale clearly does not apply to any items measuring capabilities.

Even with responses concerning sentiments, the Thurstone model would seem to apply only to certain types of statements relating to attitudes, and even there the model is in logical trouble. Attitude statements tend to fit this model only if they are "double-barreled," only if they say two things, one of which is good and the other bad. This can be seen by a careful analysis of the three attitude statements given earlier. In item 2, the subject is asked to agree simultaneously with two hidden statements:

I sometimes go to church.
I probably would not go to church if it were not for a fine ritual service with good music.

Item 3 is "triple-barreled." To agree with it, the subject must agree that the church is paternal, benevolent, and distasteful. The three modifiers add up to a moderately negative attitude toward the church. It is possible to construct such items only by subtly building two or more statements into what is ostensibly one statement. This type of item not only is very difficult to construct, but tends to be ambiguous to subjects. Some subjects respond to one of the hidden statements and some subjects to another. In a more exaggerated form, this ambiguity is evidenced in the following double-barreled statement:

The church is a wonderful, horrible institution.

Another important criticism of nonmonotone probability models is that it is very difficult to think of items for the ends of the scale that would fit. This is illustrated with item 1 in the previous example. Who could have so positive an attitude toward the church that he would *disagree* with the statement, "I believe the church is the greatest institution in America today"? Such items necessarily are monotone, continuing to rise as one reaches higher and higher levels of the attribute.

In summary, nonmonotone probability models conceivably apply only to certain types of items for the measurement of attitudes, and there are better ways to construct attitude scales.

Monotone models with specified distribution forms. In some of the models that concern monotone trace lines, it is assumed that the trace lines fit a particular statistical function. Most frequently it has been assumed that the function is a *normal ogive.* (A normal ogive is a cumulative normal distribution.) In Figure 9.12 are shown three items having normal-ogive trace lines. The important feature of a normal-ogive trace line is that it is much more discriminating at certain levels of the attribute than it is at neighboring levels. The zone where discrimination is good is that below the steeply ascending part of the curve. The steeper the section of the curve, the higher is the biserial correlation of that item with the attribute. If that section were vertical, the "tails" would disappear, the item would correlate perfectly with the attribute, and a collection of such items would form a Guttman scale. As items correlate less and less with the attribute, the S shape tends to flatten toward a straight line and the slope approaches the horizontal.

The normal-ogive model is appealing for two reasons. First, it makes good sense intuitively. Thus, for each item, one can think of a critical zone on the attribute where there is considerable uncertainty concerning how people will respond. As one moves away from that zone in either direction, the uncertainty is markedly reduced. Persons below that zone will predominately fail the item, and persons above it will predominately pass. An increasing slope of the trace line over some zone is more to be expected than, say, a straight line.

The second reason for the appeal of this model is that it has very useful mathematical properties that permit the deduction of many important principles (Lord, 1952a). For example, the sum of any number of normal ogives is also a normal ogive, and the exact shape and slope of the latter can be predicted from the ogives which are summed. Then if one obtains a scale by summing scores on individual items (e.g., enumerating the number correct), the average scores or sums of scores form a normal-ogive relationship with the attribute. (The sum of probabilities for any number of normal ogives over a point on an attribute would be the expected sum of scores on the test as a whole for persons at that point.) This means

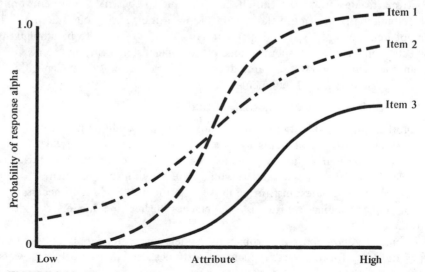

FIGURE 9.12   Three items with normal-ogive trace lines.

that summing scores on items to obtain total scores (which is the usual approach) produces a scale that is *not* linearly related to the attribute. However, in practice this is a very slight danger, because even if the trace lines do form normal ogives, the curves are so flat that they are hard to distinguish from straight lines. Also, when items are combined that vary considerably in difficulty, combined normal ogives look less S shaped than if all items are equally difficult. For these two reasons, even if one accepts the normal-ogive model, it is reasonable to assume that total test scores have an approximately linear relationship with the attribute.

There are many other interesting deductions from the normal-ogive model. The most discriminating collection of items for any particular point on the attribute would be those items whose sum of ogives is as steep as possible over that point. This fact permits some interesting deductions about the relations among discrimination at a point, difficulty of items, and correlations of items with total scores (Lord, 1952b). Other interesting deductions from this model concern the amount of measurement error (unreliability) for a test corresponding to different points on the attribute.

In addition to the normal ogive, other statistical functions have been proposed for trace lines. The function that has achieved most use in this respect is the logistic curve. To the naked eye the logistic curve and the normal ogive are very much the same. The advantage of the logistic curve is that it is much easier to work with mathematically. Very much the same deductions are made from both types of curves.

An important point to grasp in discussing monotone models with specified distribution forms is that these models have not led to ways of scaling persons other than by the conventional approach, which is to sum scores on items. Thus if one is scaling spelling ability, these models do not argue against the conventional method of scaling, which is to count the number of words correctly spelled. The situation is the same with all other attributes. What these models do is to permit some important deductions about the psychometric characteristics of measures that are obtained by summing item scores, and for that purpose, they have proved very useful.

Monotone models with unspecified distribution forms. Finally we arrive at the model that underlies most efforts to scale people (and lower animals). The model makes three major assumptions. First, it is assumed only that each item has a monotonic trace line. It is not assumed that all items have the same type of monotonic curve. Second, it is assumed that the sum of trace lines for a particular set of items (the trace line for total test scores) is approximately linear: that is, even if items do not have the same type of monotonic trace line, it is assumed that departures from linearity tend to average out as items are combined. A family of such trace lines is shown in Figure 9.13. The sum of these trace lines is shown in Figure 9.14, which is the trace line of expected scores on a four-item test.

The third assumption is that the items as a whole tend to measure only the attribute in question. This is the same as saying that the items have only one factor in common. The implication is that total scores on the particular collection of items summarize all of the information about psychological attributes that is inherent in the item scores.

The three assumptions discussed above constitute the *linear model,* or, as it is frequently called, the *summative model.* It is said to be "linear" for two reasons. First, it is assumed that the sum of item scores has an approximately linear

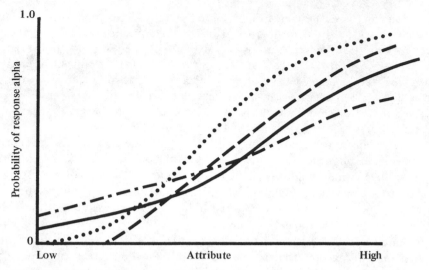

FIGURE 9.13   A family of four items with monotone trace lines.

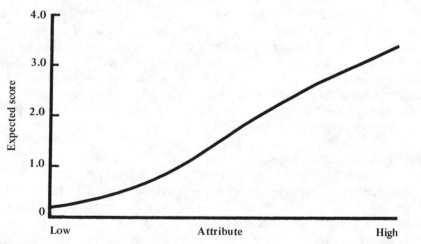

FIGURE 9.14   Expected scores on a four-item test—the sum of trace lines in Figure 9.13.

relationship with the attribute in question. Second, and more important for the sake of the name, the model leads to a *linear combination* of items. A simple sum of variables is a linear combination of variables, and a simple sum of item scores is a linear combination of those scores.

If one looks carefully at psychological measures, he will see that in nearly all cases they consist of summing scores over items. Spelling ability is measured by summing scores over items, that is, by simply counting the number of words correctly spelled. In paired-associate learning, the amount learned by each person is measured by counting the number of pairs correctly recalled. In a measure of attitudes toward the United Nations, a total score is obtained by summing the number of agreements to positive statements and the number of disagreements with negative statements.

The linear model applies to multipoint items as well as to items which are scored dichotomously. Reaction time in a particular experiment would be determined by averaging the reaction times for a subject in a block of trials. Total scores on an essay examination in history would be obtained by summing scores on individual questions. Attitudes toward the United Nations would be obtained by summing the ratings of 10 statements of a seven-step scale of agreement-disagreement.

It is not difficult to thing of psychological measures that fit the linear model; rather, it is difficult to think of measures that do not fit the model. In this chapter we have come a long way around to the conclusion that the most sensible way to measure psychological attributes of people is to sum scores on items. The essence of the linear model is that it does not take individual items very seriously. It recognizes that the individual item has considerable specificity and measurement error. It does not make stringent assumptions about the trace line. The only assumption made is that each item has some form of monotonic trace line, and even that is not a strict assumption, since some of the items could have slightly curvilinear trace lines and a linear relationship of total scores with the attribute would still be obtainable.

The remainder of this chapter and the following are based mostly on the linear model. This model makes sense and works well in practice. At the present time there is no serious challenge on the scene for the scaling of people with respect to psychological attributes.

TEST CONSTRUCTION

Previously, the summative (or linear) model was accepted as the best available approach to the measurement of individual differences among people. The model stipulates that test scores are to be obtained by summing scores over items. The items can be weighted or unweighted, and either they can all have positive signs in the combination or some can have negative signs. All these possibilities are subsumed under the concept of a linear combination of test items.

Whereas it will be convenient to speak of "test construction," the principles in this chapter apply to all forms of psychological measurement, for example, to physiological measures of anxiety, to measures of social activity in classroom groups, and to measures of delinquent behavior. The principles apply to any measure that is obtained from a linear combination of individual responses, items on mental tests constituting only a special case. The principles apply to measures of capability and sentiments; and they apply both to dichotomous items and to items scorable on more than two points.

Depending on the way tests are used, one of three standards of validity applies: predictive validity, content validity, or construct validity. (A detailed discussion of test validity may be found in Chapter 10.) As will be discussed more fully later in the chapter, the methods of test construction used for measures intended to have predictive validity and for those intended to have construct validity should be the same. Somewhat different methods of test construction are required, however, for instruments that depend primarily on content validity. First, brief mention will be made of principles concerning the construction of measures intended to have

content validity, and then the remainder of the chapter will be devoted to principles concerning the construction of measures intended to serve the other two functions.

Construction of Achievement Tests

The achievement test is the most obvious example of a measure that requires content validity. The term "achievement test" will be used in a general sense to refer to (1) examinations in individual courses of instruction in schools of all kinds and at all levels, (2) standardized measures of achievement used routinely by all the instructors in a particular unit of instruction, (3) commercially distributed tests of achievement used throughout the country, and (4) achievement tests constructed specifically for various types of evaluation research. Such measures of achievement are very frequently employed at all levels of education up through graduate school and professional training, in civil service examinations, and in special training programs in military establishments and in industry.

Achievement tests are prominently featured in many forms of evaluation research. An example would be in a city-sponsored program of involving volunteer men in the rehabilitation of delinquent boys. Among other measures that would be used to determine the success of the program, one probably would need to employ achievement tests concerning information volunteers acquired about school regulations, local law enforcement facilities, matters concerning drug usage, current social forces among teenagers, and other information that would be helpful in the work with delinquent youth. Another example of the place of achievement tests in evaluation research is in programs of the federal government to assist the people of underdeveloped countries. In the course of training such individuals, it would be expected that they would learn a great deal about the human and material aspects of the regions to which they would be sent. Specially constructed achievement tests would be very useful for that purpose. Comprehensive achievement tests would be important aspects of any program of evaluation research which concerned some type of training, even the special types of training mentioned in the two examples above, or the more general type of training involved in any school situation.

The test plan. Ensuring the content validity of an achievement test by an explicit plan for constructing the test is more appropriate than determining the content validity after the test is constructed. If representative persons who are to use the test agree in advance on the appropriateness of the plan, arriving at an acceptable instrument is mainly a matter of technical skill and applied research.

The major part of the test plan is an outline of content for the instrument which is to be constructed. Since content validity depends on a rational appeal to an adequate coverage of important content, an explicit outline of content provides a basis for discussing content validity. For example, an outline of content for a comprehensive achievement test to evaluate the success of a Head Start program would need to indicate whether or not a section on "study skills" was to be included. If it was determined that such a section was appropriate, it would also be necessary to list the aspects of study skills that would be covered, for example, use of the dictionary and locating topics in reference books.

In addition to the outline of content, the plan should describe the types of items to be employed, state the approximate number of items to be employed in each section and each subsection of the test, and give examples of the types of items to be used. The plan also should state how long the test will take to administer, how it will be administered, how it will be scored, and the types of norms that will be obtained.

When the plan is completed, it is reviewed by numerous persons, including teachers, subject-matter experts, administrative officials, and specialists in educational and psychological measurement. Many suggestions may be made for changes, and the revised plan is resubmitted to reviewers. It is hoped that the plan eventually developed is one that receives general approval from reviewers.

Of course, such an elaborate plan would be undertaken only for achievement tests that were to be used for large evaluation programs such as for Head Start or Get Set. At the other extreme, an instructor probably would not develop an elaborate plan for constructing a course examination (an achievement test) which was to be used only with his students. But even in this case it is wise for the instructor to make an outline of the intended coverage. This will provide a basis for judging the adequacy of coverage, and a discussion of the outline with fellow instructors will help ensure content validity.

Test items. Of course, a test can be no better than the items of which it is composed. A good plan represents an *intention* to construct a good test, but unless items are skillfully written, the plan never materializes. Although there are some rules for writing good items (see Nunnally, 1972, 2nd ed., chap. 6), writing test items is an art few people seem to master. Most frequently, items are marred by two shortcomings. First, they are ambiguous, because they fail to "aim" students adequately toward the type of response required. A classic example is, "What happened to art during the fifteenth century?" The question is so vague that the student could take many different directions on an essay examination and could legitimately select several different alternatives on a multiple-choice item. A second major fault is that items often concern trivial aspects of the subject matter. To write items that are unambiguous and to write them as quickly as possible, it is tempting to populate tests with items concerning dates, names, and simple facts. Most instructors will agree that the memory for simple details is not the important thing to be measured; what is important is to measure various aspects of "reasoning with" the subject matter. But regardless of the type of item employed, it takes considerable skill to write items that adequately measure a true understanding of principles.

There is a choice as to which type of item will be employed, including short-answer essay questions, longer essay questions, and numerous types of objective items. Among objective items, the multiple-choice item is considered the best for most purposes. For three reasons, commercially distributed achievement tests rely almost solely on multiple-choice items. First, they are very easy to administer and score. Second, expert item writers who are highly skilled at composing such items are available. Third, when multiple-choice items are skillfully composed, they can accurately measure almost anything. Time and again it has been shown

that a test composed of good multiple-choice items correlates with an essay test of the same topic almost as highly as the reliability of the latter will permit. Since the multiple-choice test typically is much more reliable than the essay test, the conclusion is inescapable that the objective test is more valid. This relationship tends to hold even with material where intuitively it would not seem possible, for example, in comparison of a multiple-choice test for the pronunciation of a foreign language with scores given on oral exercises.

Although in some instances it logically would be very difficult to employ multiple-choice items to measure achievement (e.g., English composition), most of the major achievement tests have no essay questions. In practice, though, this is not always a major disadvantage. When essay questions are used in achievement tests, they usually correlate so highly with other sections of the test that they can be omitted. Thus, for example, when essay questions are tried as measures of English composition, they tend to add little new variance to what can be explained by multiple-choice tests of vocabulary, reading comprehension, and grammar. This is partly because of a high degree of overlap between abilities required in the objective items and ability in English composition.

In addition to higher reliability and ease of scoring, another advantage of multiple-choice items is that they usually sample the topic much more broadly than would be possible on essay examinations. For example, a 50-minute classroom examination could easily employ 50 multiple-choice items without excessively rushing students, but it would be difficult to employ more than 5 one-page essay questions in the same amount of time. How well students performed on the essay questions would depend to some extent on their "luck" regarding which questions were asked, but such luck (measurement error because of the sampling of content) would tend to average out over 50 multiple-choice items. Since there is measurement error because of the sampling of content and an equally large amount of measurement error because of the subjectivity of scoring, the multiple-choice examination is usually much more reliable than the essay examination. A typical finding would be an alternative-form reliability between .60 and .70 for the essay examination and a reliability between .80 and .90 for the multiple-choice examination. Although the skillful item writer can measure almost anything with multiple-choice items, this is not true for many nonprofessionals, particularly those not familiar with principles of measurement and without considerable practice in constructing objective tests.

After test items are constructed, they should be critically reviewed. For important achievement tests, a careful review is done by a number of persons. First, the items would be reviewed by experts in test construction. They would consider each item for its appropriateness, apparent difficulty, and clarity. The items that survived that review would then be reviewed by teachers, program administrators, and other persons involved in the program being evaluated.

Item analysis. Although content validity mainly rests on rational rather than empirical grounds, results from applying an instrument do provide some important types of information. The first step in obtaining such information is to administer a large collection of items to a large sample of persons who are representative of the

individuals with whom the final test will be employed. To have ample room to discard items that work poorly, there should be at least twice as many items as will appear on the final test. All items should be administered to at least 300 persons, preferably to 1,000 or more. Because there are so many opportunities for taking advantage of chance in item analysis, unless there are at least five times as many persons as items, the results may be highly misleading. For this reason, few instructors obtain enough data for their test items to warrant an item analysis.

If computational resources are available for the purpose, the most important type of item analysis of achievement tests is done by correlating each item with the total test score. If the test has different parts for different topics (e.g., reading and science), each item should be correlated with the subscore for its section rather than with scores on the test as a whole. The proper coefficient is point-biserial, which is the product moment (PM) formula applied to the relationship between a dichotomous item and a multipoint distribution of scores.

Any item that correlates near zero with test scores should be carefully inspected. In an achievement test, it is possible for an item to correlate near zero with total scores and still be a valid item, but that rarely is the case. It is more likely that the item is excessively difficult or easy, is ambiguous, or actually has little to do with the topic. Unless there are strong grounds for deciding otherwise, such items generally should be discarded. Among the remaining items, those that correlate higher with total scores generally are the better items. They probably are less ambiguous; they cannot be very extreme in difficulty in either direction; and they will tend to make the final test highly reliable. After items have passed reviews by measurement experts and other persons, the steps in item analysis are almost identical to those in the item analysis of predictor tests and measures of constructs; consequently a more complete discussion of methods of item analysis will be reserved for a later section of this chapter.

Again it should be emphasized that item analysis of achievement tests is secondary to content validity. With achievement tests considerable pains are taken to ensure that all items have content validity *before* they are submitted to item analysis. Thus all items submitted for analysis are assumed to be good, and the analysis only provides additional information. But more important than the information obtained from item analysis is the initial decision to use a particular item in a tryout form of the test. Also, regardless of what is found in item analysis, the final decision to include or reject an item is based primarily on human judgment. For example, in each section of most achievement tests, the first several items are very easy. These are included to prevent some students from becoming discouraged and to give all students some practice with the particular type of item. Because nearly everyone correctly answers these items, purely on the basis of an item analysis these items might appear worthless.

Norms. In standardizing achievement tests, one of the most important steps is the establishment of norms. In the broadest sense of the word, "norms" are any scores that provide a frame of reference for interpreting the scores of particular persons. With achievement tests for measuring progress in elementary school, usually the set of norms would be based on scores made by a representative cross

section of students across the country. In addition it is useful to have local norms, such as norms based on samples of students in a particular locality and in a particular school. Then the score of a particular student can be compared with scores of students across the country, students in the same locality, and students in the same school.

Whether or not norms are required in evaluation research depends on the type of research. For example, if several differently treated groups are compared with one another and with a control group, there is no strong need for general test norms. The differences among the groups are directly interpretable. However, if there were no control group in that instance, the availability of norms (e.g., for reading comprehension) would considerably aid the interpretation of results.

Norms usually are expressed both in the form of transformed standard scores and as percentiles. For the former, a widely used method is to convert raw scores to a distribution having a mean of 500 and a standard deviation of 100. Essentially, a percentile indicates the percentage of persons in the normative sample that is *below* a particular score. Thus if 80% of the students score less than 122, a person with a score of 122 is at the 80th percentile. Such percentiles would be completely interpretable, however, only if no two students made the same score. Consequently in practice, percentiles are computed by dividing the total number of students tested into the number of students below a particular score plus half the students who make that score.

A strong case can be made that percentiles are easier to interpret than are transformed standard scores. The only way to accurately interpret transformed standard scores is to do some mental arithmetic to figure how many standard deviations a person is above or below the mean and how many persons would be above and below that point. Obviously, then, working with percentiles directly is easier than going through such mental gyrations.

Good norms, although important in many uses of achievement tests in evaluation research, are not highly important for predictor tests and measures of constructs. For the former, one could effectively employ a predictor test in a particular setting even if he had no idea how many people in general would score on the instrument. For measures of constructs, the major effort is to obtain reliable variance for the groups being investigated regardless of any information that might be supplied by norms. With predictor tests and measures of constructs, norms mainly are useful in indicating whether research results might have been somewhat different with different types of people, for example, effects on correlations because of restriction in range of scores.

The Criterion-Oriented Approach to Test Construction

There are two *incorrect* ways to construct tests: one is to select items according to their correlations with a criterion and the other is to select items according to their difficulty. Even if both methods are thought to be incorrect, they have been advocated and used so much in the past that it will be necessary to explain them in some detail. In this section will be discussed the criterion-oriented approach. By "criteria" are meant scores relating to some type of performance in daily life, such

as school grades, amount of sales by insurance agents, and ratings of the skill of airplane pilots.

The criterion-oriented approach evolved from the following faulty line of reasoning. First, you ask yourself, "Why construct a test?" Then you answer, "To predict a criterion." If that were so, what would be the best items for the test? Obviously, items that individually correlate well with the criterion. The more each item correlates with the criterion, the more the total test score will correlate with the criterion. According to this line of reasoning, the obvious thing to do is (1) compose a large group of items, (2) administer them to a large sample of individuals in the situation where the tests will be used, (3) correlate each item with the criterion, for example, grades in some course of training, and (4) fashion a test out of those items that correlate most highly with the criterion.

Following this line of reasoning further, there is a way to improve on the foregoing method for the selection of test items. Assuming that one has found a large number of items that correlate well with the criterion, one can further select items in terms of their correlations with one another. Should the items in the final test correlate highly with one another? According to the criterion-oriented approach, the answer is "No." This conclusion follows from the logic of multiple correlation. It will be remembered that, if a number of variables each correlate positively with a criterion, the multiple correlation is higher when the predictors correlate as little as possible with one another. The maximum multiple correlation would be obtained when the predictors had zero correlations with one another. The same logic would hold for a linear combination of items. When items have low correlations with one another and each correlates positively with the criterion, each item adds information to that provided by the other items; and when scores are summed over items, a relatively high correlation with the criterion will be found.

It will be remembered that the average correlation of an item with the other items on a test is highly related to the correlation of that item with total scores on the test. Then, according to this logic, one would select items that correlated highly with the criterion and had low correlations with total test scores. After these two sets of correlations are obtained, they can be plotted as in Figure 9.15. One then selects items from the indicated region of the figure. If there are enough items in that region, they are used to form the final test.

What is wrong with the criterion-oriented approach. By this point it must be apparent that something is badly wrong with the criterion-oriented approach. By this method one would select a polyglot group of items with low internal consistency. The estimated reliability (to be discussed in the next chapter) would be low, and consequently there would be no strong common core (factor) in the items. Since the items would tend to measure different things, there would be no rational basis for the construction of an alternative form.

The major error in the criterion-oriented approach is in the original premise that the purpose of constructing a test is to predict a *particular* criterion. This is seldom the guiding principle in constructing a test. It obviously is not the reason for constructing measures that require content validity and construct validity. In either case, if one had a criterion (whatever that would be), there would be no need to

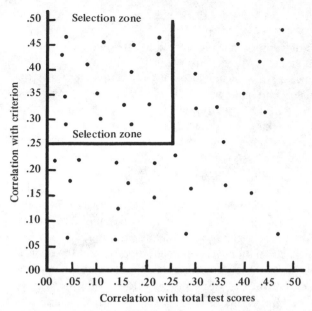

FIGURE 9.15   Scatter diagram of item correlations with a criterion and with total test scores.

construct tests. As has been argued previously, with measures that require content validity there logically is no empirical criterion. Although construct validity partly depends on correlations among different proposed measures of a construct, no one of them can be considered the criterion. Since most measures used in basic research require construct validity, the criterion-oriented approach clearly does not apply. Since in applied work there are many more uses of achievement tests (measures that require content validity) than of predictor tests, the logic obviously does not hold in most applied work.

The only sphere in which the criterion-oriented approach is not obviously inappropriate is in applied work with predictor tests. It will be shown, however, that the logic does not apply there either. It is almost always poor strategy to *construct* a test to measure a particular criterion; it is better to *select* tests of known factorial composition as potential predictors of a criterion. Instead of forming hypotheses about types of *items* that might be predictive of a criterion, it is better to form hypotheses about types of *whole tests* that might be predictive of a criterion.

There is no intention to imply here that it is wrong to construct new tests with respect to applied problems of prediction, but when they are so constructed, they should not be constructed according to the criterion-oriented approach. Each such test should be homogeneous in content. Of course, one would want to find the correlation of scores with the criterion, and if that were reasonably high, one would want to learn the factor composition of the measure by correlating it with measures of existing factors. Gradually, in this way, tests constructed for prediction problems add to what is known about factors in general.

Some will argue that the criterion usually is factorially complex and consequently can be predicted best by a factorially complex predictor test. Instead of building the factorial complexity into a particular test, however, it is far better to meet the factorial complexity by combining tests in a battery by multiple regression, in which case tests would be selected to measure the different factors that are thought to be important. If items are selected by the criterion-oriented approach, one really does not know *what* factors are being measured. Also, the importance of each factor in the test would be determined by the number of items that happened to be present for the factor, and thus would not be rationally related to the importance of the factor in the criterion. The ideal way to combine factors is by multiple regression, and this can be done only by having relatively homogeneous tests relating to each factor. With the criterion-oriented approach, one knows neither what factors are involved in the omnibus test nor what weights are being given to different factors. The fallacy is in assuming that the criterion is to be predicted with *one* test, which to be effective must be heterogeneous in content. It is far better to predict a criterion with a battery of tests, each of which is homogeneous in content.

Before concluding this section it should be made clear that the foregoing criticisms are leveled at methods of test construction based on the correlations of items with *criteria of success in daily life,* such as grades in college, amounts of sales by insurance salesmen, and ratings of effectiveness of airplane pilots. Criticisms in this section are not leveled at *all* attempts to construct tests wholly or in part by the investigation of correlations of items with some variable external to the items. An example in point is that of selecting items in terms of their correlations with a known factor of human ability or personality. This is a very useful adjunct to the methods for constructing homogeneous tests which will be discussed in a later section.

Constructing Tests in Terms of Item Difficulties

For constructing measures of constructs and measures to be used as predictors, a second *incorrect* approach concerns the selection of items in terms of their difficulties. Although the difficulty levels of items do provide important information, this information is secondary to information obtained from correlations among the items. (How to use the latter type of information will be discussed in the next section.)

It will be remembered that the difficulty of any dichotomous item (p value) is the fraction of persons tested who receive a score of 1 rather than a score of zero. On tests of ability, a score of 1 means that the individual passes the item; on nonability tests (e.g., a measure of suggestibility), a score of 1 is indicative of a high rather than a low score on the attribute. On a spelling test, a p value of .9 would mean that 90% of the persons tested passed the item, correctly spelled the spoken word or marked the correct alternative on a printed test.

In test construction, p values are important because they influence the characteristics of score distributions. The p values directly determine the mean score, the mean being the sum of the p values. The mean is only of incidental importance,

however, in the construction of tests. More important, the p values influence the shape and dispersion of test scores. (These are also influenced by the number of items and the correlations among items.) If the average p value is far removed from .5 in either direction, the distribution will tend to be skewed (particularly when the number of items is small, e.g., less than 20), and the standard deviation will tend to be small. Consequently, since it usually is desired to have approximately symmetrical distribution and to disperse people as much as possible, an argument can be made for having an average p value of .5. In addition, even if the average p value is .5, the standard deviation of test scores is larger when all the p values are near .5 rather than scattered widely above and below that point. Then, to disperse people as much as possible (to discriminate among them), one could argue that it is desirable for all test items to have p values close to .5. A test composed of items of that kind is referred to as a *peaked test.*

What is wrong with this approach. The faults in selecting items in terms of p values are not nearly so blatant as those in selecting items in terms of the criterion-oriented approach. Also, the point is not that selecting items in terms of p values is incorrect, but rather that there is a much better way to select them. Purely by selecting items so as to obtain a peaked test, one might end up with a very good instrument. If after the items were selected, they proved to have a high reliability, it might be subsequently found that the new measure related importantly with other supposed measures of a construct and/or proved effective in predicting particular criteria. If these things happened, after the fact it must be agreed that the method of test construction worked well in that instance. The important point, however, is that, a priori, there are reasons such pleasant results might not be obtained.

For reasons discussed previously, "good" items are ones that correlate well with one another. Since the correlations of items with total scores on a test are directly related to their sums of correlations with one another, it can be said that "good" items are ones that correlate highly with total test scores. This doctrine will be explained more fully in the next section, but first it will be useful to see what implications this doctrine has for the selection of items in terms of p values.

The p values only place *upper limits* on correlations of items with total scores. (The reason is discussed in detail in Nunnally, 1967: 251-252.) A p value near .5 does not *guarantee* a high correlation with total scores. In a particular analysis, it is possible to find that all the items with p values near .5 have correlations near zero with total scores and that items with p values well removed from .5 have respectable correlations with total scores. Actually, in addition to the possible advantages of having p values near .5, in some cases there are reasons for being suspicious of such items. Clearly, one would not consider it good to have true-false items with p values of .5, because that would suggest that the items were so difficult that everyone guessed. A test composed of such items would have a reliability near zero. There is even more reason to be suspicious of items on some nonability tests that have p values near .5. For example, on a personality inventory composed of agree-disagree items, any item that is highly ambiguous will tend to have a p value near .5. Since subjects are unable to understand the item, they mentally "flip coins" in giving an answer. In a sense, on personality inventories it is comforting to

find that an item has a p value somewhat removed from .5 (e.g., .7), because it at least suggests that the majority of people were able to understand the item well enough to reject or accept it.

An item on a peaked test *may* be a good item, the crucial standard being whether or not it actually correlates well with total scores on the test. It is equally possible, however, that the item might not have a high correlation with total scores. This could be either because the item is very unreliable or because it reliably measures something different from the majority of items in the test. Since the crucial consideration is how much the item actually correlates with total scores, why not select items mainly in terms of those correlations? That is what will be advocated in the next section.

Construction of Homogeneous Tests

Much of what has been said so far in this chapter argues for the construction of homogeneous tests. Only some of the most important arguments will be reiterated. It was emphasized that measurement always concerns an *attribute*. An attribute is some isolatable characteristic of organisms, some dimension of structure or function along which organisms can be ordered. Items within a measure are useful only to the extent that they share a common core, the attribute which is to be measured. The linear model was accepted as providing a reasonable approach to the construction of most measures in psychology, particularly for the construction of measures concerning individual differences among subjects. Most frequently, the model leads to a simple summation of item scores to obtain total scores. In summing scores, it is assumed that each item adds something to the others, and unless the items shared an attribute, it would not be meaningful to sum scores over items.

The major theory of reliability (discussed in the next chapter) is based on the domain-sampling model, which assumes that each test is a random sample of items from a domain. One of the major deductions from that model is that the reliability of a test composed of a sample of items is directly related to the average correlation among the items. Eventually it will be possible to understand the cardinal dimensions of human attributes only when relatively complete factor structures are known for different types of abilities and personality characteristics. The best measures of each factor will be those that correlate highly with one factor and have low correlations with other factors.

Implicit in the considerations above is the premise that tests should be as homogeneous in content as possible. (One could debate the wisdom of this statement if the average correlation among items were much higher than that found in practice.) The homogeneity of content in a test is manifested in the average correlation among items and in the pattern of those correlations. If the average correlation among items is very low (and thus the average correlation of items with total scores is low), the items as a group are not homogeneous. This may be because all the correlations are low or because a number of different factors are present in the items. In the latter case there would be a number of item clusters, each cluster being relatively homogeneous, but the clusters would have either near-zero or negative correlations with one another. The ideal is to obtain a collection of items

which has a high average correlation with total scores and is dominated by one factor only.

Factor analysis of items. Considering the last statement above regarding the ideal statistical properties of a good test, it might be thought that the ideal approach to test construction would be through factor analysis. It will be argued, however, that *constructing* tests on the basis of factor analysis usually is not as wise as investigating the factorial composition of tests after they are constructed. This is a controversial point of view, and it is recognized that those who advocate the construction of tests through factor analysis have some good points on their side.

One important reason for not beginning test construction with factor analysis is that such analyses are seldom highly successful. The results from factor analysis usually are clearest when the correlations among whole tests or individual items vary considerably. For example, if some of the correlations among tests are zero and other correlations are as high as .70, this suggests that the tests tend to divide up into clearly defined clusters, or factors. If two tests relate strongly to a factor, they are expected to correlate substantially and to have low correlations with tests that relate strongly to other factors. Then it becomes apparent that for a group of variables (either whole tests or test items) to clearly define a number of factors, there must be a wide range of correlations in the matrix. This very seldom occurs in matrices of correlations among items. On most tests the average correlation among items is less than .20, and the variance of correlations among items is small. A typical finding would be that two-thirds of the correlations were between .10 and .30. To the extent to which the variance of correlations is larger than that, it typically indicates that there is considerable sampling error because of a relatively small number of subjects being investigated. Because of the small variance in correlations among items, it usually is not possible to document clearly a number of factors by the analysis of such correlations. This is particularly so when the items are scored dichotomously. With multipoint items (e.g., rating scales), the correlations among items usually are higher than they are with dichotomous items, and correspondingly, the variance in correlations among items is greater with multipoint items. Consequently factor analyses of multipoint items have a higher probability of success.

Other reasons for not performing factor analyses of test items are (1) such analyses are extremely laborious, (2) many opportunities arise for taking advantages of chance, and (3) the factors frequently are difficult to interpret.

The hypothesis. A new measure should spring from a hypothesis regarding the existence and nature of an attribute. In some cases a formal hypothesis is deduced from a theory regarding a construct. An example would be deducing hypotheses from theories concerning the construct of anxiety. If, as many people assume, anxiety is a form of "generalized drive," many hypotheses follow regarding the attributes of people who are high in the trait (construct) of anxiety. It would be expected that people who are high in anxiety would be characterized by a relatively low ability to solve familiar problems in novel ways, for example, to write the alphabet from z to a or to solve simple arithmetic problems by a novel approach. Based on this hypothesis, one could construct a pool of items. Although in many

cases there are no formal hypotheses regarding the existence of attributes, at least the investigator should have an informal hypothesis that can be communicated to others. For example, it might be hypothesized that reliable individual differences exist in the tendency to have common rather than uncommon associations. Although the hypothesis would not be deduced from a formal theory, such individual differences, if they exist, might be important for cognitive and affective processes. The hypothesis suggests a number of types of items that might be used to measure the attribute in question. In one type of item, the subject would be given a stimulus word and two possible response words. One of the response words would be a highly common associate of the stimulus word. On each item, the subject would be required to mark the most appropriate associate. Whether the hypothesis follows from a theory or is only a "good idea," it guides the construction of items. Subsequent investigations of the items provide a test of the hypothesis.

Construction of items. One cannot know for sure how many items should be constructed for a new measure until *after* they are constructed and submitted to item analysis. If the standard is to obtain a test with an estimated reliability of .80, item analysis might show that the desired reliability can be obtained with as few as 20 items or that as many as 80 items are required. (The estimates of reliability that one would obtain in this case are based on internal consistency rather than on correlations among alternative forms or other measures. In the general case, the measure of reliability based on internal consistency is referred to as *coefficient alpha*; in the special case where the test concerns dichotomously scored items, the coefficient is referred to as KR-20. These coefficients will be discussed in detail in the next chapter.) There are some rules of thumb that can be used to determine the number of items to be constructed. Usually between 20 and 30 dichotomous items are required to obtain an internal consistency reliability of .80. Also, usually fewer multipoint items than dichotomous items are required to obtain a particular reliability. For example, it is not unusual to find a coefficient alpha of .80 for 10 agree-disagree attitude statements rated on a seven-point scale. How many more items should be constructed than the minimum required depends on what is known from previous studies about the type of item. If it were known that items of a particular type tended to have high internal consistency (e.g., items on vocabulary tests), at most no more than twice as many items would be constructed as has been found in previous studies to be required for a reliable test. In that case, to obtain a reliability of .80, 30 items probably would suffice for the final test. To provide room for the item analysis to eliminate unsatisfactory items, 60 items would be constructed initially. If very little is known about the homogeneity of items of a particular kind, it is wise to err on the conservative side and construct more items than would be the case in the previous example. For example, with the previously mentioned measure of the tendency to give common word associations, if it were desired to obtain a test with a reliability of .80, it would be wise to construct 100 items.

A somewhat different strategy in deciding how many items to construct starts by purposefully constructing a smaller number of items than is thought to be adequate, for example, constructing only 30 items when it is suspected that 30

items will be required to obtain a coefficient alpha of .80. These items are then applied to a relatively small sample of subjects (say 100), and the results are submitted to item analysis. If either the total collection of items (30) or the most homogeneous subset (say, of 15 items) has a coefficient alpha of at least .50, this indicates that it is worth the effort to construct more items, gather responses from a much larger group of subjects, and perform a more complete item analysis. The eventual labor is greater for constructing the test in stages rather than in one large step, but if the results from the first stage of the former method are very discouraging, the project can be abandoned without further loss of time and effort.

Sample of subjects. After items are constructed and before they are submitted to item analysis, they must, of course, be administered to a sample of people. So that the required types of analyses may be performed, all the items should be administered to all the people. Of course, the sample of people used in this phase of test construction should be reasonably representative of the types of people that will be studied with the eventual test. To take a very bad example, if a test is intended to be used primarily with children from eight to ten years of age, it should not be constructed on the basis of data obtained from college students. Except for such extremes, however, the subjects used in test construction need not be exactly representative of those with whom the final test will be used. Also, often a test is used with many different types of subjects (e.g., some attitude scales), and in such cases it is very difficult to ensure that the group of subjects used in test construction is highly representative of all the different groups with which the test eventually will be used.

As is true of all methods of analysis, it is not possible to say in advance exactly how many subjects should be used to obtain data for item analysis. A good rule of thumb, however, is that there should be at least ten times as many subjects as items. (This rule was mentioned previously for factor analysis. It also is a reasonable standard for all forms of multivariate analysis, such as multiple correlation.) In some cases this rule is impractical if there are more than about 70 items. For example, if there are 100 items, it might not be possible to obtain 1,000 subjects. In any case, though, 5 subjects per item should be considered the minimum that can be tolerated.

In gathering data for item analysis, one should administer items under conditions that closely resemble those under which the eventual test will be used. If subjects in the tryout sample are given all the time that they want to complete the items and one intends to place a severe time limit on the eventual test, an item analysis probably will provide very misleading information. If items for a personality inventory are being administered in an atmosphere that encourages frankness and the eventual test is to be administered in an atmosphere where subjects will be reluctant to say bad things about themselves, the item analysis will tell a faulty story.

Item-total correlations. The remainder of this section will consider methods of item analysis when most of the correlations among items (say, at least 90%) are positive. This is almost always the case in measures concerning abilities, that is, where there is a "correct" response for each item. Some of the correlations may be

very close to zero, but if the sample size is large, very few are negative. A later section will consider methods of item analysis when some of the items tend to correlate negatively with the others, as occurs on many personality inventories.

When items predominately correlate positively with one another, those with the highest average correlations are the best items. Since the average correlations of items with one another are highly related to the correlations of items with total scores, the items that correlate most highly with total scores are the best items. Compared to items with relatively low correlations with total scores, those that have higher correlations with total scores have more variance relating to the common factor among the items, and they add more to the test reliability.

The first step in item analysis, then, is to correlate each item with total scores. Thus if there are 60 items, scores are summed over items, and 60 correlations are obtained. If multipoint items are employed, the regular PM coefficient is the correct measure. If dichotomous items are employed, the correct measure is point-biserial, which is only a differently appearing version of the PM formula. The obtained coefficients are then ranked from highest to lowest. If numerous correlations are relatively high (with respect to standards that will be discussed shortly), one is "in business," and a few simple steps can be taken to obtain a final test that has (1) a desired level of reliability, and (2) a desired distribution form, this usually being a symmetrical distribution.

Although many different measures of item-total relationship can be employed in item analysis, there is a wealth of data to demonstrate that they all provide much the same information. A typical study compares four different measures of item-total relationship. Items are then ranked from highest to lowest in terms of the indices, resulting in four sets of ranks. All possible correlations are then run between the four sets of ranks, a total of six correlation coefficients. Typically it is found in such studies that the average correlation among the different indices is .90 or higher. This demonstrates that essentially the same set of items would be selected by employing any of the methods.

It is recommended that the PM correlation be used in item analysis, which with dichotomous items is point-biserial. Not only does the PM correlation give very much the same information any other measure of item-total relationship would provide, but to the extent that item selection would be slightly different by different measures, the PM correlation is logically better than the other measures.

When the PM correlation is used for item analysis, account must be taken of an artifact in such correlations. In correlating an item with total test scores, one must remember that the item is a part of the total test. This makes the correlation of an item with total scores higher than it would be if the item were correlated with scores on all other items. In the extreme case, if there were no more than five items, even if all correlations among items were zero, each item would correlate positively with total scores; but if each item were correlated with the sum of scores on the other four items, the correlations would be zero. (For the formula to correct the item-total correlation, see Nunnally, 1967: 262.)

Although it is useful to compute the standard error of the correlation coefficient and let it serve as a guide to the minimum level of item-total correlation that will be

used in the selection of items, there usually is no need to be highly concerned about the statistical significance of item-total correlations. Worries in this regard are greatly lessened by dealing with a large sample of persons, for example, very minimum of five persons per item. More important, if all or nearly all the item-total correlations are positive, as is usually the case, the only sensible hypothesis is that *all* the items actually would correlate positively with total test scores in the population of persons being sampled. When over 90% of the item-total correlations are positive, as is usually the case, one is being conservative to reject items whose correlations with total scores do not reach the .05 level of statistical significance.

Step-by-step procedures. If there are numerous uncorrected item-total correlations above .20, the remaining steps in item analysis are simple. Since about 30 dichotomous items usually are required to reach a reliability of .80, KR-20 (discussed in detail in Chapter 10) would be computed for the 30 items having the highest correlations with total scores. If the reliability is as high as desired, the item analysis is complete. If it is not, one increases the number of items, adding those items that have the next highest correlations with total scores. How many items are added depends on their correlations with total scores and on the reliability of the first set of 30 items. When the correlations with total scores are very low (e.g., .05), little can be gained by adding more items. When there are numerous additional items with correlations above .10, how many of them are added depends on how much the reliability needs to be increased. If the reliability of the original group of items is .65 and a reliability of .80 is desired, a good strategy is to add 10 items. Then KR-20 is computed for the 40 items. If the desired reliability is obtained, the item analysis is complete; if not, more items are added. If, for example, the 40-item test had a reliability of .75 rather than .80, a good strategy would be to add the next 5 items in terms of their correlations with total scores. If this did not achieve the desired reliability, one could add several more items. If at any point the reliability fails to increase or decreases, there is no use in trying out larger numbers of items.

When one wants to undertake the labors involved, a highly systematic approach to test construction is to compute KR-20 for cumulative sets of items, starting with the 5 items having the highest correlations with total scores and adding items in sets of 5. Then one can plot a curve showing the size of KR-20 for tests of different lengths. A typical curve is shown in Figure 9.16. Also shown is the expected increase in reliability from lengthening a 5-item test when the 5 items have a reliability of .40. As can be seen, the empirically obtained reliabilities are lower than the predicted results. This is to be expected, because the items that are added at each step are assumed to have the same correlations with total scores as did the original 5 items. By the method of item analysis recommended here, the first 5 items would correlate highest with total scores, and later items would correlate less with total scores. Consequently the curve of obtained reliabilities is lower than the predicted curve. Employing this approach, one would select the number of items that reached a desired level of reliability. Because this method of selecting items takes some advantage of chance, it would be well to continue adding items until KR-20 is comfortably above the reliability needed for the final test. For example, if

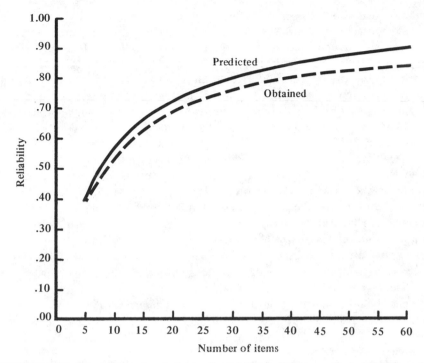

FIGURE 9.16   The predicted and obtained reliabilities of tests varying in length from 5 to 60 items when the reliability of the first 5 items is 40.

a reliability of .80 were needed in the final test, it would be wise to select enough items to achieve a KR-20 of .85 or higher. If there were no set standard for the size of the reliability, one would quit adding items when the curve began to level off, as it does in Figure 9.16 for more than 50 items.

The more complete procedure illustrated in Figure 9.16 is not necessary in most item analyses. A quicker approach with dichotomous items is to compute KR-20 for the 30 items having the highest correlations with total scores. If the desired reliability is not obtained, adding a few more items usually will suffice. If the analysis is of multipoint items, it is wise to compute coefficient alpha for the 15 items having the highest correlations with total scores, and if the reliability is not high enough, to add items 5 at a time until the desired reliability is obtained.

What should one do if this approach to test construction fails? It will probably fail if the reliability of the first 30 dichotomous items is no more than .40. Since by this point one has already used the "cream" of the items, there may not be enough good items left to reach a reliability of .80. There are three reasons the method may fail to produce a homogeneous test. The first possibility is that the items are from a domain where correlations among items are uniformly low. In that case the reliability would grow slowly as the number of items was increased, but the curve would not flatten out altogether. One could then achieve a reliable test, but it would take a very large number of items.

The second possibility is that the collection of items is factorially complex, in which case clusters of items will tend to have relatively high correlations with one another but very low correlations with members of other clusters. It usually would be very difficult to distinguish this circumstance from the first circumstance discussed. In both cases correlations with total scores would be low; KR-20 would tend to rise as more items were added, but the curve would go up very slowly.

The third possibility is that some of the items have relatively high correlations with one another but the other items have correlations near zero with all items. In that case one would have some good items to form the nucleus of a test, but the reliability could not be increased by adding items. This condition could be detected by a sudden drop-off in the size of item-total correlations as one inspected the correlations ranked from highest to lowest. This would be evidenced, for example, if the thirty-fifth item in the list had a correlation with total scores of .17 and the thirty sixth item had a correlation of only .06.

How can one recognize which of the three circumstances prevails, and what should be done after the circumstance is recognized? As was mentioned above, it is relatively easy to distinguish the third circumstance from the other two by the marked falloff in item-total correlations at some point in the list of items. If that occurs, one should study the good items and try to determine the nature of their content. Then one should try to construct more items of the same kind, administer them along with the original good items to a new group of subjects, and submit all items to the type of analysis described.

If the average item-total correlation is low, it is very difficult to tell whether this is because of the first or second circumstances. If it is caused by factorial complexity (the second circumstance), it cannot be because of the presence of only two or three strong factors. If that were the case, correlations with total scores would not be very low. Indeed, the major criticism that can be made of selecting items in terms of correlations with total scores is that the method apparently works as well when several groups of items relate strongly to different factors as it does when all items relate only moderately to the same factor. Where there are 60 items, half of which relate strongly to one factor and the other half to another factor, typically the items belonging to each factor have average correlations with one another of around .20 and with items belonging to the other factor of less than .10. In this case, regardless of the presence of two factors, all items have respectable correlations with total scores. The method of item analysis which has been discussed will select items from both factors. Thus if there are several prominent factors in the items, the problem is not so much that the item analysis will fail, but rather that it will work deceivingly well.

There is another reason the item analysis probably would not fail because of the presence of several strong factors in the items. The investigator probably would have guessed the presence of the factors and would have constructed different tests to measure the different factors. Consequently it is unlikely that he would construct an item pool containing items relating to several strong factors.

If the reliability of the first 30 dichotomous items is not above .50 and the difficulty cannot be traced to the third circumstance (marked falloff in item-total

correlations at some point in the list of items), it can be argued that factor analysis should be applied. For reasons discussed previously, this would be very laborious, and the results probably would not be very clear. The most the investigator could hope to find would be numerous rather weak factors among the items. There then would not be enough items to construct a reliable test for any of the factors found. If the average item-total correlation were low and the variance of correlations were small, the better part of valor in this circumstance might be to abandon the type of item being employed. The investigator would conclude that the attribute either did not exist or needed to be measured by a different type of item. If he were doggedly determined to continue investigating the particular type of item, his only choices would be (1) not to factor-analyze, but to construct a very long test in the hope that later it will be found to primarily measure one factor, or (2) to factor-analyze the collection of items in the hope of eventually learning how to measure one, or some, of the small factors involved.

Successive approximations. A possibility not mentioned in the previous section is that the selection of items in terms of item-total correlations can be improved by successively correlating items with subpools of the items. This can be illustrated where an analysis is being made of 100 items and only 50 of them have nonzero average correlations with the others. In this case, if it were known in advance that there were only 50 items from which to select the final group of items, the other 50 items would be removed from the analysis. If all items were correlated with total scores on the 100 items, the 50 bad items would tend to "water down" the correlations of the 50 good items with total scores. If one has the time and patience and the problem is sufficiently important, a refinement of the basic approach can be made as follows. In the first go-around, all items are correlated with total scores on all items. All items are removed that have item-total correlations which are either statistically insignificant or below some minimum value, for example, .10. For example, say that 40 items are removed from a total collection of 100. Total scores are then obtained on the remaining 60 items, and each of the 60 items is correlated with those total scores. Then KR-20 is computed for the items that stand highest in those correlations, and if the desired level of reliability is not reached, successive sets of items are added.

One could go through the above steps a number of times, each step leading to a more and more homogeneous group of items. However, it is seldom necessary to work with anything other than the original correlations of items with total scores. Usually the rank order of item-total correlations in successive sets of items refined in that way is much the same as it is for the initial item-total correlations. Where such successive refinements are sometimes required is with pools of items where many of the correlations among items are negative, as is sometimes true of items on personality inventories. This problem is discussed in a later section.

The distribution form. One of the supposed advantages of selecting items in terms of p values is that it permits control of the distribution form for total test scores. How can the same control be exercised when one selects items in terms of item-total correlations rather than p values? There is a way to control the distribution form *after* good items have been selected in terms of item correlations. The

method will be illustrated in the situation where the first 30 items in terms of item-total correlations produce the desired level of reliability but there still are more items that correlate reasonably well with total scores, say, 20 more such items. The first step would be to plot a frequency distribution for total scores on the first 30 items. If the distribution was symmetrical, the item analysis would be complete. If not, it would be necessary to study the p values of both the 30 items and the remaining 20 good items.

If the distribution is skewed toward the higher end of the continuum, it means that the test is too difficult. To make the distribution more symmetrical, some of the items in the 30-item test having low p values should be replaced by items from the remaining 20 that have p values above .5. If 5 items having p values between .2 and 3 are replaced by 5 items having p values between .5 and .7, this will tend to make the distribution symmetrical. The distribution of the new group of 30 items is then plotted, and if it is symmetrical, the item analysis is complete. If the distribution still is slightly nonsymmetrical, replacement of a few more items will solve the problem. In replacing items in this way, one must recheck the reliability at each step to make sure it is not falling below the desired standard. If it does fall slightly, then at each step in the replacement of items, several more items should be added than are removed. Thus, for example, to achieve both the desired reliability and the desired distribution form, one might end up with a 38-item test rather than a 30-item test.

Actually, though, it is quite unlikely that the distribution of scores will be markedly nonsymmetrical if items are selected purely in terms of correlations with total scores. This method tends to select items in the middle range of p values rather than those at the extremes. Since the restriction on the size of point-biserial is rather severe for items with p values below .2 or above .8, it is unlikely that items with such extreme p values will be high enough in the rank order of item-total correlations to be included in a test. Since the least restriction in point-biserial is for items having p values at .5, items with p values near .5 have a greater likelihood of having high correlations with total scores, and consequently such items tend to stand high in the rank order of item-total correlations. (It is important to remember, however, that picking items in terms of item-total correlations favors only those items with p values near .5 that actually correlate well with total scores.) Because choosing items in terms of item-total correlations tends to select items that are "average" in p value, this method of item analysis almost always produces a symmetrical distribution of scores, and consequently no further refinements are necessary. Also, one seldom seeks anything other than a symmetrical distribution.

Bipolar domains of items. The discussion in the previous section assumed that most correlations among items are positive, which usually is true for any test concerning abilities, but is not necessarily so for measures of personality, attitudes, interests, and others. For example, if an attitude scale regarding the United Nations were being constructed, one approach would be to start by writing 60 statements, of which half were thought to be favorable toward the United Nations and half thought to be unfavorable. Each item would require dichotomous, agree-disagree

responses. If all agreements were scored 1 and all disagreements scored zero, the negative statements would tend to correlate negatively with the positive statements. Then the average correlation of each item with the others would be close to zero, and thus all the items would have item-total correlations close to zero. Obviously, then, it would not be possible to select items in terms of item-total correlations, and the analyses would provide no hints as to what should be done to improve the situation.

If items are selected purely in terms of item-total correlations, the success of this method depends on the investigator's ability to devise a scoring key initially that will make the majority of correlations among items positive. In most cases this is easily done. In the previous example of constructing a measure of attitudes toward the United Nations, the investigator would score agreements with the positive statements as 1 and *disagreements* with the *negative* statements as 1. Then most of the correlations among items would be likely to be positive, and there would be no difficulty in selecting items in terms of item-total correlations. Of course, the investigator might misjudge some of the items, and consequently some items would have negative correlations with total scores. For selecting items in terms of item-total correlations, however, it is not necessary that all the correlations among items be positive, but only most of them. The method usually will work if a scoring key is devised such that 70% of the correlations among items are positive. In this case the majority of item-total correlations are positive, and some probably are sufficiently high to encourage further item analysis.

After the first attempt to devise a scoring key that will make most correlations among items positive, the next step is to rank the items in terms of item-total correlations. If at least 70% of the correlations are positive and numerous correlations are above .15, one can proceed to the next step, which is to reverse the scoring for all items having statistically significant negative item-total correlations. Thus if an item that correlated -.15 with total scores had previously been scored 1 for "agree," in the new scoring key it would be scored 1 for "disagree," and vice versa for an item with that same negative correlation which previously had been scored 1 for "disagree." The scoring would not be changed for all items having positive correlations with total scores or nonsignificant negative correlations. Next, a new set of total scores would be obtained with the new scoring key, and each item would be correlated with the new total scores. This time the number of positive item-total correlations would probably increase markedly, and the average size of the correlations would increase. If there still are numerous items having negative item-total correlations, the process can be repeated.

In most bipolar item domains, it is not necessary to go through the iterative procedure described above. Usually the investigator can intuit a scoring key that will make most correlations among items positive. This usually is easy to do with attitude scales, interest inventories, and most personality inventories. It might be necessary to go through one rekeying of the items, but seldom would it be necessary to repeat the process a number of times. But, as was said previously, even if the scoring key produces only 70% positive item-total correlations among items, the iterative approach will usually produce the needed positive item-total correla-

tions. After these correlations are obtained, rather than make only one rank order in terms of item-total correlations, it is better to make a different order for items scored "agree" (or "yes") than for items scored "disagree" (or "no"). Then one would select an equal number of items from each list to form the first trial test. For example, one would select the top 15 items from both lists and form a 30-item test. If KR-20 is not as high as desired, additional items would be added from both lists. A balanced scoring key of this kind tends to eliminate response styles such as the tendency to agree regardless of item content.

Weighting of items. The methods of item analysis discussed in this chapter assume that all items are to be weighted equally in the eventual test, and no mention has been made of the possiblity of obtaining differential weights for items. Rather than simply adding the number of correct responses on a test of ability, one could count correct responses on some items 3, correct responses on some other items 2, and correct responses on the remaining items 1. Methods have been proposed for weighting items in terms of (1) correlations with total test scores, (2) p values, (3) correlations with an outside criterion, and (4) other standards.

The crucial question in seeking differential weights for items is that of how much difference it makes to use differential weights. It would make a difference if the weighted and unweighted scores on whole tests did not correlate highly and if the reliability of the weighted test was considerably higher than the reliability of the unweighted test. However, there is overwhelming evidence that the use of differential weights seldom makes an importtant difference. Regardless of how differential weights are determined, typically it is found that on tests containing at least 20 items, the weighted test correlates in the high nineties with the unweighted test. Also, the slight increase in reliability obtained by weighing items can be matched in nearly all instances by adding several items to the unweighted test. Since it is much easier to add several items to a test than to go through the labors of determining and using differential weights for items, seeking differential weights is almost never worth the trouble.

Removal of an unwanted factor. Sometimes it is known in advance that items which are being analyzed to measure one attribute will tend to correlate with an unwanted attribute. This is the case, for example, in tests constructed to measure different factors of human ability, where experience has shown that many types of items concerning human ability tend to correlate with the factor of verbal comprehension. Since no matter what factor is being measured, the items will require some understanding of words and sentences, obtaining relatively independent measures of factors other than verbal comprehension is rather difficult.

Another example is in the construction of a measure of anxiety where previous studies have indicated that the type of item being used is likely to produce a test which will correlate substantially with measures of intelligence. This will make it somewhat difficult to perform studies on anxiety, since any results obtained will be confounded with intelligence.

An extension can be made of the method of selecting items in terms of item-total correlations to lessen the effect of an unwanted factor. One would need a larger collection of items initially than is usually required in selecting items in terms

of item-total correlations. For example, if the best guess is that a 30-item test will be required to achieve the desired level of reliability, it will be well to start with over 100 items. Each item is then correlated with total scores and with scores on the unwanted factor. To facilitate the selection of items, a scatter diagram should be made of correlations of items with both variables. The desired items are those that have relatively high correlations with total scores and relatively low correlations with the unwanted factor. Although there will tend to be few items in this category, those that correlate highly with total scores and negatively with the unwanted factor are particulary helpful in purifying the test being constructed.

After a set of items is selected from the scatter diagram, the next steps are to compute KR-20 for the collection of items and correlate the total scores on those items with scores on the unwanted factor. If the former is high and the latter is low, the item analysis is complete. If that is not the case, new items need to be added, and some compromise might have to be reached between the two considerations. If the overlap between measures of the two attributes is a particularly bothersome problem in research, it will be wise to have the reliability of the new test somewhat lower than desired to prevent the new test from correlating substantially with the unwanted factor.

Taking advantage of chance. All forms of item analysis tend to capitalize on sampling errors to make the results appear better than they will in subsequent studies. One tends to take advantage of chance in any situation where something is optimized from the data at hand. This occurs in multiple correlation, in selecting items in terms of item-total correlations, in selecting items for an equidiscriminating test, in seeking differential weights for items, and in purifying a test of an unwanted factor. Since the opportunities to take advantage of chance are related positively to the number of variables and negatively to the number of persons, it was recommended that a bare minimum in item analysis is to have 5 persons for each item, and that a safer number is 10 persons per item.

When there are at least 10 persons per item, the method of item analysis will take very little advantage of chance. A collection of items found to have a reliability of .84 might in subsequent studies prove to have a reliability of .80, but the drop in reliability is seldom more than a few points. If the exact level of reliability is a crucial issue when items are being selected, a safe procedure is to strive for a reliability at least five points above the crucial level.

The considerable amount of "playing around" with data sometimes required in constructing tests from bipolar domains of items provides more of an opportunity to take advantage of chance than is provided when items are selected in terms of the initial item-total correlations. For this reason, when dealing with such domains of items, one should strive to obtain even more than 10 persons per item if that is feasible.

To investigate the extent to which item analyses (and other forms of analysis that strive to optimize some function of the data) take advantage of chance, it has been recommended that a "holdout" group of subjects be employed. For example, if only 600 subjects are available for testing, one approach would be to base the item analysis on half of the subjects. Then KR-20 (or whatever else was being

optimized) would be computed for the first group and for the holdout group. That certainly would provide evidence about the extent to which the analysis had capitalized on sampling errors, but it would be as imprudent an approach as it would be to permit fire prevention to fall to a dangerously low level in order to invest heavily in fire-fighting equipment. If the number of subjects is limited, as it usually is, the far wiser strategy is to use every last subject in the item analysis. This way one tends to ensure in advance that the reliability (or any other function being optimized) will not fall off markedly in subsequent studies.

Speed Tests

So far in this chapter it has been assumed that test construction concerns *power tests*, that is, tests on which subjects are given about as much time as they want. Essentially one can classify a test as a power test even if there is a time limit and all subjects do not complete all items, for example, if 90% of the subjects complete all items in the allotted time. (See Nunnally, 1967, Chap. 15, for a detailed discussion of this and related matters concerning highly speeded tests.) However, some test are highly speeded, to the point where only a small percent of the subjects complete all items. Such highly speeded tests pose some special problems in test construction.

In their purest form, speed tests consist of items of *trivial difficulty*. That is, the difficulties would be trivial if subjects were given as much time as they wanted in making responses. By "trivial difficulty" is meant a p value of .95 or higher when items are administered under power conditions. One type of item that fulfills this requirement is the simple problem in addition or subtraction. If problems of this type were employed in testing normal adults, all persons would answer almost all the problems correctly if they were given as much time as they wanted. The only way, then, to obtain a reliable dispersion of scores is to employ a highly restrictive time limit, in which, for example, the average person has time to answer only about half the questions.

The rules that apply to the construction of power tests do *not* apply to the construction of speed tests. Rather, a special set of principles applies to the construction of speed tests, which will be discussed in this section.

Internal structure of speed tests. Previously in this chapter it was shown that the construction of power tests depends very much on the sizes and patterns of correlations among items. Also, in the next chapter it will be shown that the theory of reliability relates directly to the size and patterns of correlations among items. Here it will be shown that with speed tests the size and patterns of correlations among items are artifacts of time limits and of the ordering of items within a test. Consequently test construction cannot be based on the correlations of items with one another, and the reliability of speed tests cannot be based on internal consistency.

In a speed test, the average correlation among items is directly related to the amount of time allotted for taking the test. If subjects are given all the time they want, the p values of all items will be either 1.0 or close to that, and consequently the correlations among items will be either zero or close to zero. At the other extreme, if subjects are given practically no time for taking the test, the p values

will all be zero or close to zero, and consequently the correlations among items will be near zero on the average. Between these two extremes of time limits, the average p values of items range from zero to 1.0. One could, for example, experiment with time limits to obtain an average p value near .5, in which case the average correlation among items might be substantial.

In addition to the average correlation among items being related to the time limit, the patterns of correlations among items are determined by the time limit. Let us look at the case where a time limit is employed such that (1) the average p value of items is near the middle of the possible range, and (2), by methods to be discussed later, the distribution of total scores is found to be highly reliable. Suppose that one employed the methods discussed previously for constructing a power test. Essentially this consists of selecting those items that correlate highly with total scores, but on speed tests this depends directly on the ordering of items within the test. Items near the beginning of the test probably would have such high p values that they would tend to correlate very little with the other items, and consequently they would correlate very little with total scores. Items near the end of the test would have such low p values that they also would correlate very little with the other items and with total scores. In contrast, items near the middle of the test would tend to have substantial correlations with one another and with total test scores. Since, in a speed test, the ordering of items is arbitrary, the correlations of items with total scores are arbitrary, and it makes no sense to select items on the basis of item-total correlations. The construction of speed tests, then, must be based on principles other than those that apply to construction of power tests. These principles will be discussed throughout the remainder of this section.

The item pool. As is true in the construction of all tests, the first step in the construction of a speed test is to develop an item pool. Usually this is rather easily done, because the items on speed tests usually are so simple that it is easy to compose them by the dozens. Whereas previously it was possible to give some rules of thumb regarding the number of items required for the item pool for a power test, this is very difficult to do with speed tests. This is because the reliability of speed tests is not as highly related to the number of items as is that of power tests. For example, a speed test with 50 arithmetic items might be more reliable than a speed test containing 200 pairs of letter groupings. The reliability of different types of speed tests tends to be intimately related not to the number of items, but to the *testing time* required to obtain the most reliable distribution of scores. Thus if the ideal testing times for two different types of speed tests are both 15 minutes, the tests will tend to have roughly the same reliability regardless of the number of items in each. When one constructs the item pool, the number of items should depend on intuitive judgments about how rapidly the items can be answered by the average person. If later it is found that the original item pool was too small, it usually is easy to construct new items.

Time limits. Constructing a speed test consists almost entirely of finding the *time limit* that will produce the *most reliable distribution of total scores*. The amount of experimentation required to find the ideal time limit depends on previous experience with employing time limits with the particular type of item.

Say, for example, that the items consist of simple problems in subtraction and addition and the test is to be used with unselected adults. Previous experience indicates that the average adult can correctly solve such problems at the rate of two per minute. The purpose of test construction is to develop a highly reliable test of numerical computation. The experimenter thinks that a test of about 80 such items will produce a highly reliable distribution of scores. He then constructs 80 such items and performs experiments to determine the ideal time limit. Previous experience suggests that the ideal time limit would be somewhere near 40 minutes, but it is safest to perform experiments to make sure. Consequently, the experimenter administers the items with five different time limits to five different groups, the groups consisting of random selections from a larger sample of subjects. The experimenter elects to try time limits of 30, 35, 40, 45, and 50 minutes, respectively.

In the experiment above, the ideal time limit is the one that produces the most reliable distribution of scores, the reliability being determined by methods to be discussed later. Rather than perform studies of reliability at this stage, however, one can use a simpler approach which will usually produce much the same results. In a speed test the reliabilities produced by different time limits are highly related to the standard deviations of scores produced by those time limits. Consequently one selects the time limit that produces the largest standard deviation of scores. Hypothetical results from the experiment discussed above are shown in Figure 9.17. As is typically the case, the standard deviation (and thus the reliability) is highest at some point in between the extreme time limits being investigated and tapers off on either side of that point. In this case, however, the ideal time limit is 45 minutes rather than the 40 minutes originally guessed by the experimenter.

Measurement of reliability. It is not correct to measure the reliability of a speed test in terms of internal consistency, as is the case with coefficient alpha and

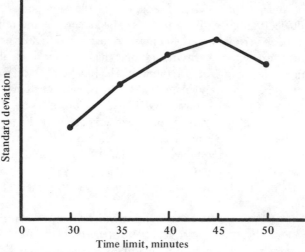

FIGURE 9.17   Standard deviation of scores on a speed test as a function of different time limits.

KR-20. (For a discussion of why coefficient alpha and KR-20 are not appropriate, see Nunnally, 1967.) The most appropriate measure of reliability is made by correlating alternative forms. Thus, in the previous example, rather than construct only one 80-item test of numerical computation, one would construct two 80-item tests. The correlation between scores on the two tests would be the best estimate of the reliability. A time-saving approximation to the alternative-form reliability can be obtained by correlating separately timed halves of only one test, which will save the labors of constructing an alternative form. In that case, even-numbered items on the test would constitute one form, and odd-numbered items the other form. The first half of the items would be administered with a time limit equal to half that employed with the test as a whole. Immediately after time is called, the second half of items would be administered with a time limit equal to half that employed with the whole test. The correlation between the separately timed halves would then be corrected to provide an estimate of the alternative-form reliability of the whole test. (This correction is discussed in Nunnally, 1967: 193-194.) The estimate usually is rather precise if (1) the trait does not change markedly over the time used for applying alternative forms, and (2) performance within a testing session is not markedly influenced by fatigue.

Factor composition. As was mentioned previously, the patterns of correlations among items in a speed test are determined almost entirely by the time limit and the ordering of items within the test. Items near the middle of the test tend to correlate more highly with other items than do items near either end of the test. Consequently, in a factor analysis, items near the middle of the test would tend to have the highest loadings on a general factor, purely because of the way items are ordered on the test. In addition, items tend to correlate more highly with items near their ordinal position on the test than they do with items further removed in the ordering. For example, the fourteenth item would probably correlate more highly with the thirteenth and fifteenth item than it would with the tenth and twentieth items. Consequently items tend to break up into different factors because of the proximity of items to one another in the test. The factor structure of speed tests is interesting from the standpoint of psychometric theory, but it tells one nothing about factors of ability, personality, and sentiment. The proper way to learn about the factors measured by speed tests is to factor-analyze whole tests *after* they have been constructed by methods discussed previously in this section.

REFERENCES

Campbell, D. T. and J. C. Stanley. *Experimental and quasi-experimental designs for research.* Chicago: Rand-McNally, 1968.

Edwards, A. L. *Techniques of attitude scale construction.* New York: Appleton-Century-Crofts, 1957.

Lord, F. M. The relation of the reliability of multiple-choice tests to the distribution of item difficulties. *Psychometrika,* 1952, 17: 181-194. (a)

———. A theory of test scores. *Psychometric Monographs,* 1952, no. 7. (b)

Nunnally, J. C. *Psychometric theory.* New York: McGraw-Hill, 1967.

———. Research strategies and measurement methods for investigating human development. Chapter in J. Nesselroade and H. Reese (eds.) *Life-Span Developmental Psychology*. New York: Academic Press, 1972.

———. Educational measurement and evaluation. 2nd ed.; New York: McGraw-Hill, 1972.

Torgerson, W. *Theory and methods of scaling.* New York: Wiley, 1958.

10

VALIDITY, RELIABILITY, AND SPECIAL PROBLEMS OF
MEASUREMENT IN EVALUATION RESEARCH

JUM C. NUNNALLY
and
ROBERT L. DURHAM

Chapter 9 was concerned with the logic and technique for constructing psychological measures from item building blocks. This chapter is concerned with some molar issues that relate to whole tests or other types of measures employed in evaluation research. In turn will be discussed methods for determining the validity of measures and principles concerning reliability. In one way or another, all of the issues discussed in this chapter concern *generalizability*. Thus, the validity of a predictor test concerns the extent to which one can generalize from scores on the test to scores on a criterion variable. Reliability concerns the extent to which one can generalize from scores on a test to scores on alternative forms of the test.

VALIDITY

After a model has been chosen for the construction of a measuring instrument and the instrument has been constructed, the next step is to find out whether or not the instrument is useful. This step is usually spoken of as determining the *validity* of an instrument. The term has some misleading connotations, but it is too well engrained in the literature to permit an easy transition to terms that more properly denote the processes involved; consequently, the term is used in this chapter, although efforts are made to sharply distinguish the different meanings which "validity" can have.

In a very general sense, a measuring instrument is valid if it does what it is

AUTHORS' NOTE: Appreciation is expressed to McGraw-Hill Book Company for permission to borrow extensively from the following book for material adapted for this chapter: J. C. Nunnally, *Psychometric theory* (New York: McGraw-Hill, 1967).

intended to do. Proper performance of some instruments is rather easily verified, for example, of the yardstick as a measure of length. It takes very little "research" with this instrument to find that resulting measurements (1) fit in perfectly with axiomatic concepts of the nature of length and (2) relate to many other variables. If all measures so perfectly met these standards, there would be little need to consider the validation of measuring instruments, but they do not. For example, whereas it might seem highly sensible to develop measures of emotions from physiological indices such as heart rate, muscle tonus, and palmar sweat, it has proved very difficult to find combinations of such indices to measure various emotions. So it is with many proposed measures in the physical, biological, and behavioral sciences: what seem to be good approaches to measurement on an intuitive basis fail to produce the desired empirical results.

Validation always requires empirical investigations, the nature of the evidence required depending on the type of validity. Validity is a matter of degree rather than an all-or-none property, and validation is an unending process. Whereas measures of length and of some other simple physical attributes may have proved their merits so well that no one seriously considers changing to other measures, most measures should be kept under constant surveillance to see if they are behaving as they should. New evidence may suggest modifications of an existing measure or the development of a new and better approach to measuring the attribute in question, for example, the measurement of anxiety, intelligence, or the temperature of stars.

Strictly speaking one validates not a measuring instrument, but rather some use to which the instrument is put. For example, a test used to select college freshmen must be valid for that purpose, but it would not necessarily be valid for other purposes, such as measuring how well students have mastered the curriculum in high school. Whereas an achievement test in spelling might be valid for that purpose, it might be nearly worthless for other purposes, such as forecasting success in high school. Similarly, a valid measure of the response to stressful experimental treatments would not necessarily be a valid measure of neuroticism or anything else. Although a measure may be valid for many different purposes, for example, as intelligence tests are, the validity with which each purpose is served must be supported by evidence.

Psychological measures serve three major purposes: (1) establishment of a functional relationship with a particular variable, (2) representation of a specified universe of content, and (3) measurement of psychological traits. Corresponding to these are three types of validity: (1) predictive validity, (2) content validity, and (3) construct validity. Examples of measures intended to serve those purposes are a test for selecting trainees for tutorial work with slow learners, a test of how much students learned in an electronics course for unskilled workers, and a measure of delinquent tendency for measuring the effectiveness of a youth training program. Each of these three types of validity will be discussed in turn.

Predictive Validity

Predictive validity is at issue when the purpose is to use an instrument to estimate some important form of behavior, the latter being referred to as the

criterion. An example is that of a test employed to select college freshmen. The test, whatever it is like, is useful in that situation only if it accurately estimates successful performance in college. The criterion in this case probably would be grade-point average obtained over four years of college. After the criterion is obtained, the validity of a prediction function is straightforwardly, and rather easily, determined. Primarily it consists of correlating scores on the predictor test with scores on the criterion variable. The size of the correlation is a direct indication of the amount of validity. Similarly with the example given above, the validity of a test for selecting trainees as tutorial workers would depend on correlations between the test and criteria concerning successful performance in the program and in actual field work after leaving training.

The term "prediction" will be used in a general (and ungrammatical) sense to refer to functional relations between an instrument and events occurring before, during, and after the instrument is applied. Thus a test administered to adults could be used to make "predictions" about events occurring in their childhood. A test intended to "predict" brain damage is, of course, intended not to forecast who will suffer brain damage at some time in the future, but rather to "predict" who does and who does not have brain damage at the time the test is administered. When a test is used to predict success in college, "prediction" properly means forecasting. Others have referred to predictive validity at those three points in time, respectively, as "post-diction," "concurrent validity," and "prediction." Using different terms, however, suggests that the logic and procedure of validation are different, which is not true. In each case a predictor measure is related to a criterion measure, and after the data are available, it does not matter when they were obtained. The nature of the problem dictates when the two sets of measurements are obtained. Thus to forecast success in college, it is necessary to administer the predictor instrument before students go to college; and to obtain the criterion of success in college, it is necessary to wait four years.

Predictive validity is determined by, and only by, the degree of correspondence between the two measures involved. If the correlation is high, no other standards are necessary. Thus if it were found that accuracy in horseshoe pitching correlated highly with success in the Peace Corps, horseshoe pitching would be a valid measure for predicting success in that program. This is not meant to imply that sound theory and common sense are not useful in selecting predictor instruments for investigation, but after the investigations are done, the entire proof of the pudding is in the correlations.

In no other area is predictive validity as important as it is in using tests to help make decisions about schooling of many kinds. In schools, predictive validity is at issue in measures of "readiness." Thus, for underage children, a test of readiness for the first grade is valid only to the extent that it predicts how well children will perform in the first grade. A test used to divide children into different ability levels is valid only to the extent that it predicts how well children will do in their different levels of instruction. A test used to select students for special programs of study in high school is valid only to the extent that it actually predicts performance in those programs. So it is with all other tests used for the selection and placement

of students: they are valid only to the extent that they serve prediction functions well.

Clear as the difference may seem, some people confuse predictor instruments with the criteria they are meant to predict. A story (a true one) will help to illustrate this confusion. A college graduate applied for entrance to a graduate training program to work toward a master's degree. He failed to score sufficiently high on an entrance examination (a predictor test) but was given special permission to enter on a trial basis. Once in training, he performed very well, doing better than most of his fellow students. Near completion of the student's training, the dean of the college insisted that the student would need to retake the entrance examination and make a satisfactory grade before his degree could be granted! Many other equally foolish examples could be given to show how predictor tests are confused with the criteria they are meant to predict.

Whereas it is easy to talk about correlating a predictor test with its criterion, in actuality obtaining a good criterion may be more difficult than obtaining a predictor test. In many cases either no criterion is available or the criteria that are available suffer from various faults, about which more will be said later in this chapter.

Validity coefficients. The validity of individual predictor instruments and combinations of predictor instruments is determined by correlational analysis and extensions of correlational analysis to multivariate analysis. (An excellent, detailed discussion of the logic and statistical methods involved is presented by Guion, 1965.) The simplest example of a validity coefficient is the correlation of an individual predictor test with an individual criterion, for example, the correlation of a test of scholastic aptitude with average grades over four years of college training.

In evaluating the worth of predictor tests, it is a mistake to think in terms of perfect correlations in any case or even of high correlations in most cases. In most prediction problems, it is reasonable to expect only modest correlations between a criterion and either an individual predictor test or a combination of predictor tests. People are far too complex to permit a highly accurate estimate of their performance from any practicable collection of test materials. Equally complex are the situations in which criterion data are obtained, for example, the immense complexity of all the variables involved in determining the average grades of students over four years of college. Considering the immense complexities of the problem, it is remarkable that some predictor tests correlate as highly as they do with criterion variables. For example, scholastic aptitude tests are as predictive of grades in college four years hence as meteorologist's predictions are of the weather in Chicago ten days in advance.

The proper way to interpret a validity coefficient is in terms of the extent to which it indicates a *possible improvement in the average quality of persons* that would be obtained by employing the instrument in question. Tests that have only modest correlations with their criteria (e.g., correlations of .30 and .40) often are capable of markedly improving the *average* performance of personnel in different positions. Of course, many mistakes would be made in predicting the performance of individuals, but on the average, persons who score high on the test perform

considerably better than persons who score low on the test. Such differences in mean performance frequently are highly important in applied settings. An example in evaluation research would be that of selecting persons for training as parole officers. A selection test that had only a modest correlation with the criterion (percentages of parolees that remained out of trouble) could be used to select future parole officers who would effect an important reduction in crime. This could be done by selecting only those persons who made high scores on the test.

Predictor tests in evaluation research. A number of cautions should be heeded regarding the use of predictor tests in evaluation research. First, one should be quite chary of using such tests unless a study of validity is planned and is feasible. Frequently, tests are employed in selection programs that later prove to have little or no validity, for example, an attractive-looking personality test for the selection of intelligence operators. Second, even if there are good intentions to validate the selection tests, adequate criteria of performance might not be available. This frequently is true in evaluation research where the purpose of the program is to improve amorphous attitudes and values. The motives of the progenitors of such programs might be the highest, but their hoped-for results are very difficult to measure. Third, selection tests really are not necessary in some programs of social improvement. In some instances, the proponents of the program are obligated to take all, or almost all, of the persons who are available or who volunteer, as is the case with many programs operated by the federal or local governments. In other instances it is both unwise and uneconomical to employ selection tests. This would be so where it would be neither dangerous nor expensive to let people ·try their hands at an activity rather than preselect them for the purpose. There is no use in trying to predict success in an activity when it is just as easy to find out in a direct manner how well people perform.

Content Validity

For some instruments, validity depends primarily on the adequacy with which a specified domain of content is sampled. A prime example would be a final examination for a course in introductory psychology. Obviously, the test could not be validated in terms of predictive validity, because the purpose of the test is not to predict something else but to *directly measure* performance in a unit of instruction. The test must stand by itself as an adequate measure of what it is supposed to measure. Validity cannot be determined by correlating the test with a criterion, because the test itself *is* the criterion of performance.

Even if one argued that course examinations should be validated in terms of correlations with other behaviors, what behaviors would serve as adequate criteria? A student might, by any standard, deserve an A in the course but never take another course in psychology or ever work in a position where knowledge from the course would be evidenced. Of course, one would expect the test to correlate with some other variables, and the size of such correlations would provide hints about the adequacy of the test. For example, one would expect to find a substantial correlation between scores on the final examination in introductory psychology and scores on the final examination in abnormal psychology (for those students

who took both courses). If the correlation were zero, it would make us suspect that something were wrong with one or both of the examinations (or with one or both of the units of instruction). However, such correlations would offer only hints about the validity of the examinations, the final proof resting on the adequacy with which content had been sampled.

There are many other examples of measures that require content validity, including all course examinations in all types of training programs and at all levels of training. All achievement tests require content validity. Examples of such tests might be a comprehensive measure of progress in school up to the end of the fourth grade or a comprehensive measure of the extent to which men performed well in a training program for electronics technicians for the physically handicapped. Because so much of evaluation research concerns training programs in which knowledge and skill are to be enhanced, measures that require content validity are frequently encountered in evaluation research.

Rather than test the validity of measures such as those above after they are constructed, one should *ensure* validity by the plan and procedures of construction. To take a very simple example, an achievement test in spelling for fourth-grade students could obtain its content from a random sampling of words occurring in widely used readers. The plan is to randomly sample from a specified domain of content, and most potential users of the test should agree that this procedure ensures a reasonably representative collection of words. In addition, a sensible procedure would be required for transforming the words into a test. It might, for example, be decided to compose items by putting each correctly spelled word in with three misspellings and requiring the student to circle the correct one. Other decisions would need to be made about ordering the items in the test and about the oral or written instructions to students. These and other details are part of the plan for selecting content and for test construction. The validity of the measure is judged by the character of the plan and by the apparent skill with which the plan has been carried out. If it is agreed by most potential users of the test, or at least by persons in positions of responsibility, that the plan was sound and well carried out, the test has a high degree of content validity. The same would hold true in evaluation research, for example, for an achievement test concerning knowledge gained in electronics training for unskilled workers or a test of how well trainee parole officers had mastered course work relating to their chosen professions.

The simple example above illustrates the two major standards for ensuring content validity: (1) a representative collection of items and (2) "sensible" methods of test construction. Of course, in most instances these standards are not so easy to judge as they were for the spelling test. Often, it is logically impossible or unfeasible to actually sample content. For example, how would one sample (in a strict sense of the word) items for an achievement test in geography? Neither the sampling unit nor the domain is well specified. One could sample sentences from textbooks and turn them into true-false items, but for obvious reasons such a test would not be adequate. Rather, what is done in such instances is to *formulate* a collection of items that broadly represents the unit of instruction. To ensure that the items actually represent the unit of instruction, it is necessary to have a detailed outline,

or blueprint, of the kinds of questions and problems that will be included. (How such outlines are developed and used is explained in a number of introductory texts on educational and psychological measurement: Cronbach, 1960; Nunnally, 1964; Thorndike and Hagen, 1961.) In such instances, judging the quality of the outline is an important part of assessing content validity.

The simple example of a random sampling of content is unrealistic in most situations for a second reason: the selection of content usually involves questions of values. Thus, for the spelling test, one might decide that it is more important to measure performance on nouns, adjectives, and verbs than performance on other parts of speech; consequently one would restrict sampling to those types of words. In an achievement test for arithmetic, one might decide that it is more important to stress questions concerning quantitative concepts than those on numerical computations. And so it is with nearly all measures based on content validity: values determine the relative stress on different types of content. Of course, where values are important, there are differences in values among people; consequently there usually is some disagreement about the proper content coverage of particular tests. Also, since values sometimes change, it can be expected that a test which is viewed today as having high content validity may not be considered so high in that regard later. The values behind the construction of a measure should be made explicit, for example, in test manuals, and it should be indicated how those values guided formulation of the test outline and the construction of items.

A second point at which content validity becomes somewhat complex is in ensuring that "sensible" methods of test construction are employed. This is not much of a problem with spelling tests, because it is relatively easy to construct items that most people will agree are satisfactory. It requires much more skill, however, to construct items in some other domains of content, for example, geography, electronics, and salesmanship training; and there often is controversy about the employment of different types of items (using the word "item" to refer broadly to questions, problems, work samples, and other evidence of accomplishment).

Even though there often are problems with ensuring content validity, inevitably content validity rests mainly on appeals to reason regarding the adequacy with which important content has been sampled and on the adequacy with which the content has been case in the form of test items. In addition there are various methods of analyzing data obtained from the test which will provide important circumstantial evidence. For example, at least a moderate level of internal consistency among the items within a test would be expected, that is, the items should tend to measure something in common. This is not an infallible guide, however, because with some subject matters, it is reasonable to include materials that tap somewhat different abilities. For example, abilities for numerical computation are not entirely the same as those for grasping some of the essential ideas about quantification, but a good argument could be made for mixing these two types of content to measure overall progress in arithmetic.

Another type of circumstantial evidence for content validity is obtained by comparing performance on a test before and after a period of training. If the test is

intended to measure progress in training, scores should increase from before to after; and the improvement in scores on individual items can be considered evidence for the validity of those items. There are, however, numerous flaws in this line of reasoning. An item can be obviously trivial yet show marked changes from the beginning to the end of the course, for example, spelling of the teacher's name. Many students would not make the correct spelling the first day of class, but nearly all would be able to spell the teacher's name correctly by the last day of class. Conversely, on some very important items, there may be little change from before to after; but that may be because of inadequate texts, unskilled teachers, or lazy students.

Another type of evidence for content validity is obtained from correlating scores on different tests purporting to measure much the same thing, for example, two tests by different commercial firms for the measurement of achievement in reading. It is comforting to find high correlations in such instances, but this does not guarantee content validity. Both tests may measure the same wrong things.

In spite of efforts on the part of some to settle every issue about psychological measurement by a flight into statistics, content validity is mainly settled in other ways. Although helpful hints are obtained from analyses of empirical findings, content validity mainly rests upon an appeal to the propriety of content and the way it is presented.

Construct Validity

Whereas up to 1950 most textbooks on measurement spoke only of predictive validity and content validity, with many different names being used to refer to the two, actually those two types of validity are mainly important only in certain types of measurement problems in applied psychology. Predictive validity is important in selecting students for college, placing soldiers in special courses of training, making decisions about the treatment of mental patients, and placing people on jobs. Content validity is important for examining progress in elementary school, studying the effectiveness of different methods for training accountants, and making decisions about the promotion of civil service workers. Whereas these and other measurement problems are of vast practical importance, such applied problems are not close to the measurement problems that occur in the basic science of psychology.

Like all basic science, psychological science is concerned with establishing functional relations among important variables. (What is an "important" variable is determined either by intuition or by the content of psychological theories.) Of course, variables must be measured before they can be related to one another in experiments; and for statements of relationship to have any meaning, each measure must, in some sense, validly measure what it is purported to measure. Examples of important variables in psychology are reaction time, habit strength, intelligence, anxiety, drive level, and degree of frustration. How does one validate measures of such variables? (Later the word "validate" will be challenged as a proper name for what is required.) Take, for example, an experiment where a particular treatment is hypothesized to raise anxiety. Can the measure of anxiety be validated as a

predictor of some specific variable? No, it cannot, because the purpose is to measure the amount of anxiety then and there, not to estimate scores on any other variable obtained in the past, present, or future. Also, the measure cannot be validated purely in terms of content validity. There is no obvious body of "content" (behaviors) corresponding to anxiety reactions, and if there were, how to measure such content would be far more of a puzzle than it is with performance in arithmetic.

In evaluation research, there are numerous examples of measures that cannot be validated entirely in terms of predictive validity or content validity. One would be a measure of criminal tendency employed in a youth training program. A second would be a measure of family adjustment used in evaluating the results of group counseling programs. A third would be measures of social adequacy used in a program of education for the mentally retarded. In these cases, the things to be measured are too global and abstract to rest entirely on predictive validity and content validity.

To the extent that a variable is abstract rather than concrete, we speak of it as being a *construct*. Such a variable is literally a construct in that it is something that the scientist puts together from his own imagination, something that does not exist as an isolated, observable dimension of behavior. This construct represents a hypothesis (usually only half-formed) that a variety of behaviors will correlate with one another in studies of individual differences and/or will be similarly affected by experimental treatments.

It is important to realize that all theories in science mainly concern statements about constructs rather than about specific, observable variables. A prime example of confusion in this regard comes from the final oral examination for a Ph.D. candidate who had investigated the effects of different drugs on how rapidly mice would swim through a water maze filled with cold water. The dependent measure was time taken to traverse the maze. The candidate spoke of the dependent measure as representing "reaction to stress," the cold water supposedly being stressful to the mice. A member of the examining committee objected to speaking of the dependent measure as representing reaction to stress and took the student to task for not sticking to a description of the experimental results purely in terms of observables, that is, mice swimming in cold water. Both the student and the committee member were partly right and partly wrong. By speaking of the dependent measure as representing reaction to stress, the student assumed that the measure had a generality far beyond the actual observables. By suggesting that science is concerned only with the particular observables in an experiment, the committee member was painting a very faulty picture. No one really cares how rapidly mice swim in cold water. The particular measure is of interest only to the extent that it partly mirrors performance in a variety of situations that all concern "stress" or some other construct.

Scientists cannot do without constructs. Their theories are populated with them, and even in informal conversation scientists find it all but impossible to discuss their work without using words relating to constructs. It is important to keep in mind not only that proposed measures of constructs need to be validated for that

purpose, but also that science is primarily concerned with developing measures of constructs and finding functional relations between measures of different constructs.

Constructs vary widely in the extent to which the domain of related observable variables is (1) large or small and (2) tightly or loosely defined. Regarding point 1, in some cases the domain of related variables is so small that any one of the few observable variables in the domain will suffice to measure the construct. This is true of reaction time, where the alternative methods of measuring are so few and so closely related that any one of them can be spoken of as measuring reaction time without doing much injustice to the "construct." At a higher level of complexity, activity level in the rat logically should be manifested in at least a score of observables, and as it turns out, some of these do not correlate well with others. At the extreme of complexity are constructs like anxiety, intelligence, and social competence, where the domains of related observables are vast indeed.

Considerations in point 1 above tend to correlate with considerations in point 2: the larger the domain of observables related to a construct, the more difficult it tends to be to define which variables do or do not belong in the domain. Thus it might be relatively easy to get agreement among psychologists about whether or not a particular observable should be related to activity level, for example, a measure of muscle tonus. The boundaries of this domain are relatively well prescribed. In contrast, for many constructs the domain of related observables has "fuzzy edges," and the scientist is not sure of the full meanings of his own constructs. Typically, the scientist holds a firm belief about some of the more prominent observables related to the construct, but beyond that he can only guess how far the construct extends. In measuring the construct of intelligence, for example, all would agree that the construct should be evidenced to some extent in various types of problems involving reasoning abilities; but it is a matter of dispute as to what extent some measures of perceptual and memory abilities should be considered part of the construct. Such is the case with most constructs (e.g., anxiety): the boundaries of the domain of related observables are not clear.

Because constructs concern domains of observables, logically a better measure of any construct would be obtained by combining the results from a number of measures of such observables than by taking any one of them individually. Since, however, the work is often tedious enough with one measure, let alone a handful, it sometimes is asking too much of the scientist to expect him to employ more than one measure in a particular investigation. Thus any particular measure can be thought of as having a degree of construct validity depending on the extent to which results obtained from using the measure would be much the same if some other measure, or hypothetically, all the measures, in the domain had been employed in the experiment. Similarly, the combined scores from a number of measures of observables in the domain can be thought of as having a degree of construct validity for the domain as a whole.

The logical status of constructs in psychology for constructs concerning individual differences is the same as that for constructs concerning the results of controlled experiments. Thus whereas the construct of intelligence is more fre-

quently discussed with respect to studies of individual differences and the construct of habit strength is more frequently discussed with respect to controlled experiments, problems of construct validity are essentially the same for both. (Of course, in different studies a construct may be investigated as the dependent variable in a controlled experiment or in terms of correlations between sources of individual differences; but most measures are predominantly used in one or the other of the two types of studies.)

If the measurement of constructs is a vital part of scientific activity, how then are such measures developed and validated? There are three major aspects of the process: (1) specifying the domain of observables, (2) determining to what extent all, or some, of these observables correlate with each other or are affected alike by experimental treatments, and (3) determining whether or not one, some, or all measures of such variables *act* as though they measure the construct. Aspect 3 consists of determining whether or not a supposed measure of a construct correlates in expected ways with measures of other constructs or is affected in expected ways by particular experimental treatments. These steps are seldom, if ever, purposefully planned and undertaken by any investigator or group of investigators. Also, although it could be argued that the aspects should be undertaken in the order 1, 2, and then 3, this order is seldom, if ever, followed. More likely, a psychologist will develop a particular measure that is thought to partake of a construct, then he will leap directly to aspect 3 and perform a study relating the supposed measure of the construct to measures of other constructs, for example, correlating a particular measure of anxiety with a particular measure of response to frustration. Typically, other investigators will develop other particular measures of the same construct, and skipping aspects 1 and 2, they will move directly to aspect 3 and try to find interesting relations between their measures and measures of other constructs. As the number of proposed measures of the same construct grow and suspicion grows that they might not all measure the same thing, one or more investigators seek to outline in writing the domain of observables related to the construct, which is aspect 1. All, or parts, of one or more such outlines of the domain are subjected to investigation to determine the extent to which variables in the domain tend to measure the same thing, which is aspect 2. The impact of theorizing with respect to aspect 1 and the research results from aspect 2 tend to influence which particular variables are studied in aspect 3.

Since most scientists work as individuals rather than being tied to some overall plan of attack on a problem, each scientist does much what he pleases, and consequently there is seldom a planned, concentrated effort to develop valid measures of constructs according to a step-by-step procedure. Instead of the domain of observables for any construct being tightly defined initially (aspect 1), more likely the nature of the domain will be *suggested* by numerous attempts to develop particular measures relating to the construct; and subsequently, some investigators will attempt to more explicitly outline the domain of content. Instead of a planned, frontal attack on the empirical investigations required in aspects 2 and 3, more likely evidence accrues from many studies of different proposed measures of the construct; and subsequently, the available evidence is accumulated and

evaluated. Hopefully the end product of this complex process is a construct (1) that is well defined in terms of a variety of observables, (2) for which there are one or several variables that well represent the domain of observables, and (3) that eventually proves to relate strongly with other constructs of interest. Some of the methods required to reach those goals are described in the following sections.

Domain of observables. Whereas, on the face of it, one might think that the scientist should outline the domain of observables before assuming that any one observable relates to a construct, this is seldom done. More frequently, scientists investigate only one observable and assume that it is related to the construct, at least for the time being. For example, there have been many studies relating the Taylor manifest anxiety scale (Taylor, 1953) to supposed measures of other constructs. The test is intended to relate strongly to other variables in a domain of behaviors constituting anxiety. Many studies have been done in spite of the fact that the domain of the construct has not been well outlined, and it is probably true that if different investigators in this area attempted to outline the domain, there would be considerable disagreement among them.

Scientists should not be criticized for assuming that particular observables relate to a construct even though the domain of the construct is only vaguely understood. In his lifetime each scientist can perform only a relatively small number of studies (100 might be the average even for very busy scientists), and consequently he does not have time to do all that is required to specify the domain of a construct, develop measures of the construct, and relate those measures to other variables of interest. As the evidence accrues from the work of different scientists interested in a particular construct, however, it is fruitful to attempt a specification of the domain of related variables.

No precise method can be stated for properly outlining the domain of variables for a construct. The outline essentially constitutes a theory regarding how variables will relate to one another; and though theories themselves should be objectively testable, the theorizing process is necessarily intuitive. Outlining a construct consists essentially of stating what one means by the use of particular words, words such as "anxiety," "habit strength," and "intelligence." In the early attempts to outline a domain, the "outline" usually consists of only a definition in which the word denoting the construct is related to words at a lower level of abstraction. An example is the early attempt by Binet and Simon (1905) to define "intelligence": "The tendency to take and maintain a definite direction; the capacity to make adaptations for the purpose of attaining a desired end; and the power of auto-criticism." Brave as such attempts are, when they define a construct with words that are far removed from specific observable variables, they do little to specify the domain in question. An example of a more clearly specified domain is that by Hull (1952) for the construct of "net reaction potential," where the specification is in terms of the observables of probability of response, latency of response, amplitude of response, and number of responses to extinction. Further specifications are made of the observables in each of the four classes of observables.

Whether or not a well-specified domain for a construct actually leads to adequate measurement of the construct is a matter for empirical investigation; but

until there is a well-specified domain, there is no way to know exactly which studies should be done to test the adequacy with which a construct is measured. In other words, the major importance of aspect 1 (outlining the domain) is that it tells you what to do in aspect 2 (investigating relations among different proposed measures of a construct).

Relations among observables. The way to test the adequacy of the outline of a domain relating to a construct is to determine how well the measures of observables "go together" in empirical investigations. In studies of individual differences, the first step is to obtain scores for a sample of individuals on some of the measures; next, each measure is correlated with all other measures. An analysis of the resulting correlations provides evidence about the extent to which all the measures tend to measure the same thing. (Essentially this is a problem in factor analysis, which is discussed briefly later in this chapter.)

In investigations of construct validity in controlled experiments, the logic is much the same as that in studies of individual differences. One investigates the extent to which treatment conditions have similar effects on some of the measures of observables in the domain. A hypothetical example is given in Figure 10.1, which shows the effects of five levels of stress (the independent variable) on four supposed measures of the construct of fear. Measures A and B are monotonically related to levels of stress, which means that they are affected in much the same way by the experimental treatments. Measure C is monotonically related to treatment levels up to level 4, but falls off sharply at level 5, and consequently measures something that is not entirely the same as that in A and B. Measure D is not related in any systematic manner to the treatment levels, and consequently it logically could not measure the same thing as measured by A, B, and C. To determine fully the extent

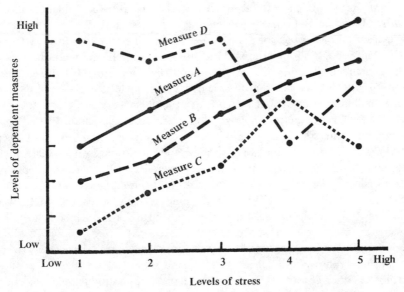

FIGURE 10.1 Effects of five levels of stress on four dependent measures.

to which these and other measures of fear "go together," it would be necessary to see how similarly they behaved with respect to other experimental treatments, for example, different levels of electrical stimulation of "fear areas" in the brains of rats.

The test of how well different supposed measures of a construct "go together" is the extent to which they have similar curves of relationship with a variety of treatment variables. It does not matter what form of the relationship is with a particular treatment variable as long as the supposed measures of the construct behave similarly. Thus, for two supposed measures of a construct, the relationship with one treatment variable could be monotonically increasing, the relationship with another curvilinear, and the relationship with another a flat line; but in all three instances the two measures of the construct would be affected much the same. If two measures were affected in exactly the same way by all possible experimental treatments, it would not matter which one was used in a particular experiment; and consequently one could speak of them as measuring the same thing. To the *degree* to which two measures are affected similarly by a variety of experimental treatments, they can be spoken of as measuring much the same thing. When a variety of measures behave similarly in this way over a variety of experimental treatments, it becomes meaningful to speak of them as measuring a construct. The measures that most consistently behave as the majority of measures do can be said to have the most construct validity.

Methods of investigating construct validity both in studies of individual differences and in controlled experiments involve correlations. Actual correlations are computed among measures of individual differences. A comparison of two curves is, in essence, a correlating of two curves, even though correlational methods might not be applied. Regardless of whether correlations are over individual differences or over levels of treatment effects, such correlations provide evidence about the structure of a domain of observables relating to a construct.

The results of investigations like those described above would lead to one of three conclusions. If all the proposed measures correlate highly with one another, it can be concluded that they all measure much the same thing. If the measures tend to split up into clusters such that the members of a cluster correlate highly with one another and correlate much less with the members of other clusters, it can be concluded that a number of *different* things are being measured. For example, in studying different supposed measures of anxiety, one might find that measures concerning bodily harm tend to go together and those concerning social embarrassment tend to go together. As a third possibility, if correlations among the measures all are near zero, they measure different things. Of course, the evidence is seldom so clear-cut as to enable one to unequivocally reach one of these three conclusions; rather, there usually is room for dispute as to which conclusion should be reached.

Evidence of the kind described above should affect subsequent efforts to specify the domain of observables for a construct and should affect theories relating the construct to other constructs. If all the measures supposedly related to a construct correlate highly, this should encourage investigators to keep working with the

specified domain of observables and should encourage continued investigation of theories relating that construct to others. If the evidence is that more than one thing is being measured, the old construct should be abandoned for two or more new ones, and theories that assume only one construct should be modified to take account of the multiplicity of constructs. If none of the variables correlate substantially with the others, the scientist has an unhappy state of affairs. Of course, it is possible that one of the measures is highly related to the construct and the others are unrelated to the construct, but it is much more likely that none of them relate well to the construct. Either the investigator must postulate an entirely new domain of observables for a construct, as, for example, when questionnaire measures of anxiety are abandoned in favor of physiological measures, or he will have to abandon the construct altogether.

Relations among constructs. In the previous section, means were discussed for studying construct validity in terms of the *internal consistency* with which different measures in a domain tend to supply the same information (tend to correlate highly with one another and be similarly affected by experimental treatments). To the extent that the elements of such a domain show this consistency, it can be said that *some* construct may be employed to account for the data, but it is by no means sure that it is legitimate to employ the construct name which motivated the research. In other words, consistency is a *necessary* but not *sufficient* condition for construct validity. A discussion of how one can, if ever, obtain sufficient evidence that a domain of observables relates to a construct requires an analysis of some of the deepest innards of scientific explanation.

First, we shall accept the assumption that it is possible to find immutable proof that a particular set of variables measures a particular construct, and we shall see what forms of evidence would be required. Later that assumption will be challenged, and different perspectives will be advocated for interpreting evidence regarding construct validity. If the assumption is accepted, sufficient evidence for construct validity is that the supposed measures of the construct (either a single measure of observables or a combination of such measures) *behave as expected.* If, for example, a particular measure is thought to relate to the construct of anxiety, common sense would suggest many findings that should be obtained with the measure. Higher scores (higher anxiety) should be found for (1) patients classified as anxiety neurotics than for unselected nonpatients, (2) subjects in an experiment who are kept threatened with a painful electric shock than for subjects not so threatened, and (3) graduate students waiting to undergo a final oral examination for the Ph.D. than for the same students after passing the examination. As another example, if a particular measure is thought to relate to the construct of intelligence, one would expect it to correlate at least moderately with grades in school, teachers' ratings of intelligence, and levels of professional attainment. So it is with all constructs: there are expected correlations with other variables and expected effects in controlled experiments.

If, according to the assumption above, it is possible to obtain immutable proof of the extent to which measures of observables measure a construct, the proof would come from determining the extent to which the measures "fit" in a network

of expected relations. First would come the test of internal consistency of elements in the domain; then there would need to be many correlational studies and many controlled experiments. To the extent to which the measures met expectations in those regards, there would be proof of construct validity.

There is an obvious logical fallacy in claiming such evidence as "proof" of construct validity. To determine construct validity, a measure must fit a theory about the construct; but to use this as evidence, it is necessary to *assume* the theory is true. The circularity in this logic can be illustrated by the following four hypotheses:

1. Constructs A and B correlate positively.
2. X is a measure of construct A.
3. Y is a measure of construct B.
4. X and Y correlate positively.

To give meat to the bones of the example, assume that A is the construct of anxiety, B is the construct of stress, X is a questionnaire thought to measure anxiety, and Y is a parameter of experimental treatments that is thought to induce stress. Even though the four hypotheses are not independent, it should be obvious that one experiment cannot test them all simultaneously. All that can be tested directly by the experiment is hypothesis 4, that X correlates positively with Y. From this one finding, it would necessary to *infer* the truth or falsity of the other hypotheses, but look at the many possibilities there are among the four hypotheses. Hypothesis 1 may be correct, but even if hypothesis 4 is correct, that would offer no direct proof for the truth of either or both hypotheses 2 and 3. Obviously X and Y could correlate positively, not because they relate to constructs A and B, respectively, but because they relate to still other constructs. As another possibility, hypothesis 2 could be correct, but if hypothesis 3 is incorrect, there would be no necessity for X to correlate with Y.

From the standpoint of inductive logic, it is apparent that the above paradigm for determining construct validity will not hold water. In the illustrative experiment, the experimenter hoped to obtain some evidence for hypothesis 2, that X is a measure of anxiety. All that can be validly tested by the experiment is whether or not hypothesis 4 is correct, whether or not X correlates with Y.

One who wanted to defend the above paradigm for testing construct validity could point out that the situation is not nearly as bleak as it has been painted. What is done in practice is to *assume* that two of the hypothesis, 1 through 3 are correct, and by performing an empirical test of hypothesis 4, to allow a valid inference regarding the remaining hypothesis. Thus, for the example above, it would be assumed that hypothesis 1 is correct, that stress does relate to anxiety. Also, it would be assumed that hypothesis 3 is correct, that the threat of painful electric shock does induce stress. If these assumptions are correct, the actual correlation between X and Y permits a valid inference regarding the truth of hypothesis 2, that X is a measure of the construct of anxiety.

One could further argue that making such assumptions in the modified paradigm above is not really so dangerous. The danger can be lessened by restricting

investigations of construct validity to those situations in which the truth of some of the hypotheses is very evident. The evidence of such truth could be based either on other experiments involving the variables, for example, prior investigations of the construct validity of electric shock as an inducer of stress, or on strong appeals to common sense. Thus in performing studies of construct validity, one relates variables in situations where the assumptions are very safe. For example, nearly everyone will agree that increases in stress should be accompanied by increases in anxiety and that the threat of painful electric shock is a form of stress. Such assumptions are made even safer by correlating a supposed measure of one construct with the supposed measure of another where the domain of the latter is both well defined and highly restricted. Thus if a supposed measure of anxiety is correlated with a supposed measure of reaction time, it is rather safe to assume that the particular measure of reaction time validly represents the construct of reaction time.

In the limiting case, construct validity concerns a hypothesized relationship between a supposed measure of a construct and a particular, observable variable. Thus it would be hypothesized that tests of intelligence should correlate positively with grades in school, teachers' rating of intelligence, and level of professional accomplishment. Such "other" variables are constructs only in the sense that there are slight variations possible in the measurement of each of these, which, though, would probably have little effect on empirical correlations. In this way one can reduce the number of hypotheses in the above paradigm from four to three. The hypothesis "Y is related to B" becomes the assumption "Y is B." Then if the assumption is very safe that A relates to B, for example, intelligence relates to progress in school, an empirical correlation of X with Y provides a safe basis of inference regarding the construct validity for the measurement of A with X. According to this point of view, studies of construct validity are safe when, and should be undertaken only when, (1) the domain of the "other" construct is well defined and (2) the assumption of a relationship between the two constructs is unarguable.

Explication of Constructs

The foregoing explanation of construct validation is the one currently accepted by many leading theorists, although perhaps the related procedures were specified in more detail than has been done by some authors. This is a workable set of standards, which provides a basis for the measurement of psychological constructs. If, however, the reader wants to go a step further in his thinking about the measurement of psychological constructs, there is a more defensible logic. Rather than referring to this logic as relating to construct validation, it would be more correct to refer to it as concerning *construct explication,* by which is meant the process of making an abstract word explicit in terms of observable variables.

The flaw in the paradigm described above is that it succinctly assumes that any construct has *objective reality* beyond that of the particular observables used to measure the construct. Thus we speak of anxiety as though it were a real variable, one to be *discovered* in the course of empirical studies. The evidence supplies

support for arguments as to whether or not *it* has been measured. One hears arguments such as, "This is not really a measure of anxiety." Inherent in these and other words used to discuss the measurement of constructs is the implicit assumption that constructs have objective reality. It is more defensible to make no claims for the objective reality of a construct name, for example, "anxiety," and instead to think of the construct name as being a useful way to label a particular set of observable variables. Then the name is "valid" only to the extent that it accurately communicates to other scientists the kinds of observables that are being studied.

A more airtight set of standards for "construct validity" starts with the definition of a set of measures concerning observables. Thus set A would be said to consist of measures of particular observables X_1, X_2, X_3, and so on, and set B would be said to consist of the particular observables Y_1, Y_2, Y_3, and so on. (The X's could be thought of as different measures of anxiety and the Y's as different measures of learning.) Construct validation (later the term will be modified), then, consists of the following steps. Through a series of empirical studies, a network of probability statements is formed among the different measures in set A, and the same is done for B. There are many ways to do this, depending on the types of empirical studies undertaken and the types of probability statements thought to be most meaningful. The most straightforward example is where individual differences on the different measures within a set are correlated with one another. Thus it might be found that X_1 correlates .50 with X_2 and .45 with X_3, and that X_2 correlates .55 with X_3. Knowing these correlations, one could make probability statements concerning scores on the three measures. If, for example, it is known that a person has a score of 20 on measure X_1, the odds can be established as to whether or not that person has a score between 40 and 60 on X_2. Although it seldom is necessary to explicitly make such probability statements about correspondences between scores on different measures, correlations among the measures directly specify the extent to which such probability statements are possible.

After all possible correlations among the individual observables have been obtained, it then is possible to deduce correlations between different combinations of variables in the set. Thus it would be possible to deduce the correlation between the sum of any three of the measures and the sum of any other three measures in the set. More important, it would be possible to deduce the correlation between any particular measure in the set and the sum of all measures that had been investigated in the set.

Gradually, in the course of many studies, more and more is learned about correlations among the measures of observables in a particular set. The total information in this regard can be spoken of as forming an *internal structure* for the elements of a set. The structure may indicate that all the variables tend to measure much the same thing, which would be support for retaining the set as it originally was defined; or the structure may be such as to indicate that two or more things are being measured by members of the set, for example, two types of anxiety. If the latter is the case, it would be appropriate to break the original set A into two sets A_1 and A_2 corresponding to those variables that actually correlate well with one another. If all the correlations among members of the set are very low, it is illogical

to continue speaking of the variables as constituting a set, and the investigator should turn his attention to other sets of variables. Regardless of which of these three conclusions is required by the evidence, eventually the evidence leads to a probability structure for the full set or for subdivisions of the set.

When the above has been accomplished, the internal consistency is known for the elements of a set A. Similarly, the internal consistency is determined for another set B. Taking the argument a step further, assume that a particular variable X_1 in A is correlated with a particular variable Y_1 in set B. Depending on the size of the correlation, it then would be possible to make many types of probability statements regarding unknown correlations between any other member of A and any other member of B. For example, if X_1 and X_2 are known to correlate highly and if Y_1 and Y_2 are known to correlate highly, finding a high correlation between X_1 and Y_1 permits a prediction of what the correlation would be between X_2 and Y_2. As another example, if the sum of all variables in A is known to correlate highly with the sum of all variables in B, it is possible to estimate the correlation between any particular variable from A and B or the correlation between any two combinations of variables from A and B. Thus there are *internal structures* for the variables in sets A and B separately and a *cross structure* between variables in the two sets. If the internal structure of any set is satisfactory, it permits the scientist to explore cross structures of that set with other sets. If such cross structures are satisfactory, scientific progress is being made: either theories are being tested or interesting discoveries are being made.

Whereas, in the ultimate analysis, the "measurement" and "validation" of constructs can consist of nothing more than the determination of internal structures and cross structures, that way of looking at it is disquieting to both the layman and the scientist. There is a need to put more meaning into the system. The scientist is not content to say only that members of set A relate to something else; he wants to say that anxiety, or a construct by another name, relates to something else. As was mentioned previously, words denoting constructs are essential to the scientist in thinking about problems, formulating theories, and communicating the results of experiments. This need for names pushes the scientist, and the layman even more, into assuming that corresponding to the name is some *real* variable which will be discovered some day. For example, some psychologists talk as though there is some real counterpart to the word "anxiety" that eventually will be found. The problem is not that of searching for a needle in the haystack, but that of searching for a needle that is *not* in the haystack.

The words that scientists use to denote constructs, for example, "anxiety" and "intelligence," have no real counterparts in the world of observables; they are only heuristic devices for exploring observables. Whereas, for example, the scientist might find it more comfortable to speak of "anxiety" than set A, only set A objectively exists, empirical research concerns only set A, and in the final analysis only relations between members of set A and members of other sets can be unquestionably determined.

Although words relating to constructs are undeniably helpful to the scientist, they also can get him into real trouble. Such words are only symbols for collections

of observables. Thus the word "fear" is a symbol for many possible forms of behavior. The difficulty is that the individual scientist is not sure of all the observables that should relate to such a word, and scientists disagree about the related observables. The denotations of a word can be no more exact than the extent to which (1) all possible related observables are specified and (2) all who use the word agree on the specification. Dictionary definitions of words concerning constructs help very little; they serve only to relate one unspecified term to other unspecified terms.

Considering the inexactness of denotations of words relating to constructs, it is not possible to *prove* that any collection of observables measures a construct. It would be much like the expedition starting out to catch a rare bird, the awrk. All scientists agree that the awrk has red wings, a curved bill, and only two toes, but everything else about the awrk is either unknown or a matter of dispute. How, then, would the expedition ever know for sure whether or not it had found an awrk? The analogy really is not farfetched: the same inconsistency is apparent in efforts to "find" measures of intelligence, anxiety, and other constructs. Looked at in this way, it logically is not possible to prove that any set of observables measure a construct.

Although, in a strict sense, "construct validity" is logically impossible, there are forms of proof that amount to much the same thing. The scientist starts with a word, for example, "anxiety," and from that he hypothesizes a set of related observables. Proof can be obtained for the internal structure of those observables by methods described previously. If some combination of the members of this set of variables relates strongly to some combination of the members of another, this is proof that the first set has explanatory power. If it is useful to refer to these two steps as "construct validation," probably no harm is done; but it is important to understand what is being proved and how the related evidence is gathered.

Ideally, one could envision a process whereby gradual refinements of a set of observables would be matched by gradual refinements of the words used to denote the set. Thus relatively inexact terms like "anxiety" and "intelligence" would be successively replaced by terms that were more denotatively exact for a set of observables, the set itself being continually refined in terms of an internal structure and a cross structure with other sets of variables. It is doubtful, though, that any terms in common parlance will ever suffice to serve this purpose, and consequently only impartial designations such as "set A" can ever meet the full test of denotative explicitness.

Strictly speaking, scientists can never be sure that a construct has been measured or that a theory regarding that construct has been tested, even though it may be useful to speak as though it has been. A construct is only a word, and although the word may suggest explorations of the internal structure of an interesting set of variables, there is no way to prove that any combination of those variables actually "measures" the word. Theories consist of collections of words (statements about natural events), and though such theories may suggest interesting investigations of cross structures among sets of observables, the evidence obtained is not so much proof of the *truth* of the theories as it is proof of their *usefulness* as guides to

empirical reality. Call it the "measurement" and "validation" of constructs if you like, but, at least as far as science takes us, there are only (1) words denoting constructs, (2) sets of variables specified for such constructs, (3) evidence concerning internal structures of such sets, (4) words concerning relations among constructs (theories), (5) which suggest cross structures among different sets of observables, (6) evidence regarding such cross structures, and (7) beyond that, nothing.

Other Issues Concerning Validity

Other names. Other authors have called the three types of validity discussed in this chapter by different names. Predictive validity has been referred to as "empirical validity" and "statistical validity"; content validity has been referred to as "intrinsic validity," "circular validity," "relevance," and "representativeness"; and construct validity has been spoken of as "trait validity" and "factorial validity."

One frequently sees the term "face validity," which concerns the extent to which an instrument "looks like" it measures what it is intended to measure. For example, an achievement test for fourth-grade arithmetic would be said to have face validity if potential users of the test liked the types of items employed. Any instrument intended to have content validity should meet that standard, but the standard is far from complete. Face validity concerns judgments about an instrument *after* it is constructed. As was discussed previously, content validity more properly is ensured by the plan of content and the plan for constructing items. Thus face validity can be considered one aspect of content validity, which concerns an inspection of the final product to make sure that nothing went wrong in transforming plans into a completed instrument.

When an instrument is intended to perform a prediction function, validity depends entirely on how well the instrument correlates with what it is intended to predict (a criterion), and consequently face validity is irrelevant. There are many instances in which an instrument looks as though it should correlate well with a criterion although the correlation is close to zero. Also, there are many instruments that bear no obvious relationship to a criterion but actually correlate well with the criterion. With prediction functions, face validity is important only in formulating hypotheses about instruments that will correlate well with their criteria. Thus even though the correlations tell the full story, it is not wise to select predictors at random. Before research is done on a prediction problem, there must be some hope that a particular instrument will work. Such hope is fostered when the instrument looks as if it should predict the criterion. Also, tests usually are more predictive of a criterion if their item content is phrased in the language and the terms of the objects actually encountered in the particular type of performance. For example, if an arithmetic test is being constructed for the prediction of performance in the operation of particular types of machines, the test probably would be more predictive if problems were phrased in terms of numbers of nuts and bolts rather than numbers of apples and oranges. For these two reasons, face validity plays a part in decisions about types of tests to be used as predictors and in the construction of items for those tests.

In applied settings, face validity is to some extent related to public relations. For

example, teachers would be reluctant to use an achievement test unless the items "looked good." Less logical is the reluctance of some administrators in applied settings, for example, industry, to permit the use of predictor instruments which lack face validity. Conceivably, a good predictor of a particular criterion might consist of preferences among drawings of differently shaped and differently colored butterflies, but it would be difficult to convince administrators that the test actually could do a good job of selecting employees.

Although one could make a case for the involvement of face validity in the measurement of constructs, to do so probably would serve only to confuse the issues. It would be better to think directly in terms of the principles stated in the previous section.

Place of factor analysis. For those who are not already familiar with factor analysis, it should be noted that it essentially consists of methods for finding clusters of related variables. Each such cluster, or factor, is denoted by a group of variables whose members correlate more highly among themselves than they do with variables not included in the cluster. Each factor is thought of as a unitary attribute (a yardstick) which is measured to greater and lesser degrees by particular instruments, depending on the extent to which they correlate with the factor. Such correlations have been spoken of as representing the *factorial validity* of measures. It would be better to speak of such correlations as representing the *factorial composition* of measures, because the word "validity" is somewhat misleading.

The factorial composition of measures plays a part in all three types of validity discussed in this chapter. Factor analysis is important in the selection of instruments to be tried as predictors. Instead of constructing a new test for each applied problem as it arises, one selects a predictor instrument from a "storehouse" of available instruments. Factor analysis can serve to construct such a storehouse of measures with known factorial composition. It then is much easier to formulate hypotheses about the possible predictive power in particular instances of particular factors rather than to formulate hypotheses about the predictive power of instruments developed ad hoc for the problem.

Factor analysis provides helpful circumstantial evidence regarding measures that are intended to have content validity. For example, a factor analysis of a battery of achievement tests might show that a test intended to measure mathematics correlates rather highly with a factor of verbal comprehension. This would suggest that the words and sentences used to phrase problems were sufficiently difficult to introduce an unwanted factor in the test, which would lead to revisions of the test for mathematics.

Factor analysis is at the heart of the measurement of psychological constructs. As was said previously, the explication of constructs mainly consists of determining (1) the internal statistical structure of a set of variables said to measure a construct and (2) the statistical cross structures between the different measures of one construct and those of other constructs. Factor analysis is used directly to determine item 1, and procedures related to factor analysis are important in determining item 2. To take the simplest case, if all the elements of set A correlate highly with one another and all the elements of set B correlate highly with one another, the members of each set then have high correlations with a factor defined by that set.

This would be evidence that the two sets, corresponding to two supposed constructs, meet the test of a "strong" internal structure. If, in addition, the two factors correlate substantially, this would provide evidence regarding the cross structure of the two sets of measures.

Factor analysis plays important parts with respect to all three types of validity, but it plays somewhat different parts with each. Regarding predictive validity, factor analysis mainly is important in suggesting predictors that will work well in practice. With content validity, factor analysis mainly is important in suggesting ways to revise instruments for the better. With construct validity, factor analysis provides some of the tools that are most useful for determining internal structures and cross-structures for sets of variables.

THEORY OF MEASUREMENT ERROR

Some error is involved in any type of measurement, whether it is the measurement of the temperature of liquids, blood pressure, or intelligence. Measurement error can be in the form of either a systematic bias or random errors. The former would be the case if a chemist had only one thermometer, and although he read it with high fidelity, the thermometer always registered two degrees higher than it should. Random error would be at work if the thermometer were accurate but the chemist nearsightedly misread it while making different measurements. A systematic bias is not important in most psychological measures. It contributes only to the mean score of all subjects being studied, and the mean is not very important in studies of individual differences and in most psychological experiments. Random errors are important in all studies, because to the extent they are present, limits are placed on the degree of lawfulness that can be found in nature. Why this is so can be illustrated with the nearsighted chemist. Suppose that when no measurement error is present there is a smooth curve relating temperature to the ratio of one chemical to another in a compound. To the extent to which random errors of measurement occur, the smooth curve will not be found, and instead the curve will appear somewhat jagged. In all areas of science, random errors of measurement tend to jumble up any form of lawfulness that exists in nature.

Random errors of measurement are never completely eliminated; but to portray nature in its ultimate lawfulness, efforts are made to reduce such errors as much as possible. To the extent to which measurement error is slight, a measure is said to be *reliable*. Reliability concerns the extent to which measurements are *repeatable*—by the same individual using different measures of the same attribute or by different persons using the same measure of an attribute. Science is concerned with repeatable experiments; and for experiments to be repeatable, any particular object in any particular circumstance must have a set quantity of any particular attribute. When one investigator can find different measurements for the object in the particular circumstance or other investigators can find different measurements with the same or different instruments, experimental results are not exactly repeatable. Thus science is limited by the reliability of measuring instruments and/or the reliability with which scientists use them.

Of course, high reliability does not necessarily mean high validity. One could, for

example, seek to measure intelligence by having children throw stones as far as they could. How far stones were tossed on one occasion might correlate highly with how far they were tossed on another occasion, and thus, being repeatable, the measure would be highly reliable; but obviously the tossing of stones would not constitute a *valid* measure of intelligence. The amount of measurement error places a limit on the amount of validity that an instrument can have, but even in the complete absence of measurement error, there is no guarantee of validity. Reliability is a *necessary* but not *sufficient* condition for validity.

It is interesting that the theory of measurement error has been developed largely in the context of psychology, and largely by psychologists. One might imagine that this is because psychological measures are plagued by measurement error, but this is only a partial explanation. Measures in other areas of science often are accompanied by as much, or more, random error than is found in psychology. For example, the measurement of blood pressure in physiological studies is far less reliable than most psychological measures, and similar examples could be drawn from the physical and social sciences. The development of the theory of measurement error by psychologists can be attributed either to an accident of history or to the fact that, being self-conscious about problems of measurement, psychologists have developed the theory of measurement error along with other advances they have made in the methodology of measurement. Among his many other contributions to psychological measurement, Charles Spearman (1904) laid the foundation stones for the theory of measurement error.

For two reasons, it is easy to overstate the importance of the theory of measurement error of psychological measurement. First, as will be shown later, measurement error usually does not harm most investigations as much as might be thought. Second, there are numerous topics regarding psychological measurement that are more important than the theory of measurement error. A large proportion of journal articles on psychological measurement and a major portion of some books on the topic have been devoted to measurement error. This is probably because the theory of measurement error is so neatly expressible in mathematical terms, in contrast to some other important issues, for example, validity, where grounds for argument are not so straightforward.

The theory of measurement error which will be presented is surely one of the most workable mathematical models in psychology. The theory can be derived with few assumptions about the nature of data, and the same formulas can be derived from quite different sets of assumptions. The theory is very "robust," in the sense that it tends to hold well even when the assumptions of the model are markedly violated. Even very elegant, highly complicated mathematical models have failed to improve substantially on the principles which Spearman gave us.

The basic issues in the discussion of measurement error are illustrated in Figure 10.2. It is assumed that each person has a "true score," one that would be obtained if there were no errors of measurement. In the figure, person A has a relatively high true score and person B has a relatively low true score. Since there is some random error in the score obtained for a person on a particular occasion, obtained scores would differ from true scores on a random basis. If it were possible to give many alternative forms of a test, for example, many different spelling tests constructed

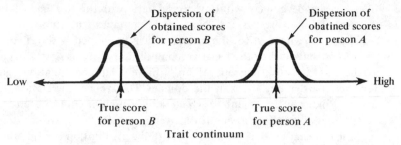

FIGURE 10.2　True scores and distributions of obtained scores for two persons.

by the same procedures, the average score on the tests would closely approximate true scores. Scores obtained from the alternative forms would be distributed symmetrically above and below the true scores. Since such random errors are expected to be normally distributed, it is expected that distributions of obtained scores will be normally distributed about true scores.

The wider the spread of obtained scores about true scores, the more error there is in employing the type of instrument. The standard deviation of the distribution of errors for each person would be an index of the amount of error. If the standard deviation of errors was much the same for all persons, which usually is assumed to be the case, one standard deviation of errors could typify the amount of error to be expected. This typical standard deviation of errors is called the *standard error of measurement*, σ_{meas}. The size of σ_{meas} is a direct indication of the amount of error involved in using a particular type of instrument.

The Domain-Sampling Model

The most useful model for the discussion of measurement error is that which considers any particular measure as being composed of *a random sample of items from a hypothetical domain of items*. An example would be a particular spelling test for fourth-grade students, which could be thought of as constituting a random sample of spelling words from all possible words appropriate for that age group. Another example would be the number of errors made by rats in a particular maze, in which case the errors made could be thought of as a random sample of the errors that would be made if there were an infinite number of turns in the maze and rats were capable of traversing an infinitely long maze. Many other examples could be given of how it is reasonable to think of a particular measure as representing a sample of items from a hypothetical domain of items.

Of course, at the outset it is obvious that the model is not entirely true to life, because strictly speaking, items are almost never actually sampled randomly; rather, items are *composed* for particular measures. The model usually does, however, lead to accurate predictions in practice. First, it is stated that the purpose of any particular measurement is to estimate the measurement that would be obtained if *all* the items in the domain were employed, for example, all the spelling words. The score that any subject would obtain over the whole domain is spoken of as his *true score*. To the extent to which any sample of items correlated highly with true scores, the sample would be highly reliable.

The model can be developed without consideration of the number of items sampled for particular measures. Each sample could contain many items, or at the lower extreme, only one item. Also, the model can be developed without concern for the type of item employed or the factorial composition of items.

Basic to the model is the concept of an infinitely large correlation matrix showing all correlations among items in the domain. The average correlation in the matrix, $\bar{r}_{ij}$, would indicate the extent to which some common core existed in the items. The dispersion of correlations about the average would indicate the extent to which items varied in sharing the common core. If the assumption is made that all items have an equal amount of the common core, the average correlation in each column of the hypothetical matrix would be the same, which would be the same as the average correlation in the whole matrix. Keep in mind that the assumption is not necessarily that all correlations in the matrix are the same, but rather that the sum of correlations, or average, of each item with all the others is the same for all items. The latter is a much less restrictive assumption than the former.

If the above assumption holds, it is possible to compute directly (not just estimate) the correlation of any particular item with the sum of all items in the domain. (These and other deductions from the domain sampling model are presented in detail in Nunnally, 1967, chaps. 6 and 7.) The result is as follows:

$$r_{1t} = \sqrt{\bar{r}_{1j}} \qquad\qquad [1]$$

where 1 = scores on item 1

    t = true scores in domain

    $\bar{r}_{1j}$ = average correlation of item 1 with all items in domain

The correlation r_{1t} of item 1 with true scores in the domain (the sum of all items in the domain) would equal the square root of the average correlation of item 1 with all other items. The formula above is the foundation of the theory of measurement error, and from it can be deduced many principles concerning reliability.

Multi-item measures. Equation 1 above concerns a hypothetical domain of items, but in nearly all research the concern is with whole tests composed of numerous items. The model can be easily extended to take care of this. The infinitely large matrix of correlations among items can be thought of as divided into groups, each containing h items. The sum of scores on each group of items would constitute a test. If items were randomly sampled to compose the tests, correlations among different tests would tend to be the same. Such randomly sampled collections of items are said to constitute *randomly parallel* tests, since their means, standard deviations, and correlations with true scores differ only by chance. If it is assumed that the average correlation of each test with the sum of all other tests is the same for all tests, one can start back with Equation 1 and insert standard scores for whole tests rather than for individual items:

$$r_{1t} = \sqrt{\bar{r}_{1j}} \qquad\qquad [2]$$

where 1 = scores on test 1

    t = true scores in domain

    $\bar{r}_{1j}$ = average correlation of test 1 with all tests in domain

The same formula results whether one is considering individual items or whole tests, no matter how many items are in each of the whole tests. (It should be kept in mind that the average correlation among whole tests will be larger than the average correlation among items, and consequently correlations with true scores will be higher for the whole tests.)

By convention, the average correlation of one test, or one item, with all tests or items in the domain is called the *reliability coefficient*, which will be symbolized as r_{11} for variable 1, r_{22} for variable 2, and so on. Then the square root of r_{11} equals the correlation of item 1 or test 1 with true scores in the domain.

Estimate of reliability. If the assumption made previously regarding correlations among elements of a domain is correct, the correlation of any test with true scores is precisely equal to the square root of $\bar{r}_{11}$, which is not an estimate, but an actual determination. Of course, in practice one never knows $\bar{r}_{11}$ exactly, because it is not possible to generate an infinite number of tests. Consequently $\bar{r}_{11}$, and thus $\bar{r}_{1t}$, can be only *estimated* in practice. An estimate of $\bar{r}_{11}$ will be symbolized as r_{11}, which is the conventional symbol for the reliability coefficient.

Obviously r_{11} is a better estimate of $\bar{r}_{11}$ when the former is obtained by averaging the correlations of test 1 with a large, rather than a small, number of tests from the domain. If the tests were obtained actually by randomly drawing items from the domain, the key assumption regarding correlations among tests would be approximately correct. The average correlation of test 1 with a number of other tests would then be an estimate of the average correlation of test 1 with all tests in the domain. For example, the average correlation between one spelling test and five other spelling tests with the same number of items would be an estimate of $\bar{r}_{11}$, and the square root of that would be an estimate of the correlation between test 1 and hypothetical true scores in spelling. What usually occurs in practice is that test 1 is correlated with only one other test (test 2), and the correlation is symbolized as r_{11}, which is taken as an estimate of $\bar{r}_{11}$. (It could be symbolized equally well as r_{22} and taken as an estimate of the squared correlation of test 2 with true scores in the particular domain.) When only one correlation is taken as an estimate of a hypothetical infinite number of correlations, however, it rightly should be questioned how efficient such estimates are, as will be considered in a later section.

The importance of the reliability coefficient. Care has been taken to explain that r_{1t} is equal to the square root of $\bar{r}_{11}$ and to show how r_{1t} is estimated by the square root of r_{11} (the average of any number of correlations between test 1 and other tests from the domain, including the "average" of only one such correlation). Once a good estimate of r_{11}, and thus a good estimate of r_{1t}, is obtained, many important principles can be developed about measurement error. In this section it will be assumed that a precise method of estimating $\bar{r}_{11}$ is being used in particular problems; in later sections the precision of such estimates in different circumstances will be discussed. Assuming, then, that $r_{11} = \bar{r}_{11}$, r_{1t} equals the square root of r_{11}.

The scores on a particular test are often spoken of as *fallible scores,* "fallible" because there is a degree of measurement error involved. In contrast, true scores are, in that sense, infallible. Although r_{1t} is the correlation between an existing variable and a hypothetical variable rather than between two existing variables, it can be used in mathematical derivations in the same way that any correlation can.

One can visualize a scatter diagram showing the relationship between the fallible scores on any test and true scores. This is illustrated in Figure 10.3. Then, according to what has been learned about correlational analysis, the line of best fit for estimating true scores from fallible scores would be obtained as follows:

$$z_{t'} = r_{1t}z_1 = \sqrt{r_{11}}z_1 \qquad [3]$$

where $z_{t'}$ = estimates of true standard scores

z_1 = standard scores on fallible measure

r_{1t} = correlation of fallible scores with true scores

r_{11} = reliability coefficient for variable 1

More about the estimation of true scores will be given in a later section. The important point here is that r_{1t} can be placed in the usual equations for correlational analysis. It is particularly important to realize that, since the square of any correlation equals the variance in one variable explainable by variance in another variable, r_{1t}^2 equals the percentage of true-score variance explainable by a fallible measure. Then it can also be said that r_{11} equals the same percentage of true-score variance in the fallible measure. This percentage takes on even more meaning when the fallible measure is expressed as deviation scores or raw scores rather than as

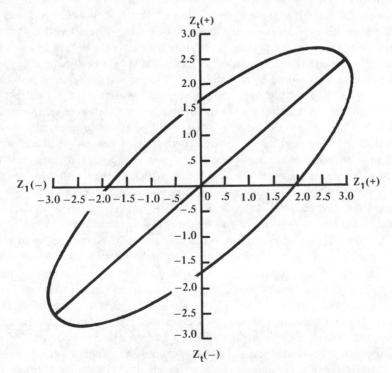

FIGURE 10.3   Regression line and scatter contour for hypothetical relationship between obtained scores and true scores.

standard scores. In the former two instances, the reliability coefficient could be expressed as follows:

$$r_{11} = \frac{\sigma_t^2}{\sigma_1^2}$$ [4]

where σ_1^2 = variance of variable 1

σ_t^2 = variance of variable 1 explainable by true scores

What Equation 4 shows is that r_{11} equals the amount of true-score variance in a measure divided by the actual variance of the measure. This way of viewing the reliability coefficient opens the door to the development of many principles concerning measurement error, but before those principles are developed, another model will be described for deriving the same principles.

Factorial composition. It sometimes is said that the domain sampling model which has been described for considering measurement error assumes that all items measure one factor only. Strictly speaking, this is not correct. This model would hold if items were equally divided between two factors, for example, if half the items in the domain concerned spelling and the other half concerned arithmetic. In the domain-sampling model, random samples from this two-factor domain would tend to correlate the same with one another. True scores would consist of combined ability in spelling and arithmetic. The square root of average correlations among sample tests would approximate the correlation of individual tests with true scores, which is the key deduction from the model. All other formulas for measurement error could be derived for this two-factor domain. The model would hold as well if instead of two kinds of items relating to two factors, all items were compounded in equal proportions of a number of factors. For example, if each item simultaneously measured anxiety, reaction time, and muscle coordination, all items would tend to correlate much the same with one another, and consequently the average correlation among 20 or more of them would serve well to represent the average correlation that would be obtained among much larger numbers of them.

The domain-sampling model would still hold even if half a dozen factors were randomly scattered among the items. In this case some of the items would be dominated by one factor only, some would share two or more factors, and some would share the variance of all factors involved. The reliability estimate would not be as precise as it would be if only one factor dominated the items, but predictions from the models would still hold.

The domain-sampling model concerns the extent to which one "anything" correlates with an infinite number of other "anythings." This correlation is estimated by taking the square root of the average correlation of one "anything" with a number of other "anythings," or the square root of the correlation with only one other "anything." All the mathematical properties of the domain-sampling model hold regardless of the factorial composition of the items.

The factorial composition of items is important in two ways. First, to the extent that the items diversely measure a number of factors rather than only one factor,

correlations among items are likely to be rather heterogeneous in size. As will be discussed more fully in the next section, the more homogeneous the correlations in the domain are, the more precise are estimates of correlations with true scores. Consequently even though the domain-sampling model leads to *unbiased* estimates of correlations with true scores when the domain is factorially complex, such estimates might be accompanied by a considerable amount of *content-sampling error*.

The second important consideration regarding factorial composition is that, in actual investigations, the *intention* is to investigate a domain of items that principally concerns one factor. No one is, or should be, interested in studying the internal consistency of a polyglot domain of test materials. As has been mentioned previously, the purpose in the development of a new measure is to tap a unitary attribute. Even though the model holds when items concern more than one factor, the problem is more meaningful and estimates of reliability are more precise when items are dominated by only one factor.

Precision of Reliability Estimates

At a number of places so far the question has arisen as to the precision of reliability estimates from the domain-sampling model. Such estimates are precise to the extent that different random samples of items correlate the same with true scores. If an item correlated exactly the same with all other items in the domain, the correlation with any other item would be a precise indication of reliability. If all items in the domain correlated exactly the same with one another, all items would have exactly the same correlation with true scores, which would equal the square root of the typical correlation. To the extent that correlations among items in the domain vary, there is some random error connected with the average correlation found in any particular sampling of items. For example, if item 1 had correlations with other items in the domain ranging from .10 to .30, the average correlation of item 1 with a number of other items randomly selected from the domain would provide a relatively precise estimate of the reliability of item 1. In contrast, if such correlations ranged between -.30 and .60, the average correlation of item 1 with the other items might give only a rough approximation of the reliability.

Related to the precision of estimates of reliability is a double problem of sampling, that concerned with the sampling of people and that concerned with the sampling of items. It is all but impossible to consider both problems of sampling simultaneously. For this reason, it is said that measurement theory is a "large sample" theory, in which it is assumed that sufficient numbers of persons are studied so that this source of sampling error is a minor consideration. This is necessary not only to simplify measurement theory, but also because the precision required in measurement theory cannot tolerate large doses of sampling error because of a small number of subjects. Consequently, in this discussion it will be assumed that a minimum of 300 persons are employed in studies of measurement error, in which case the sampling error because of the sampling of people will be a minor consideration. In the theory of measurement error, the concern is with the *sampling of items*.

A domain of items is of interest only if the average correlation among items is positive. If the average correlation is zero or near zero, the items as a group have no common core, and it is not sensible to consider them as measuring a unitary attribute. Assuming that the average correlation is positive and sufficiently higher than zero to encourage further investigation, the next point of interest is the relative homogeneity of correlations. As was mentioned previously, it is hoped that the correlations will be relatively homogeneous. Whatever the case, there will be a distribution of correlations about the average value. An approximate statistical model will help to evaluate the influence of that distribution on the precision of estimates of reliability. The model assumes that correlations are normally distrib-uted about the average value and statistically independent of one another, both of which assumptions are known to be at least slightly incorrect. If the average correlation is positive, a random distribution of correlations about that average tends to be skewed rather than strictly normal. Also, correlations in a matrix are not independent of one another. For example, the correlation of item 1 and item 2 is not independent of the correlation of item 2 and item 3. When, however, correlations are as low as they usually are among test items (typically ranging between .10 and .40), those assumptions are violated only slightly, and consequently the model probably will hold well in practice.

As will be explained more fully in a later section, regardless of the number of items sampled from a domain to obtain a test, the reliability of the test is directly related to the average correlation among those items. Longer tests have higher reliability coefficients than shorter tests, but in both cases the reliabilities of the tests are deducible from the average correlations among their items. This being so, the precision with which the reliability is estimated for any test is a direct function of the precision with which the average correlation of items in a test estimates the average correlation of all items in the domain. If such correlations are normally distributed in the domain, an approximate standard error for the estimation of $\bar{r}_{ij}$ is obtained as follows:

$$\sigma_{\bar{r}_{ij}} = \frac{\sigma_{r_{ij}}}{\sqrt{\tfrac{1}{2}k(k-1)-1}} \qquad [5]$$

where $\sigma_{\bar{r}_{ij}}$ = standard error of estimating $\bar{r}_{ij}$ in whole domain

$\sigma_{r_{ij}}$ = standard deviation of distribution of actual correlations within test

k = number of test items

Equation 5 is merely an adaptation of the customary formula for the standard error of the mean, in which case people, rather than items, would be sampled. In that instance the standard error of average scores for people would equal the standard deviation of scores divided by the number of persons minus 1. In Equation 5, each correlation is considered analogous to a score made by one person. The standard deviation of correlations within a test is taken as an estimate of the standard deviation of correlations in the whole domain. At first glance, the denominator of Equation 5 may look complicated, but it is only the square root of the number of possible correlations among k items minus 1, the 1 being subtracted to obtain the

proper "degrees of freedom." In a correlation matrix, there are k^2 terms. From this must be subtracted the k diagonal 1's. What remains must be divided by 2, because each correlation appears twice in the matrix. Proper manipulation shows that these steps end with the finding that the number of off-diagonal coefficients either above or below the diagonal is ½k(k - 1). Thus when 1 is subtracted from this number, the proper degrees of freedom appear under the radical in the denominator.

What is immediately apparent from the formula is that the error of estimating $\bar{r}_{11}$ is directly related to the standard deviation of correlations among items. Also apparent from an inspection of the denominator is that the precision (the inverse of the standard error) of estimating $\bar{r}_{11}$ is directly related to the number of test items. Thus an important principle is deduced: Not only are longer tests more reliable (which will be proved later), but also their estimates of reliability are more precise than are those for shorter tests.

A typical situation is that in which the average correlation among items is .20 and the standard deviation of correlations is .10. Then the standard error for estimating $\bar{r}_{ij}$ from a 10-item test is obtained as follows:

$$\sigma_{\bar{r}_{ij}} = \frac{.10}{\sqrt{(5 \times 9) - 1}}$$

$$= \frac{.10}{\sqrt{44}}$$

$$= \frac{.10}{6.63} \qquad [6]$$

$$\sigma_{\bar{r}_{ij}} = .015$$

In any sampling problem, the expectation is that 95% of sample means will lie in a band stretching from approximately two standard errors below the population mean to two standard errors above it. The analogous expectation here is that, for random samples of items, the average correlation among items will be distributed in a like manner. Using this logic, if the average correlation among items in a domain is .20 and the standard deviation of correlations is .10, the standard error for average correlations obtained from 10-item tests is only .015. Then the expectation is that 95% of the sample values lie between approximately .168 and .232. If in this instance there were 40 items on each test, the standard error would be only .0036! What is illustrated in the above example is that, even when tests have as few as 10 items, reliability estimates are rather precise. When there are as many items as appear on most tests, the sampling error because of the selection of items is vanishingly small. The reason for this precision is that as the number of items is increased, the number of correlations among items increases at a rapid rate, the factor being that appearing in the denominator of Equation 6. For example, there are 780 possible correlations among 40 items. One then obtains approximately the same precision for estimating the average correlation that would be obtained in sampling people if 780 subjects were used in the study. Thus, in most measurement

problems, there is very little error in the estimation of reliability that could be attributed to random error in the selection of items. A very important point is that if two tests supposedly from the same domain correlate less with one another than would be predicted from the average correlation among items within each test, the difference usually is caused not by random errors in the selection of items, but by either sampling error because of the number of persons or systematic differences in the way items are obtained for the two tests. In other words, when this occurs in a large sample of persons, the indication is that the two tests are representative of somewhat different domains of content, a point which will be discussed more fully later.

It should be kept in mind that if, for example, the average correlation in a sample of 40 items is .20, the estimated correlation of total scores on the test with true scores will not be .20, but considerably higher than that (exactly how much will be discussed later). A confidence zone for the reliability of the whole test can be obtained by extrapolating the upper and lower bounds of the confidence zone for the average correlation among items on the test. This can be done with Equation 7 which will be discussed later. First, the lower bound of the confidence zone for the average correlation among items is placed in the formula, which provides a lower bound of the confidence zone for the reliability r_{11} of the whole test. Next, the upper bound of the confidence zone for the average correlation among items is placed in the formula, which provides an estimate of the upper bound of the confidence zone for the reliability of the whole test. Although confidence zones for whole tests are larger than confidence zones for individual items, if the test has as many as 40 items, the confidence zone usually is surprisingly small.

If the assumptions of the domain-sampling model hold and the numbers of persons and test items are relatively large, there is practically no error in estimating the correlation of a collection of items with true scores. Henceforth it will be assumed that those conditions hold and consequently we shall speak of determining rather than estimating various statistics regarding measurement error.

It should be reiterated that the foregoing principles concerning the precision of reliability estimates are based on an approximate model which does some injustice to actuality by assuming that correlations among items in a domain are normally distributed and statistically independent of one another. As was mentioned previously, however, these assumptions hold reasonably well for the usual correlations among test items; consequently formulas based on those assumptions should provide useful information about the amount of error to be expected in estimating the reliability coefficient in particular investigations.

Variances of items. In this chapter the basic formulas for reliability were derived on the assumption that all items are expressed as standard scores, but in practice items are rarely standardized before they are summed to obtain test scores. One might wonder if such differences in variances that exist among items would disturb the principles that have been developed so far. For example, since dichotomous items will not all have the same p value and thus will not all have the same variance, this might introduce difficulties for the domain-sampling model. In fact, it does not. The model could have been developed from the covariances among items as

well as it was from the correlations among items, and the same principles would have resulted. Also, it is clear that differences in p values of items usually have very little effect on the precision of reliability estimates, particularly if the number of items is 20 or more. This was made quite clear in a study by Cronbach and Azuma (1962), in which they randomly sampled artificial items having a range of p values. They found that such random variation in p values had very little effect on the reliability estimates.

Deductions From the Domain-Sampling Model

When the domain-sampling model is accepted as a useful foundation, it is possible to deduce many principles regarding measurement error. These principles are useful both for the development of measurement theory and for handling problems of measurement error in research.

Test length. As was mentioned previously, the reliability of scores obtained on a sample of items from a domain increases with the number of items sampled. Thus the individual item would be expected to have only a small correlation with true scores; a 10-item test might correlate .50 with true scores, and a 100-item test might correlate above .90 with true scores. The rate at which the reliability increases as a function of the number of items can be deduced from the following formula (which is derived and discussed in more detail in Nunnally, 1967: 191-194):

$$r_{kk} = \frac{k\bar{r}_{ij}}{1 + (k-1)\bar{r}_{ij}} \tag{7}$$

where r_{kk} = the reliability of a test

k = numbers of items

average $\bar{r}_{ij}$ = the average intercorrelation of items in the test of length k

It is hard to overestimate the importance of Equation 7 for the theory of measurement error. An example will serve to show what can be learned from applying the formula. If in a 20-item test the average correlation among items is .25, these values could be substituted in Equation 7 as follows:

$$r_{kk} = \frac{20 \times .25}{1 + (19 \times .25)}$$

$$= \frac{5.00}{1 + 4.75}$$

$$= \frac{5.00}{5.75} \tag{8}$$

$$r_{kk} = .87$$

Previously it was shown that r_{kk} is the square of the correlation of scores on a collection of items with true scores. Consequently, in the above example, the

correlation with true scores would equal the square root of .87, which is .93. Thus it can be seen how a highly reliable total test score can be obtained from items that correlate only .25 with one another on the average.

Although r_{kk} was introduced as a way of obtaining the correlation of a collection of items with true scores, it has considerable meaning in its own right. It is the expected correlation of one k-item with other k-item tests drawn from the same domain. Thus r_{kk} is the *reliability coefficient* for a k-item test determined from the *intercorrelations* of *items* on the test. In many ways this is the most meaningful measure of reliability.

Equation 7 holds regardless of the size of units that are added. All one needs to know is the average correlation among the units. Thus the formula would hold if the k units being combined were pairs of items, groups with 10 items in each, or groups with 1,000 items in each. If the assumptions of the domain-sampling model hold, one will come to approximately the same conclusion about the reliability of a test with a particular number of items regardless of the number of items in each unit which is combined to obtain the final test. For example, for 40-item test, rather than estimate the reliability by placing the average correlation among items in Equation 7, a different approach would be to divide the 40 items randomly into four groups of 10 each. The average correlation among the four groups of items would be inserted in Equation 7, with k equaling 4 rather than 40. The estimated reliability of the 40-item test would be approximately the same by the two approaches.

One of the most frequent uses of Equation 7 is with respect to the split-half measure of reliability. For this, the items of a test are divided in half, and the two half-tests are correlated. The question is then one of what would be the reliability of the whole test. When only two samples of items from the domain are being added, Equation 7 reduces to

$$r_{kk} = \frac{2r_{12}}{1 + r_{12}} \qquad [9]$$

where r_{12} = correlation between two half-tests

r_{kk} = reliability of whole test

The above is the well-known Spearman-Brown formula for estimating the reliability from the correlation of split-halves of a test.

Reliability of an item sample. The logic developed in the previous section for determining the effect of test length on reliability can be extended to determine the reliability of any particular sample of items. It was shown that the reliability depends entirely on the average correlation among items and the number of items. These values could be substituted in Equation 7 to obtain the reliability for any particular test. In practice, however, it is tedious to compute all correlations among items or other units being summed. A much easier way to obtain the same results is discussed below.

Whereas up to this point it has proved convenient to work with standardized scores, in actual computations it is more convenient to work with the covariances

among items rather than with their correlations. Also, as was mentioned previously, the assumption that all items have the same variance (same p value for dichotomous items) is a potential source of imprecision in the estimation of reliability. All the formulas and principles that have been developed could have been developed on the basis of the average covariance among items. In that case Equation 7 would change to

$$r_{kk} = \frac{k}{k-1} \left(\frac{\bar{C} - \Sigma \sigma_i^2}{\bar{C}} \right)$$ [10]

where k = the number of items on the test

$\bar{C}$ = the sum of elements in the variance-covariance matrix for items

$\Sigma \sigma_i^2$ = the sum of item variances

The variance of total scores on a test equals the sum of elements in the variance-covariance matrix for the items of which the test is composed. Thus Equation 10 may be rewritten as:

$$r_{kk} = \frac{k}{k-1} \left(\frac{\sigma_y^2 - \Sigma \sigma_i^2}{\sigma_y^2} \right)$$ [11]

It also can be written as

$$r_{kk} = \frac{k}{k-1} \left(1 - \frac{\Sigma \sigma_i^2}{\sigma_y^2} \right)$$ [12]

Equation 12 is one of the most important deductions from the theory of measurement error. In that form it is referred to as *coefficient alpha*. Although it may look very different, coefficient alpha is identical to Equation 7 for estimating the reliability of a k-item test when (1) the average covariance among items is employed in the latter rather than the average correlation among items and (2) the average of the item variances (pq values for dichotomous items) is substituted for 1 as the first item in the numerator of Equation 7. All these considerations converge to justify the statement that coefficient alpha is a very important formula in the theory of reliability. It represents the expected correlation of one test with an alternative form containing the same number of items. The square root of coefficient alpha is the estimated correlation of a test with errorless true scores. It is so pregnant with meaning that it should routinely be applied to all new tests.

When, as is usually true, an investigation is being made of the reliability of a test composed of dichotomous items, coefficient alpha takes on the following special form:

$$r_{kk} = \frac{k}{k-1} \left(1 - \frac{\Sigma pq}{\sigma_y^2} \right)$$ [13]

The first step in determining the reliability of a test composed of dichotomous items is to find the p value for each item, which is then multiplied by 1 - p. These products are then summed. The second step is to compute the variance of scores on

the total test, which is then divided into the sum of pq values. After this is subtracted from 1, the result is multiplied by the ratio of the number of test items to the number of test items minus 1. This version of coefficient alpha is referred to as "Kuder-Richardson Formula 20" (KR-20). It is easy to compute, and there is no excuse for not computing it for any new measure.

Another way of looking at coefficient alpha will serve to further indicate its importance. It will be remembered that the reliability coefficient of any test is the estimated average correlation of that test with all possible tests with the same number of items which are obtainable from sampling a domain. Thus coefficient alpha is the expected correlation of one test with another test of the same length when the two tests purport to measure the same thing. Coefficient alpha can also be derived as the expected correlation between an actual test and a *hypothetical* alternative form, one that may never be constructed. If the actual test is called x and the hypothetical test is called y, then the total covariance matrix for all items on the two tests can be schematized as follows:

	x	y
x	C_x	C_{xy}
y	C_{xy}	C_y

where C_x = the covariance matrix for the items in test x

C_y = the covariance matrix for the items in test y

C_{xy} = a matrix containing all possible cross-covariances between items on the two tests

From the domain-sampling model, it is expected that the average diagonal term in C_x is the same as that in C_y and the average off-diagonal elements in the two matrices are the same. Also, it is expected that the average element throughout C_{xy} equals the average off-diagonal element in C_x. Thus coefficient alpha can be derived from the correlation of sums as follows (with a bar symbolizing the process of summing the elements in a matrix):

$$r_{xy} = \frac{\bar{C}_{xy}}{\sqrt{\bar{C}_x}\,\sqrt{\bar{C}_y}} \qquad [14]$$

According to the model, C_x approximately equals C_y, so the equation can be rewritten as

$$r_{xy} = \frac{\bar{C}_{xy}}{\bar{C}_x} \qquad [15]$$

According to the model, the average coefficient in C_{xy} (and thus the sum of coefficients) is derivable from C_x. First, it would be necessary to subtract from C_x the variances of items lying on the diagonal. Then it would be necessary to inflate

the result by the factor developed previously, that is, $k/(k-1)$. This then brings one right back to coefficient alpha. It is at the heart of the theory of measurement error.

Variance of true and error scores. Previously it was shown that the reliability coefficient can be expressed as follows:

$$r_{11} = \frac{\sigma_t^2}{\sigma_x^2}$$

The reliability coefficient equals the ratio of true-score variance to the actual variance of the measure. Then it is apparent that

$$\sigma_t^2 = r_{11}\sigma_x^2$$

and that

$$\sigma_t = \sqrt{r_{11}}\,\sigma_x \qquad\qquad [16]$$

Unless x is perfectly reliable, the variance of true scores will be less than the variance of obtained scores by a factor of r_{11}. Since error scores are uncorrelated with true scores, it follows that

$$\sigma_x^2 = \sigma_t^2 + \sigma_e^2 \qquad\qquad [17]$$

These facts might lead one to the erroneous conclusion that, generally speaking, reliable tests tend to have smaller standard deviations than unreliable tests have. Just the reverse is true. A look back at coefficient alpha (Equation 12) will show why this is so. The larger the average covariance among items, the more reliable is the test. When the sum of covariance terms is zero, the reliability is zero. It will be remembered that the variance of a sum equals the sum of variances *plus* the sum of all covariances in the covariance matrix. The variance of a totally unreliable test equals the sum of variances only. Consequently the more reliable the test, the larger is the variance of test scores. If, for example, two 20-item tests have the same average pq value, the one with the larger variance is more reliable.

It is true that the error variance adds to *whatever reliable variance is present,* but it also is true that the reliable variance adds to whatever error variance is present. Since, in a completely unreliable measure, the variance of scores equals the sum of the variance of items, this places a limit on the size of the measurement error that can be present. As the test becomes reliable, the covariance terms become positive, and as the covariance terms are made larger, the variance of test scores becomes larger. Whereas there is a severe limit on the size of the variance of errors, there is a much less severe limit on the sum of covariance terms. For example, in the typical 30-item test with moderately high reliability, the covariances among items contribute at least three times as much to the variance of tests scores as do the item variances. Thus it is seen that reliable tests tend to have large variances of total scores relative to that found on unreliable tests of the same length.

Estimation of true scores. Since the square root of r_{11} (r_{1t}) is the estimated correlation of obtained scores with true scores, it can be used to estimate true

scores from obtained scores. When variables are expressed as deviation scores, the regression equation for estimating one from the other is as follows:

$$y' = \frac{\sigma_y}{\sigma_x} xy^x$$

The problem to be considered is the estimation of true scores t from obtained scores x. Previously it was shown that the standard deviation of true scores equals $\sqrt{r_{xx}}\sigma_x$ (r_{xx} being the reliability of x). Then estimates of true scores can be obtained as follows:

$$t' = \frac{\sigma_t}{\sigma_x} (r_{xt})x$$

$$= \frac{\sqrt{r_{xx}}\sigma_x}{\sigma_x} (r_{xt})x \qquad [18]$$

$$= \sqrt{r_{xx}} (r_{xt})x$$

Since r_{xt} equals the square root of r_{xx},

$$t' = \sqrt{r_{xx}} \sqrt{r_{xx}} x$$

$$= r_{xx} x \qquad [19]$$

Estimates of true scores are computed by multiplying obtained deviation scores by the reliability coefficient.[1]

Although Equation 19 is the best least-squares estimate of true scores from *linear* regression, it was not assumed in the domain-sampling model that tests in the domain necessarily have linear regressions with true scores. There are models for measurement error that lead to the conclusion that the regression of true scores on obtained scores frequently is nonlinear (but always monotonic); such models are discussed by Lord (1959). The assumption of linear regression of true scores on obtained scores is not crucial for most of the principles derivable from the domain-sampling model, for example, the effect of test length on reliability, but it is crucial for the development of any relatively simple methods for the estimation of true scores. (Some of the models that permit nonlinear regression of true scores on obtained scores are so complex as to be understood and appreciated only by the ultra specialist in the study of measurement error.) Consequently in this section it will be assumed that the regressions are linear.

As is true in any correlational analysis, obtained scores must be *regressed* to obtain a best least-squares estimate of true scores. Hidden in this fact is an important principle: *Obtained scores are biased estimates of true scores.* Scores above the mean are biased upward, and scores below the mean are biased downward. The further scores are in either direction from the mean of obtained scores, the more, in an absolute sense, scores are biased. As a group, people with high obtained scores have a preponderance of positive errors of measurement, and the opposite is

true for people who have low obtained scores. In one sense this fact makes little difference. Estimated true scores correlate perfectly with obtained scores; they both have means of zero, and the shapes of distributions are identical. For these reasons, in most investigations there is nothing to be gained by estimating true scores. The only practical importance of estimating true scores is in setting confidence zones for the effects of measurement error on obtained scores, which will be discussed in the next section.

The fact that obtained scores are biased raises an important theoretical point. If one actually had true scores, these could be used in the usual regression equation for estimating obtained scores. To simplify the problem, imagine that both true scores and obtained scores were standardized, in which case the regression equation would be given as

$$z_{x'} = r_{xt} z_t$$ [20]

where $z_{x'}$ = estimates of obtained standard scores for x

z_t = true scores

r_{xt} = correlation of true and obtained scores

Subtracting values of $z_{x'}$ from the actual values of z_x would provide the errors of estimation, which are the errors because of unreliability. It will be remembered that such errors of estimation correlate zero with the variable used to make the estimates (true scores), which is another way of stating the assumption that error scores are uncorrelated with true scores. But it also should be remembered that errors of estimate do correlate with the variable being estimated, in this case with obtained scores. The amount would be as follows:

$$r_{xe} = \sqrt{1 - r_{xt}^2}$$
$$= \sqrt{1 - r_{xx}}$$ [21]

Thus it would be found, for example, that if x had a reliability of .64, obtained scores would correlate .60 with error scores. The correlation would be positive, because high obtained scores are biased upward and low obtained scores are biased downward. In spite of the obvious conclusion that errors must correlate positively with obtained scores, it is surprising how often this point is overlooked or misunderstood.

ASSESSMENT OF RELIABILITY

Whereas the previous section presented the theory of reliability, this section will discuss principles for applying the theory in empirical research. Also, some additional formulas will be developed for problems that frequently occur in the investigation of the effects of measurement error on research results. All of the formulas presented in this chapter are derivable from the domain-sampling model.

Previously it was said that measurements are reliable to the extent that they are repeatable and that any random influence which tends to make measurements

different from occasion to occasion is a source of measurement error. The domain-sampling model was offered as a way of investigating such random sources of error. Each test is considered as a random sample of items from a domain, and measurement error is present only to the extent that samples are limited in size. Thus if the average correlation among items is positive, a very long test is always a highly reliable test, the degree of reliability being estimated by Equation 7. This line of argument assumes that all measurement error is because of content sampling. But is content sampling the only factor that prevents measurements from being exactly the same on two occasions? First we shall look at some of the factors that reduce the repeatability of measurements, and then we shall see if these can be adequately handled by the domain-sampling model.

Sources of Error

In practice there are many factors that prevent measurements from being exactly repeatable, the number and kind of factors depending on the nature of the test and how the test is used. It is important to make a distinction between errors of measurement that cause variation in performance from item to item within a test and errors that are manifested only in variation in performance on different forms of a test given at different times. Errors of the former kind can easily be handled by the domain-sampling model, but a modification of the model is necessary to handle errors of the second kind.

Variation within a test. The major source of error within most tests arises from the sampling of items. According to the domain-sampling model, each person has a particular probability of correctly answering each item, depending on his true score and the difficulty of the item for people in general. In the simplest case, if a person has an average true score and all the items have p values of .5 for people in general, that person has a probability of .5 of correctly answering any item chosen at random from the domain. He would be expected to correctly answer half the items on any test drawn from the domain, but that expectation would be accompanied by some error. The more items in each test, the less would be the error. The same logic can be extended to items that have no "correct" responses, for example, to items concerning agreement and disagreement with statements. Each person can be thought of as having a set probability of agreeing with each statement, which in turn would lead to an expected number of agreements with a sample of items. Depending on the number of items in each sample, there would be some variability in scores from test to test.

The error because of the sampling of items is entirely predictable from the average correlation among items. Consequently coefficient alpha would be the correct measure of reliability for any type of item, and the special version of that formula, KR-20, would be used with dichotomous items.

On multiple-choice tests, guessing is a source of measurement error. If, for example, an individual does not really know the answer to two questions, he might pass one and fail the other purely because of guessing. Guessing causes some variation in performance from item to item, which tends to lower the test reliability. Guessing is easily handled by the domain-sampling model. The domain can

be thought of as consisting of multiple-choice items. The typical correlation among such items would allow an estimate of the reliability of any sample of items. Guessing would serve to lower the typical correlation, but once that typical correlation were estimated from the correlations within a test, it could be used to estimate reliability.

In addition to guessing, many other factors produce variation in scores from item to item within a test. Halfway through a test, a person might get a headache, and this would tend to lower his scores on the remaining items. A person might intend to mark alternative a for a particular item, but purely as a clerical error, mark alternative b instead. Another person might inadvertently skip an item which he could have answered correctly. Halfway through a test, a person might realize that he misinterpreted the test instructions regarding how to respond to items, and not having time to go back to earlier items, he would do better on the remaining items than on the earlier items. Even if a person actually knew the answer to a question, he might give the wrong answer because he accidentally misread "is not an example of" as "is an example of." There are many other factors that produce errors within tests.

To some extent errors of scoring can be assessed within a test. On objective tests, errors of scoring are purely mechanical, but since they tend to lower correlations among items, they are within the scope of the domain-sampling model. On some tests the scoring is largely subjective, as in essay examinations or in most projective tests. The element of chance in the scores given on such tests provides a source of measurement error. Measurement error is caused by fluctuations in standards by the individual grader and by differences in standards of different graders. For the individual grader, such errors are manifested within a test if each item is graded *independently* of other items. For example, on an essay examination the instructor might grade all responses to question 1, then grade all responses to question 2, and so on. If such scores are independent, the average correlation among the items can be used to obtain an accurate estimate of reliability. Although it infrequently occurs, if half the items are scored by one person and the other half are independently scored by another person, the average correlation among items will provide an estimate of the reliability.

All the errors that occur *within* a test can be easily encompassed by the domain-sampling model. The assumptions of the model can be extended to the case where situational influences are randomly "assigned" to the items. Thus not only would each person be administered a random sample of items from the domain, but also each item would be accompanied by a random set of situational factors. Then whether or not a person passes any item drawn at random from the domain is a function partly of the happenstance of which item is selected and partly of the happenstance of the situational factors that accompany the item. All such sources of error will tend to lower the average correlation among items within the test, but the average correlation is all that is needed to estimate the reliability.

Variation between tests. If alternative forms of a test are administered two weeks apart, almost never will the two sets of scores correlate perfectly. The domain-sampling model provides a prediction of the correlation. This prediction

takes account not only of the sampling of content, but also of many sources of errors within each testing session. There are, however, three major sources of error intervening between administrations of different tests that are not precisely estimated from the average correlation of items within each test. The first is because of systematic differences in content of the two tests. The model envisions an actual sampling of items from a hypothetical domain, but of course, in practice items are composed rather than drawn from a hat. For example, two spelling tests independently composed by two persons might emphasize different kinds of words. Then the correlation between the two tests might be less than would be predicted from the average correlation among the items within each test. Similarly, alternative forms of a measure of attitudes toward the United Nations might be systematically different in content, and consequently the correlation between the two forms would be less than that predicted by the domain-sampling model.

A second factor causing variation in scores on some tests from one occasion to another is the result of scoring subjectivity. For example, on an essay examination or a projective test, the same examiner might give somewhat different scores to the same persons, and ever larger differences would be expected between the scores given by two examiners. Previously it was said that some of the error because of the subjectivity of scoring by one person could be estimated from the correlation among items within one test if items are scored independently, but this might tap only part of the error. The scorer might change his standards somewhat from one occasion to another. For example, between the two testings, the projective tester might come to regard a particular type of response as more pathological than he previously had regarded it. Previously it was said that if different parts of a test are independently scored by different examiners, the average correlation among all items would be indicative of the error entailed in using different examiners; but since two examiners rarely collaborate in that way, there is an unassessed amount of error because of the examiner who "happens" to score responses for a particular person. Then the average correlation among items on a test scored by one person would tend to overestimate the correlation between alternative forms scored by different persons.

Another source of variation in test performance from one occasion to another is actual change with regard to the attribute being measured. A person might feel much better on one occasion than on another, might study in the domain of content, or might change his attitude toward the United Nations. It is reasonable to think there is some fluctuation in abilities from day to day, depending on a host of physiological and environmental factors. Even more to be expected are variations in moods, self-esteem, and attitudes toward people and issues. Such changes in people would tend to make correlations between alternative forms less than what would be predicted from the average correlations among items on each test.

Systematic differences in content of tests and variations in people from one occasion to another cannot be adequately handled by a model which is based on the random sampling of items. For adequately handling these factors, the model must be extended to consider the random sampling of *whole tests,* in which case the tests are thought of as being randomly sampled for particular occasions and

correlations among tests are permitted to be somewhat lower than would be predicted from the correlations among items within tests. In that case the average correlation among a number of alternative forms administered on different occasions, or the correlation between only two such forms, would be a better estimate of reliability than that provided by coefficient alpha or KR-20.

Estimation of Reliability

Because measurement error is an important issue in the use of any measurement method, investigations of reliability should be made when new measures are developed. Following are some recommendations regarding how such investigations should be undertaken.

Internal consistency. Estimates of reliability based on the average correlation among items within a test are said to concern the "internal consistency." This is partly a misnomer, because the size of the reliability coefficient is based on both the average correlation among items (the internal consistency) and the number of items. Coefficient alpha is the basic formula for determining the reliability based on internal consistency. It, or the special version applicable to dichotomous items (KR-20), should be applied to all new measurement methods. Even if other estimates of reliability should be made for particular instruments, coefficient alpha should be obtained first.

Coefficient alpha sets an upper limit to the reliability of tests constructed in terms of the domain-sampling model. If it proves to be very low, either the test is too short or the items have very little in common. In that case there is no need to make other estimates of reliability (e.g., correlation of alternative forms), because they will prove to be even lower. If, for example, coefficient alpha is only .30 for a 40-item test, the experimenter should reconsider his measurement problem.

Even though potentially there are important sources of measurement error that are not considered by coefficient alpha, it is surprising what little difference these sources of measurement error usually make. This is particularly so if the test instructions are easily understood and there is little subjectivity of scoring. If coefficient alpha for a particular test is compared with the correlation between alternative forms and at least 300 persons are studied, the two coefficients typically are very close. If, say, the former is .85, it might be found that the latter is .80, but it is rare to find the latter as low as .60. There are exceptions, which will be discussed in the next section, but reliability estimated from internal consistency is usually very close to the reliability estimated from correlations between alternative forms.

Coefficient alpha provides a good estimate of reliability in most situations, since *the major source of measurement error is the sampling of content.* Also, previously it was shown that reliability estimates based on internal consistency actually consider sources of error that are based not, strictly speaking, on the sampling of items per se, but on the "sampling" of situational factors accompanying the items.

Alternative forms. In addition to computing coefficient alpha, with most measures it also is informative to correlate alternative forms. Usually the forms would be administered about two weeks apart. This would provide time for variations in

ability and attitude to occur. If the correlation between alternative forms is markedly lower than coefficient alpha, say, by as much as 20 points, it indicates that considerable measurement error is present because of some combination of the three sources of error mentioned previously: systematic differences in content, subjectivity of scoring, or large variations in people over short periods of time. Investigations can be made to determine which of these factors is causing the reduction in reliability.

To investigate variation in scores over short periods of time (two weeks), the correlation obtained on one group of subjects with a two-week interval between testings can be compared with the correlation between forms when they both are administered on the same day. If the correlation between forms administered on the same day is much higher than that between forms administered two weeks apart, it indicates that the trait being measured tends to fluctuate somewhat over short periods of time. In one sense this is not measurement error, since such changes need not be random. For example, a measure of moods would be expected to change somewhat from one occasion to another, because we all have ups and downs in that regard. Usually, however, the effort is to measure some relatively enduring characteristic, one that at least stays relatively stable over a period of two weeks. Consequently, for most purposes, such variations in traits over short periods of time *act* like measurement error in that they tend to attenuate correlations with other variables.

If the correlation between alternative forms administered two weeks apart is low and the correlation between those administered on the same day is equally low, the indication is not that people are changing over time, but that the two forms have largely different types of content. If the average correlation among the items on one form is higher than that among items on the other form, one form is more reliable than the other. This would suggest that something went wrong in the construction of one of the forms. The decision might be to construct a new form and then correlate that with the existing reliable form.

If the average correlation within the two test forms is substantial, but the average cross-correlation between items in the two forms is low, it indicates that the two forms reliably measure somewhat different traits. For example, if the average correlation wtihin each of the two sets of items were .20 and the average correlation between items in the two sets were .10, it would indicate systematic differences in content. This should lead the investigator to think more carefully about the intended domain of content. An inspection of the content might make it evident why the forms differ, which could lead either to emphasizing in the future the type of content in one of the forms or to seeking a type of item that bridges the gap between the two types of content.

It is somewhat more difficult to determine the measurement error because of subjectivity of scoring. Let it be assumed that differences in content of the two forms and variations over short periods of time have been ruled out as major sources of unreliability by the methods described above. Then a separate set of comparisons would be needed for each scorer. Each would score responses to alternative forms given (1) two weeks apart to one group of subjects and (2) on the

same day to another group of subjects. If correlations between scorers are high for both groups, it indicates that there is little unreliability from any source, including that because of subjectivity of scoring. If the correlation for the two-week interval is substantially less than the correlation for tests taken on the same day, it indicates that scoring is reliable but the trait varies over short periods of time. If both correlations are low in a number of studies made of different scorers, it is difficult to tell whether the measurement error is because of subjectivity of scoring or some other factor. Since in essence the scorer is "a part of the item," there is no easy way to pick apart the contribution of scoring to the measurement error. There would be many hints as to the possible unreliability of scoring, such as (1) good reason to believe that the trait actually exists, for example, intelligence; (2) the existence of reliable objective tests of the trait; and (3) considerable variability in the reliability of raters. If the measurement problem is important and it is felt necessary to continue employing subjective methods of scoring, the rules for scoring should be improved. If this results in an increased reliability, it is indicated that unreliability of scoring contributed to the earlier amount of measurement error.

If raters do tend to agree with themselves when scoring the same subjects on alternative forms, another question which arises is whether or not there is measurement error because of differences in scoring by different scorers. This can be easily determined by correlating scorings of alternative forms by different scorers. It is sometimes found that scorers develop their own idiosyncratic methods of scoring, and although each scorer is consistent in employing his method, the scorers do not agree with one another. This works like other sources of measurement error to attenuate relations found between variables in research.

The need to investigate alternative forms of a measure depends very much on the type of measure. Where the domain of content is easily specified, where there is little subjectivity in scoring, and where people tend to vary little over short periods of time, coefficient alpha will provide an excellent estimate of reliability. This is the case, for example, for most tests of aptitude and achievement. It is necessary to investigate alternative forms if the trait is suspected to vary considerably over relatively short periods of time, as would be true for measures of moods and some measures of attitudes. In some cases the experimenter is challenged to compose alternative forms to satisfy others that there is a definable domain of content. This occurs with some projective techniques, such as the Rorschach, where there is some question as to whether or not it is possible to construct an alternative form. If an alternative form cannot be constructed, it is not possible to define the domain of content, and there is no way to accurately communicate what is being measured; furthermore, it is doubtful that anything of importance is being measured.

Other estimates of reliability. Coefficient alpha and correlations between alternative forms (under the various conditions mentioned previously) are the basic estimates of reliability. There are other ways of estimating reliability which, though not recommended for most measurement problems, are frequently encountered in research reports. Instead of employing coefficient alpha or KR-20, one may estimate reliability from various subdivisions of a test. The most popular method is the *split-half* approach, in which items within a test are divided in half and scores

on the two half-tests are correlated. Usually the items are halved by placing the even-numbered items in one group and the odd-numbered items in the other group. There are many other ways to make the division, for example, randomly dividing items into two groups or separately scoring the first and second halves of the items. After the correlation is obtained, it must be corrected by Equation 9 to obtain the reliability coefficient.

The difficulty with the split-half method is that the correlation between halves will vary somewhat depending on how the items are divided, which raises some questions regarding what *the* reliability is. Actually, it is best to think of the corrected correlation between any two halves of a test as being an estimate of coefficient alpha. Then it is much more sensible to employ coefficient alpha than any split-half method. The split-half method is useful when the items are not scored dichotomously, but on three or more points. In that case it is not possible to use the KR-20 version of the coefficient alpha. With KR-20, it is very easy to obtain the p values for items and thus the variances of items; but if the number of items is large and computer services are not available, it might prove excessively time-consuming to compute variances for multipoint items (which would be required for coefficient alpha). It is much easier to separately score odd and even items, correlate the two sets of scores, and make the necessary correction (Equation 9).

There are many other ways to obtain reliability estimates from subdivision of items. For example, the items can be randomly divided into four equal parts. The average correlation among the four sets of scores can be placed in Equation 7 to obtain an estimate of the reliability of the whole test. There would, however, be nothing to gain by such methods of estimating reliability. The results would serve only to estimate coefficient alpha. If items are scored dichotomously, there is no excuse for not computing KR-20. If items are scored on more than two points, it is wise to compute coefficient alpha. When saving computational time is an important consideration, the corrected correlation between odd and even items will provide a good approximation of coefficient alpha.

One appropriate use of the split-half method is in measuring variability of traits over short periods of time when alternative forms are not available. For example, the odd items can be given as one test on the first occasion, and the even items can be given as an alternative form on the second occasion. The corrected correlation between the two sets of scores will indicate the relative stability of the trait over that period of time. The result will be an accurate estimate of the correlation to be found between alternative forms if (1) the items are not markedly affected by fatigue, (2) there are enough items in each half-test to provide a precise estimate of reliability (at least 20), and (3) the actual alternative forms do not differ systematically in content. It is better actually to construct alternative forms and correlate them, but if that is not feasible, the split-half measure over time can be employed instead.

In place of using the alternative-form method for determining reliability, the *retest method* can be used, in which the same test is given to the same people after a period of time. Except for certain special instances, there are serious defects in employing the retest method. The major defect is that experience in the first testing

will influence responses in the second testing. To the extent that responses to the first testing are remembered, they will tend to be repeated on the retest. Also, the individual will tend to repeat his work habits and make much the same guesses on items where he is unsure. This works to make the correlation between testings higher than it would be for alternative forms.

Another difficulty with the retest method is that it does not fit very well into the domain-sampling model. In the model, the reliability of any test is strictly a function of the average correlation among items. As was mentioned previously, estimates derived from that model, for example, KR-20, tend to be approximately the same as correlations actually obtained between alternative forms. The reason the retest method does not fit the model is that the retest correlation is only partly dependent on the correlation among items within a test. Thinking back about principles concerning the correlation of sums will show why this is so. Even if the items within each testing correlated zero on the average with one another, it still would be possible to obtain a positive correlation between scores in the two testings. The numerator of the correlation of sums is the sum of all the cross-covariances (correlations, if scores are standardized) between the two sets of items being summed. Even if all the cross-correlations between different items were zero, each item might correlate well with itself on the two testings. Such correlations would be expected to be much higher than those usually found between different items, and they could produce a substantial correlation between retests.

If coefficient alpha is low for a test, a relatively high correlation between retests should not be taken as an indication of high "reliability." As has been mentioned in a number of places, a test should "hang together" in the sense that the items should correlate with one another. Otherwise it makes little sense to add scores over items and speak of the total scores as measuring any attribute. The major information supplied by the retest method is "negative": if the retest correlation is low, the alternative form correlation will be even lower. If a test does not even correlate with itself when administered on two occasions, it is hopeless to seek other evidence of reliability and hopeless to employ the test in research.

It is recommended that the retest method generally not be used to estimate reliability, but there are some exceptions. In some types of measures, the retest probably would not be markedly affected by the first testing. This would tend to be true, for example, if an individual were required to rate the pleasantness of 200 designs. The sheer number of ratings would make remembering the ratings of individual designs very difficult, and consequently the retest would be largely independent of the earlier testing. Also, scores would be more nearly independent if there were a long time between testings, say, six months or more.

Long-range stability. Previously it was said that alternative forms should be administered about two weeks apart to permit short-range fluctuations in abilities and personality characteristics to be manifested. Another issue concerns the stability of scores over relatively long periods of time—upward of six months. If, for example, alternative forms given six months apart correlate less than those given two weeks apart, in a sense the difference is not because of "error," but because of systematic changes in people. As was mentioned previously, what is considered error and what is considered systematic change depends on the way measurement

tools are used. If a measure is intended to represent the *relatively enduring* status of a trait in people, it would need to remain relatively stable over the period in which scores were employed for that purpose. A good example is the IQ, which is considered by most people to be a relatively enduring characteristic of the individual, something that might change gradually over a period of years, but not markedly in a period of only one year. If an earlier measurement is used at a later time either to make practical decisions about people or to make decisions about the outcomes of research, then to the extent that the trait being measured has not remained stable, measurement error will reduce the validity of the decisions. As a practical example, if scores on intelligence tests given in the second year of high school are used to make decisions about college entrance for students two years later, the effectiveness of such decisions will be limited by (among other things) the extent to which the trait of intelligence has remained stable during that time. If the correlation between alternative forms of the test over that period of time were very low, some bad mistakes would be made in advising students about college. If, for example, on the earlier testing the student has an IQ of 130 and no later testing is made, it would be tempting to encourage the student strongly to enter college. But suppose that an alternative form of the test is administered near the end of high school and the student's IQ is only 95; with this new evidence in hand, it would be a bad mistake to recommend college training strongly.

As an example of how long-range instability can attenuate research results, suppose that an experiment is being conducted to measure the effect of anxiety on difficult learning tasks. Also, suppose that the test of anxiety is administered six months prior to the learning tasks. If the retest correlation or correlation with an alternative form over the six-month period were low, the possible results from using the first test would be highly attenuated. Of course, instead of relying on measures administered much earlier, it is far better to make measurements shortly before practical decisions are to be made about people or shortly before they are used in experiments.

Aside from questions of measurement error, long-range stability is an important research issue in its own right, as, for example, in studies of the growth and decline of human abilities. Some have accused measurement specialists of assuming that psychological traits remain largely stable throughout life and, thus, that very little can be done to improve people. Such a philosophy is not at all necessary for the theory of measurement error. The theory would hold as well if people changed markedly in their characteristics from day to day; but if that occurred, it would make chaos out of efforts to make practical decisions about people and to find general principles of human behavior. People do change, but fortunately, in most traits they change slowly enough to allow valid uses of psychological measures in daily life and in research investigations.

Uses of the Reliability Coefficient

In the previous section it was shown that it is meaningful to think of a test as having a number of different coefficients of reliability, depending on the major sources of measurement error that are considered. In practice, however, it is useful to speak of *a* reliability coefficient for a test which summarizes the amount of

measurement error expected from using the instrument. In most cases this should be the correlation between alternative forms administered about two weeks apart. If there is an element of subjectivity in the scoring, the alternative forms should be independently scored by different persons. If, for example, five persons score the first form and five other persons score the second, the average correlation between the two sets of scores (25 correlations in this instance) would provide a good reliability coefficient. If alternative forms are not available, the corrected correlation between split-halves given two weeks apart can be used as the reliability coefficient. When alternative forms are not available and testing subjects more than once is not feasible, coefficient alpha can be used as the reliability coefficient.

The major use of the reliability coefficient is in communicating the extent to which the results obtained from a measurement method are repeatable. The reliability coefficient is one index of the effectiveness of an instrument, reliability being a necessary but not sufficient condition for any type of validity. In addition there are other uses that can be made of the reliability coefficient; the major uses are discussed in the following sections.

Corrections for attenuation. One of the most important uses of the reliability coefficient is in estimating the extent to which obtained correlations between variables are attenuated by measurement error. The correction for attenuation is shown below:

$$\bar{r} = \frac{r_{12}}{\sqrt{r_{11}r_{22}}}$$

In this case, $\bar{r}_{12}$ is the expected correlation if both variables are perfectly reliable. If the correction is to be made for only one of the two variables, the reliability coefficient for only that variable will appear under the radical in the denominator.

There is some controversy about when the correction for attenuation should be applied. One could argue that the correction for attenuation provides a way of fooling one's self into believing that a "better" correlation has been found than that actually evidenced in the available data. Another justifiable criticism of many uses of the correction for attenuation is that the so-called correction sometimes provides a very poor estimate of the correlation actually obtained between variables when they are made highly reliable. This can occur if a poor measure of reliability is made, in terms of principles discussed previously, and if the reliability coefficient is based on a relatively small number of cases (less than 300). That poor estimates are often obtained is illustrated by the fact that corrected correlations sometimes are greater than 1.00!

If, however, good estimates of reliability are available, there are some appropriate uses of the correction for attenuation. The most important use is in basic research, where the corrected correlation between two variables is an estimate of how much two traits correlate. In an investigation of the correlation between anxiety and intelligence, for example, the real question is that of how much the two traits go together. If the two measures have only modest reliability, the actual correlation will suggest that the two traits go together less than they really do.

Another important use of the correction for attenuation is in applied settings

where a test is used to forecast a criterion. If, as often happens, the criterion is not highly reliable, correcting for unreliability of the criterion will estimate the real validity of the test. Here, however, it would be wrong to make the double correction for attenuation, since the issue is how well a test actually works rather than how well it would work if it were perfectly reliable. In prediction problems, the reliability of the predictor instrument places a limit on its ability to forecast a criterion, and the correction for attenuation cannot make a test more predictive than it actually is. The only use for this double correction would be in estimating the limit of predictive validity of the test as both test and criterion are made more and more reliable.

Since perfect reliability is only a handy fiction, results from applying the foregoing formula for the correction for attenuation are always hypothetical. It is more important to estimate the increase in the correlation between two variables when the reliability is increased by any particular amount. A formula for doing this is as follows:

$$\bar{r}_{12} = r_{12} \sqrt{\frac{r_{11}'r_{22}'}{r_{11}r_{12}}} \qquad [22]$$

where $\bar{r}_{12}$ = estimated correlation between two variables if reliabilities are changed

r_{22}' = changed reliability for variable 2

r_{22}' = changed reliability for variable 2

The use of Equation 22 can be illustrated in the situation where two tests correlate .30 and each test has a reliability of .60. If the reliability of each test is increased to .90, the expected correlation between the more reliable tests would be obtained as follows:

$$\bar{r}_{12} = .3 \sqrt{\frac{.9 \times .9}{.6 \times .6}}$$

$$\bar{r}_{12} = .45$$

The formula also can be used to estimate what the correlation would be if both reliabilities were *lowered*. This is useful when it is necessary to employ shortened versions of longer tests. If the reliabilities are known for both the longer tests and the shortened versions and the correlation is known between the longer tests, the reliabilities of the shortened tests can be placed in Equation 22 as r_{11}' and r_{22}' the reliabilities of the longer tests as r_{11} and r_{22}. Equation 22 applies equally well when the reliability of one test is increased and the reliability of the other is decreased. If the reliability of only one of the two variables is to be changed, Equation 21 becomes

$$\bar{r}_{12} = r_{12} \sqrt{\frac{r_{11}'}{r_{12}}} \qquad [23]$$

This version of the formula is useful in estimating how much the correlation of the predictor test with a criterion will change if the reliability of the test is either increased or decreased by particular amounts.

What should be evident from inspecting the formulas concerning corrections for attenuation is that such corrected correlations seldom are dramatically different from the actual correlations. Thus, in the example above, a dramatic increase in the reliability of each test from .60 to .90 resulted in an increase in correlation from .30 to only .45. Such a difference is important, but it is much less than intuitively might be thought to occur. As another example, if the correction is made for only one variable and the reliability is increased from .60 to .80, a correlation of .30 would be expected to rise only to .35. The author once heard a colleague suggest that some low correlations found in a study probably would have been much higher if test reliabilities had been higher. The average correlation was about .15 and the average reliability was about .60. Even if the average reliability of the tests is increased to .90, the average correlation would be less than .25. The colleague had in mind an increase in average correlation to .40 or .50, which could not possibly occur.

Confidence zones. The standard error of estimating obtained scores from true scores is computed as it is in all correlational problems. In the general case, the standard error of estimating one variable in deviation-score form (x) from another variable in deviation score form (y) is

$$\sigma_{est} = \sigma_x \sqrt{1 - r_{xy}^2}$$

If x is a set of obtained scores and y is a set of true scores, the formula is

$$\sigma_{est} = \sigma_x \sqrt{1 - r_{xt}^2} \qquad [24]$$
$$= \sigma_x \sqrt{1 - r_{xx}} = \sigma_{meas}$$

The standard error of estimating obtained scores from true scores is called the *standard error of measurement* and is given the special symbol σ_{meas}.

The standard error of measurement is the estimated standard deviation of obtained scores if any individual is given a large number of tests from a domain. It then is useful in establishing confidence zones for scores to be expected on many alternative forms of a test. It was pointed out, however, that it is incorrect to establish such confidence zones symmetrically about the score that a person makes on a particular test. If, for example, an individual has an IQ of 130 on a particular test and the σ_{meas} is 5, it is incorrect to say that the 95% confidence zone for that person extends from 120 to 140 ($130 - 2\sigma_{meas}$ to $130 + 2\sigma_{meas}$). Even though the practice in most applied work with tests has been to center confidence zones about obtained scores, this practice is incorrect, because obtained scores tend to be biased, high scores tending to be biased upward and low scores, downward.

Before establishing confidence zones, one must obtain estimates of unbiased scores. Unbiased scores are the average scores people would obtain if they were administered all possible tests from a domain, holding constant the number of items randomly drawn for each. These are true scores, which are estimated as follows:

$$t' = r_{xx}X \qquad [25]$$

In the previous example, the individual with an IQ of 130 would have a deviation score x of 30. If the reliability were .90, his estimated true score t' would be 27 in deviation-score units. Adding back the mean IQ of 100 would give an estimated true score of 127 in units of IQ. Then the correct procedure would be to set the 95% confidence zone as extending from two standard errors of measurement below 127 to two standard errors above 127. With a σ_{meas} of 5, the zone then would extend from 117 to 137. If a person were administered a large number of alternative forms of the test, 95% of the obtained scores would be expected to fall in that zone, and the expected average of the obtained scores would be 127 (not 130).

In most applied work with tests, there is little reason for estimating true scores except for the establishment of confidence zones. Since estimated true scores correlate perfectly with obtained scores and making practical interpretations of estimated true scores is difficult, in most applied work it is better to interpret the individual's obtained score. The estimated true score would be used only to obtain the center for a confidence zone. Thus, in the example above, the individual would be said to have an IQ of 130, with the 95% confidence zone extending from 63 to 83. Actually, such assymmetrical confidence zones have a real practical advantage: they continually remind people that scores obtained on any test tend to be biased outward on both sides of the mean.

In contrast to applied work with tests, there seldom is need in basic research to estimate true scores or establish confidence zones. In basic research the major concerns are with how much the measurement error lowers correlations and how much it increases the error components in statistical treatments. It is sometimes necessary in basic research to consider the effect of measurement error on the mean of a group of obtained scores. This would be true, for example, if extreme groups on a measure were subjected to an experimental treatment and then either a retest were made or an alternative form were applied. The gain or loss scores for individuals, and the average gain and loss scores for the two groups, would be partly determined by regression effects from measurement error. In essence what one must do is estimate average true scores for the two groups on both tests and then see if the average change is different for the two groups. Except for this special problem, however, in basic research there is little to be gained by estimating true scores or establishing confidence zones.

Effect of dispersion on reliability. It should be realized that, since the reliability coefficient is a correlation coefficient, the size of the reliability coefficient is directly related to the standard deviation of obtained scores for any sample of subjects. Previously it was shown that the reliability coefficient could be expressed as follows:

$$r_{xx} = 1 - \frac{\sigma_{meas}^2}{\sigma_x^2} \qquad [26]$$

The variance of the errors of measurement is expected to be at least approximately independent of the standard deviation of obtained scores. In other words the

standard error of measurement is considered to be a fixed characteristic of any measurement tool regardless of the sample of subjects under investigation. Then it is apparent that the reliability coefficient will be larger for samples of subjects that vary more with respect to the trait being investigated. An example would be in studying the reliability of scores on a test used to select college freshmen. If the correlation between alternative forms is used as the measure of reliability and the correlation is computed only for persons who actually were accepted for college, the correlation will be less than it would have been if persons who were not permitted to enter college had been included in the study.

A look back at Equation 26 will indicate how estimates can be made of how much the reliability would change if the variance of obtained scores were either larger or smaller. If, for one sample, the variance of errors were 2.0 and the variance of obtained scores were 8.0, the reliability would be .75. If a new sample had a variance of 10.0, the variance of errors would be expected to remain at 2.0, and consequently the reliability would be .80. Thus after the standard error of measurement is found for one sample, it is easy to estimate what the reliability would be in another sample with either a larger or smaller standard deviation of scores.

Even though it is important to keep in mind that the reliability varies with the dispersion of scores, this does not alter the direct meaning of the reliability coefficient in any particular sample of people. The reliability coefficient is the ratio of true-score variance to obtained-score variance. If that ratio is small, measurement error will attenuate correlations with other variables and will make it difficult to find significant effects with statistical treatments. If the total group of subjects in a study has a standard deviation of scores which is not much larger than the standard error of measurement, it is hopeless to investigate the variable. Approximately this condition has occurred in some studies. For example, in some studies of creativity, investigations have been made of only those children who had IQs of at least 120. With the children preselected in this way, the standard deviation of IQs in the group being studied would not be much larger than the standard error of measurement for the measure of intelligence. Then if IQs for the preselected groups are correlated with scores on tests of creativity, the correlations obviously will be very low.

Making Measures Reliable

Of course, doing everything feasible to prevent measurement error from occurring is far better than assessing the effects of measurement error after it has occurred. Measurement error is reduced by writing items clearly, making test instructions easily understood, and adhering closely to the prescribed conditions for administering an instrument. Measurement error because of subjectivity of scoring can be reduced by making the rules for scoring as explicit as possible and by training scorers to do their jobs. On the better individual tests of intelligence, even though the scorer is a potential source of measurement error on some items, rules for scoring are so explicit and scorers usually are so well trained that very little measurement error is present. Of course, the ideal always is to completely remove subjectivity in scoring, but for practical reasons, that sometimes is difficult to do. For example, in studies of discrimination learning experimenters have been inter-

ested in "observing responses" in the rat, the tendency for the rat at the choice point in a T maze to look back and forth a number of times before making a choice. Conceivably, the number of such observing responses could be objectively recorded with a complex set of instruments, but if different scorers agree reasonably well on the numbers of observing responses made by different rats, the presence of some subjectivity in the scoring may be preferable to the expense and awkwardness of employing objective instruments. Still, though, the ultimate ideal in science is to have measures that are unaffected by errors of human judgment.

Test length. The primary way to make tests more reliable is to make them longer. If the reliability is known for a test with any particular number of items, the following formula can be used to estimate how much the reliability would increase if the number of items were increased by a factor k:

$$r_{kk} = \frac{kr_{11}}{1 + (k - 1)r_{11}} \qquad [27]$$

If, for example, the reliability of a 20-item test is .70 and 40 items from the same domain are added to the test (making the final test three times as long as the original), the estimated reliability of the 60-item test will be

$$r_{kk} = \frac{3(.7)}{1 + (3 - 1).7} = .88$$

The only assumption in employing Equation 27 in this case would be that the average correlation among the 20 items in the shorter test be the same as the average correlation among the 60 items in the augmented test. The assumption would be violated if old items and new items differed systematically in content (if they were from somewhat different domains) or if they differed in reliability (if the average correlation in one set were higher than that in the other set). In spite of these sources of imprecision, it is surprising how accurately the effects of test length on reliability are usually estimated by Equation 27. This is particularly so if the shorter test contains at least 20 items. (As will be remembered, the precision of the reliability estimate is directly related to the number of test items.) In employing the equation, k need not be a whole number. For example, one could lengthen a 20-item test by 12 items, which would make k 1.6.

Equation 27 also can be used to estimate the effects on reliability of shortening a test. In this case k equals the number of items in the shorter test divided by the number of items in the longer test, r_{kk} is the estimated reliability of the shortened test, and r_{11} is the reliability of the longer test. In the previous example, one could work backward from the reliability of .88 for the 60-item test and estimate the reliability of a 20-item test. Then, by placing .88 as r_{11} in Equation 27 and making $k = \frac{1}{3}$, one recovers the original reliability of .70 for the 20-item test. For either lengthening or shortening a test, the precision of the estimate obtained from Equation 27 depends mainly on the number of items in the *shorter* test. To take an extreme case, one would not expect a very precise estimate if the known reliability of a 5-item test were used to estimate the reliability of a 40-item test, or vice versa.

Since Equation 27 shows the test reliability to be a direct function of the

number of test items only, one might wonder how it can give accurate estimates where there are other sources of measurement error in tests, for example, variation in scores over short periods of time. As was argued previously, many such sources of error are considered by the domain-sampling model. Coefficient alpha is sensitive not only to the sampling of items but also to sources of measurement error present within the testing session. The alternative-form measure of reliability can be made sensitive to all sources of error, including subjectivity of scoring and variations in abilities and personality characteristics over short periods of time. If coefficient alpha is placed in Equation 27, the estimated coefficient alpha for a longer or shorter test takes into account the sampling of items and numerous sources of error in the testing situation. If the correlation between alternative forms is placed in Equation 27, the estimate takes account of variations over short periods of time and any factors that have been systematically varied for the two testings, for example, using different scorers for the two tests. A good estimate would then be obtained of the alternative-form reliability for a longer or shorter test over the same period of time and with the same factors systematically varied. For these reasons, Equation 27 is not blind to sources of error other than those because of the sampling of items per se. Coefficient alpha placed in Equation 27 usually gives a good estimate of the coefficient alpha that will be obtained from a lengthened or shortened test. If the alternative-form reliability is placed in Equation 27, it usually will give a good estimate of the alternative-form reliability for a longer or shorter test. Since coefficient alpha usually is a good estimate of the alternative-form reliability, when the former is placed in Equation 27, it usually will give a good estimate of the correlation to be expected between alternative forms with any particular number of items.

An inspection of Equation 27 shows that if the average correlation among items in a domain is positive, no matter how small, then as the number of items in a test is made larger and larger, the reliability necessarily approaches 1.00. If the average correlation is positive, the correlation between any two samples of items (r_{11}) is expected to be positive. If numerator and denominator of Equation 27 are divided by k, and k is allowed to approach infinity, r_{kk} approaches 1.00. At first glance this might seem to be an easy way to obtain highly reliable tests, but often in practice Equation 27 estimates that to reach even a moderately high reliability a huge number of items would be required. A conversion of Equation 27 can be used to estimate the number of items required to obtain a particular reliability:

$$k = \frac{r_{kk}(1 - r_{11})}{r_{11}(1 - r_{kk})}$$

[28]

where r_{kk} = desired reliability

r_{11} = reliability of existing test

k = number of times test would have to be lengthened to obtain reliability of r_{kk}

In the situation where a 20-item test has a reliability of .50, the estimated lengthening required to obtain a reliability of .80 is found as follows:

$$k = \frac{.8(1 - .5)}{.5(1 - .8)} = \frac{.4}{.1} = 4$$

Thus the estimate is that to reach a reliability of .80 an 80-item test would be required. In many cases it would be feasible to use a test of that length, but let us see what happens when a 40-item test has a reliability of only .20 and a reliability of .80 is desired:

$$k = \frac{.8(1 - .2)}{.2(1 - .8)} = \frac{.64}{.04} = 16$$

It is estimated that 640 items would be required to reach a reliability of .80. Unless the items were of a kind that could be administered very quickly, a test of that length would be impractical in most applied work and in most experiments. Thus one can see that if the average correlation among items in a domain is very low (e.g., only .05), the correlations between samples of items will not be large, and to obtain high correlations would require a prohibitively large number of items in each sample.

Standards of reliability. What a satisfactory level of reliability is depends on how a measure is being used. In the early stages of research on predictor tests or hypothesized measures of a construct, one saves time and energy by working with instruments that have only modest reliability, for which purpose reliabilities of .60 or .50 will suffice. If significant correlations are found, corrections for attenuation will estimate how much the correlations will increase when reliabilities of measures are increased. If those corrected values look promising, it will be worth the time and effort to increase items and reduce measurement error in other ways.

For basic research, it can be argued that increasing reliabilities beyond .80 is often wasteful. At that level correlations are attenuated very little by measurement error. To obtain a higher reliability, say of .90, strenuous efforts at standardization in addition to increasing the number of items might be required. Thus the more reliable test might be excessively time-consuming to administer and score.

In contrast to the standards in basic research, in many applied settings a reliability of .80 is not nearly high enough. In basic research, the concern is with the size of correlations and with the differences in means for different experimental treatments, for which purposes a reliability of .80 for the different measures involved is adequate. In many applied problems. a great deal hinges on the exact score made by a person on a test. If, for example, in a particular school system children with IQs below 70 are placed in special classes, it makes a great deal of difference whether the child has an IQ of 69 or 70 on a particular test. If a college is able to admit only one-third of the students who apply, whether or not a student is in the upper third may depend on only a few score points on an aptitude test. In such instances it is frightening to think that any measurement error is permitted. Even with a reliability of .90, the standard error of measurement is almost one-third as large as the standard deviation of test scores. In those applied settings where important decisions are made with respect to specific test scores. a reliability of .90 is the minimum that should be tolerated, and a reliability of .95 should be considered the desirable standard.

Reliability of Linear Combinations

So far this discussion of reliability has been concerned with the reliability of particular traits (e.g., spelling ability), as manifested in the average correlation among items. Another issue is that of the reliability of linear combinations of measures of different traits. An example of such a linear combination would be the total score on an achievement test battery for elementary school children, which would be the sum of scores obtained on separate parts of the tests for spelling, arithmetic, word usage, and others. This simple linear combination can be depicted as

$$y = x_1 + x_2 + x_3$$

Then the question is that of estimating the reliability of y from a knowledge of the reliabilities of the x variables and the covariances among them.

Problems concerning the reliability of linear combinations occur very frequently in evaluation research. One was illustrated above concerning the sum of scores on achievement tests. Of course, achievement tests are used very widely in evaluation research. Another example is that of employing multiple regression to estimate a criterion variable from a battery of tests. An example is that of employing a battery of several tests to select pilot trainees in the Air Force. The prediction of the criterion variable would be by a linear combination of the test scores. The scores would be differentially weighted in terms of the extent to which they added to the other variables in the linear combination.

Another example of a linear combination of scores employed in evaluation research is that of using several measures to explicate a construct, such as the construct of criminal tendency or the construct of social competence. Either an unweighted or weighted sum of several measures would be used to provide an estimate of the construct. Because of the prevalence of linear combinations of scores in evaluation research, it is important to consider the reliability of such linear combinations.

At first thought it might seem that the reliability of the linear combination could be estimated by coefficient alpha. For this, the sum of the variances of the x variables would be divided by the variance of y, the quotient would be subtracted from 1, and the result would be increased by the factor concerning the number of "things" being summed (see Equation 12). This could be done, but the result would be quite erroneous unless the x variables were all measures of the same trait, for example, alternative forms of a test of spelling ability. The reliability of samples of items from the *same* domain depends entirely on the average correlation among the samples, but this does not hold for samples of items from *different* domains. Suppose that, in the example concerning three subtests of an achievement test, each test had a respectable reliability, but the three all correlated zero with one another. In that case coefficient alpha would lead to the conclusion that the sum of the three tests had a reliability of zero, but that would be absurd.

The actual reliability of a linear combination would be determined by correlating alternative forms of the linear combination. Thus if there were alternative forms of the test battery, each with tests of spelling, arithmetic, and so on, the

alternative forms could be administered approximately two weeks apart. The correlation between total scores on the two occasions would be a good measure of reliability for the linear combination.

In cases where alternative forms are not available or administering them is not feasible, an estimate of the alternative-form reliability can be obtained by a special set of formulas. (Derivations of these formulas and principles for applying them are discussed in detail in Nunnally, 1967, chap. 7. Here some of the major principles and formulas will be briefly discussed.) The most general formula is one that applies regardless of whether one is working with raw scores, deviation scores, or standard scores. It is as follows:

$$r_{yy} = 1 - \frac{\Sigma \sigma_i^2 - \Sigma r_{ii} \sigma_i^2}{\sigma_y^2}$$ [29]

With this formula, one would need to compute only the variance of the linear combination (y) and the standard deviation of each variable in the linear combination and to have foreknowledge of the reliability of each variable. A concrete example would be in the case where (1) the variances of three variables are 1, 2, and 3, respectively; (2) the reliabilities are .60, .70, and .80, respectively; and (3) the variance of the sum of the three variables is 12. The reliability of the sum would be obtained as follows:

$$r_{yy} = 1 - \frac{(1 + 2 + 3) - (.6 + 1.4 + 2.4)}{12}$$

$$= 1 - \frac{6 - 4.4}{12}$$

$$r_{yy} = .87$$

If, as is usually true, variables were placed in the form of standard scores before they were summed, the following formula can be used instead of Equation 29

$$r_{yy} = 1 - \frac{k - \Sigma r_{ii}}{\sigma_y^2}$$ [30]

where k = the number of variables being summed

r_{ii} = the sum of the reliability coefficients for the variables being summed

σ_y^2 = the variance of the sum

The standard-score version of the formula for the reliability of a sum can be illustrated in the case where three variables being summed each have reliabilities of .60 and each pair correlates .50. Then k = 3, and the sum of reliabilities equals 1.8. The variance of y would equal k + (6 X .50) (there being six off-diagonal elements in the correlation matrix). The result would be as follows:

$$r_{yy} = 1 - \frac{3 - 1.8}{6} = .8$$

Going back to Equation 30, one can see that in the special case where only two sets of standard scores are summed, the following special formula can be used:

$$r_{yy} = 1 - \frac{2 - r_{11} - r_{22}}{\sigma_y^2} \qquad [31]$$

Where each of the two variables being summed has a reliability of .60 and the correlation between the two is .50, the computations are as follows:

$$r_{yy} = 1 - \frac{2 - 1.2}{3} = .73$$

The variance of y equals the sum of the elements in the correlation matrix for only two variables, which equals 2.0 plus two times the correlation between them. This makes the denominator of the fraction on the right equal 3.0.

Weighted sums. The method for estimating the reliability of a sum can be extended to the case of weighted sums. A weighted sum of variables expressed as standard scores would be as follows:

$$y = b_1 z_1 + b_2 z_2 + b_3 z_3$$

The variance of y would equal the sum of all elements in the weighted correlation matrix. The diagonal elements would consist of squared weights, and each off-diagonal element would consist of the correlation between two variables multiplied by the products of the weights for the two variables. The sum of elements in this matrix would be divided into the sum of elements in the matrix corresponding to the variance of the sum of true scores. The off-diagonal elements would be the same in the two matrices, but in the latter the diagonal elements would consist of squared weights multiplied by reliability coefficients. Then Equation 30 could be modified to obtain the following formula for the reliability of a weighted sum of variables expressed as standard scores:

$$r_{yy} = 1 - \frac{\Sigma b_i^2 - \Sigma b_i^2 r_{ii}}{\sigma_y^2} \qquad [32]$$

where b_i = weight for variable z_i

r_{ii} = reliability of variable z_i

To apply Equation 32, one would first obtain the variance of the sum of weighted standard scores, which would be the denominator of the expression on the far right of the equation. For the numerator, the sum of squared weights would be obtained. The square of each weight would be multiplied by the corresponding reliability, these would be summed, and the sum would be subtracted from the sum of squared weights. Then it would be only a simple problem in arithmetic to obtain the reliability of the linear combination.

When variables are expressed as deviation scores or raw scores rather than as standard scores, Equation 32 can be modified as follows to obtain the reliability of the weighted sum:

$$r_{yy} = 1 - \frac{\Sigma b_i^2 \sigma_i^2 - \Sigma b_i^2 \sigma_i^2 r_{ii}}{\sigma_y^2} \qquad [33]$$

Equations 32 and 33 can be applied equally well in the case where some of the weighted variables have minus signs in the linear combination.

Principles concerning the reliability of linear combinations. Because linear combinations of variables are encountered so frequently in practice, it is important to look at some principles that govern their reliability. The multiple-regression equation is a weighted linear combination of variables, weighted so as to correlate as highly as possible with a criterion variable. In factor analysis, factors consist of linear combinations of variables, and most other methods of multivariate analysis deal with linear combinations of variables. Consequently the reliability of a linear combination of variables is an omnipresent issue in psychological measurement.

Although previously it was said that the reliability of a sum cannot be estimated by coefficient alpha (Equation 12), a reinspection of the basic formula for the reliability of a linear combination (Equation 29) will show that the two formulas look very similar. In the former there is a multiplier in which the number of test items is divided by the number of test items minus 1, but otherwise the two equations look much alike. The difference is that, in the formula for the reliability of a linear combination, the sum of reliabilities multiplied by variances is subtracted in the numerator of the ratio from the sum of variances. Thus the reliabilities of the variables tend to increase the reliability of a linear combination over that which would be predicted from coefficient alpha.

When the correlations among items are all zero, coefficient alpha is necessarily zero. However, in that case, the reliability of a linear combination need not be, and usually is not zero. When the correlations are zero, the reliability of a linear combination is computed as follows:

$$r_{yy} = \frac{\Sigma r_{ii}}{k} \qquad [34]$$

Equation 34 leads to the important deduction that when the variables in a sum of standard scores correlate zero, the reliability of the sum is the average reliability of the variables. Thus if three variables expressed as standard scores had reliabilities of .60, .70, and .80, and correlations among the three variables were all zero, the reliability of the sum would equal .70. This would hold even if some of the variables had negative signs in the sum. Obviously Equation 34 also applies when the *average* correlation is zero (excluding the diagonal elements in the matrix).

If, as is usually true, the average correlation is positive, the higher the average correlation, the higher the reliability of the linear combination. To understand this rule, one must make a very careful distinction between correlations among variables *before* they are placed in linear combinations and *after* they are placed in linear combinations. The reason this distinction is so important is that the correlation between two variables before they are placed in a linear combination is reversed in sign if they are given *different* signs in the linear combination. In the simplest case, if two variables have a positive correlation and a linear combination is formed by

subtracting one from the other, obviously the correlation changes from positive to negative. So far all the discussion of the reliability of linear combinations has concerned correlations *after* linear combinations are formed. To prevent confusion in that regard, all formulas were developed so that sums or averages of correlations did not explicitly appear. Instead, the correlations among variables in the linear combination were "hidden" in the variance of the linear combination. Of course, when actually computing the variance of a linear combination, one would add or subtract variables depending on their signs in the combination. When that is done, the correct value is obtained for the variance of y. The remaining terms in the computing formulas are reliabilities for variables expressed as standard scores and both reliabilities and variances for sets of deviation scores. Since these are always positive, regardless of the signs variables are given, there is no way to become confused about the proper use of the formulas. All of the formulas in this section on the reliability of linear combinations hold as well when some of the variables which are "summed" are actually subtracted rather than added. Also, where variables in the linear combination are weighted rather than left unweighted, the formulas hold equally well when some of the weights are negative and others are positive. The formulas automatically take account of all these possibilities.

There is, however, considerable value in looking at correlations among variables *before* they are placed in linear combinations. This will show how much reliability is expected from a particular linear combination. Here is an extreme case. If two variables correlated .60 and each had a reliability of .60, then if one variable were subtracted from the other (Equation 31), the reliability of the linear combination would be zero. Obviously such a linear combination would be worthless. Less extreme cases occur frequently in practice. Where the reliabilities were each .80 and the correlation between the two variables was .60, the reliability of the difference between the two variables would be only .50. In both cases the same reliability would have resulted if before variables were combined, the correlations were negative, and both variables were given a positive sign in the combination.

Since the reliability of a sum increases with the size of the average correlation among variables, any set of signs in a linear combination that maximizes the positive sum of correlations will maximize the reliability. The problem is illustrated in the following correlation matrix for six variables:

	1	2	3	4	5	6
1	1.0	+	+	−	−	−
2	+	1.0	+	−	−	−
3	+	+	1.0	−	−	−
4	−	−	−	1.0	+	+
5	−	−	−	+	1.0	+
6	−	−	−	+	+	1.0

The matrix is meant to illustrate correlations among variables *before* they are placed in a linear combination. Variables 1, 2, and 3 form a set whose members all correlate positively, and the same is true for variables 4, 5, and 6. All correlations between members of the two sets are negative. If a linear combination were formed in which all six variables had positive signs, the sum of the elements in the above matrix would be the variance of the linear combination. The size of the reliability of the linear combination is positively related to the size of the variance of the linear combination, and thus it is positively related to the sum of correlations among variables. If, in the example above, all variables were given positive signs, there would be more negative correlations than positive correlations, and consequently the sum of correlations might be either near zero or even negative. In this example, one could obtain the maximum reliability for any possible linear combination by giving negative signs to all three variables in *either* set, (but not both). If one chose to give negative signs to variables 4, 5, and 6, all correlations among the three would remain positive and would not change in size. They would remain positive because all three variables would still have the *same* sign. The important difference would be that the signs of all correlations between the two sets of variables would change from negative to positive. Then all correlations in the matrix would be positive, the variance of the linear combination would be at a maximum, and the reliability of the linear combination would be at a maximum.

The problem is seldom as neat as in the example discussed above; however, an inspection of correlations among variables *before* they are placed in a linear combination will often indicate that a planned linear combination of variables would not be very reliable and that a different linear combination would be much more reliable. Of course, maximization of reliability is seldom the most important goal either in basic research or in applied work. For example, in the former, if a hypothesis concerns how much *better* people do on the sum of three measures than they do on the sum of three other measures, in the linear combination there is no choice but to give positive signs to the first three variables and negative signs to the other three variables. An inspection of correlations among the variables might, however, show that such a linear combination would have a very low reliability, in which case the study would be doomed before it started.

NOTE

1. Comparing Equation 19 with Equation 3 may seem to present an inconsistency: the reliability coefficient is used in the latter, but the square root of the reliability coefficient is used in the former. This is not really an inconsistency, because the purpose in Equation 3 was to estimate true scores in standard form (standard deviation of 1.0). In Equation 19, account is taken of the fact that the standard deviation of true scores is less than that of obtained scores, and consequently the two equations are slightly different. The results obtained from Equation 19 are more easily interpreted in most situations.

REFERENCES

Binet, A. and T. Simon. Méthodes nouvelles pour le diagnostic du niveau intellectuel des anormaux. *Année Psychologie,* 1905, 11: 191-244.

Cronbach, L. J. *Essentials of psychological testing.* Rev. ed.; New York: Harper and Row, 1960.

Cronbach, L. J. and H. Azuma. Internal-consistency reliability formulas applied to randomly sampled single-factor tests: An empirical comparison. *Educational & Psychological Measurement,* 1962, 22: 645-666.

Guion, R. M. *Personnel testing.* New York: McGraw-Hill, 1965.

Hull, C. L. *A behavior system.* New Haven, Conn.: Yale University Press, 1952.

Lord, F. M. An approach to mental test theory. *Psychometrika,* 1959, 24: 283-302.

Nunnally, J. C. *Educational measurement and evaluation.* New York: McGraw-Hill, 1964.

———, *Psychometric theory.* New York: McGraw-Hill, 1967.

Spearman, C. "General intelligence" objectively determined and measured. *American Journal of Psychology,* 1904, 15: 201-293.

Taylor, Janet A. A personality scale of manifest anxiety. *Journal of Abnormal and Social Psychology,* 1953, 48: 285-290.

Thorndike, R. L. and E. Hagen. *Measurement and evaluation in psychology and education.* New York: Wiley, 1961.

V

DATA COLLECTION THROUGH INTERVIEWS AND RECORDS

11

INTERVIEWING IN EVALUATION RESEARCH

CAROL H. WEISS

INTRODUCTION

Much of the information for evaluation research comes from interviews. It is largely through interviews that the evaluator finds out about the characteristics of program participants, their knowledge, attitudes, and behaviors, both before the program and afterward. Through interviews he obtains data from program staff about program expectations and inputs; through interviews he knows from clients' family, teachers, employers, physicians, and others about long-term effects of the program.

Forty years of research on interviewing have amply demonstrated that interview responses contain some measure of inaccuracy, even on simple questions like age and possession of a telephone. On complex questions or those that are socially sensitive, invalidity can run very high indeed. Researchers continue to use interviewing as a basic methodology largely because (1) it is the most convenient way to obtain much of the data they need, and (2) all other techniques for obtaining information are also subject to bias and inaccuracy.

Three Interviewing Issues

In evaluation research, there are special problems in interviewing. This chapter discusses three issues in the use of the interview to obtain research data that are particularly serious when the data are used to evaluate how effectively a program is meeting its objectives.

Validity. The first issue is the validity of response. Although some component of error is inevitable in interview responses, the tendency toward inaccuracy is likely to be increased in evaluation studies because:

(1) There *is* a "right" answer. Unlike most other studies, the hypothesis of the evaluator is clear to sophisticated respondents and probably to less sophisticated respondents as well. The hypothesis inevitably is that the program "worked."

(2) In evaluations of programs of direct service (e.g., training, health care, education), interviewing often takes place in the same setting in which the respondent is accustomed to receiving service. Furthermore, the interviewer may be on the staff of the service agency or working under its auspices. She may therefore be identified with the agency in the respondent's mind.

The combination of a "right" answer and the identification of the interviewer with those who have a stake in having the answer come out "right" presents special perils to response accuracy.

(3) The respondents in evaluation studies are usually people who, almost by the definition of "needing service," are in stressful circumstances. They are likely to be poor, or sick, or delinquent, or to have some other socially disapproved characteristic. To the extent that this affects their ability to articulate their views and their willingness to be candid, interviewing is more difficult and responses are less valid.

Selection of Interviewers. In most research, there are two parties who have an investment in the interview: the research staff and the respondent. In evaluation research, a third party enters the scene: the program staff. They have a series of legitimate concerns about the interview: it should not antagonize the client, it should not interfere with more important activities, it should not raise doubts about certain aspects of agency operations or staff performance, and so on.

Evaluators must work out coexistence arrangements with program staff if they are to have access to sources of information. One of the issues around which negotiations often take place is: Who is to do the interviewing? Shall it be program staff or research staff? Social workers or research interviewers? There are important questions about the characteristics that interviewers should have to maintain the agency's confidence and at the same time obtain valid data from respondents.

Maintaining Contact and Cooperation. In evaluation research, the design frequently requires follow-up of participants over a lengthy period of time to find out about the survival of program effects. Ways have to be found to locate people when they move, and to maintain their interest and cooperation with the study. Techniques have been tried with varying degrees of success in both endeavors, and we shall review the state of the art.

ALTERNATIVES TO INTERVIEWING

Before turning to interviews as the sole way to collect evaluation data (a decision that has become almost automatic among evaluators in certain traditions), thought should be given to alternative methods. Some of these have advantages in cost, time, and appropriateness of the data for the evaluation question.

Webb and his associates (1966) believe that noninterviewing methods have an advantage in validity as well. They urge researchers to make more use of unobtrusive methods to collect information, where the presence of the interviewer does not affect responses. They give such ingenious examples as measurement of the wear in the tiles in front of exhibits in a museum to judge their relative popularity. Even the more prosaic of us can use such nonreactive methods as inspection of agency records, and such less reactive techniques as mail questionnaires, telephone surveys,

group interviews, and participant observation. Each of these reduces the salience of the interviewer, and thereby decreases whatever biases she induces.

But interviewers are not only sources of danger to the data; they provide such important services as increasing the response rate, motivating people to answer each question, supplying common definitions, giving a structure of meaning to the study. Thus, each data collection technique has its own set of advantages and disadvantages. A brief tour through them may provide the evaluator with grounds for making decisions on data collection techniques.

Use of Records

One of the greatest advantages of using records is the saving in cost. If the information needed for evaluation already exists, as it may in hospitals, schools, employment agencies, social agencies, personnel departments, prisons, and the like, the study is considerably ahead in time, effort, and money. Even if the data are not recorded or coded in categories relevant to the study, it is worth expending a fair amount of time to make the necessary adaptations, for example, reading through narrative case records to extract the necessary information.

Sometimes there is a problem obtaining access to what are regarded in the organization as confidential files. In this event, it may be possible to designate one member of the research staff as the special "bonded" investigator, and in that way secure the confidence of the agency. Or the cognizant department can be used to supply the data itself, using code numbers or code names in such a way that later data can be matched.

While the use of agency records has many desirable features, the general experience unfortunately is that they are often incomplete, out-of-date, and painfully inaccurate. Entries are undated. Names are variously spelled. Gaps are unaccounted for. Even where records meet the standards for accuracy of the operating agency (and this is by no means always the case), they may not meet research canons. Sometimes there are special interpretations or shortcuts, known only to one or two old-time employees, that belie the face data. The evaluator is well advised to do assiduous checking before trusting available records.

Another major disadvantage of records is that they contain what somebody else needs to know, not necessarily information most germane to the evaluator's questions. Information, for example, on values, attitudes, and knowledge will rarely appear. Where these are important components of the evaluation, record data are unlikely to advance the study.

Inaccuracy and irrelevance are good reasons for abandoning the idea of using records. But before the evaluator does so, another possibility can be considered: instituting better record-keeping procedures so that appropriate data are routinely and continuously collected. If the evaluation hinges on clear and relatively simple indicators, the evaluator can accomplish the study purpose in this way and also provide a continuing legacy for program operators. Good data will be available, provided that the system is maintained, for a variety of uses beyond research, including ongoing management decision-making.

So far we have been talking about using the records of the agency involved in the

program. For follow-up purposes, it may also be possible to take advantage of outside records, such as police records, school test scores, employment records. Here, of course, confidentiality is a *must*. Often the only access is to aggregate statistics. But for follow-up, these may well be usable. Some agencies have adopted data systems that supply tabular data to researchers who convince them of the worth of their research and pay the data costs. The evaluator supplies the names (and/or background characteristics) of persons whose status he is interested in, and asks the agency to run tables from its records by sex, age, length of time in program, or whatever other variables are deemed important. Such tables preclude the identification of individuals, but allow analysis of the relation of program participation to the specified indicator.

Obviously it is preferable for the researcher to have control over the data, and where vows of confidentiality will work, they should be given. But there are cases where the value of record data is so great that it is worth settling for aggregate statistics. For example, the Social Security Administration on occasion has made available for research purposes the employment histories of subjects (e.g., numbers of quarters worked, wages received— up to the social security ceiling, industry code), in tabular from such that no table cell includes fewer than five cases. The Internal Revenue Service will reportedly respond to important bona fide research requests in similar fashion. The 1970 Census provided special newsletters and instructions for those who want to retrieve Census information on specified cases. In all these instances, the costs are relatively low and the data of irreplaceable value.

A particularly engaging feature of using official agency data for follow-up is the possibility of extracting "control group" data from the same records. If a control group was selected at the start of the program, the same data can be collected about them as about program participants. Even had there been no true randomly assigned control group, a pick-up "contrast group," matched on some important characteristics, can be constructed after the fact directly from the follow-up records. For example, the readmission of program participants to hospitals can be compared with readmissions of nonparticipants of similar age, prior length of stay, race, socioeconomic status.

Mail Questionnaires

The mail questionnaire is probably the least costly method of original data collection. The range of questions it can deal with is extensive. If it is well conceived and clearly worded, even people with little education can and will respond; thus the 1970 Census relied largely on mail returns.

The chief problem is the rate of nonresponse and the consequent bias in the data. Those responding to the questionnaire are likely to differ from nonrespondents in important but unspecified ways. The data will not be representative of the responses of the whole population surveyed.

In general, older people, those with less education, and women are less likely to return questionnaires. Cobb, King, and Chen (1957), reporting on differences between respondents and nonrespondents in a morbidity survey, found lower participation from older people and less well-educated people. Kivlin (1965),

studying a rural population, reported that nonrespondents were older, had adopted fewer farming innovations, had less formal education, and were less likely to belong to organizations.

A variety of techniques can be used to increase the response rate. The effectiveness of many of them has been studied by researchers. They include efforts to enlist cooperation before or with the mailing, such as preliminary interviewing or personal contact by the sponsor (Skipper and Ellison, 1966), announcement letters preceding the questionnaire (Heaton, 1965), accompaniment of the questionnaire by personally typed letters on letterhead (Roeher, 1963), stamped return envelopes (Robin, 1965; Roeher, 1963), and small cash offerings for questionnaire return (Kephart and Bressler, 1958). Others are follow-ups after the initial distribution—by post cards at various intervals after the questionnaire mailing (Nichols and Meyer, 1966), by personal interview follow-up (Hansen and Hurwitz, 1946), by phone call (Roeher, 1963). Generally, follow-ups were more effective than introductory inducements (even the cash reward of a quarter). About the most successful technique reported was the use of a postcard as the questionnaire form (Boek and Lade, 1963), which achieved almost complete return. But this form of questionnaire has obvious limitations.

Careful pretesting is essential before a questionnaire goes out into the field. Questions and words that hold one meaning for the researcher may be interpreted very differently by respondents. An interviewer on the scene can find this out, but with a mail questionnaire there is little feedback, and the researcher may be misled. Particularly when evaluation deals with members of a group whose traditions and experience are off the middle-class path, such as addicts or ghetto youth, there is much room for misunderstanding. For example, in a study of blue-collar wives (not a very off-beat population), Komarovsky (1964) found words variantly interpreted: "talk" meant a long discussion, "quarrel" meant something very violent, "pleased with yourself" implied being conceited or stuck-up, having your husband "surprise you" always meant a gift and not an act, "help" meant money.

Even with careful formulation of questions and assiduous pretesting, there are limits to the amount and kind of data collectible by questionnaire. A long questionnaire by its sheer bulk turns off many people. Unless the respondent is very highly motivated (by interest in the subject, feelings of loyalty to the organization, or for some other reason), he is not likely to answer 20 pages of questions.

Nor is he generally willing to write long narrative answers. Most questionnaires, accordingly, precategorize the possible responses and ask for a check in the proper box. The evaluator has to know the universe of answers well enough to list them properly, and rarely can go into much depth about the antecedents and consequences of each contingency. Complex issues are hard to cover well by questionnaires.

Telephone Surveys

Telephone surveys have much to recommend them. Interviewer travel is eliminated and costs reduced. When no one answers, unlimited call-backs are possible, and at all hours of the day. Sudman states that in many cases there is an increase in

the quality of the interviewer's performance "since the interviewer is more at ease working from the comfort of her home while the respondent is more candid than he would be in a face-to-face interview." (Sudman, 1967: 58.)

The most important recent development to make telephoning useful to research on a more-than-local basis is Wide Area Telephone Service (WATS). Special rates are offered for service to specified areas. Interviewers generally call from a central location and can be supervised on the spot. Assael and Eastlack (1966) see the major benefits of the use of WATS in survey research as sampling precision, control over what the interviewer asks respondents, and quality control over the interviewer's performance.

Even sensitive information appears to be accessible by phone. Coombs and Freedman (1964) used the telephone for reinterviews of their original Detroit sample in a study of fertility and contraceptive behavior. They completed 1,274 interviews by phone out of a sample of 1,304. Hochstim (1967), comparing responses to personal interview, phone interview, and mail questionnaire, found negligible differences; on questions about use of liquor, women were slightly more apt to acknowledge drinking when asked by phone than by either of the other methods.

On the other hand, some investigators have found greater inaccuracies in telephone surveys. In a study of alterations and repairs to residential property, Kildegaard (1965) reports that a subsample of telephone interviews produced responses less complete than those obtained through personal interviews.

Moreover, not everyone has a phone. Families too poor to have phones are missed completely. Of those with phones, not all list phone numbers in public directories, and it is not clear to what extent unlisted numbers differ from others (Brunner and Brunner, 1971). Random-digit dialing offers a way to sample all numbers—listed and unlisted—from any given telephone exchange (Glasser and Metzger, 1972). Nevertheless, as Judd (1966) warns, use of telephone interviews imposes sampling limitations that may be inconsistent with the purposes of the study. Particularly when poor people are to be interviewed, as they are in some evaluations, it is impossible to rely exclusively on survey by telephone, or the data will be severely biased by exclusion of the most deprived.

No one has systematically investigated the effects of the length of an interview by telephone. It seems possible that, without face-to-face contact, the respondent's attention cannot be sustained for as long a period of time. (This evidently does *not* apply to teenagers.) But an engrossing topic or skilled interviewing may overcome the tendency to lose interest. There is little evidence on either side of the issue, but some research organizations are successfully using telephones for interviews as long as 90 minutes (*Survey Research*, 1973).

For program staff, whom evaluators often need to interview in order to learn about program process, and for employers and other VIPs who can provide information on program outcomes, telephoning can be the best way to get access. So much of their business is conducted by phone that they are accustomed to and skilled in appropriate response patterns.

Group Interviews

Interviewing two to a half dozen or more respondents at a time can be viewed as "more bang for the buck," a saving in time and money. But the group interview is generally selected as a data collection technique when specific information about individuals is less important than obtaining the consensus of opinions of a group.

How good an approximation of individual opinions do group interviews provide? Chandler (1954) used group interviewing of workers in a study of labor-management relations in a midwestern community. Comparing responses in the group interview on questions regarding management and union to responses given in private interviews, she reports "a rather close correspondence between these two groups of materials was revealed. Still, the 'group opinions' that could be distilled from the discussions were not a completely accurate reflection of the private feelings of the various individuals: at times the expression of these feelings seemed to be modified or suppressed in the presence of the group" (Chandler, 1954: 27). For the group leader, public and private opinions were in closest correspondence.

Other investigators tend to agree on the effect of group pressure. A study of top-ranking business executives found that when respondents invited colleagues or subordinates to sit in on the interview, colleagues confirmed one another and subordinates were afraid to talk (Kincaid and Bright, 1957). As Banks (1957) concludes, group interviewing gives different results from individual interviewing. Neither is "true" or "false"; they are tackling different problems.

The nature of the differences is illustrated in three studies. Becker (1956) found that medical students interviewed in the presence of other students tend to be cynical. Alone they will talk of idealistic motives. Both types of feelings exist, but the group norms affect which feeling is expressed in the group situation. Similarly, gang boys assent to middle-class values readily in private, but voice lower-class values when fellow gang members are present. Again, both sets of values are probably real (Short and Strodtbeck, 1965). Old people are more conservative in attitudes on the extended family when their adult children are present, less conservative when their spouse is present (Taietz, 1962). As anthropologists have known since their earliest days among primitive people, the nature of the audience always affects what a speaker says, how he says it, or whether he speaks at all (Paul, 1953).

Special values have been found in group interviewing. Thus Goldman (1962) found that it offered advantages over individual interviewing in: (1) the stimulation of new ideas, (2) the opportunity for direct observation of the group process, (3) an understanding of the temporal dynamics of attitudes and opinions, and (4) spontaneity and candor. Obviously such advantages are very special and only tangentially related to the usual purposes of interviewing. Hare and Davie (1954) were talking about the more common purposes of research when they concluded that group interviewing is a useful scouting device preliminary to construction of a formal personal-interview study. Some researchers report, too, that there are respondents who are uncomfortable and inarticulate in the presence of an interviewer, such as black teenagers. In a group interview they will open up, since they

are supported by their fellows and can direct their comments as much to each other as to the figure in authority.

Group interviewing then is effective for collecting information and opinions if the special pressures toward conformity to group norms are recognized (or even desirable in the research).

In evaluation studies, the device has been particularly effective in collecting opinions on participants' responses to the program and their expectations for the post-program future.

Participant Observation

Participant observation involves the researcher (or his agents) in the daily life of people under study. Either openly as a researcher or covertly in some disguised role, the observer notes things that happen, listens to what is said, and questions people over a period of time. In this way, he gets beneath the surface of events and participates in the experiences of the people studied.

There are obvious advantages to such an approach. Participant-observers are not likely to be misled by dissembling respondents. They are there. They learn to understand how differences in perception and in motivation affect what is reported and they are able to check the distortions against events. Further, they are not apt to run aground on "sensitive" questions that interviewers cannot or prefer not to talk about. They can use their knowledge of specific incidents to face an issue and force the respondent to clarify what he means.

Participant observation is also a learning technique in speech and usage. Unlike the interviewer, who deals in the currency of the researcher's words, the participant-observer learns the meanings of the respondents' words and patterns of speech with great precision through study of their use in context and through exploration of their implications and nuances. By immersion in it, he learns the native language, along with the native values, mores, and style of life (Becker and Geer, 1957).

Participant observation has its greatest rewards when the subjects of study are sufficiently different from the usual breed to warrant this kind of attention, when there is a homogeneous community or group to observe, and when the purpose of the study is the understanding of the *system* of behavior and the interrelationships within it. Rarely is it used to collect the kind of specific, discrete items of data that many evaluations use as indicators of program effectiveness. Rather it would help to enrich concrete data by deeper knowledge of why people act as they do in the context of their own life situations.

There are drawbacks. One is cost, since a good deal of time is used hanging around the street corners, hospital wards, meeting halls, and shops. Nor is the technique routine. It takes people with perceptiveness and empathy, as well as knowledge of research and theory, to write a *Street Corner Society* (Whyte, 1955) or *Tally's Corner* (Liebow, 1967).

Further, while participant observation decreases the likelihood of *respondents'* misreporting (through the check of on-the-spot observation), it gives the *observer* wide latitude. As Schwartz and Schwartz (1955) point out, the observer is subject

to the operation of unconscious factors, such as anxiety, that affect what he sees and how he sees. There are also the influences of personal interests, values, and orientations. His feelings toward the research situation, his sympathy or antipathy toward the group under study, even his personal stability, affect the observer's findings. Some participant observers have become so caught up in the activities in the field that they become all participant and non-observer.

Anthropologists, who rely heavily on participant observation, are aware of the dangers of distortion in this method of research. But anthropological field work must involve a personal factor that operates consciously and boldly. Perhaps, as Gans (1962) has said, the best thing to do is to make the researcher's own biases and preconceptions clear at the outset, and let the reader supply his own correctives.

VALIDITY OF RESPONSE

When people speak of getting valid answers from interviews, they often mean little more than that the answers are accurate. Validity means more than that. Valid answers, when reduced to quantitative terms, actually provide a measure of the concept they purport to measure. Thus, the burden of establishing or improving response validity falls not only on the interviewer and the respondent, but also on the researcher who develops concepts, devises measures, writes questions, and manipulates the consequent data.

Data can be reliable without being valid. Reliability has to do with stability. Respondents may give the same answer over and over, even when it is wrong. Data can also be valid without being reliable. The measure measures what it says it does, but does it poorly. Answers distribute about the true mean, but because of the coarseness of the measuring instrument, the variance is large.

Having said these things, which are true and important, we shall now proceed to ignore them and concentrate primarily on accuracy of interview responses. Other chapters in the Handbook deal with other issues of research validity.

No social data, whether obtained by interviewing or through any other human technique, are totally accurate. Students of interviewing are particularly aware of the perils to validity. Ever since interviewing became a sizable enterprise, investigators have studied the extent of error in interview responses. The error reported has varied from minuscule on factual, value-free, public-knowledge questions to enormous on private and sensitive topics.

It is not always easy to foretell which questions will cause the greatest trouble. Among some groups, reporting of illegitimate births (Greenleigh Associates, 1965) or drug use (Robins and Murphy, 1967) is evidently acceptable and relatively easy. At other times and in other places, there is significant error in the reporting of age, education, doctors' visits, and length of employment.

Every evaluator seeks to minimize the degree of interview error in his study. In evaluation research, because of the authority relationships between participants and the program, the known direction of desirability of response, and often the nature of the subject matter, response accuracy is under special stress. The following

sections look first at the sources of error in the interview and then at some specific problems and what to do about them.

Sources of Error

Inaccuracy creeps into interview data through a number of channels. Figure 1 diagrams the interrelationships among the potential sources of error: (1) predispositions of the respondent, (2) predispositions of the interviewer, (3) the procedures used in the study, and (4) the interaction between respondent and interviewer.

Predispositions of the Respondent. Some of the predispositions of the respondent that may lead him to err in the interview are:

He is suspicious or hostile to research, its auspices, or its purposes.

He is suspicious or hostile to the group (for example, whites, social workers) from which the interviewer comes.

He is indifferent and unmotivated to cooperate.

He lacks information on the subject under inquiry.

He lacks self-insight, perspective, cognitive skills.

His language ability is limited.

He misunderstands the role of the respondent, reinterprets it in more familiar terms (for example, client to public assistance investigator, suspect to policeman, host to guest) and applies inappropriate norms.

He is deferential to others or to authority in general.

He wishes to present himself or his group in socially desirable terms.

He wishes to present himself in terms that are expected of him by society.

He has an acquiescent personality.

He wants to conceal damaging information (because it is ego-damaging, because it violates norms, or would incur penalties).

In the case of evaluation, he wants to make a good impression on the program people. Or he wishes to have the program look good (or possibly bad).

The reasons for misreporting can be classified in many ways. Cannell and Kahn (1968) summarize them under categories of *accessibility* (of the information to the

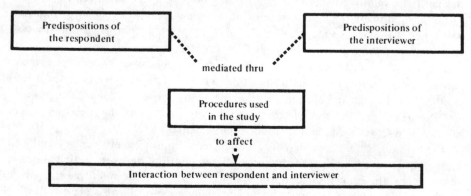

FIGURE 11.1   Sources of error in the interview.

respondent), *cognition,* and *motivation.* Another way to look at them is in terms of their effect. Some sources of error lead to random misreporting; others lead to bias in one direction. The random misreport reduces reliability, but if errors tend to cancel each other out, they are not a serious threat to validity. It is the directional bias that is most troublesome to research.

Which kinds of motivation lead to which kinds of error? Obviously people's motives are complex and interrelated. But cautiously and tentatively let us over-simplify. Faulty memory probably gives rise to errors in both directions, as does indifference to the interview and the research and lack of interest in cooperating.[1] Because of lack of information or interest in the interview, some respondents will overstate the importance of their job functions, or the school achievement of their child, or their expenditures, while others will understate. This conclusion, of course, assumes that the person does in fact hazard an answer. If he lacks information or interest, he may also fail to report at all—not report visits to the doctor, not report part-time jobs. Such behavior biases the data toward understate-ment. Health studies attempting to discover the prevalence of chronic diseases or the numbers of hospitalizations find that interviews miss out on significant chunks of data.

Bias in one direction or the other can also arise from acquiescence, deference, from the desire to live up to stereotyped expectations of one's group, from the desire to present oneself (or one's group or program) in a good light, and from the wish to avoid censure. Because the respondent consciously or subconsciously is trying to approximate some fictional version of himself, error will tend to go in one direction. Of course, many of these motives are interrelated in complex ways. We will take a closer look at them in a later section.

Predispositions of the Interviewer. The interviewer on his side comes to the interview with his own attitudes, expectations, and prejudices.

He may be uncomfortable with the people whom he is interviewing.

He may shy away from confrontations with the issues of the study.

He may be ill at ease in the environment in which he is working.

He may be unable to establish rapport with the respondent.

He may be so intent on establishing rapport that he slights the interviewing task.

He may lack understanding of the language and the life around him.

He may have strong opinions on the subject under study and allow them to influence what he hears.

He may have stereotyped expectations of what the people are like and what they will say.

In what is probably the first study of interviewer effect on response, Stuart Rice published a paper in 1929 on "contagious bias in the interview." He was doing a study of destitute men in flophouses. He found that one of his interviewers consistently received the answer from the men that it was drink that had led to their downfall. Another interviewer received answers that blamed social and eco-nomic conditions. Investigation showed that the first interviewer was a prohibi-tionist and the second interviewer, a socialist (Rice, 1929).

Unlike the respondent, the interviewer is to some degree under the researcher's control. He is recruited, hired, trained, and supervised by the research staff. Through these processes, he can be expected to shed some of his dysfunctional predilections. So while there is still cogency in the view of the interviewer as a "significant but uncontrolled variable" in research, the control can be improved. We discuss some means for improvement in the section on Training and Supervision of Interviewers.

Procedures of the Study. Here we come to the part of the study most directly under the researcher's control. Clearly no researcher adopts procedures he knows will contribute to response error. But very little evidence exists about the effects of different procedures on misreporting, and decisions are often made on other grounds.

The procedures of the interview strongly influence the ground on which the respondent and interviewer meet, the ways they perceive each other, and the latitude they have for interaction. Procedures thus help to determine whether the proclivities of each party are, or are not, expressed in the interview.

Some of the procedures that will be important are:

The manner in which the study is introduced and explained.
The grounds on which the respondent's cooperation is sought.
The discussion of the sponsorship and auspices of the study.
The wording of the questions.
The choice of answers allowed to the respondent (e.g., checklists, free narrative response).
The order and placement of questions.
The length of the interview schedule.
The method of recording answers (e.g., notes, verbatim, tape recorder).
The place in which the interview is held.
The presence of other people during the interview.
The use of proxy respondents (one person reporting about others).
Paying the respondent for the interview.

Long, complicated interviews, replete with questions that make little sense in terms of the person's experiences or vocabulary, will reduce cooperation and probably increase error. Using one person as an informant about other members of his household also increases the likelihood of error. Asking questions on socially sensitive topics (e.g., addiction to narcotics) makes a respondent more apt to misreport (but when these types of questions are the very stuff of evaluation, they cannot be lightly dropped). We will discuss several of the procedures further in a later section.

Interaction between Respondent and Interviewer. Reduced to its elements, the research interview is a conversation between two people in which one person has a purpose: getting information. The interviewer knows how to go about getting the information (he has been trained, he has a schedule, etc.); the respondent has to learn what is expected of him and how to play his part as he goes along.

Many people understand the purposes and norms of interviewing, largely because

of publicity about opinion polls and market studies. But many people do not. In either event, the immediate presence of the interviewer is the most salient feature of the interview situation, and how he acts and what he says will have great impact. An interviewer, for example, who is embarrassed about asking a certain question (income, contraceptive methods used) will have more trouble getting answers than will the interviewer who has no anxiety about the question.

Part of the interviewing lore holds that it is essential for the interviewer to establish good rapport with the respondent. In this view, the closer the interview comes to a warm, intimate relationship, the better will be the caliber of the data. Obviously it is essential that there be enough rapport so that the respondent agrees to answer the study questions. But whether, beyond that point, the interviewer should try to be friend and confidante is open to question. Some recent evidence, which is discussed further in a later section, suggests that too close a relationship reinforces the respondent's bent to seem more socially desirable than he is, and thus imperils the validity of the data.

Factors That Affect Response Validity

Social Desirability of Responses. It is a commonplace of interviewing that when "interviewed directly concerning behavior about which there is a strong expectation of social approval or disapproval, respondents tend to err in the direction of idealizing their behavior" (Maccoby and Maccoby, 1954). The more serious the social sanctions, the more pervasive is the tendency to gloss over, scrub up, and lie.

Very few questions are totally immune to the biasing effects of social desirability. Thus, women are significantly less accurate than men at reporting their ages to the Census (Myers, 1954). Voting is consistently overreported (Parry and Crossley, 1950-51; Miller, 1952; Freeman, 1953; and Weiss 1968). Contributions to philanthropic appeals are reported by sizable numbers of people for whom no record of a contribution can be found (Parry and Crossley, 1950-51). Union members overreport their attendance at union meetings (Dean, 1958). Trainees inflate the number of sessions they have attended in a leadership training program (Hagburg, 1968).

Income reporting is the main exception to the drift toward the desirable. In the United States, income is generally underreported. Whether for fear of the Internal Revenue Service or not to "show off," for reasons of superstition or faulty memory, study after study shows people reporting less income than they actually earn. Even welfare recipients (David, 1962) and recipients of social security benefits (Haber, 1966) report lower payments than they receive.

Evaluations are probably particularly susceptible to interview error. To many of the questions, there is a "right" answer, namely, that the program had beneficial effects. Accommodating respondents, seeing the intent of the questions, are apt to play up the positive.

Sometimes there are conflicts between reporting behavior that is socially acceptable in the respondent's own reference group and reporting behavior that program sponsors would like to hear. Thus in traditional societies such as Pakistan, India, and Jamaica, the use of contraceptives tends to be underreported, particularly by

women (Rowntree and Pierce, 1961; Green, Gustafson, and Begum, 1968). Juvenile gang members report more delinquency when their peers are present than when they face an interviewer alone.

What can be done to reduce the biasing effects of social desirability on response? Some things are obvious: the interviewer should show complete acceptance of any answer, however deviant it may be. He might do well to follow the style of the worldly wise Kinsey interviewer who conveys the impression that he has heard everything and is surprised at nothing. Second, the interviewer should reassure each person that his answers are confidential. Nobody will find out what he said; only aggregate totals and percentages will be reported.

Some gimmicks have been used to underscore the confidentiality of interview responses. The interviewer can give the respondent the question on a sheet of paper and ask him either to mail it back anonymously in a stamped, addressed envelope, or to drop it into a locked "ballot box" that the interviewer carries with him. There are reports that the sealed envelope technique improves the accuracy of financial reporting (Lansing, Ginsburg, and Braaten, 1961: 187).

Even more elaborate statistical techniques have been devised to assure confidentiality of each individual's responses to sensitive questions. Warner (1965) proposes that the researcher present the respondent with two complementary statements, for example, I have had an abortion/I have never had an abortion. The respondent uses a randomization device to choose which statement she will respond to, responds "true" or "false" to the chosen statement, but does not tell the interviewer which statement she has responded to. The researcher can compute aggregate data later on the basis of the probability of choosing each statement. Greenberg, Abernathy, and Horvitz (1970) successfully used a variation of Warner's technique in a large-scale survey. Instead of two complementary statements, respondents were presented with two different questions, one that was potentially embarrassing and another that was innocuous. The interviewer was unaware which question respondents were answering. Boruch (1972) compared the traditional direct method and Greenberg's techniques with his own method of asking the respondent to lie or tell the truth (depending on the roll of a die) for each question. His results on a survey of marijuana use among college students suggest that the indirect methods have limited usefulness in reducing misleading responses.

Another way to diminish the effects of social desirability bias would be through careful question construction. Instead of asking for yes-no, agree-disagree, true-false answers, the researcher presents alternative answers, each of which has equivalent social desirability value. As Smith suggests, this is extremely difficult to do (D. H. Smith, 1967); difficulties are compounded when different respondent groups perceive the levels of social desirability differently (Dohrenwend, 1966). But even rough approximations can accomplish a fair amount. For example, when alternative choices are presented, acceptable reasons for "unacceptable" replies can be included, for example, "Did not attend because of family obligations."

There is a technique for correcting for social desirability bias after the data are in. A short scale of items measuring social desirability is included in the interview. Then the questions that show a significant relationship with the social desirability

scale are tagged for correction. High scorers on the social desirability scale are the ones whose answers will be corrected. Corrections are made by shifting the answer of each high scorer one or more steps away from the more desirable end of the response scale. David H. Smith (1967) reports that his use of such a procedure increased the association between the dependent variable and the corrected data items.

Another way of handling bias is discussed in the section on Question Form, namely, the use of indirect and projective questions.

Acquiescence, Deference, and Desirability. An extensive literature exists in psychometrics on the tendency of some respondents to exhibit an acquiescent response set, that is, to agree with statements or respond affirmatively to questions irrespective of content. Some investigators view this phenomenon as a personality characteristic. Couch and Keniston (1960), in a study using 61 Harvard under-graduates as subjects, demonstrated that "yea-sayers" (acquiescent respondents) are individuals with weak ego controls who are characterized by a cluster of personality variables including impulsivity, dependency, anxiety, mania, anal pre-occupation, and anal resentment. A factor analysis of the individual items yielded a major dimension of stimulus acception versus stimulus rejection which was central to the agreeing-disagreeing response set.

Since that ground-breaking paper, much work has been done on acquiescent response set, and recurrent controversies have flared. Elliott (1961), studying airman trainees, showed that acquiescence was not a simple effect but rather the result of a complex interaction of item content and respondent aptitude. Respondents with high aptitude generally showed the least tendency toward acquiescence. Items relating to personal prestige when stated negatively did not evoke much acqui-escence. McGee (1962) concluded that no general trait of response acquiescence exists independent of the content and form of the measuring instrument.

Edwards (1961), Jackson and Messick (1962), and Foster (1961), among others, aver that social desirability is a more potent source of response bias than acqui-escence. The respondent's desire to "look good" is dominant. Only when questions are ambiguous or confusing, or the interview situation particularly threatening, does acquiescent response set become salient.

A number of investigators have looked at acquiescence specifically in the interview context. They find that lower class respondents, particularly Negroes, are more likely to display acquiescent biases (Dohrenwend, 1966). Hare's (1960) study of mothers of premature infants found that Negro respondents gave a higher number of agreeing responses even when the responses were inconsistent with each other. He concluded that the Negroes' lower economic and educational level contributed to their lack of understanding of the items and thus to their tendency to agree with them. A study of child-rearing attitudes (Radin and Glasser, 1965) similarly found more acquiescence among Negro mothers, and concluded that their difficulty in comprehending many of the items contributed to acquiescence.

Both of the latter studies as well as others (e.g., Lenski and Leggett, 1960) attribute much acquiescent behavior to another feature of the interview, the presence of the high-status interviewer. Poor people, they say, are apt to show

deference to a person of higher status, particularly if he appears to be in a position of authority.

It seems likely that acquiescence in the interview is not a pure personality trait but is influenced by comprehension of the material and by the social desirability of the response. Several techniques are available to the researcher to deal with the phenomenon. One is to pose all agree-disagree items in both the positive and negative form. Random halves of the study group receive the alternative forms. Then the two sets of replies are averaged (O'Neill, 1967). Even better is to avoid questions with yes-no, agree-disagree answers. The respondent can be presented with positive and negative statements (and if desired, a range of statements in between the extremes) and asked to choose the statement that comes closest to his opinion. There are also correction procedures, analogous to those discussed for social desirability response set, that statistically reduce the tendency toward extreme acquiescence.

Language in the Interview. In evaluation studies, many of the respondents are poor people, people of minority cultures, people under stress. In evaluation interviews, then, there are apt to be problems in communication. Since the validity of the data obtained depend in part upon the respondent's ability to understand the interviewer's questions and to give relevant replies, which in turn are fully grasped by the interviewer, commonality of language plays a vital role. Investigators have described some of the verbal limitations and habits of speech that militate against clear communication. At the simplest level, Komarovsky (1964) found that words mean different things in different groups.

At a somewhat higher level of complexity, differences in language reflect different patterns of perceiving and thinking. Observers have described the poor person's concentration on the specific and the concrete and his difficulties with abstractions and introspection (e.g., Riessman, 1962; Hollingshead and Redlich, 1958; Myers and Roberts, 1959). Gordon, in her study of multiproblem families in Harlem, notes that "questions that were concrete drew concrete responses, whereas the more general or philosophic questions either evoked nothing or responses so general as to be meaningless" (Gordon, 1965: 29-30). For example, the Harlem mothers could not understand a question asking them to choose among the different explanations offered for the existence of poverty.

Similarly, a study using the Parental Attitude Research Inventory (PARI) with poor Negro mothers found that the concepts of the language were too complex. It was necessary to give substitutes for many of the words. There were particular discrepancies between low- and middle-class mothers in interpretation of "suffer," "strict," and "hard job." (Radin and Glasser, 1965). Furthermore, it has been demonstrated that among the poor, members of the most disorganized families tend to be the poorest respondents (Geismar and La Sorte, 1963).

Schatzman and Strauss (1955) contrasted the responses of 10 middle-class and 10 lower-class white Arkansans on their experiences during a tornado. There were considerable disparities between the classes in their ability to see things from different perspectives and to clarify experiences. Lower-class respondents almost without exception described events as seen through their own eyes. They did not

take different perspectives, as did the middle-class people, and describe the actions of others from the vantage point of the actor.

Moreover, they were relatively insensitive to the interviewer and his lack of understanding and congruent imagery. They assumed that their perceptions represented reality and they felt little need to explain, qualify, or illustrate. They were particularly sparse with motivational themes, evidently assuming that it was quite clear why people did what they did. Unlike higher-class respondents, they neither explained nor elaborated on the reasons for their behavior. Regarding generalizations about groups of persons or entire organizations, they were "relatively or even wholly inarticulate." They spoke in particularistic terms, almost never in classifications. Their notions of the organizational structure of the community were rudimentary.

The authors emphasize that for the lower-class respondent, the interview with a middle-class interviewer involves cross-class communication. He is used to talking about personal experiences only to listeners who share a great deal of experience and symbolism with him and with whom he can safely assume that words and gestures are assigned similar meanings. But in the interview, these assumptions break down.

They raise the question of whether the lower-class person actually perceives in abstract and classificatory terms but is unable to mobilize the verbal skills to convey his perceptions across class lines. Tentatively they conclude "that speech does in some sense reflect thought," and that the multiple perspectives and generalizing skills common to the middle-class are likely to be absent.[2] (Schatzman and Strauss, 1955; also revised in Adams and Preiss, 1960).

Bernstein carries the analysis of lower-class language usage further (Bernstein,[*] 1964, reprinted in Riessman, Cohen and Pearl, 1964). He distinguishes between the elaborated code of the middle and upper classes and the restricted code of much of the lower working class. The restricted code assumes shared interests and identifications and a cultural identity held and accepted by members of the group. The child who learns the restricted code perceives language not as a medium for communicating the experience of separateness and difference, not as a means "for a voyage from one self to another," but as a relatively impersonal signaling of the concrete here and now. The intent of others is taken for granted. There is little need to elaborate on the unique experience of the individual. The code strengthens solidarity with the group by restricting signaling of personal differences, abstract relationships, or feelings and motivations.

To the extent that lower-class speech corresponds to this formulation, the implications for the interview are important. Respondents will demonstrate not only simplified speech structure and a narrow range of vocabulary, but difficulty in separating individual experiences out of the common cultural frame. Generalized and abstract questions will elicit little meaningful response. Attempts to collect information on intent, purpose, and values— unless questions are very carefully constructed—will founder on issues of meaning. For the future of social research, it will be important to discover to what extent, and with what groups, such a restricted lower-class speech code obtains.

The observation that lower-class respondents are not sensitive to the reactions of the listener—which Komarovsky (1964), too, illustrates— is particularly striking. This runs counter to much previous commentary (e.g., Pomeroy, 1963). If poor respondents lack the psychic mobility for putting themselves in another's place, if they assume congruent perceptions of identifications, interests, and motives, then does it lead to the expectation that they will be relatively immune to biasing effects of the interviewer? What seems likely is that they are clearly aware of social norms in broad terms, but in personal interaction, they may be susceptible only to the grossest cues from another individual. The possibilities that this holds true, even in activities more laden with social sanctions than living through a tornado, seem worth exploring.

Other social groups besides the poor have their own special vocabularies and patterns of speech. Researchers who have studied homosexuals, prisoners, narcotics addicts, and business executives have written about the special problems of communication. From their experiences, several principles can be derived. Obviously the first is to know enough about perceptions, understandings, and vocabularies to frame relevant and appropriately worded questions. The second is to avoid limiting the response choices unless you are sure that you share common vocabularies and understandings with the respondent.

There has been debate in the literature about using the local idiom in the interview. Alksne (1960), who studied narcotics addicts, found that using the addicts' argot help to increase their cooperation. Similarly, Ward and Kassebaum (1965), who studied a women's prison, found that use of the prison lexicon simplified the interview by relieving the respondent of the onus of translating prison terms into respectable language. In a study of business executives, Dexter (1956) found that it was important to use terms compatible with the respondent's ideological position. He was talking about international trade policy and found that questions expressed in the liberal vocabulary evoked resistance and hostility from his respondents. Kinsey, Pomeroy, and Martin (1948) insist on the necessity of idiomatic speech in interviews on sex behavior.

On the other side of the argument, Pomeroy (1963), while agreeing with the value of mastering the respondent's argot, cautions that improper use of the vernacular does more damage than not using it at all. William Whyte in *Street Corner Society* (1955) mentioned that his informants objected to his adopting their speech. They felt that street language was inappropriate for his role. Maccoby and Maccoby (1954) believe that changing the wording of questions to fit different respondents ruins the context and comparability of responses and endangers the validity of the study.

It seems clear that questions stated simply and in terms that have both familiarity and personal relevance to the respondent will receive more meaningful answers. In evaluation research, it becomes a challenge to the researcher to frame his questions appropriately without sacrificing the conceptual richness of his study.

Question Form. Two of the perennial issues in developing interview schedules are when to use open as against closed (fixed-alternative) questions, and whether and when to use indirect rather than direct questions.

Closed questions are easy to answer. The choices are given and the respondent picks the one that fits his views. Such questions are likely to evoke little resistance from even the poorly motivated respondent. Marquis, Marshall, and Oskamp (n.d.) found that the most structured questions received the most complete responses while less structured questions got less complete answers. For many classificatory and informational purposes, closed questions provide sufficient information.

But closed questions make a number of assumptions, chief among them that the options provided for response are relevant and exhaustive and fit the respondent's frame of reference. When these conditions do not obtain, then the respondent is being prodded into giving an invalid answer. Of course this effect may depend on the subject of the interview. The Marquis et al. study found that, on items with low salience, structured questioning resulted in complete but less accurate responses; but on high salience items, structured questioning had no effect on accuracy.

Researchers often prefer using some open-ended questions, particularly when they are unsure of what the perspectives of respondents are likely to be or when they are not confident that they know the full range of potential answers. Open questions hedge against misconstruing respondents' replies, and allow new information into the study. Too many open narrative answers—which have to be deciphered, read, and coded before they can be punched on to cards—are probably inefficient. Reports of one experiment show, too, that open-ended questions do not necessarily produce deeper or more valid data (Dohrenwend, 1965). Another researcher (Collins, 1970) suggests that interviewer recording of open-ended responses frequently leads to systematic bias.

It is in the early exploratory phases of research that open questions are most useful for learning the lay of the land. As the researcher's knowledge grows, he can set fixed answers for more and more of his questions. There will probably always be a few open questions (if only to give the talkative a chance to sound off), but the well-informed closed question can effectively capture even subtle and complex points.

An interesting technique, the random probe, has been suggested (Schuman, 1966) as a way of assessing whether closed answers are valid. Each interviewer is required to carry out follow-up probes with each respondent on a set of items randomly selected from the interview schedule. The probe follows immediately after the respondent has selected one of the given responses. The interviewer asks him to "explain a little" of what he had in mind when he chose his answer. Answers to the probe indicate how well the meaning and intent of the respondent correspond with those of the listed responses. Belson (1967) has used very similar methods to gauge respondents' understandings and misunderstandings of question wording.

Another issue in questionnaire construction is the use of direct and indirect questions. Direct questions are clear-cut, straightforward, and involve few risks of inference between question and answer. But there are times when indirection is touted. Such circumstances include: asking about socially undesirable topics, where the respondent would be loath to talk about his own experiences or behavior; asking about material that may be repressed by emotional barriers; asking about

stimuli that are complex and perhaps differentially perceived by researcher and respondent (Cannell and Kahn, 1968).

Three main indirect approaches can be used. The first is the anonymous third person, for example, "Would another trainee have problems in understanding the lectures?" Respondents often express more anxieties in terms of somebody else than they do for themselves. The inference that is made is that they are really expressing their own concerns.

A second approach is using questions that contain latent as well as manifest content. This includes many of the attitude scales in social research. The respondent answers in terms of the obvious content of the items, whereas the interpretation is based on assumptions and hypotheses of which he is unaware.

A third approach uses stimuli of ambiguous meaning. Projective tests (e.g., TAT) fall in this category. The meaning is inferred by the researcher.

Indirect measures carry clear perils of invalidity, that is, that they do not in fact measure the factor they purport to measure. There is little empirical evidence to support their assumptions. Whether other considerations outweigh this rather crucial shortcoming is a decision every researcher must make for himself. In evaluation research, when the credibility of findings is an important element in determining whether anybody takes them seriously and uses them as a basis for program decisions, extra caution may be in order.

The Use of Tape Recorders in the Interview. In some studies tape recorders have been used to record respondents' answers. Advocates of the procedure cite a host of advantages, including: (1) freeing the interviewer to concentrate on the interview conversation, (2) improving the fullness and quality of response recording, (3) avoiding interviewers' selectivity in picking and choosing what they will record (and misrecord!), (4) checking up on interviewers' interpretation of correct interviewing procedures. Other people worry that the introduction of mechanical recording increases nonresponse and inaccuracy; the respondent becomes a self-conscious actor tailoring his story for the benefit of the machine and the listening presences behind it.

A number of studies have investigated the effects of tape recording. They agree that there is little evidence that the use of recorders increases resistance to the interview, decreases or destroys rapport, or alters respondents' answers (Bucher, Fritz, and Quarantelli, 1956; Maccoby and Maccoby, 1954). Belson (1967) found that the use of tape recorders during survey interviews slightly increased the accuracy of response. Confirming evidence of respondents' acceptance of tape recorders comes from clinical and counseling situations (Kogan, 1950; Redlich, Dollard, and Newman, 1950).

Tape recorders are apt to be particularly useful when long, complex, open-ended interviewing goes on. Thus they are suited to exploratory interviews when the researcher is seeking depth and richness of information in order to develop insights and hypotheses; pretest interviewing, when the focus is on systematic analysis of the proposed instrument; intensive unstructured or nondirective interviewing, where the recorder allows the interviewer to devote full attention to the details and nuances of response (Bucher, Fritz, and Quarantelli, 1956).

The main drawback is the cost. While the machines are not very costly, there are large expenses in transcribing the tapes. Another consideration is time. Transcription of tapes can be a lengthy process. Also, coding from verbatim transcripts takes appreciably longer than more routine coding work.

There are also occasional problems with mechanical breakdowns. When the machine fails, and the interviewer—unaware of the problem—neglects to take notes, the whole interview is generally lost. Errors in transcription not infrequently bedevil the enterprise, sometimes making gibberish out of whole sections of the tape.

Tape recording then appears a happy resource in selected circumstances. It is useful particularly when the researcher wants to capture rich and complex information. There are other special cases when it is a handy adjunct, for example, when the performance of interviewers is itself the object of study, or when the style of response (word usage, pauses, sentence length, etc.) is being investigated, or when the particular interviewing staff has trouble recording answers. Because of its cost, it is not likely to be efficient for relatively routine survey interviews.

Paying the Respondent. In the past few years, since studies of the poor have increased in number, the suggestion has increasingly been advanced that respondents should be paid. Sometimes the advocate of payment cites the need to enlist people's support in order to increase the response rate. Sometimes he talks in terms of fairness: people (particularly poor people) deserve payment for their time and effort. Payment to respondents is not uncommon, although it remains controversial.

Sometimes paying respondents is seen as a way of increasing the accuracy of their answers. There are researchers who believe that payment puts the relationship between respondent and interviewer on a clear-cut commercial basis. This is a better basis, easier to define and better understood, than the ambiguous one of social science investigator. Therefore, by clearing away the confusion, payment might well lead to better response (Dotson, 1954). Payment, it is said, also shows that the interviewer sets a high value on the information asked for. Thus, it encourages the respondent to take the inquiry more seriously (Lansing, Ginsburg, and Braaten, 1961: 120).

Other researchers dislike the idea of payment. First of all, it increases study costs. If it becomes sufficiently widespread, respondents may come to insist on getting paid before they open the door—or their mouths. There are doubts, too, about the effects on validity. If a person is being paid, he may feel constrained to give value in the form of obligingly invalid data.

Little evidence exists on the effects of payment. In a study of consumer finances, a group of people known to have savings accounts were selected, and half the group were offered ten dollars to participate in interviews; half were not paid. The hypothesis was that those who were paid would be more willing to be interviewed and would give more complete and accurate information. Results denied the hypothesis. The response rate was actually lower among the paid group, and there was no appreciable reduction in response error (Lansing, Ginsburg, and Braaten, 1961: 187).

SELECTION AND TRAINING OF INTERVIEWERS

Of all the means to ensure the high quality of interview data, probably the most important—and most accessible to the researcher's control—is the selection and training of interviewers. A good interviewer is a necessary (if not sufficient) condition for the collection of complete and accurate information.

In the choice of interviewers, the evaluator faces a number of questions:

Should program staff be enlisted to conduct interviews?

Should men or women conduct interviews?

Should interviewers be matched to respondents by sex or race?

Is it wise to hire local people, indigenous to the program population, to do the interviewing?

What kind of training should be offered?

How closely supervised should the interviewing be?

Let us look at a number of these issues.

Program Staff or Research Staff as Interviewers

In an evaluation study the suggestion is often advanced that members of the program staff should conduct interviews. Sometimes the reason is that expenses can be minimized if program people interview in their spare time. Occasionally the power hierarchy in the agency suggests that research should not build up new functions and new staff. Whatever the practical considerations, the use of program staff for interviewing has effects on the completeness and objectivity of the data.

All other things being equal, program staff tend not to want to fill out researcher's interview forms. Their role is service, and almost by definition the role demands inhospitability to time-consuming data collection activities. There are also cases where they believe that their traditional methods of record-keeping satisfy operating needs, whereas artificially structured and coded research data do not (e.g., La Sorte, 1968). When assigned to interview members of control groups, program interviewers are apt to find the task an even more blatant waste of their time. They are being completely distracted from the service to clients that is their specialty.

Despite their reluctance, program operators have been assigned to interviewing in numbers of evaluation studies. When they are, they often find it hard to keep their two roles separate. If as interviewer they locate need or ignorance, as program operator they want to correct it. The conflicts and tensions that beset program staff engaged in research interviewing have been described (e.g., Fellin, 1963; Mudd and Froscher, 1950). They become anxious about making (research) demands on troubled people when they were trained to provide help. Their role becomes ambiguous, not only to the client but to themselves, and there are occasions when they are under great strain to coopt the research to meet program aims.

It is sometimes considered advantageous to use program staff as interviewers because they have special talents in establishing rapport with the disadvantaged (e.g., Radin and Glasser, 1965; Smith, 1959, Geismar and La Sorte, 1963; DeSainz, 1962). While this may be true in service settings, the research interview sets

different and restrictive conditions. Research questions may be intrusive on privacy and deal with uncomfortable matters. The questions usually must be asked in specified sequence with specified wording. The latitude for the program operator's sensitivity to operate is small; his professional skills are undercut by the rigidity of the research interview framework. Program people find that one of the most uncongenial aspects of research interviewing is the need for strict adherence to research procedures that jeopardize their rapport with clients. Instead of having the program side contribute good relations to the research, the research interview imperils the program operators' rapport with clients, a matter of considerable value and pride to the practitioner.

In the normal course of events, program staff tend to become less conscientious and exacting about interview procedures over time, even when indoctrination sessions continue to stress the purposes and contributions of evaluation. Nor is this progressive relaxation necessarily an indictment of program staff, who have their own values and goals. La Sorte (1968: 224) reports an instance where researchers could well have modified the requirements to make the "caseworkers' dual role more palatable," but they were "unable and unwilling to depart from standardized textbook research procedures . . . [B]oth the action staff and the research staff had opposed vested interests with trained incapacities which blocked all attempts at convergence of interests and techniques." He points out that when action and research co-exist, it is usually action staff who are asked to make all the concessions and research staff who reap all the profit through publication, recognition, and career advancement.

That there are incompatibilities between the program orientation and the evaluation orientation is indisputable. If much of the evidence is drawn from social work contexts, social workers are not unique. Similar differences in perspective have been noted, if more impressionistically, for other professionals. The operative factor appears to be that of role: there is an inevitable difference between the aloof objective evaluator and the engaged provider of services. To ask program personnel to depart from their personalistic (and often clinical) orientation to assume the role of neutral research interviewer can work to the detriment of both service and research. The possibility of distortion, conscious or unconscious, by committed practitioners is only one of the perils.

Nevertheless there remain occasions when there is nobody around but program people and no money to hire interviewers. In such a situation, the evaluator either uses program interviewers or gets no data. The best advice in this spot appears to be: (1) Analyze data requirements very carefully and strip them to essentials. (2) Then put a great deal of effort into persuading and training program staff to collect the few key items. (3) Keep a careful watch over the completeness and accuracy of the data turned in. (4) Proselytize unremittingly, and be willing to take on some of the drudgery of data collection on request. It is often opined, although evidence is lacking, that demonstrating the worth of the data for practical program purposes will increase program staff's cooperation. It should be true. Then part of the proselytizing activity will involve demonstrating to program staff how the evaluation data will help to improve the program.

Since reliance on program operators as interviewers is fraught with difficulties, the better course is probably the employment of interviewers responsible directly to the evaluator. Such a course improves the chances that the canons of research are adhered to. However, evaluators themselves are not always insulated from emotional involvement with the success of strategies of intervention in a particular program. Their interviewers may "catch" their preconceptions (cf. Rosenthal, 1966). One of the reasons candid researchers cite for their unduly rigid adherence to textbook methodologies is the fear of becoming coopted by the program and almost unwittingly bending the data.

Moreover, interviewers are working on program staff's turf and interviewing program staff's "cases." The frictions that are internal in the case of the interviewer-program operator may be externalized and turned into frictions between program staff and interviewers (cf. Rodman and Kolodny, 1965). Rules of the road have to be worked out with minimal interference with program activities. However painful it is for evaluators to forego the midyear interviews, the 40 questions that deal with nonprogram variables and tertiary effects, and the other intrusions into program service time, there is solace in remembering that evaluators, like most researchers, collect more information than they ever analyze.

In most cases, program has priority, in the sense that the program can go on without evaluation,[3] whereas the evaluation cannot survive the disintegration of the program. This does not imply, of course, that evaluators should compromise away the validity of their data. There are conditions necessary for valid interviewing that are nonnegotiable. Nevertheless, a sense of humility and respect for the work of others, and a reasonable accommodation in time and place, can often win the requisite support for the interviewing staff.

What is the effect on the *respondent* of using program staff or using research staff as interviewers? In an evaluation study of treatment for alcoholics, Smith (1959) reports that social workers possessed a number of skills that equipped them for successful interviewing. Their resources included knowledge of mental illness, understanding of interpersonal interaction and psychodynamic concepts, ability to accept negative attitudes from respondents, understanding of the ethics of confidentiality. In a study of multiproblem families, Geismar and La Sorte (1963) report that the caseworker interviewers were "ready to give helpful advice when requested" and thus were able to maximize rapport with respondents. Another helpful feature is that the biasing effects of interviewer's race can be eradicated when the interviewer has a second relationship with the respondent, such as psychiatrist-patient, or social worker-client (Womack and Wagner, 1967; Bryant et al., 1966). This may occur because the two parties to the interview are more concerned with the second relationship than with the interview. Thus, racial differences become less salient. But this situation is obviously a mixed blessing to the researcher. Negative consequences of using program staff are cited by La Sorte (1968) who reports caseworkers resisted following the researchers' interviewing procedures and therefore produced erroneous and inadequate data. It would seem that program staff can gain respondents' collaboration, but perhaps at the expense of the validity of the data.

As far as the respondent's perception is concerned, there is very little evidence of the effect of the affiliation of different interviewers. It seems possible that a program participant will be more willing to cooperate with a program staff person. He may have a sense of gratitude and obligation. Particularly once he leaves the program, recognition of the program operator may lure him back for the interview. On the other hand, in cases where the participant's program experience has been frustrating or unpleasant, the program staffer will not be welcome as an interviewer. In such a case, however, it is uncertain that even "neutral" interviewers will stand a better chance of securing the interview.

We can only speculate that the use of program staff as interviewers may maximize respondents' bent to be accommodatingly inaccurate. It is a pervasive enough suspicion to warrant hiring nonprogram people—wherever circumstances allow—to do the evaluation interviewing.

The Good Interviewer

Who make the best interviewers, men or women, young people or older people, those with more or less education? Studies have been conducted for 40 years to identify the "good interviewer."

On occasion, researchers have reported statistically significant relationships between interviewers' effectiveness and their age, sex, education, husband's occupation, income, amount of free time, previous interviewing experience, and other assorted characteristics. Unfortunately both for neatness and for the researcher seeking guidance, few studies agree. Thus, for example, Hanson and Marks (1958) found that among Census interviewers, age was related to interview quality: younger interviewers tended to omit a greater number of Census entries than older interviewers. Sudman (1967), in a study of 400 NORC female interviewers, discovered no relationship between age and quality of interviewing. Similarly no consistent pattern between the sex of interviewers and their performance has emerged (Colombotos, 1969).

Many researchers, believing that interviewers' attitudes may be more influential than their demographic characteristics, have studied the effects of attitudes and opinions. Again, results have been contradictory. For example, NORC found that enthusiasm for interviewing was associated with poorer performance (Sudman, 1967). The Berkeley Survey Research Center found enthusiasm associated with better performance (Nicholls, 1965).

One of the problems in identifying "the good interviewer" has clearly been the lack of agreement on what constitutes good interviewing, that is, the criterion for quality. Some of the criteria that have been used to judge good interviewing are: the rate of *contact* with prospective respondents, the *interview completion* rate, the rate of *question completion,* and the frequency of *clerical error* (inconsistancies, inadequate or ambiguous entries, etc.) Rarely has there been a measure of response validity, for example, a check of the answers obtained against independent accurate information.

In the few studies that have included validity measures, there has been almost no correlation between accuracy of response and other measures of interviewer com-

petence (Nicholls, 1965; Hauck and Steinkamp, 1964). In fact, there is little association among any of the criterion measures. As Nicholls (1965: 7) concludes about accuracy, completion, and clerical error, " . . . these three principal dimensions of interviewer performance appear to be virtually orthogonal." In these circumstances, it is not surprising that identification of "the good interviewer" has proved elusive.

Is there any conclusion to be drawn from studies of interviewer characteristics and attitudes? Probably the most important are:

(1) Interviewers can bias survey data. The experience of Rice (1929) and his prohibitionist and socialist interviewers was mentioned earlier.

(2) Good training can curb the more rampant effect of interviewers' opinions. Interviewers' expectations of what a respondent will say, which Hyman found an even greater source of bias than his/her own opinions (Hyman et al., 1954), can also be muted through careful training. Very few recent studies even investigate the impact of interviewer opinions. One of the few that did (Cannell, Fowler, and Marquis, 1968) found little relationship between interviewers' attitudes and expectations and the answers they obtained; they explicitly credit interviewer training with holding personal bias at bay.

(3) The process of bias is subtle and pervasive. Even with good training, possibilities remain for the intrusion of interviewers' attitudes on the data. Cahalan et al. (1947) found that the format of the question made a difference; interviewers who qualified their own answers were more likely to detect similarly qualified answers from respondents. Shapiro and Eberhart (1947) found that an interviewer's opinions affected his acceptance of partial answers and his decision of whether to probe for a fuller reply. The extensive work of Rosenthal and his colleagues in the allied field of "experimenter effect" cautions against ignoring the effects of the interviewer. Their fascinating series of studies demonstrate that experimenters in laboratory experiments introduce noticeable biases. In one study, a group of student experimenters was told that the rats that they were running through mazes had been bred to be fast learners. Another group of students was told that their rats (although actually indistinguishable) were dull learners. The experimenters with "fast rats" got fast results; the "dull rats" had slow results. In some way the students had communicated their expectations to the laboratory animals. In another study, laboratory assistants were randomly assigned to experimenters who had definite expectations of experimental outcomes. The assistants were not told the expectancies, but they came to have the same hypothesis as their own experimenters and get similar results (Rosenthal, 1963). In a widely publicized study Rosenthal demonstrated in an elementary school that teachers' expectations of pupils' achievement can affect children's achievement scores (Rosenthal and Jacobson, 1968).

In sum, studies on interviewers have demonstrated the likelihood of biasing effects but they have not yielded consistent data on the relationship between interviewer characteristics or opinions and the quality of response data. They provide at best equivocal guidance to the selection of interviewers, whether the researcher is concerned with clerical accuracy, completion rate, or validity of response.

But if interviewer characteristics turned out to be an unrewarding subject of study, there was another possible focus of attention: the match between the interviewer and the respondent. The interviewer , after all, is only one party in a two-party set. Considerable attention therefore has been given to the effects on response of similarities and differences between interviewer and respondent.

Match between Interviewer and Respondent. A frequent assumption is that there should be close correspondence between interviewer and respondent, particularly in class, race, sex, and age. Let us take a brief look at the evidence.

In one of the rare studies on matching by social class alone, Katz (1942) compared responses of low-income Pittsburgh residents to blue-collar and white-collar interviewers. They gave more liberal (i.e., pro-labor) responses on labor issues, government ownership, and voting behavior when the interviewer was blue-collar than when he was white-collar. The assumption is that these answers were more valid. Likewise in Cosper's (n.d.) study of drinking habits, similarity in class and education between interviewers and respondents led to more frequent reports of heavy drinking—again, presumably more accurate data.

As for matching by race, Cantril (1944) and Stouffer (1950) demonstrated that in the 1940s Negroes gave different responses to Negro and white interviewers. Hyman showed that in the same period Southern Negroes gave a significantly higher proportion of acceptable answers on questions pertaining to the war effort to white interviewers than to black interviewers (Hyman et al., 1954). Pettigrew (1964) found that Negroes in Boston more often told black interviewers than whites that they agreed with items measuring militancy and racial victimization. Similarly, Price and Searles (1961) and Williams (1963), reporting on the same study in North Carolina, found that blacks gave more conservative answers to whites on such questions as educational aspirations for their children and feelings about lunch counter sit-ins. The "threat potential" of the questions was an important factor. It was on high-threat items that lower-class respondents gave more acceptable answers to whites; replies to low-threat items did not manifest similar differences. After reviewing some of the literature on racial matching, Sattler (1970) suggests that respondents give replies that conform to racial stereotypes to different-race interviewers to avoid generating threat or hostility.

Further support for the premise that race-matching reduces bias comes from studies with white respondents. Whites gave significantly more prejudiced answers to whites than to Negro interviewers on questions about race relations (Summers and Hammonds, 1966), the effects on property values of Negroes moving into a neighborhood (Athey et al., 1960), and social relationships among high school students of different races (Bryant, Gardner, and Goldman, 1966). In fact, some studies suggest that race matching is more important to white respondents than to blacks. Whites apparently do not work as hard at supplying information when interviewed by blacks. In a health study both whites and Negroes reported higher utilization of health facilities to white interviewers than to black interviewers, but the lowest rate of use was reported by whites to black interviewers (Loewenstein and Varma, 1970). Coble (1971) found that whites had lower response rates and higher refusal rates when approached by black interviewers, while blacks showed no such differences. Furthermore, whites expressed greater personal and political

efficacy when interviewed by whites than by blacks, whereas blacks interviewed by blacks showed relatively small increase on the same efficacy items.

But while some studies of cross-race interviewing show that responses are often distorted, other studies yield different conclusions. In a study of adults in New York City, no differences were obtained in the number of psychiatric symptoms reported by black respondents to black and to white interviewers (Dohrenwend, 1966). In New Haven, a study of family functioning discovered that black respondents gave fuller information to white than to black interviewers (Weller and Luchterhand, 1968). The authors interpret the result as a strain toward privacy. There was a high probability in a city with a small black section that the black interviewer would know people who knew the respondent. Whites were remote and thus safer to talk to.

Supporting observations have been made by David (1962) and Gordon (1965), who found that white interviewers received full and frank information from black respondents on nonracial subjects. It appears likely that the subject of the interview has an important influence on bias. Where race relations is the topic of inquiry, or matters sensitive to racial norms, then bias is clearly likely. On other subjects, particularly in recent years and outside the South, the race of the interviewer apparently makes little difference to the respondent. One year after massive racial violence, a sample of the black population of Detroit gave almost identical responses to white and black interviewers on a wide range of questions, including such sensitive questions as experience of racial discrimination (Schuman and Converse, 1971). Only on a narrow band of items regarding militancy and hostility to whites did black and white interviewers obtain different responses. Black interviewers got more militant answers than white interviewers particularly from black respondents of low socioeconomic status (SES). Higher SES blacks gave much the same responses to questions of militancy to white and black interviewers (perhaps because they perceived the white interviewers as less of a threat). Thus white interviewers received data which suggested that high SES blacks were more militant and hostile than low SES blacks, while black interviewers found the two groups much the same. Other data from the same study suggest that this difference is due to underreporting militancy to the white interviewers rather than to overreporting to blacks.

A few investigators have looked at "race" matching for other ethnic groups. Several studies have used white interviewers with Mexican-American or Puerto Rican populations (e.g., Freeman, 1969) but present no data on variation due to ethnicity of interviewer. Welch, Comer, and Steinman (1973) attempted to look at this question. They found few differences in the responses of Mexican-Americans in two Nebraska communities to Anglo or Mexican-American interviewers, or to a combined Anglo-Chicano team of interviewers. These few differences disappeared when education and age were controlled. In this case respondents were given their choice of Anglo or Chicano interviewers beforehand so that these results may not generalize to a no-choice situation. But Welch and her colleagues do offer some encouragement to the white researcher hesitant to enter Spanish-speaking com-

munities. Data on the reponses of other racial and ethnic groups to different interviewers would obviously be helpful to investigators who work with polyglot urban populations. Current evidence suggests that, on a limited range of race-related questions, matching interviewers to respondents is advisable in the cause of accuracy. But for most questions in most places at most times, a good interviewer is a good interviewer.

Matching on Sex and Age. What about matching interviewers to respondents by sex? Again results are inconsistent. In a study in Baltimore in 1947, responses to two items on sexual attitudes were analyzed by sex of interviewer and respondent. It was not the "matched" set that reported more candid answers, but the respondents of male interviewers; women interviewers tended to receive more puritanical answers from both men and women (Hyman et al., 1954: 156). Women interviewers have been less successful on other studies as well. A community health survey in New York found that male interviewers generally received higher reports of psychiatric symptoms from both men and women (Colombotos, Elinson, and Loewenstein, 1968). Women interviewers received more socially desirable responses (i.e., less drinking) from men on Cosper's study of drinking practices and from problem drinkers on the Cisin et al. (1965) study of drinking habits. Women also received "desirable" responses from both men and women on Loewenstein and Varma's (1970) study of use of health facilities (i.e., higher utilization).

On the other hand, Benney, Riesman, and Star (1956) investigated the combined effects of sex and age on responses to a mental health survey. They concluded that the least inhibited communication on sexual topics takes place between young people of the same sex, that is, young men talking to young male interviewers and young women talking to young women interviewers. The most inhibited communication was between persons of the same age but different sex. Discussing the work of the Institute for Sex Research, Pomeroy notes that the one female interviewer on the staff has been equally as effective as the males with both men and women respondents. Proper training is the key (Pomeroy, 1963).

A study of attitudes of adolescent girls used only women interviewers, and analyzed the effects of interviewers' age. Older adolescent girls (16-18 years old) tended to give more independent, "unacceptable" responses to young interviewers than to older ones. But personality factors made a difference. Young interviewers who were formal and stiff did not receive as many "improper" responses, whereas friendly middle-aged interviewers could "get with" their respondents. Psychological characteristics of the interviewer can mediate the definition of the situation and bridge the age and authority gap (Ehrlich and Riesman, 1961).

On the basis of such studies, there is only fitful support for matching interviewers by sex and age. Matching apparently is important primarily when the particular characteristic is germane to the topic under investigation. Further, whatever the objective attributes of the parties to the interview, the interviewer may be able to alter the respondent's perception of the situation by his behavior.

Indigenous Interviewers? In recent years, particularly in evaluation and research involving antipoverty and community development programs, indigenous inter-

viewers (i.e., poor, usually black or Spanish-speaking, members of the target population) have been used as interviewers. In some circles, use of indigenous interviewers is highly recommended.

A number of advantages are hypothesized:

(1) Contact. Indigenous interviewers, it is averred, are better at making contact and getting the interview, both because they are trusted and because they can explain the purpose and importance of the interview in terms meaningful to local residents.

(2) Validity. The expectation is that poor people (and by extension any members of the "program" population) will give more valid answers to someone like themselves.

(3) Language and style. Indigenous interviewers know the feelings and the argot, and will better elicit and understand the respondent's answers.

(4) Involvement. When local people work on surveys, advocates say, they build the sense that the research belongs to the people served and to the community.

(5) Mediation. Local interviewers can serve as mediators and interpreters not only from the research staff to the people, but also from the people to the research staff.

(6) Jobs. Jobs as interviewers provide dignified work and income to local people.

Whether or not all of these propositions hold true, there are times when conditions make it advisable to engage members of the target population as interviewers. But let us cast a critical eye over the assumptions.

That there can be benefits in contact and interview completion is clear. A dramatic example was reported by Werner (1963) who, as a prisoner, received a higher rate of questionnaire return from his fellow prisoners than did the prison staff researcher. (Members of the prison staff, on the other hand, did not answer his questionnnaires at all.) Good results in cooperation and performance are reported in some large community surveys when indigenous interviewers are employed (Weinberg, 1971; Schwartz, 1970).

Improvement in validity through the use of indigenous interviewers is less obvious. Two studies indicate that close similarity in both race and class between interviewer and respondent leads to *less valid* data (Weiss, 1968; Dohrenwend, Colombotos, and Dohrenwend, 1968). The interview becomes a social exchange, where the norms of polite intercourse prevail rather than the norms of accurate reporting. Weiss reports that when similarity in class and race is accompanied by *close rapport* between interviewer and respondent, the perils to valid data are most severe. Study directors and field supervisors of studies of the poor rated the performance of interviewers matched by both race and class, race alone, and neither race nor class. Their ratings indicated that when interviewers were similar to respondents in both race and class, they were least able at obtaining valid responses (Weiss, Bauman, Rogers, 1973).

Interviewers who come from the target population may not have enough of what

Merton has called the "stranger value" that facilitates easy communication. If the respondent knows the interviewer, or knows somebody who knows him, he is likely to feel constrained in answering sensitive questions (cf. Weller and Luchterhand, 1968).

Indigenous interviewers are no doubt better tuned in to the language and response style of the respondents. Where they are dealing in a strictly structured schedule, with questions formulated in the evaluator's words, it is important that they be equally adept in the evaluator's language. They have to know both languages well if they are to fulfill the translation function.

Interviewers drawn from the target population might perhaps be able to increase the community's sense of involvement with the study and to meditate between the study and the studied. In the past, there is little evidence that either of these things has happened, beyond the very narrow circle of the interviewer's friends. It takes more than the interviewer's good will and helpfulness to interpret the purpose, usefulness, and meaning of an evaluation study to the "community" (whatever group this may be in a particular case), and to involve them and make them care about its results and implications for further programing. This is a tall order, and cannot be left to the off-hours of interviewers. Matching by race and class does not qualify interviewers "to do the job of an anthropologist" (U.S. Department of Labor, 1969). Involvement of a community with a study requires forethought, planning, and careful structuring; it takes professional time, adequate rewards, constant communication with a variety of leaders and groups, and *authentic* and continuous attention to the needs and wishes of the local population. Local interviewers can help, if and when such responsibilities are clearly spelled out and scheduled as part of their jobs. But "community involvement" by no means is an automatic benefit of hiring indigenous interviewers.

The attraction of jobs as interviewers to a "program population" varies. Some people see the work as short-term, part-time, and not well-paid. Interviewing is not a well-recognized occupational category with its own career line and future. Some people find the time schedule, the tasks, and the meticulous following of trivial-seeming directions uncongenial; they become discouraged when respondents are repeatedly not at home, refuse to answer, or react negatively to the interviewer and his role. Some studies that have employed indigenous interviewers report extremely high turnover. On the other hand, there are people who enjoy the work, like the flexibility of the timing, and need the money. But as a contribution to economic well-being, interviewing jobs can be oversold.

Weiss, Bauman, and Rogers (1973) surveyed directors of 194 studies of the poor concerning interviewer performance. Some used indigenous interviewers while others did not. Comparing indigenous interviewers with interviewers matched by race alone or not matched, study directors rated indigenous interviewers lowest on ten out of twelve measures of performance. The exceptions were establishing rapport with respondents and locating hard-to-reach respondents. Nonmatched interviewers (generally white and middle class) were rated highest on ten of the twelve items, with race-matched interviewers usually falling in the middle. The worst problems reported with indigenous interviewers were on the technical side of the job: doing

interviews and submitting forms promptly, recording answers, probing, following interview specifications, and asking the questions as written. However, experience has a powerful mediating effect. Indigenous interviewers with previous interviewing experience were rated much closer to the race-matched and nonmatched staffs on performance scores, without sacrificing their talent for establishing rapport.

If our support for the use of indigenous interviewers has been temperate, it is well to recognize that some circumstances may make the procedure essential. When respondents are foreign-speaking, it is obviously essential to have interviewers with idiomatic command of the language. (This, however, does not necessarily mean that interviewers be of the same class and geographical neighborhood as the respondents.) Further, in some communities militancy has closed down access to researchers. Some black people are tired of being studied "like guinea pigs," while nothing is really done to improve their lot and the money goes into the pockets of the researchers. In these cases, white interviewers will certainly not be welcome, and it may be good policy to hire local black people, not only as interviewers but as members of the research staff (at as high a level as they are qualified or can be trained for). Naturally, such a course will, in the end, be useful only if the purpose and use of the evaluation study are (1) compatible with the interests of the community and (2) so perceived by them. Phoniness and co-optation will not suffice. More is needed than token ethnic representation on the staff. If evaluators wish to do a study that is consonant with the goals and values of the target population, they must engage in sustained dialogue and cooperative planning, not merely in using indigenous people to front for the study. Evaluations that reflect participant values as well as the values of officialdom will derive only from continued involvement and exchange with community groups (Hessler and New, 1972; Moore, 1972-1973).

Interviewer Training

Interviewer training is one of the main, if not *the* main, assurance of response quality. It is essential that interviewers understand two things perfectly: (1) the purpose of the study, the meaning of each question, and what kinds of data they are to get, and (2) their role in the interview, how they are to behave, what kinds of things they should and should not say, and the kinds of reactions they can and cannot evince.

For experienced interviewers, training may be relatively short, but even here, question-by-question review of the interview schedule cannot be scanted. For inexperienced interviewers, a week of training may not be too much. Not only should instruction be given and trainees' questions answered, but there should be ample time for practice interviews in front of the class, with commentary and advice from the group. In addition, it is often advisable for each new interviewer to go out (with a fellow novice or a supervisor) to conduct "real" interviews and bring them back for careful review. (One of the by-products of this procedure is the opportunity to screen out people who are really unsuited to the job.) Time spent in forestalling problems is more productive than trying to pick up the pieces afterward.

When members of the service population are used as interviewers, special techniques may need to be introduced. More detail may be needed in training, more learning-by-doing. Some aspects that are usually taken for granted must be carefully spelled out. Cannell and his colleagues at the Michigan Survey Research Center are working on computer-assisted instruction for interviewers that will make explicit the assumptions and understandings often glossed over.

Continuing supervision is also a must. The best results are obtained when the supervisor has an office right on the scene (or close enough to be readily available), and every day checks the scheduling, goes over completed interviews, corrects errors, provides moral support and encouragement, offers advice, goes out and helps with difficult cases.

Wilner, Walkley, Pinkerton, and Tayback (1962) report a particularly detailed supervisory plan that enabled their study to survive eleven waves of interviews of 1,000 poor Negro families for three years. First, interviewers brought schedules in within three days of completion, and the supervisor reviewed them immediately and told the interviewer about any errors. Then there were weekly staff meetings to discuss problems with interviewing and errors in recording. At least once a week, the supervisor observed an interview and recorded her version of the respondents' replies for later comparison. Routinely, interviewer variability tabulations were done to see that no interviewer was getting answers markedly and consistently out of line. Finally, supervisors conducted a systematic re-enumeration of a fourth of all interviews in each 10-week period with abbreviated forms. Of such meticulousness is quality made.

MAINTAINING CONTACT AND COOPERATION

Evaluation studies often require follow-up of participants over a period of time sufficient to gauge the perseverance of program effects. Since Americans move about a great deal, it takes planning and skill to locate them for second- and third-wave interviews. Ways have to be found, too, to engage their interest in the evaluation enterprise and ensure their participation.

Where the kinds of follow-up data needed as indicators of program success are available in records (e.g., school grades, hospital discharges, parole revocations, jobs held), it is worth a lot of trouble to retrieve them therefrom. Validity is apt to go up as costs go down (see: Alternatives to Interviewing). But often the only way to get follow-up data is by interview, and when this is so, plans should be made even before the first interview is held to facilitate later follow-up.

How serious is case loss? Olendzki (1965) reports that 37% of the New York City welfare recipients in her study moved during the year between the first and second interviews. Another study, evaluating the effects of public housing on Negro families in Baltimore, found that 74% of the control families in the slums moved during the three-year study period—from one to seven times apiece (Wilner, Walkley, Pinkerton, Tayback, 1962). Many of the families leave no forwarding addresses.[4]

The best available study on panel mortality shows that, even within a general

sample of the urban population, losses are selective. The people who are lost on later waves of interviews are disproportionately younger, non-homeowners, with lower incomes (Sobol, 1959). If only the stable families are reinterviewed, the effects of the program cannot be accurately assessed. The panel is no longer representative of the original population.

A number of remedies have been used to overcome the loss of respondents over time. Eckland (1968) reports that, with appropriate techniques, panels have survived almost intact for over ten years, although some of the groups he cites were special and highly motivated, such as high school graduating classes, and few were poor or troubled.

First, all possible "anchoring" data should be collected in the first interview. This would include names of friends or relatives who will know the respondent's whereabouts, identifying information such as date of birth, social security number, driver's license number, and other registration numbers. Too heavy a dose of such questions is unwise. The character of the interview may change to that of interrogation, with overtones of the credit investigator or the police. But as many identifying questions should be asked as adroit schedule construction can carry.

Friends, neighbors, and relatives can be routinely canvassed. The post office provides some little-known services for locating individuals even after the mail forwarding period has expired. Eckland mentions, for example, that the post office will institute a record search at five cents per name. It is also possible to consult address directories, records of utility companies, welfare agencies, employment services, departments of motor vehicles, and certain federal agencies. Service can also be bought from credit bureaus, at fairly steep rates, to track lost cases.

One promising idea, which does not appear to have been tried in practice, is to hire a "panel maintenance" person, whose job is to keep track of respondents. He would call, send out postcards, or visit respondents at frequent intervals, find out about planned moves before they occur or very shortly afterward, and start checking while the trail is still warm. The task might be assigned to someone already on staff or to a part-time person (perhaps a member of the sample population).

There are other problems in maintaining a panel besides the respondents' moving away without leaving an address. Inevitably some of the original respondents refuse to participate in later interviews. Refusals, particularly when the subject matter of the study is either uncomfortable or boring, cannot all be converted into responses, no matter how persuasive the interviewer. There are indications that some types of people refuse to answer interviewers' questions when they find the questions offensive. The more compliant respondents are poor people, women, younger people, and residents of the Northeast and South Central regions (Hartmann, Isaacson, and Jurgell, 1968).

To maintain cooperation with the study, our suggested "panel maintainer" might listen to gripes about the interviews, report back to study staff about respondents' views and complaints, and help improve communication and overcome problems. Furthermore, the respondent group might be told that they will be asked, at the end of the data collection, to offer their advice on interpretations and

implications of the data. Argyris (1952) reports a series of meetings extending for almost a year with a group of interview respondents to develop interpretations of study data and suggest strategies for change. He found the process fruitful for interpretation, but we do not know whether it would work well as a lure for *participation* in the interviews.

Mid-study reporting of study results to participants probably *would* increase participation and involvement. But such a procedure runs a high risk of contaminating respondents' perceptions, knowledge, and opinions, making them different in important ways from non-sample members. (Or if the total participant population is studied, this would add a stimulus other than the program to which the interviewees are responding.) Therefore, it seems the better part of valor to schedule feedback and discussions of results only after all the data are in.

There is a final problem in maintaining panel participation that deserves mention in the evaluation framework. A category often turns up in research reports called "respondents unavailable." This catch-all classification includes respondents who die, become institutionalized, go into the armed forces, are too ill or deaf or disturbed or senile or drunk to be interviewed, as well as those who are chronically not at home. Rarely are the reasons distinguished in study reports. It seems not irrelevant to "program effects" to know the rates at which panel members succumb to the varied ills (or benefits) that make up unavailability. In other words, efforts should be made to ferret out and report the reasons for disappearance from the panel.

NOTES

1. One study (Weiss, 1968) suggests that respondents whom interviewers see as indifferent or hostile in the interview give no more misinformation—and probably less—than more "cooperative" respondents.

2. Riesman, who listened to the same tapes, offers a different, motivational interpretation. He says that, for many of the respondents, the problem they wanted to discuss with the interviewer was why the disaster had hit and why it killed those it did and spared others. When the interviewer refused to discuss this issue, they resignedly gave minimum information and made no attempt to put themselves in the listener's place (Riesman, 1964, quoted in Richardson, Dohrenwend and Klein, 1965).

3. Except for "social experiments" or "pilot" programs undertaken to test the viability of new program concepts, where funds for the project are contingent upon systematic evaluation.

4. Through careful preplanning, these studies located most of the movers.

REFERENCES

Adams, R. N. and J. J. Preiss, (eds.) *Human organization research: field relations and techniques.* Homewood, Ill. Dorsey, 1960.

Alksne, Harold. Interviewing the narcotic addict. Paper presented at the meeting of the American Association for Public Opinion Research, 1960, summarized in *Public Opinion Quarterly,* 1960, 24 (3): 473-474.

Argyris, Chris. Diagnosing defenses against the outsider. *Journal of Social Issues,* 1952, 8, 24-34.

Assael, Henry and J. O. Eastlack, Jr. Better telephone surveys through centralized interviewing. *Journal of Advertising Research,*1966, 6: 2-7.

Athey, K. R., J. E. Coleman, A. P. Reitman and J. Tang. Two experiments showing the effect of the interviewer's racial background on responses to questionnaires concerning racial issues. *Journal of Applied Psychology,* 1960, 44 (4): 244-246.

Banks, Joe A. The group discussion as an interview technique. *Sociological Review,* 1957, 5: 75-84.

Becker, Howard S. Interviewing medical students. *American Journal of Sociology,* 1956, 62 (2): 199-201.

––– and Blanche Geer. Participant observation and interviewing: a comparison. *Human Organization,* 1957, 16 (3): 28-32.

Belson, William A. Tape recording: its effect on accuracy of response in survey interviews. *Journal of Marketing Research,* 1967, 4: 253-260.

Benney, Mark, David Riesman and Shirley Star. Age and sex in the interview. *American Journal of Sociology,* 1956, 62 (2): 143-152.

Bernstein, Basil. Social class, speech systems and psycho-therapy. Pp. 194-204 in Riessman, Cohen, and Pearl (eds.) *Mental health of the poor.* New York: Free Press, 1964.

Boek, Walter E. and James H. Lade. A test of the usefulness of the postcard technique in a mail questionnaire study. *Public Opinion Quarterly,* 1963, 27 (2): 303-306.

Boruch, Robert F. Relations among statistical methods for assuring confidentiality of social research data. *Social Science Research,* 1972, 1: 403-414.

Brunner, James A. and G. Allen Brunner. Are voluntarily unlisted telephone subscribers really different? *Journal of Marketing Research,* February 1971: 121-124.

Bryant, Eugene C., Isaac Gardner, Jr., and Morton Goldman. Responses on racial attitudes as affected by interviewers of different ethnic groups. *Journal of Social Psychology,* 1966, 70 (1): 95-100.

Bucher, Rue, Charles Fritz, and E. L. Quarentelli. Tape recorded interviews in social research. *American Sociological Review,* 1956, 21: 359-364. (a)

–––. Tape recorded research: some field and data processing problems. *Public Opinion Quarterly,* 1956, 20 (2): 427-439. (b)

Cahalan, Don, V. Tamulomis and H. W. Verner. Interviewer bias involved in certain types of attitude questions. *International Journal of Opinion and Attitude Research,* 1947, 1 (1): 63-77.

Cannell, Charles F. and Robert L. Kahn, Interviewing. Pp. 526-595 in Gardner Lindzey and Elliot Aronson (eds.) *The handbook of social psychology,* vol. 2. 2nd ed.; Reading, Mass.: Addison-Wesley, 1968.

Cannell, Charles F., Floyd J. Fowler, Jr., and Kent H. Marquis. The influence of interviewer and respondent psychological and behavioral variables on the reporting in household interviews. *Vital and Health Statistics,* 1968, series 2, no. 26.

Cantril, Hadley. *Gauging public opinion.* Princeton: Princeton University Press, 1944. Chapter 8.

Chandler, Margaret. An evaluation of the group interview. *Human Organization,* 1954, 13 (2): 26-29.

Cisin, Ira, Arthur Kirsch, and Carol Newcomb. An experimental study of sensitivity of survey techniques in measuring drinking practices. Social Research Project, George Washington University, 1965.

Cobb, Sidney, Stanley King and Edith Chen. Differences between respondents and non-respondents in a morbidity survey involving clinical examinations. *Journal of Chronic Diseases,* 1957, 6: 95-108.

Coble, JoAnne. Results of the pilot study racial match experiment. Pp. 179-197 in John B. Lansing et al. *Working papers on survey research in poverty areas.* University of Michigan: Institute for Social Research, 1971.

Collins, W. Andrew. Interviewers' verbal idiosyncracies as a source of bias, *Public Opinion Quarterly,* 1970, 34: 416-422.

Colombotos, John. Personal versus telephone interviews. *Public Health Reports,* 1969, 84 (9): 773-782.

———, Jack Elinson and Regina Loewenstein. Effect of interviewers' sex on interview responses. *Public Health Reports,* 1968, 83 (8): 685-690.

Coombs, Lolagene and Ronald Freedman, Use of telephone interviews in a longitudinal fertility study. *Public Opinion Quarterly,* 1964, 28: 112-117.

Cosper, Ronald. Selection bias and interviewer effect in a survey of drinking practices. Unpublished, n.d.

Couch, Arthur and Kenneth Keniston. Yeasayers and naysayers: agreeing response set as a personality variable. *Journal of Abnormal and Social Psychology,* 1960, 60: 151-174.

David, Martin. The validity of income reported by a sample of families who received welfare assistance during 1959. *Journal of the American Statistical Association,* 1962, 57 (321): 680-685.

Dean, Lois R. Interaction, reported and observed: the case of one local union. *Human Organization,* 1958, 17 (3): 36-44.

DeSainz, Doris. The public health nurse as research interviewer. *Nursing Outlook,* 1962, 10: 514-516.

Dexter, Lewis A. Role relationships and conceptions of neutrality in interviewing. *American Journal of Sociology,* 1956, 62: 153-157.

Dohrenwend, Barbara Snell. Some effects of open and closed questions on respondent answers. *Human Organization,* 1965, 24 (2): 175-184.

———, John Colombotos, and Bruce P. Dohrenwend. Social distance and interviewer effects. *Public Opinion Quarterly,* 1968, 32 (3): 410-422.

Dohrenwend, Bruce. Social status and psychological disorder: an issue of substance and an issue of method. *American Sociological Review,* 1966, 31: 14-34.

Dotson, Floyd. Intensive interviewing in community research. *Journal of Educational Sociology,* 1954, 27: 225-230.

Eckland, Bruce K. Retrieving mobile cases in longitudinal surveys. *Public Opinion Quarterly,* 1968, 32: 51-64.

Edwards, Allen L. Social desirability or acquiescence in the MMPI: a case study with the SD scale. *Journal of Abnormal and Social Psychology,* 1961, 63: 351-359.

Ehrlich, June Sachar and David Riesman. Age and authority in the interview. *Public Opinion Quarterly,* 1961, 25 (1): 39-56.

Elliott, Lois Lawrence. Effects of item construction and respondent aptitude on response acquiescence. *Educational and Psychological Measurement,* 1961, 21: 405-415.

Fellin, Phillip. The standardized interview in social work research. *Social Casework,* 1963, 44: 81-85.

Foster, R. J. Acquiescent response set as a measure of acquiescence. *Journal of Abnormal and Social Psychology,* 1961, 63: 155-160.

Freeman, Donald. A note on interviewing Mexican-Americans. *Social Science Quarterly,* 1969, 19: 909-918.

Freeman, Howard E. A note on the prediction of who votes. *Public Opinion Quarterly,* 1953, 17: 288-292.

Friedlander, Frank. Emerging blackness in a white research world. *Human Organization,* 1970, 29 (4): 239-250.

Gans, Herbert J. *The urban villagers.* New York: Free Press, 1962.

Geismar, Ludwig L. and Michael A. La Sorte. Research interviewing with low-income families. *Social Work,* 1963, 8 (2): 10-13.

Glasser, Gerald J. and Gale D. Metzger. Random-digit dialing as a method of telephone sampling. *Journal of Marketing Research,* 1972, 9: 59-64.

Goldman, Alfred E. The group depth interview. *Journal of Marketing.* 1962, 26: 61-68.

Gordon, Joan. The poor of Harlem: social functioning of the underclass. New York: Office of the Mayor, Interdepartmental Neighborhood Service Center, 1965. Offset.

Green, Lawrence W., Harold C. Gustafson and A. Iqbal Begum. Validity in family planning

surveys: disavowed knowledge and use of contraceptives in a panel study in East Pakistan. Paper presented at the Annual Meeting of the Population Association of America, 1968.

Greenberg, B. G., J. R. Abernathy and D. G. Horvitz. A new survey technique and its application in the field of public health. *Millbank Memorial Fund Quarterly*, 1970, 39-55.

Greenleigh Associates. *Diagnostic survey of tenant households in the West Side urban renewal area of New York City.* New York: Greenleigh, 1965.

Haber, Lawrence D. Evaluating response error in the reporting of the income of the aged: benefit income. *Proceedings of the Social Statistics Section,* American Statistical Association, 1966: 412-419.

Hagburg, Eugene. Validity of questionnaire data: reported and observed attendance in an adult education program. *Public Opinion Quarterly,* 1968, 32: 453-456.

Hansen, Morris H. and William N. Hurwitz. The problem of non-response in sample surveys. *Journal of the American Statistical Association,* 1946, 41: 517-529.

Hanson, Robert H. and Eli S. Marks. Influence of the interviewer on the accuracy of survey results. *Journal of the American Statistical Association,* 1958, 53 (283): 635-655.

Hare, Paul A. Interview responses: personality or conformity? *Public Opinion Quarterly,* 1960, 24: 679-685.

——— and James S. Davie. The group interview. *Sociology and Social Research,* 1954, 39: 81-87.

Hartmann, Elizabeth L., M. Lawrence Isaacson and Cynthia M. Jurgell. Public reaction to public opinion surveying. *Public Opinion Quarterly,* 1968, 32: 295-298.

Hauck, Mathew and Stanley Steinkamp, *Survey reliability and interviewer competence.* Urbana: University of Illinois Press, 1964.

Heaton, Eugene R. Increasing mail questionnaire returns with a preliminary letter. *Journal of Advertising Research,* 1965, 5: 36-39.

Hessler, Richard M. and Peter Kong-Ming New. Research as a process of exchange. *American Sociologist,* 1972, 7 (2): 13-15.

Hochstim, Joseph R. A critical comparison of three strategies of collecting data from households. *Journal of the American Statistical Association,* 1967, 62: 976-989.

Hollingshead, A. B. and F. C. Redlich. *Social class and mental illness.* New York: Wiley, 1958.

Hyman, Herbert H., William J. Cobb, Jacob J. Feldman, Clyde W. Hart and Charles H. Stember. *Interviewing in social research.* Chicago: University of Chicago Press, 1954.

Jackson, Douglas M. and Samuel Messick. Response styles in the MMPI: comparison of clinical and normal samples. *Journal of Abnormal and Social Psychology,* 1962, 65: 285-299.

Josephson, Eric. Resistance to community surveys. *Social Problems,* 1970, 18 (1): 117-129.

Judd, Robert C. Telephone usage and survey research. *Journal of Advertising Research,* 1966, 6: 38-39.

Kahn, Robert L. and Charles F. Cannell. *The dynamics of interviewing.* New York: Wiley, 1957.

Katz, Daniel. Do interviewers bias poll results? *Public Opinion Quarterly,* 1942, 6 (2): 248-268.

Kephart, William M. and Marvin Bressler. Increasing the responses to mail questionnaires: a research study. *Public Opinion Quarterly,* 1958, 22: 123-132.

Kildegaard, Ingrid C. How consumers misreport what they spent. *Journal of Advertising Research,* 1965, 5: 51-55.

Kincaid, Harry V. and Margaret Bright. Interviewing the business elite. *American Journal of Sociology,* 1957, 63: 304-311.

Kinsey, Alfred C., Wardell B. Pomeroy and Clyde E. Martin. *Sexual behavior in the human male.* Philadelphia: W. B. Saunders, 1948.

Kivlin, Joseph E. Contributions to the study of mail-back bias. *Rural Sociology,* 1965, 30: 322-326.

Kogan, Leonard. The electrical recording of social casework interviews. *Social Casework,* 1950, 31: 371-378.

Komarovsky, Mirra. *Blue collar marriage.* New York: Random House, 1964.

Lansing, John B., Gerald P. Ginsburg and Kaisa Braaten. *An investigation of response error.* Urbana: University of Illinois Press, 1961.

La Sorte, Michael A. The caseworker as research interviewer. *American Sociologist,* 1968, 3 (3): 222-225.

Lenski, Gerhard E. and John C. Leggett. Caste, class and deference in the research interview. *American Journal of Sociology,* 1960, 65 (5): 463-467.

Liebow, Elliot. *Tally's corner.* Boston: Little, Brown, 1967.

Loewenstein, Regina and Andre Varma. Effect of interaction of interviewer and respondent in health surveys. Paper given at AAPOR, May 1970.

McGee, Richard K. The relationship between response style and personality variables. *Journal of Abnormal and Social Psychology,* 1962, 64: 229-233.

Maccoby, E. E. and Nathan Maccoby. The interview: a tool of social science. Pp. 449-487 in Gardner Lindzey (ed.) *Handbook of social psychology.* Vol. 1. Cambridge: Addison-Wesley 1954.

Marquis, Kent H. An experimental study of the effects of reinforcement, question length, and reinterviews on reporting selected chronic conditions in household interviews. Survey Research Center, University of Michigan, 1969.

–––. James Marshall, and Stuart Oskamp. Accuracy and completeness of testimony as a function of kind of question, interrogation atmosphere, and item content. N.d.

Miller, Mungo. The Waukegan study of voter turnout prediction. *Public Opinion Quarterly,* 1952, 16: 381-398.

Moore, Joan W. Letter to the editor. *SSSP Newsletter,* 1972-73, 4 (2): 37-38.

Mudd, Emily Hartshorne and Hazel Bazett Froscher. Effects on casework of obtaining research material. *Social Casework,* 1950, 31: 11-17.

Myers, J. K. and B. H. Roberts. Family and class dynamics in mental illness. New York: Wiley, 1959.

Myers, Robert J. Accuracy of age reporting in the 1950 United States census. *Journal of the American Statistical Association,* 1954, 49: 826-831.

Nicholls, William L., II. Dimensions of interviewer performance in the survey. Paper presented at the 60th meeting of the American Sociological Association, 1965.

Nichols, Robert C. and Mary Alice Meyer. Timing postcard followups in mail questionnaire surveys. *Public Opinion Quarterly,* 1966, 30: 306-307.

Olendzki, Margaret C. Welfare medical care in New York City: a research study. Ph.D. dissertation. University of London, 1965.

O'Neill, Harry W. Response style influence in public opinion surveys. *Public Opinion Quarterly,* 1967, 31: 95-102.

Parry, H. J. and Helen M. Crossley. Validity of responses to survey questions. *Public Opinion Quarterly,* 1950-51, 14: 61-80.

Paul, Benjamin D. Interview techniques and field relationships. In A. L. Kroeber et al. (eds.) *Anthropology today.* Chicago: University of Chicago Press, 1953.

Perry, Stewart E. and Lyman C. Wynne. Role conflict, role definition, and social change in a clinical research organization. *Social Forces,* 1959, 38 (1): 62-65.

Pettigrew, Thomas F. *A profile of the Negro American.* Princeton: Van Nostrand, 1964.

Pomeroy, Wardell B. The reluctant respondent. *Public Opinion Quarterly,* 1963, 27, (2): 287-293.

Price, Daniel O. and Ruth Searles. Some effects of interviewer-respondent interaction on responses in a survey situation. *Proceedings of the Social Statistics Section,* American Statistical Association, 1961: 211-221.

Radin, Norma and Paul H. Glasser. The use of parental questionnaires with culturally disadvantaged families. *Journal of Marriage and the Family,* 1965, 27: 373-382.

Redlich, Fredrick, John Dollard, and Richard Newman. High fidelity recording of psychotherapeutic interviews. *American Journal of Psychiatry,* 1950, 107: 42-48.

Rice, S. A. Contagious bias in the interview. *American Journal of Sociology,* 1929, 35 (3): 420-423.

Richardson, Stephen A., Barbara Snell Dohrenwend, and David Klein. *Interviewing.* New York: Basic Books, 1965.

Riessman, Frank. *The culturally deprived child.* New York: Harper, 1962.

Robin, Stanley E. A procedure for securing returns to mail questionnaires. *Sociology and Social Research,* 1965, 50: 24-35.

Robins, Lee N. and George E. Murphy. Drug use in a normal population of young negro men. *American Journal of Public Health,* 1967, 57: 1580-1596.

Rodman, Hyman and Ralph L. Kolodny. Organizational strains in the researcher-practitioner relationship. Pp. 93-113 in Alvin Gouldner and S. M. Miller (eds.) *Applied sociology: opportunities and problems.* New York: Free Press, 1965.

Roeher, G. Allen. Effective techniques in increasing response to mailed questionnaires. *Public Opinion Quarterly,* 1963, 27: 299-302.

Rosenthal, Robert. *Experimenter effects in behavioral research.* New York: Appleton-Century-Crofts, 1966.

———. On the social psychology of the psychological experiment: the experimenter's hypothesis as unintended determinant of experimental results. *American Scientist,* 1963, 51: 268-283.

——— and Lenore Jacobson. *Pygmalion in the classroom.* New York: Holt, Rinehart and Winston, 1968.

Rowntree, Griselda and Rachel M. Pierce. Birth control in Britain, part I: attitudes and practices among persons married since World War I. *Population Studies,* 1961, 15: 3-31.

Sattler, Jerome. Racial 'experimenter effects' in experimentation, interviewing and psychotherapy. *Psychological Bulletin,* 1970, 73: 137-160.

Schatzman, Leonard and Anselm Strauss. Social class and modes of communication. *American Journal of Sociology,* 1955, 60: 329-338.

Schuman, Howard. The random probe: a technique for evaluating the validity of closed questions. *American Sociological Review,* 1966, 31: 218-222.

——— and Jean M. Converse. The effects of black and white interviewers on black responses in 1968. *Public Opinion Quarterly,* 1971, 35: 44-68.

Schwartz, David A. Coping with field problems of large surveys among the urban poor. *Public Opinion Quarterly,* 1970, 34 (2): 267-272.

Schwartz, Morris and Charlotte Green Schwartz. Problems of participant observation. *American Journal of Sociology,* 1955, 15: 343-353.

Shapiro, S. and J. C. Eberhart. Interviewer differences in an intensive interview survey. *International Journal of Opinion and Attitude Research,* 1947, 1 (2): 1-17.

Short, James F., Jr. and Fred L. Strodtbeck. *Group process and gang delinquency.* Chicago: University of Chicago Press, 1965.

Skipper, James K., Jr. and Margaret D. Ellison. Personal contact as a technique for increasing questionnaire returns from hospitalized patients after discharge. *Journal of Health and Human Behavior,* 1966, 7: 211-214.

Smith, David H. Correcting for social desirability response sets in opinion-attitude survey research. *Public Opinion Quarterly,* 1967, 31: 87-94.

Smith, Eugenia V. Field interviewing of problem drinkers. *Social Work,* 1959, 4: 80-86.

Sobol, Marion G. Panel mortality and panel bias. *Journal of the American Statistical Association,* 1959, 54: 52-68.

Stouffer, S. A. et al. *Measurement and Prediction.* Vol. 4. Princeton: Princeton University Press, 1950.

Sudman, Seymour. Quantifying interviewer quality. *Public Opinion Quarterly,* 1966-67, 30: 664-667.

———. *Reducing the cost of surveys.* Chicago: Aldine, 1967.

Summers, Gene F. and Andre D. Hammonds. Effect of racial characteristics of investigator on self-enumerated responses to a Negro prejudice scale. *Social Forces,* 1966, 44 (4): 515-518.

Survey Research. Interviewing in telephone surveys. 1973, 5 (1): 9-13.

Taietz, Philip. Conflicting group norms and the 'third' person in the interview. *American Journal of Sociology,* 1962, 68: 97-104.

U.S. Department of Health, Education, and Welfare. The influence of interviewer and respondent psychological and behavioral variables on the reporting in household interviews,

prepared by C. F. Cannell, F. J. Fowler and K. H. Marquis. *Vital and Health Statistics,* 1968, ser. 2, no. 26.

U.S. Department of Labor. *A compilation of papers on data gathering in manpower research.* Washington: Operational Research Group, Office of Manpower Research, September 1969.

Ward, David A. and Gene G. Kassebaum. *Women's prison.* Chicago: Aldine, 1965. Appendix: 228-261.

Warner, Stanley L. Randomized response: a survey technique for eliminating evasive answer bias. *Journal of the American Statistical Association,* 1965, 60: 63-69.

Webb, Eugene J., Donald T. Campbell, Richard D. Schwartz, and Lee B. Sechrest. *Unobtrusive measures: non-reactive research in the social sciences.* Chicago: Rand-McNally, 1966.

Weinberg, Eve. *Community surveys with local talent: a handbook.* Chicago: National Opinion Research Center. University of Chicago, 1971.

Weiss, Carol H. Interviewing low-income respondents. *Welfare in Review,* 1966, 4 (8): 1-9.

———, Validity of welfare mothers' interview responses. *Public Opinion Quarterly,* 1968, 32 (4): 622-633.

———, Interaction in the research interview: the effects of rapport on response. *Proceedings of the Social Statistics Section,* American Statistical Association, 1970: 17-20.

———, L. J. Bauman and T. F. Rogers. *Practices of research organizations in surveys of the poor.* Bureau of Applied Social Research, Columbia University, April 1973.

———. Respondent/interviewer interaction in the research interview: abstracts. National Technical Information Service, U.S. Department of Commerce, PB-204 597, April 1971.

Welch, Susan, John Comer, and Michael Steinman. Interviewing in a Mexican-American community. *Public Opinion Quarterly,* 1973, 37: 115-126.

Weller, Leonard and Elmer Luchterhand. Interviewer-respondent interaction in negro and white family life research. *Human Organization,* 1968, 27 (1): 50-55.

Werner, Dane. Measuring the motive. Pp. 99-104 in National Institute of Mental Health, *Experiment in culture expansion,* 1963.

Whyte, William F. *Street corner society.* Chicago: University of Chicago Press, 1955.

Williams, James Allen, Jr., *Interviewer-respondent interaction: a study of bias in the information interview.* Ph.D. dissertation. University of North Carolina at Chapel Hill, 1963.

Wilner, Daniel M., Rosabelle Price Walkley, Thomas C. Pinkerton, and Matthew Tayback. *The housing environment and family life.* Baltimore: Johns Hopkins Press, 1962.

Womack, William M. and Nathaniel Wagner. Negro interviewers and white patients. *Archives of General Psychiatry,* 1967, 16: 685-692.

ACKNOWLEDGEMENT

For their assistance in review of the literature, I wish to thank Mary Mayer and Florence Rosenstock, who worked on the original chapter for this Handbook in 1969, and Janet Weiss who worked to update it in 1972.

12

EVALUATION THROUGH MEDICAL RECORDS AND RELATED INFORMATION SYSTEMS

ABBOTT S. WEINSTEIN

New York State Department of Mental Hygiene

EVALUATION OF GENERAL HEALTH AND MENTAL HYGIENE PROGRAMS

Traditionally in medicine, individual physicians and other therapists have assessed for themselves how well individual patients responded to particular treatment procedures. In a very different way, evaluation of overall service programs have been attempted indirectly through statistical analysis of data ennumerating the various kinds of patients and their movement into and out of treatment facilities.

Evaluation of health and mental health programs has broadened in scope and scale in keeping with the broadened mission of the programs themselves. For example, it is no longer adequate for the operators of facilities for the disabled to consider only those individuals who come to them for service. In the finest traditions of the public health field, their responsibility is extended to the needs of the general population including those who are not currently being served. Thus, with a broadened notion of "accountability," there is, consequently, a broadened set of criteria for evaluation.

As a practical matter, it is fortunate that much of the information needed to evaluate the treatment of individual patients is the same information needed to treat these patients, and it is this same information that must be assembled for statistical analyses of groups of patients. Thus, with imaginative use of modern information handling resources, it is possible to have a given piece of information recorded only once and used any number of times for a variety of purposes.

[397]

PURPOSES OF AN INFORMATION SYSTEM FOR
MENTAL HYGIENE FACILITIES

In general, the purposes of an information system for facilities serving the mentally disabled can be summarized as follows:

1. To aid the clinician in serving individual patients;
2. To aid the facility director in managing the operation of the facility;
3. To aid the state or county mental health authority in developing and in monitoring overall programs in a system of service;
4. To aid researchers in the fields related to mental disability.

At each of these levels, evaluation is a basic ingredient.

KINDS OF DATA NEEDED

While data about individuals served and the services they receive are the heart of the information system, other data must also be available.

The medical record provides information about patients including their personal characteristics, their problems, the services they received, the outcome of their treatment program, legalities, and the like. The information system should also include data about (a) facility staff including their activities on behalf of the general community as well as activities with and for patients, their skills and disciplines, and personnel administrative information; (b) the facility organization; (c) the facility buildings including their nature, size, location, and condition; (d) other resources used by the facility including food, medication, clothing, and other supplies and equipment; (e) finances and costs; (f) the geographic area served including the size of the area, the number of its residents and their characteristics, the transportation network, services available and auspices, social resources and social "morbidity," identifiable "consumer groups," political organization, and so on. In addition, it is essential to obtain insight regarding the numbers and characteristics of individuals *not* served.

Clearly, much of the information needed is available only from sources outside a given treatment facility and includes not only other treatment facilities and agencies within the basic system of service (e.g., facilities primarily for the mentally disabled), but also facilities and agencies in related areas (e.g., general health, welfare, education, correction and social service).

KINDS OF DATA NEEDED TO SERVE INDIVIDUAL PATIENTS

To serve a patient and to evaluate that service, the following data are needed:

1. *Admission Information*
   Who is the patient?
   Where is he from?
   What is he like? What are his general social and economic resources?
   Who sent him?
   What prior service has he received?

What and where was the most recent service?

How long was that service?

What's "wrong" with the patient, i.e., what are his problems?

How serious are the problems?

What unit or program is he assigned to?

2. *Information During Services*

What are the plans for dealing with each of his problems?

What programs is he participating in? What programs has he participated in?

What services is he receiving? What services has he received?

What staff provided these services?

How is he doing with respect to each of his problems? Has the nature of his condition or problems changed? How?

Has the treatment plan changed? How? Why?

3. *Information at Conclusion of Service*

What was done for the patient for each of his problems?

Is further care indicated? If so, was the patient referred? Where?

Who was responsible for paying?

What was the patient's disability?

What was his condition on termination with respect to each of his problems?

4. *Information after Service*

How is the former patient doing? Is he working? How does he get along with others? How does any current symptomatology compare with that exhibited during service?

How long has it been since his service at the facility?

Is he receiving service elsewhere? How long has it been since his most recent service? What service has he received since termination? What was his condition and adjustment during the period between termination and his current service?

Answers to the questions under headings 1, 2, and 3 above should be in any basic medical record system. The reporting systems used by the New York State Department of Mental Hygiene (DMH) and the Multi-State Information System for Psychiatric Patients (MSIS) include this information. A procedure is currently developed by the DMH to follow up samples of patients who have left each facility so that the questions in 4 may be answered. These questions (4) could best be answered by communication among providers of service with a cooperative reporting system in which all facilities serving an area participate.

KINDS OF DATA NEEDED TO OPERATE AND MONITOR PROGRAMS

To operate and to monitor programs, the following data are needed:

1. *General Questions*

What is the facility doing?

What are other parts of the overall system of service doing?

How is the system working?

2. *Specific Questions*

How many patients were: Admitted to the facility? Added to each unit? Serviced by each unit? Removed from each unit? Terminated from the facility?

Where were they from? How many were from each part of the catchment area? From outside the area? How many catchment area residents were served by others? Within the area? Outside the area?

What were the clients like? How many males and females? How many children, adolescents, adults, geriatrics? How many were single, married, separated, widowed? How many lived alone? Lived with parents, children, spouse? How many had low incomes, large families, little education? How many were from groups with identifiable special needs?

Who referred them to the facility? How many came on their own? Referred by friends? From other agencies?

What prior service have they received? How many had prior inpatient service? Outpatient? Public mental hospital? Service at this facility? By private psychiatrist? Other?

What was the most recent service? How much time elapsed since the most recent prior service? How many patients sought service within one month, six months, over one year after termination from prior service? How does this compare for patients terminated from each unit? For those referred elsewhere? For those not referred?

What problems and disabilities did the patients have? How many were psychotic? How many had problems at home, with spouse or children? How many had problems on the job or in school? Had physical problems? Had antisocial behavioral problems? Abused drugs? Abused alcohol?

How serious are these problems? How long had they been apparent? How many patients could be classified as having severe problems? On admission? During service? On termination? On readmission?

What services were provided? To which groups of patients?

What staff provided these services? How many contacts of each type were there by individual staff members, disciplines, or teams? With which groups of patients? How much time was provided?

What were the dollar costs?

What changes took place in patients' condition? How many had changes in activities, problems, needs? What kinds of changes? How many had no changes?

What was the outcome of service? How many patients were terminated with no further care indicated and how many withdrew? After how many visits? How many were referred to mental hospitals, to private physicians, to others? After completion of service, upon follow-up, how many patients were working or carrying out other responsibilities? How many were getting along well with others? How many had no change in symptomatology since termination? How many showed improvement or deterioration? How many had no need for further service, for how long? How many

sought further care at this facility? At other facilities? How long after
termination? What service was provided?

What was spent in terms of staff hours by each discipline or team for each of
these groups of patients, per episode?

What were the dollar costs per patient served, per visit, and per total episode,
for patients terminated with no further care indicated? For other groups?

Where did the money come from? How much from fees, paid by whom? How
much from federal, state and local government? How much from voluntary sources?

For the services provided by other facilities to catchment area residents, what
were the total staff investments in time and total dollar costs?

What was the total volume of service and cost, for all catchment area
residents? Per total episode? Per individual served? For each priority
group?

What was the total volume of service and cost of service provided by the
facility to nonresidents of the catchment area?

What groups in the catchment area were not served or not fully served? What
priority groups were not fully served?

What would it have required to serve them, in terms of staff, satellite
locations. transportation assistance, arrangements with other facilities?
What would this cost? What nonpriority groups might have service post-
poned, provided elsewhere, or not provided? What resources would this
make available for priority groups?

How have all of these data changed since a year ago? Two years ago? By
quarter, or month? What direction are they taking? What caused the
changes? How could specific changes be brought about? By individual
facility action? By federal, state or local governmental action? By local
citizen or "consumer" action?

How do the various catchment areas compare in terms of answers to the
above questions?

Statistics drawn from patient records, carefully interpreted, should suggest
answers to many questions; but for a number of them, patient statistics must be
related to data from staff activity reports, cost accounting reports, payroll, fiscal
records, state and local mental health authorities, and general population census.
While these data can *suggest* answers, statistics alone cannot describe or evaluate a
program but rather can help identify appropriate directions for qualitiative consideration, thus adding a degree of perspective not otherwise possible.

KINDS OF DATA NEEDED TO DEVELOP PROGRAMS

Questions to be answered in order to develop programs are listed below along
with indications of sources for the needed data.

1. *What is the facility's catchment area like in general?*
   How many people live in it? In what parts of it? What are they like (especially
   in terms of characteristics associated with need for health or mental health

services, such as age, income, ethnicity, mobility, family size, marital status)?

Sources: U.S. Census of Population, 1970; local intercensal estimates or special enumerations.

What are the formal and informal social and political organizations in and for the area?

Sources: Local organizations and individuals.

What are the physical characteristics of the area and its parts (such as size; shape; housing type, quality, and distribution; population density; transportation network; industrial, domestic and recreation areas)?

Sources: U.S. Censuses of Population and Housing, 1970; local maps; state and local planning agencies; local chambers of commerce.

2. *What resources are there?*

What health, mental health, education, and other "people" resources serve the area? Are available to serve the area? In the area? Accessible to the area? In the facility organization? In other organizations? (In terms of existing or potential facilities, staff, buildings, space.)

What fiscal resources are available? What resources are currently being used?

Sources: State and local health and mental hygiene and related agencies; National Institute of Mental Health Inventory.

3. *What are the mental health needs of the area?*

What services are being provided? To residents of each part of the area? Compared to other areas? By the facility? By others? (In terms of numbers and characteristics of patients in relation to numbers and characteristics of the general population.)

Sources: Patient Information System; U.S. Census of Population, 1970; local intercensal estimates of special enumerations.

What services are sought but not provided? How many who request service are turned down? Referred elsewhere?

Sources: Patient Information System.

What "indicators" are there of mental morbidity in the area? For example, in terms of high-risk groups for whom special needs have been identified: the disadvantaged (in terms of income, ethnicity, level of education), the highly mobile, the aged, those living in high crime or delinquency areas?

Sources: U.S. Censuses of Population and Housing, 1970; local population studies, data on unemployment, crime, delinquency and other topics from state and local governmental agencies.

Which of the needs should the facility itself try to meet directly? With what priorities? Which needs should be met by others? What organization of resources might meet these needs? On what timetable? How can the

facility meet its responsibilities to be "accountable" for the needs of the catchment area?

Sources: Facility board and staff; other service providers; "consumer" groups; state and local mental health authorities; data from Patient Information System and other sources noted above.

STRUCTURE OF THE PATIENT INFORMATION SYSTEM

The major body of information on patients is maintained at the treating facility which has the basic responsibility for recording and maintaining information needed to provide service to clients and to document the service provided. (Later discussion will show how the computer can assist facilities in both clinical and administrative responsibilities.) This discussion begins with a description of the basic statewide reporting system for facilities serving the mentally disabled, and will move through successively greater levels of detail which augment the basic system.

The information system on patients consists of three levels which were developed and are being operated modularly. Level one consists of a basic set of information which is reported by all facilities operated, licensed, and/or funded by the DMH. Currently, there are more than 1,000 reporting units—state and local, public and private, inpatient and outpatient—with about 500,000 admissions per year (see Table 12.1). The second and third levels add modular components to the basic level so that the specialized needs of particular types of programs can be reflected (e.g., facilities for the mentally retarded) or so that additional medical record components can be automated for facilities which elect to report in greater detail.

The system is constructed with two general types of information, (1) "events" or transactions and (2) "enhancements." An *event* is a simple fact that something happens, such as an admission, a movement from one inpatient ward to another, a placement in family (foster) care status, an outpatient clinic visit, a death, a termination. An *enhancement* is descriptive information about the patient or the service he receives, such as the patient's date of birth, marital status, area of residence, previous service, diagnosis, or the length of an outpatient visit. The basic system includes reports of both events and enhancements; the other levels include additional reportable events and/or enhancements.

For convenience, events can be recorded in two major ways so as to identify (1) "statuses" and (2) "activities." A *status* can be defined as a program, location, or service classification which applies to an individual patient over a period of time, while an *activity* is defined as an incident of service. A patient is reported as entering into a status by an event and as leaving the status by another event. Between these two events, the patient is considered to be in that status. For an activity, however, each instance of the activity is reported by a separate event. For example, a client may be in "outpatient status" for a period of time. During this time, he may make a number of "outpatient visits" each of which is reported as an event.

TABLE 12.1   NUMBER OF FACILITIES OR UNITS FOR THE MENTALLY DISABLED,
NEW YORK STATE, 1973

Type of Facility or Unit	Number of Facilities or Units
Total	1,033
Inpatient Services	177
Hospitals	120
General hospitals–psychiatric units	65
State hospitals–adult units	27
State correctional hospitals	1
Licensed hospitals	16
State hospitals–alcohol units	8
Local–alcohol units	2
State hospitals–narcotic unit	1
State children's hospitals	12
Schools for the retarded	45
State schools	18
Licensed schools	26
State correctional facility	1
Outpatient, Partial Care, and Rehabilitation Services	724
Clinics	478
Local–unrestricted	202
State hospitals–adult	27
Local–adult	45
Local–court	10
State hospitals–alcohol	6
Local–alcohol	26
State children's hospitals	12
Local children's hospitals	94
Bureau Child Guidance (NYC)	8
State schools	15
Local–retardation	8
Local–emergency	25
Partial care units	104
State facilities	27
Local facilities	66
State children's hospitals	11
Rehabilitation units	67
State facilities	11
Local facilities	56
Day training centers	64
Detoxification centers	11
Halfway Houses	19
Hostels	11
Other Facilities	30
Family Care	52*
State hospitals	34
State schools	18
Community MH Centers**	20

* Number of facilities with residents in family care homes, not the number of homes.
** The numbers of units of mental health centers are also included with the respective types of
service.

At the simplest level, a reporting system could reflect a single status, such as "inpatient," and would count only those events that enter patients into that status and remove them from it. Such events would consist of admissions, discharges, and deaths.

As more statuses are defined and as more distinctions are made among ways of entering and leaving statuses, the system can be expanded in either of two ways: by identifying additional events or by adding descriptive enhancements. Thus, instead of (or in addition to) statuses, the system can record activities beginning with, for example, "day care visit" and extending to any number of services, such as "medication" or even the specifics of a prescription. Also "enhancements," such as patient characteristics which would be recorded upon admission, during a periodic review, or with respect to a treatment plan, can be added.

Consider the following example. A patient may be "admitted" (an event) to "outpatient status" and later "removed" (an event) from that status; during the period between the two events, the patient is *in* "outpatient status." This information, however, does not reflect the degree to which the patient is served while in the particular status. Some information about the volume of service received, such as number of visits, can be obtained by a summary on an enhancement form completed upon removal from the status (see Figure 12.3, item 23). Even this approach does not reflect just when the visits occurred during the patient's tenure on the status. This can be captured by recording the specific activity of each individual visit as an event. Going further, each visit "event" can be "enhanced" by recording the services provided during the visit (e.g., medication, group session) and/or the length of the visit (Figure 12.4).

Thus, the information maintained and produced by the system consists of data regarding *individuals* served and statistics about *groups* of individuals served. This distinction is relevant with respect to the mechanics of the reporting system and the respective responsibilities of those who contribute to it. For example, data can be provided from a reporting facility either in the form of information regarding individual patients or in the form of summary statistics.

OUTLINE OF MAJOR INPUTS TO THE PATIENT INFORMATION SYSTEM

The basic inputs to the patient system which are required of even the smallest, single-unit, locally operated facility consist of (1) a monthly summary statistical form, (2) a form for each patient admitted, and (3) a form for each patient terminated. Additional reporting requirements regarding staff activity and costs are described below.

The Monthly Statistical Report Form

The Monthly Statistical Report, a basic input form, shows the number of patients enrolled at the beginning and at end of the month and the numbers of admissions, terminations, and patient visits (for an outpatient facility) or the number of inpatient days (for an inpatient facility) during the month. A slightly more detailed version of this form (Figure 12.1), which is used for each unit of

LS-2C (6/72)

NEW YORK STATE DEPARTMENT OF MENTAL HYGIENE
MONTHLY STATISTICAL REPORT (UNITS)

Send one copy to the New York State Department of Mental Hygiene and one copy to the County Mental Health Board by the 5th working day after the close of the month.

FACILITY NAME

FACILITY CODE

FOR THE MONTH AND YEAR OF

19

UNIT NAME

UNIT CODE

A STATISTICAL SUMMARY

1	NUMBER OF PATIENTS OR CLIENTS ON ROLLS AT BEGINNING OF MONTH If number on rolls (line 1) is different from last month's "End-of-Month" (line 8), show adjustments in Section E and enter line 20 figure on line 1	
2	NUMBER OF PATIENTS OR CLIENTS ADMITTED DURING THE MONTH	
3	OTHER ADDITIONS TO THE UNIT DURING THE MONTH	
4	SUBTOTAL (line 1 plus line 2 plus line 3)	
5	NUMBER OF PATIENTS OR CLIENTS TERMINATED DURING THE MONTH	
6	OTHER REMOVALS FROM THE UNIT DURING THE MONTH	
7	SUBTOTAL (line 5 plus line 6)	
8	NUMBER OF PATIENTS OR CLIENTS ON THE ROLLS AT END OF MONTH (line 4 minus line 7)	

B WAITING LIST

9	NUMBER OF PATIENTS OR CLIENTS ON WAITING LIST AT END OF MONTH (If none, enter 0)	

C INPATIENT OR RESIDENTIAL UNITS

10	NUMBER OF PATIENT OR CLIENT DAYS IN THE UNIT DURING THE MONTH	

D NON-INPATIENT UNITS (e.g., clinics, day hospitals, other non-residential units)

11	NUMBER OF PATIENT OR CLIENT VISITS DURING THE MONTH	
12	NUMBER OF INDIVIDUAL PATIENTS OR CLIENTS WITH ONE OR MORE VISITS DURING THE MONTH	

E ADJUSTMENTS - COMPLETE THIS SECTION ONLY IF LINE 1 IS DIFFERENT FROM LINE 8 ON LAST MONTH'S REPORT

13	NUMBER OF PATIENTS OR CLIENTS REPORTED ON ROLLS AT END OF PREVIOUS MONTH (line 8 of last month's report)	
14	NUMBER OF ADMISSIONS NOT PREVIOUSLY REPORTED ON AN LS-2C	
15	NUMBER OF OTHER ADDITIONS TO THE UNIT NOT PREVIOUSLY REPORTED ON AN LS-2C	
16	SUBTOTAL (line 13 plus line 14 plus line 15)	
17	NUMBER OF TERMINATIONS NOT PREVIOUSLY REPORTED ON AN LS-2C	
18	NUMBER OF OTHER REMOVALS NOT PREVIOUSLY REPORTED ON AN LS-2C	
19	SUBTOTAL (line 17 plus line 18)	
20	ADJUSTED TOTAL OF PATIENTS OR CLIENTS ON THE ROLLS AT END OF PREVIOUS MONTH (line 16 minus line 19) Enter here and on line 1 above	

COMPLETED BY (TYPED OR PRINTED NAME AND TITLE)　　　　DATE

FIGURE 12.1　Monthly Statistical Report form.

multicomponent facilities, also shows the numbers of "additions" to and "re-. movals" from the unit for individuals already admitted to the facility as a whole.

The Monthly Statistical Report form is initiated by the central computer, which prints the facility name and code, the month to which the report will refer, and the number of patients or clients on the facility or unit rolls at the beginning of the month (i.e., the number reported as of the end of the month on the previous month's report), and then is sent to the respective facilities. This procedure has aided substantially in improving reporting and reducing reporting errors by providing an automatic reminder when the report should be completed and by providing a previously reported and checked number as a reference.

The monthly statistical form is an example of a summary statistical report which provides data which are assembled at the facility and which are combined into basic statistical reports for the state as a whole and its individual geographic areas (Table 12.2). In some states or jurisdictions or for some groups of facilities within particular jurisdictions, reports of this nature might be adequate and practical for many purposes. Where the system includes additional reporting such as the submission of individual forms for each client, the Monthly Statistical Report form serves the further function of providing control totals against which the numbers of individual client forms can be checked. Checks of this nature, or some alternative means of verifying the inclusion of all individual documents, are essential in any sound record system; however, the data reported on the summary forms are obviously limited in flexibility, and they are augmented substantially by reports on individual clients.

Admission and Termination Forms

The Admission Form, MS-5 (Figure 12.2), and the Termination Form, MS-5A (Figure 12.3), are required for each client seen one or more times at any facility for the mentally disabled which is operated, funded in whole or in part, or certified (licensed) by the New York State Department of Mental Hygiene.[1] These forms were developed as part of the Multi-State Information System on Psychiatric Patients, and they have been used in a number of states since 1968.[2]

The Admission and Termination forms are provided for local facilities (those not operated directly by the state) in four-part sets, including an original and a copy for each of the two forms. The first 17 items on the Admission and Termination forms are identical, and the form sets are arranged so that these entries are carboned onto the Termination Form when they are made on the Admission Form. When these entries have been completed, the Termination Form pages are separated from the Admission Form pages and retained until the client's termination. The Admission Form is completed; the original is sent to Albany; and the copy is retained in the client's facility record (local facilities are not required to include client's names or social security numbers on the forms). In Albany, the equivalent of a punched card is keyed from the items at the top of the form plus item 37, and a second card is produced by scanning the rest of the form (items 18 through 36) on IBM #1232 Optical Mark Page Readers. When the Termination Form is completed and submitted, often some time later, that form is entirely scanned. The information for the client is combined on the computer by use of the "Consecutive Number" which

TABLE 12.2 STATISTICS ON PSYCHIATRIC, RETARDATION, ALCOHOLISM AND
NARCOTIC SERVICES LOCATED IN ALBANY COUNTY AND FOR RESIDENTS OF
ALBANY COUNTY SERVED IN STATE FACILITIES, FISCAL YEAR ENDED
MARCH 31, 1972

Type of Service	No. of Units	Additions During Period	Avg. Daily Inpatients	No. of Visits	No. of Pat. Days
Grand Total, Catchment Area	25	6,454	433	143,775	157,712
Inpatient Services	9	1,406	317	---	115,372
Hospital Units	5	1,368	194	---	70,659
Gen. Hosp. Psych. Units	1	1,136	58	---	21,018
State Hosp. Adult. Serv.	1	139	130 #	---	47,268 #
Hudson River	1	139	130 #		47,268 #
State Corr. Hospitals	0	---	---	---	---
Priv. Mental Hospitals	0	---	---	---	---
State Hosp. Alcoholic Units+	2	89*	NA	---	NA
Local Alch. Inpat. Rehab.	0	---	---	---	---
Local Alch. Detox. Unit**	0	---	---	---	---
State Hosp. Narc. Units	0	---	---	---	---
State Children's Hosp. & Units	1	4	6 #	---	2,373 #
Hudson River Child. Unit	1	4	6 #	---	2,373 #
Schools for the Retarded	4	38	123	---	44,713
State Schools	2	23	54 #	---	19,528 #
Private Schools for Retarded	2	15	69	---	25,185
Outpatient Clinic Services	11	4,374	---	64,633	---
Local Unrestricted Clinics	1	1,362	---	5,831	---
State Hosp. Adult Services	1	782	---	20,969	---
Local Adult Clinics	1	697	---	10,296	---
Local Court Clinics	0	---	---	---	---
State Hosp. Alch. Service	0	---	---	---	---
Local Alch. Clinics**	1	NR	---	NR	---
Local Drug Clinics	3	272	---	252	---
Children's Hosp. & Units	0	---	---	---	---
Local Children's Clinics	3	1,080	---	27,285	---
State School Clinics	0	---	---	---	---
Local Retardation Clinics	0	---	---	---	---
DACC Clinic	1	181	---	NR	---
Partial Care	3	359		16,679	
State Hospitals–Adult	1	345	---	9,246	---
Local Facilities–Adult	0	---	---	---	---
Children's Hospitals	0	---	---	---	---
Local Facilities–Children	2	14	---	7,433	---
Rehabilitation	1	153	---	47,055	---
Special Schools/Headstart	0	---	---	---	---
Day Training Centers	1	14	---	15,408	---
Halfway Houses	0	---	---	---	---
Hostels	0	---	---	---	---
Residential Treatment Centers	0	---	---	---	---
Family Care	---	148	116	---	42,340
State Hospitals	---	78	62	---	22,630
State Schools	---	70	54	---	19,710
Other Facilities	0	---	---	---	---
Mental Health Centers	0	---	---	---	---

Includes only those patients admitted from area in last five years.
+ Alcoholism units have no catchment areas, but area is served primarily by 2 units.
* Admissions with alcoholism diagnoses to hospitals with alcoholism units.
** During Fiscal Year 1973 a detoxification unit and alcoholism clinic was opened at St. Peter's Hospital. The alcoholism clinic at Albany Med. Ctr. (NR) was closed.

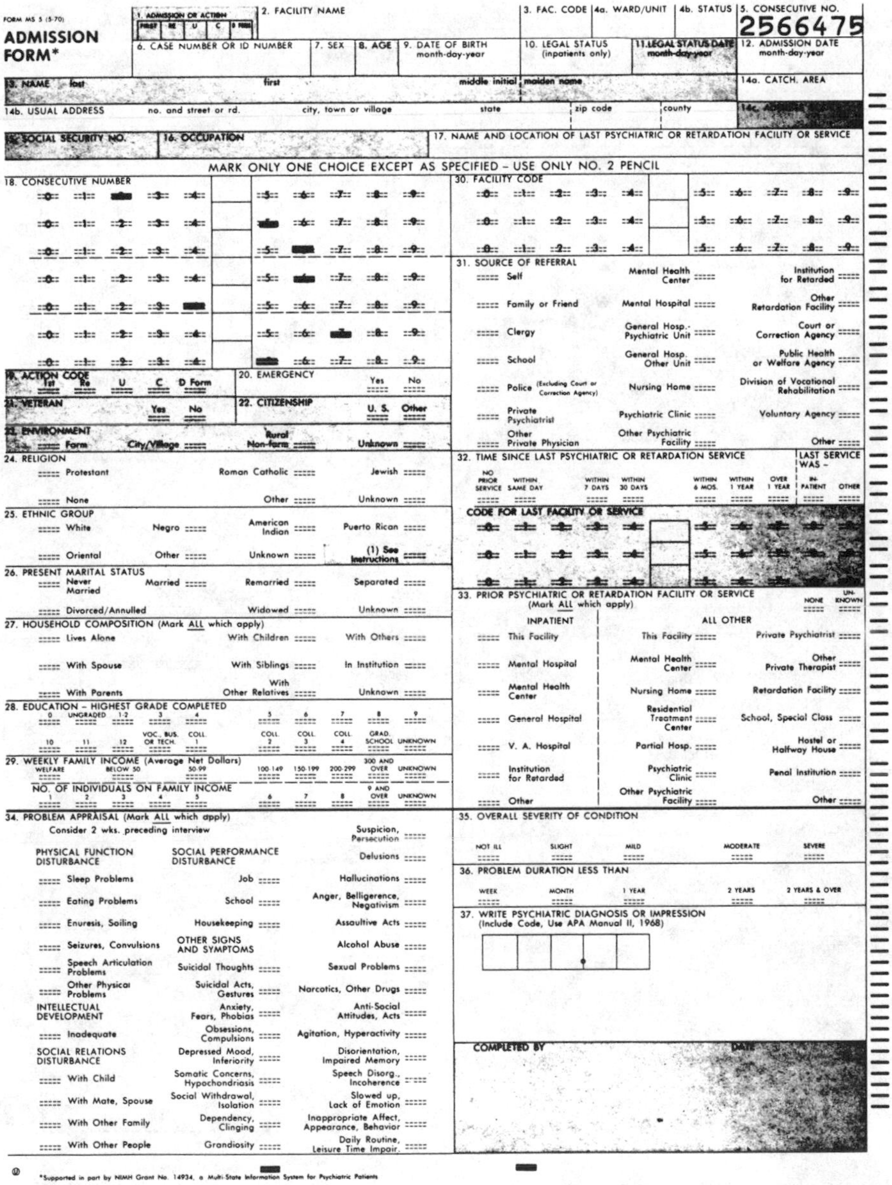
FORM MS 5 (5-70)

ADMISSION FORM*

1. ADMISSION OR ACTION: FIRST | RE | U | C | D FORM
2. FACILITY NAME
3. FAC. CODE
4a. WARD/UNIT
4b. STATUS
5. CONSECUTIVE NO. 2566475
6. CASE NUMBER OR ID NUMBER
7. SEX
8. AGE
9. DATE OF BIRTH month-day-year
10. LEGAL STATUS (inpatients only)
11. LEGAL STATUS DATE month-day-year
12. ADMISSION DATE month-day-year
13. NAME last first middle initial maiden name
14a. CATCH. AREA
14b. USUAL ADDRESS no. and street or rd. city, town or village state zip code county
14c. [illegible]
15. SOCIAL SECURITY NO.
16. OCCUPATION
17. NAME AND LOCATION OF LAST PSYCHIATRIC OR RETARDATION FACILITY OR SERVICE

MARK ONLY ONE CHOICE EXCEPT AS SPECIFIED – USE ONLY NO. 2 PENCIL

18. CONSECUTIVE NUMBER: 0 1 2 3 4 5 6 7 8 9 (seven rows)
19. ACTION CODE: 1st | Re | U | C | D Form
20. EMERGENCY: Yes | No
21. VETERAN: Yes | No
22. CITIZENSHIP: U. S. | Other
23. ENVIRONMENT: Farm | City/Village | Rural Non-farm | Unknown
24. RELIGION: Protestant | Roman Catholic | Jewish | None | Other | Unknown
25. ETHNIC GROUP: White | Negro | American Indian | Puerto Rican | Oriental | Other | Unknown | (1) See Instructions
26. PRESENT MARITAL STATUS: Never Married | Married | Remarried | Separated | Divorced/Annulled | Widowed | Unknown
27. HOUSEHOLD COMPOSITION (Mark ALL which apply): Lives Alone | With Children | With Others | With Spouse | With Siblings | In Institution | With Parents | With Other Relatives | Unknown
28. EDUCATION – HIGHEST GRADE COMPLETED: 0 | UNGRADED | 1-2 | 3 | 4 | 5 | 6 | 7 | 8 | 9 | 10 | 11 | 12 | VOC., BUS. OR TECH. | COLL. 1 | COLL. 2 | COLL. 3 | COLL. 4 | GRAD. SCHOOL | UNKNOWN
29. WEEKLY FAMILY INCOME (Average Net Dollars): WELFARE | BELOW 50 | 50-99 | 100-149 | 150-199 | 200-299 | 300 AND OVER | UNKNOWN
NO. OF INDIVIDUALS ON FAMILY INCOME: 1 | 2 | 3 | 4 | 5 | 6 | 7 | 8 | 9 AND OVER | UNKNOWN
30. FACILITY CODE: 0 1 2 3 4 5 6 7 8 9 (three rows)
31. SOURCE OF REFERRAL: Self | Mental Health Center | Institution for Retarded | Family or Friend | Mental Hospital | Other Retardation Facility | Clergy | General Hosp.-Psychiatric Unit | Court or Correction Agency | School | General Hosp. Other Unit | Public Health or Welfare Agency | Police (Excluding Court or Correction Agency) | Nursing Home | Division of Vocational Rehabilitation | Private Psychiatrist | Psychiatric Clinic | Voluntary Agency | Other Private Physician | Other Psychiatric Facility | Other
32. TIME SINCE LAST PSYCHIATRIC OR RETARDATION SERVICE: NO PRIOR SERVICE | WITHIN SAME DAY | WITHIN 7 DAYS | WITHIN 30 DAYS | WITHIN 6 MOS. | WITHIN 1 YEAR | OVER 1 YEAR
LAST SERVICE WAS – IN-PATIENT | OTHER
CODE FOR LAST FACILITY OR SERVICE: 0 1 2 3 4 5 6 7 8 9 (three rows)
33. PRIOR PSYCHIATRIC OR RETARDATION FACILITY OR SERVICE (Mark ALL which apply): NONE | UNKNOWN
INPATIENT: This Facility | Mental Hospital | Mental Health Center | General Hospital | V. A. Hospital | Institution for Retarded | Other
ALL OTHER: This Facility | Private Psychiatrist | Mental Health Center | Other Private Therapist | Nursing Home | Retardation Facility | Residential Treatment Center | School, Special Class | Partial Hosp. | Hostel or Halfway House | Psychiatric Clinic | Penal Institution | Other Psychiatric Facility | Other
34. PROBLEM APPRAISAL (Mark ALL which apply) Consider 2 wks. preceding interview
PHYSICAL FUNCTION DISTURBANCE: Sleep Problems | Eating Problems | Enuresis, Soiling | Seizures, Convulsions | Speech Articulation Problems | Other Physical Problems
INTELLECTUAL DEVELOPMENT: Inadequate
SOCIAL RELATIONS DISTURBANCE: With Child | With Mate, Spouse | With Other Family | With Other People
SOCIAL PERFORMANCE DISTURBANCE: Job | School | Housekeeping
OTHER SIGNS AND SYMPTOMS: Suicidal Thoughts | Suicidal Acts, Gestures | Anxiety, Fears, Phobias | Obsessions, Compulsions | Depressed Mood, Inferiority | Somatic Concerns, Hypochondriasis | Social Withdrawal, Isolation | Dependency, Clinging | Grandiosity | Suspicion, Persecution | Delusions | Hallucinations | Anger, Belligerence, Negativism | Assaultive Acts | Alcohol Abuse | Sexual Problems | Narcotics, Other Drugs | Anti-Social Attitudes, Acts | Agitation, Hyperactivity | Disorientation, Impaired Memory | Speech Disorg., Incoherence | Slowed up, Lack of Emotion | Inappropriate Affect, Appearance, Behavior | Daily Routine, Leisure Time Impair.
35. OVERALL SEVERITY OF CONDITION: NOT ILL | SLIGHT | MILD | MODERATE | SEVERE
36. PROBLEM DURATION LESS THAN: WEEK | MONTH | 1 YEAR | 2 YEARS | 2 YEARS & OVER
37. WRITE PSYCHIATRIC DIAGNOSIS OR IMPRESSION (Include Code, Use APA Manual II, 1968)
COMPLETED BY | DATE

*Supported in part by NIMH Grant No. 14934, a Multi-State Information System for Psychiatric Patients

FIGURE 12.2 Admission Form, MS-5.

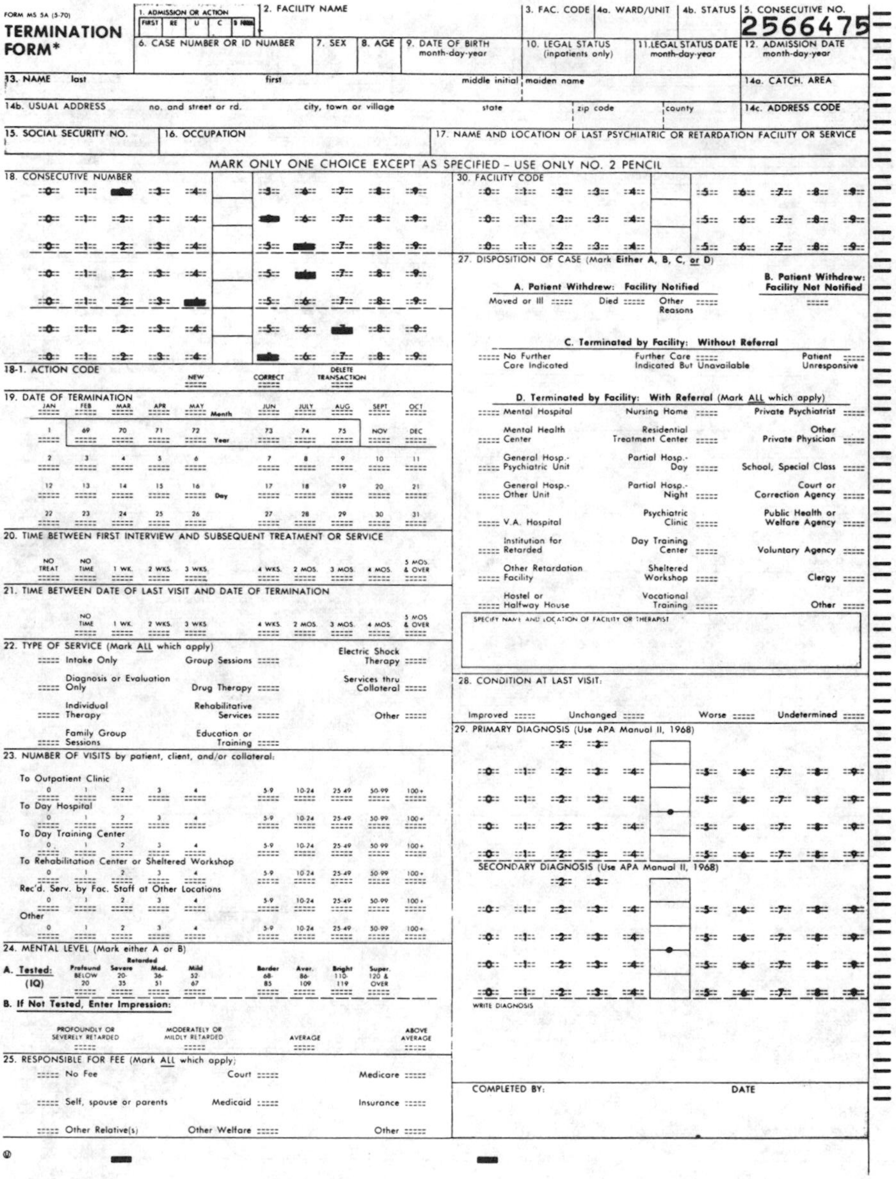

FORM MS 5A (5-70)

TERMINATION FORM*

1. ADMISSION OR ACTION: FIRST | RE | U | C | D
2. FACILITY NAME
3. FAC. CODE
4a. WARD/UNIT
4b. STATUS
5. CONSECUTIVE NO. 2566475
6. CASE NUMBER OR ID NUMBER
7. SEX
8. AGE
9. DATE OF BIRTH month-day-year
10. LEGAL STATUS (inpatients only)
11. LEGAL STATUS DATE month-day-year
12. ADMISSION DATE month-day-year
13. NAME last / first / middle initial / maiden name
14a. CATCH. AREA
14b. USUAL ADDRESS no. and street or rd. / city, town or village / state / zip code / county
14c. ADDRESS CODE
15. SOCIAL SECURITY NO.
16. OCCUPATION
17. NAME AND LOCATION OF LAST PSYCHIATRIC OR RETARDATION FACILITY OR SERVICE

MARK ONLY ONE CHOICE EXCEPT AS SPECIFIED – USE ONLY NO. 2 PENCIL

18. CONSECUTIVE NUMBER (0–9)

18-1. ACTION CODE: NEW / CORRECT / DELETE TRANSACTION

19. DATE OF TERMINATION: Month: JAN FEB MAR APR MAY JUN JULY AUG SEPT OCT NOV DEC; Year: 69 70 71 72 73 74 75; Day: 1–31

20. TIME BETWEEN FIRST INTERVIEW AND SUBSEQUENT TREATMENT OR SERVICE: NO TREAT / NO TIME / 1 WK. / 2 WKS. / 3 WKS. / 4 WKS. / 2 MOS. / 3 MOS. / 4 MOS. / 5 MOS. & OVER

21. TIME BETWEEN DATE OF LAST VISIT AND DATE OF TERMINATION: NO TIME / 1 WK. / 2 WKS. / 3 WKS. / 4 WKS. / 2 MOS. / 3 MOS. / 4 MOS. / 5 MOS. & OVER

22. TYPE OF SERVICE (Mark ALL which apply): Intake Only / Group Sessions / Electric Shock Therapy / Diagnosis or Evaluation Only / Drug Therapy / Services thru Collateral / Individual Therapy / Rehabilitative Services / Other / Family Group Sessions / Education or Training

23. NUMBER OF VISITS by patient, client, and/or collateral: To Outpatient Clinic / To Day Hospital / To Day Training Center / To Rehabilitation Center or Sheltered Workshop / Rec'd. Serv. by Fac. Staff at Other Locations / Other — 0 / 1 / 2 / 3 / 4 / 5-9 / 10-24 / 25-49 / 50-99 / 100+

24. MENTAL LEVEL (Mark either A or B)
A. Tested: (IQ) Retarded: Profound BELOW 20 / Severe 20-35 / Mod. 36-51 / Mild 52-67 / Border 68-85 / Aver. 86-109 / Bright 110-119 / Super. 120 & OVER
B. If Not Tested, Enter Impression: PROFOUNDLY OR SEVERELY RETARDED / MODERATELY OR MILDLY RETARDED / AVERAGE / ABOVE AVERAGE

25. RESPONSIBLE FOR FEE (Mark ALL which apply): No Fee / Court / Medicare / Self, spouse or parents / Medicaid / Insurance / Other Relative(s) / Other Welfare / Other

30. FACILITY CODE (0–9)

27. DISPOSITION OF CASE (Mark Either A, B, C, or D)
A. Patient Withdrew: Facility Notified — Moved or Ill / Died / Other Reasons
B. Patient Withdrew: Facility Not Notified
C. Terminated by Facility: Without Referral — No Further Care Indicated / Further Care Indicated But Unavailable / Patient Unresponsive
D. Terminated by Facility: With Referral (Mark ALL which apply) — Mental Hospital / Nursing Home / Private Psychiatrist / Mental Health Center / Residential Treatment Center / Other Private Physician / General Hosp.-Psychiatric Unit / Partial Hosp.-Day / School, Special Class / General Hosp.-Other Unit / Partial Hosp.-Night / Court or Correction Agency / V.A. Hospital / Psychiatric Clinic / Public Health or Welfare Agency / Institution for Retarded / Day Training Center / Voluntary Agency / Other Retardation Facility / Sheltered Workshop / Clergy / Hostel or Halfway House / Vocational Training / Other
SPECIFY NAME AND LOCATION OF FACILITY OR THERAPIST

28. CONDITION AT LAST VISIT: Improved / Unchanged / Worse / Undetermined

29. PRIMARY DIAGNOSIS (Use APA Manual II, 1968)

SECONDARY DIAGNOSIS (Use APA Manual II, 1968)

WRITE DIAGNOSIS

COMPLETED BY: DATE

FIGURE 12.3 Termination Form, MS-5A.

is preprinted in item 5 in Arabic numbers for keying and in machine-readable numbers in item 18 of both forms for scanning. [3]

The Admission Form includes a basic, elementary entry for each of the major questions asked of clients upon admission or shortly thereafter, providing a summary of the client's characteristics at a level which might be appropriate for a medical record face sheet. To meet the service needs of the facility, however, many of the entries on the Admission Form would be expanded in the record maintained at the facility. The detail of the information included would vary for different types of facilities or units. The Admission and Termination forms were designed to cover the broad range of facilities serving the mentally disabled (including the mentally ill, the developmentally disabled, and those with alcohol or drug problems). For many subgroups within this broad spectrum, it would be preferable to have separate specialized forms. While much of the basic data would be relevant for any groups, there are obviously some questions which would be more appropriate for, say, children than for the elderly. This problem and some practical approaches to it are discussed later. [4]

While some basic information is needed for every individual served, it would make little sense, for example, to inquire into a client's education upon admission to an alcohol detoxification unit.

An attempt has been made to make the forms applicable in large-volume, short-contract programs such as emergency rooms by identifying a limited number of required items. To simplify the mechanisms of recording in such units, an abbreviated form, which consists of a combined one-page subset of the more detailed Admission and Termination forms, has been printed.

For many years, an admission to outpatient clinic service was defined as occurring "when the facility accepted psychiatric responsibility for the client." Inasmuch as such a definition excluded some major segments of the system of service, an admission has been defined in the New York State reporting system as occurring when a client discusses his problems face-to-face with a facility employee whether further service is provided or not (this would not include general inquiries such as those handled by receptionists).

Reports for individuals who are seen briefly but "not admitted" should be covered because, first, even a brief discussion of personal problems constitutes a service which, in many instances, can have real meaning to the person involved; second, data on the characteristics of those seen briefly are extremely valuable in assessing the needs for service by potential clients; third, the totality of brief services often comprises an appreciable part of the program.

Intra-Facility Movements

In many multicomponent facilities, such as mental health centers and others that provide more than one type of service (e.g., inpatient, outpatient, and day care), the reporting system is simplified as follows: When a patient is admitted to the facility, an Admission Form is completed. When he is removed from the unit to which he was admitted and added to another unit, a simple list is submitted monthly for each unit of the facility showing the consecutive numbers and dates

for all additions to and removals from that unit. A Termination Form is not completed until the patient is removed from the facility as a whole.

In a number of multicomponent facilities, particularly where communication between the units is not well developed, this listing procedure has not proven effective. Moreover, even where the communication among units is reasonable, problems occur when patients who are referred from one unit to another fail to report to the new unit. In this situation, a Termination Form should be completed after a reasonable period of time either by the old or by the new unit. In some facilities, because of the logistics involved, the staff have opted to complete the Termination Form each time a patient leaves a unit and to submit a new Admission Form each time he enters a unit.

The definitions and procedures of the system are such that a patient need not be removed from one unit or status in order to be added to another unit or status as patients often receive appropriate services simultaneously from more than one unit. The system thus permits multiple enrollments within a facility. For example, a resident of a halfway house (one unit) might receive services at the outpatient clinic (another unit) at the same time.[5]

Basic Level for State-Operated Facilities

Because the DMH has additional administrative responsibilities for the facilities it operates, the information system for these has a number of features which go beyond those required for locally operated facilities. These responsibilities, aside from the overall direction and evaluation, include such "housekeeping" services as notifying patients of their legal rights on a periodic basis, monitoring the expiration of legal authorizations for inpatient care, aiding in the maintenance of clinical records, billing for patient care, cost accounting, and distributing supplies.

State-operated facilities use the same Admission Form as that used by local facilities; however, as noted earlier, state facilities use a Disposition Form for terminating patients. The form consists largely of item 27 from the Termination Form (see Figure 12.3) plus an item on "expected residence." In addition to reporting removals from inpatient or outpatient care, this form is also used as a document to effect transfers between state facilities. The Disposition Form omits such items covered on the Termination Form as numbers of visits and final diagnoses, because these are reported separately.

Basic patient movement events are reported on either of two forms: a Daily Supervisor's Report for inpatient or residential units and an Outpatient Daily Service Record (Figure 12.4) for other units. The Daily Supervisor's Report consists of a listing of all entries into and exits from a given unit and has a section for balancing the number of entries and exits with the number of clients on the rolls at the beginning and at the end of the day. The Daily Supervisor's Report is used primarily for intra-facility operations with a "by-product" copy which is used for reporting to the central system.

The events recorded on the Daily Supervisor's Report identify the beginning and the end of *statuses*. Basic events reported for outpatients on the Outpatient Daily Service Record (Figure 12.4) reflect individual *activities*, such as "clinic visit,"

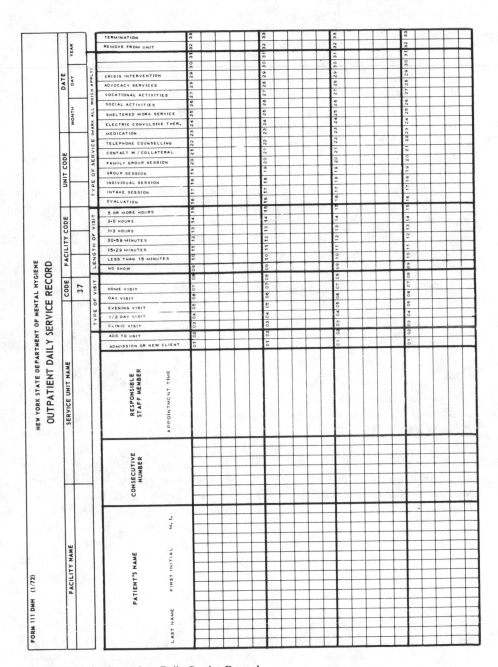

FIGURE 12.4 Outpatient Daily Service Record.

"day-care visit," or "home visit," in addition to identifying entries into and exits from outpatient units. This form also includes "enhancements" recording the length of each visit and the services provided.

In identifying activities, the reporting for outpatient programs is at a more in depth level than reporting for inpatient programs. Some indication of the particular services provided to inpatients however is reflected by the type of wards in which they are served and by "enhancements" on the clinical forms discussed above. "Ancillary services," which are now reported for individual patients from nine Department facilities, include such activities as x-ray, lab work, and dental work. These services are being covered initially as part of the cost system (outlined later), but the procedures were designed to meet clinical and medical record needs at the same time. The system at Rockland has for many years assembled information on psychopharmological treatment to individual inpatients.

For state facilities, in addition to the initial diagnosis or impression which is reported on the Admission Form, a separate Psychiatric Diagnosis form (Figure 12.5) is submitted whenever diagnoses are made or changed. Thus any number of additional diagnoses may be added to the system for a given patient, with up to three diagnoses on each form. Specialized versions of this form are used for the mentally retarded and to cover physical diagnoses.

A number of administrative forms which are part of the basic system for state facilities will not be discussed here. These include legal papers to support inpatient admission, forms to change legal statuses, transmittal forms which accompany batches of forms submitted, and the like.

Clinical Forms

The basic system for state facilities includes two forms which have substantial management value. These are a Mental Retardation Client Survey form (Figure 12.6) used for all clients of the State Schools for the Retarded, and a Patient Progress Note form used for state hospital inpatients hospitalized three months or longer.

The Mental Retardation Client Survey form is completed (a) upon application for admission to either residential or nonresidential service and (b) every six months for clients receiving service. When a client's six-month examination is due, the form is initiated on the computer which prints the client's name and other identifying data and the machine-readable institution code, ward number, and client consecutive number. Programming is under way to include the printing of other data, such as date of birth, ethnic group, and intelligence level, so that manual entries would be made for these items only if the previous information was incorrect or when a new test has been administered. After preprinting, the forms are distributed to facility staff for completion in the wards or units serving the respective clients. The form is printed in two-part sets so that a copy remains in the client's record at the facility while the original is sent to Albany for processing. In addition to the Mental Retardation Client Survey form, the computer initiates a quarterly Case Review form which is completed at and retained in the facility but is not entered in the central system.

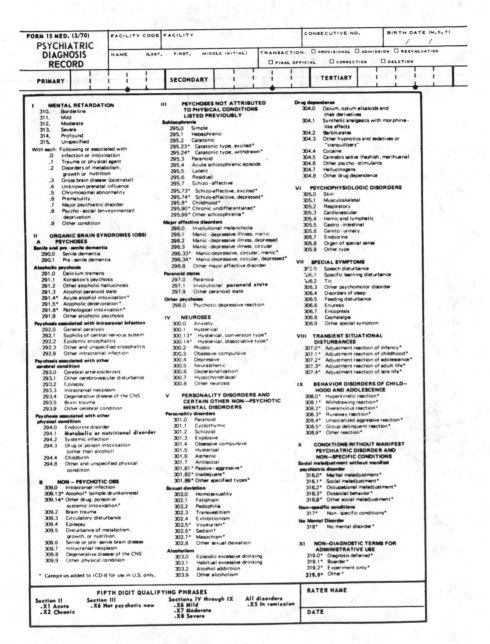

FIGURE 12.5   Psychiatric Diagnosis Record form.

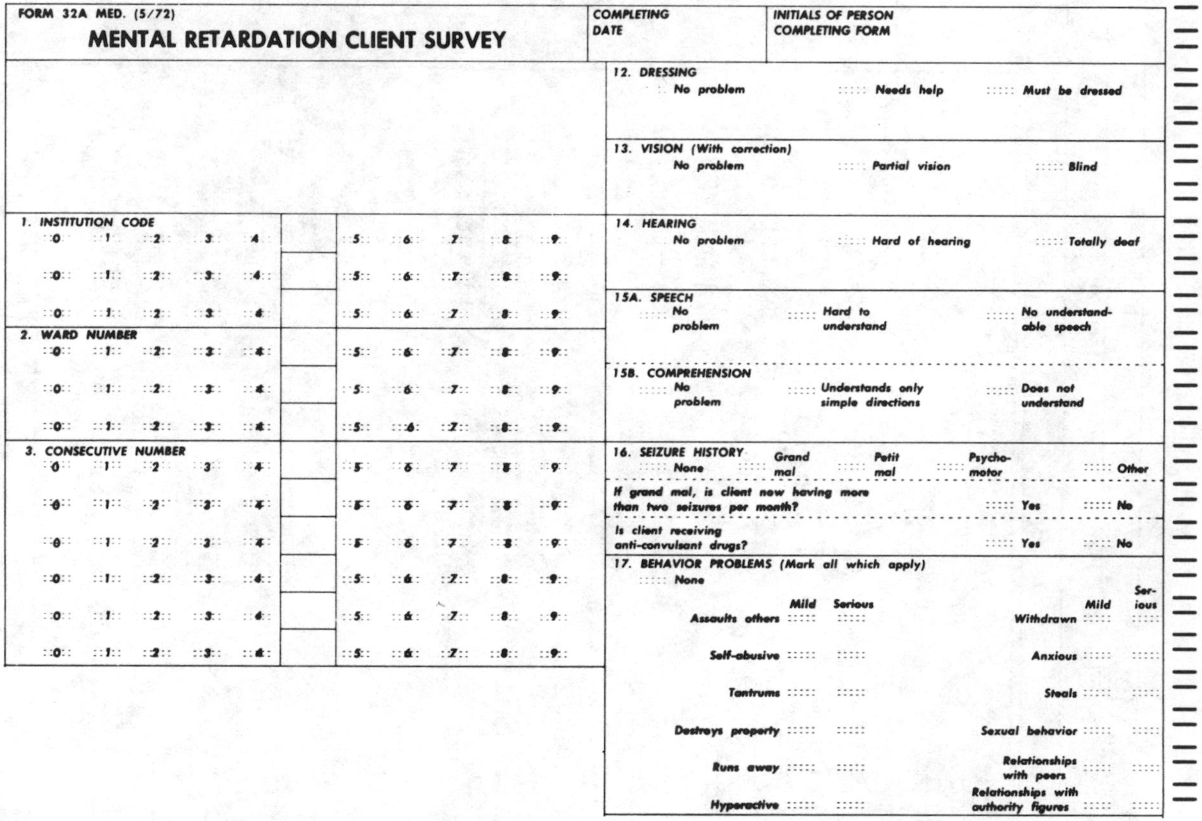

FORM 32A MED. (5/72)

MENTAL RETARDATION CLIENT SURVEY

COMPLETING DATE

INITIALS OF PERSON COMPLETING FORM

1. INSTITUTION CODE
0 1 2 3 4 5 6 7 8 9
0 1 2 3 4 5 6 7 8 9
0 1 2 3 4 5 6 7 8 9

2. WARD NUMBER
0 1 2 3 4 5 6 7 8 9
0 1 2 3 4 5 6 7 8 9
0 1 2 3 4 5 6 7 8 9

3. CONSECUTIVE NUMBER
0 1 2 3 4 5 6 7 8 9
0 1 2 3 4 5 6 7 8 9
0 1 2 3 4 5 6 7 8 9
0 1 2 3 4 5 6 7 8 9
0 1 2 3 4 5 6 7 8 9
0 1 2 3 4 5 6 7 8 9

12. DRESSING
No problem — Needs help — Must be dressed

13. VISION (With correction)
No problem — Partial vision — Blind

14. HEARING
No problem — Hard of hearing — Totally deaf

15A. SPEECH
No problem — Hard to understand — No understandable speech

15B. COMPREHENSION
No problem — Understands only simple directions — Does not understand

16. SEIZURE HISTORY
None — Grand mal — Petit mal — Psycho-motor — Other

If grand mal, is client now having more than two seizures per month? — Yes — No

Is client receiving anti-convulsant drugs? — Yes — No

17. BEHAVIOR PROBLEMS (Mark all which apply)
None

	Mild	Serious		Mild	Serious
Assaults others			Withdrawn		
Self-abusive			Anxious		
Tantrums			Steals		
Destroys property			Sexual behavior		
Runs away			Relationships with peers		
Hyperactive			Relationships with authority figures		

FIGURE 12.6 Mental Retardation Client Survey form.

FIGURE 12.6 (Continued)

4. DATE OF BIRTH

MONTH: Jan, Feb, Mar, April, May, June, July, Aug, Sept, Oct, Nov, Dec

DAY: 1–31

YEAR

5. ETHNIC GROUP
- White
- Negro
- Puerto Rican
- Oriental
- American Indian
- Other

6. MOST RECENT IQ TEST
- None
- Binet
- Kuhlman
- Wechsler
- Other
- Unknown

Year tested — Earlier — Unknown

IQ Score (Use 99 for 99 or more)

7. INTELLIGENCE LEVEL (See instructions)
- Normal
- Borderline
- Mild
- Moderate
- Severe
- Profound

9. AMBULATION
- Walks freely
- Walks with difficulty
- Uses wheelchair only
- Non-ambulatory

10. TOILET TRAINING
- Fully trained
- Partially trained
- Not trained

11. EATING
- Socially acceptable
- Uses utensils but messy
- Feeds self with fingers
- Needs help
- Must be fed
- Tube fed

18. CURRENT PROGRAMS (Mark all which apply)

None

Program	Hours per week
	1-5 / 6-10 / 11-20 / 21-30 / Over 30
Pre school class	
School classes	
Adult education	
Home economics classes	
Prevocational training	
Vocational training	
Sheltered workshop	
Job on grounds	
Job off grounds	
Occupational therapy	
Physical therapy	
Speech therapy	
Language development	
Intensive therapy	
Recreation Dept. activities	
Volunteer program	

STATE OF NEW YORK
DEPARTMENT OF MENTAL HYGIENE

The Patient Progress Note for state hospitals is processed in a similar manner except that for this form a narrative note is printed by the computer listing the information marked on the form. This note is sent to the hospital for filing in the patient's medical record, where it replaces the copy of the form itself. The content of this form is being revised as of this writing, and it will be replaced by a slightly modified version of the Periodic Evaluation Record (Figure 12.7) which was designed for the Multi-State Information System by Drs. Robert Spitzger and Jean Endicott of the Department of Mental Hygiene Biometrics Research Unit and Columbia University. The revised form will add items on psychiatric drugs and physical illnesses. There are two versions of the Periodic Evaluation Record, one for long-term inpatient settings and one (called the Community Version) for outpatient programs and short-stay inpatient settings. The Community Version differs in the section on "Activities," and adds items on "Adequacy of Housing" and "Financial Problems" (Figure 12.8). Most of the items on the two versions are a subset of the items on a longer (four-page) form, the Mental Status Examination Record, which along with a number of other clinical forms, is processed at Rockland Psychiatric Center for states and facilities which opt to report on a more detailed clinical level (Spitzer and Endicott, 1970-71; Spitzer and Endicott, 1971; and references in note 2).

The Periodic Evaluation Record includes the "medical" portion of the quarterly update of a medical-social plan such as that required for medicaid. The "social" portion will be covered on another form which is now being redesigned after review by program staff.

SOME MAJOR OUTPUTS OF THE PATIENT INFORMATION SYSTEM

Information from the various inputs referring to a given client is stored and manipulated by the computer so as to produce outputs which combine data drawn from multiple inputs. Outputs of the patient information system can be described in terms of a number of dichotomies which are characteristic of automatic data processing and statistical systems in a wide range of applications. These dichotomies include:

1. Recurring or periodic reports vs. ad hoc reports;
2. Printed or "hard-copy" reports vs. machine-readable outputs;
3. Statistical tabulations vs. listings;
4. Numerical vs. verbal reports;
5. Tables vs. graphs.

The different types of reports can be described best by reference to some representative examples.

Recurring or Periodic Reports

As of this writing, there are 37 different printed reports produced by the patient information system on a periodic basis ranging from weekly to annually. In addition, a number of recurring outputs from this system, ordinarily on computer

Form MS 8 (7/69)

PERIODIC EVALUATION RECORD (PER) *

Read instructions on reverse side.

| Patient's last name | First name | M.I. | Facility | Ward |

IDENTIFICATION
Case or consecutive no.

Facility code

Rater code

Last day of week being evaluated

	Jan	Feb	Mar	Apr	May	Month	Jun	Jul	Aug	Sep	Oct
1	69	70	71	72	Year	73	74	75		Nov	Dec
2	3	4	5	6		7	8	9	10	11	
12	13	14	15	16	Day	17	18	19	20	21	
22	23	24	25	26		27	28	29	30	31	

Sex: male / female

TRANSACTION: Initial evaluation / reevaluation / partial reevaluation / correction / deletion

APPEARANCE (neat) none slight mild mod marked
Unkempt

Weight: underweight / average / overweight | gaining losing

Ambulation disturbance: walks with assistance / must use wheel chair / bedridden

PSYCHOMOTOR ACTIVITY very retarded / retarded / average / accelerated / very accel

GENERAL ATTITUDE, BEHAVIOR none slight mild mod marked
Uncooperative

Withdrawn

Inappropriate

Impaired functioning in goal directed activities

Suspicious

Anger (overt): none slight mild mod marked / physically destructive / assaultive

MOOD AND AFFECT
Depression: none slight mild mod marked / inappropriate euphoric

Anxiety: flat labile

QUALITY OF SPEECH, THOUGHT
Productivity: mark reduc / reduced / average / increased / marked increase

Incoherence: none slight mild mod mark / evasive blocking / loosening of associations

Irrelevance: grandiosity / inadequacy / phobia

CONTENT OF SPEECH AND THOUGHT
obsessions   compulsions   suicidal ideation

distrustfulness   bizarre thoughts   ideas of reference

Delusions: none slight mild mod marked / persecutory somatic

SOMATIC FUNCTIONING AND CONCERN
Physical health: very good / good / only fair / poor / very poor

Appetite: very poor / poor / normal / excessive / very exces / to eat requires urging help

Insomnia: none slight mild mod marked / sleeps excessively

Severe sensory impairment (organic): visual / hearing

Other symptoms: psycho-physiological / incontinence / seizures

Unwarranted concern with physical health: none slight mild mod mark

HALLUCINATIONS: none slight mild mod marked / auditory visual

ORIENTATION DISTURBANCE Time: unknown none slight mild mod mark
Place
Person

MEMORY DISTURBANCE Recent: unknown none slight mild mod mark
Remote

JUDGMENT ABOUT FUTURE PLANS: no plans (or) very good / good / only fair / poor / very poor

POTENTIAL FOR Suicide: unsure / not significant / low / mod / high / very high

Physical violence: unsure / not significant / low / mod / high / very high

MANAGEMENT
Staff attention required: almost none / very little / fair amount / considerable / because of behavior / phys ill / unauthorized leave / suicide / violence

Special observations

Permitted to leave (by himself): neither ward or facility / ward / facility

Permitted to leave (with escort): neither ward or facility / ward / facility

ACTIVITIES
Social conversation: pract never / rarely / occasional / often / very often

Family contact: no family available (or) pract never / rarely / occasional / often / very often

Has visitors at facility: pract never / rarely / occasional / often / very often

Sees people outside facility: pract never / rarely / occasional / often / very often

Works (hours/week): 1-5 / 6-10 / 11-20 / 21-30 / 31+ / for pay / no pay

Interest in voluntary leisure time activities: none / little / fair / average / considerable

organized recreation: writes letters / religious activities / reads / watches TV

games with other people: organized patient groups / hobbies

OVERALL SEVERITY OF ILLNESS: not ill slight mild mod mark

CHANGE IN CONDITION: marked impr / improved / stable / variable / worse / during past week month

RATER HAS WRITTEN COMMENTS: below / elsewhere

Signature   Date

COMMENTS

* Developed by Robert L. Spitzer, M.D., and Jean Endicott, Ph.D., Biometrics Research, N.Y.S. Department of Mental Hygiene, with the assistance of the Multi-State Information System for Psychiatric Patients Project Supported by N.Y.S. Department of Mental Hygiene, C29820 and NIMH Grant 14934.

FIGURE 12.7   Periodic Evaluation Record.

ACTIVITIES		goes to school				keeps house	
Works (hours/week)	1-5 6-10		11-20 21-30 31+			for pay	no pay
Work performance (if working)		very good	good	only fair		poor	very poor
Doesn't work at all because of (or)		Amount of time working limited by					
physical illness		psychopathology				looking for work	
household responsibilities		going to school				his retirement	
Involvement in voluntary leisure time activities		consid erable	mod erate	only fair		little	none
Good friends	many several	a few	only one		none	prefers being alone	
Heterosexual adjustment		very good	good	only fair		poor	very poor
frigidity		potency disturbance				homosexual behavior	
Marital adjustment (if married)		very good	good	only fair		poor	very poor
Pleasure out of life		a great deal	consid erable	mod erate		little	none
ADEQUACY OF HOUSING	?	very good	good	only fair		poor	very poor
FINANCIAL PROBLEMS	?	none	slight	mild		mod	mark
OVERALL SEVERITY	not ill slight mild	mod	mark	severe		among most	extreme
CHANGE IN CONDITION	marked im- lm-impr proved	stable	vari-able	worse		during past week month	

::::: RATER HAS WRITTEN COMMENTS ELSEWHERE

Signature   Date

FIGURE 12.8   Community Version of Periodic Evaluation Record.

tapes or disks, serve as inputs to other systems such as the DMH billing and cost systems.

Currently, the major output for state-operated programs is the monthly DMH Statistical Report (Tables 12.3-12.6). These tables refer to state mental hospital patients, excluding children's units, alcohol units, and a narcotic unit, which are covered in comparable tables on other pages of the Statistical Report. The Report also includes comparable tables for the state facilities for the mentally retarded and other developmentally disabled. The Statistical Report begins with a table (Table 12.3) which covers both outpatient and inpatient activity to emphasize the shifting role of the state hospitals from largely residential care to a strong general community involvement. Newer reports, similar to those illustrated in Table 12.2, cover locally operated programs in the same tables with state-operated programs in order to reflect the movement in New York State toward a single system of service.

Tables 12.4-12.6 cover state hospital inpatient services. Table 12.4 shows the number of inpatients at the end of the month with an indication of which hospitals exceed their "program goal occupancy" (a reasonable bed capacity), the change in the size of the inpatient population during the month, the percentages of the inpatient population in major age and length-of-stay groups, and several "turnover" rates. Table 12.5 is a traditional inpatient movement table. Table 12.6 shows changes in the number of resident patients during the past month and year and comparisons of admissions, net releases, and inpatient deaths for the most recent 12-month period and the previous 12-month period. This table provides a brief "annual report" each month.

The Statistical Report tables for children's hospitals and units and alcohol and narcotic units are identical to those for state hospitals. The tables for the state schools for the retarded are also the same except for the percentage distributions of the resident population. Here, instead of the age and length-of-stay groups shown for the other facilities, percentages are presented for age groups under 21 and for those 21 and over, for two major mental level groups (those with IQs of less than 36 and those with IQs of 36 and over).

The Statistical Report is distributed to about 1,300 individuals in the state facilities, in other state and local governmental agencies, and others. While this report does provide a summary of activity for facilities as a whole and for some major specialized areas, it does not refer specifically to the individual treatment units and wards which comprise the overall facilities. To meet the needs of these units, most of which relate to particular local geographic areas or offer specialized services, additional Statistical Report tables are produced on a monthly basis. For inpatient units, tables like Table 12.4 and Table 12.5 are produced for each facility, with separate rows for each ward and treatment unit. The data covered in Table 12.4 are particularly useful for characterizing and comparing wards and treatment units, in terms of number of patients, major characteristics, and "turnover." For non-inpatient units, tables for each facility and each treatment unit are produced showing the number of individuals served, additions, removals, visits, services by major type, and visits per individual.

TABLE 12.3   NEW YORK STATE DEPARTMENT OF MENTAL HYGIENE STATISTICAL REPORT FOR OCTOBER[1] 1973
SUMMARY OF ALL SERVICES FOR DEPARTMENT FACILITIES, STATE HOSPITALS

Facilities	Additions[2]	Number of Individ. Served	Non-Inpatient[1] Number of Visits by Type				Total Number of Services	Inpatient[1]		
			Total	Partial Care	Out-Patient	Home		Additions	Resident & Leave End of Mo.	Number on Fam. Care End of Mo.
All Services	1,679	31,217	110,124	35,912	60,827	13,385	198,113	3,716	63,377	6,786
State Hospitals	1,182	24,869	78,981	25,792	43,517	9,672	148,995	2,956	39,526	3,810+
Binghamton	22	591	1,678	674	650	354	3,495	130	1,113	379
Bronx	61	1,675	5,348	1,723	3,313	312	9,191	274	647	25
Brooklyn	63	1,858	4,961	608	4,251	42	9,377	133	1,516	0
Buffalo	54	1,269	3,040	999	1,290	751	5,591	126	820	604
Capital District*	101	754	3,359	843	2,118	398	6,138	4	---	43
Central Islip	50	1,090	2,437	360	1,937	140	4,867	194	2,839	17
Creedmoor	64	3,181	9,492	4,742	4,699	51	18,444	157	2,264	0
Elmira*	24	321	2,619	1,428	878	313	7,710	0	---	125
Gowanda	35	632	3,243	1,215	1,351	677	4,745	47	1,163	177
Harlem Valley	67	534	2,757	1,273	739	745	4,212	84	2,264	110
Hoch Psych	12	605	1,260	367	863	30	3,179	86	103	0
Hudson River	3	788	3,035	154	1,331	1,550	4,949	134	2,551	360
Hutchings Psych $	118	838	4,735	2,445	2,133	157	8,177	72	75	22
Kings Park	10	573	1,178	213	797	168	2,572	128	3,974	41
Man-Dunlap	8	814	1,581	154	1,392	35	2,756	141	698	0
Man-Kirby	7	476	1,152	57	905	190	1,880	97	582	0
Man-Meyer	24	412	1,966	537	1,404	25	4,007	89	513	26
Marcy	52	475	1,455	370	843	242	2,551	75	1,789	118
Mid-Hudson	---	---						51	213	
Middletown	46	807	2,136	665	1,220	251	3,528	102	1,465	415
N.E. Nassau	9	340	917	357	488	72	1,820	60	117	20
Pilgrim	27	993	1,263	39	949	275	2,173	229	6,982	158
Psych. Institute		No Reports						53	93	0
Rochester	17	567	1,776	432	1,108	236	2,396	161	1,773	114
Rockland	73	1,246	4,324	704	2,736	884	7,791	72	2,660	124
South Beach	130	1,680	6,591	2,450	3,867	274	11,680	35	36	0
St. Lawrence	66	982	4,111	2,401	1,128	582	10,580	75	882	446
Utica	10	850	1,223	80	721	422	2,175	92	1,265	217
Willard	29	518	1,344	442	406	496	3,011	55	1,129	269

1   Numbers shown on pages i, ii, iii, are for September for purposes of comparing inpatient with non-inpatient data.
2   Additions include admissions and new clients.
*   Presently eot providing inpatient service.
+   State Hospital Family Care includes Children's, Alcoholic, and Narcotics Services.
$ Hutchings Psychiatric formerly known as Syracuse Psychiatric Hospital.
N.B.   Some facility non-inpatient figures may be low because of late reporting.

TABLE 12.4 NEW YORK STATE DEPARTMENT OF MENTAL HYGIENE MONTHLY STATISTICAL REPORT FOR OCTOBER 1973, STATE HOSPITALS # #

	Res. & Lv. Patients End of Period	Change Since Beg. of Period	Average Daily Resident Patients	% of Res. & Lv. Patients — Years of Age				% of Res. & Lv. Patients — Years from Adm.			Patients Under Treatment**	Percent of Patients Under Treatment — Additions	Releases #	Deaths	Trans. Out
				<16	16-20	21-64	>64	<1	1-2	>2					
Total	39,145+	-355	38,515	<1	2	51	47	15	5	80	42,832	7.8	5.9	0.7	0.5
Binghamton	1,120+	+26	1,086		3	41	56	20	5	75	1,244	12.1	8.3	0.6	0.2
Bronx	648	+2	591		9	73	18	59	9	32	964	33.0	16.6	0.2	0.2
Brooklyn	1,520+	+3	1,452	<1	2	63	34	24	6	70	1,710	11.3	9.4	0.5	0.1
Buffalo	801+	-33	795	<1	1	45	54	17	6	77	953	12.5	12.0	1.8	0.1
Cap. Dist. Psy.	0		0								1	100.0	100.0	0.0	0.0
Central Islip	2,784+	-56	2,777	<1	2	38	60	10	5	85	3,047	6.8	5.6	1.3	1.1
Creedmoor	2,252	-17	2,202		4	59	38	24	8	68	2,470	8.1	6.5	0.6	0.0
Gowanda	1,129	-31	1,126	<1	1	32	67	11	4	84	1,219	4.8	4.1	1.0	2.0
Harlem Valley	2,175+	-89	2,198	<1	1	45	54	6	4	90	2,336	3.1	5.4	0.6	0.4
Hoch Psy.	91	-11	88		8	88	4	87	9	4	185	44.9	42.2	0.0	1.6
Hudson River	2,516+	-34	2,506	<1	1	45	53	9	3	88	2,692	5.3	5.0	0.8	0.1
Hutchings Psy.	69	-6	65		10	78	12	93		7	163	54.0	47.2	0.0	0.0
Kings Park	3,962+	-9	3,919	<1		54	44	7	3	90	4,135	4.0	2.4	0.6	0.8
Man-Dunlap	671+	-25	637		3	67	30	39	10	52	820	15.1	9.3	1.6	3.2
Man-Kirby	610+	+30	554	<1	2	78	20	43	8	50	730	20.5	9.7	0.0	2.1
Man-Meyer	480	-27	451	<1	5	72	22	42	12	46	618	18.0	13.6	0.0	1.9
Marcy	1,773+	-12	1,728	<1	2	47	49	12	6	82	1,867	4.4	3.7	0.5	0.1
Middletown	1,471+	+4	1,462	<1		41	58	12	3	84	1,566	6.3	4.3	0.6	0.3
Mid-Hudson	218	+7	211	<1	10	89	<1	89	11	<1	264	20.1	11.4	0.0	6.1
N.E. Nassau Psy.	121	+4	107	8	26	54	12	78	7	16	174	32.8	22.4	0.6	1.1
N.Y. Psych. Inst.	113	+19	97	4	18	71	8	79	18	4	159	40.9	20.8	0.0	0.0
Pilgrim	6,913+	-66	6,881			53	47	9	4	87	7,193	3.0	2.4	0.7	0.2
Rochester	1,767+	-4	1,694	1	2	50	47	18	6	76	1,933	8.4	6.3	0.8	0.1
Rockland	2,614	-45	2,616		2	58	40	6	2	92	2,737	2.8	3.4	0.7	0.1
South Beach	61	+25	54		8	87	5	95	2	3	114	68.4	34.2	0.0	0.0
St. Lawrence	868	-15	857		3	40	57	15	5	80	961	8.1	8.7	0.5	0.1
Utica	1,257+	-8	1,238	<1		46	53	12	4	84	1,378	8.2	6.0	1.0	0.1
Willard	1,141	+13	1,123	<1		34	65	10	2	88	1,199	5.9	3.8	1.0	0.0

Period of this report is 10/1/73 to 10/31/73.

+ Number of patients in unit exceeds program goal occupancy.
# Releases = Direct discharges + Placements to CC + Placements to EC.
# # Excludes Children, Alcoholic & Narcotics services.
** Res. and Lv. patients at beginning of period plus all additions during period.

TABLE 12.5 NEW YORK STATE DEPARTMENT OF MENTAL HYGIENE MONTHLY STATISTICAL REPORT FOR OCTOBER 1973, STATE HOSPITALS ##

	Res. & Lv. Patients End of Period	Additions to the Unit				Removals from the Unit							Ward Transfers Out #		
		Total	Adm.	Trans. In	Returns	Total	Died	Dir. Disch.	To CC	To EC	To ESC	Trans. Out	Total	Intra Svc.	Inter Svc.
Total	39,145+	3,332	2,423	208	701	3,687	311	2,035	273	234	624	210	4,150	2,391	1,759
Binghamton	1,120+	150	130	2	18	124	7	82	3	18	12	2	68	6	62
Bronx	648	318	210	5	103	316	2	151	4	5	152	2	110	110	0
Brooklyn	1,520+	193	175	4	14	190	9	160	1	0	18	2	118	50	68
Buffalo	801+	119	64	15	40	152	17	58	7	49	20	1	404	228	176
Cap. Dist. Psy.	0	1	1	0	0	1	0	0	0	1	0	0	0	0	0
Central Islip	2,784+	207	165	30	12	263	39	166	3	1	19	35	356	144	212
Creedmoor	2,252	201	161	7	33	218	15	145	16	0	41	1	265	156	109
Gowanda	1,129	59	43	9	7	90	12	45	1	4	4	24	78	18	60
Harlem Valley	2,175+	72	33	8	31	161	15	71	31	25	9	10	198	59	139
Hoch Psy.	91	83	72	5	6	94	15	75	3	0	13	3	0	0	0
Hudson River	2,516+	142	89	2	51	176	21	79	33	22	19	2	272	157	115
Hutchings Psy.	69	88	73	2	13	94	0	73	0	4	17	0	50	50	0
Kings Park	3,962+	164	96	33	35	173	23	62	37	0	16	35	140	138	2
Man-Dunlap	671+	124	80	28	16	149	13	75	1	0	34	26	50	50	0
Man-Kirby	610+	150	116	12	22	120	0	69	2	0	34	15	47	47	0
Man-Meyer	480	111	75	14	22	138	0	84	0	0	42	12	3	3	0
Marcy	1,773+	82	64	1	17	94	9	58	8	3	14	2	255	157	98
Middletown	1,471+	99	77	3	19	95	10	51	3	13	14	4	68	25	43
Mid-Hudson	218	53	52	1	0	46	0	30	0	0	0	16	0	0	0
N.E. Nassau Psy.	121	57	46	3	8	53	1	34	4	1	11	2	4	4	0
N.Y. Psych. Inst.	113	65	48	0	17	46	0	33	0	0	13	0	0	0	0
Pilgrim	6,913+	214	160	13	41	280	53	151	16	7	42	11	766	459	307
Rochester	1,767+	162	118	2	42	166	15	97	18	6	29	1	261	142	119
Rockland	2,614	78	60	5	13	123	19	66	16	11	9	2	137	136	1
South Beach	61	78	70	0	8	53	0	39	0	0	14	0	13	13	0
St. Lawrence	868	78	53	0	25	93	5	37	23	24	3	1	109	29	80
Utica	1,257+	113	48	3	62	121	14	22	36	24	24	1	144	70	74
Willard	1,141	71	44	1	26	58	12	22	7	16	1	0	234	140	94

Period of this report is 10/1/73 to 10/31/73.

+ Number of patients in unit exceeds program goal occupancy.

Excludes transfers to other institutions.

Excludes Children, Alcoholic & Narcotics services.

TABLE 12.6　NEW YORK STATE DEPARTMENT OF MENTAL HYGIENE MONTHLY STATISTICAL REPORT FOR OCTOBER 1973, STATE HOSPITALS #

Facilities	Res. & Lv. Patients	Res. Pat. Change		Admissions		Net Releases		Deaths	
		In Month	In 12 Months	Most Recent 12 Months ##	Previous 12 Months	Most Recent 12 Months	Previous 12 Months	Most Recent 12 Months	Previous 12 Months
Total	39,145	-355	-5,926	27,422##	27,821	27,296	26,339	3,950	4,709
Binghamton	1,120	+ 26	- 149	1,132	1,075	1,008	993	132	148
Bronx	648	+ 2	- 9	2,136	2,207	1,777	1,948	29	34
Brooklyn	1,520	+ 3	- 245	1,480	1,290	1,542	1,252	135	168
Buffalo	801	- 33	- 428	804	873	885	792	188	237
Central Islip	2,784	- 56	- 804	2,209	4,485	2,401	4,394	439	607
Creedmoor	2,252	- 17	- 460	1,862	1,685	2,035	1,809	237	327
Gowanda	1,129	- 31	- 257	518	492	516	434	133	144
Harlem Valley	2,175	- 89	- 636	478	553	856	489	223	246
Hoch Psy.	91	- 11	- 1	913	891	834	799	1	3
Hudson River	2,516	- 34	- 356	1,239	1,321	1,324	1,250	254	288
Hutchings Psy.	69	- 6	+ 35	859	383	788	357	0	1
Kings Park	3,962	- 9	- 366	1,058	756	1,240	916	280	275
Man-Dunlap	671	- 25	- 137	1,267	1,246	1,237	1,164	134	152
Man-Kirby	610	+ 30	- 65	925	856	814	797	9	17
Man-Meyer	480	- 27	- 158	955	836	829	666	8	13
Marcy	1,773	- 12	- 262	745	1,018	769	978	162	218
Middletown	1,471	+ 4	- 188	861	968	765	830	152	176
Mid-Hudson	218	+ 7	+ 10	591	495	394	200	0	0
N.E. Nassau Psy.	121	+ 4	+ 6	670	585	608	565	1	3
Pilgrim	6,913	- 66	- 568	2,372	1,876	2,214	1,735	675	783
Psy. Institute	113	+ 19	+ 20	425	342	409	302	1	2
Rochester	1,767	+ 4	- 86	1,126	853	1,088	899	155	206
Rockland	2,614	- 45	- 509	794	1,046	1,043	1,290	220	278
South Beach	61	+ 25	+ 39	231	10	185	6	0	0
St. Lawrence	868	- 15	- 175	675	631	696	552	124	105
Utica	1,257	- 8	- 93	628	631	597	568	135	136
Willard	1,141	+ 13	- 84	464	417	442	354	123	142

#　Excludes Children's, Alcoholic, and Narcotics Services.
##　Includes 5 Admissions to Capital District Psychiatric Center.

Ad Hoc Reports

The information system provides nonrecurring analyses, tabulations, and reports. Whether for the system of service as a whole or for an individual facility, it is literally impossible to provide for all of the data needs in recurring reports; however, many questions can be answered from the extensive computer files which have been developed to facilitate their use in answering a wide range of questions to meet immediate and changing needs, as well as to provide recurring outputs. In addition, many questions can be answered by assembling data clerically from a number of different, previously produced outputs.

Special requests for data arise from DMH divisions, facilities and offices; local, state, and federal agencies; governmental and university researchers; the press; concerned citizens' groups; students; and so on. The work performed in responding to such requests ranges from quoting a few items of data over the telephone or xeroxing a table to fairly elaborate studies. During July 1973, the most recent month for which overall work load data are available as of this writing, 218 requests from 140 different persons were received by the DMH statistical office.

In addition to varying greatly in scope, content, urgency, and predictability, the procedures used to respond to special requests vary greatly depending on the availability of data, which are stored in a variety of forms, and on the availability of trained staff. The selection of the approach depends on a weighing of alternatives: clerical processing of data previously run for another purpose, use of specially developed generalized "table-making programs" by statistical staff, programming of extract files to enable statisticians to use the available table-making programs, and/or programming directly to produce the data needed.

While the content of ad hoc requests differs from month to month, some insight into the nature of this activity can be obtained from a list of some of the projects which were in process during July 1973:

1. Statements on numbers of persons served and recent trends in services for the mentally ill and mentally retarded were prepared for press releases issued from the governor's office.

2. An analysis of the ethnic composition of employees of Department facilities and units was prepared for the Department's Affirmative Action Committee. Similar but less elaborate data were reported to the federal government, as required.

3. An analysis of length-of-stay patterns and discharge volume during the past 24 months by county of patients' residence was prepared for a number of state hospitals. This was necessary to respond to charges by a group of hospital employees and by the Civil Liberties Union that administrative changes during a specified period had resulted in major reductions in the numbers of patients discharged.

4. Statistics were assembled for the State Department of Health on admissions to state and local facilities with drug-related diagnoses or problems during the period 1966-1972.

5. Alcoholism prevalence was estimated and needs for services were projected for each of the state's 62 counties for 1979 and 1984.

6. Projections of the general population and units of service by auspicis were prepared for each of the state's 13 planning regions for 1979 and 1984, for use in developing a Capital Plan.

7. Listings of residents of the state schools for the retarded by county of residence, showing the name, other identifying data, mental level, and degree of ambulation were prepared for each school to be used to plan, develop, and operate programs to meet the needs of these individuals at the state and local levels.

8. Analyses of services to state and local patients by ethnic group were provided in response to requests by legislators and citizens' groups. Longer-term analyses in this area are being conducted to monitor and identify differential levels of service for the various groups.

9. A wide variety of data on volume of service, waiting lists and costs were assembled for a joint State University and Department project to develop productivity measures for evaluating mental retardation programs.

10. Data on state and local day-care services for the elderly were assembled for the State Office of the Aging.

11. A number of similar statistical tables and/or computer listings of residents of particular counties being served by state or local programs were prepared showing various characteristics, such as age group, type of disability, place of residence within the county, for use by several county mental health departments and Department facilities for program planning, operation, and monitoring.

12. Special tabulations of state school residents with hearing and/or visual handicaps were prepared to support an application for special federal funds for the handicapped.

13. An extensive analysis was conducted to compare the length of stay in state hospitals and the length of stay out of the hospitals for patients leaving. (For the initial report on this continuing study, see Weinstein, DiPasquale and Winsor, 1973).

14. A study was designed and data were assembled to collaborate with the State Health Department in a study of deaths from colon cancer and other causes comparing the data for the general population with those for patients of state institutions. Death rates are being related to characteristics of patients, institution diets, and other variables over a period of years. This study will update and extend an earlier one conducted jointly by the two departments (Katz et al., 1967).

From time to time, a number of requests for ad hoc analyses or reports tend to be similar for various counties, catchment areas, or program groups. When they are, and when widespread need for special data is anticipated, the provision of such data is consolidated to the extent practical. When identified needs are expected to

continue, consideration is given to developing recurring reports to meet these needs. There are practical dangers in developing too many recurring reports, however, since they can lose much of their value as conditions change, and experience has shown that it is difficult to discontinue them.

Printed versus Machine-Readeable Outputs

It was noted earlier that the patient information system produces recurring outputs on magnetic tapes or disks which are, in turn, inputs to other systems such as the Department's billing and cost systems. The data on the tapes or disks are readable only by the computer, although some data are printed so that staff can check and control the various processes.

Some printed outputs are themselves machine-readable. For example, the Mental Retardation Client Survey form (Figure 12.6) and the Patient Progress Note described earlier are initiated on the computer which prints background identifying data, such as the patient's name for staff use, but which also prints machine-readable codes to identify the patient and the facility to the computer when the forms are returned from the facility for processing.

Statistical Tables versus Listings

Table 12.7 is a statistical table summarizing data assembled from the Mental Retardation Client Survey Form (Figure 12.6) for Willowbrook State School, showing the number of residents by degree of toilet training, feeding ability, and ambulation, for each major intelligence level and age group (a second page, not shown here, completes the table for the remaining intelligence levels). Similar tables are issued for each state school and for the other items covered in the periodic review, and comparable data are issued in the form of percentages. Table 12.8 shows one page of a listing which includes similar information on each individual resident. While listings may contain information that can be summarized in the form of statistical aggregates, the purposes of the two types of presentation differ.

Lists of individual patients (or residents) are issued for a variety of management or administrative procedures, such as grouping patients by geographic area of residence or major disability to facilitate the operation of programs of service or to check for errors in reporting. For example, in planning, organizing, and effecting transfers of state school residents into treatment units associated with individual counties, lists similar to Table 12.8 have been prepared showing the residents from the respective counties who were currently in the various wards within each facility. To help prepare for an assessment of the appropriateness of each individual for transfer to particular units, additional data were shown for each individual on the listing. Residents were grouped first by mental (intelligence) level (i.e., profound, severe, moderate, mild, etc.); for each mental level, they were grouped by degree of ambulation; for each degree of ambulation, they were grouped by ward location; and for each ward, names were listed in alphabetical order (on Table 12.8, names are blocked out in order to maintain confidentiality). In addition, the lists show the sex, identifying numbers, dates of admission and birth, county and place of residence (within New York City, for example, the local health area code is shown),

TABLE 12.7   MRRS TABLE NO. 2: TOILET TRNG., EATING, AMBULATION, BY AGE, INTELLIGENCE LEVEL, AND SCHOOL AGE AS OF 10/1/72 (STATE SCH RES/LV, 10/72)

Willowbrook 276	Total	Fully Train	Part Train	Not Train	Inv-Blank	Eating Total	Accep Table	Messy	W/ Fingers	Needs Help	Must Feed	Tube Fed	Inv-Blank	Ambul Total	Walks Frely	Walks W/Dif	Wheel Chair	Non Ambul	Blank
Major Total	4,887	2,280	711	1,607	229	4,887	2,093	1,224	212	142	1,167	5	44	4,887	3,089	735	308	700	55
Under 5	77	2	2	61	12	77	3	5	0	1	64	2	2	77	9	1	5	59	3
5 - 11	1,005	205	126	615	59	1,005	257	213	44	23	451	1	16	1,005	497	103	67	314	24
12 - 15	628	233	110	255	30	628	223	171	30	10	187	0	7	628	386	90	47	100	5
16 - 20	908	442	149	272	45	908	409	226	43	23	203	1	3	908	579	160	64	100	5
21 - 24	629	318	101	173	37	629	282	163	36	17	123	0	8	629	411	119	35	58	6
25 - 34	803	481	148	151	23	803	407	228	40	32	89	1	6	803	594	115	39	46	9
35 - 44	399	269	71	49	10	399	223	119	13	15	29	0	0	399	303	56	28	10	2
45 - 64	368	276	54	26	12	368	244	85	3	16	18	0	2	368	263	76	19	9	1
65 & Up	70	54	10	5	1	70	45	14	3	5	3	0	0	70	47	15	4	4	0
Profound	2,018	458	354	1,100	106	2,018	430	514	141	51	854	4	24	2,018	1,004	328	135	521	30
Under 5	41	1	0	34	6	41	1	0	0	0	37	2	1	41	1	0	1	37	2
5 - 11	541	43	40	423	35	541	64	85	33	9	337	1	12	541	194	55	40	237	15
12 - 15	312	55	62	178	17	312	55	90	19	7	137	0	4	312	160	45	28	75	4
16 - 20	440	123	95	204	18	440	111	121	36	10	159	1	2	440	224	100	32	80	4
21 - 24	259	75	49	117	18	259	68	73	17	8	89	0	4	259	152	51	7	45	4
25 - 34	238	73	63	96	6	238	58	84	22	10	63	0	1	238	148	40	13	36	1
35 - 44	108	42	32	30	4	108	34	40	9	4	21	0	0	108	73	18	11	6	0
45 - 64	68	38	13	15	2	68	32	20	3	3	10	0	0	68	47	14	3	4	0
65 & Up	11	8	0	3	0	11	7	1	2	0	1	0	0	11	5	5	0	1	0
Severe	1,518	807	269	369	73	1,518	782	368	58	55	244	1	10	1,518	1,082	187	95	141	13
Under 5	29	0	2	22	5	29	0	3	0	0	25	0	1	29	4	1	3	20	1
5 - 11	362	108	77	158	19	362	140	101	10	8	100	0	3	362	237	40	12	66	7
12 - 15	211	104	32	66	9	211	93	57	10	2	46	0	3	211	152	27	11	20	1
16 - 20	248	157	39	41	11	248	146	59	7	7	29	0	0	248	192	26	15	14	1
21 - 24	183	109	30	33	11	183	107	38	15	6	17	0	0	183	130	30	16	7	0
25 - 34	272	173	53	35	11	272	156	66	14	16	17	1	2	272	210	34	16	9	3
35 - 44	102	75	15	9	3	102	67	22	2	7	4	0	0	102	80	9	11	2	0
45 - 64	94	69	16	5	4	94	65	16	0	7	5	0	1	94	65	18	9	2	0
65 & Up	17	12	5	0	0	17	8	6	0	2	1	0	0	17	12	2	2	1	0
Moderate	567	442	52	55	18	567	404	111	3	21	26	0	2	567	414	82	45	23	3
Under 5	5	1	0	4	0	5	2	3	0	0	0	0	0	5	3	1	1	0	0
5 - 11	66	37	7	21	1	66	31	21	1	4	9	0	0	66	47	6	5	7	1
12 - 15	70	51	11	7	1	70	48	17	0	3	2	0	0	70	49	12	5	4	0
16 - 20	102	81	4	10	7	102	77	17	1	3	4	0	0	102	76	12	12	2	0
21 - 24	73	57	6	7	3	73	47	11	1	6	7	0	1	73	44	17	9	3	0
25 - 34	109	94	10	3	2	109	85	19	0	2	2	0	1	109	88	11	9	1	0
35 - 44	65	54	8	2	1	65	54	9	0	1	1	0	0	65	51	9	2	2	1
45 - 64	69	60	5	1	3	69	54	12	0	2	1	0	0	69	50	14	2	2	1
65 & Up	8	7	1	0	0	8	6	2	0	0	0	0	0	8	6	0	0	2	0
Mild	350	298	26	18	8	350	257	76	2	7	5	0	3	350	273	52	16	4	5
Under 5	0	0	0	0	0	0	0	0	0	0	0	0	0	0	0	0	0	0	0
5 - 11	22	14	0	7	1	22	17	0	0	0	1	0	0	22	14	2	5	0	0
12 - 15	24	19	1	3	1	24	20	3	0	0	1	0	0	24	17	5	2	0	0

TABLE 12.8 RICHMOND COUNTY PERSONS RESIDENT IN OR ON LEAVE FROM STATE SCHOOL NO. 276, WILLOWBROOK

Mental Level	Ambulation	Ward Number	Name of Patient	Sex	ID. No.	Consec Number	Date of Admisn.	Date of Birth	Residence	IQ
Severe	Walks Freely	261		Male	1170790	015167	4/13/71	5/65	43 04000	28
Severe	Walks Freely	284		Female	1170899	015292	9/22/71	11/64	43 01000	27
Severe	Walks Freely	322		Female	0865598	006336	5/1/56	8/35	43 00000	22
Severe	Walks Freely	763		Male	0872141	009131	10/26/59	10/55	43 01000	34
Severe	Walks Freely	772		Male	1114636	014642	3/20/69	12/62	43 09100	28
Severe	Walks Freely	783		Male	1024547	014119	4/6/67	1/65	43 05000	30
Severe	Walks Freely	784		Male	1114529	014523	12/5/68	8/66	43 09100	34
Moderate	Non-Ambulatory	154		Female	0876832	010890	2/1/62	6/59	43 04000	41
Moderate	Wheel Chair	111		Female	0815751	001755	7/27/34	1/17	43 00000	46
Moderate	Walks With Diff.	093		Male	0836148	005375	1/16/55	4/34	43 00000	37
*Moderate	Walks With Diff.	273		Female	0874399	010203	3/3/61	7/55	43 03000	34
Moderate	Walks With Diff.	322		Female	0862205	005314	3/8/55	12/12	43 00000	49
Moderate	Walks With Diff.	771		Male	1127052	015009	8/10/70	4/60	43 09000	36
Moderate	Walks Freely	052		Male	0872105	009089	10/8/59	9/56	43 09100	42
Moderate	Walks Freely	052		Male	1119330	015059	10/14/70	8/59	43 03000	50
Moderate	Walks Freely	054		Male	0893023	013561	2/4/65	9/52	43 03000	51
Moderate	Walks Freely	054		Male	1114619	015373	3/11/69	8/57	43 07000	40
Moderate	Walks Freely	092		Male	0868915	007984	7/25/58	7/43	43 07000	49
Moderate	Walks Freely	092		Male	0859380	003813	5/14/53	8/14	43 00000	47
Moderate	Walks Freely	092		Male	0865641	006385	5/21/56	8/12	43 00000	48
*Moderate	Walks Freely	092		Male	1066239	014267	11/9/67	4/51	43 02000	62
Moderate	Walks Freely	092		Male	0853224	001363	8/8/50	7/34	43 00000	38
Moderate	Walks Freely	093		Male	0866175	007671	1/21/58	12/41	43 00000	41
*Moderate	Walks Freely	094		Female	0854659	002646	5/28/51	11/42	43 00000	37
Moderate	Walks Freely	112		Female	0842082	007034	5/19/44	9/34	43 00000	09
Moderate	Walks Freely	191		Male	1066233	014258	10/23/67	2/32	43 03000	42
Moderate	Walks Freely	193		Male	0847199	009717	7/7/60	5/33	43 04000	37
Moderate	Walks Freely	202		Male	0820159	015207	10/22/33	11/24	43 00000	36

* Notice disagreement in this case between mental level reported by the school and IQ reported by the school.

and the IQ. Where the mental level and the IQ reported are inconsistent, the computer indicates this by an asterisk and a footnote (Table 12.8).

For the purposes of overall program planning or monitoring, it is ordinarily more convenient and, for many applications, necessary to use the aggregate statistics. Listings can include counts of, say, the numbers of patients in the respective groupings, but statistical tables provide the advantages of having the data assembled and arranged in a convenient and manageable form for comparing groupings, cross-classifying variables, including derived measures, such as percentages and rates, and summarizing alternative groupings or arrangements.

Numerical versus Verbal Reports

The output examples shown so far include illustrations of reports produced in both numerical and alphabetic form. The distinction being highlighted here is between reports which are, for the most part, aggregates for groups of subjects such as patients or staff and those which are verbal summaries relating to individual subjects, such as individual patient medical record notes.

Figure 12.9 shows a "patient history note" for an individual patient based on the data reported on his admission and termination forms. In contrast, Figures 12.10 and 12.11 show comparable data in the aggregate for all patients admitted to and terminated from "unrestricted clinics" (that is, outpatient clinics which do not limit service to specialized groups such as children or alcoholics) in New York City during 1972.

Tables versus Graphs

In general, statistical outputs are more easily produced in tabular form, but many analyses and comparisons can be made more effectively by means of graphic or visual representations. For example, Table 12.9 compares exit rates and reentry rates [6] for each New York State hospital for the 1971 fiscal year.[7] One check as to whether reentry rates are related to exit rates was made by a standard scatter chart which shows that, except for three hospitals (represented by the three X's toward the upper right side of the graph), there was no appreciable relationship between the two sets of rates. While this type of graph gives the clearest picture of the overall relationship, it does not provide a convenient reference to particular hospitals.

Figure 12.13 presents an alternative representation which has the advantage of showing the ordinal position or "ranking" of the individual hospitals with respect to one of the two variables, in this case the exit rates, while providing a general indication of the relationship between the exit and reentry rates. This form of graphic presentation is a compromise which sacrifices some clarity in measuring the overall relationship between the exit and reentry rates in order to show the relative position of the individual hospitals. Such a compromise is sometimes advisable, particularly when the number of units covered is too large to permit identifying each unit clearly. When the number of units to be identified is small enough, they can be identified on the "scatter chart" itself, as was done with the major

(text continues on p. 436)

****** PERSONAL DATA ******

	MALE
JOHN DOE	U. S. CITIZEN
ENVIRONMENT	CITY / VILLAGE
DATE OF BIRTH	01/23/17
	NEGRO
	PROTESTANT
	MARRIED
	COMPLETED EIGHTH GRADE
WEEKLY FAMILY INCOME (NET)	$50 – $99
	TWO INDIVIDUALS ON INCOME
HOUSEHOLD COMPOSITION	SPOUSE

****** ADMISSION DATA ******

DATE OF ADMISSION	06/24/70
CONSECUTIVE NUMBER	0671372
ADMITTED TO	ROOSEVELT HOSP CMHC–ALCOH DRUG ABUSE
REFERRED BY	UNSPECIFIED UNIT OF GENERAL HOSPITAL
PRIOR PSYCHIATRIC TREATMENT	NONE
TIME SINCE LAST SERVICE	NO PRIOR SERVICE
LAST TREATMENT FACILITY	NONE
PROBLEM APPRAISAL	SLEEP PROBLEMS
	EATING PROBLEMS
	SOC PERF DISTURB WITH JOB
	OBSESSIONS, COMPULSIONS
	ALCOHOL ABUSE
PROBLEM DURATION	OVER TWO YEARS
OVERALL SEVERITY OF ILLNESS	SEVERE

PROVISIONAL DIAGNOSIS
ALCOHOL ADDICTION

****** TERMINATION DATA ******

DATE OF TERMINATION	11/01/73
RECEIVED	DIAGNOSIS OR EVALUATION ONLY
NUMBER OF VISITS	
TO OUTPATIENT CLINIC	NONE
TO DAY HOSPITAL	THREE
TO DAY TRAINING CENTER	TWO
TO REHABILITATION CENTER	NONE
SERVICE AT OTHER LOCATIONS	NONE
OTHER	NONE
DISPOSITION OF CASE	
PATIENT WITHDREW	UNSPECIFIED REASONS

FIGURE 12.9   Patient history note, Roosevelt Hospital, case number 3083551.

TOTAL, UNRESTRICTED CLINICS NYC

ADMISSION STATISTICS FROM 01/01/72 TO 12/31/72 AS OF 08/09/73

	NUMBER	%
ADMISSNS	41502	100
MALE	19149	46
FEMALE	22037	53
UNDER 12	6270	15
12-15	3907	9
16-20	3910	9
21-64	24352	59
65+	2996	7
VETERAN	1089	3
EMERGNCY	3685	9
WHITE	22297	54
NEGRO	7468	18
P/RICAN	6015	14
A/INDIAN	19	*
ORIENTAL	217	1
OTHER	459	1
UNK, BLNK	5027	12
PROTSTNT	5820	14
R/CATH	13943	34
JEWISH	8051	19
OTHER	1221	3
NONE	998	2
UNK, BLNK	11469	28
NEV-MAR	19027	46
MARRIED	9942	24
REMARRD	307	1
DIV-ANN	1935	5
SEPARTD	3435	8
WIDOWED	1569	4
UNK, BLNK	5287	13
EDUCATION		
NONE	1007	2
UNGRADED	693	2
1-3	2746	7
4	1019	2
5	936	2
6	1106	3
7	1074	3
8	1807	4
9	1659	4
10	2043	5
11	1957	4
12	5911	14
VOC-BUS	547	1
COLL-1	1154	3
2	1251	3
3	561	1
4	1613	4
GRAD SCH	926	2
UNK, BLNK	13593	33

	NUMBER	%
REFERRED BY		
SELF	9819	24
FAM,FRND	7493	18
CLERGY	353	1
SCHOOL	5105	12
POLICE	661	2
PVT PSYC	633	2
OTHER PHYS	2459	6
CENTER	755	2
MENT HOS	1045	3
GENH PSY	1215	3
GENH OTH	4234	10
NUR HOME	22	*
PSY CLIN	683	2
OTH FAC	371	1
IN RETAR	12	*
OTH RETD	40	*
COURT	395	1
PH WELF	829	2
DVR	231	1
VOL AGCY	692	2
OTHER	1749	4
UNK, BLNK	2700	7
TIME SNCE LAST SVC		
0 PR SVC	17358	42
SAME DAY	416	1
1-7 DAYS	1661	4
8-30 D.	2086	5
1-5 MOS	2200	5
6-11 MOS	2127	5
1 YR +	5106	12
LAST SVC	–	
INPATNT	2838	7
OTHER	6623	16
WEEKLY INCOME		
WELFARE	8323	20
UNDER 50	1573	4
50-99	2892	7
100-149	4066	10
150-199	2764	7
200-299	2033	5
300+	926	2
UNK, BLNK	18925	46
HOUSEHOLD COMP		
ALONE	5365	13
SPOUSE	9677	23
PARENTS	14436	35
CHILDREN	10315	25
SIBLINGS	8822	21
OTH-REL	1896	5
OTHERS	2062	5
INSTUTN	166	*
UNK,BLNK	4776	12

	NUMBER	%
PRIOR SERVICE		
NONE	15635	38
UNK,BLNK	10233	25
INPATIENT		
THIS FAC	1442	3
MENT HOS	3683	9
CENTER	412	1
GEN HOS	1592	4
VA HOS	210	1
IN RETAR	69	*
OTHER	300	1
ALL OTHER		
THIS FAC	2923	7
CENTER	1439	3
NUR HOME	14	*
R TR CTR	155	*
PART HOS	197	*
PSY CLIN	2424	6
OTH PSY	696	2
PVT PSYC	2814	7
OTH THER	810	2
RETD FAC	133	*
SCHL SPC	444	1
HOST H/W	62	*
PENAL	121	*
OTHER	1795	4
DIAG IMPRESSION		
RETARDED	770	2
SENIUM	136	*
ALCOHOL-		
PSYCHOS	76	*
OTH OBS	18	*
OTH ALC	513	1
DRUGS-		
PSYCHOS	32	*
OTH OBS	1 19	*
OTHER	863	2
OTH OBS-		
PSYCHOS	139	*
NONPSY	240	1
SCHIZ	3895	9
AFFECTIV	465	1
OTH PSY	384	1
NEUROSES	5067	12
PERSONTY	2750	7
PSY-PHYS	409	1
TRAN-SIT	3227	8
BEHAVIOR	884	2
MALADJUS	1029	2
NO MENT	596	1
UNDIAG	10711	26
PHYSICAL	5	*

	NUMBER	%
PROBLEM APPRAISAL		
PHYSICAL		
SLEEP	8597	21
EATING	4356	10
WET/SOIL	744	2
CONVUL	527	1
SPEECH	1361	3
OTH PHYS	4614	1
INTELLECTUAL		
ADQUAT	2239	5
SOCIAL RELATIONS		
CHILDREN	4402	11
SPOUSE	7547	18
OTH FAM	9460	23
OTHERS	9719	23
SOC PERFORMANCE		
JOB	6047	15
SCHOOL	8016	19
HOUSKPNG	2589	6
OTH SIGNS/SYMP		
SUIC THT	3690	9
SUIC ACT	1912	5
ANX FEAR	13902	33
OBSESSN	2473	6
HYPOCHON	3521	8
S WITHDR	6853	17
DEPEND	4651	11
GRANDIOS	806	2
SUSPICN	3740	9
DELUSNS	1948	5
HALLUCNS	1973	5
ANGR/BEL	6474	16
ASSAULTV	1651	4
ALCOHOL	2063	5
SEXUAL	3227	8
DRUGS	2909	7
ANTISOCL	1767	4
AG HYPAC	3936	9
DISORIEN	1859	4
INCOHERE	995	2
SLOWED	2913	7
INAP A&B	3504	8
ROUTINE	4609	11
BLANK	4785	12
SEVERITY		
NOT ILL	1047	3
SLIGHT	2090	5
MILD	7645	18
MODERATE	17427	42
SEVERE	4973	12

* LESS THAN .5 %

NEW YORK STATE
DEPT. OF MENTAL HYGIENE

NOTE: SUMS OF INDIVIDUAL ITEMS MAY NOT EQUAL TOTALS DUE TO UNREPORTED AND/OR MULTIPLE ENTRY ITEMS.

FIGURE 12.10 Aggregate patient history data from New York City unrestricted clinics, 1972.

TOTAL, UNRESTRICTED CLINICS NYC

TERMINATION STATISTICS   FROM 01/01/72 TO 12/31/72   AS OF 08/09/73

	NUMBER	%
TERMNTNS	27949	100
MALE	12891	46
FEMALE	14900	53
UNDER 12	3446	12
12-15	2528	9
16;20	3066	11
21-64	17090	61
65+	1780	6
TYPE OF SERVICE		
INTAKE	4328	15
EVALUATN	5517	20
INDIV	12512	45
FAM GRP	2563	9
GROUP	2391	9
DRUG	3682	13
REHABIL	456	2
ED, TNG	329	1
ECT	201	1
COLLAT	1120	4
OTHER	1013	4
BLANK	588	2
NUMBER OF VISITS TO FACILITY/UNIT		
MEDIAN	3	
0	4264	15
1	5124	18
2	2857	10
3	1789	6
4	1428	5
5-9	3599	13
10-24	3767	13
25-49	1917	7
50-99	1097	4
100+	460	2
OTHER LOCATIONS		
0	—	
1	2456	9
2	642	2
3	374	1
4	309	1
5+	1232	4
TIME, 1ST INTERV TO 1ST TREAT/SVC		
NO TRTMT	5531	20
NO TIME	8566	31
1 WEEK	4130	15
2-4 WKS	5022	18
2-3 MOS	1279	5
4 MOS +	998	4

	NUMBER	%
TIME SINCE ADMIS		
MEDIAN	203 DAYS	
MEAN	306 DAYS	
SAME DAY	991	4
1 6 DAYS	2158	8
7-13 D	1105	4
14-20 D	1318	5
21-27 D	504	2
1 MONTH	2146	8
2 MOS	1702	6
3-5 MOS	3354	12
6-11 MOS	6975	25
1 YEAR	4786	17
2 YEARS	1769	6
3-4 YRS	848	3
5-9 YRS	237	1
10 YRS +	56	*
TIME, LAST VISIT TO TERMINATION		
NO TIME	4096	15
1 WEEK	2015	7
2-4 WKS	5451	20
2-3 MOS	4468	16
4 MOS +	8943	32
PRIMARY DIAGNOSIS		
RETARDED	741	3
SENIUM	141	1
ALCOHOL-		
PSYCHOS	67	*
OTH OBS	13	*
OTH ALC	361	1
DRUGS-		
PSYCHOS	15	*
OTH OBS	15	*
OTHER	751	3
OTH OBS-		
PSYCHOS	131	*
NONPSY	269	1
SCHIZ	3315	12
AFFECTIV	351	1
OTH PSY	346	1
NEUROSES	4483	16
PERSONTY	3162	11
PSY-PHYS	428	2
TRAN SIT	3138	11
BEHAVIOR	976	3
MALADJUS	1039	4
NO MENT	534	2
UNDIAG	4227	15
PHYSICAL	3	*

	NUMBER	%
MENTAL LEV -TESTED		
RETARDED		
PROFOUND	22	*
SEVERE	65	*
MODERATE	105	*
MILD	230	1
NOT RETARDED		
BORDERLN	685	2
AVERAGE	1325	5
BRIGHT	324	1
SUPERIOR	194	1
MENT LEV -IMPRESSN		
PROF-SEV	64	*
MOD-MILD	774	3
AVERAGE	14463	52
ABOVE AV	2365	8
SECNDARY DIABNOSIS		
RETARDED	72	*
SENIUM	8	*
ALCOHOL-		
PSYCHOS	2	*
OTH OBS	3	*
OTH ALC	62	*
DRUGS-		
PSYCHOS	1	*
OTH OBS	1	*
OTHER	95	*
OTH OBS		
PSYCHOS	18	*
NONPSY	25	*
SCHIZ	129	*
AFFECTIV	42	*
OTH PSY	68	*
NEUROSES	416	1
PERSONTY	376	1
PSY-PHYS	73	*
TRAN SIT	123	*
BEHAVIOR	48	*
MALADJUS	92	*
NO MENT	15	*
UNDIAG	90	*
PHYSICAL	—	

	NUMBER	%
DISPOSITION		
WITHDREW		
MOVE-ILL	1162	4
DIED	166	1
OTHER	6368	23
UNKNOWN	6331	23
NO REFERRAL		
NO NEED	3265	12
UNAVAIL	444	2
UNRESPON	2450	9
REFERRED TO		
MENT HOS	463	2
CENTER	624	2
GENH PSY	948	3
GENH OTH	368	1
V A HOSP	34	*
IN RETAR	30	*
OTH RETD	59	*
HOST H/W	12	*
NUR HOME	57	*
R TR CTR	124	*
DAY HOSP	38	*
NITE HOS	3	*
PSY CLIN	722	3
TRNG CTR	28	*
SHEL W/S	25	*
VOC TRNG	81	*
PVT PSYC	589	2
OTH PHYS	149	1
SCHL SPC	280	1
COURT	35	*
PH/WELF	74	*
VOL AGCY	322	1
CLERGY	10	*
OTHER	963	3
CONDITN LAST VISIT		
IMPROVED	8771	31
UNCHANGD	10441	37
WORSE	485	2
UNDETERM	3449	12
RESPNSIBLE FOR FEE		
SELF, FAM	11305	40
OTH RELA	110	*
COURT	16	*
MEDICAID	4830	17
OTH WELF	390	1
MEDICARE	220	1
INSUR	1065	4
OTHER	362	1
NO FEE	3507	13
BLANK	5720	20

* LESS THAN .5%
NOTE: SUMS OF INDIVIDUAL ITEMS
NOTE: SUMS OF INDIVIDUAL ITEMS MAY NOT EQUAL TOTALS DUE TO UNREPORTED AND/OR MULTIPLE ENTRY ITEMS.

NEW YORK STATE
DEPT. OF MENTAL HYGIENE

FIGURE 12.11　Aggregate patient history data for New York City unrestricted clinics, 1972.

TABLE 12.9 EXIT RATES[a] AND REENTRY RATES[b] NEW YORK STATE HOSPITALS
AND CHILDREN'S HOSPITALS, YEAR ENDED MARCH 31, 1971

Hospital	Number of Additions	Exit Rate	Number of Removals	Reentry Rate
TOTAL	41,531	55.9	42,308	27.7
Binghamton	1,487	63.9	1,434	20.3
Bronx	2,817	66.7	2,966	28.9
Brooklyn	1,915	49.2	2,044	26.2
Buffalo	2,078	59.6	2,058	25.6
Central Islip	5,158	58.5	4,923	35.0
Creedmoor	2,805	53.0	3,209	23.2
Gowanda	619	38.1	606	19.5
Harlem Valley	888	40.0	786	24.4
Hoch Psych.	852	81.6	906	36.0
Hudson River	1,742	60.7	1,684	29.3
Kings Park	1,222	38.0	1,395	27.0
Manhattan-Dunlap	556	43.5	734	21.5
Manhattan-Kirby	643	41.7	666	26.1
Manhattan-Meyer	994	32.4	1,076	24.4
Manhattan-Narcotics	771	68.5	766	4.8
Marcy	1,631	42.9	1,519	25.1
Middletown	1,600	55.8	1,558	22.0
N.E. Nassau	424	58.7	502	30.9
Pilgrim	3,069	43.8	2,973	33.0
N.Y. Psychiatric Institute	626	61.3	613	23.5
Rochester	2,158	60.6	2,225	29.0
Rockland	1,892	42.8	1,937	25.6
St. Lawrence	1,388	74.3	1,295	28.2
Suffolk Psychiatric	1,898	86.2	2,075	37.2
Syracuse Psychiatric	375	91.2	426	35.7
Utica	872	57.1	898	23.8
Willard	403	56.1	384	22.9
Bronx Children's Hosp.	24	0	7	0
Queens Children's Hosp.	372	25.0	384	23.7
Rockland Children's Hosp.	93	20.4	130	19.1
Sagamore Children's Hosp.	138	10.9	107	27.1
W. Seneca Children's Hosp.	21	23.8	22	13.6

a. Percent of hospital additions (admissions plus returns from convalescent care) discharged (excluding deaths) within two months.
b. Percent of discharges (direct discharges plus placements on convalescent care) who return to a state hospital within six months.

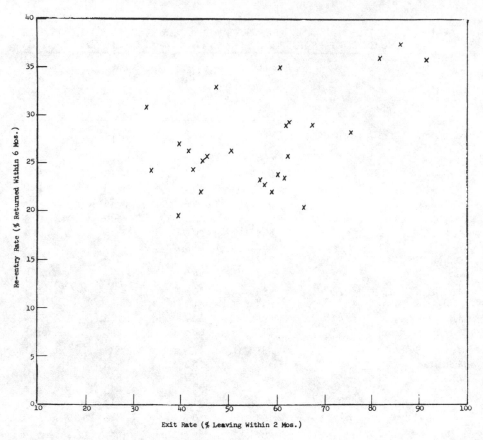

FIGURE 12.12 Scatter chart showing reentry rates versus exit rates by hospital for the year ended March 31, 1971.

diagnostic groupings shown in Figure 12.14. Here the number of X's is small enough so that the diagnostic terms on the chart do not obscure the general relationship.

Effective graphic analysis, although done manually in most settings, can be computer produced. In addition to plotting and graph drawing devices, the computer is often used to produce bar-type graphs such as those shown in Figures 12.15 and 12.16 which were drawn from the UCLA Biomedical series (Sperry Univac, 1973).[8]

OUTLINE OF STAFF ACTIVITY AND COST SYSTEMS

In evaluating (as well as in planning and operating) treatment programs and the system of service of which they are a part, it is necessary to know not only what was done for whom and what was its outcome, but also who did it and how much it cost. In order to reflect staffing and costs, the patient information system is

LENGTH OF STAY IN AND OUT OF HOSPITALS, BY HOSPITAL
FISCAL YEAR 1971

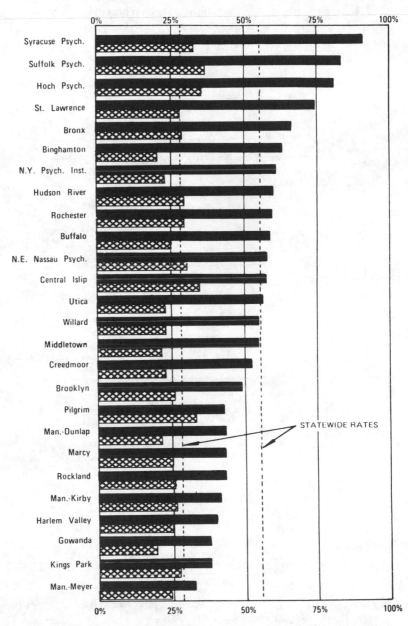

FIGURE 12.13   Bar graph comparing length of stay in and out of hospitals, by hospital, for fiscal year 1971.

augmented by other systems which provide data on staff activity in identified "service groups" (i.e., cost centers, in cost accounting terminology). These service groups reflect both direct services to patients (such as inpatient, outpatient, day care, direct service at other locations, sheltered living, client education, and sheltered workshops) and indirect services (such as general education and consultation, staff training, research, and administration). The system allocates staff time, by discipline, to the various service groups and distributes staff costs and other costs to the respective groups. Outputs relate staffing and cost data for the various groups, by facility unit and local geographic area, to comparable data on services provided from the patient information system.

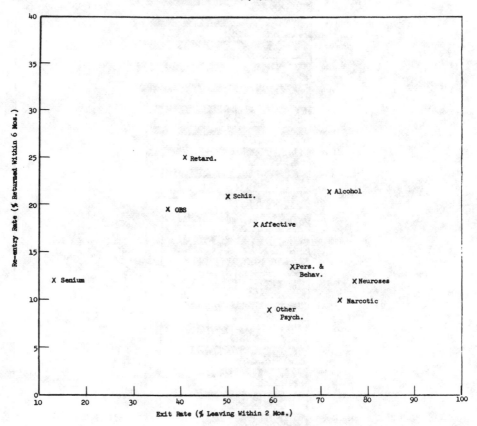

FIGURE 12.14   Scatter chart showing reentry versus exit rates, by psychiatric diagnosis, for the year ended March 31, 1971.

Data on staff activity in local facilities is to be obtained by means of a worksheet form, Figure 12.17, which will be completed by each staff member to cover one week's activity each quarter. The data from the worksheet forms will be aggregated to obtain totals for each service group for each major discipline. Using the

UPPER ENDPOINT		CELL FREQ	PCT	CUMM FREQ	PCT
	5 10 15 20 25				
	+ +				
149	+	0	0.0	0	0.0
	—				
174	—	0	0.0	0	0.0
	+ X				
199	+ X	1	1.0	1	1.0
	—XX				
224	—XX	2	2.0	3	3.0
	+ XXXXXXX				
249	+ XXXXXXX	7	7.0	10	10.0
	—XXXXXXXXXXXXXXXXXXXXXXXXX				
274	—XXXXXXXXXXXXXXXXXXXXXXXXX	25	25.0	35	35.0
	+ XXXXXXXXXXXX				
299	+ XXXXXXXXXXXX X	13	13.0	48	48.0
	—XXXXXXXXXXXXXXXX				
324	—XXXXXXXXXXXXXXXX	16	16.0	64	64.0
	+XXXXXXXXXXXXXXX				
349	+ XXXXXXXXXXXXXXX X	15	15.0	79	79.0
	—XXXXXXXXXX				
374	—XXXXXXXXXX	10	10.0	89	89.0
	+ XXXXXXX				
399	+ XXXXXXX	7	7.0	96	96.0
	—X				
424	—X	1	1.0	97	97.0
	+ X				
449	+ X	1	1.0	97	97.0
	—X				
474	—X	1	1.0	99	99.0
	+				
499	+	0	0.0	99	99.0
	—X				
	—X	1	1.0	100	100.0
	5 10 15 20 25				

VARIABLE   7 CHOL 52

GROUP   1 A

```
N            100.0000
MEAN         308.7300
VARIANCE     3109.4038
ST. DEV.     55.7620
```

FIGURE 12.15 Computer-produced graph, UCLA Biomedical Series (Sperry Univac, 1973).

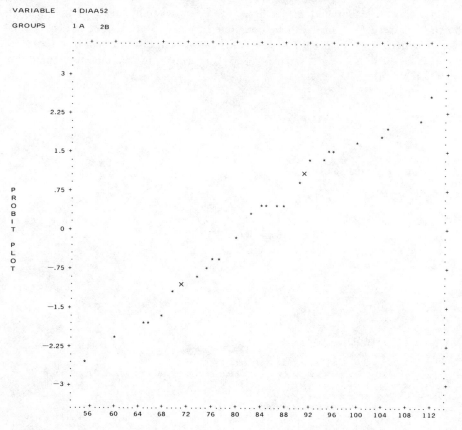

FIGURE 12.16   Computer-produced graph, UCLA Biomedical Series (Sperry Univac, 1973).

percentages of time devoted to the various service groups, expenditures will be allocated to the respective groups. By relating costs of operating each service group to the volume of services provided in that group, costs per unit of service are derived. Cost data by facility and unit, service group and geographic area are developed separately for programs for the mentally ill, the developmentally disabled, and those dealing with alcohol problems. Figure 12.17 is a simplified version of a form used for the past two years to allocate staff time for mental health centers in New York State. The new form and the cost allocations have been piloted in 20 facilities with favorable results.

The Department's cost system for state-operated facilities is considerably more elaborate than that outlined above for locally operated facilities. While the systems are compatible, the state system (which was designed by Price Waterhouse and Department staff) has a far greater number of cost centers than the dozen service groups identified for local facilities. In addition, the state system allocates each employee's actual salary payments to the individual cost centers based on previously reported allocations of time. Also, each type of administrative and overhead

403 DMH (8/73) (Pilot Study)

STAFF ACTIVITY SURVEY

	WEEK BEGINNING:	MONTH	DAY	YEAR

A) FACILITY _____   CODE

　　NAME OF STAFF MEMBER _____   I. D. NO.

　　DISCIPLINE _____   CODE

DISCIPLINE CODES

		B) PAYROLL: (CHECK ONE)	STATE	[1]

01	PSYCHIATRIST	08	PHYSICAL THERAPIST
02	PEDIATRICIAN	09	SPEECH THERAPIST
03	OTHER PHYSICIAN	10	OCCUPATIONAL
04	PSYCHOLOGIST		THERAPIST
05	SOCIAL WORKER	11	TEACHER
06	REGISTERED NURSE	12	OTHER DIRECT SERVICES
07	REHAB. COUNSELOR		PROFESSIONAL
		13	MENTAL HYGIENE AIDE

LOCAL [2]

SHARED [3] - [ ] % LOCAL SHARE

C) TYPE OF STAFF:　　REGULAR STAFF [1]
　　(CHECK ONE)

　　　　TRAINEE, RESIDENT, OR INTERN [2]

　　　　REGULARLY SCHEDULED VOLUNTEER [3]

E) SERVICE GROUP	DAY OF THE WEEK (ENTER HOURS WORKED BY SERVICE GROUP)							
	MON	TUES	WED	THUR	FRI	SAT	SUN	TOTAL
1) DIRECT SERVICE								
INPATIENT								
OUTPATIENT CLINIC								
DAY CARE								
SHELTERED LIVING								
CLIENT EDUCATION								
SHELTERED WORKSHOP								
DIRECT SERVICE AT OTHER LOCATION								
2) OTHER SERVICES								
CONSULTATION AND EDUCATION								
RESEARCH								
STAFF TRAINING								
ADMINISTRATION								
3) AUTHORIZED LEAVE								
TOTALS								

FIGURE 12.17　Staff Activity Survey form.

cost is distributed to the various cost centers according to a rationale related to that type of cost. For example, heating costs are allocated based on the size of the areas being heated, and food costs are allocated based on the number of meals served. Initially, the system for local facilities will distribute all administrative and overhead costs based on the distribution of staff time.

The system which will be required for local facilities is less elaborate than that which is being operated for state facilities. The latter system has a wide range of uses from the establishment of billing rates to planning and evaluation. The local system must cut across the differing accounting systems, auspices, and affiliations which exist for some 1,000 public and private reporting units in 62 counties in such

a way as to permit individual facilities to produce the cost distributions in the form of summary reports without sending the various worksheet documents to Albany for processing.[9]

In addition to the data on staffing which are assembled as part of the cost systems, staffing data are assembled monthly on summary statistical reports which show the number of billed and vacant positions in each title at each Department facility. These data are summarized and issued as part of the Department's Monthly Statistical Report, as shown in Table 12.10 for the state hospitals. (Similar pages are issued for the other state facilities.)

A central state personnel information system, which has been in development for several years is in its final "debugging" stages. This system, which will cover all state departments, will tap the standard administrative personnel forms and assemble central computer records for each employee and position.

DEVELOPMENT OF THE INFORMATION SYSTEM

The information system has its roots in the medical records systems which have been maintained in one form or another in treatment facilities for centuries and in statistical reports which have been assembled for medical records and other sources at least since the early nineteenth century.

From 1843, when the first New York State mental hospital was opened in Utica, until 1889, the state mental hospitals were independent organizations. Each hospital maintained its own medical record system and published statistics reflecting its operations in separate annual reports. In 1889, the state hospitals were brought together under a three-member State Commission in Lunacy. In its first annual report for the year 1889, the Commission published an impressive statistical summary of the operations of the then existing seven state hospitals and included trend data covering the period from 1843 to 1889.

In 1911, the Commission appointed its first full-time director of statistics, Dr. Horatio Pollock, who centralized the statistical reporting system in Albany. In addition to summary statistical reports from each hospital, reports on individual patients were initiated on cards which were hand-sorted and tabulated.

In 1944, Dr. Pollack was followed by Dr. Benjamin Malzberg, who achieved internation renown as a pioneer in the development of extensive statistical tabulations and analyses of the characteristics of the hospitalized mentally ill in New York State. Among his many contributions, Dr. Malzberg, continuing the work he began with Dr. Pollock, led the way in the application of life table techniques (including cohort analyses) to mental hospitalization, and he introduced punch card processing to the Department. Beginning in 1943, punch cards were maintained for each patient on the books, admission, discharge, death, and transfer, for all mental institutions operated or licensed by the Department.

Beginning in 1954, Robert Patton greatly expanded the statistical and punch card systems on patient activity for Department-operated and licensed institutions, and he added systems on outpatient clinics and other community services. Mr. Patton introduced sophisticated uses of patient-related statistics in administrative decision-making and in long-range planning.

In 1960, a digital computer was used by the Department for the first time when the cohort studies were processed on an IBM 650 at Rensselaer Polytechnic Institute in Troy. In 1964, the separate patient billing and statistical systems were combined into a far more efficient single patient information system. In 1964 after conducting some analyses and testing of the new system on a computer (IBM 1401) at the State Department of Motor Vehicles, the Department of Mental Hygiene became one of the first users of the central computer installation at the State Office of General Services.

As part of a major reorganization of the Department of Mental Hygiene early in 1966, the Director of Statistics and Data Processing became a member of the Commissioner's Cabinet. At the time, steps were taken toward combining the statistical and medical records systems, including establishment of much needed positions for Medical Record Librarians and the development of the automated Patient Progress Note.

Beginning in 1966, basic forms for reporting admissions and terminations were designed. This work was expedited considerably by a five-year $6,500,000 grant from the National Institute of Mental Health for the development of the "Multi-State Information System for Psychiatric Patients (MSIS)" (see note 2).

Although in retrospect the basic system which was developed for the state drew heavily upon the then existing New York State system for its content, its actual development took place *in* the treatment facilities rather than in the Department's Central Office. Department and MSIS grant-funded staff worked together with local agency and facility staff in a cross section of facilities to identify the information needed. Drafts of the forms for the basic system were designed, discussed with representatives of treatment programs, governmental agencies, and universities, and subsequently revised to reflect recommendations by this group. The revised drafts were then sent to all potential reporting facilities and to each county mental health board and were tried on a pilot basis prior to installation statewide.

The basic system was installed on October 1, 1968, in about 450 local (community) facilities, and all facilities licensed, approved, and/or funded through state aid were required to report. In addition to covering outpatient clinics, the new procedures covered general hospital psychiatric units, partial care units, rehabilitation centers, sheltered workshops, day training centers, halfway houses, hostels, mental health centers, and other multi-component facilities. After the first two months of actual statewide use in local facilities, questionnaires were sent to all reporting facilities and extensive meetings were held with professional groups, including District Branches of the American Psychiatric Association; the State Hospital Association; a special advisory committee representing general hospitals; county and city mental health departments; individual facilities (including both staff and boards of directors); Department program divisions and staff offices; research units; universities; and other New York state and federal agencies to assess the forms. Revisions were again made in the forms to reflect the advice of respondents and advisory committees, and to meet the needs of other collaborating MSIS states.

After implementation in the local facilities, the new admissions forms were

TABLE 12.10 NEW YORK STATE DEPARTMENT OF MENTAL HYGIENE MONTHLY STATISTICAL REPORT FOR OCTOBER 1973, STATE HOSPITALS[1]

	All Employees			Psychiatrists		Other Phy.		Psychologists		Social Workers		Occ. Therapy		Phy. Therapy	
	Filled	Vac.	% Vac.	Filled	Vac.	Filled	Vac.	Filled	Vac.	Filled	Vac.	Filled	Vac.	Filled	Vac.
Total	35,839	4,126	10.3	1,032	174	203	62	335	127	930	215	573	138	78	36
Binghamton	1,275	133	9.4	29	4	6	1	9	4	29	3	24	2	5	1
Bronx	1,411	101	6.7	87	4	16	2	45	3	88	15	38	4	1	0
Brooklyn	1,755	194	10.0	55	13	7	4	30	5	76	17	30	4	4	3
Buffalo	1,308	191	12.7	40	8	9	2	7	2	36	8	29	3	3	0
Cap. Dist. Psy*	110	49	30.8	14	3	1	0	5	3	12	9	0	4	0	0
Central Islip	2,551	372	12.7	71	14	13	4	16	8	28	15	37	8	7	6
Creedmoor	2,756	373	11.9	77	7	20	7	19	21	59	19	37	13	3	1
Elmira Psy*	143	90	38.6	5	4	1	1	10	5	9	7	7	3	0	1
Gowanda	1,064	167	13.6	9	7	11	4	9	7	15	10	24	5	4	0
Harlem Valley	1,633	115	6.6	22	7	9	3	9	3	21	7	22	3	2	1
Hoch Psy	216	39	15.3	12	0	1	0	4	3	13	3	6	0	0	0
Hudson River	1,857	215	10.4	46	10	10	3	13	2	38	5	31	6	6	2
Hutchings Psy	444	98	18.1	15	8	3	0	6	17	26	9	8	6	2	0
Kings Park	2,469	226	8.4	77	10	15	1	10	3	27	5	37	8	6	3
Manhattan	551	84	13.2	5	0	0	0	2	0	3	1	1	0	0	0
Man-Dunlap	581	88	13.2	36	6	16	2	9	2	38	5	11	3	3	2
Man-Kirby	439	56	11.3	42	4	1	1	10	3	36	11	9	4	3	0
Man-Meyer	507	37	6.8	28	4	1	1	13	2	46	3	13	3	0	0
Marcy	1,439	124	7.9	31	6	8	3	7	1	33	9	28	5	2	2
Middletown	1,144	131	10.3	35	6	4	0	5	4	25	6	14	0	4	1
Mid-Hudson	226	15	6.2	5	0	0	0	3	0	4	1	4	0	3	0
N.Y. Psy$	400	58	12.7	21	6	4	0	2	0	5	4	5	1	3	1
N.E. Nassau Psy	258	13	4.8	11	0	1	0	9	0	14	1	6	3	0	0
Pilgrim $$	4,037	302	7.0	99	5	12	6	9	3	41	7	40	24	11	6
Rochester	1,283	176	12.1	31	7	10	2	10	3	35	6	18	3	2	0
Rockland	2,320	136	5.5	62	5	7	1	19	4	36	7	40	2	3	0
St. Lawrence	1,009	82	7.5	12	3	7	5	11	4	28	5	12	5	1	1
South Beach	503	204	28.9	14	5	1	0	25	11	64	3	4	7	0	2
Utica	1,036	105	9.2	25	10	4	4	3	2	23	5	15	3	2	2
Willard	1,114	152	12.0	16	3	5	5	6	3	22	9	21	5	4	3

1 "State Hospitals" excludes Children's Units, Alcoholic Services, and Narcotics Services.
* Presently not providing residential services.
$ Figures for June 21, 1973; current reports not received.
$$ Figures for August 30, 1973; current reports not received.

TABLE 12.10 (continued)

	Recreation		Rehab.		Education		Nursing		Patient Care		Other Clin.		Support		Research	
	Filled	Vac.	Filled	Vac.	Filled	Vac.	Filled	Vac.	Filled	Vac.	Filled	Vac.	Filled	Vac.	Filled	Vac.
Total	464	83	215	76	122	22	3,116	542	16,698	1,153	986	124	10,961	1,365	126	9
Binghamton	17	2	10	3	5	3	139	16	574	52	30	2	398	40	0	0
Bronx	43	6	13	0	5	0	81	9	580	27	32	5	376	25	6	1
Brooklyn	29	2	23	10	4	0	207	17	766	38	52	9	472	72	0	0
Buffalo	16	3	8	5	4	3	115	20	634	53	37	8	370	76	0	0
Cap. Dist. Psy*	0	1	8	3	4	0	15	5	19	8	1	1	28	12	0	0
Central Islip	32	7	6	2	6	1	196	39	1,243	145	74	8	817	115	5	0
Creedmoor	28	4	30	9	19	7	132	95	1,460	85	92	12	772	92	8	1
Elmira Psy*	9	4	7	3	1	1	9	5	26	16	7	6	52	34	0	0
Gowanda	14	3	9	1	2	0	143	23	403	35	34	9	387	62	0	0
Harlem Valley	11	1	1	0	7	1	109	10	855	21	48	9	517	49	0	0
Hoch Psy	6	6	0	0	0	0	23	4	98	5	4	0	49	14	0	1
Hudson River	22	3	2	2	6	0	190	31	786	50	52	6	653	94	2	1
Hutchings Psy	19	1	10	4	6	0	52	16	137	14	10	4	144	19	6	0
Kings Park	25	5	8	0	0	0	208	26	1,221	54	73	6	762	105	0	0
Manhattan	0	3	15	9	3	1	6	0	15	3	9	1	475	66	17	0
Man-Dunlap	13	9	0	1	1	0	80	29	293	16	27	3	54	18	0	0
Man-Kirby	13	5	1	0	1	0	25	1	254	11	9	0	43	12	0	0
Man-Meyer	15	0	0	1		0	30	5	298	6	9	0	53	7	0	0
Marcy	17	0	8	0		0	156	15	643	50	33	3	460	29	3	0
Middletown	19	1	11	2	10	0	114	23	531	31	27	1	354	56	0	0
Mid-Hudson	4	0	0	0	2	0	10	1	108	8		0	86	5	0	0
N.Y. Psy $	3	0	0	0	0	0	40	18	47	13	24	2	193	9	51	4
N.E. Nassau Psy	10	0	2	0	6	0	24	4	116	5	5	0	54	0	0	0
Pilgrim $$	16	7	0	2		2	278	16	2,360	134	106	9	1,064	82	0	0
Rochester	16	3	9	0	8	2	138	25	587	55	30	0	389	72	0	0
Rockland	21	2	6	1	9	0	161	12	1,159	36	61	7	713	58	23	1
St. Lawrence	5	4	4	0	3	0	141	14	413	17	32	5	340	21	0	0
South Beach	9	0	20	14	1	1	48	32	141	86	15	1	156	44	5	0
Utica	10	0	0	0	4	2	121	8	461	22	26	3	342	44	0	0
Willard	22	0	4	2	2	0	125	23	470	57	29	4	388	33	0	0

1 "State Hospitals" excludes Children's Units, Alcoholic Services, and Narcotics Services.
* Presently not providing residential services.
$ Figures for June 21, 1973; current reports not received.
$$ Figures for August 30, 1973; current reports not received.

installed over a four-year period in the remaining facilities. During this same period, clinical forms were developed through an Ad Hoc Committee on Medical Forms which met regularly at Rockland State Hospital. This committee included representatives from facilities and agencies throughout the Northeast, and major contributions were made by Spitzer and Endicott (1970-71, 1971).

Implementation of a reporting system such as that outlined here cannot be done effectively without personal interaction among statistical, data processing systems, and medical records staff and clinical personnel. State and grant staff were assigned specifically to work with staff of facilities and county mental health departments to help the facilities tool up their internal record systems to facilitate reporting and, where possible and desired locally, to use the reporting forms in the work of the facilities themselves. It is acknowledged that these liaison activities could have benefitted greatly from the assignment of more staff than were available.

After the system is installed, it is essential to maintain ongoing liaison between the reporting facilities and the central processing agency—and, obviously, within the facilities, between the medical records staff and the clinical staff. This contact is maintained by statistics clerks who call individual facilities as needed to clarify instructions, to reconcile discrepancies, or to inquire about missing reports. More difficult questions are handled by statisticians or administrative analysts directly with facility staff or with the assistance of the Department's program divisions. A strong relationship is necessary on a continuing basis because the system, its definitions, and its procedures cannot remain static. Moreover, even when the system's written instructions and procedures do not change, there is a continuing need to interpret the instructions to changing facility staff who themselves operate in a continually changing environment. In addition, strong interaction is needed to make effective use of the outputs at the state, county, and facility levels.

COMPLICATING ISSUES

Scope and Complexity of the System of Service

Development, operation, and use of the information system is complicated substantially because it must reflect a wide range of variables, from many varied facilities serving many different patients under varied auspices—public and private, state and local. There are, in addition, differing levels of interest and involvement by various facilities which are reflected in a diversity of emphasis on administrative management concerns, on clinical interventions, on training, or on research. Not the least of the problems is that the system of service delivery is undergoing major changes in operational and geographical arrangements. In addition, the turnover of staff in clinical and medical records units requires continuing training and orientation with respect to records and reporting procedures.

A major problem arises because the effective system of service is actually broader than the "official" system of service which is directly operated or supervised by the Department of Mental Hygiene. While the information system proper covers the facilities over which the Department has some supervisory or regulatory authority, it does not include reports from related resources such as the public

schools, other health and welfare agencies, and private practice. An attempt has been made to reflect these "interfaces" on the reporting forms by indicating prior services and source of referral for individuals admitted to reporting facilities.

Recently, increasing attention has been focused on housing in the community patients who leave inpatient care in state hospitals. Many discharged patients have no homes, and appreciable numbers are placed in or find their way to proprietary boarding homes or single-room units of various sorts. Currently, measures have been introduced in the state legislature to require the licensure of some kinds of homes and the monitoring of placements of discharged mental patients in facilities other than the former patients' own homes or apartments. There are complex issues regarding responsibilities for former hospital patients and the civil rights of these citizens to go where they please, and it will probably take some time to resolve these issues in operational detail. However, it is clear that the effective scope of the system of service is being extended, and this will have to be reflected in the information system.[10]

Overlapping Information Systems

Problems also arise where other, overlapping information systems exist, and steps have been taken wherever possible to avoid duplications in reporting requirements. Cooperative efforts with local and federal governmental agencies have helped to consolidate the various reporting requirements by making some compromises in attempts to meet the needs at the respective levels. However, duplications appear to be inevitable in many situations. For example, general hospital psychiatric units are part of the system of service for the mentally disabled, but they are also part of their respective general hospitals. These hospitals have their own overall requirements which must cover general medical and surgical needs in a variety of specialties. Within the mental disability field itself, other information systems have been developed and are still being developed for local areas and for specialized needs. For example, the New York City Department of Mental Health and Mental Retardation Services operates a system which requires local facilities receiving public funds to prepare monthly "Levels of Service" reports showing for each discipline the number of staff hours and the number of sessions devoted to each major service modality. The Nassau County Mental Health Board requires a monthly report on the activity of each staff member, and the Suffolk County Department of Health Services is currently planning to adapt for its use a staff activity system which has been operated in the State of Illinois (VanHoudnos). The Multi-State Information System offers forms and procedures for reporting both services received by a patient and on services delivered by individual staff. These, and a number of developments elsewhere (e.g., Elpers), indicate a major interest in data on staff activity at a fairly detailed level.

In each of the special systems, the local system adds to the basic state system in a modular way. In most cases this involves using the state Admission and Termination forms and providing for supplementary reporting to the respective local agency. In a few cases, such as an elaborate reporting system for alcoholism facilities in New York City, an agreement has been made to permit the local agency

to collect all of the information needed by both agencies and to send computer tapes with the required data to the state. Similar arrangements are made for some local agencies and state research units which are interested in obtaining additional outputs on a recurring or on an ad hoc basis.[11]

The Multi-State Information System on Psychiatric Patients. The system being used by the New York State Department of Mental Hygiene was developed in part by the Multi-State Information System for Psychiatric Patients and is being used in a number of other states. The relationship with the Multi-State project made it necessary to compromise in a number of areas to meet the needs of other states as well as those of New York and to develop the system so that its major elements can be processed on different kinds of computer equipment.

The system operated by New York State and the Multi-State Information System operated at Rockland State Hospital use exactly the same Admission and Termination forms; also other basic data in the systems are generally compatible. However, the systems differ in mechanics and in emphasis. The state system has input forms mailed to Albany from over 1,000 reporting units and mails outputs to an even larger number of sites. The multi-state system operates essentially through terminals at remote locations with inputs and outputs transmitted over telephone lines. The systems differ in emphasis in that the multi-state system has more clinical components while the state system is more administratively oriented. Although the users of the two systems have generally common needs, joint development has been hampered considerably by the fact that the two systems use different computer hardware, operating systems, file structures, and programming languages (see note 2).

Psychiatric Case Registers. Two counties within New York State have psychiatric case registers. Basically, a case register is a statistical reporting system with the added requirement that a single identification number is issued for each person in the reporting system. This permits tracing pathways through the various elements in the system of service and provides for the identification of duplications in services (Bahn et al., 1966).

The state system links episodes for individuals served by state-operated facilities; but for locally operated facilities, information reflecting the flow from one facility to another is limited to a few items on the Admission and Termination forms. While this level of information gives some insight into interfacility flow, it cannot answer the kind of questions about duplications of service in parallel or in series which case register are designed to cover. A unique identifier for each individual served in the 1,000 reporting units in New York State could possibly be accomplished efficiently enough by using social security numbers. (The Social Security Administration has recently indicated a willingness, previously absent, to aid in checking and in providing social security numbers on a timely basis for clients who lack numbers or who do not know them.) However, the statewide system does not require locally operated facilities to identify their clients by name or by social security number, since such indentification would be considered by many a breach of confidentiality.

The most comprehensive psychiatric case register in the United States has been operated since 1960 in Monroe County, New York, which includes the city of

Rochester (Gardner et al., 1963; Miles and Gardner, 1966; Gardner and Babigian, 1966; Babigian, 1972; and Gardner et al., 1973). This register includes data on each episode of care provided in the county, including reports from all state and local treatment facilities and from private psychiatrists. The Register was developed and is operated by the University of Rochester Department of Psychiatry and the Monroe County Department of Mental Health Services. Major funding was provided by the National Institute of Mental Health for nine years and by the State Department of Mental Hygiene thereafter. The Monroe County Register offers a unique opportunity to study changes in the system of service during the period since 1960 in a large county with urban, suburban, and rural areas. The county includes four catchment areas, two of which have mental health centers which were opened during the period covered by the Register. Moreover, the county is medically self-contained, with negligible proportions of its residents receiving psychiatric services in other counties.

A case register has been operated for Dutchess County residents for many years by Ernest Gruenberg of the State Department of Mental Hygiene and of Columbia University. However, until recently, this register did not cover all facilities serving the county, and it was necessary to use different input forms for various facilities. The Dutchess County Register has been "retooled" substantially over the past few years, and it has several features not included elsewhere. For example, this register uses the state reporting forms which provide a greater depth of information than that available in other registers. In addition, by being related directly to the statewide system, it includes data on services to Dutchess County residents at facilities outside the county. Also, this register reflects migrations of Dutchess County residents and deaths of register-subjects which occur after the conclusion of service episodes. The register is maintained on a timely basis and, possibly most important, it has the potential of being used directly as an adjunct of the medical record systems of the state and local facilities serving the county. Most recently, the register has been utilizing the Multi-State Information System through a terminal link to Rockland State Hospital.

Confidentiality

In the development and operation of the medical record and information systems, no single issue has received as much attention as that of confidentiality and the rights of patients to privacy. The issues of confidentiality have direct relevance to medical records and information systems in a number of respects which have a fundamental bearing on their structure and day-to-day operation.

When a patient "confides" to a therapist, the information he provides is kept confidential in a pristine sense only as long as the therapist does not share this information with anyone else for any purpose. As a practical matter, the context of confidentiality is extended as soon as the therapist records any notes which include the information confided and which may be available to other individuals on his staff or on the staff of facilities with which he is affiliated. The therapist's secretary, the nurse, other members of the "treatment team," and employees of the facility's medical records unit are obvious examples of extensions of the confi-

dential context. Other extensions include reviews by the Joint Commission on Accreditation of Hospitals.

In a properly run medical records unit, great care is exercised to ensure that confidential information is provided only to individuals who have a legitimate right to see it. Provisions are made for obtaining the written consent of patients authorizing the facility to make information from the patient's medical record available to others for general purposes, and in some facilities, the requirements for informed consent are quite specific for particular purposes. For a statewide reporting system, the context of confidentiality is extended beyond the facility itself especially for those facilities operated by the Department of Mental Hygiene, which are required to include patients' names on reports to the central office.

In developing and operating an information system dealing with the mentally disabled, or any group for that matter, a balance must be achieved between the need to know particular items of information and the dangers of knowing this information. Unfortunately, society still places a stigma on individuals who have received psychiatric treatment. Too many people have been denied appropriate employment, housing, or other rights because of public or private misunderstanding and confusion regarding the nature of mental disability. Paradoxically, insisting on secrecy regarding the fact of treatment contributes to this stigma in society; regrettably, it would seem necessary to do so for the immediately foreseeable future. In New York and in a number of other states, recent legislation has considerably strengthened the protections of confidentiality (New York State Mental Hygiene Law, Section 15.13). [12]

In defining the context of confidentiality as covered both by legislation and prudent policy, a few distinctions should be noted. First, there is a distinction between (a) the fact that someone received service and (b) clinical information. While there has always been a strict prohibition against the release of clinical information from the Department's central office without the informed consent of the patient, the fact of admission to a state hospital was a matter of public record until 1965. New legislation which was effective January 1, 1973, placed further very specific limitations upon the revelation of even the fact of hospitalization. In this connection, a distinction is made between information provided from the Department's central office and that provided from the facility itself. While the fact of hospitalization may not be reported from the central office except for very specific purposes and with the consent of the Commissioner, the facilities themselves are free to exercise a greater degree of judgment regarding the fact that an individual is currently hospitalized.

For the statewide reporting system, there are distinctions between the requirements for state-operated and locally operated facilities. While names of patients are not required on reports from locally operated facilities, they are required for facilities operated by the Department of Mental Hygiene. Primarily, this is because the Department has responsibilities to carry out administrative and management functions and to evaluate the facilities it operates directly. These responsibilities are on a qualitatively different level from those the Department sets for facilities it certifies (licenses) or supports in part through state financial aid to localities. For example, in addition to obvious administrative functions such as billing for patient

care and cost accounting, the central computer is used to issue notices of patients' rights on a periodic basis, to notify the facilities regarding the expiration of legal retention periods for involuntary patients, and to initiate and process periodic clinical forms. In addition, the effective monitoring and evaluation of programs operated by the Department requires the linking of stays in its various units.

There are distinctions between inpatient and outpatient services with respect to confidentiality. Recognizing that even voluntary inpatient care involves some sacrifice on an individual's freedom, the law has provided elaborate protections to safeguard his physical freedom. However, these protections involve further extensions of the context of confidentiality. For example, in New York State, the Mental Health Information Service has been established by law as an arm of the courts to protect the rights of individuals hospitalized as inpatients in any state or local, public or private hospital or other institution or unit for the mentally disabled. To carry out these regulatory functions, the law requires that copies of legal admission papers and other notifications be sent to the Mental Health Information Service on a timely basis. At the same time, the existence of such an agency has made it possible to eliminate a previous requirement that general hospital psychiatric units send copies of legal admission papers to the State Department of Mental Hygiene.

Although there have been strong feelings for many years regarding the rights of patients to privacy, these feelings have gained new expression and a greater visibility in recent years because of a number of concomitant developments. Abuses of computer "data banks" in other fields have properly received increasing attention from Congress, the media, and others. It is perhaps natural to wonder whether these abuses carry over into the Department of Mental Hygiene. Although the computer has been used for many years to process data about patients, and conventional punch card equipment was used for this purpose even earlier, attention was focused upon the use of modern data processing equipment in 1968 when the reporting forms were redesigned for optical scanning. The very appearance of the new forms serves to remind their users of the presence of the computer. It should be noted that the computer is not in reality the prime danger to privacy: index card files have existed for a long time, and such files could very easily be understood by an unauthorized intruder if he could gain physical access to them.

The extension of the state reporting requirements to outpatient clinics and to general hospital inpatient units, which include patients of private practitioners, contributed substantially to the general concerns. At that time, meetings were under way with professional societies and others to clarify the nature and purpose of the reporting requirements. Issues related to confidentiality dominated these discussions, and much of the general concern persisted even though the names of patients were not required for locally operated facilities.

While the extension of the system from outpatient clinics to inpatient units contributed to the concern in the local and private sector, the opposite was true within the state-operated system itself. With the growth of outpatient programs conducted by the state facilities, the staff of these facilities, who are employees of the Department of Mental Hygiene, voiced very strong objections to the reporting of clients' names to the Central Office. Although considerable effort has been made to explain the need for this information at the central level of the Department,

objections have persisted and suit has been brought by a group of Department employees and patients to enjoin the Department from assembling this information centrally.

The Department believes that it is necessary to include the names of patients of Department facilities in the central reporting system in order to carry out the Department's responsibilities to bill for patient care. (Alternative procedures would require billing by each facility; a careful assessment of these alternatives has been made and it has been found that the costs of this approach would be substantially greater than the cost of the central billing operation.)

The identification of patients served by Department facilities is necessary also in order to monitor the operation of these programs on an ongoing basis. For example, one measure (among many) of the outcome of services in outpatient programs involves the proportions of patients served by various units who are subsequently admitted to inpatient care. A review of the characteristics of these individuals, the programs in which they were involved, and the nature and duration of the subsequent inpatient care is considered by the Department an essential component of information needed to evaluate these programs.

While the concerns regarding confidentiality and the rights of clients to privacy have been given more vocal expression with the healthy arrival of a "new breed" of young people into the field, the expressed concerns are by no means limited to this younger group. Many people who have been around the field for a long time remember vividly abuses of the rights of clients to privacy which afflicted some social services registers and some other allied systems over a period of years. Within the state hospital system, the fingerprinting of inpatients was still required by law as recently as 1972. It is often charged erroneously that the Department gives information about patients to the State Motor Vehicles Department, the Civil Service Department, prospective employers, political parties for campaigning, bill collectors, and others. While none of these charges is true, they continue to be made and their persistence has contributed substantially to a feeling of mistrust on the part of clinical staff who are required to report.

To minimize the "dangers of knowing" the names of patients at the central departmental level, the statutory protections have been strengthened greatly, as noted above. In addition, continuing emphasis is placed on confidentiality through-out the processing procedures. For example, when forms have been processed, they are destroyed by shredding, and staff is reminded regularly about the need for confidentiality and their responsibilities under the law.

In summary, while maintaining strict protections for the rights of patients to privacy within the confidential context, it is necessary to extend the confidential context beyond the facility walls for a number of specific purposes. These purposes include the protection of other rights of patients, such as the right to personal freedom and the right to the best possible treatment or service.

Format of Clinical Outputs

In designing clinical output notes for inclusion in patients' medical records, questions arose as to whether these notes should be issued in narrative style, a more

cryptic "telegraphic" style, or whether a copy of the input form itself should be included in the medical record. A decision was reached early that no attempt would be made, for the present, to store the whole medical record in the computer. Thus, the computer would aid in maintaining "hard copy" (i.e., printed) records, but it would not replace the medical record folder as the primary repository.

Narrative notes were proposed because they were generally similar to the traditional medical record notes with which clinicians were familiar (see Figure 12.18 and the references in note 2). Data from the structured forms were entered into the computer in code; the computer stored the codes and converted these to sentences with appropriate syntax. The narrative style had the same disadvantages as the traditional notes in that the significant points were buried in verbiage. More important, in forming sentences and paragraphs, possibly independent entries on the form were juxtaposed so that the computer notes in some cases implied unintended relationships among the various clinical observations.

A cryptic or telegraphic style output was designed for the Patient Progress Note (Figure 12.19) in order to take advantage of the structure inherent in the form itself. By stripping the output of unnecessary verbiage, the note made it easy to find any particular fact. Also, the cryptic format will facilitate the inclusion of information from a series of periodic inputs in an arrangement which will show change from one periodic review to the next. In addition to making it easier to detect changes over time, this arrangement will have the advantage of facilitating comparisons with similarly arranged aggregate statistics for groups of patients.

To assess the acceptance of the two styles by clinical staff, the progress notes for two state hospitals were issued in both versions for over six months. After this period, the relative advantages were discussed at meetings of all staff at the two hospitals. Although their clear preference had been for the narrative version before they used the forms over a period of time, a substantial majority opted for the cryptic style after their experience with both versions.

Many feel that a copy of the form itself is preferable to a computer printed note in the patient's record. This viewpoint has merit so long as the outputs merely rearrange information reported on the form; however, when information contributed on a number of different forms is summarized, the computer output adds a dimension which is not available on the forms themselves.

Complete Reporting versus Sampling

In assembling statistics from medical records, there has always been some sort of "sampling." For example, in assessing the operation of hospitals, use has been made of autopsy findings as a means of verifying general diagnostic procedures. Recognizing that it was not practical or advisable to perform autopsies on all patients who died in the hospital, conclusions were based on those who were autopsied, and "autopsy rates" (the percentages autopsied) were used among the indicators of the quality of the hospital's overall procedures. This approach would not qualify as sampling in a technical statistical sense, since the selection of subjects for autopsy depends on such biasing factors as the demands of the law with respect to deaths which occur under unusual circumstances or the willingness of the next-of-kin

```
PATIENT PROGRESS NOTE FOR 04/18/69          DOE, JOHN
                                            HOSP NO: 012 345
BINGHAMTON STATE HOSPITAL                    WARD: 051
ID NUMBER: 012 34 56                         AGE: 86
ADM DATE: 12/13/14                           MALE
                                             BLACK
LEGAL STATUS: RETEN                          SINGLE

PRIMARY DIAGNOSIS:
     295.10     SCHIZOPHRENIA, HEBEPHRENIC TYPE.
```

THE PATIENT IS CONFINED TO BED AND IS NOT AT ALL INTERESTED IN
PLANNED ACTIVITIES. THE PATIENT'S MOTOR ACTIVITY HAS DECREASED, AND
HE IS USUALLY UNTIDY. THE PATIENT IS UNDERWEIGHT AND HE SHOWS A
WEIGHT LOSS SINCE LAST OBSERVATION; HIS EATING HABITS ARE POOR.
SERIOUS SOMATIC PROBLEMS ARE EVIDENT.

THE PATIENT IS OFTEN COOPERATIVE, BUT OFTEN WITHDRAWN AND
SOMETIMES INCONTINENT.

HIS AFFECT IS FLAT, AND HIS MOOD IS DEPRESSED. HIS ADJUSTMENT
TO HOSPITALIZATION IS GOOD, BUT INSIGHT INTO HIS OWN ILLNESS IS
IMPAIRED. IN GENERAL, HIS JUDGMENT IS IMPAIRED, AND HE PLANS POORLY
FOR THE FUTURE. THE PATIENT'S SPEECH IS IRRELEVANT. VERBAL
PRODUCTIVITY IS BELOW AVERAGE. HE IS ORIENTED AS TO PLACE AND PERSON
BUT NOT AS TO TIME. BOTH RECENT AND REMOTE MEMORY ARE IMPAIRED. THE
PATIENT HAS BELOW NORMAL INTELLECTUAL ABILITY, AND HIS ABILITY FOR
ABSTRACT THOUGHT IS IMPAIRED.

NEUROTIC SYMPTOMS INCLUDE TENSION AND ANXIETY.

THE PATIENT MAY HAVE VISITORS.

```
SIGNATURE ------------------------------------------ DATE ___ /___ /___
```

```
                                            PHYSICIAN NO. 021
```

FIGURE 12.18   Narrative Patient Progress Note.

```
PATIENT PROGRESS NOTE FOR 04/18/69              DOE, JOHN
                                                HOSP NO: 012 345
BINGHAMTON STATE HOSPITAL                        WARD: 051
ID NUMBER: 012 34 56                             AGE: 86
ADM DATE: 12/13/14                               MALE
                                                BLACK
LEGAL STATUS: RETEN                              SINGLE

PRIMARY DIAGNOSIS:
     295.10     SCHIZOPHRENIA, HEBEPHRENIC TYPE.

   GENERAL HEALTH - BED PATIENT. SERIOUS SOMATIC PROBLEMS. UNDERWEIGHT.
        WEIGHT LOSS. POOR EATING HABITS.

   ACTIVITIES - NONE. GENERALLY NOT INTERESTED.

   PHYSICAL APPEARANCE - DECREASED MOTOR ACTIVITY. UNTIDY.

   GENERAL BEHAVIOR - RARELY OR NEVER HOSTILE OR AGGRESSIVE. OFTEN
        COOPERATIVE AND WITHDRAWN. SOMETIMES INCONTINENT.

   ADJUSTMENT TO HOSPITALIZATION - GOOD.

   INSIGHT INTO ILLNESS - IMPAIRED.

   GENERAL JUDGMENT - IMPAIRED.

   FUTURE PLANNING - POOR.

   EMOTIONAL REACTION - FLAT AFFECT. DEPRESSED MOOD.

   PRIVILEGES - VISITORS.

   STREAM OF MENTAL ACTIVITY - IRRELEVANT.

   VERBAL PRODUCTIVITY - BELOW AVERAGE.

   SENSORIUM - ORIENTED AS TO PLACE AND PERSON. DISORIENTED AS TO TIME.
        RECENT AND REMOTE MEMORY ARE IMPAIRED. ABSTRACT THINKING IS
        IMPAIRED. BELOW NORMAL INTELLECTUAL ABILITY.

   THOUGHT CONTENT - NEUROTIC SYMPTOMS INCLUDE TENSION AND ANXIETY.

   SPECIAL PRECAUTIONS -

   CHANGE DURING LAST MONTH -




        ---------------------------------     ----------
        PHYSICIAN                             DATE

                                             PHYSICIAN NO. 021
```

FIGURE 12.19   Cryptic Patient Progress Note.

under any ordinary circumstances. However, the approach is one example of using less than a complete population in order to draw inferences about that population.

In developing an information system, the relative advantages of sampling versus assembling data about the whole population of interest must be considered. For many purposes, a carefully designed and monitored sampling procedure can produce more accurate data than those which could be assembled for the whole population involved, given limited resources available to assemble and process the data. For example, in a procedure being designed by the Department of Mental Hygiene to inquire into the "outcome" of treatment programs (discussed below), a sample of patients terminated from each treatment program will be followed in order to assess their functional status after a fixed period of time.

While a sampling approach can be adequate for many purposes, the degree to which it can answer each of the questions must be considered. Obviously, sampling from among patients would not meet the need of maintaining a medical record for each patient. In addition, sampling is likely to be inadequate where the number of individuals in the population is small and the number of variables to be covered is large. For example, consider the task of monitoring the system of service for residents of each geographic catchment area. In answering some basic questions about the overall characteristics of individuals admitted from a catchment area as a whole, the absolute number of individuals admitted to service from that area would ordinarily be large enough to support sampling for this purpose. However, in answering questions about subgroups, the size of the particular groups becomes too small for practical sampling very rapidly. Where the degree to which service is provided by each facility or unit to each part of the catchment area and to each segment (e.g., age group, ethnic group, disability group) of the general population living in that area must be monitored, there appears to be no useful substitute for reporting basic data on each individual served. To the extent that the data reported can be a by-product of the medical record system, the overall costs attributable to the reporting system can be reduced considerably.

RECOMMENDATIONS FOR THE FUTURE

From Description to Evaluation

While a term like evaluation is often used with respect to the products of medical records and information systems, many of these products are descriptions. This is not to minimize the contributions of this work, for it is necessary to describe before evaluating. The New York State Information system is designed, in part, to help describe the system of service, its operation and service. To use this system to evaluate the service programs in a formal sense, specific criteria will have to be developed.

The variables or "questions to be answered" which were outlined at the beginning of this chapter were selected and enumerated to suggest the general dimensions of the information which should be covered in the system. Naturally, these questions and the outputs designed to answer them reflect at least this writer's understanding of the collective values of the field. If the data elements of

the information system afford a reasonable description of the system of service, what remains is to identify explicit degrees of desirability and undesirability in terms of the various data elements and their combinations. At present, the assessment of desirability is ordinarily done on a general level, and more often than not, the value implications of the data are left to the judgment of the reader. For example, in producing measures such as "exit rates" and "reentry rates," no attempt has been made to suggest just what the respective rates *should* be. More work is needed in order to develop norms and ranges for groups of patients or clients with various combinations of characteristics and needs.

Problem Oriented Medical Records

The Problem Oriented Medical Record is one of the most promising developments in the structure of medical records. Pioneered by Weed (1969) in general medicine and adapted by Grant (Grant and Maletsky, 1972; Smith, Hawley and Grant, 1974) in psychiatry, this approach appears to avoid many of the difficulties that have plagued the traditional medical record format in practice.

The Problem Oriented Record consists of four main parts:

1. A *"data base"* contains the traditional body of information regarding a patient and his characteristics such as medical and social history, difficulties and strengths, and prior treatment. This information is assembled from a variety of sources, including the patient and others familiar with him, medical records of prior service, lab reports, staff observations, and so on. The data base is not necessarily in structured form, but it can include structured components. Provision is made for identifying a minimum body of information which should be present in the data base for particular groups of patients.

2. A *"problem-list"* identifies the patient's problems based on the original data base and subsequent information, and lists each of the problems in the form of a brief descriptive title, with a number, the date the problem was presented, and when appropriate, the date it is resolved. The problem number has no ordinal meaning but serves as a sort of index in the record. Problems listed should be based on observed or reported situations rather than on conclusions which involve some conceptual analysis. However, where a conceptual conclusion such as a diagnosis appears with sufficient clarity, it can be included in the problem list. The problems which can be listed go beyond the sphere which might be reflected in a medical or psychiatric diagnosis. For example, in addition to signs and symptoms, role descriptions, functional levels, and the like, the problems can reflect difficulties in the treatment process, such as "Will not take his medicine" or "Often misses appointments."

3. *"Treatment plans"* are developed and recorded in relation to the specific problems listed. Each part of the treatment plan recorded in the record is headed by the number and title of the problem which that part of the plan is designed to alleviate. Ideally, the plan should indicate in operational terms, where possible, the immediate and longer range goals with respect to the given problems.

4. *"Progress notes"* are entered with respect to a particular problem. Beginning with the problem number and title, a progress note might have up to four parts,

identified by the acronym "SOAP." "S" stands for *subjective* information such as that related by the patient or others; "O" stands for *objective* information such as direct clinical observations stated in factual terms, or the results of lab reports; "A" represents the *assessment* of this information by the clinician; and "P" represents the *plan* or modification of the plan for the specific problem, based on the information and its assessment.

While the plan would ordinarily be revised by a clinician or a treatment team (it is hoped, in concert with the patient), Grant encourages the entry of progress notes by any employee or volunteer (including nonclinical support staff at any level) who might make an observation about a patient. While the problem oriented record does facilitate entries by a wide variety of staff, the rules with respect to which staff would be authorized to make record entries are within the province of the individual facility.

A conceptual formulation such as a diagnosis of the patient's condition (s) is not inconsistent with this approach although some have characterized the traditional format (simplistically, I believe) as "the diagnostic approach" in distinguishing it from the problem oriented approach. The latter not only permits conceptual formulations, but it facilitates the orderly development of such formulations as work progresses.

It is well known that the traditional medical record is not used as actively as it might be in the treatment process; this fact has been verified by a recent detailed study conducted by the Department of Mental Hygiene. The problem oriented record appears to offer a format which can make the record an integral part of the treatment process itself to the benefit of both the patient and the clinician.

The problem oriented record has further benefits in that it facilitates evaluation on a number of levels. First, the arrangement of the information aids in ongoing evaluation of the patient's condition and his treatment by the clinician and by those responsible for the medical management of the facility. For example, the explicit dynamic relationship of the problem, plan, and progress can lead directly to analyses such as those of Kiresuk (Kiresuk and Sherman, 1968) whereby each patient's progress is charted with respect to a number of targets which are developed specifically with and for him. As knowledge is gained, some general classification of problems might be used so that programs for groups of patients can be monitored.

Evaluation at a different level, which is facilitated greatly by the problem oriented record, involves the audit of the record system itself. The structuring of the problem oriented record makes it economically feasible to check individual records on a continuing basis using such elementary criteria as the inclusion of the required minimum data base, the presence of a problem list, the relationship of plans to problems, and the relationship of progress notes to problems. More sophisticated evaluation of the records and the treatment process is also facilitated, for example, where one can inquire into the validity of the plan with respect to the problem it is intended to ameliorate.

The advantages of the problem oriented approach and the deficiencies of the

traditional records (as used in most settings) combine to make a compelling case for moving to the problem oriented record as promptly as is feasible. In doing so, it should be clear that many of the difficulties of the traditional records, or *any* records in practice, cannot be attributed to the system per se but to misuses or "non-uses." It is essential that the new system be installed in an orderly manner with a heavy commitment by the staff at all levels.

One approach to installing the new system, which seems most appropriate, is being taken by a group in a consortium of local, state, and federal (VA) psychiatric facilities in the Albany area. This group was assembled by Alan Kraft who heads the consortium and is chaired by Bernardo Gaviria, a psychiatrist who works in the consortium and in private practice. A manual (Gaviria and Pratt, 1973) was developed, and the new system was introduced, first in one VA inpatient ward, then in several other units of the consortium which represent a cross section of programs. Regular meetings of the treatment unit chiefs and records staff are held to discuss the developments, resolve problems, evaluate progress, and consider extensions or revisions. The manual developed by Gaviria has been adapted for a developmental disabilities facility by McNabb (1973) of the Monroe Developmental Center in Rochester.[13]

Based on a careful assessment of the present state of the art, it is recommended that a good *manual* problem oriented record system be installed before an attempt is made to install an automated system on any large-scale basis. Work on automated problem oriented systems is proceeding (as it should) under Grant at the University of Vermont, Laska at Rockland (Pulier, Honigfeld, and Laska, 1972; Honigfeld, 1972) and others. Automation, properly developed, can facilitate the retrieval of medical records information for clinical needs and permit the grouping of data regarding numbers of patients for analysis.

Two problems raised by automation may serve to illustrate the nature of some issues which require resolution before large-scale installation of an automated system should be attempted. A major strength of the manual problem oriented approach is the freedom it gives the staff to identify problems in their own terms specifically for a given patient, without reference to a hierarchical classification. If an automated system were to require the use of a lengthy catalogue of terms and codes, this would undoubtedly stultify and retard its acceptance by some if not most of the clinical staff (who can make or break the system). The automated systems being developed at Vermont and Rockland permit unstructured verbal entries along with structured ones, at the option of the staff member. However, if the systems should prove in practice to contain too heavy a proportion of unstructured entries, the requirements for computer capacity would be greater than most facilities could afford at the present level of data processing technology.[14] The system could be developed with some compromises, such as permitting the clinical staff to record problems in a free verbal form but having a medical record technician code the problems for entry into the computer.

A second kind of problem raised by medical records automation involves the added difficulties which this can make for the protection of confidentiality. For

example, a heavily automated record system, such as that at the University of Vermont, uses cathode ray tube terminals (similar to television screens) through which record entries are made and retrieved as needed by staff. The terminals are spread throughout the hospital at a number of strategic locations. This makes any information stored in the records available to most hospital employees. Proper safeguards should be developed to limit the availability of particular bodies of information to appropriate staff.

Follow-up and "Outcome"

Relatively little has been done on a large-scale, continuing basis to review patients after completion of service. The case registers and the Department's analysis of length of stay out of the state hospitals are attempts to reflect "outcome" on a partial and indirect level such as by studying the characteristics of those who return to treatment within given periods compared to those who do not return. While these approaches have been instructive, they do not inquire directly into the status and functioning of individuals who do *not* return to treatment.

One attempt, which has been carried out in the Department of Mental Hygiene under the direction of Borys Kobrynski (Assistant Commissioner for Geriatric Services), involves a quarterly follow-up of individuals who are examined by geriatric screening teams and referred either to state hospitals or elsewhere. Figure 12.20 shows the screening form (developed by Kobrynski and Department systems staff) which is used along with the Admission Form (Figure 12.2) in the initial contact and in each follow-up contact made by screening team staff. Sections A and B are completed for first contacts and Sections A and C for follow-ups. If any information covered in Section B is found to have changed, that item is also completed during the follow-up. Work of this type should be extended well beyond the area of geriatric screening.

For the past eight months, a Department task force headed by Elizabeth Markson has been working to develop procedures for reviewing patients upon admission, during service, upon termination, and (for a sample of those terminated) at finite points after termination. A draft form is undergoing initial pilot testing and review, with a 1974 target for implementation in Department facilities. The new form must be melded into the existing information system without imposing duplication, and although it is being developed and piloted initially as if it were an independent instrument, its content and mission overlap those of the existing periodic clinical forms. While the overlap can probably be handled by some basic systems work, a second problem presents a new kind of challenge. Specifically, the new form implies new operational activities on the part of facility staff. At present, patients are not followed up systematically after termination. To identify the level of functioning of groups of terminated patients, facility staff will have to locate and question a representative, preselected sample of these former patients. All of the forms previously designed have been related to existing facility procedures.

The questions being considered are simple enough to be asked by paraprofessional staff, possibly by telephone. While publication of the complete form would

be premature as of this writing, examples of the kind of questions being considered can be found in Figure 12.6, the Mental Retardation Client Survey form, items 9-15B. Other items would cover current living arrangements, treatment, social functioning, and behavior. It should be clear that the information and the procedures being considered will not necessarily measure "outcome" specifically. With the large number of factors involved during and after service, it would not be possible to attribute a patient's functional level to the treatment process alone. However, the data assembled would permit some comparisons between facilities or treatment programs for former patients with given sets of characteristics and allow monitoring of changes over time. Many issues remain to be resolved: the content of the form; the use of collaterals in addition to the former patients; the type of staff to use; the time period after termination, and so on.

A Consolidated Information System for a Unified System of Service

During the past century and a half, statistics assembled for mental disability facilities, with relatively few exceptions, have been segmented with separate presentations for facilities of a given type. For example, there are separate tables for such groups as state hospital inpatients, state school residents, local outpatient clinic terminations, and state hospital outpatients. Tables 12.4-12.6 and 12.10 are examples of such presentations.

Over the past several years, it has been clear that, while comparative statistics for facilities of a given type are useful and necessary for many purposes, the data assembled in this manner do not reflect the system of service and the part each type of program plays in it. Even for the state-operated facilities themselves, the traditional separate focus on inpatient care has failed to reflect the range of services provided by these facilities—and there has been great difficulty in reorienting state budget staff, the press, and others to think of treatment programs as relating to something more than inpatient beds. Table 12.3 is one attempt to combine outpatient and inpatient data in the same table.

To meet the needs of a modern system of service, it is necessary to move from primarily facility-oriented presentations to statistics which relate primarily to geographic service areas and which show the volume of service provided for the respective areas by all types of programs, state and local, public and private, inpatient and other. Table 12.2, one example of such a presentation, shows indicators of the volume of service provided by facilities located in Albany County. Inasmuch as state-operated facilities are often located outside the geographic areas they are intended to serve, the data shown for state facilities relate specifically to residents of Albany County, regardless of the state facility's location. Volume of service is indicated by additions (i.e., admissions to facilities, plus movements into units of multi-component facilities); the number of visits to non-inpatient units (including visits by facility staff to clients at other locations); and the number of patient days for inpatient or residential units. Note that no attempt is made to combine outpatient visits and inpatient days.

Inasmuch as those serving a catchment area are accountable for services to

COMPLETE SECTION A FOR FIRST CONTACTS AND FOR FOLLOW-UP CONTACTS - USE ONLY A NO. 2 PENCIL

STAT 12 (1/73)
NEW YORK STATE
DEPT. OF MENTAL HYGIENE
GERIATRIC
ASSESSMENT FORM

1. TYPE OF CONTACT
1 FIRST CONTACT
2 FOLLOW-UP CONTACT

2. FACILITY NAME

3. FAC. CODE

4. PATIENT CONS. # OR TEL. CONTACT #

5. PATIENTS NAME: LAST FIRST M.I.

6. SEX

7. AGE

8. DATE OF BIRTH MO. DAY YR.

9. DATE OF THIS CON. MO. DAY YR.

SECTION A

10. FACILITY CODE
0 1 2 3 4 5 6 7 8 9
0 1 2 3 4 5 6 7 8 9

11. COUNTY OF PATIENTS CURRENT RESIDENCE

FOR CENTRAL OFFICE USE
ACTION CODE 1ST RE U C D FORM

12. LOCATION OF ASSESSMENT (WHERE CONTACT WITH THIS PATIENT OR WITH THE PATIENTS CARETAKER WAS MADE)
0 PRIVATE HOME
DOMIC. INST. (HOME FOR THE AGED, HOSTELS, ETC.)
0 FOSTER CARE HOME OR FAM. CARE HOME
HLTH. RELATED FACILITY
0 NURSING HOME
5 OUTPATIENT PSYCH. FAC.
GEN'L HOSP. PSYCH. UNIT
5 GEN'L HOSP. OTHER UNIT
STATE MENT. HOSPITAL
5 MAIL CONTACT
9 OTHER LOCATION (SPECIFY IN 18A)
TELEPHONE CONTACT
NO. OF TELEPHONE CONTACTS THAT WERE MADE 1 2 3 4+ UNKNOWN

13. PATIENTS CONSECUTIVE NO. - ENTER LEADING ZEROS IF NECESSARY IF THE CONTACTS BEING REPORTED WERE TELEPHONE CONTACTS - ENTER "T" IN THE 1ST BOX & USE THE DIGIT TC#
0 1 2 3 4 5 6 7 8 9
0 1 2 3 4 5 6 7 8 9
0 1 2 3 4 5 6 7 8 9

COMPLETE SECTION B FOR FIRST CONTACTS AND FOR CHANGES DURING FOLLOW-UP CONTACTS

14. IF SEEN IN A GENERAL OR MENTAL HOSPITAL, OR OUTPATIENT FACILITY INDICATE PATIENT'S CURRENT RESIDENCE
PRIVATE HOME
HLTH. RELATED FACILITY
NURSING HOME
DOMIC. INST.
FOSTER/FAMILY CARE
OTHER (SPEC. IN 18A)

16. SOURCE OF INCOME
FAM. OR FRIENDS
WELFARE
EMPLOY. (SELF OR SPOUSE)
SOCIAL SECURITY
OTHER (SPEC. IN 18A)
SAVINGS
OTHER PENSION
UNKNOWN

HEALTH SERVICES COVERAGE
MEDICARE A
MEDICAID
OTHER HLTH. INS.
MEDICARE B
BLUE CROSS/SHIELD
UNKNOWN

15. REASON PATIENT IS REFERRED FOR ASSESSMENT (MARK ALL WHICH APPLY)
CONFUSED, DISORIENTED POOR MEMORY
DEPRESSION SUICIDAL TENDENCIES
MEDICAL PROBLEM
WANDERS AWAY
PARANOID DELUSIONS HALLUCINATIONS
FAMILY PROBLEM
INCONTINENT
AGITATED NERVOUS, ANXIOUS
FINANCIAL PROBLEM
NEEDS TO BE FED
HOSTILE AGGRESSIVE
OTHER PROBLEM

17. RECOMMENDED FOR ADMISSION TO PSYCH. HOSP. (INPATIENT CARE) YES NO
IF 'YES' - INDICATE TYPE STATE MUN VOL VA PRIV. PROP.

FIGURE 12.20 Screening form (developed by Kobrynski and Department Systems staff) used along with the Admission Form (Figure 12.2) in initial contact and in each follow-up contact made by screening team staff.

FIGURE 12.20 (Continued)

18. TYPES OF CARE

MARK AS OPTIMAL THE TYPE OR TYPES OF CARE THAT ARE MOST NEEDED BY THE PATIENT, WHETHER OR NOT THE TYPE OF CARE IS AVAILABLE. MARK AS AVAILABLE THE TYPE(S) OF CARE THAT IS NEEDED AND CAN BE PROVIDED WHETHER OR NOT THE TYPE OF CARE IS OPTIMAL. IF A PARTICULAR TYPE OF CARE IS BOTH OPTIMAL AND AVAILABLE, MARK BOTH SPACES.

SECTION B

	OPTIMAL	AVAILABLE
STATE MENT HLTH HOSP INPATIENT	0	1
GEN'L HOSPITAL-PSYCH. DIV.-INPATIENT	0	1
GEN'L HOSPITAL-OTHER UNIT-INPATIENT	0	1
PRIV. PSYCH. HOSPITAL INPATIENT	0	1
COMM. MENT. HLTH. CENTER INPATIENT	0	1
OUTPATIENT PSYCH SERVICE		
DAY TREATMENT CENTER		

	OPTIMAL	AVAILABLE
OUTPATIENT MEDICAL CARE	5	6
NURSING HOME		
HLTH. RELATED FACILITY (INTERMEDIATE CARE)	5	6
DOMIC. INST. (HOME FOR THE AGED, HOSTEL, ETC.)		
FOSTER CARE OR FAM. CARE HOME		

18A. OTHER: MARK HERE AND SPECIFY.

LOCATION OF ASSESSMENT (#12).

SOURCE OF INCOME (#16).

OTHER NEEDS (#18).

LIVING AT HOME:

	OPTIMAL	AVAILABLE
NO ADDITIONAL CARE	0	1
HOME CARE NURSING AND/OR HEALTH AIDE	0	1
HOUSEKEEPER	0	1
SOCIAL ACTIVITIES	0	1
FINANCIAL ASSISTANCE	0	1
BETTER HOUSING	0	1
TRANSPORTATION		
OTHER (SPEC. IN 18A)		

PATIENTS RESIDENCE (#14).

REGULAR FOLLOW-UP BY GERIATRIC TEAM

	OPTIMAL	AVAILABLE
TWICE WEEKLY OR MORE	5	6
AT LEAST WEEKLY		
AT LEAST EVERY OTHER WEEK	5	6
AT LEAST MONTHLY	5	6
OTHER (SPEC. IN 18A)		

COMPLETE SECTION C FOR ALL FOLLOW-UP CONTACTS

19. SERVICES PROVIDED SINCE LAST CONTACT

SECTION C

SERVICES OF GERIATRIC TEAM	NURSING HOME	HOME CARE:
OUTPATIENT PSYCH. CARE	HLTH. RELATED FAC.	VISITING NURSE
DAY TREATMENT CENTER	DOMIC. INST. (HOME FOR AGED ETC.)	HOME HLTH. AIDE
OUTPATIENT MED. CARE	FOSTER HOME OR FAM. CARE	HOMEMAKER
GEN. HOSP.-PSYCH. INPATIENT UNIT	FINANCIAL ASSIST.	TRANSPORTATION
GEN. HOSP.-OTHER INPATIENT UNIT	BETTER HOUSING	OTHER (SPECIFY IN REMARKS)
MENT. HOSPITAL INPATIENT	SOCIAL ACTIVITIES	

20. PATIENT'S CONDITION

PATIENTS COND. IN REMISSION	COND. IMPROV.	COND. DETERIORATED	NO CHANGE

21. IF CARE NEEDS HAVE CHANGED, INDICATE THE REASON BELOW

PATIENT HAS CHANGED	ENVIRONMENT HAS CHANGED	OTHER CHANGE (SPEC. IN ITEM 22)

ALSO COMPLETE APPROPRIATE PARTS OF SECTION B ABOVE

22. REMARKS:

COMPLETED BY: _____   DATE _____

residents of the area, data are produced to show the numbers and proportions of clients from the area and from other areas. As an example, Table 12.11 shows the percentages for each area facility. Here the proportions of admissions are used as indicators; other presentations are based on the numbers and proportions of visits and patient days.

For a long time, statistics which cut across facility types and auspices were confined, with few exceptions, to a small number of psychiatric case registers such as that noted above for Monroe County. More recently, community mental health centers, in developing information systems to cover their own operations, have necessarily covered their range of services which include inpatient, outpatient, partial care, etc. However, even for the center itself, it is not sufficient to assemble data only for the programs it operates. Accountability now applies to all segments of the general population, whether served by the center or by others—or not served at all. In many catchment areas, even very large mental health centers provide only

TABLE 12.11 NUMBER AND PERCENT DISTRIBUTION OF ADMISSIONS TO FACILITIES LOCATED IN ALBANY COUNTY BY RESIDENCE IN OR OUT OF CATCHMENT AREA BY TYPE OF SERVICE AND FACILITY, FISCAL YEAR ENDED MARCH 31, 1972

Type of Service and Facility	Total	Inside Catchment	Outside Catchment
Total	6,454	71.4	28.6
Inpatient	1,406	65.3	34.7
Albany Medical Center	1,136	57.6+	42.4
Hudson River S. H.	143	100.0	- - -
Marcy S. H. Alch. Unit	24	100.0	- - -
St. Lawrence S. H. Alch. Unit	65	100.0	- - -
Valatie Dev. Ctr.	23	100.0	- - -
Cobb Memorial	4	NA	NA
St. Colman's	11	NA	NA
Outpatient	4,374	76.9	23.1
Albany Ment. Hlth. Ctr.	1,362	91.8	8.2
Cap. Distr. Psych. Ctr.	782	66.3	33.7
Albany Med. Ctr.	697	89.1	10.9
Albany Med. Ctr. Alch. Cl.	NR	NR	NR
Albany Drug Abuse	98	85.9	14.1
Albany Meth. Clinic	141	83.7	16.3
Hope House	42	73.8	26.2
Albany Child Guid.	174	86.6	13.4
Albany Study Ctr.	857	60.0	40.0
LaSalle School	49	53.1	46.9
Albany Rec. Ctr.	235	21.7	78.3
Partial Care	359	66.9	33.1
Albany Home for Child.	2	0.0	100.0
LaSalle School	12	90.9	9.1
Cap. Distr. Psych. Ctr.	345	66.3	33.7
Other	167	52.1	47.9
Albany Co. ARC	14	85.7	14.3
Menands Workshop	153	49.3	50.7

+ Based on residence of 1971 admissions.

a portion of the services given to residents of the area. Table 12.12 shows that for one catchment area (the Metropolitan Hospital Community Mental Health Center area in New York City), the center itself served only half of the admissions from the catchment area in 1972. This is not to imply that a center should necessarily serve all of the clients from the area directly. The important consideration is that, to be accountable for services to the area's residents, one must know about much more than the immediate activities of one facility.

In order to develop a prototype analysis of the system of service for given geographic areas, the National Institute of Mental Health, Biometry Branch, contracted with the New York State Department of Mental Hygiene[15] to conduct a study first for the Metropolitan CMHC catchment area and then for 12 additional areas, urban and rural, with and without centers. This project drew upon the information system outlined in this chapter, then verified the data by checking facility records, and augmented the available data by interviews with staff of agencies, including those outside the system of service proper. In particular, the project developed the informational model which is being applied to all of the service areas of the state.

The informational model outlined in the study report (Weinstein, Hanley and Strode, 1972), in far more detail than is possible in this chapter, includes (1) a description of the area and its parts, in terms of its location and physical characteristics, size, general physical appearance, public transportation, and general population characteristics; (2) characteristics of the facilities located in the area; (3) characteristics of area residents served by facilities inside and outside the area, and (4) state hospital trends reflecting changing numbers and characteristics of patients from the area. Table 12.13 is an example of a table designed to reflect services to area residents by type and location of facility, in this case by age group. Additional tables in a similar format cover the other patient characteristics included on the Admission Form (Figure 12.2).

TABLE 12.12 TRENDS IN ADMISSIONS TO PSYCHIATRIC FACILITIES, RESIDENTS OF METROPOLITAN CMHC CATCHMENT AREA BY TYPE OF SERVICE FISCAL YEARS 1971-1972

Fiscal Year Ended March 31, 1972	Inpatient Units					Other Services				
	Total	Metro. CMHC	State Hosp.	Priv. Hosp.	Other	Total	Metro. CMHC	Bureau of Child Guidance	Court	Other
Number										
1972	1,674	832	282	161	399	4,339	2,186	646	252	1,255
1971	2,005	770	472	176	587	4,777	2,323	707	306	1,441
Percent										
1972	100.0	49.7	16.9	9.6	23.8	100.0	50.4*	14.9	5.8	28.9
1971	100.0	38.4	23.5	8.8	29.3	100.0	48.6*	14.8	6.4	30.2

* Excluding Bureau of Child Guidance and Court Clinics, Metropolitan Outpatient Services accounted for 63.5% of all other service admissions in 1972 and 61.7% in 1971.

TABLE 12.13   SERIES 1 NUMBER AND PERCENT DISTRIBUTION OF ADMISSIONS BY TYPE, AUSPICES AND LOCATION OF FACILITY, FISCAL YEAR 1972

	Total Area Adms	Ages							
		< 18	18-24	25-34	35-44	45-54	55-64	65-74	75+
Total, Residents of metropolitan catchment area	6,028	24.1	17.3	23.8	17.4	9.2	4.6	1.8	1.7
Facilities located in metropolitan catchment area	4,107	22.5	16.7	23.7	19.0	10.0	4.9	1.6	1.6
Metro, CMHC-Individuals admitted	2,054	11.0	20.4	27.0	20.7	11.8	5.5	1.9	1.8
Inpatient									
Gen. Hosp. Psyc. Unit	942	4.1	21.1	28.7	23.2	12.1	5.8	2.7	2.4
Metropolitan CMHC	832	2.1	20.9	29.5	24.6	12.6	5.6	2.3	2.4
Other	110	19.1	22.7	22.7	12.7	8.2	7.3	5.5	1.8
Manhattan State Hospital	245	6.9	14.3	31.4	26.9	9.8	6.9	2.4	1.2
Dunlap	5	20.0		20.0	20.0		40.0		
Kirby	181	7.2	13.3	29.8	30.4	10.5	5.5	2.2	1.1
Meyer	59	5.1	18.6	37.3	16.9	8.5	8.5	3.4	1.7
Outpat. Clinics, Inc. Emg. Rooms									
Metropolitan CMHC	2,104	10.7	18.6	26.4	22.2	12.5	6.1	1.7	1.7
Locally oper. exc. BCG and court	255	69.8	9.8	11.8	5.1	2.4	.8		.4
Bur. of Child Guidance (BCG) State Operated	468	98.3	.9						.9
Partial Care Facilities									
Metropolitan CMHC	82	1.2	30.5	46.3	15.9	4.9	1.2		
Other locally operated State Operated	11	9.1	63.6	18.2	9.1				
Facilities located outside metropolitan catchment area	1,921	27.7	18.5	24.2	14.1	7.4	3.9	2.3	1.9
Inpatient									
Gen. Hosp. Psyc. Unit	289	22.2	19.8	28.1	11.1	9.0	4.2	3.8	1.7
Private Mental Hospital	162	4.9	11.7	19.1	21.0	8.6	9.9	11.1	13.6
Private School for Retarded	7	57.1	42.9						
State Mental Hospitals	39	20.5	7.7	28.2	23.1	10.3	7.7	2.6	
Civil	38	21.1	7.9	28.9	21.1	10.5	7.9	2.6	
Correctional	1				100.0				
State Schools for Retarded	5	60.0		20.0			20.0		
Outpat. Clinics, Inc. Emg. Rooms									
Locally oper. exc. BCG and court	931	19.2	23.3	30.4	13.6	7.9	3.6	1.4	.9
Bur. of Child Guidance (BCG)	178	96.6	2.8						
Court Clinics State Operated	252	31.5	15.3	20.2	22.2	8.1	2.4	.4	.6
Partial Care									
Locally Operated	13	38.5	15.4	23.1	23.1				
State Operated									
Rehab./Sheltered Workshop	32	9.4	21.9	9.4	34.4	15.6	9.4		
Day Training Centers	10	60.0	40.0						
Halfway Houses or Hostels									
Other	3	100.0							

In going forward with the system outlined in this chapter, the first series of new tables being produced is an expansion of Table 12.2 with the following columns:

Number of Admissions or Additions
Number of Individuals Served Per Month
Residential Units—
    Number of Inpatient Days
    Removals Per Individual Served Per Month
Non-Residential Units—
    Number of Visits
    Visits Per Individual Served Per Month
Staff
    Total Number
    Number of Direct Service Staff
    Ratio of Individual Clients to Direct Service Staff
Expenditures

These data will be shown for the state as a whole and each geographic area by service group (see Figure 12.17 for service groups) and facility, for each mental disability group (mental illness, mental retardation, alcoholism). Further break-downs will show comparable data for major age groups and for residents of the respective service areas. A prototype test table covering some of these items for each county has been programmed and produced.

Analysis of Differences in Use of Mental Disability Services

For many years, it has been known that different levels of service have been provided in various mental health programs to groups of individuals with differing characteristics which are not necessarily intrinsic to their clinical condition. It has been known that some socioeconomic variables such as income, education, housing, occupation, recency of migration, and others have a strong bearing not only on the type of facility in which an individual might be served but also on the type of service he is likely to receive within the given facility. However, it is also known that these variables are highly interrelated with ethnic group and a variety of cultural characteristics which are associated with ethnic group.

Statistical analysis of ethnic group differences in level of service has been hampered by the coarseness of the measures used, for the most part, to reflect volumes of service provided, for example, numbers of admissions, numbers of resident inpatients. These measures, when related to the number of individuals in the general population with comparable characteristics, have provided rates which have generally been higher for the black and the Puerto Rican population than for the white population. Interpreted uncritically, these data would lead to the conclusion that the volume of service provided to the black and Puerto Rican population was, if anything, greater than that provided to the white population.

In the catchment area study (noted above) being conducted, analyses based on admission volumes are being enhanced by analyses based on numbers of visits to outpatient programs and numbers of patient days in inpatient programs for the

major ethnic groups (and groups reflecting other population characteristics). The pattern of admission rates by ethnic group has been found to be altered materially when numbers of visits are considered. In general, in many programs, the average number of visits by black and Puerto Rican clients is appreciably fewer than the number of visits by white clients. Based on the statistics available, differences are shown among the proportions of the black, Puerto Rican, and white populations, who are referred to other programs upon termination, who complete service with no further care indicated, and most significant, who withdraw from service after one or two visits.

Analyses such as this have obvious substantive significance in considering the degree to which important segments of the population are served. In addition, this kind of analysis helps in the interpretation of the measures developed to describe and to evaluate the system of service and its component programs.

Identifying Met and Unmet Needs for Service

Record and information systems such as those described here are based on services provided, and they do not provide direct measures of unmet needs. Even the follow-up information noted above does not reflect the needs of individuals who have not recently received service. Direct assessments of met and unmet needs are made by a number of field studies or household surveys, such as those conducted or discussed by the Dohrenwends at Columbia (Dohrenwend and Dohrenwend, 1969; Dohrenwend, Egri and Mendelsohn, 1971; and Dohrenwend, 1970). Nationwide household surveys are conducted on an ongoing basis by the National Center for Health Statistics.

Although information systems based on treated clients do not measure unmet needs directly, they can provide indirect indicators of possible unmet needs by identifying geographic areas or population groups which the system appears to serve unevenly. Using basic epidemiological techniques, the degree of service to area residents can be reviewed by calculating rates obtained by dividing such numbers as (a) admissions, patient days or visits for particular demographic groups, by (b) the general population with the respective demographic characteristics. Such rates, when calculated for the individual geographic areas, permit the identification of areas which are "low" compared to comparable areas, for particular groups or facilities. Further inquiry into the reasons for differences in the apparent levels of service can identify groups of areas for which additional services or different services should be considered. Approaches such as this, while falling short of a direct assessment, are feasible and economical.

Table 12.14 presents, as one example of this approach, a comparison of admission rates per 10,000 general population for the Metropolitan CMHC catchment area and its parts, with the borough of Manhattan and the state as a whole as reference "norms." The higher admission rates to state hospitals from Manhattan in particular and highly urban areas in general is well known historically. A comparison of the admission rates for the catchment area total with those for the individual health areas shows that the rate for the catchment area as a whole can be misleading where the catchment area is as heterogeneous as the one under study. For example,

TABLE 12.14   ADMISSION RATES PER 10,000 GENERAL POPULATION FOR
RESIDENTS OF METROPOLITAN CMHC CATCHMENT AREA, BOROUGH OF
MANHATTAN AND NEW YORK STATE BY TYPE OF FACILITY
FISCAL YEAR ENDED MARCH 31, 1971

Area	Total	State Hospitals	Private Hospitals	Gen. Hosp. Psych. Units	Outpatient Services
New York State	176.6	20.2	4.5	33.3	118.6
Borough of Manhattan	443.1	39.0	7.2	94.1	302.8
Metropolitan CMHC Catchment Area	343.4	23.9	8.9	68.7	241.9
Health Area - 21	452.4	33.8	1.6	82.5	334.5
- 25	488.7	44.5	1.8	99.3	343.1
- 26	604.1	37.3	2.5	124.1	440.2
- 28.1	579.1	31.4	2.5	113.7	431.5
- 28.2	248.5	14.7	14.7	47.4	171.7
- 33	390.8	24.5	4.5	76.8	285.0
- 36	140.3	12.1	17.7	33.2	77.3
- 37	229.8	20.5	12.9	49.6	146.8
- 38	146.6	8.3	15.1	27.6	95.6

the rate of 343.4 admissions per 10,000 general population in the catchment area as a whole is far less than the rate of 443.1 for the borough as a whole. However, for each of the first four health areas, the admission rate was higher than that for the borough; and for two of the areas, it was substantially higher. The general population of these four contiguous health areas includes very high proportions of the disadvantaged who are largely non-white and Puerto Rican with low incomes, limited formal education, and crowded living conditions. The admission rates for these areas were substantially higher than those for the rest of the catchment area for each of the major facility types shown, except for the private mental hospitals (Weinstein, Hanley and Strode, 1972).

This analysis was extended by calculating rates for a variety of population characteristics and for more detailed facility types, by location of the respective facilities. Table 12.15, which shows one initial step in this extension, includes a comparison of the admission rates by age group for residents of the catchment area as a whole, by facility type, reflecting the general location of facilities as inside or outside the catchment area. While a full discussion of the implications of these data is beyond the scope of this chapter, one major observation should be noted. Specifically, there was a highly significant decrease in admission rates for the older age groups compared to the rates for the younger groups for all but the private mental hospitals. In 1968, the New York State Department of Mental Hygiene announced a policy in conformity with 1965 revisions in the State Mental Hygiene Law, to the effect that individuals should not be admitted to mental hospitals unless they had a bonafide psychiatric condition (Kobrynski and Miller, 1970). Previously large numbers of individuals were admitted with primary medical conditions or other problems of aging which were not predominantly psychiatric in nature. Since 1968, the annual number of admissions of patients over 65 years of age to the state hospitals was reduced by well over 50%. As a result of this

TABLE 12.15 NUMBER, PERCENT DISTRIBUTION, AND RATE PER 10,000 GENERAL POPULATION OF ADMISSIONS TO PSYCHIATRIC FACILITIES FROM METROPOLITAN CMHC CATCHMENT AREA (CA) BY AGE AND TYPE OF FACILITY FISCAL YEAR ENDED MARCH 31, 1971

Age (Years)	Admissions Total	Inpatient Services						Other Services					
		Total	In CA Metropolitan	In CA Mt. Sinai	Out of CA	State Hosp.	Priv. Lic. Hospitals	Total	Metropolitan	Bureau of Child Guidance	Court Clinic	Other In CA	Other Out of CA
Number													
Total	6,782	2,005	770	105	482	472	176	4,777	2,323	707	306	256	1,185
Under 18	1,587	158	28	19	73	24	14	1,429	211	702	130	154	232
18 - 24	1,206	434	155	21	141	92	25	772	420	4	42	23	283
25 - 34	1,640	535	213	36	122	138	26	1,105	647	1	57	52	348
35 - 44	1,150	400	176	9	85	101	29	750	515	0	40	13	182
45 - 54	585	213	107	6	37	46	17	372	264	0	25	9	74
55 - 64	351	143	56	7	15	42	23	208	162	0	6	3	37
65 - 74	162	75	18	2	8	22	25	87	66	0	5	0	16
75 & Over	101	47	17	5	1	7	17	54	38	0	1	2	13
Percent													
Total	---	100.0	38.4	5.2	24.0	23.6	8.8	100.0	48.6	14.8	6.4	5.4	24.8
Under 18	---	100.0	17.7	12.0	46.2	15.2	8.9	100.0	14.8	49.1	9.1	10.8	16.2
18 - 24	---	100.0	35.7	4.8	32.5	21.2	5.8	100.0	54.4	0.5	5.4	3.0	36.7
25 - 34	---	100.0	39.8	6.7	22.8	25.8	4.9	100.0	58.5	0.1	5.2	4.7	31.5
35 - 44	---	100.0	44.0	2.2	21.2	25.3	7.3	100.0	68.7	0.0	5.3	1.7	24.3
45 - 54	---	100.0	50.2	2.8	17.4	21.6	8.0	100.0	71.0	0.0	6.7	2.4	19.9
55 - 64	---	100.0	39.2	4.9	10.5	29.3	16.1	100.0	77.9	0.0	2.9	1.4	17.8
65 - 74	---	100.0	24.0	2.7	10.7	29.3	33.3	100.0	75.9	0.0	5.7	0.0	18.4
75 & Over	---	100.0	36.2	10.6	2.1	14.9	36.2	100.0	70.4	0.0	1.8	3.7	24.1
Rate Per 10,000 General Population													
Total	343.4	101.5	39.0	5.3	24.4	23.9	8.9	241.9	117.6	35.8	15.5	13.0	60.0
Under 18	306.2	30.5	5.4	3.7	14.1	4.6	2.7	275.7	40.7	135.4	25.1	29.7	44.8
18 - 24	566.2	203.8	72.8	9.9	66.2	43.2	11.7	362.4	197.2	1.8	19.7	10.8	132.9
25 - 34	479.7	156.5	62.3	10.5	35.7	40.4	7.6	323.2	189.2	0.3	16.7	15.2	101.8
35 - 44	461.6	160.5	70.7	3.6	34.1	40.5	11.6	301.1	206.7	0.0	16.1	5.2	73.1
45 - 54	280.4	102.1	51.3	2.9	17.7	22.0	8.2	178.3	126.5	0.0	12.0	4.3	35.5
55 - 64	176.7	72.0	28.2	3.5	7.6	21.1	11.6	104.7	81.6	0.0	3.0	1.5	18.6
65 - 74	102.8	47.6	11.4	1.3	5.1	13.9	15.9	55.2	41.9	0.0	3.2	0.0	10.1
75 & Over	114.7	53.4	19.3	5.7	1.1	8.0	19.3	61.3	43.1	0.0	1.1	2.3	14.8

reduction, a higher percentage of those who were admitted were subsequently discharged alive from the hospitals and a smaller percentage died in the state hospitals (Weinstein and Maiwald). Nevertheless, it is perhaps surprising that the admission rates shown in Table 12.15 for the older age groups, beginning with the group from 45 to 54 years of age, were actually *lower* than the rates for the younger age groups. While it was anticipated in establishing the new admissions policy that there would be some decrease in the admission rates for the older groups from their previous very high levels, it was not anticipated that these rates would actually fall below those for younger groups.

While the phenomenon of lower admission rates for the older groups for the state hospital is explainable in part by a change in policy, it is not clear why this same phenomenon appears for Metropolitan Hospital and for general hospitals outside the catchment area. It will be necessary to study the alternative loci of care to the elderly, including nursing homes and other programs, before more is known about services, particularly residential services, provided to this group.

In addition to this kind of inquiry which is made possible by combining client and general population data for small areas, general population data for such areas can be used effectively in other ways. For example, for some items of information, such as that on family income (Figure 12.2, item 29), the data are reported very poorly. Many clinical staff in public facilities do not inquire into personal finances, particularly upon admission. In many if not most small geographic areas (such as health areas or census tracts), the bulk of the general population have similar economic characteristics. Thus, some inferences can often be made about the income level of residents, as a group, from the respective areas.

Regrettably, approaches based on general population data suffer increasingly as the date of the most recent decennial census becomes more remote. Intercensal estimates or projections are made by a number of agencies, but these are ordinarily confined to relatively large geographic areas. Such projections are of questionable dependability for individual age groups or other subgroups in areas as small as most counties. Until more frequent population enumerations are made, one must use the general population data which he can acquire, and where necessary, modify these data as well as possible to reflect the major shifts which occur.

Centralization versus Decentralization of Processing

In developing an information system to cover the sphere described in this chapter, a maze of interrelated decisions must be made regarding at just which points and in what form the various processing steps should take place. The bulk of the information needed is recorded at the facility, and much more of this information is used at the facility than at the county, state, or federal level. However, some of the processing procedures can be carried out more efficiently with the aid of a computer, and relatively few facilities have their own computers. Even where a facility has access to a computer, the necessary systems analysis and programming support is lacking more often than not. In addition, although one facility may be served by a computer system, the information system should cover all of the facilities serving residents of a given geographic area. Thus, centralized processing at

some level will probably be needed indefinitely. This level need not necessarily be the state, however, and it is quite possible to foresee a number of county or intra-state regional processing centers which would serve their respective areas and send a subset of data to the state.

In a centralized reporting system, there are some considerations which must be faced whether or not a computer is used. For example, there are a number of clerical procedures which could be carried out either locally or centrally. These include such steps as entering residence codes or checking and reconciling errors. Some errors are detected by the computer, and these may include such difficulties as incorrect case numbers, inconsistent entries, illogical events, missing items, and data out of arithmetic balance. Clerically detectable errors could include incorrect codes, illegible entries, and some internal inconsistencies.

In the State Department of Mental Hygiene, a cadre of statistical clerks in the Central Office enters a number of codes on the forms, checks for errors, and reconciles these errors with facility staff. This arrangement facilitates training and supervision of the coding and checking procedures and permits some economies of scale. The intra-facility procedures are designed so that, if the appropriate steps are carried out at the facility, the number of errors detected centrally should be almost negligible. It would be possible to delegate to the individual facility the responsibility for the accuracy of reported data. However, this does not answer the questions as to what would happen when appreciable errors were not in fact corrected. For the many purposes discussed earlier, the Department has an obvious interest in accurate information.

While some facilities lack computers or adequate data processing staff support, some facilities have access to sophisticated equipment and support staff. The degree to which such resources are available has a direct bearing on the extent to which the computer can assist in clinical activities. For many clinical procedures, it would take too long to mail forms to a central point and receive outputs by mail. If the computer is to be used for many clinical activities, it must be readily accessible throughout the facility, and the system should be capable of rapid response. While relatively inexpensive terminals are available, these terminals require rather cumbersome input procedures, particularly where a sizable volume of information must be entered. In addition, in many present settings, as noted earlier, the proliferation of terminals makes it more difficult to provide safeguards needed to ensure confidentiality. The terminals installed by the Multi-State system are more elaborate than many, and they accept inputs by scanning (as well as by key punching). However, these terminals are too expensive to install at more than one location within a facility. Given the rate the data processing field has progressed, the foreseeable future should bring significant advances in the capability of terminals with reductions in their cost.

For many purposes, including planning, monitoring and operating facilities and systems of service, and some clinical applications, it is currently feasible and reasonably economical to use terminals such as those supported by the Multi-State Information System at Rockland or a number that are available commercially. Where a local agency or a facility is interested in operating an information system

which goes beyond the scope of the statewide system, and where the agency or facility cannot justify a computer of its own, terminals such as these should be considered seriously. However, computerization should not be considered unless adequate technical staff is readily available on an ongoing basis.

Residence Coding

To assemble data for the geographic areas of clients' residence, it is necessary to enter residence codes into each client's record in the information system. These codes can be quite simple, identifying fairly large areas such as counties or cities, or detailed, when relatively small areas must be identified. If small areas are identified, a marked increase in the cost of the coding can be expected.

In the information system described here, residence is coded on the Admission Form MS-5 (Figure 12.2) as follows: The address code in item 14c consists of six digits, of which the first two identify the county. In New York State the county is the major unit of local government which is responsible for services to the mentally disabled; in some other states or areas, a different code might be appropriate. The codes for the remaining four digits differ from county to county depending on local needs. For example, for some large counties, census tracts are coded, while in others, the city, town (township), or incorporated village is coded. For New York City, which consists of five counties with over 7,000,000 people, the codes refer to local health areas which range from about 15,000 to about 35,000 in general population. New York City health areas consist of groups of census tracts, thus permitting the assembly of census data for each area.

Data for intra-county catchment areas can be assembled in either of two ways: Where the areas coded can be combined to identify catchment areas, the computer is programmed to assemble the data in this manner. However, in some counties, the residence areas identified in the information system are not sufficiently specific to denote the catchment areas. In these cases, a one-digit catchment area code can be entered in item 14a of the Admission Form. Such a code to identify the catchment area is advisable even where more detailed health area or census tract codes are used, for three reasons: First, in many cases the small area codes for particular clients cannot be identified or are found to be invalid, while the catchment area can generally be identified. Second, it is reasonable to request the facilities to enter catchment area codes, while experience has shown that the more difficult small area coding has often been done very poorly at many facilities. Third, it is more efficient even for computer processing to use the simpler catchment area code for outputs which do not identify the individual subareas.

Some complications have arisen in using census tract codes, which can total six digits, in the four-digit space available. Ordinarily it is not necessary to use cumbersome recoding procedures to convert the six digits into four-digit codes, because for most counties, only four of the six digits are needed to identify any given tract. In general, outside mammoth counties such as those in New York City, the first and fifth digits are not needed.

Coding small areas such as census tracts is more expensive than coding on a broader level. This is because, for small areas, one must look up the address for each

client in a lengthy code book in order to do the coding. Where the residence code is based on larger areas such as the county, city, or town, the code lists are very much shorter and more easily used. Computer programs have been written by the U.S. Bureau of the Census and others to enable the computer to assign census tract codes. However, these programs necessarily require entering the addresses into the computer, and unless the address would be entered into the computer system for other purposes, the cost of the punching, verifying, and processing the address would more than offset the cost of coding the address clerically.

Where the cost of coding census tracts is considered excessive, useful compromises are possible and advisable. The codes used in New York for many counties (reflecting city, town, and village) are adequate for many purposes. One very practical compromise would involve using Postal Zip Codes. It would be reasonable to request the facilities to include the Zip Code on the reporting forms, and census data related to Zip Code areas are available. It should be recognized that Zip Code areas were drawn solely to facilitate the postal system, and the mail routes do not necessarily relate to homogeneous population groups or reflect "neighborhoods." In some cases, by combining city or other readily available codes with the Zip Codes, useful groupings can be made inexpensively. There would be other advantages in using Zip Codes more widely, such as in drawing and identifying catchment area boundaries in large counties. It would be far easier to tell potential facility clients that the facility serves people living in particular Zip Code areas than to describe the service areas in terms of more complicated boundaries such as those based on groups of census tracts.

Whatever code is used for clients' residence, it has become clear that it is not sufficient in the state system to record the residence only upon admission. Although newly admitted patients are now discharged quite soon after admission, they do not always return to the area from which they were admitted. For instance, where the state hospital is not physically located in the county it serves, as is true in many areas in New York, some patients take up residence near the hospital upon discharge. In some counties, this has led to additional pressures upon the local welfare system and other agencies. To document the migration of patients upon discharge and to plan and monitor postdischarge programs on their behalf, the county and catchment area of residence as of discharge will be coded and entered into the system.

Reducing the Reporting Burden

Fundamentally, an information system should include no more elements than those needed to carry out the purposes of the system. While it is easy to identify a large number of items which *could be* useful sometime, it is most important to recognize that the staff of operating facilities have much to do in order to carry out their primary mission, the provision of service. There is a need to balance the value of a particular datum with the effort required to record it. Among the large variety of facilities in the overall system of service, many are required to report to a number of different agencies with overlapping but slightly different data elements and consequent duplications of effort. Modifications are currently being made or considered to reduce the recording burden still further.

Alternative versions of the Outpatient Daily Service Record (Figure 12.4) have been developed to meet the specialized needs of particular groups of facilities. For example, for units such as day training centers or sheltered workshops, which have a reasonably stable clientele who make frequent visits to the facility, one version of the form permits the listing of the clients once a month with a column allotted to each day of the month for checking attendance. Quite a different version has been developed for the New York State Psychiatric Institute which uses a separate form for each visit, initiated by a plastic plate at the facility. In this version, the form is printed in three-part sets, with one copy for the facility, one for the Central Office, and part of one copy for the client. It is not clear that this version reduces the amount of work required to use the form, but this approach should improve the accuracy of the identification numbers entered and it has the potential of providing a copy for the patient's medical record. The Multi-State Information system also provides alternate versions of a number of forms (including forms for reporting direct and indirect services by staff). While the use of alternative versions of forms complicates the central processing procedures, such flexibility should be considered where possible in developing the system; the costs involved in staff time at the facilities are at least as significant as those involved at the central level.

To reduce the recording burden at the facility level, Department staff are currently reevaluating the use of scanning for processing the Admission and Termination forms, and possibly others. There is little doubt that it is easier to record on a form for keypunching than for scanning on the type of optical mark page readers available to the Department. More advanced optical scanning equipment would permit using less restrictive forms than the scannable forms shown above, but this equipment is many times more expensive and cannot be justified based on current applications alone. There are several reasons for believing that "old fashioned" forms suitable for keypunching could be completed with less effort at the facilities. First, it is easier to enter standard Arabic numbers on a form than to enter the machine-readable marks. This is true especially where several digits are involved. Second, it is easier to make check marks in boxes than to enter the machine-readable marks between the small parallel lines. Third, if a form is damaged slightly by wrinkling or tearing, or by smudging or other stray marks, it can still be keypunched (a reasonable number of such forms can be tolerated) but not scanned. Fourth, if inadvertently a ball-point pen rather than a number 2 pencil is used, or inadvertently a carbon copy instead of the original is submitted, the form can be used for keypunching. At the Central Office, while there would be some increase in the cost of keying rather than scanning, this increase would be offset partly by savings in clerical time now required to review and "clean up" the forms for scanning. In addition, nonscannable forms are much more flexible and more easily designed or revised. They can be printed much more quickly; almost any printer can produce them; and the saving in printing costs would be substantial.

Systems Choices

The information system outlined here is only one example of an approach to assembling data from medical records for a variety of purposes, including evaluation. In general, questions like those listed earlier would have to be answered in

any system of service, and the structure of the patient information system may be applicable fairly generally even where different data elements are used. However, it is obvious that other systems might come closer to meeting particular needs, and the field offers many variations on the theme presented here. Attention is directed to the references in note 14 and to Bloom, 1972; Elpers; Kleffel, 1972; National Institute of Mental Health, 1969; and Person, 1969.

It is clear that there are a number of systems available with various strengths and weaknesses for particular settings or applications. It would seem that, for the development of new systems, the point of diminishing returns has been passed. Anyone interested in modifying his current system or installing a new one is strongly advised to review the now extensive field carefully, and if possible, to select from existing systems components which may meet his needs. Where appropriate, new input or output components can be added to existing systems. If the temptation to embark on the design of entirely new systems is resisted successfully, more time will be available to develop new and more useful outputs using the plethora of data elements which are now assembled, stored, and too often, not tapped.

Whatever systems or components are selected, the medical record and information system should not be considered static. Although changes are costly and should not be made frivolously, medical record and information systems should be as flexible as possible, and they should periodically be reevaluated. As experience is gained, as the information-handling technology advances, and as the system of service changes, revisions in the record and information system will be necessary.

CONCLUSION

In this chapter, attention was directed to medical records and related information systems as major sources of data for use in describing and evaluating services to individuals and to groups. Emphasis was placed on the complex of agencies, facilities, and staff which together comprise a system of service for residents of defined geographic areas. The notion of accountability for the needs of each area's general population was stressed and the impact of this responsibility on the content, development and use of medical records and information systems was described and illustrated.

One information system was outlined in detail. This system was designed for fields serving primarily the mentally disabled, but its structure, procedures, and approach to analysis, and many of its data elements may be useful in related fields such as general health, education, and social services.

Throughout this report, references were made to applications at the facility, local governmental, and state levels. Before concluding, reference should be made to the work at the federal level, over a long period of years, by the Biometry Branch and others at the National Institute of Mental Health in stimulating and supporting the kind of development described above, in assembling data from the myriad information systems in the different states, and in demonstrating the usefulness of this information (for example, Kramer, 1966; National Institute of Mental Health; Bass, 1972; Person, 1969).

The references cited in this chapter were chosen in general as illustrative of approaches which are practical and sufficiently economical for consideration by a broad range of possible users. No attempt was made to present an exhaustive list: extensive bibliographies are available from NIMH, NIH, National Library of Medicine, and the like. In particular, no reference was made to a large number of imaginative and sophisticated evaluative studies which have been conducted using medical records and information systems as sources but which are beyond the technical level which most facilities or agencies can employ in the near future.

ACKNOWLEDGMENTS

The author wishes to acknowledge the contribution of many individuals who have regularly, over a period of years, recorded, assembled, processed, and used the information described in this chapter. This includes staff in the clinical and medical records units of state and local facilities and statistical, clerical, and data processing staff in the New York State Department of Mental Hygiene. Special thanks are due to Robert Patton for the strong foundation he provided and for his continued support. Major credit is due to Frederick Winsor and Donald Greene for their work in the development and operation of the patient information system and to Albert Maiwald for helping many people to use its products. Special credit is due to John Burke for the design and implementation of the subsystem for Department outpatient units and to Ken Miller for a number of contributions to better medical records and reporting procedures. The Department is indebted to Morton Kramer, Carl Taube, and Earl Pollack of NIMH, who served as project officers for the NIMH-supported studies noted above and made those projects possible. In the development of the cost system for state facilities, Peter Barbagelata represented the Department. The task force developing the cost system for local facilities and adapting the patient information system for unified services is headed by Edward Skelly. Other acknowledgments are spread throughout this chapter, but space does not permit giving credit to the large number of people who contributed to the subjects discussed.

NOTES

1. The Admission Form is identical for state-operated and locally operated facilities. A simpler version of the Termination Form is used by state-operated facilities because most of the data on the local form are reported on other forms during the course of service at state facilities.

2. The Multi-State Information System on Psychiatric Patients was developed in part by NIMH Grant No. MH 14934-03. The Principal Investigator was Eugene Laska, Ph.D., Director of the Information Sciences Division, Rockland Research Center, Rockland State Hospital, Orangeburg, New York. This chapter's author was Co-Principal Investigator from 1967 to 1972. See Laska et al , 1972; Laska, Logemann and Weinstein, 1971; and IBM, 1973.

3. Slightly different procedures for processing these forms are employed for facilities, mostly outside New York State, which use remote terminals to computers at the Rockland Research Center. See references listed in note 2.

4. While this chapter deals with *medical* records and related information systems, the term "medical" is used here in a general sense for convenience to apply also to nonmedical services

for the mentally and developmentally disabled. Similarly, the term "patient" is used in a general sense to apply to any client of a facility in this broad field and related fields and "inpatient" applies to any facility resident. No intention to limit this discussion to a medical model should be inferred.

5. When a patient is served by more than one unit at a time, the information system should provide for identifying the unit, team, or clinician who has the primary responsibility for the patient's care. Currently, the primary unit or therapist is not distinguished from the other unit(s) in the central system, but it should be noted in the patient's record at the facility. The possibility of identifying the primary unit in the central system is being studied.

6. Exit rates are defined as the percentages of hospital additions (admissions plus returns from convalescent care, a "trial discharge") who leave the hospitals alive within two months. Reentry rates are the percentages of removals (direct discharges plus placements on convalescent care) who return to the hospitals within six months.

7. For a discussion of the relationships between length of stay in and out of state hospitals in terms of a number of variables, see Weinstein, DiPasquale and Winsor, 1973.

8. Further discussion and examples of graphic approaches to analyzing and presenting data can be found in National Institutes of Health, 1970; U.S. Army Finance School, 1963; some texts on statistics such as Croxton, Cowden and Klein, 1967; and publications by computer firms.

9. For more detailed descriptions of the state and local cost systems, write to the New York State Department of Mental Hygiene, 44 Holland Avenue, Albany, N.Y., 12208. For other cost systems, see Cooper, 1973; Elpers; Nelson, 1973; Salsbery and McCullough, 1971; and Sorenson and Phipps, 1971.

10. A number of additional complications arising from the scope and complexity of the system of service have not yet been addressed specifically in the Department's information system. For example, the information system relates to individual clients, but in a number of programs, a "case" is considered as consisting of several members of a family. At the same time, most facilities do consider their case loads as consisting of individual clients, and some common denominator is needed in order to make comparisons across programs and areas. Moreover, reimbursing agencies ordinarily pay for care to individuals, not families. Present methods used for reflecting individual and family frames of reference in the same information system are cumbersome and should be improved.

11. A special complication is presented where State and local staff work jointly in the same facility or unit. Current plans call for requiring all such units to use the Outpatient Daily Service Record (Figure 6) which is now used only by State-operated facilities (local facilities would not be required to include clients' names). Instead of entering check marks in the columns indicating the services provided, a number "1" would be entered for State staff and a "2" for local staff. This will permit allocating the activity for monitoring and for reimbursement.

12. For a discussion of the confidentiality issues regarding states (other than New York) which process information through terminals to the computers at Rockland, see Curran et al., 1973.

13. Copies of the manuals are available by writing the Department of Mental Hygiene, 44 Holland Avenue, Albany, N.Y. 12208. For further references to problem oriented medical records in psychiatry, see *Hospital & Community Psychiatry*, Jan. 1974, 25(1).

14. The issues involving verbal entries into the computer versus coded entries are not limited to problem oriented records. For a system using primarily verbal entries, see Eiduson, 1966. For other references to medical record automation in general, see Brosin et al., 1969; Butkus et al., 1974; Fisher, King and Shernoff, 1972; Glueck et al., 1972; Glueck and Luce, 1968; IBM, 1973; Laska et al., 1972; Laska, Logemann and Weinstein, 1971; Laska et al., 1967; Plasman, 1972; Spitzer and Endicott, 1971; Spitzer and Endicott, 1970-71; and Ulett et al., 1973.

15. Contracts HSM 42-72-53 (SA) and HSM 42-73-63 (OP), Changes in Patterns of Use of State Mental Hospitals and other Mental Health Services.

REFERENCES

Babigian, H. M. The role of psychiatric case registers in the longitudinal study of psychopathology. *Life History Research in Psychopathology,* 1972, University of Minnesota Press.

Bahn, A. K., E. A. Gardner, L. Alltop, G. Knatterud, and M. Solomon. Admission and prevalence rates for psychiatric facilities in four register areas. *American Journal of Public Health,* 1966, 56(12).

Bass, R. D. *A method for measuring continuity of care in a community mental health center.* DHEW Publication No. (HSM) 72-9109, 1972.

Bloom, B. L. Human accountability in a community mental health center: report of an automated system. *Community Mental Health Journal,* 1972, 8(4).

Brosin, H. W. et al. Computers in psychiatry. *American Journal of Psychiatry,* Jan. 1969 Supplement, 125(7)

Butkus, D., J. Powell, C. Souders, and A. Boroskin. *Individualized data base, manual of reports.* IDP Publication Series No. 5, Neuropsychiatric Institute, Pacific State Hospital, Pomona, California, Jan. 1974.

Cooper, E. M. *Guidelines for a minimum statistical and accounting system for community mental health centers.* DHEW Publication No. (ADM) 74-14, 1973.

Croxton, F. E., D. J. Cowden, and S. Klein. *Applied general statistics.* 3rd ed. Library of Congress Catalog No. 67-15187, 1967, 60-120.

Curran, W., E. Laska, H. Kaplan, and R. Bank. Protection of privacy and confidentiality. *Science,* Nov. 1973, 182(4114).

Dohrenwend, B. P. Psychiatric disorder in general populations; problem of the untreated "case." *American Journal of Public Health,* June 1970, 60: 1052-1064.

――― and B. S. Dohrenwend. *Social status and psychological disorder: a causal inquiry.* New York: Wiley, 1969.

Dohrenwend, B. P., G. Egri, and F. Mendelsohn. Psychiatric disorder in general populations: a study of the problem of clinical judgment. *American Journal of Psychiatry,* April 1971, 127(10): 1304-1312.

Eiduson, B. T. Replacing traditional records by event reports. *Hospital and Community Psychiatry,* March 1966, 17(3).

Elpers, J. R. The practical development and implementation of management information systems for community mental health programs. Orange County Department of Mental Health, Santa Ana, California.

Fay, H. J. and A. Norman. Modifying the problem-oriented record for an inpatient program for children. *Hospital & Community Psychiatry,* Jan. 1974, 25(1): 28-30.

Fisher, G., J. King, and E. Shernoff. Do-it-yourself computer reports in the medical record department. *Medical Record News,* June 1972, 43(3): 31-38.

Gardner, E. A. and H. M. Babigian. A longitudinal comparison of psychiatric service. *American Journal of Orthopsychiatry,* October 1966, 36(5).

Gardner, E. A., H. C. Miles, A. K. Bahn, and J. Romano. All psychiatric experience in a community. *Archives of General Psychiatry,* Oct. 1963, 9.

Gardner, E. A., H. C. Miles, H. C. Iker, and J. Romano. A cumulative register of psychiatric services in a community. *American Journal of Public Health,* Aug. 1973, 53(8).

Gaviria, B. and D. F. Pratt. *Problem-oriented medical records: instruction manual for problem-oriented recordkeeping in psychiatric services.* Veterans Administration Hospital, 113 Holland Ave., Albany, N.Y., Jan. 1973.

Gilandas, A. Implications of the problem-oriented record for utilization review and continuing education. *Hospital & Community Psychiatry,* Jan. 1974, 25(1).

Glueck, B. C., et al. Computers in psychiatry. *Psychiatric Annals,* Dec. 1972, 2(12).

Glueck, B. C. and G. Juce. The computer as psychiatric aid and research tool. *Mental Health Program Reports, No. 2,* Feb. 1968, DHEW Public Health Service, 353-372.

Grant, R. L. and B. M. Maletsky. Application of the Weed system to psychiatric records. *Psychiatry in Medicine,* 1972, 3.

Honigfeld, G. *Problem-oriented psychiatric records—manual and automated.* Information Sciences Division, Research Center, Rockland State Hospital, Orangeburg, N.Y. 10962, 1972.

IBM. *The multi-state information system for psychiatric patients.* IBM Data Processing Division, 1133 Westchester Ave., White Plains, N.Y., GK20-0607-0, April 1973.

Katz, J., S. Kunofsky, R. E. Patton, and N. C. Allaway. Cancer mortality among patients in New York mental hospitals. *Cancer,* 1967, 20(12).

Kiresuk, T. J. and R. E. Sherman. Goal attainment scaling: a general method for evaluating comprehensive community mental health programs. *Community Mental Health Journal,* 1968, 4(6).

Kleffel, D. *A statistical information program for utilization review in extended care facilities.* DHEW Publication No. HSM 72-6500, 1972.

Kobrynski, B., and A. Miller. The role of the state hospital in the care of the elderly. *Journal of the American Geriatrics Society,* 1970, 18(3).

Kramer, M. Mental health statistics of the future. *Eugenics Quarterly,* 1966, 13(3).

Laska, E., G. Logemann, G. Honigfeld, A. Weinstein, and R. Bank. The multi-state information system. *Evaluation,* 1972, 1(1).

Laska, E., G. W. Logemann and A. S. Weinstein. The multi-state information system for psychiatric patients. *Transactions of the New York Academy of Sciences,* Dec. 1971, 33(8), 780-790.

Laska, E., A. Weinstein, G. Logemann, R. Bank and F. Breuer. The use of computers at a state psychiatric hospital. *Comprehensive Psychiatry,* Dec. 1967, 8(6).

McNabb, N. A. *POR in developmental disabilities: preliminary instruction manual for problem-oriented recordkeeping in developmental disabilities services.* Monroe Developmental Services, Rochester, N.Y., Aug. 1973.

Miles, H. C. and E. A. Gardner. A psychiatric case register: the use of a psychiatric case register in planning community mental health services. *Archives of General Psychiatry,* June 1966, 14: 571-580.

National Center for Health Statistics. U.S. Dept. of H.E.W., *Vital and health statistics,* Series 11: Data from the National Health Survey.

National Institute of Mental Health. *Community mental health center data systems-a description of existing programs.* Public Health Service Publication No. 1990, 1969.

National Institutes of Health. *Manual of statistical presentation.* DRG Statistical Items, Jan. 1970 Ed., No. 10.

National Institute of Mental Health. *Statistical notes.* Series published by Biometry Branch, Survey and Reports Section, Rockville, Md.

Nelson, C. A. *An integrated management information system.* Hennepin County MH/MR Area Program, 527 Park Ave., Minneapolis, Minn., June 1973.

Person, P. H. *A statistical information system for community mental health centers.* PHS Publication No. 1863, 1969.

Plasman, F. B. The medical record—the basis for an automated information system. *Medical Record News,* June 1972, 43(3): 15-21.

Pulier, M., G. Honigfeld, and E. Laska. *Psychiatric record-keeping: an analysis of current trends.* Information Sciences Division, Research Center, Rockland State Hospital, Orangeburg, N.Y. 10962, 1972.

Salsbery, D. L. *Accounting guidelines for mental health centers and related facilities.* Edited by P. M. McCullough. Western Interstate Commission for Higher Education, Boulder, Colo., 1971.

Sehdev, H. S. Adapting the Weed system to child psychiatric records. *Hospital & Community Psychiatry,* Jan. 1974, 25(1): 31-32.

Smith, L. C., C. J. Hawley, and R. L. Grant. Questions frequently asked about the problem-oriented record in psychiatry. *Hospital & Community Psychiatry, Jan. 1974, 25(1): 17-22.*

Sorensen, J. E. and D. W. Phipps. *Cost-finding and rate-setting for community mental health centers.* Association of Mental Health Administrators, 2901 Lafayette Ave., Lansing, Mich., Dec. 1971.

Sperry Univac Computer Systems. *Series 70, program application, statistical system, BMDP series.* Systems Publications, Building 214-1, Cinnaminson, N.J., Jan. 1973.

Spitzer, R. L. and J. Endicott. An integrated group of forms for automated psychiatric case records. *Archives of General Psychiatry,* June 1971, 24.

——— Automation of psychiatric case records. *International Journal of Psychiatry,* 1970-71, 9: 604-621.

U.S. Army Finance School. *Statistical presentation,* Fort Benjamin Harrison, Ind., July 1963.

Ulett, G. A., I. W. Sletten, A. Ameiss, and W. A. Thompson. Realities and prospects for the use of computers in psychiatric hospital management. *Psychiatric Annals,* Jan. 1973, 3(1).

Vanhoudnos, H. M. *An automated community mental health information system. Region 3B Management Information, Adolf Meyer Center, Decatur, Ill.*

Weed, L. L. *Medical records, medical education, and patient care.* Press of Case Western Reserve University, Cleveland, 1969.

——— Medical records that guide and teach. *The New England Journal of Medicine,* 1968, 278(11, 12).

Weinstein, A. S., D. Dipasquale and F. Winsor. Relationships between length of stay in and out of the New York state mental hospitals. *American Journal of Psychiatry,* Aug. 1973, 130(8).

Weinstein, A. S., A. T. Hanley, and R. L. Strode. *Services to the mentally disabled of the Metropolitan Hospital community mental health catchment area in New York City.* USDHEW—HSM Contract 42-72-53, N.Y.S. Dept. of Mental Hygiene, 44 Holland Avenue, Albany, N.Y., 1972.

Weinstein, A. S. and A. Maiwald. Trends in the New York State mental hospital population, admissions and length of stay. *The Willard State Hospital Centennial Symposium,* Hanover, N.J., Sandoz Pharmaceuticals, in Press.

Weinstein, A., and R. Patton. Trends in "chronicity" in the New York State mental hospitals. *American Journal of Public Health,* June 1970, 60(6).

Williams, D. H., S. Jacobs, A. Debski, and M. Revere. Introducing the problem-oriented record on a psychiatric inpatient unit. *Hospital & Community Psychiatry,* Jan. 1974, 25(1): 25-28.

VI

EVALUATION THROUGH SOCIAL ECOLOGY

13

PSYCHOLOGY, ECOLOGY AND COMMUNITY:
A SETTING FOR EVALUATIVE RESEARCH

STANLEY LEHMANN

New York University

The growing need for the field of psychology to address itself to current human problems is still being met with traditional reluctance if not, on occasion, with outright resistance. The great majority of psychologists still prefer to practice their discipline within the confines of the laboratory or consulting room. This has led to a profusion of microtheories which have not provem themselves adequate to the task of suggesting solutions or even approaches to the major social problems of the day. By virtue of these same deficits, the field has largely failed to supply adequate models for the evaluation of the ameliorative attempts that have been launched. As a result, such attempts have frequently been poorly conceptualized in the first place and are not likely to lead to meaningful evaluative studies. Researchers intent on evaluation are seen as intrusive critics who are more prone to produce negative appraisals than constructive suggestions. This sorry state of affairs places the scientist-researcher at odds with the activist-innovator so that neither benefits from the experience of the other and the field suffers as a consequence.

The subdiscipline of community psychology has arisen in large part as a response to these conditions. Although community studies abound in anthropology and sociology, they are nearly nonexistent in psychology. The field of mental health,

AUTHOR'S NOTE: Dr. Lehmann is Associate Professor of Psychology at New York University and Associate Research Scientist with the New York State Department of Mental Hygiene. His research interests lie in the areas of community mental health and reactions to stress. The writing of this paper was supported by the New York State Department of Mental Hygiene which sponsors the Community Research Program at New York University.

[485]

however, has forced a realization that the social context of behavior cannot be ignored. Studies like those of Hollingshead and Redlich (1958) and Faris and Dunham (1963) were important milestones in making this point. More recently, Barker (1968) has provided a powerful argument for cataloging the relationships between situations and all forms of behavior. Yet, in spite of the ever-ready acknowledgment of environmental influences on behavior, little systematic attention has been paid to man's behavioral habitat: the community in which he lives.

The contemporary passion for ecology derives more from a sense of impending disaster than from a true understanding of the interrelationships between living organisms and their environments. We are appalled by the eutriphication of a stream that accrues to our economic or aesthetic disadvantage just as we are appalled by social unrest that threatens an accustomed way of life. Neither case is necessarily an instance of natural disorder. In fact, each is more likely to represent a process change that renders the system more viable. Whether or not it is to our liking is quite a different matter. A similar confusion intrudes on our understanding of deviant behavior so that we cannot tell whether we are dealing with a specific individual disorder, a collective social disorder, or a result of social censure. To a considerable extent, these differences arise from isolated viewpoints which do not adequately integrate the individual, behavioral, and social aspects of a complex system. It is perhaps most obvious in the field of mental health that these differences must be resolved before substantial progress can be made.

PSYCHOLOGY

Laboratory research became an early hallmark in the history of psychology and, curiously for a natural science, naturalistic observation lost out in respectability to the laboratory. Rigor was interpreted in such a way that most of the influences that affect behavior had to be excluded from consideration because they interfered with the studied manipulations of a laboratory science. Clinical psychology which attempts to deal with the individual in depth also resorts to the relative isolation of the consulting room in order to achieve some sort of conceptual purity. What is lost, however, is a good deal that is relevant to the behavior of an individual or a class of individuals in the context in which they usually behave. Rigor could as easily be defined as the necessity to consider all of the manifold factors that influence behavioral outcomes. The relative ease of the exclusionary methodology as compared with the methodological problems of a holistic approach has probably disposed the science to favor the first course. A great deal has been learned through the independent manipulation of single variables in a protected setting. The considerable body of knowledge that has been accrued by the field comes almost exclusively from this methodology, but the continued growth of psychology requires expansion of these limited horizons.

Such exhortations as these are not new. H. S. Murray (1938), W. Koehler (1938), and K. Lewin (1951) have advocated broadening the concerns and methods of psychology. Recently, the cause has been joined by others (Ring, 1967; McGuire, 1967; Barker, 1968; Williams and Raush, 1969). This does not constitute an appeal to abandon laboratory science but to extend the concerns of this science

to the broader arena in which behavior takes place. The field of clinical psychology has done this to some extent by incorporating the newly developed methods of family therapy and its involvement in milieu therapy. Laboratory and field studies are not only compatible but essential to one another. Finesse can be obtained in the laboratory and the consulting room, but finesse is only applicable where it fits. The world outside the laboratory and the consulting room is the unique testing ground for the theories and observations developed in protected settings. Unfortunately, the fit between the two is often less than one would like, and consequently psychology is accused of not being relevant. While part of the difficulty stems from the lack of effort to extend findings *en vitrio* to the world *en vivo,* another part stems from omitting an initial phase of scientific investigation: the careful and systematic observation of nature. Such observation provides a knowledge of the distribution of phenomena and their interrelationships and can lead to theory building which is productive and non-trivial. This is not to say that science must be concerned only with problems of immediate practical importance. The history of science demonstrates that this has seldom been the major preoccupation of scientists, and it is probably also true that science would have been a good deal less productive had it been the case. Nevertheless, there is good reason to believe that the best questions come from an observation of nature rather than from the existence of a convenient methodology.

ECOLOGY

Ecology, as a well developed biological science, is based on the premise that living organisms must be studied in relation to the other organisms with which they coexist and in relation to the nonorganic setting which they occupy. Man is no exception, and the biological and environmental concomitants of his existence are beginning to be appreciated. Psychologists have been paying increasing attention to the environmental surround (Barker, 1968; Proshansky, Ittelson and Rivlin, 1970; Wohlwill and Carson, 1972; Ittelson et al., 1974; Moos and Insel, 1974) but this does not always produce a consistent ecological point of view. Barker, for example, presents a well-documented ecological theory but tends to lose the importance of interactions by concentrating on the environmental settings. He makes the striking observation that there are some situations in which almost 100% of the behavior can be predicted from the setting but fails to note the important qualification that the participants must share a communality of experience. Although there is a noticeable conformity of behavior among the spectators at a baseball game, it is unlikely that a foreigner would share in this conformity.. Even more important is the fact that he would probably not select the setting in the first place. Membership in some sort of shared community is part of the ecological framework. This is one aspect of the ecological model that removes it from the overly simple cause and effect paradigm so familiar in psychology.

Reductionism, not to be confused with determinism, has led to a philosophy of science where ecological considerations are largely ignored. Where every effect is assumed to have a unique and unitary cause, questions can be answered by singular

antecedent events. This is translated into experimental design where only one element is varied at a time or in clinical psychology becomes a search for the precipitating condition common to a given syndrome. Although it is easy to accuse these ideas of being overly simplistic, it must be admitted that they have perservered because they are frequently heuristic. A striking example is the periodic table of elements based on a trinity of fundamental particles which have long since lost their immutable properties. In psychology, the quantum theory of intelligence is another example. The prediction of responses from the number of reinforced trials or the assignment of response tendencies, such as conformity, from prior behavior samples follows from a conception of human behavior as an aggregate of some type of behavioral fundamental particle. Such concepts are heuristic so long as a static state of affairs continues to exist. This is to say, given that just about everything stays the same, an individual will continue to behave much as he has done in the past. Of course, everything seldom remains quite the same but, since an important behavioral dynamic is to maintain as stable an equilibrium as possible, the effect is to produce a consistency where such predictions are possible.

The ecological model is based on the observation that organisms living together in an environment will become adapted to their habitat and to each other in such a way that their essential needs are met. An interlocking system of mutual interdependence, such that the organisms contribute to the maintenance of the environment and to each other, tends to ensure the continuity of the species. The sedentary pond is the classic example of a balanced or "climax" ecosystem where the flora and fauna that inhabit it live together in a relatively enduring system of mutual support (see Amos, 1970). It is the nature of the ecosystem to tend toward a state of equilibrium by way of a series of stages or "successions" so long as conditions external to the system are reasonably constant and appropriate. The popular concern over pollution reflects the fact that changing conditions may alter the natural ecosystem so that it no longer provides the resources that were previously available. In like manner, social change, mental illness, behavioral deviations, and many other phenomena of interest to contemporary psychology often represent states of disequilibria where the convenient fiction of a dynamic equilibrium no longer holds.

Human beings, like all other organisms and along with them, live in an ecosystem. Ultimately they are dependent upon natural resources in one form or another but they are distinctive from most other organisms in the extent to which they have transformed and modified their environment. To a very large extent, the modern urban human environment is man-made. Men live in concrete cities with central heating, air conditioning, and rapid transit, and their food arrives in plastic packages at the end of a vast technological food chain. They do not have to live entirely at the whim of nature but are instead, very much at the whim of each other. By far the most important features of the man-made environment are the institutionalized behaviors called social and cultural. They represent collective behavioral adaptations that have become part of the ecosystem. Anthropologist A. L. Kroeber (1939) noted the parallel between cultural forms of North American tribes and the ecological areas in which they lived. Some anthropologists have taken

the position that many, if not most, social customs can be ultimately related to environmental adaptation (Vayda, 1969). As early as the 1920s, the Chicago School of Sociology under Park and Burgess charted the association between behavior and the urban environment. With the development of the study of human ecology, the distinction between the natural and the social environment became blurred since it was evident that they mutually affected one another (Alihan, 1938). Social patterns derived from environmental adaptations influence other behavioral interactions which lead to a changed environment and so the process continues. For the behavioral scientist today, human ecology is largely social ecology.

COMMUNITY

Bioecologists call the minimal network of organisms and their natural resources that are mutually interdependent a community. In human ecology, this minimal functional unit may coincide with the popular notion of a geographic community where people live, reproduce, work, and shop together, or it may be poorly localized in space. The sedentary pond is a highly localized community but that of a migrating species may be very diffuse. Functional, rather than geographic integrity is the defining characteristic of the community. For the psychologist, the community is the arena in which the individual acquires his behavioral patterns and carries out the major functions of his life. During his lifetime, an individual may live in a number of different communities and some of them, especially if they are urban, may have little local identity. Nonetheless, at any given time, he is in interaction with a number of significant others who influence his behavior, help to satisfy his needs, are influenced by him in turn, and who, along with his physical environment, make up his community. The community must work out mutually adaptive behaviors and roles to support the majority of its members if it is to endure. Once it has achieved a functional integrity with sufficient diversity to sustain its membership, it will tend to maintain the functional organization it has achieved. As a mutually reactive system, the community will absorb or minimize change insofar as possible. This tendency often results in the phenomenon known as "cultural lag," but it also provides enduring behavior patterns and a more stable environment with which to cope. The well balanced ecological community is a natural accommodation which affords its members the maximum opportunity for survival.

Practical concerns with social problems, mental illness, and growing evidence of a general malaise have generated an interest in community psychology. As an area of specialization, it is loosely defined and consists mostly of the conviction that individual problems are inseparable from community problems. As working tenets, it supports a host of ideas such as "intervention," "outreach," "catchment areas," and others which signify good intentions more than anything else. The concept of community has remained not only largely undefined but also largely ignored. What passes for community obeys a logic that is more often political than geographic and seldom possesses any functional integrity. The idea of a catchment area is frequently the ecological equivalent of a fisherman's net.

The analogy with bioecology suggests that a human community adequately defined can be a valid and useful concept. Functional interdependencies establish the form and extent of a viable community. Because it is difficult to imagine a circumscribed human community as a closed system, its boundaries must be assumed to be permeable and fluid. Since function is a defining concept, there may be distinctive but overlapping communities. In addition, function will determine differing levels of organization among community structures (Suttles, 1972). The biological analogy of cells, organs, and systems (Thomas, 1974) demonstrates that systems exist within hierarchies of other systems, and they too have their functional interdependencies. This conceptualization of organization may seem to become rapidly overwhelming, but essentially it is little more than the recognition of the system in which human behavior takes place. Within such a system it is possible to study the individual, the family, the community, or the social order, but each of these is somewhat of an abstraction without taking into account the matrix in which it is embedded or the components which make it up. Thus the nets cast by intervention, outreach, and catchment areas should follow the networks of functional interrelationships rather than administrative fiat, political history, or geography.

INNOVATION

The conceptual model developed here is an attempt to provide a framework within which to both ask and answer questions in a way which will lead to the development of a unified and useful body of knowledge. It has been posited that human behavior takes place in a social and physical context to which it is responsive and which imposes both directions and limitations. This context can best be understood as a community in which individuals occupy an extensive variety of niches which represent the functional interrelationships of the system. Change is brought about by a new configuration or combination of components rather than by the presence or absence of independent conditions. The high degree of interdependency within the system can either deter or promote change. As a mutually reactive system, there is a strong tendency to maintain a dynamic equilibrium or state of homeostasis. On the other hand, once a new configuration begins to evolve, the entire system must move to a new level of equilibrium to accommodate it. Innovation, then, must operate within this set of dynamics. In dealing with individuals, it may be quite feasible to work within the quasi-stable systems of family and community. If, however, a systems change seems to be required, not only must a good deal of inertia be overcome but a new configuration of those systems must be anticipated. Even individual changes can have systems ramifications so that one has to be prepared to deal with a somewhat different situation from that which originally existed. It is therefore frequently necessary to think of innovation not in terms of pre-existing condition but in terms of an outcome condition.

Recognition of these factors has increasingly oriented service delivery toward the community with the intention of promoting more effective change and, following the model of public health, to exercise a preventive influence. The first question

which arises if one is going to address himself to the community is, "What is the community?" This is not an easy question to answer, for multiple communities are likely to be involved in the attempt to deliver services to a cohort of individuals (Panzetta, 1971). If mental health services are at issue, the relevant community comprises those who are mentally ill, their families, their friends, their employers, and those who are prone to be high risks. Overlapping this community, and in hierarchical relationships to it, are the other organizations and agencies also concerned with these individuals. While such a community is relatively easy to specify, it is a good deal more difficult to identify. Here, appropriate research can be immensely valuable. Unfortunately it is usually missing so those who propose to deliver services must also endeavor to identify their potential clientele. Then, of course, they must somehow involve them in the service delivery system, an enterprise fraught with complications (Hersch, 1972). Whoever the targeted clientele, there is a great likelihood that they will self-select themselves to some extent so the community actually being served may or may not be like the one that was anticipated. Even an elementary record system can provide some feedback on this question but more elaborate information gathering can provide valuable data on the potential client population and their needs. What is needed to round out the picture at this point is some idea of what those who are not in the client population are like. This is a logical first step in outreach since it is always possible that the primary target population is not being overly responsive or that some more serious or more numerous associated needs are not being met. A relatively simple technique for doing this is to visit a sample of the immediate neighbors of known clients (Lehmann, 1970). There is a good probability that these neighbors share much in common with the clients and can reveal something about the non-clients as well as about the impact of the service delivery system itself. This information can and should have an important influence on the ultimate delivery of services. It should also be clear that research is a compatible and useful part of the innovative process.

Innovation means change and is instrumented by a change agent who needs an imposing variety of skills as an administrator, scientist, educator, and politician. His job is especially difficult because he has no well-organized body of knowledge or technology to fall back on and the community in which he is working is equally inexperienced (Iscoe, 1974). There is also a mission with its goals and means, the latter usually being better defined than the rest. This in itself constitutes a problem since the means should logically derive from the ends rather than the other way about as is frequently the case. The objectives, more or less clearly defined, will be to change behavior either of individuals or groups with the intention of enhancing human welfare and will involve some form of intervention to modify the environment, change existing interrelationships, or to provide additional options. Any such intervention must alter, to some extent, the system on which it is operating with the consequence that behaviors and conditions other than those targeted may be modified and, because the newly created context is different from the original, those behaviors and conditions may not respond as anticipated. The unexpected and highly debated results of moving slum dwellers into new high-rise apartments is a case in point. The change not only affects the physical environment but social

patterns, communication channels, and acquired life-styles so the requirements of adaptive behavior are forcibly altered. The result, often enough, is a breakdown of such behaviors and the physical environment, which is seen as the culprit, receives the reprisals and the well-intentioned innovators are defeated and disaffected.

A knowledge of the system relations that describe the ecology of human behavior is invaluable for establishing the locus of a planned change and for previewing the possible consequences of the change. An ecological system may be changed at many points, but the point at which the change is incurred will influence the outcome. A desired behavioral change can come as the result of direct modification of behavior, of a change in the setting, of a change in the consequences of the behavior, or a change in the internal state of the actor. A child can be discouraged from stealing cookies by preventing access to the cookie jar, by hiding the cookie jar, by spanking him, or by inculcating in him a sense of guilt for so doing. Any of these measures may end the act of stealing cookies, but the overall consequences may be radically different. An ecological conceptualization can increase the number of available alternatives for instigating a desired change. Schwitzgebel (1970), for example, has noted that technological change regularly produces drastic alterations in behavioral systems and suggests this device as a means of effective planned change. Technological change usually represents process change and thus is pervasive as well as forceful. Under such circumstances it is especially important to be able to appraise the range of possible consequences.

The history of the utilization of DDT provides a useful cautionary tale about attending to only a part of a system being manipulated. The complexity of the human ecosystem makes it improbable that all conceivable consequences will be foreseen, but an understanding of the system will help in knowing where to look for problems. The cookie-snatching child whose behavior has been impeded will have other forms of redress depending upon how he is blocked, and the behavioral scientist should be able to anticipate some of the likely possibilities. The moral for the innovator is that planned innovation should be much more carefully worked out and considered in a much broader range than is commonly done. Unfortunately social reforms are characteristically designed with a good deal less care than that which goes into designing a bridge although the latter is infinitely less complex. Here again, effective teamwork between the researcher and the designer can begin to develop a comprehensive body of knowledge which will lead to the technology needed to produce planned and predictable change.

EVALUATION

Innovations are, almost by definition, experimental for they represent an untried attempt to produce a change. Evaluation research represents the effort to determine the effects of the innovation, but it can address itself to much more than the questions of what went right and what went wrong. Since social innovation tends to be a complex process, it is helpful to document as carefully as possible what when on. The need to identify the population sample involved (who they are and who they are not) has already been discussed briefly. Because this sample is seldom homogeneous, it is useful to also examine subgroupings. Cost effectiveness and

operational questions can be as important as methodological and conceptual ones. The not unnatural foreboding of administrators, well characterized by Campbell (1969), often tends to keep evaluation research at the level of monitoring and record keeping; but there is a wide range of services it can perform and, properly presented, it need not be threatening. The fact that it goes under the name of applied research implies another limitation that is misleading. The appelation "applied" refers to the need to know and the prospect of immediate utility, but it does not prevent it from being theoretical as well. The ecological context of innovation and evaluation that is advocated here is a theoretical framework with important implications for the study of behavior in any setting. The field setting is a convenient arena in which to try out the formulations of scientific psychology. It is, in fact, the ultimate testing ground for which the laboratory is only the drawing board.

In certain respects, evaluative field research looks like any other kind of research. The social innovation under investigation is a manipulation applied to a selected sample of an assumed population. It is hypothesized that those treated in this fashion will turn out differently in some predictable way from those who are not. In other ways, however, this procedure is necessarily different from that applied in the laboratory. There are almost always a substantial number of possibly salient variables that are not and cannot be rigorously controlled. Frequently it is difficult or impossible to come by an adequate control group, and the nature of the situation may prohibit some kinds of measurements that would otherwise be desirable. These difficulties and others weaken the research design so that the effects have to be stronger in order to be observed. On the other hand, field research has the advantage of dealing with authentic behavior in its normal setting so that what is going on is more apt to be salient in the lives of the participants and hence the effects are more likely to be strong. Nevertheless, anything that helps strengthen the design is all to the good. Control groups are invaluable if at all possible. It should be noted in passing that control groups do not mean that someone is denied an assumed valuable treatment since alternative treatments can serve as controls. It should be further noted in passing that if the treatment were known to be the best one could do, evaluative research would be redundant. The same could be said of randomization of treatment which is another powerful research device. Perhaps the commonest hazard of real life research is the imposition of simultaneous multiple treatments either advertently or inadvertently. Not only does this confound the attribution of effects, but the several treatments may interact with each other quite differently from how they would behave alone or in other combinations. If multiple treatments are to be investigated and they cannot be assigned to different groups, they can at least be strung out in a time series so that their individual and joint effects can be appraised. Methods are available for handling such contingencies (Campbell, 1969; Campbell and Stanley, 1966). Correlational techniques, such as multiple regression, cannonical correlations, cross-lag correlations, and path analysis, can be employed where strict experimental paradigms are not possible; but no statistical technique can make up for a deficient design.

If, at this point, good design can be counted upon as a given, it is time to look at the virtues of the ecological model for evaluative research. Normal variation is a prominent feature of an ecological system; thus, control and comparison conditions arise as a consequence of natural alterations. Systematic variations among variables represent the working equations of the system and, as these change, the inner workings reveal themselves. Techniques such as epidemiology, social area analysis and ethology (discussed respectively by Susser, Struening, Cassell in this part) make full use of these natural variations and in so doing have provided important theoretical and applied contributions. In social innovation, the variations are to some extent man-made and hence less likely to be judiciously chosen than when nature has done the selection. As with poor research design, the effects will be less strong but presumably nature has not obliged in providing the desired change so that we are left with the responsibility for doing so. Nevertheless, techniques like those noted above (and including ethnomethodology; Garfinkel, 1967) or modifications of them are valuable for locating changed system relationships in order to evaluate and understand the changes. Man-made interventions will effect not only specific, isolated variables but will change the working equations of the system. Looking for changes in relationships within the changed system or comparing those relationships with a comparable part of the unchanged system can be a more sensitive way of assessing differences than by looking for changes in discrete variables. It has the added advantage that secondary effects and unforeseen consequences are more apt to be discovered. While recent policy and administrative protocol in community mental health has produced powerful first order effects which can be seen in length of hospital stay and the number of hospital beds occupied, other and related trends can be found in the number of single room occupancies and the attendant problems of medical and social welfare along with concentrations of other forms of social pathology. A more profound knowledge of community dynamics than we now possess is required to understand these relationships adequately. This information could come from well-designed, specialized community studies, such as an exploration of the careers of mental patients, but until such information is available, it will have to come from cautious analyses of epidemiological and social area studies. This is the same sort of material that is needed for intensive planning and designing of social innovation and for anticipating the broad range secondary effects. Thus research and innovation are highly congruent enterprises.

The researcher is often seen as an outsider by those inside the service delivery system, but he neither belongs on the outside nor is it possible for him to remain on the outside. Just as social innovation becomes part of the need-resource network of the community, the research enterprise becomes part of the internal service delivery system and the external community. Unobtrusive techniques have been devised to minimize the effects of research on that which is being researched (Webb et al., 1966), but the mere knowledge that research is going on affects the process. The concept of action research (Sashkin et al., 1973) incorporates the investigative process into the service delivery system. Research provides new channels of information which optimally become part of the natural feedback network of the

community action program. The program of social innovation, like the community itself, is an open system and it is dependent upon outside input to maintain a dynamic equilibrium. Von Bertalanffy (1962) has postulated that open systems, unlike closed systems, are not subject to entropy but in fact tend toward greater differentiation (negative entropy) because of constant external input. It is tempting to look at communities such as the Shakers and Mennonites which have behaved more like closed systems and have not flourished under changing conditions. Integrated feedback loops, both positive and negative, are an essential part of a natural ecosystem in maintaining a functional balance. In nature this is a slow and circumspect process and so should it be in human intervention. Reliable and carefully evaluated data can feed back into the system to prevent harmful excesses, to maximize desired effects, and to enable it to respond to the changes that it has introduced.

Research is necessary to maintain the viability of a natural ecosystem upon which an intervention has been imposed. Within the natural system, feedback networks, information channels, and control mechanisms exist in abundance. Population explosions, for example, are readily handled by disease, famine, and changes in mortality and fertility rates. It is precisely because these natural mechanisms are not to our liking that we invent our own means of control but to do so effectively we must incorporate the necessary regulatory devices. Research is no luxury. We must first understand the workings of the system so that we can intervene effectively. Then we must provide efficient channels for information exchange, the means for processing this information and responding to it appropriately. The dichotomy between pure and applied, theoretical and evaluative research is not useful here. Nor is the dichotomy between innovation and research a useful one. Unless the process is an integrated one, it has little chance of survival. The mostly unmourned memory of the Great Society is proof enough of this.

REFERENCES

Alihan, M. A. *Social ecology*. New York: Columbia University Press, 1938.

Amos, W. H. Teeming life as a pond. *National Geographic*, 1970, 138: 274-298.

Barker, R. G. *Ecological psychology*. Stanford: Stanford University Press, 1968.

Bertalanffy, L. V. General systems theory: A critical review. *General Systems*, 1962, 7: 1-20.

Campbell, D. T. Reforms as experiments. *American Psychologist*, 1969, 24: 409-429. (See Chapter 5 of this Handbook.)

———, and J. C. Stanley. *Experimental and quasi-experimental design for research*. Chicago, Rand McNally, 1966.

Faris, R. E. L. and W. H. Dunham. *Mental disorder in urban areas*. New York: Wiley, 1963.

Garfinkel, H. *Studies in ethnomethodology*. Englewood Cliffs, N.J.: Prentice-Hall, 1967.

Hersch, C. Social history, mental health and community control. *American Psychologist*, 1972, 27: 749-754.

Hollingshead, A. B., and F. Redlich. *Social class and mental illness*. New York: Wiley, 1958.

Iscoe, I. Community psychology and the competent community. *American Psychologist*, 1974, 20: 607-613.

Ittelson, W. H., H. M. Proshansky, L. G. Rivlin, G. H. Winkel, and D. Dempsey. *An introduction to environmental psychology*. New York: Holt, Rinehart & Winston, 1974.

Koehler, W. *The place of value in a world of facts.* New York: Liveright, 1938.

Kroeber, A. *Cultural and natural areas of native North America.* Berkeley: University of California Press, 1939.

Lehmann, S. Selected self-help: A study of clients of a community social psychiatry service. *American Journal of Psychiatry,* 1970, 126: 1444-1454.

Lewin, K. *Field theory in social science.* New York: Harper & Row, 1951.

McGuire, W. J. Some impending re-orientations in social psychology: Some thoughts provoked by Kenneth Ring. *Journal of Experimental Social Psychology,* 1967, 3: 124-139.

Moos, R. H., and P. M. Insel, (eds.) *Issues in social ecology.* Palo Alto, Calif.: National Press Books, 1974.

Murray, H. A. *Explorations in personality.* New York: Oxford University Press, 1938.

Panzetta, A. F. The concept of community. *Archives of General Psychiatry,* 1971, 25: 291-297.

Proshansky, H. M., W. H. Ittelson, and J. C. Rivlin. (eds.) *Environmental psychology.* New York: Holt, Rinehart & Winston, 1970.

Ring, K. Experimental social psychology: Some sober questions about some frivolous values. *Journal of Experimental Social Psychology,* 1967, 3: 113-123.

Sashkin, M., W. C. Morris, and L. Horst. A comparison of social and organizational change models: Information flow data use processes. *Psychological Review,* 1973, 80: 510-526.

Schwitzgebel, R. L. Behavior instrumentation and social technology. *American Psychologist,* 1970, 25: 491-499.

Suttles, G. D. *The social construction of communities.* Chicago: University of Chicago Press, 1972.

Thomas, L. *The lives of a cell.* New York: Viking Press, 1974.

Vayda, A. P. An ecological approach in cultural anthropology. *Bucknell Review,* 1969, 17: 112-119.

Webb, E. J., D. T. Campbell, R. D. Schwartz, and L. Sechrest. *Unobtrusive measures: Nonreactive research in the social sciences.* Chicago: Rand McNally, 1966.

Willems, E. P., and H. L. Raush, (eds.) *Naturalistic viewpoints in psychological research.* New York: Holt, Rinehart & Winston, 1969.

Wohlwill, J. F., and D. H. Carson. *Environment and the social sciences.* Washington, D.C.: American Psychological Association, 1972.

14

EPIDEMIOLOGICAL MODELS

M. SUSSER

Columbia University

In current definition, epidemiology is the study of the distribution and determinants of states of health in human populations. The modern epidemiologist
studies the occurrence, the evolution, and the causes of health disorders, maintains
surveillance over trends, and seeks methods to prevent or control their occurrence.
For these purposes, the enumeration of health disorders is a first step; and the next
step is the study of their relationship to society and habitat, that is, the way they
vary in the population and the attributes and circumstances with which they are
associated.

Populations are central to epidemiological study. Whereas case studies deal only
with numerators, population studies give the numerators meaning by relating the
cases to the population from which they are drawn, thus, creating a standard of
comparison, without which no conclusion can be reached on the abnormality or
distinctiveness of any phenomenon.

Epidemiology shares this procedure, in a general way, with other sciences that
study populations, for instance the social sciences, human biology, and population
genetics. The study of populations also involves the study of society, for states of
health do not exist in a vacuum apart from people. People form societies, and any
study of the attributes of people is also a study of the manifestations of the form,
the structure, and the processes of social forces.

The disciplines studying society differ one from another in the selection of the
particular substance of study. At the same time, by differentiating itself through its
choice of states of health, epidemiology shares common ground with other medical
sciences. It differs from other medical sciences in that the unit of observation is

populations and not individuals. Epidemiology brings into medicine, with this unit of observation, another level of organization.

The level of organization of populations and societies introduces a set of variables[1] over and above those germane to individuals. These variables are complex and numerous, and their use in medicine creates a body of knowledge about states of health different from that obtained in clinical and laboratory medicine and complementary to it. The study of disease in individuals can suggest the nature of the disordered state of functioning and its progress through time. Studies of individuals cannot determine, even in a series of cases, the limits of the disorder in relation to normality or securely predict its onset, progress, and outcome. To garner this knowledge the epidemiological method, which provides data both sufficient in number and chosen in a manner that permits meaningful comparisions, must be used. Only by such comparisons is it possible to comprehend all the aspects of a disease process at different points in time. The spectrum to be comprehended starts with the antecedent factors that cause disease, moves to the precursors that may enable the prediction and prevention of disease, and passes through the full span of clinical manifestations, course, and eventual outcome.

SURVEY METHOD

The survey is the general method that establishes the real relation between two or more variables in a population in numerical terms (Hyman, 1955). Surveys rely on the information that can be elicited and collated from existing sources (not only records, but people who can say how they feel or what happened). The survey sets up suitable mechanisms to collect the information. In its broad sense, the term survey can be made to include the *secondary analysis* of existing data collected for purposes other than the study in hand, for instance, from registers of vital statistics, from hospital records, and from censuses. For example, in the London of 1662, parishes reported deaths by cause in weekly "bills of mortality." Originally intended as a plague warning to allow the wealthier classes time to leave the city, the aggregated figures were used by John Graunt (1662) to study the population in relation to the environment. He found differences in mortality between the sexes and between urban and rural areas, noted changes in causes of death over time, and offered statistical interpretations of his findings. His approach to the study was that of secondary analysis of existing data accumulated in registers. More commonly, the term describes the planned collection of data for a specific study by means of the *field survey.*

One use of surveys is *descriptive,* to set our norms and limits of the distribution of variables in numerical terms. Surveys quantify the attributes of populations, of environments, and of periods of time. They provide an understanding of a selected problem, its size, its nature, among whom and where it is to be found, and, indeed, whether the problem exists.

A second use of surveys is *explanatory* or *analytical:* to compare different populations in relation to environments and trends in time and to account for the variations between them. To explain relationships and establish causes, specific variables or combinations of variables must first be conceived and then isolated, and

the effects of their presence or absence predicted. In the explanatory survey, the prediction or hypothesis is tested by seeking out circumstances in which the effects of the presence and absence of the supposed cause can be observed and compared. The comparisons can be made as valid as possible through the proper use of techniques of sampling (the numerators in the rates compared relate to denominators that represent known populations), techniques of data collection (as much information as needed is obtained and is unbiased, replicable, and means what we say it does), and of research design (an efficient means of answering the question one aims to answer is used).

The essence of the analytical survey is the comparision of similarities and dissimilarities in the past, the present, or the awaited experience of populations. The field survey is most often retrospective. The retrospective survey is commonly a *case-control* study and starts with the case of established disorder (MacMahon and Pugh, 1970). Thus, a population of cases that manifests given effects is chosen for observation, and the history of supposedly causal past events and experiences in the population is compared with a control population that does not manifest the effects. The prospective survey is normally a *cohort* study and starts with the experience thought to give rise to disorder. Thus, a population exposed to a given experience is chosen for observation, and the development of cases in that population is compared with a control population not so exposed.[2] In either case, the survey is influenced by events. A survey can exercise no direct control over the variables that are the object of study; it must exploit and observe the unfolding of the natural and the social environment through history.

The survey and the epidemiological or social experiment share the basic design of the survey method by which the effects of different group experiences are compared. Thus, a survey, even if done from records after the event, to some degree approximates the epidemiological experiment by the way in which it reconstructs the past experience of the population. The essential comparisons made in case-control, cohort, and experimental studies can all be represented in the fourfold table such as Table 14.1.

The cells of the table represent the frequency in a population with which both a manifestation or effect (the dependent variable) and an experience or hypothetical cause (the independent variable) occur both separately and together. In other words, the table represents the degree to which the two variables are associated with each other. The letters a, b, c, and d stand for the numbers of individuals in each cell. Whatever the study design, the cells of the table show all four possible combinations of any two characteristics in a survey population.

TABLE 14.1

Independent Variable	Dependent Variable		Total
	Present	Absent	
Exposed	a	b	a + b
Unexposed	c	d	c + d
Total	a + c	b + d	a + b + c + d

In a case-control study, individuals are first identified, and classified into case and control groups by the presence or absence of the manifestation under study. In the table, the group of cases is represented by a + c, the group of controls by b + d. The frequencies of the independent variable in the two groups are then compared. That is,

$$\frac{a}{a+c} \text{ is compared with } \frac{b}{b+d}$$

A higher frequency or exposure in the group of cases points to the association of the two study variables.

In cohort and experimental studies, individuals are first identified and classified according to whether they were exposed or not to the experience under study. In the table the group exposed is represented by a + b, the unexposed control group by c + d. The frequencies of the dependent variable among both groups is then compared. That is,

$$\frac{a}{a+b} \text{ is compared with } \frac{c}{c+d}$$

Here a higher frequency of cases in the exposed group points to the association of the two variables.

CONCEPTS OF ENVIRONMENT

The results a survey can yield follow strictly from the nature and specificity with which steady variables are conceived and isolated. Different concepts of reality lead to the selection of different types of variables. In science generally, as in other areas of study, concepts play a major role in determining modes of thought. Concepts are the organizing principles by which facts are brought together and woven into a coherent whole. Concepts thus determine the particular explanations sought for the phenomena observed and even the phenomena chosen for observation. Early in the nineteenth century, medicine and the public health movement were dominated by the miasma theory of Sydenham and others that foul emanations from impure soil and water cause disease. At that time, investigation sought to prove the ill effect of miasma; prevention tried to eliminate the sources of miasma in slums and poor sanitation. Thus Edwin Chadwick published the Report on the Sanitary Condition of the Labouring Population of Great Britain in 1842 (MacMahon and Pugh, 1970). This work, inspired by the "miasma" theory, relates area mortality to drainage. After Jacob Henle had formulated the conditions that needed to be met to prove the germ theory (Rosen, 1937) and, some twenty years later, Louis Pasteur had demonstrated the existence of microorganisms, a quite different course of investigation was followed. Microorganisms became the object of the search for causes, and containment of their spread the object of prevention.

Yet the concepts of miasma and of germs both proved effective when applied to disease prevention. Evidently different theories can often work equally well as guides to action. Assumptions lie behind all scientific theories; the governing

assumptions of a faulty theory may be sufficiently general to permit a broad range of effective action within its terms. In brief, concepts and theory enable predictions to be tested and choices to be made among paths of action. But different theories can lead to equally successful action in the same situation. One theory is better than another only when it is faced with more specific tests which require narrower assumptions, which the less effective theory cannot meet. Although justified by both the miasma theory and the germ theory, sanitation prevents only one broad class of infectious diseases. Immunization chemotherapy, and antibiotics are needed to prevent others. The concept of the *environment* as a source of disease goes back to the Hippocratic writings. In the book, *Ave, Nube, Places,* the authors speculated on the relationship between disease and the physical environment of climate, water, soil, and prevailing winds. In doing so, they distinguished the environment from the *host,* as represented by the individual constitution. Only in the seventeenth century, however, did it become apparent with the world of John Graunt that understanding of the environment required the numerical approach to populations, as surveys. Quantitative studies of disease mortality became the foundation of the Public Health movement. Thus Edwin Chadwick's famous Report May 1842 is a compilation of many local surveys. The quote below, from Chadwick (1842: 151), is set out on the model of a "before and after" experiment and describes the condition of the population of Wisbech by mortality rates before its exposure to the experience of living in an area that had been drained, and again after. The independent variable postulated as cause is drainage; the dependent variable is deaths.

On reference to a very perfect account of the baptisms, marriages, and burials, in Wisbech, from 1558 to 1826, I find that in the decennial periods, of which 1801, 1811, and 1821, were the middle years, the baptisms and burials were as under:

	Baptisms	Burials	Population in 1801
1796 to 1805	1627	1535	4710
1806 to 1815	1654	1313	5209
1816 to 1825	2165	1390	6515

In the first of the three periods the mortality was 1 in 31; in the second, 1 in 40; in the third, 1 in 47; the latter being less than the mean mortality of the Kingdom for the last two years. (See *Registrar General's Second Report,* p. 4, folio edition.) These figures clearly show that the mortality has wonderfully diminished in the last half century, and who can doubt but that the increased salubrity of the fens produced by drainage is a chief cause of the improvement.

A more sophisticated research design than control by the "before and after" comparison of an environment was the comparison by Chadwick (1842: 103) of a drained area with an undrained area at three parallel points in time. This comparison provided a control for the historical factors, presumably shared by both areas, that might have brought about a decline in mortality and protected against wrongly attributing such a decline in the drained area to drainage. Writes Chadwick,

The following has been the proportion of deaths to the population in the two towns:

	Beccles	Bungay
Between the years 1811 and 1821	1 in 67	1 in 69
Between the years 1821 and 1831	1 in 72	1 in 67
Between the years 1831 and 1841	1 in 71	1 in 59

You will therefore see that the rate of mortality has gradually diminished in Beccles since it has been drained, whilst in Bungay, notwithstanding its larger proportion of rural population, it has considerably increased.

The Ditchingham Factory may have given a greater increase of population to Bungay than I have allowed for, but on the other hand, the Roman Catholics and the Independents bury many of their dead in their own ground, which I have not calculated upon. Since writing the above, I have been over to Bungay, to examine more particularly the state of its drainage, which is much worse than I had any idea of. If their population should much increase, their mortality will increase much faster.

The numerical approach to the understanding of public health problems related to the environment taken by Chadwick was followed by epidemiologists throughout the nineteenth century, and by the end of the century was well established in epidemiological thinking.

The discovery of microorganisms and their effects thus gave impetus to the search for specific agents that caused specific conditions. This search still continues. At the same time, from the standpoint of the development of causal models, this great spurt in medical research diminished awareness of the rarity of one-to-one relationships and of the complex relationships between causes and effects that exist in the real world. The concept of specific agents as causes of disease enlarged knowledge, but the concept was adequate only up to a point. Like the miasma theory, the germ theory failed to explain many medical observations and had to be rethought before further advance became possible.

Pasteur's work and thought opened up another major area of research, that of immunity and host resistance. In 1880, Pasteur developed immunizing procedures in chicken cholera and produced immunity by inoculating hens with attenuated organisms—a method he extended soon after to anthrax, swine erysipelas, and rabies.

The many developments around the idea that resistance to specific infections depended on specific immune mechanisms again emphasize the importance of the initial concept. By 1798 Edward Jenner had managed to publish his paper (refused by the Royal Society) on smallpox vaccination, in which he put an observation of folk medicine to scientific test. But until the concept of immunity was clearly formulated, the practice of vaccination was confined to the one condition in which Jenner had discovered it to be effective. Between the development of smallpox and diphtheria immunization there was the lapse of a century. New concepts were a prerequisite for generalization from the particular practice of smallpox vaccination to the practice of immunization against a wide range of diseases.

From the point of view of the epidemiologist, the focus on the host is an

important element of the concept of immunity. The host had always been the prime object of medical study by the nature of medicine as a social institution concerned with the care of sick individuals. But the concern had been with the manifestations of disorder rather than the host's own capacity to shape the manifestations of disorder.

AGENT, HOST, AND ENVIRONMENT

For many investigators of the early era of microbiology, the physical environment became all important in the search for the specific agents that caused specific diseases. The environment tended to be seen as a source, or a vehicle, of specific agents rather than as a shaping force with many interacting elements.

Epidemiologists of the time emphasized infectious diseases, often to the exclusion of all other diseases from their interests. Their professional responsibilities for the prevention and control of disease, however, obliged epidemiologists also to investigate the environmental sources of infectious agents and modes of transmission of infection. Their work demanded a broad concept of disease that syntehsized the triad of agent, host, and environment.

Schistosomiasis, or bilharzia, will serve to illustrate[3] the use and limitations of these three elements in a causal analysis. The life cycles of the agent, the flatworms *Schistosoma mansoni* and *Schistosoma haematobium* alternate between man and certain species of snails (see Figure 14.1).

Man is the primary host in which *S. mansoni* and *S. haematobium* undergo their adult and sexual life; they embed themselves in no other mammal. Each subspecies of schistosome also has an intermediary host and seeks out various snail species as hosts of predilection. The free-living forms that alternately infect humans and snails can exist only in water. Thus, the life cycle of the schistosome could not have evolved if man had not habitually dwelt, bathed, and excreted in the vicinity of pools or slow-running streams infested by snails. Human beings are part of the ecology of the schistosome, and human ways of life made their infection by the schistosome possible. This epidemiological model can be represented as a simple causal sequence of events between agent, host and environment. (Figure 14.2).

The necessary environment of the intermediate forms of the schistosome is quiet waters. The snails that are host to these intermediate forms also need or prefer special environments. The human host of the schistosome can survive in most environments, but man perfers some environments to others, and he changes the environment to suit himself. Man developed tools, family life, and the social organization of group society; he came to live in increasingly dense aggregates of people. These developments in turn modified the relationship between the schistosome and its human hosts.

Bilharzia is mentioned in a papyrus of ancient Egypt, and signs of it have been found in mummies. In modern Egypt, social and economic development, by altering the physical environment, have given a new advantage to this disease of antiquity. When water use and excretion remain promiscuous in the absence of sanitation, then the closer the settlement to water and the denser it is, the heavier

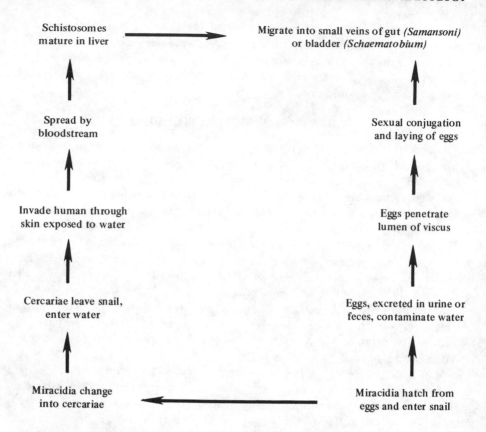

FIGURE 14.1   Exhibit 3: Life cycle of schistosoma.

the rate of infection in a population. The traditional form of irrigation in Egypt was to collect the flood waters of the Nile in basins, to water fields from the basins once a year, and to allow the land to dry out in the off season. Nowadays, the waters of the Nile are collected in huge reservoirs, and water is released gradually over the whole year through a network of canals. This perennial system of irrigation makes better use of the land, produces more food, and creates a favorable environment for the people, so that more of them survive to live there. At the same time, the irrigation system creates an environment permanently damp and full of vegetable matter that is favorable to snails and cercariae. In this new environment created by economic development, habits of water use and excretion remained the same as the population grew, and the prevalence of bilharzia rose. In the areas where the traditional form of irrigation is practiced, the rate of infection is about 6% among the population. In areas watered from the reservoirs, it is often 60%.

Even in this example, chosen for its simplicity, there are complex relations between agent, host, and environment. The environment and, in this instance, the prevalence of the agent itself can alter the response of the host to the agent. Many

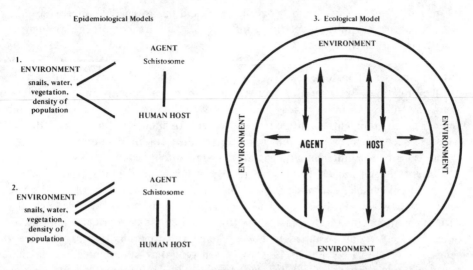

FIGURE 14.2   Exhibit 4: Schistosomiasis: epidemiological and ecological models.

Egyptian adults show little reaction to bilharzia infection, and it seems that they acquire a degree of resistance from frequent exposure in their youth. Persons newly exposed to the parasite do not show such resistance and have more severe reactions. When Napoleon's troops were billeted in the Nile delta during his Egyptian campaign, they apparently suffered marked reactions to bilharzia, as did British troops in Egypt in World Wars I and II. Thus immunity to an infecting agent varies in populations with opportunities for exposure, with previous experience of infection, and with age at first exposure. Resistance to infection probably varies also with other factors unrelated to the agent, such as nutrition.

The epidemiology of bilharzia is further complicated by the fact that, while the reactions of the human host to infection are modified by the pervasiveness of the agent in the environment, the host population in turn influences the pervasiveness of the agent by its role in distributing it. The host population exposes snails to infection through promiscuous excretion, eliminates snails or the vegetation on which they depend, or alters its own habits of excretion and bathing.

The simple sequential causal model (Figure 14.2.1) has developed into a model in which the triad of agent, host, and environment are engaged in processes of reciprocal interaction (Figure 14.2.2). A complex ecological model (Figure 14.2.3)[4] is a still better representation of reality: agent and host are engaged· in continuing interactions with an enveloping environment.

ABSTRACTING VARIABLES FROM ECOLOGICAL MODELS

In the ecological model, the interrelationships are appropriately described by terms like "web," "network," or "configuration." Nearly all the interactions among factors in the particular system already examined are reciprocal and multiple, and

the terms "agent," "host," and "environment" and the associated concepts, can be used to describe ecological relationships though they are not precise enough to describe causal relationships.

The triad of agent, host, and environment helped epidemiologists to focus on different classes of factors, especially with communicable disease, and so to tease out their relations. But when the elements of all three components interact, analysis in terms of cause becomes clumsy. The activity and survival of both host and agent depend on environment, are altered by it, and in turn alter the environment. Before a disease becomes manifest with a characteristic distribution in a population, many elements of the triad interact with each other in manifold fashion.

Current genetic models (Edwards, 1969) have developed in a way remarkably similar to epidemiological models. Few characteristics are now attributed to single genes, as they were in the simple and elegant Mendelian model. For instance, the heritable components of a characteristic that has a continuous distribution, say IQ or blood pressure, are assumed to be polygenic and to result from a number of genes at several loci on the chromosome. Each gene may be polymorphic, in that each gene may express itself in different forms and each form in different degrees. These many forms of expression allow for a subtle and complex interaction of heredity with the environment. The interaction produces change and diversity in the characteristics and health disorders of populations.

Thus current genetics, in common with epidemiology, uses models of multiple causality. Even where the heritable component of a particular characteristic appears to be large, the models are compatible with dramatic changes in the frequency of the characteristic produced by change in the environment. The current rates of occurrence of tuberculosis and rheumatic fever, diseases for which a genetic element seems established, have dwindled to a small fraction of the rates that existed a half-century ago. The scale and rate of these changes indicate that they are environmental in origin. Current genetic models allow for such interaction of genetic forms with environmental forces.

To handle these complexities, variables must be conceived in a way that makes them accessible to being counted, qualified, and manipulated. Ecological systems or, at any rate, segments of systems, can be simplified to models comprised of related variables. The function of such models is either to predict or to represent, and thus help develop and clarify statements about causal relationships.

The *predictive* function is perhaps the most widespread use of explicit model building. Such models begin with the relationships between variables known to exist in present and past trends. From these relationships future trends can be extrapolated and predicted within estimated margins of error. The assumption (not always valid) is made that known relationships will remain constant and hold in the future and that past trends will continue.

Predictive models are an essential aid to planning, a process that aims to devise rational responses to estimated future needs. A rational response implies that one makes particular choices among courses of action in the expectation that what follows from the choice can to some degree be predicted. Planning proceeds,

therefore, by predicting the effects of various interventions using assumptions about causal relationships. In terms of variables, the planner assigns alternative values to the various independent variables included in the system, and he then assesses the effects of these alternatives on the dependent variables (Navarro and Parker, 1970).

The *representational* function of models is to represent existing or postulated relationships in simplified form. The representations serve at least three sub-functions: organizing, mediating, and analyzing.

The *organizing* function of models is illustrated in the previous discussion of epidemiological and ecological models. Such models organize and synthesize a complex of related factors into coherent forms (see Figure 14.2).

The *mediating* function of models is less familiar. The model reveals the common ground between formulations that appear distinct or even disparate at first sight. The ecological model for schistosomiasis developed in the preceding discussion has such a mediating function. The model mediates between the traditional epidemiological formulation of agent, host, and environment and the multivariate formulations that quantify the relationships among the many variables of the ecological system.

The *analyzing* (explanatory) function involves models that pose alternatives among the possible relations between variables. The scientific procedure is then to test the consistency of the alternative explanations, hypotheses, and theories in particular situations. An ideal test will eliminate one or more of the competing hypotheses.

The work of MacDonald (1957) will serve to illustrate how complex ecological relations, set out in Figure 14.2 for schistosomiasis, can be reduced to a system of variables that can be handled and analyzed by epidemiologists. Writes MacDonald (1965):

> A following set of programmes . . . completes these observations by testing over a long period, 20 years, the effects of equal reduction in contamination, snails, exposure, and worm longevity by treatment, supported by reduction of exposure, to a degree at which some of them at least would be expected to produce ultimate eradication. The effect of reduced contamination to one 15,000th of excreta reaching water, which represents a very high standard of sanitation, is virtually negligible over the entire period. The effects of snail control and control of exposure in the form of entry to water are virtually identical during most of the period of fall, though during the later stages control of exposure is somewhat more effective, resulting in a slightly earlier disappearance of the infection. Ultimate disappearance following either of these methods is delayed for over 20 years, throughout all of which effective measures would have to be carried out, and even improvement to a level approaching perfection would only slightly reduce the time involved, to 14 or 15 years, owing to the long mean length of life postulated for the worms, 3 years. By contrast, the combination of systematic treatment with either reduction of exposure or snail control produces a rapid result, the final effects of which are visible between 4 and 5 years after the start.

In his schistosomiasis model (Figure 14.3), MacDonald introduced four main sets of variables:

1. A fertility factor measured the over-all output of eggs by the schistosome infecting the human host. The chance of the worms sexually pairing and producing eggs depends on the worm load in the body systems of the human host and on the longevity of the worms.
2. A contamination factor measured the number of schistosome eggs introduced into the local water. This factor depends on the number of excreted eggs carried into the water (determined by the excretory habits and methods of sanitation of the human hosts).
3. A snail factor measured the output of cercariac by infected snails. This factor depends mainly on the density of the susceptible snail population in the water contaminated by schistosome eggs. Snail density determines the chances of a snail's being infected by the miracidia generated by the eggs, as well as the number of cercariac excreted by the snails into the water.
4. An exposure factor measured the chance of cercariae excreted by the snail's infecting the human host. This factor depends on the number and extent of the contacts with infected water made by potential hosts.

MacDonald used his model to predict the effectiveness of several approaches to eradication of the disease in a community. He found that there was a critical number of worms in a given environment, a "break point," above which numbers would increase until they reached a stable infection level and below which numbers would decrease and disappear. Exhibit 14.3 illustrates the effects of four different control programs on the prevalence of the human host population. The model predicted that sanitation alone would prove ineffectual, that the most effective approach would prove to be a combination of measures intensively applied at a local level, and that the most rapid benefits at the least cost would be the improvement of mass therapeutic methods. Although the predictions of this model have not been tested and validated, as have those of other models, predictions seem to be in rough accord with past experience of preventive programs.[5]

Whereas the success of some disease eradication programs has encouraged model builders, the failures have instructed them. These failures are of two main types:

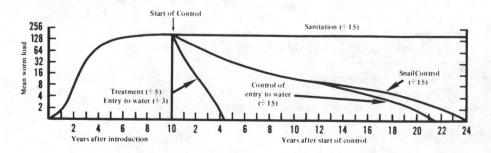

FIGURE 14.3   Exhibit 5

biological and mathematical. On the biological side, the models cannot be universal. The processes of transmission are not everywhere the same, and as a result, programs that work in Ceylon do not work in Ethiopia. On the mathematical side, the models are too simple to encompass all the relevant variables, that is, immunity, vector resistance, and human migration. Social and political contexts are often not quantifiable. In addition, for models that try to represent causal sequences, the time dimension is especially significant. Processes evolve through time, and adequate models that must simulate the continuing unfolding of interacting events often need the assistance of electronic computers, a tool only recently available.

While the merits of various models may be argued, it is agreed that the concept of abstract variables with general properties is a heuristic one for epidemiologists.

SYSTEMS AND ORGANIZATIONAL LEVELS

Any multivariate model is an abstraction from a system, as a segment of a system. The concept of a "system" implies a set of factors connected with each other in terms of a coherent structure or coherent function. The circulatory system comprises heart and blood vessels; the nervous system comprises the brain, spinal cord, and the peripheral and autonomic nerves. The human body is a system in itself at a higher and more complex level of organization than each of the physiological systems of the body. Society comprises a system of persisting and ordered relationships at a still more complex level of organization. The universe is a system of vast and cosmic scale; the DNA molecule, or any atom, a system of minuscule scale.

Systems define the limits of a particular level of organization and the structure and function within those limits. Because the factors contained in the system are related and connected, change or activity in one sector of the system is likely to have an effect on another sector.

Systems also relate to one another; they contain each other like the boxes of a Chinese conjuring trick. The universe has a simultaneous existence, and each level of organization is encompassed by a more complex level or organization. Atoms are encompassed by molecules, molecules by chromosomes, chromosomes by cells, and cells by tissues. Organs and physiological systems are encompassed by individuals and individuals by social groups.

All these systems are linked. The conceptualization and isolation of 26 systems and subsystems is solely for purposes of study and understanding. Thus the limits of the systems and subsystems studied are defined by those dimensions of time, place, and structure that contain the independent and dependent variables selected. The subsystem, thus, begins with the independent variables and ends with dependent variables. The focus of study may be, so to speak, horizontal and confined to a single level of organization. If the study cuts vertically across levels, the focus will include more than one level.

DIRECT AND INDIRECT CAUSE

One of the problems of inference posed by a study that cuts across levels of organization, or indeed by any complex system of variables, is the question of

direct and indirect cause. Associations between cause and effect are direct or indirect according to those decisions of research design or analysis that define the variables to be included in the system or in the segment of the system under study.

The cause is direct if a change in the causal factor (or independent variable) is capable of producing a change in an effect (or dependent variable) with two critical provisos: First, that there are no known intervening variables; and second, that cause and effect relate to the same level of organization within a system.

The cause is indirect when either of the two provisions is not satisfied: Either a sequence of linked factors exists or another level of organization is interposed between the cause under study and its outcome. If the first proviso is not satisfied, there is a known sequence of linked factors that intervenes between the independent and dependent variables included in the defined causal system chosen for study, and the system can be represented as follows:

$$X_1 \longrightarrow X_2 \longrightarrow X_3 \cdots\cdots Y$$

For example, breathing air polluted by cigarette or other smoke (independent variable X_1) causes damage to the respiratory epithelium (intervening variable X_2); this damage increases the susceptibility of the epithelium to infection (intervening variable X_3) and results in chronic bronchitis (dependent variable Y).

The second proviso implies that a cause is indirect if the causal factor on one level of organization in a system is related to an effect located at a different level of organization indicated by the unit of observation used. The unit may be, for example, country, state, residential area, household, or individual. Thus the circumstances of social class could be said to be a direct cause of the variation of mortality rates. This conclusion could be reached by showing that area mortality rates vary consistently with the social class composition of areas, even when such other known factors as age and sex, which influence mortality rates, are controlled. However, individuals represent a different level of organization from social groups. To try to attribute the death of an individual to his social class position is at once to become aware that additional factors must intervene between social position and causes of death. The analyst is nudged, as it were, into stating hypotheses to explain the links between social class and the causes of individual deaths.

Chadwick's report (1842) related area mortality to drainage. Drainage was the causal factor, mortality, the outcome in local communities defined by administrative area. In these tables, Chadwick examined independent and dependent variables relating to phenomena located at the same level of organizational complexity, that is, as defined by administrative area.

In terms of the system Chadwick had chosen to isolate for analysis, he had discovered a direct relationship, a relationship that both the time-order of the variables and the replication of the results across the country suggested was causal. With these findings, therefore, he had grounds enough to go ahead and institute area sanitation nationwide without doing violence to causal logic. The method of sanitation Chadwick introduced probably saved more human lives than any other single health measure up to the post-World War II era. The success of his policy, propounded on the basis of a mistaken etiological theory, was more than a lucky accident. The policy was based on an entirely reasonable inference of causality.

William Farr was involved with these problems during the same historical period and made his great contribution as chief statistical medical officer of the General Registry Office in London starting in 1832. The outstanding historical value of these British statistics, even though they were started later than some others in Europe, rests on the fact that from the beginning Farr collected and analyzed the data for specific causes of death. Thus, by specifying the cause of death, he advanced the process of refinement of variables and opened up a new field of investigation and analysis vital statistics.

In his analyses of the vital statistics of England and Wales, Farr examined specific causes of death in relation to many independent variables. Table 14.2 is Farr's tabulation of the correlation between altitude and deaths from cholera (Farr, 1852: lxiv), the most feared scourge of the times.

Commented Farr, "The difference between the number of persons to an acre in the mean of 38 districts, and in all London, as separately calculated, arises in consequence of several districts of large area being thrown into the divisor in the latter case, while the effect of taking the mean of 38 districts is to render the population of each district of equal amount."

In this analysis, Farr set out a direct ecological relationship of the type used by Chadwick. He took the hypothesized environment cause, altitude, as the independent study variable and related it to cholera death rates as the dependent variable. Both the independent and dependent variables were characteristics of administrative areas and are thereby units at the same level of organization.

From this analysis, however, Farr concluded wrongly that "elevation of habitations reduces the effects of cholera to insignificance." The relationship Farr

TABLE 14.2 CHOLERA MORTALITY AND ALTITUDE. A. LONDON DISTRICTS
ARRANGED ACCORDING TO THE ELEVATION OF THEIR SOIL. B. MORTALITY FROM
CHOLERA IN LONDON TO 10,000 OF THE POPULATION, AT SIXTEEN DIFFERENT
ELEVATIONS FROM 0 TO 350 FEET.

| | | Observed Average | | | | | |
| | | Annual mortality to 10,000 persons living | | Number of persons to | | Average annual value of | |
Number of districts	Elevation in feet above Trinity high-water mark	Cholera (1849)	All causes (1838-44)	An acre	A house	Houses	House and shop room to each person	Poor rate in the of house rent 1842-43
							£	£
16	Under 20	102	251	74	6.8	31	4.645	.072
7	20 - 40	65	237	105	7.6	56	7.358	.071
8	40 - 60	34	235	184	8.5	64	7.342	.056
3	60 - 80	27	236	152	8.8	52	6.374	.049
2	80 - 100	22	211	44	7.7	38	5.183	.036
1	100	17	227	102	9.8	71	7.586	.043
1	350	8	202	5	7.2	40	5.804	- - -
Mean of 38 districts		66	240	107	7.6	46	5.985	.064
All London		62	252	29	.7	40	5.419	.063

observed was local and not general. The lower reaches of the Thames, as it flowed through London, became increasingly contaminated by sewage. The contaminated water supply that caused most of the cholera in London was thereby brought into association with low altitude. Thus, Farr had developed a testable hypothesis, but he had not searched far enough for instances to contradict it. Although Chadwick was right and Farr wrong in inferring the causes of high mortality in certain areas, both had developed legitimate hypotheses from their observations of *ecological units.* From there, however, neither could go further in establishing direct causes of death in *individuals* because the unit of observation was not individuals but the population of defined administrative areas, a different organizational level.

Like Farr, John Snow began his studies of cholera with data relating cholera deaths to administrative areas; at that level of organization, he postulated water supplies contaminated by sewage as the causal factor. But Snow took his hypothesis much further. About thirty years before Koch and Pasteur described the "Vibrio" as the agent in cholera, he postulated an invisible, self-reproducing living agent as the cause of the manifestations of cholera in individuals. So precise a hypothesis about individuals implied a linked sequence of events between data for areas and data for individuals which could not be tested at the level of organization of admininstative areas.

Snow demonstrated the precision of his hypothesis by extending his investigations to other levels of organization where the units of observation were smaller than administrative areas. Early in his studies, Snow tabulated cholera mortality rates of the 1849 outbreak for the districts of London in rank order, and set against these rates the company responsible for the water supply. Snow showed an obvious association of the water supplied by the Southward and Vauxhall and the Lambeth Waterworks with the high rates of death from cholera (Table 14.3, from Snow, 1855: 62-63). This was a direct relationship at the ecological level.

Snow pointed out that five years later, in the 1853 outbreak, a change had come about: the Southwark and Vauxhall Company water supply was still associated with high cholera mortality, but the Lambeth supply seemed not to be (Table 14.4, from Snow, 1855: 69). Snow found that the Lambeth Company had moved its waterworks to a point higher up the Thames, thus obtaining a supply of water free from the sewage of London. William Farr had provided this lead for Snow in his weekly return of births and deaths from the General Registry Office.

Now by narrowing his focus down to a different level of organization, namely, households, Snow produced his most convincing evidence of the relationship of water supply to individual cholera deaths. These studies illustrate the principle that, as soon as the dependent variable is observed and specified at a level of organization different from the independent variable, the postulated causal relationship is made indirect. Thus, in trying to relate the water supply to areas of deaths in households, Snow was dealing with an indirect relationship. Between area water supply and household deaths, there had to be intervening factors at the household level. The next logical step in investigation was to reveal these factors.

As is often true in epidemiological studies, obtaining the data relating to this smaller and more refined unit of observation required Snow to conduct a special

TABLE 14.3 MORTALITY FROM CHOLERA, AND THE WATER SUPPLY, IN THE DISTRICTS OF LONDON IN 1849
(DISTRICTS ARE ARRANGED IN THE ORDER OF THEIR MORTALITY FROM CHOLERA)

District	Population mid-1849	Deaths from cholera	Deaths by cholera to 10,000 inhabitants	Annual value of house & shop room to each person in £	Water supply
Rotherhithe	17,208	352	205	4.238	Southwark and Vauxhall Water Works, Kent Water Works, and Tidal Ditches
St. Olave, Southwark	19,278	349	181	4.559	Southwark and Vauxhall
St. George, Southwark	50,900	836	164	3.518	Southwark and Vauxhall, Lambeth
Bermondsey	45,500	734	161	3.077	Southwark and Vauxhall
St. Saviour, Southwark	35,227	539	153	5.291	Southwark and Vauxhall
Newington	63,074	907	144	3.788	Southwark and Vauxhall, Lambeth
Lambeth	134,768	1,618	120	4.389	Southwark and Vauxhall, Lambeth
Wandsworth	48,446	484	100	4.839	Pump wells, Southwark and Vauxhall, river Wandle
Camberwell	51,714	504	97	4.508	Southwark and Vauxhall, Lambeth
West London	28,829	429	96	7.454	New River
Bethnal Green	87,263	789	90	1.480	East London
Shoreditch	104,122	789	76	3.103	New River, East London
Greenwich	95,954	718	75	3.379	Kent
Poplar	44,103	313	71	7.360	East London
Westminster	64,109	437	68	4.189	Chelsea
Whitechapel	78,590	506	64	3.388	East London
St. Giles	54,062	285	53	5.635	New River
Stepney	106,988	501	47	3.319	East London
Chelsea	53,379	247	46	4.210	Chelsea
East London	43,495	182	45	4.823	New River
St. George's, East	47,334	199	42	4.753	East London
London City	55,816	207	38	17.676	New River
St. Martin	24,557	91	37	11.844	New River
Strand	44,254	156	35	7.374	New River
Holborn	46,134	161	35	5.883	New River
St. Luke	53,234	183	34	3.731	New River
Kensington (except Paddington)	110,491	260	33	5.070	West Middlesex, Chelsea, Grand Junction
Lewisham	32,299	96	30	4.824	Kent
Belgrave	37,918	105	28	8.875	Chelsea
Hackney	55,152	139	25	4.397	New River, East London
Islington	87,761	187	22	5.494	New River
St. Pancras	160,122	360	22	4.871	New River, Hampstead, West Middlesex
Clerkenwell	63,499	121	19	4.138	New River
Marylebone	153,960	261	17	7.586	West Middlesex
St. James, Westminster	36,426	57	16	12.669	Grand Junction, New River
Paddington	41,267	35	8	9.349	Grand Junction
Hampstead	11,572	9	8	5.804	Hampstead, West Middlesex
Hanover Square & May Fair	33,196	26	8	16.754	Grand Junction
London	2,280,282	14,137	62	---	

TABLE 14.4   CHOLERA DEATH RATES BY CHIEF WATER COMPANIES SUPPLYING
DISTRICTS, GROUPED BY SOURCES OF COMPANY WATER

| Water companies | Sources of supply | Aggregate of districts supplied chiefly by the respective companies | | |
		Population	Deaths by cholera in 13 weeks ending Nov. 19	Deaths in 100,000 inhabitants
(1) Lambeth and (2) Southwark and Vauxhall	Thames, at Thames Ditton and at Battersea	346,363	211	61
Southwark and Vauxhall	Thames at Battersea	118,267	111	94
(1) Southwark and Vauxhall (2) Kent	Thames, at Battersea the Ravensbourne in Kent; ditches and walls	17,605	19	107

field survey. It so happened that the overlap of the water supply provided by the two companies was so intimate that an ideal opportunity for observation was created. Snow described the situation:

> . . . As there is no difference whatever, either in the houses or the people receiving the supply of the two Water Companies, or in any of the physical conditions with which they are surrounded, it is obvious that no experiment could have been devised, which would have been devised, which would more thoroughly test the effect of water supply on the progress of cholera than this, which circumstances placed ready made before the observer.
>
> The experiment, too, was on the grandest scale. No fewer than three hundred thousand people of both sexes, of every age and occupation, and of every rank and station, from gentlefolks down to the very poor, were divided into two groups without their choice, and, in most cases, without their knowledge; one group being supplied with water containing the sewage of London, and, amongst it, whatever might have come from the cholera patients, the other group having water quite free from such impurity.
>
> To turn this grand experiment to account, all that was required was to learn the supply of water to each individual house where a fatal attack of cholera might occur.

The data from the investigation carried out by Snow are shown in Table 14.5 (Snow, 1855: 86).

Here the Southwark and Vauxhall Company consumers were at a relative risk of cholera deaths of more than 8 to 1 compared with Lambeth Company consumers. The conviction arising from this study is greatly strengthened by the direct relation shown between independent and dependent variables with a smaller unit of observation. Despite the epidemiologist's insistence on studying populations, his ultimate

TABLE 14.5 CHOLERA DEATH RATES BY COMPANY SUPPLYING
HOUSEHOLD WATER

Company	Number of houses	Deaths from cholera	Deaths in each 10,000 houses
Southwark and Vauxhall Company	40,046	1,263	315
Lambeth Company	26,107	98	37
Rest of London	256,423	1,422	59

concern is with health, disease, and death as it occurs in individuals. In the analyses by district, there was no way of knowing if all individuals were exposed to the same water supply. In Snow's analysis persons grouped in households and exposed to particular water supplies are specified with great precision. The distribution is almost in imitation of random assignment.

Snow's work stands as a classic in epidemiology. By his procedures of method and inference, he solved a major problem and established a model for all who followed him. He was careful to seek out the intervening links of indirect causal chains, including the indirect relationships created by moving from one level of organization to another and by intervening variables. Thus Snow was able to reinterpret the variable contaminated water (which had confounded Farr's work and led him into the error of attributing cholera mortality to residence at low altitude) as the intervening variable between cholera mortality and place or residence.

In epidemiology and the social sciences, turbulence, willfulness, and low levels of predictability are manifest characteristics of the subjects of study. By the same token, the process of causal analysis, central to all science, is here most crucial.

NOTES

1. A variable is an abstract term representing a particular property (e.g., age, sex, or income) of the units under observation (e.g., persons or groups of persons). Thus, a variable is a measure comprising all the differing values or qualities of the property among the units under the study (e.g., "males" and "females" are the values of the property "sex" in the unit "persons"). An effect is a dependent variable and a cause is an independent variable.

2. Cohort studies need not be prospective in relation to the position of the investigator in time. The criteria by which the study populations, or cohorts, are selected for entry to observation must be attributes or experiences that precede the events to be studied among them, but it is feasible and often economical to reconstruct study populations and the events that befell them from historical records.

3. There are many cases in New York City, all imported from elsewhere. That schistosomiasis should appear in New York, the epitome of the megalopolis, is a commentary in itself on the intimate relations between social forces and the distribution of disease.

4. The main distinction between epidemiology and ecology is that, while epidemiology is centered on the state of health of man, ecology is not anthropocentric but embraces the interrelations of all living things. Epidemiology could be described as human ecology, or that large part of human ecology relating to states of health.

5. In China the story seems to be a different one. The disease caused by Schistosoma japonicum is reported to be serious and even devastating. Eradication is known to be complicated, and various approaches are being used. Mass treatment is being undertaken; night soil

is collected and stored until the heat generated kills the excreted ova; and snails are destroyed by filling in old canals or burying the snails on the banks. The attack is carried out by the technique of the "human sea," by which many thousands of people are mobilized in communal effort. Several country districts are reported to have been cleared by these means, with dramatic improvement in the people's health (Horn, 1969; Cheng, 1971).

Chairman Mao wrote about this problem: "After reading in the *People's Daily* of how schistosomiasis was wiped out in Yukiang County, so many fancies crossed my mind that I could not sleep. In the warm morning breeze, as sunlight fell on my window, I looked toward the distant sourthern sky and in my happiness wrote the following lines." His poem, "Farewell to the God of Plague," refers to a famous physician, Hua To, and to two mythical emperors, Yao and Shun.

> Green streams, blue hills—but all to what avail?
> This tiny germ left even Hau To powerless;
> Weeds choked hundreds of villages, men wasted away;
> Thousands of households dwindled, phantoms sang with glee.
> On earth I travel eighty thousand li a day,
> Ranging the sky I see myriad rivers,
> Should the cowherd ask tidings of the God of Plague,
> Say; Past joys and woe have vanished with the waves.
> The spring wind blows amid ten thousand willow branches,
> Six hundred million in this sacred land all equal Yao and Shun.
> Flowers falling like crimson rain swirl in waves at will;
> Green mountains turn to bridges at our wish;
> Gleaming mattocks fall on heaven-high peaks;
> Mighty arms moved rivers, rock and earth.
> We ask the God of Plague; Where are you bound?
> Paper barges aflame and candlelight illuminate the sky.

REFERENCES

Chadwick, E. (1842) *Report on the Sanitary Condition of The Labouring Population of Great Britain.* Reprinted 1965; Edinburgh: Edinburgh University Press.

Cheng, Tien-Hsi (1971) Schistosomiasis in Mainland China: A Review of research and control programs since 1949. *Amer. J. Trop. Med. & Hyg.* 20: 26-53.

Edwards, J. H. (1969) Familial Predisposition in Man. Pp. 58-64 in C. E. Ford and H. Harris (eds.) *New Aspects of Human Genetics.* London: British Medical Bulletin, vol. 25.

Farr, W. (1885) *Vital Statistics: A Memorial Volume of Selections From the Reports and Writings of William Farr.* Edited by N. Humphries. London: Sanitary Institute.

——— (1852) *Report on the Mortality of Cholera in England in 1848-49.* London: H. M. Stationery Office.

Graunt, J. (1662) *Natural and Political Observations.* Made upon the Bills of Mortality (London: T. Roycraft). Reprinted 1939 (Baltimore: John Hopkins Press).

Horn, J. S. (1969) *Away With All Pests.* New York: Monthly Review Publications. Pp. 94-106.

Hyman, H. (1955) *Survey Design and Analysis.* New York: Free Press.

MacDonald, G. (1965) The Dynamics of Helminth Infections, with special Reference to Schistosomes. *Trans. Roy. Soc. Trop. Med. Hyg.* 59(5): 489-506.

——— (1957) *The Epidemiology and Control of Malaria.* London: Oxford University Press.

MacMahon, B., and T. F. Pugh. *Epidemiology: Principles and Methods.* Boston: Little, Brown.

Navarro, V. and R. D. Parker. (1970) Models in health services planning. Pp. 181-198 in W. W. Holland (ed.) *Data Handling in Epidemiology.* London: Oxford University Press.

Rosen, G. (1937) Social aspects of Jacob Henle's medical thought. *Bull. Inst. Hist. Med.* 5:509-37.

Simon, J. (1890) *English Sanitary Institutions.* London: Cassell.

Snow, J. (1855) *On the Mode of Communication of Cholera.* 2nd ed., much enlarged; London: J. Churchill. Reprinted 1936 as *Snow on Cholera* (New York: Commonwealth Fund).

Wilcocks, C. (1962) *Aspects of Medical Investigation in Africa.* London: Oxford University Press.

15

SOCIAL AREA ANALYSIS AS A METHOD OF EVALUATION

ELMER L. STRUENING

As interest in the specialities of community medicine and community mental health has evolved, emphasis has been placed on the delivery of comprehensive health and mental health services to populations residing in defined geographic or catchment areas. Service delivery systems are assumed to be responsible for the health and mental health status of the residents of their catchment areas. Although the effectiveness of service delivery systems is partially dependent upon the quality of their relationships with catchment area populations or communities, the understanding of this interaction has yet to receive serious attention in the literature of program evaluation. As a result, our knowledge of the determinants of the selective use of health and mental health facilities by catchment area populations and of the effectiveness of these facilities in maintaining the health status of their communities according to accepted epidemiological criteria is still in the early stages of development (McKinlay, 1972; Williams and Ozarin, 1968).

Ideally, representatives of service delivery systems and elected members of their catchment areas would formulate a hierarchy of priorities as a guide to the use of available resources. Within the limits of a stated budget, the specific objectives of the service system would be derived from ordered priorities and stated, in operational terms, as meaningful questions to be answered by evaluation research studies. The results of such studies would then be used for deciding whether or not the service system meets its stated objectives. If it does not, theoretically sound changes in the service delivery system would be in a constant state of systematic change, guided by feedback from evaluation studies, with the general goal of evolving to a system of optimal effectiveness.

This ideal state of affairs seldom, if ever, exists in our health and mental health delivery systems. As a consequence the field of evaluation research has not produced a well-developed applied science complete with a comprehensive set of

AUTHOR'S NOTE: A portion of this chapter was published in the International Journal of Health Services, 1974, 4 (3), and is reprinted by permission of the publisher: Baywood Publishing Company, Inc.

constructs and their reliable and valid measures. Nor has it developed a systematically acquired body of knowledge acceptable to the scientific community and
sufficiently general to apply in a variety of settings without question. What appears
to be available are methods, measures, and concepts primarily borrowed from other
disciplines and applied in an unsystematic manner to a variety of problems in a
variety of settings. The time is ripe for the development of general evaluation
methodologies which have application in a number of settings so that an accumula-
tive set of substantive findings can be generated.

The general purpose of this chapter is to describe and demonstrate a methodology designed to promote the understanding of relationships between health and
mental health delivery systems and residents of the catchment areas they serve.
Emphasis is placed on explaining the selective use of services and evaluating the
effects of change as it is introduced into the service system. Principles of epidemiology, the methodology of modern social area analysis, and selected multivariate
statistical methods are discussed and integrated into a set of procedures for
evaluating health and mental health delivery systems with catchment area responsibilities. The role of evaluation research is briefly discussed; three levels of evaluation are defined. A brief history of social area analysis is given, with illustrations of
area analysis in descriptive, correlational, and controlled evaluation studies.

THE ROLE OF EVALUATION RESEARCH

Evaluation research is generally thought of as a speciality within the applied
sciences, with general emphasis placed on assessing the effectiveness of human
service systems and with particular focus on the relative effectiveness of their
treatment, service, or educational programs. Evaluation studies are generally preoccupied with providing answers to carefully formulated questions and not with
testing hypotheses or with making predictions derived from theories. While the
formulation of hypotheses regarding the outcomes of evaluation should help to
conceptualize the study in greater depth, leading to the important issue of why, for
example, differential reactions to treatment occur, this is seldom done. This
approach to evaluation may partly explain the superficial nature of many evaluation studies. As the knowledge of this field grows, producing well-defined constructs, organized into meaningful theories capable of predicting (health and mental
health) relevant behavior, it seems likely that evaluators will make more direct use
of theory in conceptualizing studies, or at least be more aware of the theoretical
assumptions implicit in their work.

The role of evaluation research differs from that of conventional research in its
explicit attempt to make value judgments. Evaluation research goes beyond hypothesis testing, if it is concerned with that at all. It is generally directed toward
determining what is most effective, valuable, desirable, or useful, rather than simply
whether or not a hypothesis was supported. It is concerned with the determination
of relative value.

This concern of evaluation research with the relative value of human endeavor
places it squarely in the middle of social and political controversy. Evaluation takes

place in a social and organizational context and is therefore influenced by the particular value orientations, vested interests, and political forces which surround each study. On one hand, properties of this social and organizational context may greatly facilitate the conduct and use of the implications of the evaluation study; on the other hand, the social and political forces may impede the conduct of the study and, in the extreme, distort or suppress the results. Thus the political and social climates of evaluation studies are potentially stormy and, to be successfully completed, require a thorough understanding of the context in which they are to be conducted.

The above conditions suggest that the project directors of evaluation studies must possess attributes somewhat different from the laboratory oriented scientist. For a detailed discussion of how politics and values are involved in evaluation research, please see chapters by Weiss, and those by Sjoberg and by Gurel in Volume II in this *Handbook*. These chapters document in some detail the sources of cooperation and conflict in the evaluation process. Whatever conditions obtain, it seems important to move toward objective, quantifiable methods of evaluation which are sufficiently relevant to answer important questions about the effectiveness of human service delivery systems and convincingly accurate to all parties involved in the evaluation process.

A DEFINITION OF EVALUATION RESEARCH

In the limited perspective of this chapter, the subject matter of evaluation research is restricted to the evaluation of human service systems. Even within this limited sphere, evaluation research is complex in nature and does not lend itself to simple and precise definition. It is insufficient to reduce it to the classical experimental method because, as a developing discipline, much work needs to be done in the conceptual, descriptive, and measurement aspects of development. A definition should include the range of activities currently involved and necessary to promote growth of the discipline.

Evaluation research is defined as the application of scientific principles, methods, and theories to identify, describe, conceptualize, measure, predict, change, and control those factors or variables important to the development of effective human service delivery systems.

The definition of *effective* at both the construct and operational levels involves both the theoretical and value orientations of those engaged in the evaluation process. These orientations influence the *selection* or *development* of outcome or criterion variables, the interpretation of results, and the implications of the results for changing the service delivery system. Controversy arising from evaluation studies probably derives more from differences in the value orientations of those with vested interests, such as administrators and evaluators, than from the specific problems of actually doing the study.

Evaluation research is conceived at four levels: (1) descriptive, (2) correlational or comparative, (3) experimental, and (4) theory construction. Theory is implicated, either implicitly or explicitly, at all four levels.

Descriptive evaluation research is preoccupied with *what is* and *how much,* or the descriptive statistics of the measure of an important construct or characteristic. It is concerned with the comprehensive description of human service systems, their component parts and programs, the populations they serve, and the environments in which the populations live. This requires the creation of conceptual frames of reference and the development of constructs and their operational definitions of measures. Evaluation research, like the social sciences from which it borrows, suffers from an abundance of overlapping and poorly defined constructs which are either inadequately defined or defined by a number of measures with questionable psychometric properties. As a result the evaluator often finds it necessary to develop appropriate measures or to use those of marginal utility that are available in the literature. Thus evaluation research, as a field in the early, developmental stages, will find it necessary to expend considerable energy at the descriptive level before moving to correlational and experimental studies.

The correlational or comparative level of evaluation is concerned with relationships among measures developed at the descriptive level. Critical examination of relationships among measures describing a health or mental health delivery system may raise meaningful questions which can be answered by subsequent experimental studies or may result in immediately useful causal inferences regarding, for example, the implications of social status in the use of service facilities. While inferences from correlations or the comparison of groups from a population of interest may provide valuable insights into the what goes on, for example, in a service delivery system, experimental studies are needed to understand the value of new and innovative programs relative to established programs.

The experimental approach to evaluation is generally viewed as the most important type of evaluation research. The general logic of the experimental design requires the comparison of experimental and control groups, to which subjects were randomly assigned, on a measure of change on some outcome variable of interest, such as symptom reduction. Experimental usually implies something new or innovative. Therefore, experimental designs are usually concerned with discovering the relative effectiveness of new approaches to a problem compared with older, more traditional approaches. Thus, while descriptive and correlational studies yield valuable information about a service delivery system or a treatment modality, results of the more rigorous experimental studies are needed to demonstrate the effectiveness of innovation as a basis for introducing change into the delivery system.

The fourth level of evaluation, that of theory construction, is generally not accepted as the province of evaluation research. As an applied science, the role of evaluation research is restricted to the application of that which is already known or accepted to a particular problem. However, as previously indicated, that which is already known or developed is frequently inadequate. Populations investigated in university settings, frequently representing only a narrow segment of society, are too restricted to produce results on which comprehensive theories of behavior can be constructed. Therefore, it seems that theories of behavioral change could fruitfully grow out of evaluation studies focused on those influences or treatments designed to produce change. Most health and mental health systems hope to

promote physical, intellectual, and emotional growth, or change, in all populations involved in their delivery systems. In both client and community populations there is a desire to educate toward the prevention of disease and mental illness and toward the appropriate use of health and mental health facilities. In the staff population there is an ever-present need to acquire and apply new knowledge so that health and mental health delivery systems reflect the latest advancements in the many relevant disciplines. This difficult enterprise requires the integration of disparate theories of behavior and behavioral change from clinical, social psychological, sociological, and anthropological frames of reference and the cooperation of theoretical and applied scientists if the final results are to be useful to the evaluator. At the rate that universities and human service delivery systems are joining forces to develop a comprehensive theory of behavior relevant and useful to understanding the behavior of the general population, it seems important for evaluation researchers to become more interested in the theoretical sources of their applied work, and in theory construction, if evaluation research is to evolve into a mature discipline.

ISSUES IN SERVICE DELIVERY: A BASIS FOR ASKING QUESTIONS

With the above definitions in mind, we turn now to selected issues in service delivery to catchment area (CA) populations which provoke meaningful questions that can be answered by different levels of evaluation research, using the methodology of social area analysis.

The Issue of Equity

Equity is defined as serving all citizens of a CA according to their medical and mental health needs. This implies the design and deployment of competent service delivery systems that are effectively used by all populations, especially those at high risk, in both preventive and secondary roles. To achieve the goal of equity in service delivery, information about the health and mental health status of the CA population is needed. Planners, administrators, and evaluators must have reasonably accurate information about the distribution of health and mental health problems in subpopulations (usually defined by age and sex) as they vary over geographical subareas comprising the CA if they are to design effective programs related to the pattern of risk in the CA. Generation of this type of information involves the disciplines of epidemiology and demography. By revealing the relevant characteristics of the CA as they vary over subareas, both in frequency and rate format, the descriptive level of evaluation is illustrated.

The Issue of Context

Community medicine and mental health professionals involved in service delivery are becoming more aware that the social, physical, and normative context in which people live affects their health and behavior in important and subtle ways. To understand the health and behavior of a population, it now seems necessary to understand the particular environments in which the people live. Over large cities

there is enormous variability in housing, transportation, medical services, income, refuse collection, family stability, spatial mobility, sociocultural values, life-styles, belief systems about the causes of mental and physical illness, and so forth, all of which bear some relationship with the health and mental health status of the citizen population. Relationships among selected characteristics of environments and the health and mental health status of their residents provide a basis for causal inference with implications for designing strategies of intervention that will reduce incidence and prevalence rates. Inferences made from patterns of relationships illustrate the correlational level of evaluation.

The Issue of Change

Human service systems often become committed to, and subsequently defensive about, their particular style of service delivery. To improve service effectiveness, there is a need to experiment with new or alternative forms of service delivery by comparing their relative effectiveness with currently used methods under controlled experimental conditions. Thus the introduction of change in service systems requires evaluation research studies at the third level if change is to be systematic and rational rather than haphazard and unplanned.

The Issue of Theory

With the rebirth of interest in ecology, the role of environment as it effects man is receiving increased attention. A particular aspect of this interest is the relationship of environments with the health and mental health of their inhabitants. A still more specialized facet are the conceptions and attitudes of people about the prevention and treatment of physical and mental disorders and their selective use of facilities responsible for treating these disorders. As yet our knowledge in these areas is fragmented, inconsistent, and controversial. There is a need for dynamic theories linking the well-being and behavior of people to characteristics of their environments, especially behavior relevant to self care and the use of services. Well-designed experimental evaluation studies carried out in a variety of settings may provide a worthwhile basis for constructing such theories.

Community medicine and community mental health, then, are experiencing the growing pains of early development, particularly with respect to relationship between the service delivery system and the community to be served. A number of important questions on such issues as the equity, effectiveness, and accountability of service systems occur as one conceptualizes the interaction and interdependence between service systems and their CA populations. While a considerable literature has partial answers for some of the questions, the need for a body of organized knowledge, based on the systematic observation of service-community relationships, is unmet.

The following section provides a sample of three types of questions which might occur as one attempted to understand the environment of CA residents, the facilities providing them with medical and mental health services, and the nature of their interactions.

A SAMPLE OF MEANINGFUL QUESTIONS

Questions of Description

Demography. What are the major demographic characteristics of the CA which, according to the literature, are likely to be related to the health and mental health status of CA residents? To what extent do these characteristics vary over subareas, such as census blocks or tracts of the CA?

Epidemiology. What are the major health and mental health problems observed in the CA and how do their rates vary over subareas and among various subpopulations of the CA? To what extent do age-specific death rates vary over the subareas of the CA?

Physical Environment. What is the quality of the environment surrounding the citizens of the CA, including factors, such as housing, transportation, and refuse collection, which are hypothetically linked to, for example, general morale and the use of service facilities.

Social Context. What are the dominant belief systems and levels of knowledge about physical and mental illness, their nature, cause and cure?

Community Resources. What support systems, in the form of family structures, extended families, ethnic cohesion, religious groups, social welfare agencies, social and political clubs, and so forth, exist in the CA and provide avenues of education, communication, and help during crisis situations.

Questions of Relationship or Comparison

Poverty and Health. To what extent do measures of poverty account for variability in rates of disease in various subpopulations of the CA?

Sociocultural Factors and Facility Use. To what extent does variation in sociocultural values over subareas of the CA account for variation in the use of health services?

Social Class and Mental Health. Is variability in the inpatient/outpatient ratio of mental health service use over the subareas of the CA primarily a function of variability in social class variables?

Environment and Mortality. Which characteristics of subareas of the CA play the most important role in predicting age-specific mortality rates?

Family Structure and Mental Disorders. With age controlled, is marital status a significant factor in the mental health of the CA population? Is marital status an important variable in predicting the use of mental health facilities?

Ethnicity and Use of Mental Health Facilities. Is variation in ethnic composition over the subareas of the CA an important variable in predicting the use of mental health facilities?

Transportation and Facility Use. Are the location, quality, and efficiency of transportation facilities important determinants of the use of health and mental health facilities?

Family Structure, Poverty, and Infant Health. What is the relative contribution of variables measuring family structure and poverty in accounting for variability in rates of premature birth and neonatal and postneonatal mortality?

Questions of Change or Experimentation

Facility Location. Is proximity a factor in the use of health and mental health facilities? Does the installation of new clinics in areas of high risk result in serving more citizens at a reduced cost per service rendered?

Education. Are recent mothers more likely to seek a postpartum examination following exposure to a health education program?

Training. Do inservice training programs for paraprofessionals, which carry the immediate reward of high school or college credit, increase the morale and effectiveness of this category of personnel?

Service Delivery Style. Do components of service organized as teams function more effectively than components in which staff members are organized along occupational categories?

Monitoring of Drugs. Do education programs for staff members, focused on drug characteristics and their appropriate prescription and evaluation, result in more effective treatment? Do drug education programs for patients, including the purpose of the drugs, its potential benefit, and possible side effects, result in fewer complaints, greater compliance with instructions, and more rapid recovery rates among patients?

Patient Role. In controlled experiments does the education of patients to be inquiring and knowledgeable about their medical and mental problems and clear about their roles in the treatment and recovery program make a difference in terms of time and rate of recovery?

Answers to the above questions can be provided by different levels of evaluation research studies using a variety of strategies and methods. We turn now to the methods of modern social area analysis, an objective and systematic methodology for understanding characteristics of small geographic areas and their resident populations. In the following sections, social area analysis will be defined and illustrated at the descriptive, correlational, and experimental levels.

THE METHODOLOGY OF SOCIAL AREA ANALYSIS

Review articles on the historical development of this methodology will be found in Cartwright (1969) and Bell (1967). Objective procedures for developing indexes from census tract data were published by Shevky and Williams (1949). Modifications of these procedures appeared in Shevky and Bell (1955). In the same year Tryon (1955) published a monograph in which multivariate statistical procedures were applied to identify salient dimensions in a correlation matrix of census variables and to relate these dimensions, describing characteristics of citizens living in defined areas (census tracts), to their voting behavior, rates of mental illness, and other forms of behavior. These methods, generally referred to as social area analysis, are most comprehensively presented in Tryon and Bailey (1970).

Within the limits described here, social area analysis is defined as a set of integrated procedures designed to study characteristics of groups or subpopulations of people who live in defined geographical areas, such as census tracts, census blocks, enumeration districts (Houser and Duncan, 1959) or "natural" neighbor-

hoods or communities. More specifically, the interest is in characteristics or attributes which meaningfully differentiate areas or their resident populations, and have important relationships with the health status of residents. The relationships of variables describing groups and their environments with variables describing their health status provide a basis for inferring causal priorities and for planning intervention programs.

It is, of course, meaningful to conceptualize and measure properties of groups or subpopulations living in defined geographical areas just as one conceptualizes and measures properties of individuals or objects. For example, a group could be described in terms of the percent of its members completing college; similarly, an individual in the same age range could be described on the same dichotomous variable: completed college versus did not complete college. In a similar manner the group being described is one of a sample of groups representing some population of groups, while the individuals represent some known population of individuals. Our purpose is to make valid conclusions about either population from studying a sample drawn from it. It is incorrect to make conclusions about populations of individuals from the study of a sample of groups. To do so constitutes a kind of error that is known as the "ecological fallacy."

Measures of properties of groups can be appropriately manipulated to answer specific questions or to test hypotheses. For example, measures of two characteristics of a sample of groups could be correlated to estimate the magnitude of the relationship of the two characteristics in the population of groups. In an urban setting, the correlation of age-corrected death rates with rates of overcrowded housing or poverty income, with a sample of census tracts as the units of observation, would provide some insight into the relationship between environment and health. The relationship of premature births with the percent of mothers using medical facilities during pregnancy, observed over the health areas of New York City, provides preliminary information on the importance of appropriate health care and identifies those areas of the city where intervention in the form of more effective facilities or health education programs is needed. Following intervention, changes in the use of medical facilities and the subsequent changes in prematurity rates, if they occur, can be observed. The effectiveness of types of intervention can also be compared if the target areas and populations are similar.

A HYPOTHETICAL APPLICATION OF SOCIAL AREA ANALYSIS

To apply the above procedures to a CA served by a health service, let us imagine the area occupied by approximately 400,000 people, subdivided into 100 census tracts with a mean population of about 4,000 residents per block. N, or the number of areas, is equal to 100 or the 100 groups of people which compose both the sample and population of interest. Subgroups from each of the 100 areas, such as all women giving birth during a certain time period, could be selected for study, in which case the number of observed groups would again be 100.

To limit our perspective, let us assume that our primary concerns are with the health of pregnant women, newborn babies, and people over 65 years of age, and with the selective use of health services by these groups.

Describing the Catchment Area

Our first step might be the location of target populations, their distribution over the CA, their predicted increase or decrease in size over time, and salient health characteristics and living conditions. Birthrates vary widely over the areas of large cities, and it is important to locate areas of the CA where rates are especially high and where pregnant women and newborns are at high risk (Struening et al., 1973). While high birthrates are generally associated with such factors as high premature birthrates and high infant mortality rates, this may not be true for a limited area of a large city.

In conceptualizing the effective delivery of services, consideration of both birth concentration and the possible increase or decrease in the number of births may be important. Trends in the latter may be derived from birth figures of the past ten years, usually available through vital statistics. Such factors as mobility, the building of new housing, and the relaxation of abortion laws may have important and unanticipated influences on birthrate changes. Living conditions, such as overcrowded housing and poverty income, and family disorganization, as indicated by divorce and separation rates, are, as characteristics of area populations, generally strongly associated with high rates of low birth weight and infant mortality (Struening et al., 1973). Since extremely low birth weight is associated with developmental problems and subsequently with learning problems, the medical planner can anticipate that a range of services will be required to meet the needs of this high-risk group. The issue of the possibility of prevention, as compared with the extensive, long-term treatment often required by children with developmental problems, is important in the planner's deliberations (Stein, Susser, and Guterman, 1973).

A health problem of increasing dimensions is effective service delivery to older citizens, many of whom live well beyond 75 years and are not able to make the difficult trip to outpatient services. Thus, transportation or easy access to medical services is a major factor of effective service to the elderly. The breakdown of the extended family and the low social value placed on the elderly are additional influences affecting treatment of the elderly. The specific family situation is apparently extremely important; widows generally die at higher rates than married subjects at the same age levels (Kraus and Lilienfeld, 1959). In New York City approximately 19% of the men over 65 are widowed, while approximately 54% of the women over 65 are widowed. Over 65% of the men over 65 are married while 31% of the women over 65 are married. Approximately 10% of either group did not marry and another 5% reported divorce or separation status.

Rates of widowhood for both men and women over 65 vary greatly over the census tracts of New York City: 10 to 43% for men and 41 to 68% for women. Thus, the living situations of the elderly, easily available in census data, have important implications for service delivery administrators. Although the relative importance of these implications must be derived from empirical studies relating, for example, widowhood status to appropriate use of medical facilities, data describing the living conditions and social context of the elderly are available though such sources as social welfare statistics, census records, and vital statistics.

The records kept by a health service can provide a useful description of the client or patient population. By noting the age, sex, and census tract of residence of each client over a given time period, frequency of use of each age-sex combination can easily be determined. Rates of use can be computed by dividing the number of clients from each corresponding census tract, yielding a comparable set of rates and a basis for identifying high- or low-use populations in the CA. The rates of use by more specific categories of clients can easily be obtained by dividing, for example, the number of women clients over 65 by the number of women of that age category in each census tract. Study of this distribution of rates will readily identify those areas with high, low, and average use patterns. Results of such work might provoke the testing of a hypothesis that married women over 65 are more likely to use the health services than are widowed women of the same age range. If marital status is recorded in client files, rates of use by the two groups could be compared in each census tract. It may be that the hypothesis will hold only in certain census tracts where, for example, many of the widows are living alone and thus do not have someone to help them get to the doctor.

In summary, descriptive statistics tell a limited but useful and sometimes hypothesis-provoking story. Frequencies, the result of simply counting, tell the administrator how many in each meaningful category are in the community as potential users and in the client's files as actual users. Variations in rates of use, linked to subareas of the CA, identify high-user and low-user areas and suggest the hypothesis of differential risk levels or perhaps inappropriate use of services. Rates of certain categories, such as premature birth or neonatal death, take on meaning by comparison with national or city standards. Assuming relatively high rates, the politically astute administrator may use these data to increase his budget or secure federal funding.

Although descriptive statistics as a primitive form of evaluation are useful and provocative of further inquiry, they also have definite limitations. They provide answers to questions of "what is" or "how many," but offer little basis for the important questions of "why" and "of what relative importance are causal factors?" That is, descriptive statistics provide only a weak basis for causal infer-ence and the identification of causal priorities.

We turn now to more powerful forms of statistical analysis to provide a firmer basis for causal inference and the development of intervention strategies.

Studies Involving Comparison and Correlation

Let us first consider the issue of the selective use of health services by catchment area residents. Clinicians and administrators involved in service delivery and plan-ning may have specific ideas or hypotheses regarding the selective use of services. The evaluator or epidemiologist may derive hypotheses from environmental stress theory or the role of family structure in appropriate health care.

Dependent variables would be selected from service system records. As pre-viously indicated age, sex, and the census tract of residence are essential in describing the client population using the services over a given time period. Additional classification data, such as marital status, occupation, services rendered,

diagnosis, and so forth, may provide further understanding of the relative importance of factors related to service use in selected categories of clients. The client
population should be sufficiently large so that census tracts are represented
by reliable and valid samples which, ideally, differentiate census tracts on continua
of frequency and rate.

Dividing service users by two categories of sex and five categories of age would
result in 10 dependent variables. If both frequency and rate formats are used, we
would have 20 variables describing each of the 100 census tracts in terms of the use
of medical services. Totals for each sex, and a grand total expressed as frequencies
and rates, would yield a total of 26 variables.

Our next job is to develop a rationale for selecting variables which have the best
chance of predicting variability in rate of service use for the ten categories of users.
This is the time for conjecture and the raising of questions. Do elderly people living
in areas with high rates of single-room occupants fail to use medical services? Do
pregnant unmarried teenagers shy away from medical examinations? Is distance a
factor in seeking treatment, or is the convenience of mass transportation? Is the
median education level of women aged 14-44 in census tracts related to their use of
medical facilities during pregnancy? Is the rate of movement of people into census
tracts from outside the state a factor in their use of the medical services? Is the rate
of marital stability a factor in the use of medical services by women aged 20-44?
Are high death rates directly or inversely related to high rates of service use? Is
ethnicity related to rates of service use, especially when English is not the preferred
language?

The above questions are examples of those that might occur to clinicians,
administrators, evaluators, epidemiologists, and perhaps a sample of clients as they
think about characteristics of census tract populations which might affect the use
of medical services. In seeking answers to these questions, or in testing this set of
hypotheses, measures of the designated variables would be derived from census
data, vital statistics, social welfare data, and other sources to form a set of
independent variables. That is, we are interested in those characteristics of census
tract populations and subpopulations which account for variability in rates of
medical service use for ten categories of clients composed of age-sex combinations.

For illustrative purposes, let us consider variables in rate format only. All
independent variables would be expressed in percentages, such as the percentage of
women between 20 and 44 who have not completed high school, the percentage of
people who have migrated from another state, rates of death for men between 45
and 64, and so forth.

Next, a 33 by 33 correlation matrix with 13 dependent and 20 independent
variables in rate format would be computed, resulting in 528 correlation coefficients. A systematic examination of results could start with relationships among the
dependent variables to assess the extent to which census tracts are ranked in
approximately the same order by the 13 use-rate variables. Is medical service use a
unidimensional phenomenon, or are, for example, rates for men uncorrelated with
rates for women over the 100 census tracts? Are use rates for the elderly related to
use rates for the very young? If, for example, use rates for elderly men are

correlated with use rates for elderly women at a magnitude of 0.85 or above, the two variables could possibly be combined in future work. Use rates for small children would almost certainly be highly correlated and could be combined without loss of information. Thus, correlations among the 13 dependent variables would clarify the organization and structure of medical use rates over census tracts as influenced by the age and sex classification system (Struening et al., 1970).

The relationships among the 20 independent variables could be studied for the same structural properties. Study of the patterns of relationship among the 20 variables will almost certainly indicate several groups of variables with moderate to high correlations within each group and relatively low correlations among variables with different group membership. Each variable group will probably define a meaningful construct such as social alienation or socioeconomic status. The procedures of cluster analysis (Tryon and Bailey, 1970) and factor analysis (Comrey, 1973; Harmon, 1967) effectively identify the important dimensions measured by the 20 variables. By using either this formal and objective method of scaling or more subjective, judgmental methods of variable clustering, the groups of variables can be combined into variable composites or factor/cluster scores with high reliability. In previous studies of the dimensionality of census data, theoretically meaningful constructs were inferred from the groups of highly correlated variables. For example, Bloom (1968) identified and combined census variables into four cluster scores which described the census tracts of Pueblo, Colorado, and defined the following constructs or terms: socioeconomic affluence, young marrieds, social isolation, and social disequilibrium. The above procedure can be reversed by selecting census tract variables to define constructs which are theoretically or empirically related to health status and the use of medical facilities.

Regardless of the particular approach, it is possible to reduce a sample of census variables to somewhere between four and nine highly reliable, theoretically meaningful, and relatively independent composite scores which comprehensively describe the environments of census tract residents.

By reducing, through factor or cluster analysis, the 20 independent variables to five composite scores and by eliminating one of the 13 dependent variables by combining rates of use by very young (age 0-5) males and females, we have a manageable set of 17 variables which describe census tracts and their respective client populations. These variables may be statistically manipulated to answer questions or test hypotheses.

We might first tackle the general question: to what extent do characteristics of census tracts predict the selective use of medical services? Patterns of relationship of the five independent composite variable scores with each service delivery variable should provide at least partial answers to the question: Why do residents of certain tracts make extensive use of medical services while residents of other tracts make minimal use of the services? The five independent variables may play strikingly different roles in predicting service use rates by the very old and the very young. Social isolation may be dominant in the very young. Studies of this type are sparse, and there is little or no organized knowledge based on replicated results which might guide the evaluator. However, common sense, a sensitive ear to the ideas of

service clinicians, and interpretations of even fragmentary results of other studies will help to make the results meaningful, raise additional questions, and provide one type of information for changes in service delivery.

More rigorous and comprehensive data analysis procedures may of course be applied to this data set of 17 variables observed on the 100 census tracts. Using multiple regression procedures, one could estimate the extent to which differences among residents of census tracts on variables of service use could be accounted for by a weighted, linear combination of the five independent composite scores which describe the environments of the census tract residents. Such analyses would establish the degree of predictive power which characteristics of the environment have in accounting for differences in the rate of service use over tracts. Again, it would be of interest to observe the relative weight which each independent variable receives in accounting for rate differences.

Partial correlation coefficients, where four of the five independent variables are held constant, would help determine the importance of one characteristic of the environment in accounting for rate differences when the other four characteristics are partialled out or held constant. Application of this procedure would result in five partial correlation coefficients as one more basis for inferring causal priorities.

Study and interpretation of the above results should provide a reasonably firm basis for designing changes in service delivery. It may at times be wise to test inferences regarding the cause of service use rates by surveying populations of census tracts with low, medium, and high rates of use. Such medical-sociologic surveys would be excellent training for students in health occupations. All results, considered within the political-economic context in which service delivery takes place, should lead to change. The next section presents a strategy for evaluating the effects of change.

THE EXPERIMENTAL EVALUATION OF INNOVATION

Kurt Lewin is among those credited with the statement that the best way to understand a social system is through attempting to change it (Marrow, 1969). The foregoing sections have provided methods for describing communities divided into geographic areas and for inferring causal priorities in the use of health services. Assuming that change is desirable in a particular area of health care, how do we procede, using social area analysis methodology? The logic of experimentation dictates that we influence, or attempt to change, similar populations with different stimuli or programs and observe the relative change in the populations being compared. Within a social area analysis framework, similar populations are defined as residents of areas with similar profiles on a number of characteristics which comprehensively describe the area residents.

To follow through with our hypothetical study of the residents of 100 census tracts, let us assume that the rates of seeking a physical examination following the delivery of a child are below a desirable level and that the health service is committed to doing something about it. However, the health service would also like to know the most effective method of convincing this population of recent mothers

to obtain a thorough postpartum examination. Recent figures indicate that approximately 50% now complete the examination. Two methods of influence are developed. One, method A, is a personal letter from the subject's doctor urging her to return for the examination, stressing its importance and also assuring her that in all probability there will be no problem. The second method, labeled B, involves a visit to the subject's home by a congenial, mature woman, trained as an obstetric assistant, who talks with the subject, conveying to her essentially the content of the letter sent in method A. A third method, method C, is the one currently used in the hospital, where a nurse discusses the importance of the postpartum examination with the subject during her hospital stay.

Areas of the CA with similar profiles on both the independent and dependent variables previously described would be identified by profile analytic methods, referenced in Fleiss and Zubin (1969) and applied by Tryon and Bailey (1970). Census tracts with very similar profiles would be assigned to methods A, B, and C, resulting in three experimental areas with highly similar characteristics. In addition, rates of postpartum examination would be computed for each experimental area to assure us of essentially similar populations on this variable.

Following a pilot study to test the methodology, the study would be implemented and changes would be observed in the two experimental groups relative to each other and to the control group. After the collection of sufficient data to make valid conclusions, additional changes in the health delivery system could be made to encourage proper health care following the birth of a child. Such changes might include the installation of a satellite clinic in an area of high birthrates or the training of a home visiting team to provide home examinations to mothers unable to make clinic visits. The message of the visiting woman could be varied to determine whether its influence varies with different types of women. An interesting study of this type was completed by Lehmann (1970).

A similar type of evaluation strategy could, of course, be applied to estimate the effects of change in the delivery of mental health services. The effectiveness of satellite clinics, sensitive to the sociocultural values and life-styles of their clients and area residents, could be evaluated by comparing their service use patterns with those of more traditional clinics providing services to residents living in similar areas. The influence of different types of mental health education programs, placing emphasis on the early detection or prevention of mental disorders, could be evaluated by comparing the types of services requested by clients from similar areas, but participating in different mental health education programs.

A key issue in providing mental health services is for example, the source of referral of clients. The referral network is one important connection between the service system and the community it serves. The nature of the referral network is a function of both the type of community served and the service delivery style.

If, for example, a large proportion of clients are brought in by the police and require hospitalization, while out-patient services receive minimal use, the service system would be dominated by in-patient services where clients request service only when their mental disorders are severe or they are forcibly brought in by the police. If, on the other hand, a large proportion of clients came to out-patient services

accompanied by a relative or friend and referred by a family member or social organization in the community, then a different style of service delivery is manifest.

If one makes the assumption that referral sources are related to levels and types of mental disorders received, and subsequently, to the pattern of services rendered, then service administrators could ask a number of pertinent questions: With what pattern of services should I spend allocated funds in order to best serve the mental health needs of CA residents? Is it possible to alter referral sources so that service dollars play a more preventive role? Is it possible to attract clients through new referral sources before their level of disorder is severe enough to require hospitalization? Can rates of hospitalization for discharged patients be lowered by developing referral sources and making more effective use of out-patient and rehabilitation services? What role can consultation and educational services play in developing more effective referral networks?

Once referral sources and patterns of service have been conceptualized as important issues, plans for changing selected aspects of service delivery procedures or for creating new referral sources can be developed. The effects of introducing these changes into program components serving a given area could be compared over time, in a time series design, to see if desirable results, in terms of referral source and services rendered, are achieved.

In a more rigorous experimental framework, planned changes to improve referral sources and to increase preventive services could be introduced to a defined area while an area with a very similar resident and client population continued the usual style of service delivery. Changes in referral source and services rendered could be compared at various time intervals to estimate the efforts of planned change.

It would take little effort to think of additional factors that could conceivably play important roles in service delivery. The social area method, in the experimental framework, involves the introduction of new methods of service delivery to similar areas in order to observe their relative effectiveness in achieving some service delivery goal or standard of performance.

Application of social area analysis need not be limited to relationships between service delivery systems and their CA populations and organizations. A study of Brandon in the second volume of this Handbook illustrates area analysis applied to New York City. This study identifies the relative role of social area characteristics, type and cost of services, and proximity of services in predicting the rate of use of inpatient and out-patient services by selected age-sex populations residing in 338 health areas of New York City. In Chapter 11, Brandon clearly indicates the complexity of factors which influence the selective use of services by applying multiple regression procedures to area or aggregate data. Chein (1963) in New York City and Cartwright and Howard (1966) in Chicago have applied social area analysis to the study of deviant behavior, while as previously mentioned, Tryon (1955) has used the same approach in relating area characteristics to voting behavior. Studies by the author and colleagues (1970) have analyzed the relationships of area attributes to the health, mental health and behavior of area residents. Work by Bloom (1968) and Levy and Rowitz (1973) illustrate the use of area analysis with psychiatric hospitalization as the dependent variable.

SUMMARY

Systematic study is needed to provide understanding of the complex relationships between human service delivery systems and the populations they serve. More generally planners and administrators need to know more about situational or environmental factors which influence the health, mental health, and behavior of people experiencing those situations or environments.

Because our level of knowledge regarding the successful fit of characteristics of groups to be served with the style of human services rendered is fragmentary and inconclusive, it seems that all levels of evaluation—descriptive, comparative or correlational, and experimental—are urgently needed. It is hypothesized that theory construction will take on a more important, integrative role as empirical development progresses. Appropriate applications of social area analysis, particularly focused on the experimental evaluation of the effects of innovation, promise to add to our understanding of area populations, their selective use of human service delivery systems, and the types of changes needed to make services optimally effective.

REFERENCES

Bell, W. Urban neighborhoods and individual behavior. In *Problems of Youth: Transition to Adulthood in a Changing World*, edited by M. Sherif and C. W. Sherif. Chicago: Aldine, 1967.

Bloom, B. L. An ecological analysis of psychiatric hospitalizations. *Multivariate Behavioral Research*, 1968, 3(4): 423-464.

Cartwright, D. S. Ecological variables. Pp. 155-218 *in Sociological Methodology*, edited by E. F. Borgatta. San Francisco: Jossey-Bass, 1969.

Cartwright, Desmond S. and Kenneth Howard. Multivariate analysis of gang delinquency: I Ecologic influences. *Multivariate Behavioral Research*, July 1966, 1: 321-371.

Chein, I. *Some Epidemiological Vectors of Delinquency and Its Control: Outline of a Project.* Research Center for Human Relations, New York University, 1963. Mimeo.

Comrey, A. L. *A First Course in Factor Analysis.* New York and London: Academic Press, 1973.

Fleiss, J. L. and J. Zubin. On the methods and theory of clustering. *Multivariate Behavioral Research*, 1969, 4(2): 235-250.

Harman, H. H. *Modern Factor Analysis.* Chicago: University of Chicago Press, 1967.

Hauser, P. M. and O. D. Duncan. (eds.) *The Study of Population.* Chicago: University of Chicago Press, 1959.

Kraus, A. S. and Lilienfeld. Some epidemiologic aspects of the high mortality rate in the young widowed group. *J. Chron. Dis.*, 1959, 10 (3): 207-218.

Lehmann, S. Personality and compliance: A study of anxiety and self-esteem in opinion and behavior change. *J. Pers. Soc. Psychol.*, 1970, 15 (1): 76-80.

Levy, L. and L. Rowitz, *The Ecology of Mental Disorder*. Behavioral Publications, New York, 1973.

McKinlay, J. B. Some approaches and problems in the study of the use of services—An overview. *J. Health Soc. Behav., 1972, 13(2): 115-152.*

Marrow, A. J. *The Practical Theorist: The Life and Work of Kurt Lewin.* New York: Basic Books, 1969.

Shevky, E. and W. Bell. *Social Area Analysis.* Stanford: Stanford University Press, 1955.

Shevky, E. and M. Williams. *The Social Areas of Los Angeles: Analysis and Typology.* Berkeley and Los Angeles: University of California Press, 1949.

Stein, Z., M. Susser, and A. Guterman. Screen programme for prevention of Down's syndrome. *Lancet,* 1973, 1(7798): 305-310.

Struening, E. L., S. Lehmann, and J. G. Rabkin. Context and behavior: A social area study of New York City. In *Behavior in New Environments,* edited by E. B. Brody. Beverly Hills, Calif.: Sage Publications, 1970.

Struening, E. L., J. G. Rabkin, and H. Peck. Migration and ethnic membership in relation to social problems. In *Behavior in New Environments,* edited by E. B. Brody. Beverly Hills, Calif.: Sage Publications, 1970.

Struening, E. L., J. G. Rabkin, P. Cohen, G. Raabe, G. Muhlin and J. Cohen. Family, ethnic and economic indicators of low birth weight and infant mortality: A social area analysis. *Ann. N. Y. Acad. Sci.,* 1973, 218: 87-107.

Tryon, R. C. *Identification of Social Areas by Cluster Analysis.* Berkeley and Los Angeles: University of California Press, 1955.

– – –. Predicting group differences in cluster analysis: The social area problem. *Multivariate Behavioral Research,* 1967, 2: 453-475.

– – –. Comparative cluster analysis of social areas. *Multivariate Behavioral Research,* 1968, 3(2): 213-232.

– – – and D. E. Bailey. *Cluster Analysis.* New York: McGraw-Hill, 1970.

Williams, R. H. and L. D. Ozarin (eds.) *Community Mental Health.* San Francisco: Jossey-Bass, 1968.

16

SOCIAL SCIENCE IN EPIDEMIOLOGY:
PSYCHOSOCIAL PROCESSES AND "STRESS"
THEORETICAL FORMULATION

JOHN CASSEL

University of North Carolina

In the pursuit of one of its central objectives, epidemiological enquiry has consistently sought to identify those factors in mans' environment that influence his health. For most of its recorded history the focus has been on physico-chemical factors, supplemented, since the discovery of microorganisms, by microbiological agents thought to be directly pathogenic to the human organism. The increasing recognition of the inability of these factors to explain the occurrence of many diseases of modern societies, or at best to afford a very partial explanation, has led to a search for new categories of environmental factors potentially capable of producing disease. Guided by the elaboration of the stress concept of disease, as originally formulated by the work of Cannon (1935), Selye (1946), and Harold Wolff (1950), recent investigators have postulated that one of the hitherto overlooked features of the environment of potential importance in disease etiology is the presence of other members of the same species. In other words, the concept of the environment for epidemiological purposes has been expanded from the physical and microbiological to include the social.

Despite increased efforts however, attempts to document the role of social factors in the genesis of disease have led to conflicting, contradictory, and often confusing results. There is today no unanimity of opinion that social factors are important in disease etiology, or if they are, which social processes are deleterious, how many such processes there are, and what the intervening links between such processes and disturbed physiological states may be. In part this unsatisfactory state of affairs is a function of the methodological difficulties inherent in such studies, particularly the difficulties of measuring in any precise form such relatively intan-

Reprinted from International Journal of Health Services, 1974, *4* (3), with permission of the publisher: Baywood Publishing Company, Inc.

gible processes. To a larger extent, and underlying these methodological difficulties are, I believe, inadequacies in our theoretical or conceptual framework. The purpose of this paper is to make these inadequacies as explicit as possible, present an alternative point of view and some of the evidence supporting this view, and discuss the research and intervention strategies that such a view would dictate.

As indicated above, much of the research into the role of social factors in disease etiology has been based upon implicit or explicit notions derived from stress theory. While there can be no doubt that the concept of stress has made a significant contribution to our ideas about the nature of disease and its causes, the uncritical subscription to these ideas and often eroneous interpretation of the theory as propounded by its originators has led, frequently, to inappropriate research strategy and contradictory findings.

First, it is important to recognize the semantic difficulties surrounding the use of the word "stress." In the hands of Selye and Wolff, the originators of this term as applied in a scientific sense to medicine, stress was envisaged as a bodily state, not a component of the environment. Thus Wolff states, "I have used the word stress in biology to indicate that state within a living creature which results from the interaction of the organism with noxious stimuli or circumstances i.e. it is a dynamic state within the organism; it is not a stimulus assault, load symbol, burden, or any aspect of environment, internal, external, social or otherwise." While both Selye and Wolff demonstrated that this stress state (evidenced by neuroendocrine changes) can be produced by a variety of noxious stimuli, physical as well as psychological, neither investigator attempted to define the characteristics or the properties of these nonphysical (psychological and/or social) noxious stimuli. Despite such formulations, subsequent investigators have tended to apply the term "stress" to these postulated noxious social or psychological stimuli, often quoting Selye and Wolff for their justification. The use of the word "stressor" to indicate the environmental noxious stimulus and "stress state" or, more frequently, "stress disease" to indicate the postulated consequences of such exposure clarifies the semantic difficulty but highlights the more important conceptual issue. Stated in its most general terms, the formulation subscribed to (often implicitly) by most epidemiologists and social scientists working in this field is that the relationship between a stressor and disease outcome will be similar to the relationship between a microorganism and the disease outcome. In other words the psychosocial process under investigation is envisaged as a stressor capable of having a direct pathogenic effect analogous to that of a physico-chemical or microbiological environmental disease agent. The corrollaries of such a formulation are that there will etiologic specificity, each stressor leading to a specific stress disease, and there will be a dose response relationship, the greater the stressor the more likelihood of disease. There is serious doubt as to the utility or appropriateness of either of these notions.

The idea that disease is produced only by exposure to the direct pathogenic action of disease agents and that, if psychosocial processes can produce disease, they do so by virtue of some direct pathogenic action ignores much of our recent understanding of the disease process and the data available in this field. Du Bos, for example, has emphasized the growing recognition that disease, even infectious

disease, does not occur solely, or even most commonly, from exposure to a new pathogenic disease agent. Du Bos (1965: 164-165) states:

> The sciences concerned with microbial diseases have developed almost exclusively from the study of acute or semi-acute infections caused by virulent micro-organisms acquired through exposure to an exogenous source of infection. In contrast, the microbial diseases most common in our communities today arise from the activities of micro-organisms that are ubiquitous in the environment, persist in the body without causing obvious harm under ordinary circumstances, and exert pathological effects only when the infected person is under conditions of physiological stress. In such a type of microbial disease the event of infection is of less importance than the hidden manifestation of the smoldering infectious process and than the physiological disturbances that convert latent infection into overt systems and pathology.

According to Du Bos, then, in a large number of cases clinical manifestations of disease can occur through factors which disturb the balance between the ubiquitous disease agents and the host that is harboring or exposed to them. Ten to fifteen years before Du Bos, Wolff was arguing that the action of physico-chemical disease agents was different from psychosocial factors in that the former had a direct pathogenic effect by damaging and distorting structure and function, while the latter acted indirectly (or, as he termed it, conditionally) by virtue of their capacity to act as signals or symbols (Wolff, 1973). If then disease can occur by virtue of a disturbance in the balance between the organism and various disease agents, as maintained by Du Bos, and if this balance is mediated largely by the neuro-endocrine system, as has been maintained by Cannon (1935) and Schoenheimer (1942) and widely accepted since, then the mechanism through which the signals and symbols produced by the conditional noxious stimuli work presumably will be by altering neuroendocrine secretions and levels in the body and thus changing the balance. As will be referred to later, there is evidence both from animal and human experiments indicating that variations in the social milieu are indeed associated with profound endocrine changes in the exposed subjects.

Viewed in this light, then, it is most unlikely that any given psychosocial process or stressor will be etiologically specific for any given disease, at least as currently classified. In other words, it no longer becomes useful to consider a subset of existing clinical entities as "stress" diseases as all diseases can in part be due to these processes. Hinkle, arguing from the biological evidence, supports this point strongly when he states: "At the present time the 'stress' explanation is no longer necessary. It is evident that any disease process and in fact any process within the living organism, might be influenced by the reaction of the individual to his social environment or to other people" (Hinkle, 1973: 43).

A more reasonable formulation thus would hold that psychosocial processes acting as "conditional" stressors will, by altering the endocrine balance in the body, increase the susceptibility of the organism to direct noxious stimuli, that is, disease agents. The psychosocial processes thus can be envisaged as enhancing susceptibility to disease. The clinical manifestations of this enhanced susceptibility will then not be a function of the particular psychosocial stressor but of the physico-chemical or

microbiological disease agents harbored by the organism or to which the organism is exposed. Presumably, the disease manifestations will also be determined by constitutional factors, which in turn are a function of genetic endowment and previous experience.

Some reasonably convincing data exist to support this point of view. For example, one of the striking features of animal studies concerned with demonstrating the health consequences of a changed social environment has been the wide range of diseases that have followed such changes. Alteration of the social environment by varying the size of the group in which animals interact while keeping all aspects of the physical environment and diet constant has been reported to lead to a rise in maternal and infant mortality rates, an increase in the incidence of arteriosclerosis, a marked reduction in the resistance to a wide variety of direct noxious stimuli, including drugs, microorganisms, and x-rays, an increased susceptibility to various types of neoplasia, to alloxan produced diabetes and to convulsions (Calhoun, 1962; Ratcliffe and Gronin, 1958; Swinyard et al., 1961; Davis and Read, 1958; Ader and Hahn, 1963; Ader, Kreutner and Jacobs, 1963; King, Lee and Vissacher, 1955; Andervont, 1944; Christian and Williamson, 1958). Thus, in animals at least, no specific type of "stress disease" appears in response to changes in the social milieu, changes that have been interpreted as "stressors." Rather the animals appear to respond with a variety of diseases, the particular manifestation being determined by factors other than the disturbed social process. The evidence from human studies is somewhat less direct but nevertheless still consistent with this idea. A remarkably similar set of social circumstances characterizes people who develop tuberculosis (Holmes, 1956), schizophrenia (Dunham, 1961; Mishler and Scotch, 1963), multiple accidents (Selye, 1946), suicide (Durkheim, 1957), and alcoholism (Holmes, personal communication). Common to all these people is a marginal status in society. They are individuals who, for a variety of reasons (ethnic minorities rejected by the dominant majority in their neighborhood, high sustained rates of residential and occupational mobility, broken homes or isolated living circumstances), have been deprived of meaningful social contact. It is perhaps surprising that this wide variety of disease outcomes associated with similar circumstances has generally escaped comment. To a large extent this has probably resulted from each investigator usually being concerned with only one clinical entity so the features common to multiple disease manifestations have tended to be overlooked. One exception to this has been the study by Christenson and Hinkle (1961). In an industrial study in the United States, they have shown that managers in a company who, by virtue of their family background and educational experience, were least well prepared for the demands and expectations of industrial life were at greater risk of disease than age-matched managers who were better prepared. They found that this increased risk included all diseases, major as well as minor, physical as well as mental, long-term as well as short-term. A further example illustrating this point is the health consequences that follow the disruption of important social relationships, particularly death of a spouse. It has been shown that widows have a death rate 3 to 5 times higher than that of married men of the same age for *every* cause of death (Kraus and Lilienfeld, 1959). It is difficult to conceive of a specific etiologic process responsible for the increased death rate from such diverse conditions as, for

example, coronary heart disease, cancer, infectious diseases, and peptic ulcer, and would appear more reasonable to consider the loss of the spouse as increasing the susceptibility of such men to other disease agents.

As will be readily appreciated, subscription to such a formulation of the role of psychosocial factors in disease etiology would have important implications from the point of view of both research and intervention strategies. As far as research is concerned it would suggest that attempts to document that certain social processes are stressors, capable of producing disease, by examining their relationship only to specific clinical entities (coronary heart disease, hypertension, or various forms of cancer, for example) or even to subsets of diseases labeled "stress diseases" are unlikely to be too useful. If the formulation is correct, certain people exposed to these stressors will develop the clinical entity under investigation. Others however will not, but will develop some other manifestation which will not have been recorded or used as evidence as to the importance of the postulated stressor. A more logical approach would be either to examine all disease outcomes related to exposure to the postulated stressor(s) or alternatively to identify subsets of the population who by virtue of their personal or environmental characteristics are known to be at high risk or specific clinical manifestations and examine the role of psychosocial stressors in facilitating the appearance of those manifestations. If this latter approach were used, it would imply that, instead of examining the role of psychosocial stressors in the genesis of coronary heart disease in a random sample of the population, for example, the study should be restricted to those who, by virtue of their elevated risk factors (blood pressure, cholesterol, cigarette smoking, etc.), are known to be at high risk to coronary heart disease and who, therefore, if they become ill, are more likely to manifest coronary heart disease than say tuberculosis.

Should such a research produce promising results, the implications for preventive intervention strategies would be profound. Before discussing these however, it is necessary to consider a further dilemma: our uncertainty as to the nature and properties of psychosocial stressors. Clarification of the outcomes to be expected from exposure to such stressors, unfortunately, provides no guide as to what these stressors are, never mind how they are to be measured.

One of the unfortunate arguments that has clouded research in this area has been the controversy as to whether such stressors are invariant, affecting all people in a similar manner, or whether they are idiosyncratic, affecting each person differently depending upon his personality, interpretation of the situation, and so forth. The position for the latter point of view (which may be summarized as "one man's meat is another man's poison") has recently been stated quite succintly by Hinkle. "In view of the fact that people react to their 'life situations' or social conditions in terms of the meaning of these situations to them, it is difficult to accept the hypothesis that certain kinds of situations or relationships are inherently stressful and certain others are not" (Hinkle, 1973: 46). Others, perhaps the majority of investigators, have treated these factors not only as if they were invariant but as if they were unidimensional, the presence of the factor being stressful with its absence being beneficial.

Quite clearly, if the idiocyncratic point of view is correct, much of the work to

identify universal or general stressors will be futile and lead to contradictory and confusing results. But equally clearly, the contrary point of view ignores the proposition that these processes do not have a direct pathogenic action but operate in their capacity as signals or symbols triggering off responses in terms of the information they are perceived to contain. And, as this perception will almost certainly be a function of the differing personalities and salience of the experience to different individuals, it is hard to accept the notion that certain social circumstances will always, or even in the majority of cases, be "stressful." This dilemma can best be resolved, I believe, by two changes in our thinking, changes that appear consistent with most of the data and conceivably explain some of the existing contradictions. The first of these is that the extent to which the postulated psychosocial processes are generally noxious versus idiocyncratic in their action is largely a function of our level of abstraction. If we can identify the characteristics or properties of those signals or symbols that generally evoke major neuro-endocrine changes in the recipients, we will have identified a general class of stressors even if the particular circumstances or relationships creating those types of signals or symbols differs for different people. Furthermore, if we can identify the attributes of this class of stressors, it may well be that the same relationships or social circumstances within a given culture (or perhaps subculture) regularly produce such a class of signals. Second, the existing data has led me to believe that we should no longer treat psychosocial processes as unidimensional, stressor or not stressor, but rather as two dimensional, one category being stressors, and another being protective or beneficial.

The evidence supporting these points of view comes from both animal and human research. As has been indicated earlier, altering the social milieu of animals by increasing the number housed together leads to marked changes in health status, even when all relevant aspects of the physical environment and diet were kept constant. The biological mechanisms through which such changes are produced have also been identified. Changes in group membership and the quality of group relationships in animals have been shown to be accompanied by significant neuro-endocrine changes affecting among others the pituitary, the adrenal-cortical system, the thyroid, and the gonads (Mason, 1959; Mason and Brady, 1964). These same endocrines are those responsible in large part for maintaining what Schoenheimer has termed the "dynamic steady state" or the organism and thus presumably its ability to withstand changes that would result from the action of disease agents. The question of concern then is what are the properties of the changes in this social milieu and are there analogues in the human social system? The usual notion that the crowding itself, that is, the physical density of the population, is responsible for the deterioration in health status has not been sustained by human studies. Despite the popularity of the belief that crowding is harmful to health, a review of the literature shows that, for every study indicating a relationship between crowding and some manifestation of poor health, there is another equally good (or bad) investigation showing either no relationship or even an inverse one (Cassel, 1971; Cassel, in press). Furthermore Hong Kong, one of the most crowded cities in the world, and Holland, one of the most crowded countries, enjoy some of the highest levels of both physical and mental health in the world (Wolff, 1950).

A careful review of the data reported from these animal studies may hold a clue to these puzzles. Apparently in animals, an almost inevitable consequence of crowding is the development of a set of disordered relationships between animals. While being manifest in a wide variety of bizarre and unusual behaviors, these disordered relationships often result in a failure of the animal to respond with anticipated responses to what were previously appropriate cues. Thus habitual acts of aggression (including "ritualized aggression" in defending the nest) or evidence of acceptance or subordination on the part of one animal fail to elicit appropriate reciprocal responses on the part of another. In social animals under wild conditions, for example, the occupier of a nest will define a zone around that nest which is "home" territory." Invasion of this territory by another animal of the same species will lead to a set of highly ritualized aggressive moves and countermoves, rarely leading to bloodshed, but culminating in one or other animal "signalling" capitulation. Under crowded conditions, apparently, the defending animal may initiate this ritual "dance," but the invading animal fails to respond in the anticipated fashion. Instead he may lie down, go to sleep, attempt to fornicate, walk away, or do something that, for the situation, is equally bizarre.

This failure of various forms of behavior to elicit predictable responses leads to one of three types of responses on the part of the animals involved, the most common of which is repetition of the behavioral acts. Such acts are, of course, always accompanied by profound neuroendocrine changes, and presumably their chronic repetition leads eventually to the permanent alterations in the level of the hormones and to the degree of autonomic nervous system arousal reported under conditions of animal crowding. The fact that these behavioral acts are, in a sense, inappropriate, in that they do not modify the situation, can be expected to enhance such hormonal changes. Under these conditions it is not difficult to envisage the reasons for the increased susceptibility to environmental insults displayed by such animals.

An alternative response on the part of some animals is to withdraw from the field, to remain motionless and isolated for long hours on end. It is apparently not uncommon, for example, to observe some mice under crowded conditions crouched in most unusual places, on top of the razor-thin edge of a partition or in the bright light in the center of the enclosure, completely immobile and not interacting with any other animals. Such animals apparently do not exhibit the increased pathology demonstrated by the interacting members (Calhoun, 1962).

The third alternative is for animals to form their own deviant groups, groups that apparently ignore the mores and codes of behavior of the larger group. Thus, "gangs" of young male rats have been observed invading nests, attacking females (the equivalent of gang rapes have been reported), indulging in homosexual activities, and the like. I am not aware of any data on the health status of these gang members, but according to this hypothesis they also should not exhibit any increase in pathology.

These observations would suggest that stressful social situations might be those in which the actor is not receiving adequate evidence (feedback) that his actions are leading to anticipated consequences. While we do not as yet have the appropriate instruments to measure in any direct fashion the extent to which such a phenom-

enon is occurring in humans, it is not unreasonable to infer that it is highly likely under certain sets of circumstances. First, it is probable that, when individuals are unfamiliar with the cues and expectations of the society in which they live (as in the case of migrants to a new situation, or those individuals involved in a rapid change of social scene, such as the elderly in an ethnic enclave caught up in urban renewal), many of their actions and the responses would fall into this category and thus, if this suggestion is correct, they should be more susceptible to disease than are those for whom the situation is familiar.

Some circumstantial evidence supporting this point of view exists. Scotch (1960, 1963) found that blood pressure levels among the Zulu who had recently migrated to a large urban center were higher than the blood pressure levels of both those who had remained in their rural tribal surroundings and those who had lived for over 10 years in the urban setting. In two independent studies, Syme, Hyman, and Enterline (1964) and Syme, Borhani, and Buechley (1965) have demonstrated that occupationally and residentially mobile people have a higher prevalence of coronary heart disease than stable populations, and that those individuals displaying the greatest discontinuity between childhood and adult situations, as measured by occupation and place of residence, have higher rates than those in which less discontinuity could be determined. Tyroler and Cassel designed a study in which death rates from coronary heart disease, and from all heart disease, could be measured in groups who were themselves stable but around whom the social situation was changing in varying degree. For this purpose they selected 45 to 54-year-old, white, male, rural residents in various counties of North Carolina and classified those counties by the degree or urbanization occurring in that locality. Death rates for coronary heart disease and all heart disease showed a stepwise increasing gradient with each increase in the index of urbanization of the county (Tyroler and Cassel, 1964). In another study, Cassel and Tyroler (1961) examined two groups of rural mountaineers working in a factory. The first of these was composed of individuals who were the first of their family to engage in industrial work, while the second comprised workers who were the children of previous workers in this factory. The two groups were drawn from the same mountain coves and doing the same work for the same pay. The underlying hypothesis was that the second group, by virtue of their previous experience, would be better prepared for the expectations and demands of industrial living than the first and would thus exhibit fewer signs of ill health. Health status was measured by responses to the Cornell Medical Index and by various indices of sick absenteeism. As predicted, the first group had higher Cornell Medical Index scores (more symptoms) and higher rates of sick absenteeism after the initial few years of service at each age.

A second set of circumstances in which this lack of feedback might occur would be under conditions of social disorganization. This, while still being far from a precise term which can be measured accurately, has proved to be a useful concept in a number of studies. In the hands of several investigators, for example, various indicators of social or familial disorganization have been related to increased rates of tuberculosis (Holmes, 1956), mental disorders (Leighton et al., 1963), deaths from stroke (Neser, Tyroler and Cassel, 1970), prevalence of hypertension

(Harburg, et al., 1969), and coronary heart disease (Syme, Hyman and Enterline, 1965). In addition this same property might well explain the stressor role often ascribed to status inconsistency (Jackson, 1962) and role conflict and ambiguity (Kahn et al., 1961). Thus the human data, while by no means confirming the utility of this postulation, is certainly not inconsistent with it and sufficiently intriguing to warrant further research along these lines.

As indicated earlier however, a fuller explanation of the potential role of psychosocial factors in the genesis of disease requires the recognition of a second set of processes. These might be envisioned as the protective factors, buffering or cushioning the individual from the physiological or psychological consequences of exposure to the stressor situation. It is suggested that the property common to these processes is the strength of the social supports provided by the primary groups of most importance to the individual. Again both animal and human studies have provided evidence supporting this point of view. Conger, Sawrey, and Turrel (1958), for example, have shown that the efficacy with which an unanticipated series of electric shocks (given to animals previously conditioned to avoid them) can produce peptic ulcers is determined, to a large extent, by whether the animals are shocked in isolation (high ulcer rates) or in the presence of littermates (low ulcer rates). Henry, Meehan, and Stephens (1967) have been able to produce persistent hypertension in mice by placing the animals in intercommunicating boxes all linked to a common feeding place, thus developing a state of territorial conflict. Hypertension only occurred, however, when the mice were "strangers." Populating the system with littermates did not produce these effects. Liddel found that a young goat isolated in an experimental chamber and subjected to a monotonous conditioning stimulus will develop traumatic signs of experimental neurosis, while its twin in an adjoining chamber, and subjected to the same stimulus, but with the mother present, will not.

The evidence from human studies is somewhat more conflicting. To a large extent I believe this to be due to a lack of recognition in many investigations that social supports are only likely to be protective *in the presence* of stressful situations. Thus the majority of studies have restricted themselves either to attempts at relating the absence of some form of social support to disease or to the effect of some postulated stressful situation but have rarely examined the joint effects of a stressful situation together with the presence or absence of social supports. Despite this there have been some studies which have produced reasonably convincing evidence implicating lack of social supports in disease occurrence. The studies, referred to above (Holmes, 1956; Dunham, 1961; Mishler and Scotch, 1963; Tillman and Hobbs, 1949; Durkheim, 1957), indicating the higher disease rates in people with marginal status probably fall into this category. Separation from the family and evacuation from London during World War II appeared more deleterious for London children than enduring the blitz with their family (Titmus, 1950). Combat studies have suggested the effectiveness of the small group (platoon, bomber crew) in sustaining members under severe battle stress (Mandelbaum, 1952). While these latter have indeed studied the effect of social supports under some form of presumed stressful situation (the blitz in one instance and combat in

the other), the exposure of individual subjects to such stressors was not in fact measured, their existence being implicit rather than explicit. In one recent study, however, both the stressors and the supports were more directly measured. Nuckolls, Cassel, and Kaplan (1972) studied the joint effects of these two processes on the outcome of pregnancy. Complete data were obtained from 170 white, married primipara of similar age and social class, all delivered by the same service. Social stresses were measured by a cumulative life-change score, a method developed by Holmes and Rahe (1967) to assess the major life changes to which an individual had had to adapt.

Social supports or, as they were termed, psychosocial assets were assessed by an instrument developed by the investigator designed to measure the subject's feelings or perceptions of herself (with particular reference to this pregnancy), her relationships with her husband, her extended family, and her immediate community in terms of the support she was receiving or could anticipate receiving. Both instruments were administered to the subjects before the 32nd week of pregnancy. After delivery, the records were reviewed blind for any evidence of complications of pregnancy or delivery. Of these patients 47% had one or more minor or major complication, a rate comparable to the 50% found in a national study using the same criteria.

Neither the life-change score alone nor the psychosocial asset score by itself was related to complications. However, when the relations between a high life-change score and complications of pregnancy were examined in the presence or absence of psychosocial assets, important associations were discovered. Of women with high life-change scores, but low asset scores, 90% had one or more complications of pregnancy, whereas only 33% of women with equally high life-change scores, but with high asset scores, had any complications. In the absence of high life-change scores, the asset scores were irrelevant.

Taken together these studies would suggest, at both the human and animal levels, the presence of another particular animal of the same species may, under certain circumstances, protect the individual from a variety of stressful stimuli. The mechanisms through which such interpersonal relationships may function have largely been a matter of speculation. Theories have however been advanced and tested, one of the more attractive ones being that of Bovard (1959, 1962). On the basis of animal studies, he suggests that stressful psychological stimuli are mediated through the posterior and medial hypothalamus leading via the release of a chemotransmitter to the anterior pituitary to a general protein catabolic effect. He further suggests that a second center located in the anterior and lateral hypothalamus, when stimulated by an appropriate social stimulus (namely, the availability of a supportive relationship), calls forth in the organism a "competing response" which inhibits, masks, or screens the stress stimulus, such that the latter has a minimal effect.

To test the notions advanced in this paper, further work obviously needs to be done to develop the instruments to measure these categories of psychosocial processes. If such research were to support these ideas, it would suggest a radical change in the strategies used for preventive action. Recognizing that throughout all

history disease, with rare exceptions, has not been prevented by finding and treating sick individuals, but by modifying those environmental factors facilitating its occurrence, this formulation would suggest that we focus efforts more directly on attempts at further identification and subsequent modification of these categories of psychosocial factors rather than on screening and early detection. Of the two sets of factors, it would seem more immediately feasible to attempt to improve and strengthen the social supports than to reduce the exposure to the stressors. A recent example of the successful use of community counselors, women without any specific training but carefully chosen on the basis of high levels of empathy, warmth, and concern, in improving the well-being of children with chronic handicapping conditions (Pless, 1971) would suggest that even in advance of any further specific knowledge such modes of intervention could be more widely tested. With advancing knowledge, it is perhaps not too far-reaching to imagine a preventive health service in which professionals are involved largely in the diagnostic aspects, identifying families and groups at high risk by virtue of their lack of fit with their social milieu and determining the particular nature and form of the social supports that can and should be strengthened if such people are to be protected from disease outcomes. The intervention actions then could well be undertaken by nonprofessionals, provided adequate guidance and specific direction were given. Such an approach would not only be economically feasible but if the notions expressed in this paper are correct, would do more to prevent a wide variety of diseases than all the efforts currently being made through multiphasic screening and multirisk factor cardiovascular intervention attempts.

REFERENCES

Ader, R. and E. W. Hahn. "Effects of Social Environment on Mortality to Whole Body–X-Irradiation in the Rat." *Psycho. Rep.*, 1963, 13: 24-215.

Ader, R., A. Kreutner and H. L. Jacobs. "Social Environment, Emotionality and Alloxan Diabetes in the Rat." *Psychosom. Med.*, 1963, 25: 60-68.

Andervont, H. B. "Influence of Environment on Mammary Cancer in Mice." *J. Nat. Cancer Inst.*, 1944, 4: 579-581.

Bovard, Everett W. "The Balance Between Negative and Positive Brain System Activity." *Perspectives Biol. and Med.*, 1962, 6: 116-127.

———. "The Effects of Social Stimuli on the Response to Stress." *Psychol. Rev.*, 1959, 66: 267-277.

Calhoun, J. B. "Population Density and Social Pathology." *Sci. Amer.*, 1962, 206: 139.

Cannon, W. B. "Stresses and Strains of Homeostasis." *Am. J. Med. Sci.*, 1935, 189: 1.

Cassel, John. "Health Consequences of Population Density and Crowding." In *Rapid Population Growth*. National Academy of Sciences, Johns Hopkins Press, 1971.

———. "The Relation of the Urban Environment to Health." *Mt. Sinai Med. J.* In Press.

——— and H. A. Tyroler. "Epidemiological Studies of Culture Change I: Health Status and Recency of Industrialization." *Arch. Envir. Health*, 1961, 3: 25.

Christenson, W. N. and L. E. Hinkle. "Differences in Illness and Prognositic Signs in Two Groups of Young Men." *J.A.M.A.*, 1961, 177: 247-253.

Christian, J. J. and H. O. Williamson. "Effect of Crowding on Experimental Granuloma Formation in Mice." *Proc. Soc. Exp. Biol. Med.*, 1958, 99: 385-387.

Conger, J. J., W. Sawrey, and E. S. Turrell. "The Role of Social Experience in the Production of Gastric Ulcers in Hooded Rats Placed in a Conflict Situation." *J. Abnorm. Soc. Psych.*, 1958, 57: 216.

Davis, D. E. and C. P. Read. "Effect of Behaviour on Development of Resistance in Trichinosis." *Proc. Soc. Exp. Biol. Med.,* 1958, 99: 269-272.

Du Bos, R. *Man Adapting.* New Haven: Yale University Press, 1965.

———. "The Human Environment in Technological Societies." *The Rockefeller Review,* July-Aug. 1968.

Dunham, Warren H. "Social Structure and Mental Disorders: Complete Hypotheses of Explanation" *Milbank Mem. Fund. Quart.,* 1961, 39: 259-310.

Durkheim, E. *Suicide.* Free Press, 1957.

Harburg, E., W. J. Schull, M. A. Schork, J. B. Wigle and W. R. Burkhardt. "Stress and Heredity in Negro/White Blood Pressure Differences." Progress Report to National Heart Institute, 1969.

Henry, J. P, J. P. Meehan and P. M. Stephens. "The Use of Psycho-Social Stimuli to Induce Prolonged Hypertension in Mice." *Psychosomat. Med.,* 1967, 29: 408-432.

Hinkle, Lawrence E. "The Concept of "Stress" in the Biological and Social Sciences." *Sci. Med. and Man.,* 1973, 1: 43.

Holmes, T. "Multidiscipline Studies of Tuberculosis." In *Personality Stress and Tuberculosis,* edited by Phineus J. Sparer. International Universities Press, 1956.

Holmes, T. H. Personal communication.

Holmes, Thomas and Richard Rahe. "The Social Readjustment Rating Scale." *J. Psychosom. Res.,* 1967, 11: 213-218.

Jackson, Elton F. "Status Consistency and Symptom of Stress." *Am. Soc. Rev.,* 1962, 27: 469-480.

Kahn, R. L., D. M. Wolfe, R. Quinn et al. *Organizational Stress: Studies in Role Conflict and Ambiguity.* New York: Wiley, 1961.

King, J. T., Y. C. P. Lee and M. B. Vissacher. "Single Versus Multiple Cage Occupancy and Convulsion Frequency in C H Mice." *Proc. Soc. Exp. Biol. Med.,* 1955, 88: 661-663.

Kraus. A. and A. Lilienfeld. "Some Epidemiologic Aspects of the High Mortality Rate in the Young Widowed Group." *J. Chronic. Dis.,* 1959, 10: 207-217.

Leighton, D. C., J. S. Harding, D. E. Macklin, A. M. Macmillan and A. H. Leighton. *The Character of Danger.* Basic Books, 1963.

Mandelbaum, D. G. *Soldier Groups and Negro Soldiers.* Berkeley: University of California, 1952. Pp. 45-48. Quoted by Everett W. Bovard (1959: 269).

Mason, J. W. "Psychological Influences on the Pituitary-Adrenal-Cortical System." *Recent Progress in Hormone Research,* edited by G. Pencus, 1959, 15: 345-389.

Mason, W. and J. V. Brady. "The Sensitivity of the Psychoendrocrine Systems to Social and Physical Environment." In *Psychiobiological Approaches to Social Behavior,* edited by D. Shapiro. Stanford University Press, 1964.

Mishler, E. G. and N. A. Scotch. "Sociocultural Factors in the Epidemiology of Schizophrenia: A Review." *Psychiatry,* 1963, 26: 315-351.

Neser. W. B., H. A. Tyroler and J. Cassel. "Stroke Mortality in the Black Population of North Carolina in Relation to Social Factors." Presented at the American Heart Association Meeting on Cardiovascular Epidemiology, New Orleans, 1970.

Nuckolls, Catherine B., John Cassel and Berton H. Kaplan. "Psycho-Social Assets, Life Crises and the Prognosis of Pregnancy." *Am. J. Epid.,* 1972, 95: 431-441.

Pless, Ivan B. "Chronic Illness in Childhood: The Role of Lay Family Counsellors." Presented at Health Services Research Conference, Chicago, Dec. 8-10, 1971.

Ratcliffe, H. L. and M. T. I. Cronin. "Changing Frequency of Arteriosclerosis in Mammals and Birds at the Philadelphia Zoological Garden." *Circulation,* 1958, 18: 41-52.

Schoenheimer, R. *Dynamic Steady State of Body Constituents.* Cambridge: Harvard University Press, 1942.

Scotch, N. A. "A Preliminary Report on the Relation of Socio Cultural Factors to Hypertension Among the Zulu." *Ann. New York Acad. Sci.,* 1960, 86: 1000.

———. "Sociocultural Factors in the Epidemiology of Zulu Hypertension." *Am. J. Publ. Health,* 1963, 52: 1205-1213.

Selye, H. "The General Adaptation Syndrome and Diseases of Adaptation." *J. Clin. Endocrinol*, 1946, 6: 117.

Swinyard, E. A., L. D. Clark, J. T. Miyahara and H. H. Wolf. "Studies on the Mechanism of Amphetamine Toxicity in Aggregated Mice." *J. Pharmacol. Exptl. Therap.*, 1961, 132: 97-102.

Syme, S. L., M. M. Hyman and P. E. Enterline. "Some Social and Cultural Factors Associated with the Occurrence of Coronary Heart Disease." *J. Chron. Dis.*, 1964, 17: 277-289.

———. "Cultural Mobility and the Occurrence of Coronary Heart Disease." *Health & Human Beh.*, 1965, 6: 173-189.

Syme, S. L., N. O. Borhani and R. W. Buechley. "Cultural Mobility and Coronary Heart Disease in an Urban Area." *Am. J. Epid.*, 1965, 82: 334-346.

Tillman, W. A. and G. E. Hobbs. "Social Background of Accident Free and Accident Repeaters." *Am. J. Psychiat.*, 1949, 106: 321.

Titmus, R. M. *Problems of Social Policy*. London: H.M. Stationery Office, 1950. Quoted by Everett W. Bovard (1959: 269).

Tyroler, H. A. and J. Cassel. "Health Consequences of Culture Change: The Effect of Urbanization on Coronary Heart Mortality in Rural Residents of North Carolina." *J. Chron. Dis.*, 1964, 17: 167-177.

Wolff, H. G. "Life Stress and Bodily Disease." *Res. Publ. Ass. Nerv. and Ment. Dis.*, 1950, 29: 3-1135.

———. Quoted in Lawrence E. Hinkle, "The Concept of Stress in the Biological and Social Sciences," *Sci. Med. and Man.*, 1973, 1: 34.

VII

DATA ANALYTIC METHODS

17

MULTIVARIATE METHODOLOGIES FOR EVALUATION RESEARCH

HERBERT W. EBER

HISTORY AND DEVELOPMENT

When the social sciences emerged from the armchair of the natural philosopher and began the application of scientific method to psychology, sociology, economics, and similar areas, the model of the scientific method was that provided by the older, "established," physical sciences. The model emphasized laboratories, equipment, rigorous experiments under controlled conditions, and most important, the study of one variable at a time, all other variables being held constant.

The young sciences accepted the model but found compliance with its requirements difficult to impossible. "All other variables" refused to become or remain constant. Actually, they had never been really constant in physics. All billiard balls are not really alike, billiard tables do not have perfect surfaces or cushions, and even astronomers had found the exasperation of the "personal equation."

However, the magnitude of error introduced by the inconstancy of "other variables" in the physical sciences was trivial during the early years; measurements themselves were of limited accuracy, and the main effects under study were so gross that their obvious parameters overshadowed the minor errors.

Not so in the social sciences. Experiments using organic subjects, animal or human, usually obtained variance of the same magnitude between subjects as between conditions. For example, comparison among the effects of several methods of memorizing showed (unwanted) differences among subjects. While Ebbinghaus solved that problem by studying primarily his own memory processes, a better solution seemed required.

Univariate statistical models provided the required technique. In general, these models were of two types, though later these were shown to be simply two ways of looking at the same thing.

[553]

The basic concept was that variance is additive and that total variance can thus be partitioned into two major components, a *lawful* part and an *error* part. Lawful was defined as resulting from the variable under study; error was that variance due to those "other variables" that refused to remain constant.

It was shown that *error* provided a basis for judging the significance of *lawful variance*. Clearly, intuitively, if *error* is so large that *lawful* is hardly perceptible by comparison, then all may be error. Conversely, if *lawful* looms large by contrast with *error*, then theory is supported (or destroyed) and the experiment has been successful. In time, the theoretical basis of such judgments was defined and codified. Statistical inference had become a handmaiden to the social (and later the physical) scientist.

The two types of models mentioned above resulted from two types of *lawfulness* that had been hypothesized. Where theory was oriented toward differences in outcome resulting from differences in the variable under examination, *lawfulness* was defined as between-groups (of subjects) variance while *error* was variance within groups. Techniques such as the t-test, and later more extensive types of "analysis of variance" resulted.

Where theory looked at relationships of two variables (perhaps an "independent" and a "dependent," perhaps not), *lawfulness* was defined as covariance of the relationship, while error was all else. Correlational techniques of many kinds were the product of this approach.

It is intuitively obvious to many students, and it can be shown both mathematically and empirically, that complete translation from one type of model to the other is simple and complete. Nevertheless, historical factors produced two "schools" of statistical thought, emphasizing different approaches to different problems, and at times each vigorously defending the "rightness" of its technology. An association of analysis-of-variance with experimental rigor versus correlational methods with naturalistic observation became historically meaningful, despite being substantively unnecessary and irrelevant.

In time, both schools grasped the larger utility of the concept that variance can be partitioned. The t-test became the F-test; analysis-of-variance became analysis-of-covariance. Simple correlation led to multiple correlation and regression theory, and in turn to factor analysis.

With the advent of the electronic computer, what had been the demanding (and even exhausting) technique used by a few became the technology available to all social (and other) scientists. The ability actually to carry out the calculations that had seemed desirable served as a spur to development. Multivariate statistical methods had arrived, and the last two decades have seen not only the development of theory, but the coming of age of a group of scientists whose familiarity with that theory permits the ready use of multivariate technology.

The mathematics of the multivariate approaches to statistical inference need not concern us in this discussion. They are not inordinately difficult, but are of interest primarily to the specialist, and the notation and precise conceptualization can become complex. Excellent treatments in as much detail as may be desired are

readily available, for example, in Cooley and Lohnes (1971), Cattell (1966), or Overall and Klett (1972).

At the level of understanding required for the user of these techniques, however, the issues are not beyond the present concern. All multivariate techniques are based upon the familiar concept that variance can be subdivided, allocated, analyzed, related to other variance, compared, and so forth. Moreover, all multivariate techniques are extensions into more general terms of concepts whose univariate antecedents were a special case. In exactly the same way that plane geometry can be conceptualized as a special case (two dimensions, Cartesian metric) of a much larger, more general family of geometries, so a t-test may be considered as a very simple, special case of discriminant functions.

Without minimizing the very real and extensive competence required of the multivariate statistician, and the large number of procedures whose judicious use can be of major help to the evaluation researcher, it is nevertheless fair to say that there are essentially only three types of problems, and two of these are alternate versions of the same thing. Understanding these three (or two) types is not difficult.

DATA REDUCTION MODELS

There is a class of problems in which the researcher has a larger number of observations than he can easily interpret. Perhaps there are multiple measurements upon a number of subjects, perhaps on a number of occasions, perhaps obtained through a number of methods. The task is to reduce this complexity to a more easily conceptualized pattern; it is not primarily a matter of statistical inference or proof.

A number of specific techniques have been developed to achieve desired types of data reduction. Factor analysis is probably the best-known name of a procedure in this area, but cluster analysis, image analysis, and component analysis all describe techniques of this type.

Important methodological issues are represented by the names of the techniques and by other issues discussed by multivariate analysts, not only in the area of technique but also in areas of philosophy of science and definition of goals. However, these are not our major concern in this chapter. Rather, we shall examine the basic (simplified) strategy of all such methods.

The basic method is the partitioning of variance and the grouping together of those variables, subjects, occasions which show relatively small variance among themselves, while showing large variation from other groupings. These things that "go together" are then conceived as a type, a factor, an influence.

At the simplest level, a reduction in complexity occurs, and this is helpful in dealing with the data. One test score on each of a dozen factors represents an easier way of describing persons than 100 test scores from as many measurements. If the analysis has been properly performed, then little useful accuracy is lost in the reduction of the number of scores, and a great deal of convenience has been gained.

On the other hand, some factor-cluster analysts are far from content with gains in convenience. They wish to use the methods to search for underlying causes, basic

types, and similar explanatory concepts. While such efforts have sometimes generated more in the way of controversy than utility, the reverse has also been true. Years of programmatic research in an area have developed conceptual structures eminently suitable for scientific theorizing (e.g., Cattell, 1965; Guilford, 1967; French et al., 1963).

In the more immediate world of evaluation research, data reduction by such techniques has classified patients or clients, analyzed demographic variables, subdivided states into regions and countries into voting blocs, suggested (multiple) production criteria, and reduced the complexity of many other problems. Whenever an evaluation specialist finds a problem with multiple variables, he is likely to perform some of these data reduction analyses to help bring the ultimate issues of the research into more manageable focus.

A (SIMPLIFIED) EXAMPLE OF DATA REDUCTION
IN EVALUATION RESEARCH

In a massive study of the Alabama Vocational Rehabilitation System, the writer (Eber, 1966, 1967) analyzed file record data from three groups of rehabilitation clients. Included among these data were various aspects of rehabilitation outcome. Substantial controversy existed at that time (and still does) regarding what may be called the "true" criterion of rehabilitation success. The results of the study may be an instructive example of the use of factor analysis, or data reduction technique, in aiding conceptual clarity.

The raw data describing each of several hundred clients included:

1. Degree of disability as judged by OASI pension decisions
2. Age
3. Work status at case closure
4. Mobility (can client get around) at acceptance
5. Mobility at closure
6. Prestige status of closure job (if any)
7. Earnings during week of closure
8. Was the counselor the job placement agent?
9. Amount of money spent for diagnosis
10. Amount of money spent for prostheses
11. Amount of money spent—TOTAL
12. Was case closed "successful"?
13. Was client alive at closure?
14. Were any services (beyond diagnosis) ever given?
15. Had client worked after the onset of disability, but before rehab acceptance?
16. Amount of wages claimed ever earned
17. Employed at follow-up?
18. Work status at follow-up
19. Earnings at follow-up
20. Public assistance at follow-up

21. Was client "happy" at follow-up?
22. Has client been reactivated?
23. Has client received "services to a closed case"?
24. Was client drawing OASI disability benefits at follow-up?

An interesting, and misleading question might be "Which of these 24 variables represents the *real* outcome criterion?" or "Which one of the 24 variables tells me, the decision maker, how well the client did?"

Some more meaningful questions could be:

A. How many "outcomes" are there? One? Two? Twenty-four?
B. If there are fewer than 24 "outcomes," how best do we define them?
C. What relationship exists, if any, between various types of outcome?

Factor analysis was performed as a way of answering the latter questions. The results are shown in Table 17.1, where an "X" represents how much a variable "belongs" in the factor and a blank, that it does not.

The first dramatic result of the analysis is a clear answer to question A. There are *two* outcome factors, not one, not twenty-four. In fact, analysis of the variables that "belong" versus those that do not suggests a clear meaning for the two factors, *short-range success* and *long-range success*.

TABLE 17.1   LOADINGS OF 24 VARIABLES ON TWO OUTCOME FACTORS

Variable	Factor	
	I	II
1. OASI benefit at intake	-XX	-X
2. Age		-XX
3. Status at closure	XXX	
4. Mobility at acceptance	XXX	
5. Mobility at closure	XXX	
6. Prestige, closure job	XXX	
7. Earnings, week of closure	XXX	
8. Counselor placement	X	
9. Money spent, diagnosis	X	-X
10. Money spent, prosthesis		-X
11. Money spent, total		-X
12. Closed "success"	XXX	
13. Alive at closure	X	
14. Ever served	X	
15. Work history after disability	X	
16. Highest claimed wage		-X
17. Employed at follow-up		XXXX
18. Status at follow-up		XXXX
19. Earnings at follow-up		XX
20. Public assistance at follow-up		-X
21. "Happy" at follow-up		XXXX
22. Reactivated?	-X	
23. "Service to closed case"	-XX	
24. OASI benefit at follow-up		-XX

Second, definition of the two factors is easily accomplished. *Short-range success* could be defined by a weighted composite of variables 3, 5, 6, 7, and 12; *long-range success* by a similar composite of variables 17, 18, 19, 21, and (–) 24.

Third, the analysis shows a correlation of .57 between the two factors. Interpretation? Short-range and long-range success are positively correlated but are not, apparently, the same thing.

Moreover, the relationship of individual variables to outcome can now be defined well enough for further study. For example, it would appear that counselor placement effort is helpful in the short run but *not* in the long-range result. If verified in a second study, such evidence could affect the way the decision maker allocates counselor effort.

It should be emphasized that the data here have been simplified, and are in fact part of a much larger, more complex study. Nevertheless, what has been cited is part of the results, and demonstrates the utility of data reduction technique to the evaluation researcher.

GROUP DIFFERENCE MODELS

This is a class of problems in which impact of independent variables upon one or more dependent variables is to be evaluated by comparisons among groups of subjects. Typically, the researcher may classify subjects into experimental and control groups, and search for evidence of impact by between-group comparison.

The basic technique is that lawful, predicted (or theoretically predictable) variance between groups is compared with random, unpredicted (perhaps unpredictable) variance within groups. The impact of treatments, programs, classifications, and so on should make the between-group variance large by comparison with the error term, and impact is judged by *how* large.

Standard statistical tests exist, based upon both theoretical and empirical evidence, that answer the question "how large is large enough?" Typically, they approach the problem in terms of the probability that differences as large as those observed could have occurred purely by chance. In this, the multivariate techniques are no different from the simpler, univariate ones. By treating the total, or at least large subsets of the data simultaneously, the multivariate methods tend to allow for the full complexity of the data to emerge in the findings. On the other hand, these techniques tend to "capitalize on chance" less than repeated univariate analysis of the same data. For example the graduate student who evaluates two groups of rats by twenty different measures, performs twenty t-tests, finds one "significant at the .05 level," reports on that one, and forgets the rest may be more apocryphal than real. Nevertheless, comparable if less obvious distortions of statistics are reported in the literature, and not always by students.

Multivariate methods are based, by and large, upon the so-called linear model. That is, multiple linear equations in multiple unknowns are solved. Often, a "best fit" of that solution is evaluated against how good the "fit" is likely to be by chance. The power of that linear model to provide "good fit" for *any* data has often been underestimated, most often by those who use the model unknowingly.

The multivariate methods for evaluating group differences have grown out of the "analysis-of-variance" model. From two groups to many; from random selection to designed, multifactorial experiments; from a single dependent variable to many; the expansion of models to include complex cases has made the techniques constantly more valuable in the sense that the simplification of the laboratory has become less and less a prerequisite.

The power and flexibility of multivariate group comparisons is well illustrated by the frequently used *multiple discriminant function*. A number of measures are obtained on each of a (it is hoped, large) number of subjects; the latter are classified into groups on the basis of the researcher's hypotheses. Each group represents some treatment or condition. The question asked is: "Within the complex multispace provided by the variables, what is the best possible separation of groups that can be achieved by giving each variable a single weight. The function gives literally an equation for the *best* such separation that can be achieved. How good is this "best" separation is then evaluated by significance tests, and the separation achieved is mathematically *removed* from the data.

The same question is asked again, but the removal of the first function rephrases it as ". . . what is the best possible *further* separation. . . ?" The process of defining a function, removing it, defining another, and so on continues until the number of functions is n-1 or k-1, whichever is smaller (n = number of variables, k = number of groups).

As might be expected from any mathematical technique that maximizes ("best"), each succeeding separation of the groups is less clear (or at least no clearer) than the one before. Each function is tested for significance, and spurious ones are dropped. The significant functions may then correspond to hypotheses about the groups.

As is true of data reduction methods, the calculations would be horrendous without electronic computers. Also, the mathematics of the model are quite demanding, and programming a computer to perform such a process is a significant job. Fortunately, none of this presents a barrier to the use of these techniques. Standard computer programs are available for most machines, and statisticians can readily arrange the use of whatever is, in their judgment, most appropriate.

AN EXAMPLE OF THE GROUP DIFFERENCE APPROACH

Miss A and Mrs. B are teachers of special classes for retarded children. A budget cut requires that only one of them be retained for the following year. They are of equal seniority and equal formal qualifications, and both desire to continue on the job. The administrator wants to find some fair basis for a choice between them; he proposes that their students' data be examined for possible evidence of the teachers' competence.

For each student, the data consist of:

Achievement test scores at entrance
Achievement test scores after the class year

Number of involvements in disciplinary problems

IQ as reported by the school psychologist, obtained before the student was exposed to Miss A or Mrs. B.

The data are shown in Table 17.2. It is suggested that the reader examine this table and evaluate the evidence before reviewing the analysis below.

Obviously, "eyeball" methods are of little help with such data. With an adding machine, one might get means, but then which ones are significant? Moreover, even if a substantial mean difference appeared in "post test" data, how much compensation would be necessary for any differences in "pre test" data? Finally, the scores are somewhat correlated, and that makes the analysis even more complex.

The relevant parts of the discriminant analysis are shown in Table 17.3; all numbers have been rounded off for ease of reading. The function tells us:

1. The best separation of Miss A's and Mrs. B's students that can be achieved is not very significant. Virtually *any real* evidence of qualifications would be

TABLE 17.2   STUDENT DATA FROM TWO SPECIAL CLASSES

		Pre			Post			Discipline	
		Reading	Spelling	Arithmetic	Reading	Spelling	Arithmetic	Problems	IQ
Miss A:	John	2	3	2	2	3	3	1	68
	Bill	0	1	1	1	2	3	5	77
	Mary	3	2	0	4	2	1	0	70
	Ann	4	4	3	4	4	4	0	74
	Alice	1	1	5	2	1	5	3	61
	Harry	2	2	4	5	2	4	1	71
Mrs. B:	Jane	2	2	4	4	1	4	0	66
	Martha	0	2	0	0	2	1	2	59
	Bob	2	6	3	2	5	4	4	78
	Allen	4	0	2	4	0	2	4	74
	Martin	0	3	2	4	2	2	1	75
	Helen	2	5	2	5	5	4	0	73

TABLE 17.3   DISCRIMINANT FUNCTION: MISS A VERSUS MRS. B

	Variable	Weight	Description
Pre	Reading	0	On this function, Mrs. B's
	Spelling	4	students are higher than
	Arithmetic	-3	Miss A's
Post	Reading	1	
	Spelling	-4	
	Arithmetic	2	**Significance**
Discipline		1	X^2 (df = 8) = 10
IQ (pre)		-1	sig = .30

better than these data provide. The significance level of .30 means that the findings would have occurred by accident 30% of the time, hardly overwhelming odds. Scientists want odds of 20:1 ($p < .05$) for *suggestive* findings; these odds are not even 3:1.

2. Even what *is* shown is a mixture of preexisting conditions and possible influence of the teachers. The largest weights in the function (pre and post spelling) suggest either that Mrs. B's students have deteriorated in this ability, or that Miss A's have improved. Inspection of the data suggests the former. It would seem that Mrs. B began with students whose arithmetic was poor, emphasized that aspect, and perhaps obtained some small improvement. While doing this, she neglected spelling, where her students pre-tested fair, and these scores deteriorated. (A better explanation is still that nothing consistent is shown by these data.)

3. The administrator is advised to look elsewhere for justification as to which teacher to retain.

RELATIONSHIP MODELS

At first glance, models that examine "co-variation," that is, co-occurring variance in two or more measures, seem quite different from group difference models. Historically, that apparent difference has been the cause of two major "schools" of statistics. In fact, however, there is little difference.

Suppose that a measure of some type has been made upon each of several hundred subjects, and that these subjects can be logically classified into three groups (perhaps "drug," "placebo," and "control"). The task is to evaluate the impact of the drug upon the measured (dependent) variable. Obviously, this is true for the group difference model.

Alternatively, suppose we define two variables in addition to the measured (dependent) one. The first such variable is "has been given *the drug*," and on this variable, members of the "drug" group are assigned a score of 1, while both "placebo" and "control" group members get a score of 0. Then, the second constructed variable is "has been given something," with a score of 1 for members of the "drug" *and* the "placebo" group, 0 for the controls.

It should be evident that all our knowledge about the subjects is now represented by three variables, one measured and two *constructed* to show group membership. What may be less evident, but is equally true, is that all statistical measures that can be derived from the original data by the *group difference* model can be as easily derived from these constructed data and the *relationship model*. Not only will the results of the analysis be the same, but the exact same numbers will be obtained, and this is true regardless of what "scores" are used to signify group membership on the constructed variables.

Conversely, we could restructure the data in another way. Let us define six groups instead of three by using the measured variable as a grouping method. Let us say that all subjects who score above the mean will be in the "high" group, all below the mean in the "low" group. Obviously, we now have six groups, in the format shown in Figure 17.4, and a simple chi-square test of statistical significance can be used.

TABLE 17.4

	Drug	Placebo	Control
High	G_{hd}	G_{hp}	G_{hc}
Low	G_{ld}	G_{lp}	G_{lc}

Note however that "high" and "low" does *not* contain all the knowledge we have of the subjects. This approach will yield *essentially similar* results, but the method of analysis is less sensitive and makes use of only part of the data.

Actually, any data of the group difference type can always be equally well represented as relationships, but not necessarily vice versa. In this sense, what appear to be distinct approaches are, in fact, quite closely related. Moreover, it is never necessary to force data into categories when, in fact, continuous measures were initially available. Such a procedure may reduce computing complexity but must, inevitably, use the information contained in the data less efficiently. With the availability of computers, complexity of calculation is, or should be, a trivial consideration in most cases.

An example of a problem falling "naturally" into the relationship model is provided by the development of a *regression equation* to predict some *criterion*. Given a (large) group of subjects whose status upon some criterion variable, presumably one of a substantive importance, is known; given further, for each subject, a number of other scores representing status on other, *predictor* variables; the questions asked are: (1) "How well can the variance in the criterion be predicted (explained?) by a composite of predictor scores?" and (2) "What is the formula for the best such composite?"

The *linear regression* model provides answers to these questions. It solves, essentially, for a "best fit" among a system of linear equations in multiple unknowns. Each equation represents one subject, with (unknown) weights given to each predictor score. If the number of equations (subjects) were exactly equal to the number of unknowns (predictor weights), an exact solution could be obtained by the methods familiar to high school algebra. With fewer equations than unknowns, the solution is impossible; with (the usual) more equations than unknowns, we obtain a "best fit," and again, the power of the linear model to obtain such a best fit is substantial.

The results of the calculations will include a multiple correlation coefficient which answers the question "How well . . ." and a set of "beta" weights which constitute the formula. Because the model must, by definition, yield a "best fit," there will be some concern about how well the formula will work with a different set of subjects. In other words, an issue of *cross validation* must be resolved, analogous to the question of chance differences among groups. Both theoretical and practical answers to this question of "shrinkage" of a multiple correlation are well

known; both use the obvious fact that data based upon a large number of observations are more stable than those based upon fewer. Good estimates of "How good . . ." can be made.

However, as with all best fit models, the ultimate proof is most convincing when a new set of data *cross validate* at an appropriate level of significance. The concept that the initial analysis yields an *hypothesis* to be tested by further study is not so often honored by social scientists as might be ideal; still, that must remain the ultimate test, in relationship models as in other (multivariate *and* univariate) approaches.

STRATEGY OF ANALYSIS

The foregoing discussion makes a strong case for the use of multivariate techniques whenever the data required for such analysis exist. They usually do exist, and simplified, univariate analysis usually requires that available data be ignored.

It is desirable, however, that the picture not be overdrawn. While it is true that simpler models usually lose information, and that the more comprehensive techniques can never yield less information than the simpler ones, this does not rule out the possibility that a simple model may yield the most effective and desirable insight for a particular problem in a specific context.

Particularly in evaluation research, the scientist's role is not exclusively one of discovering relationships that conform to the canons of rigorous inquiry. To be sure, that is part of the task, and the emphasis upon objectivity, replication (or at least replicability), conceptual rigor, and dissemination of methods *and* results are the hallmark of the scientific method. However, most research is undertaken for a purpose, and that purpose is rarely more clearly defined than in evaluation research. Someone needs or wants to use the information developed, usually as a guide to decision making.

Given that there is a consumer of research, a user of the information developed by a scientific enterprise, then the researcher's job must include the communication of his findings to their user *in such form that they are correctly understood.* The "pure" scientist, whose consumers are primarily others of his own background and interest, may legitimately communicate in as complex and rigorous a manner as may to him seem appropriate to the issue. He may, and usually will, demand of his reader such expertise as may be necessary to understand all appropriate ramifications of the findings.

The "pure" scientist assumes that the reader of his report has no limitations, either of capacity or of expertise. If the subject is best presented as a set of 47 equations, whose understanding requires intimate knowledge of a dozen esoteric mathematical concepts, then that is the way the information will be presented. The "consumer" who is not sufficiently expert to understand must either obtain the required expertise or abandon the information.

In evaluation research, and in fact in *any* applied research, findings must be communicated to a different consumer. Were that user of the information oriented toward technical and esoteric competence, he would likely have little need for the

evaluation researcher. More important, the specialization of roles in a complex society makes it unlikely that orientation toward complex scientific issues and toward sociopolitical decision making will coexist in the same person. Therefore, the evalation researcher must accept the responsibility for communication to what may best be described as the highly intelligent layman. He must present his findings without demanding that the reader share his scientific expertise. In this task, the judicious reexamination of findings by models whose results are easy to communicate may become part of the total picture.

Thus, the evaluation researcher must analyze the data from two standpoints, his own attempt to achieve the most complete and rigorous possible understanding of the results, and his need to communicate the relevant parts of those results to the consumer. The two parts of the task may well require complementary, but different, statistical models.

In his attempt to clarify the relationships underlying a set of data, the evaluation researcher most often should take advantage of the comprehensive models offered by multivariate methods. He can never, in this way, lose information. Any *legitimate* result that can emerge from univariate analysis *must* emerge at least equally clearly from the more comprehensive multivariate technology. The inclusion of additional relevant variables in an analysis will reduce the error variance. Since that error component forms the denominator in the F-ratio (or acts in an analogous manner in other statistics), valid significance levels from a univariate analysis must be at least equally significant (usually more significant) in the more comprehensive model.

The exception occurs when irrelevant variables are included, increasing the "degrees of freedom" without increasing lawful variance. In that case, what would otherwise be significant appears less so, but one must distinguish here between what was known to be irrelevant *before* the analysis and what was discovered to be irrelevant *in* the analysis. We are back to the student and his 20 t-tests, one significant at the .05 level. The decision that the other 19 are "irrelevant," *after* the analysis, is simply cheating. The multivariate result of *no significance* is correct; the apparent univariate result of significance is obviously wrong.

Thus the investigator should begin his analysis of a set of data by including the maximum permissible number of relevant variables. "Permissible" must be defined in terms of degrees of freedom. Without discussing this sometimes technical concept, it is intuitively obvious that a mathematical equation with a sufficient number of possible adjustments (degrees of freedom) can be made to fit an elephant. "Goodness of fit," upon which concept all statistical tests of significance are based, is meaningless if the data are such that a *bad* fit cannot occur.

The initial question asked of his data by the evaluation researcher should be: "Is *anything* other than random variation in the data system evident?" If the answer to that question is in the negative, further analysis is not only useless but virtually guaranteed to produce misleading results. The ability to find "meaningful and significant" results in an isolated area of the data by throwing away what is (now) defined as irrelevant is an asset to the fortune-teller. Unfortunately, that ability is not found only among such practitioners.

In his role as statistical consultant to projects where massive data sets are the rule, the author has repeatedly been impressed with the rationalization capacities of investigators (including himself). An analysis yields nonsignificant results, but the few trends that are suggested as *possible* areas for further study are "so obviously sensible and in line with theory/knowledge/intuition/clinical judgment (chose one)" that they *must* be real truths emerging from statistical obfuscation. When, by error or design, the author has reversed the signs, and thus the direction of apparent relationships of half the variables in question, the trends are still equally "obviously . . .".

Just as the power of the linear model to fit *any* data set should not be underestimated, so the capacity of the scientist to rationalize *any* results must be taken into account. The evaluation researcher must first demand of the data some solid evidence that "something other then nothing is indicated." Failure to adhere to this standard cannot help but vitiate any further evidence obtained.

Now it is a fact that real data obtained by competent observers using reasonably good measures usually show very clearly that lawful variance exists. The more comprehensive the analysis, the less chance that lawful relationships which exist will have been missed by failure of representation in the data set. This is the basis for the suggestion that comprehensive analysis by multivariate techniques is the best strategy at the beginning.

Assuming then that the comprehensive analysis has been completed and that lawful variance has been identified, the researcher next faces the task of communicating results to the user of the information. The findings must be expressed in ways that will permit the decision maker to anticipate probable consequences of various courses of action. If the decisions to be made are sufficiently important to warrant the gathering and analysis of a second data set, this final state of evaluation research can use the most powerful method of predicting results of decisions with increased accuracy.

That method is cross-validation of major hypotheses derived from the first (comprehensive) analysis. The researcher selects or produces a data set representing those major factors that emerged from the first study as candidates for action to be taken. Here now is the place for "designed experiments," for systematic variation of combinations of (few) factors. Also, here is the place for simpler statistics, for more specific but less comprehensive models.

Since the first experiment yielded proof of lawful variance, this cross-validation can focus upon the specific impact of a small number of manageable factors. The results can now be expressed in less esoteric concepts than before. Assuming that cross-validation is successful, the probable impact of action taken can be predicted fairly accurately. On the other hand, failure of cross-validation can yield dual benefits, preventing useless (or possibly even harmful) action, and permitting the researcher to clarify and correct erroneous concepts.

Thus, while a single evaluation research project usually obtains best results from a comprehensive, multivariate analysis of data, a cycle of research, incorporating more than one project, may best proceed from complex to simpler models, from comprehensive to narrower goals, from general conceptualization to precise defini-

tion. In the latter stages of the cycle, univariate or simple multivariate models achieve optimum utility.

SOME SUGGESTIONS FOR CONDUCTING, MANAGING, AND UTILIZING MULTIVARIATE RESEARCH

The complexity of the models used in multivariate procedures, and the facility with which these models can be applied through the use of electronic computers, give rise to a new type of problem which has been inaccurately but graphically described as "GIGO," namely "garbage in, garbage out." The description is inaccurate because it is not inevitably true; multivariate (and other) statistical analysis is a matter of separating the wheat from the chaff, of separating lawful variance from random variance. The suspicion that the information used may include a substantial proportion of error should not necessarily prevent the researcher from proceeding.

Social scientists are accustomed to hearing criticisms regarding the fallible nature of their data, even while some researchers who make these criticisms utilize extremely fallible data as if those data were perfect. A psychiatrist of the writer's acquaintance recently obtained, on a large sample of patients, both their age and their date of birth. Calculating age from the date of birth, and correlating that calculated age with the "age" reported by the patients, he obtained a correlation of only .91. Clearly such a simple datum as age is fallible. Similarly, it is suggested that a person's sex is by no means a clear-cut datum; otherwise, there would be no need for sophisticated chromosome tests of Olympic athletes who claim to be women but who strike observers of women's events at the Olympics as possibly being impostors.

The question is not whether there is error in the data, but whether the effects of error on the findings may be minimized, so that the meaningful variance can be given a chance to show itself. Multivariate techniques are the most sophisticated ones available for this process; however, the very sophistication and complexity of the multivariate models gives rise to some new problems against which definitive steps have to be taken by the researcher, the administrator, and the user of research findings. These problems reside in the area of the data definitions, and of the relationships between the multivariate operations performed and the application of the model to the specific case at hand.

At the simplest level, keypunchers make mistakes, and most computer programs do not successfully identify these mistakes. Many researchers are impatient with the painstaking editing of data that should be a prerequisite before an analysis is begun. Such editing is not easily done by the computer or by any other method. Often, a printed listing of the data cards and the trained eye of the researcher are the most appropriate combination in the search for ridiculous errors. There is evidence that this step is all too rarely executed.

Then there is the problem of missing data. A number of conventions are used for the representation of missing data, and there are too many cases where the user of an available computer program did not assure himself that missing data would be appropriately handled. Many programs are written in Fortran, with Fortran input and output conventions. When that is done, a blank entry among numeric data is

read as a zero, and no error message results. The researcher may well proceed, blindly unaware of the fact that missing data have occurred and have been interpreted by the computer program as scores which lie 341 standard deviations below the mean.

Conventions for representing missing data which do not utilize blanks in the data set can be equally dangerous. The ubiquitous practice of representing a missing data item by a 9, a 99, and 999, or some such "ridiculous" value can be quite effective unless the researcher neglects to tell the computer what has been done. In this case, missing data are likely to be interpreted as 300-odd standard deviations *above* the mean, and again there is no error message to tell the user that he has made a ridiculous error.

Among the conventional methods of handling missing data, once assuming that they have been properly identified as "missing," one suggestion (Cohen and Cohen, 1973) deserves special mention. Let the missing data value be replaced by the mean for that item, thus effectively neutralizing it. Then, construct another variable in which the "missingness" of the data is represented. Analyze both, and it may turn out that "missingness" is a more powerful predictor than the data value itself.

A fictional example provided by Cohen and Cohen concerns IQ data "missing" from files of students who had been classified as mentally retarded. Analysis gave strong evidence that data had not been lost on a random basis. A "retarded" student whose IQ data were missing showed strong probability of having been classified for administrative convenience rather than on the basis of the data now (years later) missing.

At a more sophisticated level than missing data is the problem of distributions which depart radically from those assumed by the statistic being used. The writer is not a purist, and has relatively little patience with compulsive discussions of the fine points regarding assumptions about the shape of data distributions which may or may not be satisfied by a particular set of scores. At the same time, gross deviations from the assumed shape of a distribution may lead to insignificant results where more careful attention to such shape would have permitted a clearer definition of the data and resulting greater ease in finding lawful variance. Here again, the very facility of the electronic computing machinery serves to obscure relationships which would be evident, perhaps painfully so, to the researcher utilizing a hand calculator.

Most multivariate (and univariate) models are built upon assumptions about the shape of the distributions and of the relationships among variables which may frequently not be true for a real set of data. However, there is a good deal of evidence in the literature that replicable and significant results maybe obtained by ignoring the shape of the data distribution. When the purpose of the study is analytic—designed to provide understanding of the relationships among variables— rather than predictive, assumption failure is most likely to lead to erroneous inference.

There are some cases in which a knowledge of the nature of the data permits rational transformations which can make the resulting numbers more readily analyzed, and which will permit lawful variance to emerge more clearly than would

otherwise be the case. One example is the logarithmic transformation, in which log X is substituted for the original observed data value X. The transformation is readily made in a computer program; it can literally be had for the asking.

There are variables used in evaluation research which have been studied and reported in the literature, and whose distribution shape is known to become more amenable to statistical and other interpretation when such a transformation is made. Examples of the log transform abound in psychophysical measurement. Within the ordinary ranges of stimulation, the relationship between perception and physical stimulation levels is virtually always best represented by the logarithmic equation. Many variables which involve human judgment of physical reality can be considered for such transforms, and similarly many growth curves which occur in nature fit this pattern quite well.

The question is not primarily one of correctness but rather of utility. Attention to the shape of the data, prior to entering them into multivariate analytic programs, can yield rich benefits in making lawful variance more visible and more easily interpreted than it would be if analytic programs were applied in a less sophisticated manner.

This leads finally to a more general point which concerns the collaboration between the administrator and user of research with the researcher himself. In general it requires repeated attempts to make clear, in the thinking of all concerned, the conceptual meaning in the substantive world of the operations that are performed upon and by the statistical model. The model, for example, permits certain kinds of transformations from the raw data variables to those derived data items which shall be analyzed. The question that must be asked, and answered, repeatedly is: "What does this operation *mean* when applied to these data?"

Our data permit correlations to be calculated, or covariance, or distance functions, or other coefficients of similarity or dissimilarity. What does each one of these represent in terms of the meaning of the data items? Which do we wish to analyze? Is there some rational basis for selecting one rather than the other?

It is at this point that general knowledge about the characteristics of various statistical coefficients and measures must be combined with intimate knowledge of the data, of how they were obtained, how they are given in the tables or cards used to represent them, and what the numbers really mean. It is suggested that the researcher should become so intimately knowledgeable in this regard that he can fully explain the impact of his statistical operations to an interested and intelligent layman. It is further suggested that those interested and intelligent laymen who function as administrators or users of research may well *insist* that this be done.

On the other hand, no serious examination of the data numbers by the researcher himself can substitute for that information regarding the data which is readily available to the substantive scientist, the administrator, the program director, and the research user. Collaborative effort stands to gain as much from these people as from the researcher's participation.

For example, in an evaluation of a rehabilitation program, the writer found that the results of a multivariate analysis failed to make the expected sense. He looked at the variables in question and found two variables which correlated .996. One

variable represented the amount of welfare payment received out of funds that included federal money; the other represented the total amount received, regardless of source. Inspection of the data prior to the discovery of ridiculous results could have shown the offending correlation coefficient just as readily at that time as later. Inspection of the raw data, could have made the state of affairs obvious before even the correlation matrix was calculated, since the two data items were in adjoining columns and the equivalence of scores for almost every client upon these two data items would have been readily perceived. When the writer reported this finding to the administrator in charge of records, he responded, "Of course! During that year, there were *no significant* welfare funds in this state that did not include federal monies! The only reason we kept both data items is because federal regulations require both to be reported." The administrator knew the true facts of the case all the time, but no one asked him. He never had a chance to volunteer the information because he did not know what was being done with the data which his staff had helped to collect.

In this instance, the error was discovered because the findings were so obviously ridiculous that they alerted the researcher to the need for closer contact with the raw data and with those who understand the nature of those data. A much more serious example would be one in which a similar but not so blatant thing happened, for which the results of the study were not ridiculous but merely wrong. Leaving aside the man-hours wasted in the obtaining of the data and in their analysis, the real harm comes from the application of erroneous results. No amount of statistical sophistication can prevent such disasters; intimate communication among those who know various aspects of the problem is the only effective preventive measure.

Finally, let it be said that multivariate technology is by no means alone in being subject to the distortions inherent in insufficient understanding of the data and of the situation represented by the numbers. However, in the application of simpler models, errors are easier to find and the researcher remains closer to his data because he does not depend upon machine processes which he could not possibly duplicate. A single bivariate distribution plot can be inexpensively obtained and readily examined by the researcher, by simply looking at it. Under those conditions, ridiculous data items (such as apparent outliers which are, in fact, erroneous representations of missing data) can be readily seen, investigated, and corrected. In a multivariate analysis, however, there may be potentially several hundred or several thousand such bivariate distribution plots, making them expensive to obtain and impossible to examine carefully. Careful mapping of complex processes upon the substantive meaning represented by the data, repeated at every step of the analysis, becomes the only effective method of quality control.

SUMMARY

Multivariate methodologies for evaluation research have been presented as extensions of familiar statistical techniques. They fall generally into three types of models: data reduction, group differences, and relationships. The equivalence in most cases of the latter two has been stressed. Some strategies of analysis have been

outlined, and suggestions for the utilization of multivariate techniques in evaluation research have been given.

The user of multivariate techniques is warned that the distance from the actual data sometimes created by the fact that a computer does the work may result in a larger number of errors in input and interpretation than when simple techniques are used. These errors may be avoided by careful examination of the raw data in combination with good communication between data analytic experts, substantive experts, and the research consumer.

REFERENCES

Cattell, R. B. *The Scientific Analysis of Personality.* Baltimore: Penguin, 1965.

Cattell, R. B. (ed.) *Handbook of Multivariate Experimental Psychology.* Chicago: Rand McNally, 1966.

Cohen, J. and P. Cohen. "A Method for Handling Missing Data in Multiple Regression/ Correlation." Paper presented at the Annual Meeting of the Society of Multivariate Experimental Psychology. November 1973.

Cooley, W. W. and P. R. Lohnes. *Multivariate Procedures in the Behavioral Sciences.* New York: Wiley, 1971.

Eber, H. W. Multivariate Analysis of a Vocational Rehabilitation System. *Multivariate Behavioral Research Monogram.* Number 66-1. For Worth, Tex.: TCU Press, 1966.

———. Multivariate Analysis of a Rehabilitation System: Cross Validation and Extension. *Multivariate Behavioral Research,* 1967, 2(4): 477-484.

French, J. W., R. B. Ekstrom and L. A. Price. *Manual of Kit for Reference Tests for Cognitive Factors.* Princeton: Educational Testing Service, 1963.

Guilford, J. P. *The Nature of Human Intelligence.* New York: McGraw-Hill, 1967.

Overall, J. E. and C. J. Klett. *Applied Multivariate Analysis.* New York: McGraw-Hill, 1972.

18

MULTIPLE REGRESSION AS A GENERAL
DATA-ANALYTIC SYSTEM

JACOB COHEN

New York University

Techniques for using multiple regression (MR) as a general variance-accounting procedure of great flexibility, power, and fidelity to research aims in both manipulative and observational psychological research are presented. As a prelude, the identity of MR and fixed-model analysis of variance/covariance (AV/ACV) is sketched. This requires an exposition of means of expressing nominal scale (qualitative) data as independent variables in MR. Attention is given to methods for handling interactions, curvilinearity, missing data, and covariates, for either uncorrelated or correlated independent variables in MR. Finally, the relative roles of AV/ACV and MR in data analysis are described, and the practical advantages of the latter are set forth.

If you should say to a mathematical statistician that you have discovered that linear multiple regression analysis and the analysis of variance (and covariance) are identical systems, he would mutter something like, "Of course—general linear model," and you might have trouble maintaining his attention. If you should say

AUTHOR'S NOTE: This work was supported by Grant No. MH 06137 from the National Institute of Mental Health of the United States Public Health Service. The author is grateful to the members of the Society of Multivariate Experimental Psychology for their constructive response when this material was presented at their annual meeting in Atlanta, Georgia, November 1966. This work profited greatly from detailed critiques supplied by Robert A. Bottenberg and Joe H. Ward, Jr., but since not all their suggestions were followed, they share no responsibility for any defects in the result. A detailed treatment of the procedures outlined here is available in Cohen and Cohen (1975).

Reprinted from Psychological Bulletin, 1968, Vol. 70, No. 6, 426-433, with permission of the publisher.

this to a typical psychologist, you would be met with incredulity, or worse. Yet it is true, and in its truth lie possibilities for more relevant and therefore more powerful exploitation of research data.

That psychologists would find strange the claimed equivalence of multiple regression (MR) and the fixed-model analysis of variance (AV) and covariance (ACV) is readily understandable. The textbooks in "psychological" statistics treat these matters quite separately, with wholly different algorithms, nomenclature, output, and examples.

MR is generally illustrated by examples drawn from the psychotechnology of educational or personnel selection, usually the prediction of some criterion (e.g., freshman grade point average) from predictors (e.g., verbal and quantitative score, high school rank). The yield is a multiple correlation (R) and a regression equation with weights which can be used for optimal prediction. The multiple R and the weights are subjected to significance testing, and conclusions are drawn about the effectiveness of the prediction, and which predictors do and do not contribute significantly to the prediction.

By way of contrast, AV and ACV are generally illustrated by pure research, manipulative experiments with groups subjected to different treatments or treatment combinations. Means and variances are found and main effect, interaction, and error mean squares computed and compared. Conclusions are drawn in terms of the significance of differences in sets or pairs of means or mean differences. More analytic yield of one or both of these systems is sometimes presented, but the above is a fair description of the respective thrusts of the two methods, and they are clearly different.

The differences are quite understandable, but the basis for this understanding comes primarily from the history and sociology of behavioral science research method and not from the essential mathematics. MR began to be exploited in the biological and behavioral sciences around the turn of the century in the course of the study of *natural* variation (Galton, Pearson, Yule). A couple of decades later, AV and ACV came out of the structure of (agronomic)experimentation, that is, of *artificial* or experimentally manipulated variation, where the treatments were carefully varied over the experimental material in efficient and logically esthetic experimental designs. The chief architect here was R. A. Fisher. These historical differences resulted in differences in tradition associated with substantively different areas and value systems in the psychological spectrum (cf. Cattell, 1966).

Yet the systems are, in the most meaningful sense, the same.

One of the purposes of this article is to sketch the equivalence of the two systems. In order to do so, it is necessary to show how nominal scales ("treatment," religion) can be used as "independent" variables in MR; the same is shown for "interactions." It is also necessary to demonstrate how multiple R^2 (and related statistics) can be computed from fixed-model AV and ACV output. Once the case is made for the *theoretical* equivalence of the two systems, the *practical* advantages of MR will be presented, which, given the foregoing, will be seen to constitute a very flexible general system for the analysis of data in the most frequently arising

circumstance, namely, where an interval scaled or dichotomous (dependent) variable is to be "understood" in terms of other (independent) variables, however scaled.

A word about originality. Most of the material which follows was "discovered" by the author, only to find, after some painstaking library research, that much of it had been anticipated in published but not widely known works (chiefly Bottenberg & Ward, 1963; Li, 1964). Thus, no large claim for originality is being made, except for some of the heuristic concepts and their synthesis in a general data-analytic system realized by means of MR.

THE EQUIVALENCE OF THE SYSTEMS:
NOMINAL SCALES AS
INDEPENDENT VARIABLES IN MR

Some of the apparent differences in MR and AC/ACV lie in their respective terminologies. The variable being analyzed (from AV and ACV) and the criterion variable (from MR) are the same, and will be called the dependent variable and symbolized as Y. The variables bearing on Y, variously called main effect, inter-action, or covariate in AV and ACV (depending on their definition and design function), and predictor variables in MR will be called independent variables, and symbolized as X_i (i = 1, 2, $\cdots$ k). Each X_i consumes *one* degree of freedom (df). In complex problems (e.g., factorial design, curvilinear analysis), it is convenient to define sets of the X_i, each such set representing a single research variable or factor.

In the conventional use of MR, the X_i are ordered quantitative variables, treated as equal interval scales. Thus, in a study of the prediction of freshman grade point average (Y), one might have X_1 = verbal aptitude score, X_2 = quantitative aptitude score, X_3 = percentile rank in high school graduating class, and X_4 = Hollingshead socio-economic status index. Thus, k = 4, and the question of sets need not arise (or, they may be thought of as four sets, each of a single variable). But what if one wanted to include *religion* among the X_i? Or alternatively, if the entering class were to be assigned randomly to four different experimental teaching systems, how would experimental group assignment be represented? More generally, how does one accommodate a purely nominal or qualitative variable as an independent variable in MR?

Imagine a simple situation in which a dependent variable Y is to be studied as a function of a nominal scale variable G, which has four "levels": groups G_1, G_2, G_3, and G_4. For concreteness, Y and G may be taken as having the following alternative meanings:

Research Area	Y		The G Set: G_1, G_2, G_3, G_4
Social Psychology	Attitude toward United Nations	Religion:	Protestant Catholic Jewish Other

Clinical Psychology	Suggestibility	Diagnosis:	Paranoid Schizophrenia
			Nonparanoid Schizophrenia
			Compulsive Neurosis
			Hysterical Neurosis

Physiological Psychology	Retention	Treatment:	Drug and Frontal Lesion
			Drug and Control Lesion
			No Drug and Frontal Lesion
			No Drug and Control Lesion

Formally, what is being posited is the assignment, not necessarily equally, of each of n cases into (four) mutually exclusive and exhaustive groups, no matter whether G is an organismic, naturally occurring variable or one created by the experimenter's manipulative efforts on randomly assigned subjects.

The expression of group membership as independent variables in MR can be accomplished in several ways, all equivalent in a sense to be later described. The intuitively simplest of these is "dummy" variable coding (Bottenberg & Ward, 1963; Suits, 1957).

Dummy Variable Coding

Table 18.1 presents various coding alternatives for the rendition of membership in one of four groups. Columns 1, 2, and 3 represent a dummy variable coding scheme. It involves merely successively dichotomizing so that each of $3(=g-1)$ of the $4(=g)$ groups is distinguished from the remainder as one aspect of G. For example, on X_1 all subjects in G_1 are scored 1 and all others, without differentiation, are scored 0. Thus, this variable by itself carries only some of the information in the G variable as a whole, for example, Protestant versus all other, or Paranoid Schizophrenia versus all other. However, the three variables coded as in Columns 1, 2, and 3 together exhaust the information of the G variable. One might think that a fourth independent variable, one which distinguishes G_4 from all others, would be necessary, but such a variable would be redundant. In the usual MR system which uses a constant term in the regression equation, it requires no more than $g-1$ independent variables (no matter how coded) to represent g groups of a G nominal scale. A fourth X_i here is not only unnecessary, but its inclusion would result in indeterminacy in the computation of the MR constants. This is an instance of a more general demand on the set of independent variables in any MR system: no independent variable in the set may yield a multiple R with the remaining inde-

TABLE 18.1 ILLUSTRATIVE CODING FOR A NOMINAL SCALE

Nominal scale variable	Columns														
	1	2	3	4	5	6	7	8	9	10	11	12	13	14	15
	X_1[a]	X_2	X_3	X_1	X_2	X_3	X_1	X_2	X_3	X_1	X_2	X_3	X_1	X_2	X_3
G_1	1	0	0	1	1	0	1	1	1	5	25	125	1	-7	0
G_2	0	1	0	1	-1	0	1	-1	-1	0	0	0	-1	-1	0
G_3	0	0	1	-1	0	1	-1	1	-1	-4	16	-64	-4	½	24
G_4	0	0	0	-1	0	-1	-1	-1	1	6	36	216	1	6	-1

a Independent variable.

pendent variables of 1.00. This constraint on the independent variables (in matrix algebraic terms, the demand that their data matrix be nonsingular or of full rank) would be violated if we introduced a fourth variable, since, in that case, any of the four X_i would yield $R = 1.00$ when treated as a dependent variable regressed on the other three. In terms that are intuitively compelling, one can see that members of G_4 are identified uniquely on the X_1, X_2, X_3 vector as 0, 0, 0, that is, as not G_1, not G_2, and not G_3, thus not requiring a fourth dichotomous X_i. G_4 is not being slighted; on the contrary, as will be shown below, it serves as a reference group. Any group may be designated for this role, but if one is functionally a control or reference group, so much the better.[1]

Before we turn to a consideration of X_1, X_2 and X_3 as a set of variables, let us consider them separately. Each can be correlated with the dependent variable Y. A set of artificial data was constructed to provide a concrete illustration. For n = 36 cases, a set of three-digit Y scores was written, the cases assigned to four groups and coded for X_i as described. The resulting product moment r's (point-biserial) were $r_{Y1} = -.5863$, $r_{Y2} = .0391$, and $r_{Y3} = .4965$. When squared, the resulting values indicate the proportion of the Y variance each distinction accounts for: $r^2_{Y1} = .3437$, $r^2_{Y2} = .0015$, and $r^2_{Y3} = .2465$. Thus, for example, the Protestant versus non-Protestant variable accounts for .3437 of the variance in Attitude toward the United Nations dependent variable, as represented in the sample.

Whether the .3437 value can be used as an estimator of the proportion of variance which G_1 versus remainder accounts for *in the population* of naturally occurring G depends on the way G was sampled. If the n cases of the sample were obtained by randomly sampling from the population as a whole so that the proportion of G_1 cases in the sample, n_1/n reflects their population predominance, .3437 estimates the proportion of variance in the natural population. However, if G was sampled to yield equal n_i in the g groups (or some other nonrepresentative numbers), the .3437 value is projectible to a similarly distributed artificial population. The statistical purist would abjure the use of r or r^2 (and R or R^2) in such instances, but if one understands that the parameters being estimated are for populations whose X_i characteristics are those of the sample, no inappropriate errors in inference need be made, and a useful analytic tool becomes available.

Although the separate r^2_{Yi} are analytically useful, our purpose is to understand the operation of X_1, X_2, X_3 as a set, since it is as a set that they represent G as the four-level nominal scale. The r^2_{Yi} cannot simply be added up to determine how much Y variance G accounts for, since dummy variables are inevitably correlated with each other. Mutually exclusive assignment means that membership in one group G_i necessarily means nonmembership in any other, G_j, hence a negative relationship. The product moment r (i.e., the phi coefficient) between such dichotomies, that is, between G_i and G_j or X_i and X_j when expressed in dummy variable form, is

$$r_{ij} = -\sqrt{\frac{n_i n_j}{(n - n_i)(n - n_j)}} \qquad [1]$$

where n_i, n_j are the sample sizes of each group, and n is the total sample size over all g groups. When sample sizes are all equal, the formula simplifies to

$$r_{ij} = -\frac{1}{g-1} \qquad [2]$$

that is, the negative reciprocal of one less than the number of groups; thus, in our running artificial example, if we assume the four groups equal in size, the phi coefficients among the X_i dichotomies are all $-\frac{1}{3}$.

The fact that the independent variables representing group membership are correlated with each other poses no special problem for MR, which is designed to allow for this in whatever guise it appears. But it does alert us to the fact that the proportions of Y variance given by the r^2_{Yi} are overlapping. If we now compute the multiple R^2 using X_1, X_2, and X_3 as independent variables, the value we find in the artificial data is $R^2_{Y \cdot 123}$ = .4458. This is interpreted as meaning that G (religion, diagnosis, or treatment group membership) accounts for .4458 of the variance in the dependent variable Y, and in the exact sense ordinarily understood.

Identity with Analysis of Variance

Consider the more familiar AV analysis of these data. The Y scores can be assembled into the four G groups and a one-way AV performed. This yields the usual sums of squares for between groups (B SS), for within groups (W SS), and their total (T SS). If we determine the proportion of T SS which B SS constitutes, we have η^2 (eta square), the squared correlation ratio. This statistic has, as its most general interpretation, the proportion of variance of the dependent variable accounted for by G-group membership, or equivalently, accounted for by the group Y means. (Unfortunately, tradition in applied statistics textbooks and courses has focused on a narrow, special-case interpretation of η as an index of curvilinear correlation. For a broader view, see Cohen, 1965, pp. 104-105 and Peters & Van Voorhis, 1940, pp. 312-325 and, particularly, 353-357).

If we compute $\eta^2_{Y \cdot G}$ for the artificial data, we find

$$\eta^2_{Y \cdot G} = \frac{B\ SS}{T\ SS} = \frac{12127.0}{27205.6} = .4458 \qquad [3]$$

Thus, our MR coding procedure yields an $R^2_{Y \cdot 123}$ exactly equal to $\eta^2_{Y \cdot G}$, interpretable as the proportion of Y variance for which G accounts. The parallel goes further. It is demonstrable that the "shrunken" or df-corrected R^2 (McNemar, 1962, pp. 184-185) is identically the same as Kelley's "unbiased" squared correlation ratio, epsilon-square (Cohen, 1965, p. 105; Cureton, 1966; Peters & Van Voorhis, 1940, pp. 319-322).

Furthermore, if one tests either of these results for significance, one obtains identically the same F ratio, for identically the same df:

For the $R^2_{Y \cdot 123}$, using the standard formula (e.g., McNemar, 1962, p. 283)

$$F = \frac{R^2_{Y \cdot 123 \cdots k}/k}{(1 - R^2_{Y \cdot 123 \cdots k})/(n - k - 1)}$$

$$= \frac{R^2_{Y \cdot 123 \cdots k}/(g-1)}{(1 - R^2_{Y \cdot 123 \cdots k})/(n-g)}$$

$$= \frac{.4458/(4-1)}{(1 - .4458)/(36-4)} = 8.580, \tag{4}$$

for numerator (regression) df = k = g - 1 = 3 and denominator (residual or error) df = n - k - 1 = n - g = 32.

The significance of η^2 is, of course the signficance of the separation of the G groups' Y means, that is, the usual AV F test of the between-groups mean square (MS):

$$F = \frac{\text{between G groups MS}}{\text{within G groups MS}} = \frac{(B\ SS)/(g-1)}{(W\ SS)/(n-g)}$$

$$= \frac{(12127.0)/(4-1)}{(15078.6)/(36-4)} = \frac{4042.33}{471.21} = 8.580, \tag{5}$$

for numerator (between G groups) df = g - 1 = 4 - 1 = 3, and denominator (within G groups, or error) df = n - g = 36 - 4 = 32.

These F ratios must be identical, since B SS = $(R^2_{Y \cdot 123 \cdots k})$ (total SS), and W SS - $(1 - R^2_{Y \cdot 123 \cdots k})$ (total SS). Formula 4 differs from Formula 5 only in that the total SS has been cancelled out from numerator and denominator.

The formulas help clarify the identity of the two procedures. We obtain another perspective on why 3(= g - 1) independent variables carry all the group membership information for 4(= g) groups, —there are only 3 df "associated with" G group membership. By either the MR or AV route the total SS (or variance) of Y has been partitioned into a portion accounted for by G group membership (or by G group Y means), and a portion not so accounted for (i.e., within group, residual, or "error"), the latter, by either route based on n - g df.

Conceptually, the F ratios can be understood to be the same because they are testing null hypotheses which are mathematically equivalent, even though they are traditionally differently stated:

$$\text{MR} : H_0 : \text{Population } R^2_{Y \cdot 123} = 0$$
$$\text{AV} : H_0 : \text{Population } m_1 = m_2 = m_3 = m_4 = m$$

If the AV H_0 is true, then knowledge of group membership and the use of group means leads to the same least squares prediction of the Y value of a given case as no knowledge, namely, the grand mean, thus one can account for none of the variance in Y by such knowledge, hence $R^2_{Y \cdot 123} = 0$, and conversely.

A full MR analysis also yields the regression coefficients and constant for the regression equation:

$$\hat{Y} = B_1 X_1 + B_2 X_2 + \cdots + B_k X_k + A \tag{6}$$

where Y is the least-squares estimated ("predicted") value of $\hat{Y}$, the B_1 are raw score partial regression coefficients attached to each X_i, and A is the regression

constant or Y-intercept, that is, the estimated value of Y when all X_i are set at zero. (Its computation is accomplished by including a "unit vector" with the X_i; see Draper & Smith, 1967.)

In any MR problem, a B_i coefficient gives the amount of the effect in Y expressed in Y units which is yielded by a unit increase in X_i. But since as dummy variables the X_i are coded 0 - 1, a unit increase means 1, membership in the group, rather than 0, nonmembership in the group. Solving for the values of the general regression Equation 6 for the artificial data, and using dummy variables, we obtain:

$$\hat{Y} = -30.34X_1 - .56X_2 + 21.22X_3 + 84.12$$

Since group membership is all-or-none, the B_i values give the *net* consequence of membership in G_i relative to G_4 for groups G_1, G_2, and G_3. Thus,

$$\hat{Y}_1 = \overline{Y}_1 = -30.34(1) - .56(0) + 21.22(0) + 84.12 = 53.78$$

$$\hat{Y}_2 = \overline{Y}_2 = -30.34(0) - .56(1) + 21.22(0) + 84.12 = 83.56$$

$$\hat{Y}_3 = \overline{Y}_3 = -30.34(0) - .56(0) + 21.22(1) + 84.12 = 105.34$$

And G_4 has not been slighted, since, substituting its scores on X_1, X_2, and X_3, we find:

$$Y_4 = \overline{Y}_4 = -30.34(0) - .56(0) + 21.22(0) + 84.12 = 84.12$$

Thus, one can understand that "B_4," the "missing" reference group's weight, is always zero, and that therefore $Y_4 = A$. The exact values of the B_i will vary, depending on which group is taken as the reference group (i.e., is coded 0, $\cdots$, 0), but the differences among the B_i's will always be the same, since they are the same as the differences between the group Y means. That is, whichever the reference group, the separation of the B_i's in the example will be the same as that among the values -30.34, -.56, +21.22 and 0. (For example, if G_1 is taken as the reference group, the new B_i are 0, 29.78, 51.56, and 30.33, and the regression constant $A = \overline{Y}_1 = 53.78$.)

Not only are the B_i meaningful, but also the multiple-partial correlations with the criterion, that is, the correlation of Y with X_i, partialing out or holding constant all the other independent variables, which for the sake of notational simplicity, we designate p_i. With dummy variable coded X_i, p_i can be more specifically interpreted as the correlation between Y and the dichotomy made up of membership in G_i versus membership in G_0, the reference group. The p_i thus give, in correlational terms, the relevance to Y of the distinction between each G_i and the reference group.

Furthermore, the p_i, B_i, and β_i (the standardized partial regression coefficient) can be tested for significance by means of t (or equivalently, F with numerator df = 1). Indeed, the null hypothesis is the same for all three, —the respective

population parameter equals zero. But for a given X_i, if any one of the three is zero, all are zero, and the value of t is identical for all three tests. For the artificial data, the results are

	X_1	X_2	X_3
B_i	-30.34	$-.56$	$+21.22$
β_i	$-.478$	$-.009$	$.334$
p_i	$-.464$	$-.010$	$.344$
t_i	-2.96	$-.05$	2.07

Thus, the G_1-G_4 distinction and also the G_3-G_4 distinction with regard to Y are significant (two tailed .01 and .05, with 32 df) while the G_2-G_4 is not. These are identically the results one would obtain for t tests between the respective Y means, using the within-group mean square (with 32 df) as the variance estimate.

The reader, having been shown the MR-AV identities, may nevertheless react, "O.K., that's interesting, but so what?" Other than the provision of correlational (or regression) values, no advantage of MR over AV is claimed for this problem. But if there were other independent variables of interest (main effects, either nominal, ordinal, or interval; interactions; covariates; nonlinear components; etc., whether or not correlated with G or each other), their addition to the G variable could proceed easily by means of MR, and not at all easily in an AV/ACV framework. This possibility is the single most important advantage of the MR procedure, and will receive further attention below.

To summarize, dummy variable coding of nominal scale data yields the multiple R^2 and F test (proportion of variance accounted for by group membership and an overall significance test) and the group Y means, but also information on the degree of relevance to Y of membership in any given group, G_i, relative to the remainder (r_{Yi}), and to a reference group in terms of either regression weights (B_i or β_i) or correlation (p_i), as well as specific significance tests on the relevant null hypotheses. The importance of dummy variable (or other nominal scale) coding lies not so much in its use when only a single nominal scale constitutes the independent variables, but rather in its ready inclusion with other independent variables in MR.

CONTRAST CODING

Another system for representing nominal data can be thought of as contrast or "issues" coding. Here, each independent variable carries a contrast (in the AV/ACV sense) among group means. Each subject is characterized for each contrast according to the role he plays in it, which depends upon his group membership. With all contrasts so represented, the MR analysis can proceed.

As an example, reconsider the representation of the G variable. We can contrast membership neither G_1 or G_2 versus membership in either G_3 or G_4. This could be substantively interpreted as, for example, majority versus minority religions, schizophrenic versus neurotic, or drug versus no-drug treatment condition. The coding or scoring of this issue may be rendered as in Column 4 in Table 18.1: the value of 1 is assigned the subjects in G_1 and G_2 and the value -1 to those in G_3 and G_4, as is

done in the computation of orthogonal contrasts in AV (e.g., Edwards, 1960). Actually, any two different numbers can be used to render this issue by itself, but there are advantages for some purposes in using values which sum to zero. The simple correlation between the dependent variable and this X_1 is a point-biserial correlation (as were the dummy variable correlations) whose square gives directly the proportion of Y variance attributable to the G_1, G_2 versus G_3, G_4 distinction. For the artificial data, the $r^2_{Y1} = .2246$ ($r_{Y1} = -.4739$). This is a meaningful value which gives the size of the relationship in the sample. This r_{Y1} can be tested for significance, and confidence limits for it (or for r^2_{Y1}) can be computed by conventional procedures.

Other issues or contrasts can be rendered as independent variables. For example, a second issue which may be rendered is the effect on Y of the G_1 versus G_2 distinction, ignoring G_3 and G_4. A third issue may be the analogous G_3 versus G_4 distinction, ignoring G_1 and G_2. These are rendered, respectively, in Columns 5 and 6 in Table 18.1. Each yields an r and r^2 with the criterion which is interpretable, testable for significance, and confidence boundable.

Beyond the separate correlations of these three contrast variables, there is the further question of what their *combined* effect is on Y. We compute the $R^2_{Y \cdot 123}$ and F and obtain *exactly* the same values as when the arbitrary or dummy variable coding was used, .4458 and 8.580 (for the artificial data). This follows from the fact that the three independent variables satisfy the nonsingularity condition, that is, no one of them gives a multiple R with the other two of unity. This is a necessary *and sufficient* condition for *any* coding of g - 1 independent variables to represent G (see next section).

As before, the partial statistics, that is, the p_i, B_i and β_i and the common t test of their significance are also meaningful. If the independent variables all correlate zero with each other, the β_i will equal their respective r_{Yi}. That this must be the case can be seen from the fact that each r^2_{Yi} represents a *different* portion of the Y variance whose sum is the multiple $R^2_{Y \cdot 123}$ and thus the relationship $R^2_{Y \cdot 123} = \Sigma r_{Yi}\beta_i = \Sigma r^2_{Yi}$ must hold. The X_i as presented in Columns 4, 5, and 6 will be mutually uncorrelated if and only if the group samples sizes are equal. If they are not equal, the correlations among the X_i will be nonzero, which means that the contrasts or issues posed to the data are not independent. Such would be the case, in general, in the example if it were religion or diagnosis which formed the basis for group membership, and the actual natural population randomly sampled. Given unequal n_i for the four samples, although it is possible to make the three contrasts described above mutually uncorrelated, the coding of Columns 4, 5, and 6 does not do so. The scope of this article precludes discussion of the procedures whereby contrasts are coded so as to be uncorrelated. We note here merely that although it is always possible to do so, it is not necessarily desirable (see below).

Since, in AV terms, the between-groups SS can be (orthogonally) partitioned in various ways, there are sets of contrasts other than the set above which can be represented in the coding. A particularly popular set is that automatically provided by the AV factorial design. If the four groups of this example are looked upon as occupying the cells of a 2 x 2 design (an interpretation to which the physiological

example of drug versus no drug, frontal lesion versus control lesion particularly lends itself), each of the usual AV effects can be represented as X_i by the proper coding. The first is the same as before, and contrasts G_1 and G_2 with G_3 and G_4, for example, the drug-no-drug main effect, reproduced as Column 7 of Table 1. The second main effect, for example, frontal-control lesion, contrasts G_1 and G_3 with G_2 and G_4 and is given by the coding in Column 8. This latter X_2 gives r_{Y2}, the (point-biserial) r for (e.g.) site of lesion with the dependent variable (e.g.) retention, and r^2_{Y2} is the proportion of Y variance accounted for by this variable.

The remaining df is, as the AV has taught us, the interaction of the two main effects, for example, Drug-No-Drug x Frontal-Control Lesion. It can always be rendered as a multiplicative function of the two single df aspects of the main effects. Here, it is simply coded as the product of each group's "scores" on X_1 and X_2 (given as Column 9 in Table 18.1): 1 x 1 = 1, 1 x -1 = -1, -1 x 1 = -1, and -1 x -1 = 1. Rendering the interaction as X_3, one can interpret it as carrying the information of that aspect of group membership which represents the *joint* (note, *not* additive) effect of the drug and frontal lesion conditions. Its (point-biserial) r_{Y3} is an expression in correlational terms of the degree of relationship between Y and the *joint* operation of drug and lesion site. r^2_{Y3} gives the proportion of Y variance accounted for by this joint effect.

In the example, these three issues are *conceptually* independent, thus it would be desirable that the X_i be uncorrelated, that is, $r_{12} = r_{13} = r_{23} = 0$. The coding values given in Columns 7, 8, and 9 of Table 18.1 will satisfy this condition if (and only if) the sample sizes of the four cells are equal. (If not, other coding, not discussed here, would be necessary.)

The conceptual independence of the issues arises from the consideration that they are both manipulated variables. When this is the case, it is clearly desirable for them to be represented as mutually uncorrelated, since then the $\beta_{Yi} = r_{Yi}$ and the $R^2_{Y \cdot 123}$ is simply a sum of the separate r^2_{Yi}. Thus, the total variance of Y accounted for by group membership is unambiguously partitioned into the three separate sources. Further, the factorial AV F test values of each of the separate (one df) effects is *identical* with the t^2 of the analogous MR partial coefficients (β_i, B_i, or p_i).

However, whether one wishes to represent the issues as uncorrelated depends on whether they are conceptually independent and the differing n_i are a consequence of animals randomly dying or test tubes being randomly dropped on the one hand, or whether they carry valid sampling information about a natural population state of affairs. Assume Y is a measure of liberalism-conservatism and reconsider the problem with the groups reinterpreted as G_1: low education, low income ($n_1 = 160$), G_2: low education, high income ($n_2 = 20$), G_3: high education, low income ($n_3 = 80$), and G_4: high education, high income ($n_4 = 100$). These unequal and disproportional n_i carry valid sampling information about the univariate and bivariate distributions of education and income as defined here, the product moment r_{12} (phi) between them (coded as in Columns 7 and 8) equalling .4714. They may also be correlated with their interaction. One would ordinarily not wish to render these effects as uncorrelated, since the resulting X_i would be quite

artificial, but rather by the coding given in Columns 7, 8, and 9, where, again, X_3 is simply the $X_1 X_2$ produuct.

Note that whether the X_i are correlated or uncorrelated, or whether the n_i are equal or unequal, *all* of these coding systems yield the same $R^2_{Y \cdot 123}$ and associated F.

Two systems of rendering nominal scale (group membership) information into independent variables have been described: dummy variable coding and contrast coding. They result in identically the same multiple R^2 (and associated F) but different per independent variable partial statistics which are differently interpreted. Either involves expressing the nominal scale of g levels (groups) into g - 1 independent variables, each carrying a distinct aspect of group membership whose degree of association and statistical significance can be determined.

Nonsense Coding

It turns out, quite contraintuitively, that if one's purpose is merely to represent G so that its R^2_Y and/or its associated F test value can be determined, it hardly matters how one codes $X_1, X_2, \cdots, X_{g-1}$. *Any* real numbers, positive or negative, whole or fractional, can be used in the coding subject only to the nonsingularity constraint, that is, no X_i may have a multiple R of 1.00 with the other independent variables.

Consider, for example, the values of Columns 10-12 of Table 1. The numbers for X_1 in Column 10 were obtained by random entry into a random number table and their signs by coin flipping. Column 11 for X_2 was constructed by squaring the entries in Column 10, and Column 12 for X_3 by cubing them. Powering the X_1 values assures the satisfaction of the nonsingularity constraint. Now, using these nonsense "scores" to code G and the same Y values of the artificial example, we find the *same* $R^2_{Y \cdot 123}$ of .4458 with associated F = 8.580!

Or, alternatively, the coding values of Columns 13, 14, and 15 were obtained by haphazard free association with a quick eyeball check to assure nonsingularity. They, too, yield $R^2_{Y \cdot 123}$ = .4458 and F = 8.580.

Why these, or any other values satisfying nonsingularity will "work" would require too much space to explain nontechnically. Ultimately, it is a generalization of the same principle which makes it possible to score a dichotomy with *any* two different values (not only the conventional 0 and 1) and obtain the same point-biserial r^2 against another variable.

Of course, the statistics per X_i, that is, r_{Yi}, p_i, B_i, β_i, are as nonsensical as the X_i. But the regression equation will yield the correct group means on Y, and, as noted, R^2 and its F remain invariant. Thus, with the aid of an MR computer program and a table of random numbers (or a nonsingular imagination), one can duplicate the yield of an AV.

Apart from its status as a statistical curiosity, of what value is the demonstration that one can simulate an AV by means of an arbitrarily coded MR analysis? Not much, taken by itself. However, despite this disclaimer, it should be pointed out that for most investigators, the yield sought from the AV of such data is the significance status of the F test on the means, which the MR provides; the latter

also "naturally" yields, in R^2, a statement of proportion of variance accounted for. True, this is identically available from the AV in η^2, but this is not generally understood and computed. The MR approach has the virtue of calling to the attention of the investigator the existence of a rho (relationship) value and its distinction from a tau (significance test) value (Cohen, 1965, pp. 101-106), an issue usually lost sight of in AV contexts (but, see Hays, 1963, pp. 325-333).

But if it hardly matters how we score G and still get the same $R^2_{Y \cdot 123}$ and F ratio, we can score it in some meaningful way, one which provides analytically useful intermediate results, that is, by dummy variable or contrast coding. For other approaches to nominal scale coding, see Bottenberg and Ward (1963) and Jennings (1967).

ASPECTS OF QUANTITATIVE SCALES AS INDEPENDENT VARIABLES

As noted in the introduction, psychologists are familiar with the use of quantitative variables as independent variables in MR. This, indeed, is the only use of MR illustrated in the standard textbooks. Thus, given duration of first psychiatric hospitalization as the dependent variable Y, and as independent variables: age (X_1), Hollingshead SES Index (X_2), and MMPI Schizophrenia (Sc) score (X_3), the psychologist knows how to proceed. But MR provides opportunities for the analysis of quantitative independent variables which transcend this very limited approach.

Curvilinear Regression

From the enlarged conceptual framework of the present treatment of MR, we would say that this analysis is concerned with the *linear* aspects of age. SES, and Sc. There are other functions or aspects of these variables which can be represented as independent variables.

It has long been recognized that curvilinear relationships can be represented in linear MR by means of a polynomial form in powered terms. The standard Equation 6

$$\dot{Y} = B_1 X_1 + B_2 X_2 + \cdots B_k X_k + A$$

is linear in the X_i. If the X_i are $X_1 = Z, X_2 = Z^2, X_3 = Z^3, \cdots X_k = Z^k$, the equation is *still* linear in the X_i, even though not linear in the Z. The result of this stratagem is that nonlinear regression of Y on Z can nevertheless be represented within the linear *multiple* regression framework, the "multiplicity" being used to represent various aspects of nonlinearity, the quadratic, cubic, etc. The provision of any given power u of Z, that is, Z^u allows for u - 1 bends in the regression curve of Y or Z. Thus Z^1 or Z provides for $1 - 1 = 0$ bends, hence a straight line, Z^2 provides for $2 - 1 = 1$ bend, Z^3 for 2 bends, etc. In most psychological research, provision for more than one or two bends will rarely be necessary.

It is the same stratagem of polynomial representation further refined to make these aspects orthogonal to each other, which is utilized in the AV, also a linear model, in trend analysis designs.

A note of caution must be injected here. Such variables as Z, Z^2, and Z^3 are in

general correlated, indeed, for score-like data, usually highly so. Table 18.2 presents some illustrative data. In this example, the correlations are .9479, .8840, and .9846. For reasons of ordinary scientific parsimony, unless one is working with a strong hypothesis, we normally think of them as a hierarchy: how much Y variance does Z account for? (.5834) If Z^2 is added to Z as a second variable, how much do both together account for? (.5949) The difference represents the increment in variance accounted for by making allowance for quadratic (parabolic) curvature. In the example, it is a very small amount, -.0115. If to Z and Z^2 we add Z^3,the multiple $R^2_{Y \cdot 123}$ becomes .5956, an increment over $R^2_{Y \cdot 12}$ of only .0007. Each of these separate increments, or the two combined can be tested for significance. In general, *any* increment to an $R^2_{Y \cdot A}$ due to the addition of B can be tested by the F ratio:

$$F = \frac{(R^2_{Y \cdot A,B} - R^2_{Y \cdot A})/b}{(1 - R^2_{Y \cdot AB})/(n - a - b - 1)} \qquad [7]$$

with df = b and (n - a - b - 1), where

$R^2_{Y \cdot A,B}$ is the incremented R^2 based on a + b independent variables, that is, predicted from the combined sets of A and B variables,

$R^2_{Y \cdot A}$ is the smaller R^2 based on only a independent variables, that is, predicted from only the A set,

a and b are the number of original (a) and added (b) independent variables, hence the number of df each "takes up."

This F test of an increment to R^2 is much more general in its applicability than the present narrow context, and its symbols have been accordingly given quite general interpretation. It is used several times later in the exposition, in other circumstances where, because of correlation among X_i, it provides a basis for judging how much a set of independent variables contributes *additionally* to Y variance accounting. Since what is added is independent of what is already provided for, this is a general device for partitioning R^2 into orthogonal portions. Since the size of such portions depends on the *order* in which sets are included, the hierarchy of sets is an important part of the investigator's hypothesis statement. The generality of Formula 7 is further seen in that Formula 4 is actually a special case of Formula 7, where $R^2_{Y \cdot A}$ is zero because no X_i are used (hence a = 0) and $R^2_{Y \cdot B}$ is the R^2 based on b (= k) df which is being tested, that is, an increment of R^2 from zero.

TABLE 18.2 ILLUSTRATIVE DATA ON POLYNOMIAL MULTIPLE REGRESSION

| Variable | Correlations (r) | | | Cumulative R^2 | Increment | pi |
	Y	Z	Z^2			
Z $(= X_1)$	.7638			.5834	.5834	.1399
Z^2 $(= X_2)$	.7582	.9479		.5949	.0115	-.0116
Z^3 $(= X_3)$	.7268	.8840	.9846	.5956	.0007	.0419

Either set may have one or more independent variables. Thus, to test the increment of Z^2 to Z alone, assuming total n = 36,

$$F = \frac{(.5949 - .5834)/1}{(1 - .5949)/(36 - 1 - 1 - 1)} = \frac{.0115}{.4051/33} = .934$$

with df = 1 and 33 (a chance departure).
To test the pooled addition of both Z^2 and Z^3 to Z,

$$F = \frac{(.5956 - .5834)/2}{(1 - .5956)/(36 - 1 - 2 - 1)} = \frac{.0122/2}{.4044/32} = .483$$

with df = 2 and 32 (also a chance result).

The need for caution arises in that if one studies the results of the regression analysis which uses Z, Z^2 and Z^3, where the solution of the partial (regression or correlation) coefficients is simultaneous, not successive, the three variables are treated quite democratically. Each is partialed from the others without favor or hierarchy. Since such variables are highly correlated, when one partials Z^2 and Z^3 from Z, one is robbing Z of Y variance which we think of as rightfully belonging to it. Table 18.2 gives the p_i of the three predictors when one treats them as a set. The values are smaller (reflecting the mutual partialing), and may be negative (reflecting "suppression" effects). Because the p_i are so small, they may well be nonsignificant (as they are here), even though r_{YZ} is significant and any of the other variables may yield a significant increment. Thus, the significance interpretation of the regression of a set of polynomial terms simultaneously may be quite misleading when the usual hierarchical notions prevail.

On the other hand, if the analyst's purpose to portray a polynomial regression fit to an observed set of data, he can solve for the set simultaneously and use the resulting MR equation. For the data used for Table 18.2, the regression Equation 6 is:

$$\hat{Y} = 11.70X_1 - .50X_2 + .25X_3 + 55.90$$

the values being the B_i regression coefficients and constant, and the X_i successively Z, Z^2, and Z^3. One can substitute over the range of interest of Z and obtain fitted values of Y for purposes of prediction or of graphing of the function.

There are other means whereby curvilinear relationships can be handled in an MR framework. Briefly, one can organize an independent variable Z into g class intervals (ordinarily, but not necessarily equal in range) and treat the resulting classes as groups, coding them by the dummy variable technique described above. This results in g - 1 independent variables, each a segment of the Z range. The resulting $R^2_{Y \cdot G}$ is the amount of Y variance accounted for by Z (curvilinearly, if such is the case) and the Y means for the g intervals, computable from the resulting raw score regression equation, can be plotted graphically against the midpoints of the class intervals of Z to portray the function.

A more elegant method is the transformation (coding) of the Z values to *orthogonal* polynomials. This has the advantages in that the resulting X_i terms representing linear, quadratic, cubic, etc., components of the polynomial regression

are uncorrelated with each other; thus each contributes a separate portion of the Y variance capable of being tested for significance. Unfortunately, this method becomes computationally quite cumbersome unless the Z values are equally spaced and with equal n_i per interval. The latter is the usual case when Z is an experimentally manipulated variable, where the standard trend analysis designs of the AV can be used (Edwards, 1960).

Finally, although the first few powers of a polynomial is a good *general* fitting function, in some circumstances, such transformations of Z as log Z, $1/Z$, or $Z^{1/2}$ may provide a better fit. Draper and Smith (1967) provide a useful general reference for handling curvilinearity (and other MR problems).

Joint Aspects or Interactions

Given two independent variables, $X_1 = Z$ and $X_2 = W$, one may be interested in not only their separate effects on Y, but also on their joint effect, over and above their separate effects. As noted above (Contrast Coding), where this was discussed in the narrow context of a 2 x 2 design, this joint effect is carried by a third independent variable, a score defined for each subject by the product of his Z and W scores, that is, $X_3 = ZW$. This variable contains this joint effect, which is identically the (first-order) interaction effect of AV, or the "moderator" effect of Saunders (1956). This identity is quite general, so that a triple interaction is carried by a triple product, say ZWV, etc. Furthermore, the above are all interactions or joint effects of *linear* aspects of the variables. The more complex interactions of nonlinear aspects, such as the linear by quadratic, or quadratic by cubic, made familiar by advanced treatments of AV trend analysis (Winer, 1962, pp. 273-278), would be represented by products of powered variables, for example ZW^2, Z^2W^3, each a single independent variable.

The presentation of joint effects as simple products in MR requires the same caution as in the polynomial representation of a single variable. (Indeed, a powered variable can be properly understood as a special case of an interaction, for example, Z^2 contains the Z by Z interaction.) If one uses simultaneously as independent variables $X_1 = Z$, $X_2 = W$, $X_3 = ZW$, the correlations of Z with ZW, and W with ZW will ordinarily not be zero, may indeed be large, and the partial coefficients for Z and W (β, B, p) will have lost to ZW some Y variance which properly is theirs (just as Z would be robbed of some of its Y variance by Z^2 and Z^3). The problem is solved as in the polynomial regression analysis: Find $R^2_{Y \cdot 123}$, the variance proportion accounted for by all three variables; then find $R^2_{Y \cdot 12}$, the amount accounted for *without* the interaction. The increment is tested for significance by the F ratio of Formula 7.

This, too, generalizes. In more complex systems, involving either more variables and higher order interactions or interactions among polynomial aspects (or both), one forms a hierarchy of sets of independent variables and tests for the significance of increments to R^2 by means of the same F ratio (Formula 7). For example, if one has three variables Z, W, and V, represented both linearly and quadratically with all their interactions, one possible way of organizing the variables is by means of the following sets:

$$A: Z, W, V$$
$$B: ZW, ZV, WV$$
$$C: ZWV$$
$$D: Z^2, W^2, V^2$$
$$E: Z^2W, ZW^2, Z^2V, ZV^2, W^2V, WV^2$$
$$F: Z^2W^2, Z^2V^2, W^2V^2$$
$$G: Z^2W^2V^2$$

One would then test $R^2_{Y \cdot AB} - R^2_{Y \cdot A}$, $R^2_{Y \cdot ABC} - R^2_{Y \cdot AB}$, etc., each by the F ratio for increments. When a set containing more than one variable is significant, one can "break out" each variable in it and test its increment for significance by the same procedure. Of course, one can elect to make all sets contain only one variable, but the number of resulting tests (in the example there would be 20) brings with it an increased risk of spuriously significant results over the complete analysis. This strategy parallels that of the AV, where the avoidance of this risk is implicit. In a 4 x 5 factorial design AV, for example, the interaction involves a single mean square based on 3 x 4 = 12 df which is tested by a single F test. One ordinarily does not test each of these 12 effects separately unless the set as a whole is significant. The principle, of course, obtains even for the main effects, involving sets of 3 and 4 df, where each set normally is tested "wholesale."

Other combinations and priorities of the X, Y, and Z variables are, of course, possible. This operation involves formulating hypotheses about what constitutes a relevant class of independent variables and the priorities of these classes. It depends not only on mechanical variance-stealing considerations, but also on substantive issues in the research and the judgment of the investigator.

Although the discussion in this section has been concerned with interactions among quantitative variables, the principles of forming interaction variables hold also for nominal variables, and for mixtures of variables. Let an "aspect" of a research variable such as religion or IQ be one of the X_i of the set which represent it. Then, for example, if the interaction of u aspects of one variable U and v aspects of another variable V are desired, one may form a total of uv interaction X_i, by multiplying each of the u aspects by each of the v aspects. Each of the resulting uv independent variables is a single (one df) variable which represents a specific aspect by aspect joint or interaction effect. Either U or V may be nominal or quantitative. Where nominal, their aspects may be dummy variables or contrasts; where quantitative, the aspects may be powered polynomial terms or missing data dichotomies (see below). One can thus generate such single interaction X_i as "majority-minority religious group by authoritarianism," "experimental group D versus control group by quadratic of stimulus intensity," etc. It is both convenient and enlightening to have each such joint aspect separately and unambiguously (but not necessarily orthogonally) represented in the set of independent variables. Their individual increment to R^2 and significance can then be determined.

Perhaps as important as being able to represent the interaction X_i in specific detail is the availability of the option *not* to represent some or all of them. The textbook paradigms for factorial design AV lead data analysts to dutifully harvest

all possible interactions of all possible orders up to the highest, whether or not they are meaningful or interpretable or, if interpretable, communicable. There emanate from psychology departments many silent prayers to the spirit of R. A. Fisher that high-order interactions will not prove significant! Obviously, one need not (indeed cannot) analyze for all possible aspects including joint aspects of variables if for no other reason than the rapid loss of df for estimating error. The need to "specify the model," that is, the set of X_i to be studied in MR has the salutary effect of requiring an incisive prior conceptual analysis of the research problem. This goes hand in hand with the flexibility of the MR system, which makes readily possible the representation of the research issues posed by the investigator (i.e., multiple regression in the service of the ego!), rather than the canned issues mandated by AV computational routines.

Missing Data

In nonexperimental, particularly survey, research, it frequently occurs that some subjects are missing data on one or more (but not all) of the independent variables under study. Typically, the data are not missing randomly, but for reasons frequently related to values for other independent variables, and particularly to values for the dependent variable under study. For example, in a study of factors associated with the rehabilitation of drug addicts, reported weekly wages on last job is used as an independent variable, among others. Some respondents claim they do not recall or refuse to respond. As another example, consider a retrospective study of the school records of adult mental retardates where the recorded IQ is abstracted for use as an independent variable but found missing in some cases. In neither of these cases can one prudently assume that the mean of these cases on the X_i in question, other X_i, and, particularly, Y is the same as that for the cases with data present. The practice of excluding cases lacking some of the data has the undesirable properties of analyzing a residual sample which is unrepresentative to an unknown degree of the population originally sampled, as well as the loss of information (viz., the *fact* of data being missing) which may be criterion relevant.

MR provides a simple method for coping with this problem. Each such variable has *two* aspects, its value (where present) and whether or not the value *is* present. Accordingly, two independent variables are constructed: X_1 is the value itself, with the mean of X_1 for those cases where it is present entered for the cases where it is missing, and X_2 is the missing data aspect, a dummy variable dichotomy coded 0-1 for absent-present. These two aspects contain all the information available in the variable. Moreover, as scored, $r_{12} = 0$, hence X_1 and X_2 are each contributing an independent portion of the Y variance.

Actually, *any* value entered for the missing data in X_1 will "work" in the sense of accounting for Y variance, that is, the $R^2_{y \cdot 12}$ will be the same. The use of the mean will uniquely result in $r_{12} = 0$, which may be advantageous interpretively. For some purposes, this advantage may be offset by using some (or any) other value, obviating the necessity of a prior computation of the mean.

The researcher, normally sensitive about tampering with data, may find the prospect of "plugging" empty spaces in his data sheet with means singularly

unappealing. He may even correctly point out that this will have the effect of reducing r_{Y1} from what r_{YX} is for the subsample having X values present. In rebuttal, it must be pointed out that the subsample is not representative of the originally defined population, and the method proposed can be thought of as reflecting the fact that the population studied contains missing data, and fully incorporates this fact as positive information.

ANALYSIS OF COVARIANCE

Viewed from the perspective of the MR system, the fixed-model ACV turns out to be a rather minor wrinkle, and not the imposing parallel edifice it constitutes in the AV/ACV framework. A covariate is, after all, nothing but an independent variable, which, because of the logic dictated by the substantive issues of the research, assumes priority among the set of independent variables as a basis for accounting for Y variance. Consider a research in educational psychology in which the Y variable is some performance measure in children, X_1 is midparental education, X_2 is family income, and G, carried by the set X_3, X_4, X_5 represents some differential learning experience in four intact classes. This situation is a "natural" for ACV (assuming its assumptions are reasonably well met). One would think of it as studying the effect of learning experience or class membership on Y, using X_1 and X_2 as covariates. Thus considered, we are asking how much variance in Y (and its significance) the variables X_3, X_4, and X_5 account for, *after* the variance due to X_1 and X_2 is allowed for, or held constant, or "partialed out" (the terms being equivalent). The form of the MR analysis to accomplish this purpose is directly suggested. Find $R^2_{Y \cdot 12345}$, the proportion of Y variance all independent variables account for. Then find $R^2_{Y \cdot 12}$, the proportion of Y variance attributable to the covariates education and income. Their difference is the increment due to group membership, which is tested for significance by the F test of Formula 7 used in a different design context above. Note that no problem arises if the four groups are defined by a 2 x 2 factorial. If X_3, X_4, X_5 are coded as in Columns 7, 8, 9 in Table 18.1 to represent the two main effects and their interaction, the respective ACV significance tests are performed by (Formula 7) F ratio tests of the increments $R^2_{Y \cdot 12345}$ - $R^2_{Y \cdot 1245}$ (for the main effect represented by X_3), $R^2_{Y \cdot 12345}$ - $R^2_{Y \cdot 1235}$ (for the main effect represented by X_4) and $r^2_{Y \cdot 12345}$ - $r^2_{Y \cdot 1234}$ (for the interaction or joint effect). Note that X_1 and X_2 are always included in the debited R^2, because of their priority in the issues as defined. This principle is readily generalized to designs of greater complexity.

That a covariate is nothing but another independent variable except for priority due to substantive considerations is evident when one considers a study formally almost identical to the above, now, however, done by sa social psychologist. Since there are four different classes and four different teachers, the classes ipso facto have had different learning experiences. But this research is concerned with the effects of parental education and income on the performance criterion, with group membership now the contaminant which must be removed, hence the covariate. Using the same set up and data, he would find $R^2_{Y \cdot 12345}$ - $R^2_{Y \cdot 345}$ as the combined effect of education and income, $R^2_{Y \cdot 12345}$ - $R^2_{Y \cdot 2345}$ as the net effect

of education (i.e., over and above that of income as well as the covariates of class membership), and $R^2_{Y \cdot 12345} - R^2_{Y \cdot 1345}$ for the net effect of income, each F-testable as before. Thus, one man's main effect is another man's covariate.

The MR approach to ACV-like problems opens up possibilities for statistical control not dreamed of in ACV. We have just seen how purely nominal or qualitative variables (class membership) can serve as covariates. Beyond this, we can apply other principles which have been adduced above: (a) Any aspects of data can, by appropriate means, be represented as independent variables. (b) Any (sets of) independent variables can serve as covariates by priority assignment in variance accounting. Thus, for example, one can make provision for a covariate being nonlinearly related to Y (and/or to other independent variables) by writing a polynomial set of independent variables and giving the set priority; or, one can carry two variables *and* their interaction as a covariate set; or, one can even carry as a covariate a variable for which there are missing data by representing the two aspects of such a datum as two independent variables and giving them priority. Finally, one can combine the priority principle with those of contrast coding to achieve analytic modes of high fidelity to substantive research aims.

The ACV assumption that the regression lines (more generally, surfaces) of the covariates (U) on Y have the same slopes (more generally, regression parameters) between groups (V) is equivalent to the hypothesis of no significance for the set of uv interaction independent variables. This hypothesis can be F-tested as a Set B following the inclusion of U and V as Set A, using Formula 7.

DISCUSSION

In the introduction it was argued that MR and AV/ACV are essentially identical systems, and so they are, at least in their theory. In the actual practice of the data-analytic art, many differences emerge, differences which generally favor the MR system as outlined above.

Before turning to these differences, a closer look at their similarity in regard to statistical assumptions is warranted. This article has concerned itself only with the fixed-model AV/ACV, wherein it is assumed that inference to the population about the independent variables is for just those variables represented (and not those variables considered as samples) and that values on these variables are measured without error. This means that in a MR whose set of X_i include quantitative variates (e.g., scores), the population to which one generalizes, strictly speaking, is made up of cases having just those X_i values, only the Y values for any given combinations of values for the X_i varying; moreover, the Y distribution (and only this distribution) is assumed normal and of equal variance for all the observed combinations of X_i values. These seem, indeed, to be a constraining set of assumptions. However, the practical effect on the validity of the generalizations which one might wish to draw is likely to be vanishingly small. It seems likely that the substantive generalizations made strictly for the particular vectors of X_i values in the rows of the basic data matrix of the sample would hold for the slightly differing values which the population would contain if the sampling is random. As for the normality and variance homogeneity assumptions for Y, the robustness of the F test under

conditions of such assumption failure is well attested to (for a summary, see Cohen, 1965, pp. 114-116). Particularly when reasonably large samples are used, itself desirable to assure adequate statistical power, no special inhibition need surround the drawing of inferences from the usual hypothesis testing, certainly no more so than in AV.

A discussion of the practical differences between MR and AV is best begun with a consideration of the nature of classical fixed-model AV. Its natural use is in the analysis of data generated by experimental manipulations along one or more dimensions (main effects), resulting in subgroups of observations in multifactor cells, treatment combinations. Each main effect is paradigmatically a set of qualitative distinctions along some dimension. These dimensions are conceptually independent of each other, and since they are under the control of the designer of the experiment, the data can, in principle, be gathered in such a way that the dimensions are actually mutually orthogonal in their representation in the data. (This condition is met by the proportionality of cell frequencies in all two dimensional subtables.) This also results in interactions being orthogonal to each other and to the main effects. Thus, the paradigm is of a set of batches (one batch per AV main effect or interaction) of qualitative independent variables, all batches mutually orthogonal.

Now, under such conditions, one *can*, as illustrated above, analyze the data by MR, but there is no advantage in so doing. The AV can be seen as a computational shortcut to an analysis by the linear model which analyzes by batches and capitalizes on the fact that batches are orthogonal. Thus, the classical fixed factorial AV is a special simplified case of MR analysis particularly suited to neat experimental layouts, where qualitative treatments are manipulated in appropriate orthogonal relationships. Later refinements allows for quantitative independent variables being exploited by trend analysis designs, but these, too, demand manipulative control in the form of equally spaced intervals in the dimension and equal sized samples per level if the computational simplicity is to be retained.

These designs are quite attractive, not only in their efficiency and relative computational simplicity, but also in the conceptual power they introduced to the data analyst, for example, interactions, trend components. They were presented in excellent applied statistics textbooks. Inevitably, they attracted investigators working in quite different modes, who proceeded to a Procrustean imposition of such designs on their research.

A simple example (not too much of a caricature) may help illustrate the point. Dr. Doe is investigating the effects of Authoritarianism (California F scale) and IQ on a cognitive style score (Y), using high school students as subjects. He is particularly interested in the F x IQ interaction, that is, in the possibility that r_{YF} differs as a function of IQ level. He gives the three tests, and proceeds to set up the data for analysis. He dichotomizes the F and IQ distributions as closely as possible to their medians into high-low groups and proceeds to assign the Y scores into the four cells of the resulting 2 x 2 fixed factorial design. He then discovers that the number of cases in the high-low and low-high cells distinctly exceed those in the other two, an expression of the fact that F and IQ are correlated. He must

somehow cope with this disproportionality (nonorthogonality). He may (a) throw out cases randomly to achieve proportionality or equality; (b) use an "unweighted means" or other approximate solution (Snedecor, 1956, pp. 385-387); or (c) "fit constants by least squares" (Snedecor, 1956, pp. 388-391; Winer, 1962, pp. 224-227), which is, incidentally, an MR procedure.

Clearly, this is a far cry from experimentally manipulated qualitative variables. These are, in fact, naturally varying correlated quantitative variables. This analysis does violence to the problem in one or both of the following ways:

1. By reducing the F scale and the IQ to dichotomies, it has taken reliable variables which provide graduated distinctions between subjects over a wide range, and reduced them to two-point (high-low) scales, squandering much information in the process. For example, assuming bivariate normality, when a variable is so dichotomized, there is a reduction in r^2_{YX}, the criterion variance it accounts for, and hence in the value of F in the test of its significance, of 36%. This wilful degradation of available measurement information has a direct consequence in the loss of statistical power (Cohen, 1965, pp. 95-101, 118).

2. The throwing out of cases to achieve proportionality clearly reduces power, but, even worse, distorts the situation by analyzing as if IQ and F scale score were independent, when they are not. Other approximations suffer from these and/or other statistical deficiencies or distortions.

If Dr. Doe uses the MR-equivalent exact-fitting constants procedure, he has still given up computational simplicity, and, of course, the measurement information due to dichotomization. If he seeks to reduce the latter and also allow for the possibility of nonlinearity of Y on X_i regressions by breakdown of IQ and/or F scale into smaller segments, say quartiles, his needs for equality of intervals and cases will be frustrated, and he will not be able to find a computational paradigm, which, in any case, would be very complicated. It seems quite clear that, however considered, the conventional AV mode is the wrong way to analyze the data.

On the other hand, the data can be completely, powerfully, and relevantly analyzed by MR. A simple analysis would involve setting X_1 = IQ, X_2 = F scale score, X_3 = (IQ)(F). By finding $R^2_{Y \cdot 123} - R^2_{Y \cdot 12}$ and testing it for significance (or equivalently, by testing the significance of p_3), he learns how much the interaction contributes to Y variance accounting and its significance. Determinations of the values of $r^2_{Y1}, r^2_{Y2}, R^2_{Y \cdot 12}, R^2_{Y \cdot 12} - r^2_{Y \cdot 1}$, and $R^2_{Y \cdot 12} - r^2_{Y2}$ and testing each for significance fully exploits the information in the data at this level. If he believes it warranted, he can add polynomial terms for IQ and F score and their interaction in order to provide for nonlinearity of any of the relationships involved.

Another practical difference between MR and AC/ACV is with regard to computation. The MR procedure, in general, requires the computation and inversion of the matrix of correlations (or sums of squares and products) among the independent variables, a considerable amount of computation for even a modest number of independent variables. It is true that *classical* AV, whose main effects, interactions,

polynomial trend components, etc., are mutually orthogonal, capitalizes on this orthogonality to substantially reduce the computation required. Whatever computational reduction there is in AV or MR depends directly on the orthogonality of the independent variables, which we have seen is restricted to manipulative experiments, and is by no means an invariant feature even of such experiments.

However, given the widespread availability of electronic computer facilities, the issue of the *amount* of computation required in the analysis of data from psychological research dwindles to the vanishing point, and is replaced by problems of programming. The typical statistical user of a typical computer facility requires that a computer program which will analyze his data be available in the program library. Such programs will have been either prepared or adapted for the particular computer configuration of that facility. Unfortunately, it is frequently the case that the available AV program or programs will not analyze the particular fixed AV design which the investigator brings. Some AV programs are wanting in capacity in number of factors or levels per factor, some will handle only orthogonal designs, some will handle only equal cases per cell, some will do AV but not ACV, some of those that do handle ACV can handle only one or two covariates. Many will not handle special forms of AV, for example, Latin squares.

On the other hand, even the most poorly programmed scientific computer facility will have at least one good MR program, if for no other reason than its wide use in various technologies, particularly engineering. All the standard statistical program packages contain at least one MR program. Although these vary in convenience, efficiency, and degree of informativeness of output, all of them can be used to accomplish the analyses discussed in this article. In contrast to the constraints of AV programs, the very general MR program can be particularized for any given design by representing (coding) those aspects of the independent variables of interest to the investigator according to the principles which have been described.

A note of caution: as we have seen, given even a few factors (main effects of nominal variables or linear aspects of quantitative variables), one can generate very large numbers of distinct independent variables (interactions of any order, polynomials, interactions of polynomials, etc.). The temptation to represent many such features of the data in an analysis must be resisted for sound research-philosophical and statistical reasons. Even in researches using a relatively large number of subjects (n), a small number of factors (nominal and quantitative scales) can generate a number of independent variables which exceed n. Each esoteric issue posed to the data costs a df which is lost from the error estimate, thus enfeebling the statistical power of the analysis.

This, ultimately, is the reason that it is desirable in research that is to lead to *conclusions* to state hypotheses which are relatively few in number. This formulation is not intended to indict exploratory studies, which may be invaluable, but by definition, such studies do not result in conclusions, but in hypotheses, which then need to be tested (or, depending on the research context, cross-validated). If one analyzes the data of a research involving 100 subjects by means of MR, and utilizes 40 independent variables, what does one conclude about 4 or 5 of them which

prove to have partial regression weights "significant" at the .05 level? Certainly not that *all* of them are real effects, when one realizes that an overall null hypothesis leads to an expectation that 5% of 40, or 2 are expected by change. But which two?

A reasonable strategy depends upon organizing a hierarchy of sets of independent variables, ordered, by sets, according to a priori judgments. Set A represents the independent variables which the investigator most expects to be relevant to Y (perhaps all or some of the main effects and/or linear aspects of continuous variables). These may be thought of as *the* hypotheses of the research, and the fewer the better. Set B consists of next order possibilities (perhaps lower order interactions and/or some quadratic aspects). These are variables which are to be viewed less as hypotheses and more as exploratory issues. If there is a Set C (perhaps some higher order interactions and/or higher degree polynomials), it should be thought of as unqualifiedly exploratory. (If there are covariates in the design, they, of course, take precedence over all these sets, and would enter first.) The "perhaps" in the parenthetical phrases in this paragraph are included because it is *not* a mechanical ordering that is intended. In any given research, a central issue may be carried by an interaction or polynomial aspect while some main effect may be quite secondary. In most research, however, it is the simplest aspects of factors which are most likely to occupy the focus of the investigator's attention. However, the decision as to what constitutes an appropriate set depends on both research-strategic issues that go to the heart of the substantive nature of the research, and subtle statistical issues beyond the scope of this article. The latter are discussed by Miller (1966, pp. 30-35).

The independent variables so organized, one first does an MR analysis for Set A, then Sets A + B, then Sets A + B + C. Each additional set is tested for the increment to R^2 by means of the F test of Formula 7. A prudent procedure would then be to test for significance the contribution of any *single* independent variable in a set only if the set yields a significant increment to R^2. A riskier procedure would be to dispense with the latter condition, but then the results would clearly require cross-validation.

NOTE

1. It is of interest to note that information about the "omitted" group, here G_4 (more generally, G_0), is readily recovered. The value for the correlation of the dichotomy for that group with *any* variable Z (r_{Z0}) is a simple function of the r's of the other variables with Z (r_{Zi}) and the standard deviations of the X_i, namely

$$r_{Z0} = (-\Sigma_{i-1}^{g-1} r_{Z_i}\sigma_i)/\sigma_0$$

where

$$\sigma_i = [n_i(n - n_i)/n^2]^{\frac{1}{2}}, \text{ similarly for } \sigma_0.$$

When all groups are of the same size, this simplifies to

$$r_{Z0} = -\Sigma_{i-1}^{g-1} r_{Zi}$$

This relationship will hold whatever the nature of Z; it need not even be a real variable, —it will hold if Z is a factor in the factor-analytic sense, unrotated or rotated, with the r_{zi} being factor loadings.

REFERENCES

Bottenberg, R. A. & J. H. Ward, Jr. *Applied multiple linear regression.* (PRL-TDR-63-6) Lackland AF Base, Texas, 1963.

Cattell, R. B. Psychological theory and scientific method. In R. B. Cattell (Ed.), *Handbook of multivariate experimental psychology.* Chicago: Rand McNally, 1966.

Cohen, J. Some statistical issues in psychological research. In B. B. Wolman (Ed.), *Handbook of clinical psychology.* New York: McGraw-Hill, 1965.

Cohen, J. & Cohen, P. *Applied multiple regression/correlation analysis for the behavioral sciences.* Hillsdale, New Jersey: Lawrence Erlbaum Associates, 1975.

Cureton, E. E. On correlation coefficients. *Psychometrika,* 1966, 31: 605-607.

Draper, N. & H. Smith. *Applied regression analysis.* New York: Wiley, 1967.

Edwards, A. E. *Experimental design in psychological research.* (Rev. ed.) New York: Rinehart, 1960.

Hays, W. L. *Statistics for psychologists.* New York: Holt, Rinehart & Winston, 1963.

Jennings. E. Fixed effects analysis of variance by regression analysis. *Multivariate Behavioral Research,* 1967, 2: 95-108.

Li, J. C. R. *Statistical inference.* Vol. 2. *The multiple regression and its ramifications.* Ann Arbor, Mich.: Edwards Bros., 1964.

McNemar, Q. *Psychological statistics.* (3rd ed.) New York: Wiley, 1962.

Miller, R. G., Jr. *Simultaneous statistical inference.* New York: McGraw-Hill, 1966.

Peters, C. C. & W. R. Van Voorhis. *Statistical procedures and their mathematical bases.* New York: McGraw-Hill, 1940.

Saunders, D. R. Moderator variables in prediction. *Educational and Psychological Measurement,* 1956, 16: 209-222.

Snedecor, G. W. *Statistical methods.* (5th ed.) Ames: Iowa State College Press, 1956.

Suits, D. B. Use of dummy variables in regression equations. *Journal of the American Statistical Association,* 1957, 52: 548-551.

Winer, B. J. *Statistical principles in experimental design.* New York: McGraw-Hill, 1962.

19

HOW REGRESSION ARTIFACTS IN QUASI-EXPERIMENTAL EVALUATIONS CAN MISTAKENLY MAKE COMPENSATORY EDUCATION LOOK HARMFUL

DONALD T. CAMPBELL
and
ALBERT ERLEBACHER

Northwestern University

Evaluations of compensatory educational efforts such as Head Start are commonly quasi-experimental or ex post facto. The compensatory program is made available to the most needy, and the "control" group then sought from among the untreated children of the same community. Often this untreated population is on the average more able than the "experimental" group. In such a situation the usual procedures of selection, adjustment, and analysis produce systematic biases in the direction of making the compensatory program look deleterious. Not only does matching produce regression artifacts in this direction, but so also do analysis of covariance and partial correlation. These biases of analysis occur both where pretest scores are available and in ex post facto studies.

It seems reasonably certain that this methodological error occurred in the Westinghouse-Ohio University study (Cicirelli, et al., 1969) and it probably has occurred in others purporting to show no effects or harmful effects from Head Start programs. The occurrence of such tragically misleading misanalyses must be attributed to the slow diffusion of the isolated warnings. These have been long

AUTHORS' NOTE: Supported in part by National Science Foundation Grant GS 1309X.

Reprinted from J. Helmuth (ed.) *Compensatory Education: A National Debate,* Vol. III of *The Disadvantaged Child.* New York: Brunner/Mazel, 1970, by permission of Brunner/Mazel.

available for the process of matching (e.g., McNemar, 1940, 1949; Thorndike, 1942; Hovland, Lumsdaine and Sheffield, 1949; Campbell and Clayton, 1961; Campbell and Stanley, 1963), and for ex post facto designs (Campbell and Stanley, 1963). But for analysis of covariance, the warning message is newer (Lord, 1960; Evans and Anastasio, 1968; Werts and Linn, 1969; see also Lord, 1967, 1969) and most references are wrong in their recommendations (e.g., Thorndike, 1942; Peters and Van Voorhis, 1940; Walker and Lev, 1953; Winer, 1962; Campbell and Stanley, 1963; McNemar, 1969).

The purpose of this essay is the didactic one of illustrating with a detailed example why these biases appear. The initial focus will be on the case of the superior control group. Subsequently, data assemblies which could misleadingly make compensatory education look effective will be discussed. Several of the sections that follow involve statistical technicalities which some readers will want to skip. It could be hoped that every reader will stick it out through the section on Matching. But however that may be, we would like to call attention of all readers to some general conclusions: (1) For the ex post facto situation to which the Westinghouse-Ohio University study was unavoidably limited, no satisfactory analysis is possible; (2) analysis of covariance in its usual forms is inadequate not only in such ex post facto settings, but also in those quasi-experimental settings where pretests are available; (3) for quasi-experiments with pretests similar in composition to the posttests, common-factor covariance adjustments developed by Lord (1960) and Porter (1967) may be appropriate. We would also like to call attention to the two nonstatistical sections at the end, especially the argument in favor of randomly assigned control groups.

For the purpose of illustration, we have generated computer-simulated data for two overlapping groups with no true treatment effect. Figure 19.1 shows the frequency distributions of these two groups. In the bottom portion are the two distributions representing the test scores obtained after the ameliorative treatment ("posttest"). It can be seen that the Experimental Group has a lower mean than the Control. However, as can be seen in the top portion of the figure, the difference between the two groups was already present prior to the treatment. The "pretest" shows precisely the same difference, except for the vagaries of random sampling.

With the data as displayed in Figure 19.1, few if any would be tempted to conclude that the treatment had any effect, helpful or harmful. However, our example is especially clear because we have kept the same means and standard deviations for the pretest and the posttest (as far as population parameters are concerned). Nevertheless we will be able to show that even in the present clear-cut instance of no treatment effects, the common quasi-experimental analysis techniques will result in serious biases.

Figures 19.2, 19.3, and 19.4 display the relationship between pretest (or covariate) and posttest scores within each group, separately and then combined. The relationships there displayed could have been reported more economically as correlation coefficients (the pretest-post correlations are .489 for the Experimental Group, .496 for the Control, where the theoretical population values are each

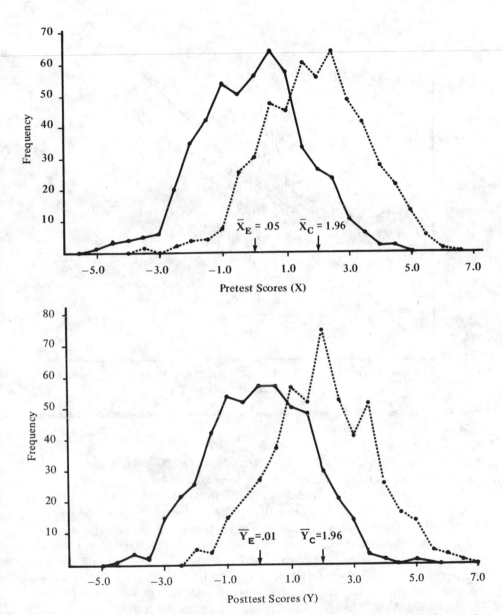

FIGURE 19.1   Pretest and posttest distributions (simulated data) for an instance of a superior Control Group (dashed lines) and no treatment effect in the Experimental Group (solid lines).

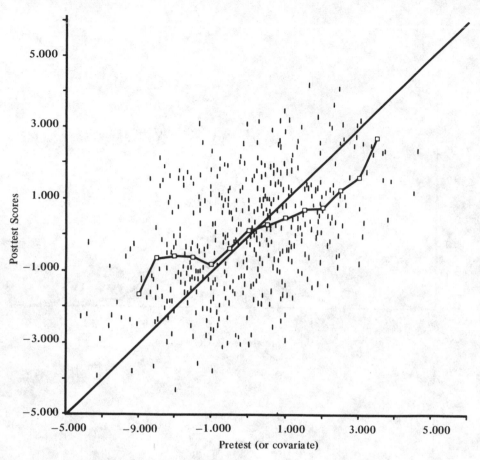

FIGURE 19.2 Scatter plot of the correlation of pretest and posttest scores for the Experimental Group.

.500); but we feel that the display of relationships as scatter diagrams provides the easiest route to an intuitive understanding of regression artifacts.

The truisms we are going to demonstrate with these simulated data are not at all specific to our mode of generating them. The similarity of pretest and posttest means and variances makes the didactic exposition easier to follow, but is not essential. Any simulation would do in which the mean difference and overlap between experimental and control group exists to the same degree in both pretest and posttest (as shown for example by the t ratio for the mean difference between experimental and control). Thus posttest means and variances could be larger than for the pretest. Or still less restrictively, any simulation will do which distinguishes between pretest values and the common factor (or true score component) shared by pretest and posttest, as by adding "error" or "unique variance" to the pretest as well as to the posttest. We believe that the reader may skip without loss the following paragraph on the details of our simulation.

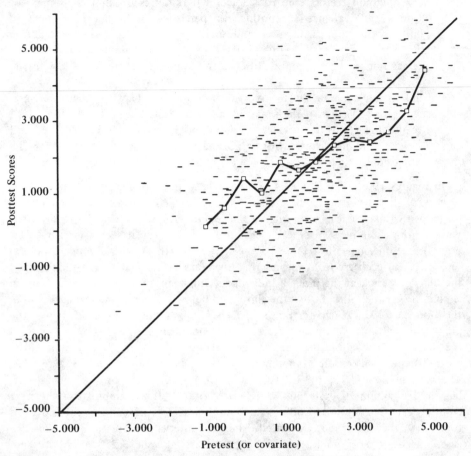

FIGURE 19.3   Scatter plot of the correlation of pretest and posttest scores for the Control Group.

The data were generated in the following way: A person's score was made up of three parts, added to each other. Thus for the pretest,

$$X_{ij} = G_{i.} + C_{ij} + E_{ij}, \text{ and}$$

for the posttest,

$$Y_{ij} = G_{i.} + C_{ij} + E'_{ij}, \text{ where}$$

X_{ij} is the pretest score of person j in Group i.

Y_{ij} is the postest score of subject j in Group i.

G_i is a group score common to all members of a group. It was taken as 0 for all members of the Experimental Group and 2 for all members of the Control Group. G is that portion of "true score" variance producing group differences.

C_{ij} is a common factor score for subject i j. It represents that component of "true score" variance accounting for persisting individual differences in ability within groups. C_{ij} was randomly chosen from a normal population with a mean of 0 and a standard deviation of 1. (In this simulation, neither pretest nor posttest contain "true score" components not shared with the other.)

E_{ij} and E'_{ij} are separate "error" scores for subject i j. They represent measurement errors. That is, if the same subject were tested again on the same test, because the test is not perfectly reliable, his E_{ij} would be different. E_{ij} and E'_{ij} were randomly chosen from a normal population with a mean of 0 and a standard deviation of 1.

In Figures 19.2, 19.3, and 19.4 there is a tally mark for each of 500 individuals in each of the highly overlapping distributions. Each "Experimental" individual is diagramed with a vertical mark, each of the generally superior "Control" individuals with a horizontal mark. For each class interval of pretest scores (width = .500 points), the mean posttest score has been plotted (the boxed or circled points) separately for each group. A meandering line connects these means. To understand the diagrams, look at the plots of individuals and means in a given area: Each mean is based upon the tallies of its type above and below it in a narrow vertical column, the boundaries of which are not shown but which can be inferred. Where the number of cases in a column was fewer than 6, no mean was plotted on the grounds that its small N would lead to misleading variability. Checking visually some of the plotted details will ensure comprehension. Begin at the left edge of Figure 19.2. The class interval -4.750 to -4.250 centered at 4.500, as read on the bottom line, has in the column it designates three cases, mean = 1.566, unplotted. The next column, centered around -4.000, with boundaries of -4.250 and -3.750, contains four cases, mean = -.2564, unplotted. The next interval, -3.750 to -3.250 has five cases, mean = -1.868, unplotted. In the next class interval, -3.250 to -2.750 there are six cases, mean = -1.643, providing our first plotted column mean, the boxed point above -3.000. From there rightward there is a plotted mean for the next 13 class intervals, plotted every .500 points, above points -2.500, -2.000, -1.500, -1.000, and so on. Small numbers still create instability, leading to the high value for the Experimental category centered at pretest +3.500, where one very high point produces a column (posttest) mean of +2.711, leading it to cross over the corresponding Control Group value, as seen in Figure 19.4.

The straight line running diagonally through Figures 19.2, 19.3, and 19.4 can be designated the identity diagonal and represents the set of values which all tallies would have taken had pretest and posttest scores been identical. Note that the line of column means for each of the groups lies below this identity diagonal in the higher range of its scores, and lies above the identity diagonal for lower half of its scores. The meandering line ideally should cross the identity diagonal at that point representing the intersection of the pretest and the posttest means. A straight line fitted by least squares to the column means would be the regression line of posttest on pretest. If the correlation were perfect, there would be no scatter, and this line would coincide with the identity diagonal. If there were zero correlation, that is if

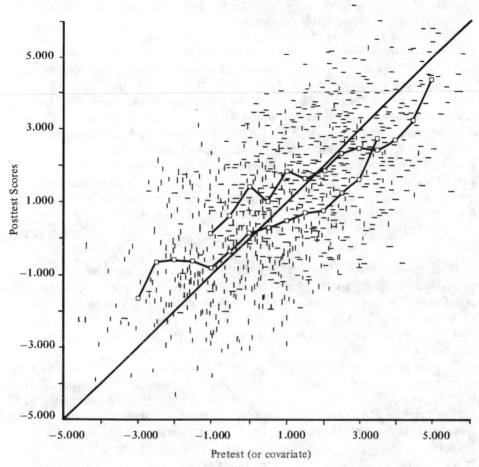

FIGURE 19.4   Scatter plot of the correlation of pretest and posttest scores for Experimental and Control Group. (Vertical tally marks represent Experimental Group children, horizontal tallys Controls)

pretest scores were totally useless in predicting posttest scores, then all column means would equal the posttest mean for the whole group (in universe values if not specific sample values) and the regression line would be perfectly horizontal. This case falls about halfway between. The correlation between pretest and posttest scores is .489 for the Experimental Group, and .496 for the Control Group, where the universe values determined by the formula for generating the scores are both .500.

In a usual presentation of regression phenomena, there would also be a presentation of the regression of pretest on posttest. However, to avoid needless visual complexity, we have omitted presentation in Figures 19.2, 19.3, and 19.4 of row means, that is of the mean pretest scores for each class interval of posttest scores. These values would be tipped away from the identity diagonal in the direction of

the vertical, would be to the left of the identity value above the means, and to the right of the identity value below the means.

The often referred to but less often understood "regression toward the mean" is portrayed in the departure of the column means from the identity diagonal. For each class of pretest scores, the corresponding mean posttest score lies closer to the overall population mean, posttest values being thereby lower in the case of high pretest values, and higher in the case of low pretest values. (This verbal statement must be made more complex for situations in which pretest and posttest have different means and variances: For each pretest class interval, the corresponding mean score on the posttest is closer in standard-deviation units to the overall posttest mean than is the pretest class interval's distance from the pretest mean in pretest standard deviation units.) Note that *just as our Experimental and Control groups have different means on both pretest and posttest occasions, they thereby also have different regression lines.* This point will be expanded below.

MATCHING

With the details of the illustration before us, we can now look at several procedures commonly used in quasi-experimental situations to attempt to compensate for pretest inequality between experimental and control groups. Most widespread of these is *matching,* an ubiquitous error so supported by common sense that it is repeatedly reinvented as the way of "controlling for" initial inequalities of group means.

We have graphed, in Figures 19.1 through 19.4, an absolutely null case, in which the supposed "treatment" applied solely to the "Experimental Group" had absolutely no effect. Suppose we attempt to examine the effect of the treatment on a matched sample. Let us start with subsamples from each population matched on a specific pretest score, for example, 1.000 (class interval from .750 to 1.250). Looking at Figures 19.2 and 19.4, we see that, for the "Experimental" sample, the posttest mean is .478, for the "Control" sample (Figures 19.3 and 19.4), the mean is 1.850, a difference in the direction of the Experimental Group's becoming worse, the Control Group's becoming better. If we expand this matched sample by taking equal numbers of experimentals in each of the overlapping class intervals, we add further replication of this same bias, easily getting a highly significant effect. The proper interpretation of this effect is that scores in each group are regressing toward different means, which is inevitable if the groups do in fact have different means. It is to be hoped that the why of this error is by now intuitively obvious from the form of display used in Figures 19.2, 19.3, and 19.4.

One reason one is so often deceived by regression artifacts in the matching situation is that the matching score and the value of the dependent variable seem to be stated in the same, but actually are in different, metric languages. In the example above, the two pretest values of 1.000 are in the language of scores selected just because they had that value. The posttest values of .478 and 1.850 are actually means of scores that have been free to vary, and all of the effects of error and independence in the relationship between pretest and posttest have been thrown into these posttest means.

We could generate the opposite picture by starting with selected, matched posttest scores of 1.000 and looking for the mean pretest score corresponding to each. While row means have not been graphed in Figures 19.2, 19.3, and 19.4, you can probably confirm by visual inspection that the row (pretest) mean for the Experimental subjects whose posttest score is in the .750 to 1.250 interval is about .505, while that for the Control Group is 1.152. If one were a trapped director of a Head Start program who had to have experimental proof for the worth of a program which he knew on other grounds to be valuable, one could probably package this last result persuasively: "Of children scoring the same at time two, the Head Start children have gained .495 points while the Control children have lost .152." For a growth situation, the actual numerical values of our illustration are of course inappropriate in having pretest and posttest means the same. Normally both groups would have gained. Let us accommodate this by adding 1.000 to all posttest scores. This gets rid of the implausible loss on the part of the Control Group. Now our trapped director can say. "Of children scoring equally on the posttest, the Head Start children have gained 1.495 points, in comparison with a gain of only .848 on the part of the Control children." We recoil at such politically motivated sophistry, yet the analysis itself is no more fallacious than the complementary one we have fallen into inadvertently by matching on the pretest. The resulting implications for social policy might even be regarded as more benign, though neither bias is defensible.

Our simulated case has been based upon the psychometrician's traditional "true score" model. Along with this goes the derivation that a "fallible" ("obtained," "manifest") score is an unbiased estimate of the true score, given the normal definition of error as uncorrelated with true score. But this is correct only for *unselected* scores, that is, for total sets of scores that have been allowed to fall freely. Where scores have been selected *because* of their manifest values, they become biased estimates of true scores in the direction indicated by regression to the mean. Matching and any other classifying for analysis by obtained scores are just such biasing processes.

The magnitude of the pseudo-effect resulting from matching depends upon two parameters: First, the higher the pretest-posttest correlation, the less the regression. In a symmetrical situation such as this, or in a less symmetrical one when expressed in z scores, r directly shows the proportion of regression, or rather of nonregression. If the pretest-posttest correlation were .90, the scores would regress 1/10th of the distance toward the mean. In our simulation, the regression is 1/2 the way to the mean. Second, the larger the difference between group means, the more regression. Verbally stated, the farther the group means are apart, the farther the matched cases will be from their respective means, hence, the more regression. Visually, it is obvious that the larger the mean difference of the two overlapping clouds of tallies in Figure 19.4, the larger the separation between the two parallel plots of column means. In our example, the differences in the means of the two groups is about 2.00, and the regression pseudo-effect concomitant with a .50 correlation is half this, or about 1.00. If the mean difference were 4.00, the regression pseudo-effect would be half of that, or 2.00.

Matching on several variables simultaneously has the same logic and bias. The use of multiple matching variables may reduce the regression artifact, but will not remove it. It reduces it insofar as the multiple correlation of the several matching variables with the posttest is higher than the simple r of a single matching variable. Matching by means of qualitative dimensions or dichotomous variables has an equivalent bias. All such matching variables turn out to be imperfect indicators of the underlying variables we would like to match on. Parents' number of years of schooling have vastly different meanings from school to school, and within the same schools and classrooms. Living in the same neighborhood or block means widely different things as far as the educational quality of the home is concerned. Regression artifacts analogous to those of Figure 19.4 emerge. There is inevitably undermatching, in the sense that the population differences which one is trying to correct by matching are undercorrected by the matching process. The initial matching in the Westinghouse-Ohio University study was of this qualitative nature. This undermatching showed up on the socioeconomic status ratings subsequently made. Had they "corrected" their initial matching by further matching on the socioeconomic ratings, this composite would still have been an imperfect indicator of underlying achievement-ability; there would still have been undermatching, with resulting regression artifacts as in Figure 19.4, in the specific direction of making Head Start look damaging. Even had they had an achievement-ability pretest to match on, as some studies including Follow Through have, matching would produce this erroneous put down.

How can one tell which direction a matching bias will take? Only by having evidence on the nature of the population differences which matching attempted to overcome. Conceivably, in reporting a matching process, the researcher might neglect to say what kind of cases he found hard to get matches for, and what kind of cases existed in surplus in the control population. If so, we could not tell. In the Westinghouse-Ohio University study it *might* have been that matches were easily found for the most disadvantaged Head Start children, and hard to find for the

TABLE 19.1   MEANS OF SIMULATED DATA

	Group	
	Experimental	Control
Pretest	-0.047	1.956
Posttest	0.006	1.961
Population Values	0.000	2.000

TABLE 19.2   STANDARD DEVIATIONS OF SIMULATED DATA

	Group		Pooled Within Groups
	Experimental	Control	
Pretest	1.644	1.602	1.625
Posttest	1.595	1.597	1.597
Population Values	1.414	1.414	1.414

TABLE 19.3   CORRELATION COEFFICIENT BETWEEN PRETEST AND POSTTEST

Group	r
Experimental	.489
Control	.496
Within Groups	.492
Population Value	.500

more advantaged ones: It *might* have been, but it was not. If it had been, then regression artifacts would have artifactually made Head Start look effective. Instead, it seems clear that, generally in the Westinghouse-Ohio University study, it was the most disadvantaged Head Starters who were hard to match and that the controls were selected from generally more able populations. The same direction of matching bias is probably prevalent in many of the small-scale studies of compensatory education also. Whereas it would probably be the case in most fields, as it is in pharmacology (Smith, Traganza and Harrison, 1969), that the less rigorously designed studies show the most favorable effects, it seems to be the reverse in compensatory education studies. For example, McDill, McDill and Sprehe (1969) review eleven studies of compensatory education. Of five using randomly assigned control groups, all show significant gains on some cognitive measures. Of five with quasi-experimental controls, only one shows a significant effect. While an examination of control group selection in each of these cases has not been done, pending that, the most plausible explanation seems to us to be the bias of the superior control group in the quasi-experimental studies.

In situations such as this where control samples are chosen to have pretest scores equaivalent to experimental samples, the question may be asked, "Since the Head Start children are an extreme group, why don't they regress toward the overall population mean just as much as do the matched controls?" Comparable questions emerge when psychotherapy applicants are matched with a control sample chosen to have equally maladjusted test scores (e.g., Campbell and Stanley, 1963; 1966: 11-12, 49-50). Why are these controls expected to regress to the population mean while the therapy applicants are not? An initial answer is that person-to-person matching on individual scores involves the misleading exploitation of score instability phenomena to a much greater degree than do the complex of processes which produced the Head Start sample or the psychotherapy applicants. These groups turn out to be extreme when measured, but were not selected on the basis of their extreme scores. It is selection on the basis of extreme individual scores that creates most strongly the conditions under which obtained scores become biased estimates of true scores.

This is not to deny some small degree of regression toward a mean of all children on the part of the Head Start children. But since the Head Start children were not selected on individual characteristics, but rather as members of neighborhoods or school districts, the degree of such regression would be trivial in magnitude in comparison with that of the control children selected because of individual attributes. The mean test level of the hundred or so children in a neighborhood is a very

stable value compared with the score of a single child. The test-retest correlation for neighborhood average, computed over all of the neighborhoods of a city, will be very high, perhaps as high as .98 or .99, even with tests for which the test-retest correlation for children within a single neighborhood is only .50. These considerations become very confusing in the abstract. But in the applied situation one can tell the direction of the bias by the specific nature of the difficulties one has in finding matches, and by the differences prior to matching in the groups from which the matched cases are sought.

ANALYSIS OF COVARIANCE

The posttest means in our simulation were .006 and 1.961 for the Experimental and Control groups, respectively. The difference, 1.955, when tested by analysis of variance gives $F (1, 998) = 374.31$ which is, of course, statistically significant. Analysis of covariance, a technique commonly prescribed and used in the Westinghouse-Ohio University study to statistically "equate" groups, yields adjusted means of .491 and 1.476 for the two groups. Although the difference between these has been reduced to .985, we obviously have a serious undercorrection which is further demonstrated by the analysis of covariance $F (1, 997) = 90.80$, which is also very large and also statistically significant. The mean difference is of the same general magnitude as that produced by matching, and again, makes the experimental treatment look damaging. Our simulation is like a pretest, rather than a qualitatively different covariate, in that it is in the same metric as the posttest. The principle of undermatching due to error and unique factors in the covariate holds just as inexorably for the case of dissimilar covariates.

This underadjustment by the analysis of covariance has commonly been overlooked, and the resulting bias makes the statistical criticisms of the Westinghouse-Ohio University study by Smith and Bissell (1970) seem trivial in comparison. While we do not have enough information to estimate the magnitude of the bias, we can confidently state its direction on the basis of the reported group differences on the socioeconomic status rating used as a covariate. We can therefore confidently conclude that, had the Head Start programs actually produced no effects whatsoever, the mode of analysis used in the Westinghouse-Ohio University study would have made them look worse than useless, actually harmful.

Porter (1969) has pointed out that, in the Westinghouse-Ohio University tests of Summer Head Start programs, 44 of 56 have outcomes in the direction of Head Start's being worse than nothing, significantly different from a 50-50 split. For the summer programs, apparently, the true gains were not sufficient to overcome the inevitable regression artifacts coming from the fact that controls were selected from a superior population. For one-year programs, on some measures at least, the regression artifacts were overcome, but with the inevitable result that the true effects were underestimated to an unknown degree.

GAIN SCORES

In our particular analysis, with its stationary pretest-posttest structure chosen for a simplicity of presentation, analysis in terms of gain scores would have avoided

TABLE 19.4   MEANS ON POSTTEST ACCORDING TO PRETEST SCORE

Pretest Score	Experimental Group		Control Group	
	n	Posttest Mean	n	Posttest Mean
5.75 − 6.25	0	- - -	1	5.098
5.25 − 5.75	0	- - -	5	3.558
4.75 − 5.25	0	- - -	13	4.375
4.25 − 4.75	2	1.774	21	3.271
3.75 − 4.25	2	.954	27	2.699
3.25 − 3.75	6	2.711	41	2.413
2.75 − 3.25	10	1.625	48	2.485
2.25 − 2.75	23	1.252	64	2.320
1.75 − 2.25	26	.773	55	1.892
1.25 − 1.75	33	.716	60	1.631
.75 − 1.25	57	.478	45	1.850
.25 − .75	64	.293	47	1.029
- .25 − .25	56	.138	30	1.412
- .75 − - .25	50	- .349	25	.611
-1.25 − - .75	54	- .813	7	.114
-1.75 − -1.25	42	- .609	4	1.058
-2.25 − -1.75	35	- .583	4	- .340
-2.75 − -2.25	20	- .631	2	- .076
-3.25 − -2.75	6	-1.643	0	- - -
-3.75 − -3.25	5	-1.868	1	-2.205
-4.25 − -3.75	4	-2.564	0	- - -
-4.75 − -4.25	3	-1.566	0	- - -

the regression artifacts which both matching and analysis of covariance generated. Applied as a t test of the difference between the mean gain scores of the total Experimental Group versus the mean gain score of the total Control Group, such an analysis would have shown no effect. As can be seen from Figure 19.1, these means would be equal, both being essentially zero. (A comparison of gain scores for only the overlapping parts of the distributions would, of course, be biased, as described under Matching.) However, gain scores are in general such a treacherous quicksand, for example, are so noncomparable for high versus low scorers within any single sample, that one is reluctant to recommend them for any purpose. More important here is that, for the setting of compensatory education, the use of gain scores would involve an assumption that is certainly wrong. Again, the bias would be to make Head Start look damaging.

In a growth situation, unlike our simulation, the posttest mean would be higher than the pretest mean, for both Experimental and Control groups, and this would be so whether or not the treatment had an effect. In this situation, the crucial assumption of gain score analysis is that the absolute amount gained would have been the same for both Experimental and Control pupils under the condition of no treatment effect. This assumption is inconsistent with the fact that the groups differ at the time of the pretest. That difference no doubt is there because of a previously more rapid rate of growth on the part of the Control Group, which would be expected to continue during the period of the experimental treatment. Figure 19.5 illustrates the situation.

TABLE 19.5 MEANS ON PRETEST ACCORDING TO POSTTEST SCORE

	Experimental Group		Control Group	
Posttest Score	n	Pretest Mean	n	Pretest Mean
6.25 − 6.75	0	- - -	1	2.877
5.75 − 6.25	0	- - -	3	4.459
5.25 − 5.75	0	- - -	4	4.406
4.75 − 5.25	1	3.266	14	3.153
4.25 − 4.75	0	- - -	16	3.746
3.75 − 4.25	2	2.036	25	2.762
3.25 − 3.75	3	1.719	51	2.719
2.75 − 3.25	14	1.420	41	2.407
2.25 − 2.75	21	1.790	52	2.256
1.75 − 2.25	29	.164	75	1.916
1.25 − 1.75	48	.340	52	1.862
.75 − 1.25	50	.505	57	1.152
.25 − .75	57	.623	37	1.338
- .25 − .25	57	- .048	27	1.143
- .75 − - .25	52	- .101	21	1.209
-1.25 − - .75	54	- .719	15	.841
-1.75 − -1.25	42	- .506	4	-1.102
-2.25 − -1.75	26	-1.281	5	- .771
-2.75 − -2.25	22	-1.623	0	- - -
-3.25 − -2.75	15	-1.259	0	- - -
-3.75 − -3.25	2	-1.971	0	- - -
-4.25 − -3.75	4	-3.325	0	- - -
-4.75 − -4.25	1	-1.966	0	- - -

In Figure 19.5 we have the growth curves for the two groups under the condition of no treatment effect. Between the ages of 4 and 5 when a treatment was given, the Control Group increased 8 units in ability while the Experimental Group increased only 4 units. This would result in an interpretation of a decrement of 4 units due to the treatment received by the Experimental Group. If a true treatment effect was actually present, it would be underestimated to the same degree. (Ommitted in this reprinting is a 4 page section on Lord's [1960] and Porter's [1967] reliability-corrected covariance adjustments.)

BIASING PROCEDURES THAT COULD MAKE HEAD START LOOK GOOD

Selecting a control group from a generally more advantaged population has made Head Start look bad. Selecting a control from a generally less able population would make it look good. There are so many combinations of conditions that would produce this bias that we may be sure it has occurred in many studies. One could make Head Start voluntary, advertising its availability, then select as controls those non-Head Start children who eventually turn up at school from the same tenements and blocks as do the Head Start alumni. In this process, the control group would probably have mothers of lower contact with community information sources and of less concern for their child's school achievement. Or one could select as controls those who initially enrolled but who attended less than one fourth of the sessions. If we look to the probable biases in quasi-experimental evaluations of

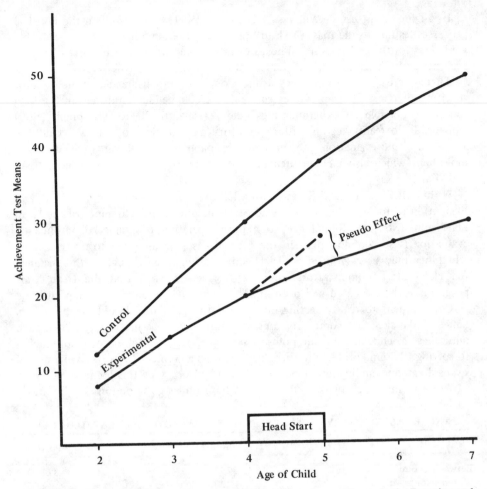

FIGURE 19.5   Pseudo effect generated by assuming the same growth rate in the Experimental Group as in a superior Control Group.

the "Sesame Street" preschooler's educational television program, they will no doubt be in this direction. In any given neighborhood, it will be the more competent homes that know of the program's existence, and make certain that their children get to see it.

SOCIAL SCIENCE'S UNREADINESS FOR APPLIED QUASI-EXPERIMENTAL EVALUATION

It is tragic that the social experiment evaluation most cited by presidents, most influential in governmental decision making, should have contained such a misleading bias. The technical and political background of this error needs discussion, particularly since it involves so much that is correct and forward looking, and has produced extremely important social experiments such as the New Jersey negative income tax experiment.

In an important essay, Williams and Evans (1969) have described the political processes leading to the massive Head Start evaluation, and have provided valuable guidelines for the proper political postures to be taken when, as must often happen, accurate evaluations show specific ameliorative programs to be ineffective.

There were political pressures from Congress for hardheaded evaluation of specific programs. These pressures can only be commended, and may in the long run make possible an experimenting society (Haworth, 1960; Campbell, 1969) which will do reality testing with exploratory modifications of its own structure. These program evaluation pressures are probably the most valuable part of a movement which also includes demands for more generalized "social indicators" and "data banks."

Within OEO the demand for evaluation led the Office of Planning, Research, and Evaluation to force evaluation of Head Start in spite of the reluctance of the Head Start administrators. Reluctance to expose operating programs to hardheaded evaluation is so common that, in the general case, a willingness to override such reluctance may be essential for social reality testing, even though in this instance the Head Start administrators were right, given the fact that the Head Start programs to be evaluated had been initiated without randomization or pretesting.

Commitment to reality testing on ameliorative programs should involve acceptance of the fact that some programs will turn out to be ineffective. When such outcomes are encountered, the political system should seek alternative approaches to solving the same problem, rather than abandon all remedial efforts. Williams and Evans do an outstanding job of clarification and advocacy on this point.

We academics are apt to assume that, where things go wrong in collaborations

TABLE 19.6 SUMMARY OF ANALYSES OF VARIANCE ON SIMULATED DATA

	Pretest	Posttest
Between Groups F	379.93	374.31
Within Groups MS	2.640	2.552
Within Groups df	998	998
Point Biserial r	.525	.522

TABLE 19.7 SUMMARY OF ANALYSES OF COVARIANCE ON SIMULATED DATA

	Type of Analysis	
	Usual	True Score
Adjusted Means		
Experimental Group	0.491	.991
Control Group	1.476	.976
Between Groups F	90.80	.01
Adjusted		
Within Groups MS	1.935	1.935
Within Groups df	997	997

between the political and scholarly communities, the failure comes from the political process, in the form of a failure to make use of our more than adequate wisdom. In this instance it was quite the reverse. As outlined in the preceding paragraphs, the political forces were positive, and if they survive or can be revived, are such as to make possible a reality-testing society. In this instance, the failure came from the inadequacies of the social science methodological community (including education, psychology, economics, and sociology) which as a population was not ready for this task. The one weakness in Williams and Evans' otherwise outstanding paper comes at this point. They state that ex post facto studies are a respected and widely used scientific procedure. While it would be hard to find any text since Chapin (1955) that has advocated them, most methodology texts are silent on the issue and condone comparable procedures. They cite "matching" as though it achieved its purpose. Warnings against matching as a substitute for randomization occur in a few texts, but probably 90% of social scientists teaching methodology at U.S. universities would approve the process. On using analysis of covariance to correct for pretreatment differences, the texts that treat the issue are either wrong or noncommital (that is, fail to specify the direction of bias), and probably 99% of experts who know of the procedure would make the error of recommending it. Note again that the competitive reanalysis of the Westinghouse-Ohio University data by Smith and Bissell (1970) repeats the original error in this regard. The prestige of complex multivariate statistics and their associated computer programs will perpetuate such mistakes for years to come, under such terms as dummy variable analysis, multiple covariate analysis of covariance, step-wise multiple regression, and the like. The deep-rooted seat of the bias is probably the unexplicit trust that, although the assumptions of a given statistic are technically not met, the effects of these departures will be unsystematic. The reverse is, in fact, true. The more one needs the "controls" and "adjustments" which these statistics seem to offer, the more biased are their outcomes.

THE CASE FOR TRUE EXPERIMENTS IN FUTURE EVALUATION OF COMPENSATORY EDUCATION

There are other possible quasi-experimental designs which avoid the biases here described although none are available for the data to which the Westinghouse-Ohio University study was limited. In a school system with good records of annual testings in the lower grades, a time series of such testings might be employed retrospectively (Campbell, 1970). Longitudinal studies which include some Head Start children offer another possibility (Campbell, 1969b). Looking to the future, by making explicit in quantified detail a policy of giving Head Start opportunity to the most needy, one could create Regression Discontinuity designs (Thistlethwaite and Campbell, 1960; Campbell, 1969a, 1969b) at the individual or school district level. Where highly similar pretests are available, where test-retest correlations are similar for experimentals and controls, and where the assumptions of homogeneous mean and variance growth are tenable, Lord's and Porter's common-factor covariance adjustments may be used with caution. But are there compelling reasons to limit ourselves to quasi-experimental designs when true experiments involving randomization would be so much more informative?

There are problems, of course, with randomization experiments. Randomization at the invitational level avoids the disappointment problem generated by randomly allocating eager applicants to the control condition. But it exaggerates the always present problem of experimental mortality inasmuch as not all those randomly invited accept the treatment. Using only those invited who accept as the experimental group produces a selection bias with favorable pseudo-effects. The unbiased solution of treating all those randomly assigned as though treated dilutes experimental effects, but is at present the recommended solution (Campbell and Stanley, 1963; 1966: 15-16). More sensitive and yet still unbiased procedures focusing on an upper edge of the experimental and control distributions rather than the whole are feasible (Campbell, 1965) and can be further developed. Randomization by neighborhoods or school districts rather than by individuals is an acceptable solution with superior external validity, but again *all* eligible children in the experimental areas must be compared with all eligible children in the control areas. While one can estimate what the magnitude of the effect would be if one could remove the dilution coming from including the untreated, the tests of significance must be made on the full samples created by randomization. These same strictures, however, apply to most quasi-experimental designs, and in particular to the very attractive Regression Discontinuity analysis.

Even though "true" experiments in the field setting are on these grounds more "quasi" than those in the laboratory, (and those in the laboratory more "quasi" than published reports and statistical treatments indicate), experiments with randomized assignment to treatments are greatly to be preferred where possible. We believe that any investigator fully attending to the presumptions he is making in using quasi-experimental designs will prefer the random assignment of children to treatments *where this is possible.*

Social ameliorative changes which are applied or made available to everyone do not readily permit the creation of control groups. These include across-the-board legal changes and television broadcasts. But those expensive remediations which are in short supply and which cannot be given everyone provide settings in which true experiments are readily possible. Once the decision makers in government and applied research are educated to their importance, they can become the standard evaluational procedure.

On the other hand, we must not create a political climate which demands that no ameliorative efforts be made unless they can be evaluated. There will be many things obviously worth doing which cannot be experimentally evaluated, and which should still be done. The shift to new math is an example. By making math achievement tests inappropriate it undermined the only convenient benchmark for its own evaluation. College education is another example, a boon for which we have almost no interpretable experimental or quasi-experimental evidence. (Since college education is given to those who need it least, the regression artifacts are biased to make it look effective.) We applied social methodologists should be alert to recognize such cases and not assume that every new program must be and can be evaluated.

On the other hand, where we can experiment and where the social costs of such experimentation are outweighed by the social value of reality testing, we should hold out for the least biased, most informative procedures.

There exist in administrators, researchers, legislators, and the general public "ethical" reluctances to random assignment. These center around a feeling that the control group is being deprived of a precious medicine it badly needs. But if it be recognized that the supposed boon is in fact in short supply, then it can be seen that the experiment has not increased the number so deprived, but has instead reassigned some of that deprivation so that the ethical value of knowing may be realized. Is randomization as the mode of such reassignment ethically defensible? It might represent an ethical cost (one nonetheless probably worth paying) if all the children in the nation had been rank ordered on need, and those most needy given the compensatory education up to the budgetary and staff limits of the program. But instead, the contrast is with a very haphazard and partially arbitrary process which contains unjust inversions of order of need far more extensive than a randomization experiment involving a few thousand children would entail. These unjust deprivations are normally not forced to our attention, and so do not trouble our ethical sensitivities as does the deprivation of the control group. But there is no genuine ethical contrast here.

Within randomization, there are some designs and stances that may ease any residual ethical burden. For example, the randomization could be limited to the boundary zone, at the least needy edge of those to be treated, and the most needy edge of the untreated. For this narrow band of children, all considered as essentially tied at the cutting point on a coarse grained eligibility score, random assignment to treatment and nontreatment could be justified as a tie-breaking process. We would learn about the effects of the program only for a narrow band of talent. We would wonder about its effectiveness for the most disadvantaged. But this would be better than nothing, and better than quasi-experimental information.

The funds set aside for evauation are funds taken away from treatment. This cost-benefit trade-off decision has already been made when quasi-experimental evaluation has been budgeted, or when funds are committed to any form of budgeting and accounting. Taking these evaluational funds, one could use nine-tenths of them for providing experimental expansions of compensatory instruction, one-tenth for measurement of effects on the small experimental and control samples thus created. Here the ethical fucus could be on the lucky boon given to the experimentals. Since evaluation money would be used to expand treatment, the controls would not be deprived. In retrospect, we are sure that data from 400 children in such an experiment would be far more informative than those from the 4,000 tested by the best of quasi-experiments, to say nothing of an ex post facto study.

REFERENCES

Campbell, D. T. Invited therapy in an archival or institutional-records setting: with comments on the problem of turndowns. Duplicated memorandum, Northwestern University, August 1965. 13 pp.

–––. Reforms as experiments. *American Psychologist,* 1969, 24(4): 409-429. (a)

–––. Treatment-effect correlations and temporal attenuation of relationships in longitudinal studies. Duplicated memorandum, Northwestern University, December 1969. 15 pp. (b)

–––. Time-series of annual same-grade testings in the evaluation of compensatory educational experiments. Duplicated memorandum, Northwestern University, April 1970.

––– and K. N. Clayton. Avoiding regression effects in panel studies of communication impact. *Studies in public communication,* Department of Sociology, University of Chicago, 1961, no. 3, 99-118. Bobbs-Merrill Reprint No. S-353.

Campbell, D. T. and J. C. Stanley. Experimental and quasi-experimental designs for research on teaching. Pp. 171-246 in N. L. Gage (ed.) *Handbook of research on teaching.* Chicago: Rand McNally, 1963. Reprinted as *Experimental and quasi-experimental design for research.* Chicago: Rand McNally, 1966. Paper.

Chapin, F. S. *Experimental designs in sociological research.* Rev. ed.; New York: Harper, 1955.

Cicirelli, V., et al. *The impact of Head Start: An evaluation of the effects of Head Start on children's cognitive and affective development.* A report presented to the Office of Economic Opportunity pursuant to Contract B89-4536, June 1969. Westinghouse Learning Corporation, Ohio University. Distributed by: Clearinghouse for Federal Scientific and Technical Information, U.S. Department of Commerce, National Bureau of Standards, Institute for Applied Technology. PB 184 328.

Evans, S. H. and E. J. Anastasio. Misuse of analysis of covariance when treatment effect and covariate are confounded. *Psychological Bulletin,* 1968, 69: 225-234.

Haworth, L. The experimental society: Dewey and Jordan. *Ethics,* 1960, 71(1): 27-40.

Hovland, C. L., A. A. Lumsdaine and F. D. Sheffield. *Experiments on mass communication.* Princeton, N.J.: Princeton University Press, 1949.

Lord, F. M. Large-scale covariance analysis when the control variable is fallible. *Journal of the American Statistical Association,* 1960, 55: 307-321.

Lord, F. M. A paradox in the interpretation of group comparisons, *Psychological Bulletin,* 1967, 68, 304-305.

–––. Statistical adjustments when comparing preexisting groups. *Psychological Bulletin,* 1969, 72: 336-337.

McDill, E. L., M. S. McDill and J. Sprehe. *Strategies for success in compensatory education: An appraisal of evaluation research.* Baltimore: Johns Hopkins Press, 1969.

McNemar, Q. A critical examination of the University of Iowa studies of environmental influences upon the I.Q. *Psychological Bulletin,* 1940, 37: 63-92.

–––. *Psychological Statistics.* New York: Wiley, 1949; 4th ed., 1969.

Peters, C. C. and W. R. Van Voorhis. *Statistical procedures and their mathematical bases.* New York: McGraw Hill, 1940.

Porter, A. C. *The effects of using fallible variables in the analysis of covariance.* Ph.D. dissertation, University of Wisconsin, June 1967. University Microfilms, Ann Arbor, Mich., 1968.

–––. Comments on some current strategies to evaluate the effectiveness of compensatory education programs, and Comments on the Westinghouse-Ohio University study. Two memoranda prepared for Robert D. Hess for use at the Symposium on "The effectiveness of contemporary education programs in the early years: Reports from three national evaluations and longitudinal studies." Annual Meeting of the American Psychological Association, Washington, D.C., August 31, 1969.

Smith, A., E. Traganza and G. Harrison. Studies on the effectiveness of antidepressant drugs. *Psychopharmacology Bulletin,* 1969 (March): 1-53.

Smith, M. S. and J. S. Bissell. Report analysis: The impact of Head Start. *Harvard Educational Review,* 1970, 40(1): 51-104.

Thistlethwaite, D. L. and D. T. Campbell. Regression-discontinuity analysis: an alternative to the ex post facto experiment. *Journal of Educational Psychology,* 1960, 51: 309-317.

Thorndike, R. L. Regression fallacies in the matched groups experiment. *Psychometrika,* 1942, 7: 85-102.

Walker, H. M. and J. Lev. *Statistical inference.* New York: Holt, Rinehart & Winston, 1953.

Werts, C. E. and R. L. Linn. Analysing school effects: ancova with a fallible covariate. Research Bulletin #69-59, Educational Testing Service, July 1969. In press, *Educational and Psychological Measurement.*

Williams, W. and J. W. Evans. The politics of evaluation: the case of head start. *The Annals,* 1969, 385 (September): 118-132.

Winer, B. J. *Statistical principles in experimental design.* New York: McGraw-Hill, 1962.

VIII

COMMUNICATION OF EVALUATION RESULTS

20

THE UTILIZATION OF EVALUATION

HOWARD R. DAVIS
and
SUSAN E. SALASIN

Appropriate utilization of evaluation can be a comfortable assumption if taken within the concepts of the cybernetic vision of the purposively guided society. In that vision a person at the helm reads the compass bearing, notes the degrees of departure from the desired course, and turns the wheel the required number of spokes to bring bearing into line with course. To carry further Campbell and Converse's analogy, the evaluator is, on more complex "vessels" of social programs, the navigator if not the helmsperson, who at least "must have a goal, current bearings, and contextual understanding of the forces about" (1972: 9). But can it be assumed, in the hurly-burly world of social program organizations, that feedback from the compas to the helm will lead to optimum fidelity between compass readings and wheel action?

CLEAR READINGS; OBSCURE ACTIONS

Evaluative data on an innovative furlough program adopted by a District of Columbia correctional institution indicate that barely 1% of inmates violate furlough in the program. Is the consequence community support for the innovation?

Within a federal applied research grant program, an evaluation of the utilization of project results indicates that only 11% are in use off the original site one year after project termination. Is corrective action quickly adopted?

Two evaluations of the Work Incentive (WIN) program of HEW indicate that the local welfare departments are not expanding the WIN program because to do so would demand substantial new funds. Is that barrier addressed?

A detailed study of the Emergency School Assistance Program showed that it

has little immediate impact on attitudes about desegregation and the smoothness of the desegregation process. Are changes made to render the program more effective?

The impact of community mental health centers on the reduction of state hospital populations is examined. The evaluation finds that there are no great differences in resident rates between those catchment areas served by CMHC's and those which are not, when pre-CMHC data for each catchment area are statistically controlled. Do new policies and practices ensure a greater impact?

Actions on evaluation results vary as do evaluations themselves: sometimes its neglect; sometimes controversy; sometimes misuse. And sometimes disregard of invalid results is a warranted action. But sometimes—perhaps more commonly than we have an opportunity to see—consequent actions are precisely and effectively appropriate.

We will attempt to examine the winds and currents, the array of forces, impinging on evaluation utilization, consider an approach to predicting their influence on a given evaluation, and propose a guideline for use by evaluators who may wish to enhance even further their contributions to the destinies of the cause they serve.

OBSERVATIONS ON THE STATE OF EVALUATION UTILIZATION

Evaluation results do achieve appropriate utilization. Richardson (1972) offers one example. Evaluation of the National Defense Education Act loans to students who undertake a career in teaching suggested that this had not been a significant incentive. It was possible to conclude, with the concurrence of the Congress, that the feature should be eliminated, and it was. Lynn (1972) gives further illustrations of HEW utilization of evaluations of major programs, ranging from evaluations of the utilization of health care services to an array of educational assistance programs. Effective utilization of evaluation among federal agencies was reported by Riecker (1974) when those agencies participated in the evaluation. Beigel (1974) illustrates how local program self-evaluations can have meaningful impact on policies and practices. Both Weiss (1972) and Ciarlo (1974) stress that the evidence of effective utilization of evaluation becomes much clearer if one maintains observation over a sufficiently extended period.

Indeed, There May be Overutilization of Some Evaluation

Mushkin (1973) has called attention to numerous instances of well-known evaluations of major programs which were methodologically or conceptually unsound. In some instances decisions to terminate or reduce programs have been justified on the basis of those evaluations. It is a clear lesson that concern over utilization must emphasize *appropriate* use rather than just greater use.

Evaluators Sometimes Face the "Oppenheimer Risk"

Weiss (1973) has pointed out that evaluators who may be progressive in their orientations and dedicated to the growth and improvement of human services may find their work being used to justify sharply conservative predecisions resulting in cutback, rather than improvement, of social programs.

The Nature of Evaluations Determines Utilization to a Significant Extent

Summative evaluations, where the investigator is asking the question "Does this program work or not?" are quite similar to research enterprises. These may not have theoretical relevance; nevertheless, their utilization routes tend to follow those of other applied research results. Consequently, there may be less concern on the part of the evaluator about the adoption of the results within the host agency. In formative evaluations, where the evaluator is asking the question "How may this program be improved?" the payoff from the endeavor is entirely dependent upon the assimilation of the results within the agency in focus.

Compliance control evaluations would seem, on the surface, to lead toward more immediate utilization of results. When a site visit is made by a certifying body to check for compliance with standards, the incentive is quite great to bring things into shape. Similarly, if utilization review finds that practices are substandard and therefore third party payments are cut off, motivation to correct the practice should be high. The trouble with compliance control evaluation utilization is that it does not assure effective outcome in terms of consumer benefits. Furthermore, some people in service programs become highly skilled in compliant noncompliance. Utilization of the evaluation may be more apparent than real when it is mandated by authority.

The same may hold true with respect to evaluations carried out by supra-ordinate agencies without collaborative involvement of the people representing the program being evaluated. For a six-month period, clippings were made of news items on higher federal agency evaluations as they appeared in the *Washington Post*. With almost formula-like precision the paragraph just before the middle of the article was devoted to disparagement of the evaluation report by a spokesman for the evaluated agency. Again, there can be no question that a display of compliance must be exhibited in those circumstances. But from what is known about the ineffectiveness of most mandated organizational change, there is reason to wonder whether supra evaluations achieve the best utilization possible. It may be leading a horse to water.

Fuddling: A Never-Fail Response to Evaluation Feedback

President Kennedy once expressed his frustration over the fact that even Presidential Orders were so commonly fed into the "Federal Fuddle Factory" never to be heard of again, at least not in recognizable form. Fuddling is an ancient and revered skill as seen by many of us who consider ourselves accomplished bureaucrats. When addressing evaluation results, the skilled fudder would not deign to contest or criticize the report. She or he may feign cheerful assimilation of the implied recommendations, but try and prove it has not been done. One who loves the art may engage in protracted exchanges of requests for, and attempts at, clarification. Your mere everyday fuddler will assume a countenance of glassy obscurity if the subject of the evaluation comes up. We do not mean to treat this phenomenon too lightly. It quite probably amounts to a great loss of the potential benefits that could be realized from evaluation. On the other hand, the quality of so many evaluations in the past has been such as to render this happening a merciful one.

Evaluations of Evaluations: Too Rare

It is unfortunate that evaluations of evaluation utilization are rare. One study reported by Windle and Volkman (1973) provides some reason for optimism, at least insofar as utilization of self-evaluation in community mental health centers is concerned. Of 189 centers responding to their survey, 70% reported a total of 249 program changes resulting from evaluation activities. Eight percent of those changes led to the elimination or reduction of practices; 21% led to expansion; 31% led to the development of new practices; and 40% resulted in change of policies or practices. (136 centers failed to respond.) The most common type of evaluation activities was monitoring center service process; the next most common was measuring changes in clients, followed by assessing efficiency, evaluation by others, assessing incidents or prevalence of mental illness, evaluation of community attitudes, and client-involved assessment, in that order.

SIGNIFICANCE OF UTILIZATION IN THE EVALUATION FIELD

Growth of interest and faith in evaluation over the past few years has been unparalleled. As community advisory and control boards have pressed for accountability evaluations, requests for technical assistance in establishing evaluation within local facilities have climbed steeply.

At the federal level evaluation of programs almost invariably has been a requirement within enactments of social programs. For example, in the anticipated legislation on a new community mental health centers act not only would national-level evaluation continue to be required but each center would dedicate 2% of its grant funds to its own program evaluation.

For the past two years, surveys of the needs of community mental health centers reveal that program evaluation was the topic above all others, about which further information was needed.

When *Evaluation* magazine was launched in 1972, the anticipation was that the readership would amount to approximately 5,000 at the most. Two years later it has climbed to 30,000.

Training and orientation programs in evaluation have been subscribed to with enthusiasm. The Conference on Evaluation in Alcohol, Drug Abuse and Mental Health Programs held in April 1974 was planned for 400 participants. The Conference was expanded to include 750 with an additional 200 applicants turned down prior to the meeting because of space limitations.

New persons coming into the field seem to have little doubt about the potential of evaluation in contributing to the fulfillment of hopes and expectancies of the many beneficiaries of social programs. But neither do they seem to question the assumption that effective utilization can be taken for granted. At a national workshop held in Florida in spring of 1974, the group of new persons to the field of evaluation preferred not to have time consumed by a consideration of utilization techniques.

At the conference on evaluation referred to, Dr. Jack Zusman, co-organizer of the conference, announced his prediction that evaluation would turn out to be a

current fad. If that proves true, one contributing factor may be a disenchantment among veteran evaluators, one growing out of evidence that appropriate utilization does not invariably follow evaluation.

Attkisson and coworkers (1973) visited more than 60 community mental health centers. They observed a generalized sentiment that "evaluation activities would not result in a net gain in program effectiveness. The consequences of this state of affairs is that managers are reluctant to invest resources necessary to effect a workable evaluation strategy, and evaluators often feel demoralized and unsupported in their roles" (Attkisson, 1973: 6).

Weiss (1973a) visited a sample of research evaluators originally for the purpose of discussing with them methodological problems in program evaluation. However, she found their frustration so great that they preferred to discuss their problems of personal relationships in their facilities rather than methodological ones. One interviewee expressed it this way: "[The project administrator] said, 'Educate me,' but he didn't sit still. He believed in research, he thought it should be done, but he had no understanding of how he should back it up or administer a combined service-research program. When I reported findings . . . he listened to me (I don't think he did more than glance at anything I'd written), but he didn't do anything about implementing the results" (Weiss, 1973a: 51).

An evaluator, who has been responsible for nearly $3 million worth of contract evaluations and who has engaged in intensive evaluation of his own, lamented to us recently that he was finding little professional satisfaction in his current work. His primary frustration stemmed from the futility of his efforts; there seemed to be so little response to the findings he supplied. As is the case with many evaluators, "Dr. A" came into the field of evaluation from research. He had gained wide respect through his many publications on the topic of personality development of a specific age group. His decision to dedicate himself to program evaluation was based upon the understandable belief that even more professional significance would be realized in that pursuit. But things turned out differently: his research studies bore theoretical relevance and accommodated his creative concepts; by contrast, his evaluation studies deal with largely ungeneralizable matters, directed by policy-makers rather than, by contrast, his own creativity. Results of his research studies were readily publishable; results of his evaluation studies seldom find open doors to publication. On reporting his research findings he received accolades from his colleagues; by contrast, on reporting evaluation studies he is apt to draw captious attacks on his methods. His research findings were used by other scientists; by contrast, he feels his evaluation findings rarely are used by anybody. In general, as he experiences it, the response to his dedicated endeavors has changed from approbation to opprobrium. Dr. A's laments describe contrasts experienced commonly by evaluators who have ventured away from the green fields of scientific discovery toward the jungle of organizational performance. It may be worth the hardships if the payoff in social significance of one's work is realized; without that, why live in the jungle?

A portion of the apparent demoralization among veteran evaluators may be attributed to the slow process of utilization of evaluation results. In the eyes of

others, many of Dr. A's findgings are highly significant in guiding policies and practices. But for many months, his findings have been underground and waiting marriage with other determinants of change, only now reemerging in different costumes. Ciarlo (1974) reports that he, too, had reached the conclusion that evaluation results were generally ignored. But after continued close observation of the careers of his findings, he is learning that a time period of about nine months must pass before things begin to happen that can be traced to the evaluation effort. Even then decision-makers may not have conscious awareness of where the seeds of change were sown.

The findings of Windle and Volkman (1973), with respect to the report of high utilization rates from community mental health center evaluators, appears on the surface to be inconsistent with Attkisson's findings about demoralization among evaluators in centers. That suggests it may be important for evaluators to modify their expectations about both the timing and form of the utilization of their results. Also, perhaps better tracer evaluations of evaluation utilization itself would offer more reinforcement to evaluators.

A second suggestion is that evaluators might extend the range of their roles to encompass change consultation.

THE NEED FOR AN EVALUATOR/CHANGE CONSULTANT ROLE

Evaluation and planned change would seem to travel hand in hand. Yet it is mystifying to see how players in each group exclude the other. Very few persons straddle both specialties. This is reflected in the results of a little exercise we carried out recently: Among 600 references on evaluation, only 5% pertained to utilization, even under the broadest interpretation of that technology. But even worse, a review of 1,200 references on utilization contained only 2 1/2% which pertained to evaluation, again even in the broadest sense. It is as difficult to see how planned change can be carried out without evaluation as it is to understand how evaluation can realize its potential without consideration of planned change.

There are problems, to be sure, in asking the evaluator to extend her or his role in this direction. As Campbell (1973) has said, "academics continue to be reluctant to get involved in evaluation research." How much greater might be their reluctance to venture beyond that into the territory of utilitarianism! But Suchman (1962) wrote: "While this debate [relative to the evaluator becoming involved in action] may have a certain legitimacy in regard to nonevaluative research, it seems to us academic when it comes to evaluation studies." Buchanan and Wholey (1972) say it another way: "Evaluators, and critics of evaluation, must move from their present pre-occupation with evaluation as an end in itself and begin to think in terms of evaluation as part of policy planning and management systems."

We are not advocating that evaluators take up the cudgels to see that their own recommendations are adopted. There may, however, be some who feel that way. (At a program evaluation meeting in Colorado, one experienced, but perhaps frustrated, evaluator proposed that studies be undertaken only on the condition

that the decision-makers agree beforehand to utilize the results as they emerged!). Guiding decision-makers in effective utilization of evaluation results would not seem to violate scientific values. Consideration of the determinants of utilization in designing evaluation hardly would create a value conflict at all. Even if evaluators were to extend their roles, significant benefits in the contributions of evaluators would be yielded.

Beyond the barrier of traditional value assumptions, others may loom in front of the evaluator considering change consultation:

(1) To employ a specific technique in deliberately bringing about change may be seen as just too Orwellian. Oh, if only the technique to be proposed were that effective! It may nudge the probability of desired change up a few percentage points, but "control" is hardly a threat. Further, anyone who institutes a new policy or practice must do the same; somehow we like to tell ourselves acceptance of change is a natural response to its goodness. The management of factors determining change must take place if it is to occur, even though employment of a technique may be denied. The overriding factor in most instances of change is power. What planned change techniques offer is an alignment of the other factors which will render the change more salutary concerned. (What comes to mind here is the state mental health director in the Midwest who announced he would fire a group of psychologists unless they stopped controlling people with those behavior modification techniques).

(2) Planned change is a poor second to power in modifying policies and practices. Power—of authority, of money, of whatever the "changee' must reckon with—is by far the most prominent instrument of change. Parents use it over children, teachers over students, employers over employees, the rich over the poor, and so on.

The change consultant may find her or his skills not altogether welcomed by some captains-of-the-ship who have been accustomed to a much quicker change model, the I-say-you-do one. But as Davis (1973) has described, change induced by power may have its problems, however underground and delayed they might be. But convincing decision-makers of this is often a difficult task. Furthermore, adopting change that specifically has been called for in evaluation results may restrict the decision-maker's degrees of freedom in responding to the multitude of persuaders within her or his organization.

(3) Planned change is hard! That was the Number One Principle listed by Fairweather and coworkers (1974) after what may be the most intensive experiment on planned change attempted so far in the human services field. There are no quick tricks in planned change. The reward of seeing desired consequences comes only after sustained effort, practice and belief in what one is about have been liberally injected into the process.

Fortunately, the reward of seeing evaluation results utilized in the service of program beneficiaries is great. Furthermore, despite the caveat about unconvinced decision-makers, the demand for consultants on planned change is growing from several quarters. The evaluator who encompasses such skills will quite surely

experience an increased sense of service. The following descriptions may serve as examples of approaches to organizing the abundant information on planned change.

Five Research-Development-Dissemination-Utilization (RDDU) Models

Five models of the RDDU process have received notable attention in the literature. The first three to be described have been set forth by Havelock (1969), among others, and the last two by Sashkin, Morris, and Horst (1973), also among others.

(a) The first is the *research, development, and diffusion model.* This model assumes there is a relatively passive target audience of consumers which will accept an innovation if it is delivered through a suitable medium, in the right way, at the right time. It calls for a rational sequence of activities from research to development to packaging before dissenimantion takes place. It assumes large scale planning, and requires a division of labor and a separation of roles and functions. Evaluation is particularly emphasized in this model, in which there is a high initial development cost and which anticipates a high payoff in terms of the quantity and quality of long-range benefit through its capacity to reach a mass audience.

(b) The second is the *social interaction model,* which is more sensitive to the complex and intricate set of human relationships, substructures and processes that are involved in the dissemination phase, and which stresses the importance of face-to-face contacts. This model implies that a user can hold a variety of positions in the communication network, and that people tend to adopt and maintain attitudes and behavior which they perceive as normative for their psychological reference group. The size of the adopting group is basically irrelevant in this model, which follows essentially the process stages of knowledge and research diffusion, with appropriate influencing strategies used at each stage.

(c) Third is the *problem-solving model,* which starts with the user's needs as a beginning point for research, with diagnosis as an essential first step in the search for solutions. The outside helper, or change agent, in this model, is largely non-directive, mainly guiding the potential user through his own problem-solving processes and encouraging him to utilize internal resources. The model assumes that self-initiated and directed change has the firmest motivation and hence the best prospect for maintenance.

(d) In the fourth model, the *planned change model,* information is considered useful only if it leads to action, and is shared between the change agent and the client. The assumptive basis of this model is that change occurs through a consciously controlled sequential and continuous process of data generation, planning, and implementation. The changes made need to be stabilized and supported.

(e) The fifth model is the *action research model.* Although similar in some respects to the problem solving and planned change models, it is most distinctive in emphasizing the development of research within the organiza-

tion. The type of research and its methodology are influenced by its concurrent conduct with the ongoing activity of the organization. The results of the research, while primarily intended for the organization itself, may prove useful to others and contribute to behavioral science itself. The model assumes the action research to be a continuous process of research, action, evaluation, and more research.

All five of the models may entail the use of a consultant. External data sources are used in the first two models. The problem-solving model uses internal data sources. The last two models employ both external and internal sources.

Training is not likely to be included in the first model, may well be included in the second, and is clearly included in the last three models.

Research activities are possible in the first and second models, but not necessarily included. Research by the client is a possible component of the problem-solving model. Planned change includes a limited form of research. The action reserach model includes several forms of research, including the evaluation of the change program, the evaluation of the change agent's functioning, and the study of the change process itself.

The Problem-Solving Dialogue Model. The *problem-solving dialogue model,* described in detail in Havelock and Lingwood (1973), builds on a problem-solving and a linkage approach to yield a highly comprehensive framework for analyzing a research development, dissemination, and utilization system.

Basically, the model may be described quite simply in terms of four components: (1) the client or *user system,* represented diagrammatically by a circle at the right; (2) the knowledge or research *resource system,* represented by a circle at the left; (3) a *need-processing system,* represennted by an arrow leading from the user system to the resource system; and (4) a *solution-processing system,* represented by an arrow leading from the resource system to the user system. The first two, it may be noted, are problem-solving systems; the last two represent the dialogue between the first two.

One may designate the system as a whole, with all the relationships among the subsystems depicted above, as the province of *macrosystem building.* The process is termed *microsystem building* when one considers actions in which many elements of the problem-solving dialogue are present simultaneously and are permitted to interact on a small scale.

Each of the components of the total dialogue system can be analyzed in great detail, according to one's purpose. Correspondingly, any real-life system can be described in terms of the dialogue system, elaborated to any degree or expressed in any appropriate manner. Research surveys may be made to cover designated provinces of the entire system, and sets of recommendations can be generated concerning chosen parts of the model.

This model has been used as the framework for studying four federal research dissemination agencies (Havelock and Lingwood, 1973), for charting eight "operational modes" reflecting various possible emphases by a research development, dissemination, and utilization agency, in examining resource linkage in educational innovations, and in determining the extent to which highway safety research

communication may be considered as representing an effective system (Havelock and Markowitz, 1971).

The National Institute of Education Model. According to a National Institute of Education Task Force on Resources Planning and Analysis (National Institute of Education, 1973), the underlying model of the Institute calls for the coordinated operation of four subsystems: (1) a monitoring system; (2) an external research and development system; (3) a linkage and support system; and (4) an internal, problem-solving operating system. The last named is the school system, in which it is posited, a good deal of problem-solving activity occurs, aided and abetted by the other subsystems of the Institute. Hence the interest in "how and by whom problems get formulated in the first place" and "the organizational life of operating systems which will affect the possibility of implanting the solution to a problem" (NIE, 1973).

Some of the considerations affecting the program and plan of the National Institute of Education may be noted:

(1) The literature on social indicators provides a source for use in the monitoring system, as does multidisciplinary knowledge. Surveys of educational practice and R&D impact thereon represent the subject matter of the monitoring process.

(2) The tendency of R&D models to borrow from the "hard sciences" may not be suited to the needs of complex social situations. A concerted series of long-range and short-range programs and projects is necessary to the realization of the system's R&D mission.

(3) The building of the linkage and support system requires a consumer information strategy, an information dissemination strategy, and a product delivery strategy.

(4) In building problem-solving capacity in the operating system, it is necessary to provide support at the teacher level, the school level, the school district level, and the school/community level.

The model clearly encourages widespread involvement in the educational improvement process, emphasizes a problem-solving approach, and calls for well-supported, coordinated effort.

Miscellaneous Contributions to Model Building. It has been noted that the process of model building with respect to research utilization is in a fluid state. The literature abounds with many closely focused, as well as widely focused, sets of ideas that may prove helpful in carrying the process to a higher level of integration and to greater fruitfulness of conceptualization. Some of the additional notions regarding model building that have come to light in the preparation of the distillation are here presented.

1. Several writers sought to set down the types or categories of models.

   a. According to Chin (1961), there are two major categories of models the practitioner may use as a diagnostic tool for planning change: the *systems model* and the *developmental model*. Chin defines the major terms used in each type of model. For the systems model these include:

system; boundary; tension, stress, and conflict; equilibrium and steady state; and feedback. The terms defined in conjunction with the developmental model are: direction; identifiable state; form of progression; forces; and potentiality.

Chin raises five questions regarding the relationship of the change agent to the model:

(1) Does the the model account for stability and change?
(2) Where does the model locate the source of change?
(3) What does the model assume about the determination of goals and directions?
(4) Does the model provide levers for effecting change?
(5) How does the model place the change agent in the scheme of things?

Each model is examined in the light of these questions. Chin asserts that a third model for change is emerging, one that incorporates features from both the systems and developmental models. In this model, direct attention is paid to the induced forces producing change.

b. Bennis (1963) refers to three approaches to planned organizational change: (1) the *equilibrium model,* according to which the mechanism for change is tension release through anxiety reduction; (2) the *organic model,* in which the mechanism for change is power redistribution and conflict resolution; and (3) the *developmental model,* whereby the mechanism for change is the transformation of values.

All three approaches have a deep concern with applying social knowledge to create more viable social systems, a commitment to action, as well as a research role for the social scientist, and a belief that improved interpersonal and group relationships will ultimately lead to better organizational performance.

c. Hage and Aiken (1970) distinguish between the *"mechanical model"* and the *"organic model"* commonly referred to in the sociology of organizations in describing two "ideal" types of organizations manifesting, respectively, "static style" and "dynamic style."

2. A number of writers have presented models depicting particular aspects of the research development, dissemination, and utilization process.

a. Glaser and Ross (1971), for example, identify four models of *advocacy formation:* (1) the *fiat model;* (2) the *platonic* (rational appeal) *model;* (3) the *apostolic model;* and (4) the *conversion model.* Each is related to methods used to achieve advocacy.

Advocacy by fiat, or change by force of power, administrative regulation, or law, leads to change resulting from decisions of those in authority, as in military, hierarchical, and bureaucratic organizations.

The *platonic model* assumes that potential users can be persuaded through education and rational appeal to use particular research-based

information or innovative procedures. As evidenced by both Fairweather (1973) and Glaser and Ross (1971), this approach apparently leads to intellectual adoption more than to behavioral modification.

The *apostolic model* attempts to stimulate conviction and motivation toward behavioral change through testimony and personal presentation and discussion in addition to written persuasion. Glaser and Ross (1971) found that many potential innovators appeared to appreciate intellectual stimulation afforded by such discussions, but the discussions did not necessarily dissipate the participants' doubts concerning implementation.

The *Conversion model* has a stronger emotional component, seemingly based on a more profound reordering of the conceptual frame of reference, with conversion facilitated by firsthand participation in an experience with a mutually reinforcing group of peers.

b.   Fairweather (1971) has developed a *model of experimental social innovation.* In his delineation of the attributes of social innovative experiments, he starts with the *definition* of a significant social problem whose basis includes engaging in naturalistic field observations (diagnosis) to describe the parameters of the problem in its actual community setting. The next step, *innovation,* creates and formulates different solutions as innovative subsystems. These subsystems then go through the process of *comparison,* whereby an experiment is designed to determine the efficacy of the different subsystems in solving the social problem. The innovative subsettings are implanted in appropriate social contexts so that they can be evaluated in their natural habitat. In the *evaluation* phase, the subsystems are continued in operation for several months or even years to allow for adequate outcome and process evaluation.

Throughout, participants in the subsystems are responsibly included, and a cross-disciplinary approach is employed, the social problem determing the fields and subject matter encompassed. Fairweather (1973) considers social innovative research to be the only humanitarian approach with social subsystems in which individuals function. While the model utilizes research in a natural setting, it follows the logical stages of (1) concern; (2) diagnosis; (3) formulation of alternatives; (4) implementation; and (5) evaluation.

c.   *Scientific communication as a system* is summarized by Menzel (1966) under five topical statements:

(1) Acts of scientific communication constitute a system.
(2) Several channels may act synergistically to bring about effective transmission of a message.
(3) Informal and unplanned communication plays a crucial role in the science information system.
(4) Scientists constitute publics.

(5) Science information systems serve multiple functions, including exhaustive search, reference, research stimulation, and scientist re-education.

d. Shannon's *information theory* is used by Dahling (1962) to illustrate the spread of an idea through an amazing number of disciplines, including: computer science, electronics, psychiatry, psychology, engineering, educational psychology, biology, physiology, radar, linguistics, biosociology, library work, optics, education, statistics, social science, and journalism, in the order enumerated.

A BRIEF INTRODUCTION TO INFORMATION
AND MODELS ON PLANNED CHANGE

Since 1955 the number of references dealing with planned change has grown from some 400 to over 20,000. Much of the literature consists of asserted notions. A large portion of the contributions are derived from observations and experiences. Some are research-based. Few are reports of experiments.

The proliferation of views staggers the imagination: There are the approaches of Lippitt, of Jenkins, of Jung, of Watson and Greiner, of Reuben, and Havelock, and Rogers, and Glaser. There are those labeled as theories of Zaltman-Duncan-Holbek, and of March and Simon, and of Burns and Stalker, and of Harvey and Mills, and of Wilson, and of Hage and Aiken. There are the processes of problem-solving; of research, development, and diffusion; of social interaction; of linkage; of reward structure; and of action research, and on to conflict theory and intervention theory.

For the reader sufficiently concerned, the following volumes may help provide order to the vast array of available information (all represent quite comprehensive overviews):

A Distillation of Principles on Research Utilization Volume I. DHEW Publication No. (HSM) 73-9148 GPO. $2.00.

An Annotated Bibliography on Research Utilization Volume II. DHEW Publication No. (HSM) 73-9149 GPO. $2.00.

A Manual on Research Utilization. DHEW Publication No. (HSM) 73-9147 GPO. $ .45.

Ronald G. Havelock and Mary C. Havelock, *Training for Change Agents* (Ann Arbor: University of Michigan, 1973).

Gerald Zaltman, Robert Duncan, and Jonny Holbek, *Innovations & Organizations* (New York: Wiley, 1973).

THE MOVE-OUT TIME

Fairweather has popularized for the change field the old military term "move-out time." It calls attention to the fact that in successful change inevitably action must occur. We face the same in this consideration of the Evaluator/Change Consultant role. Contemplation and review are necessary, but we have come to the point where we must answer the question "What plan is there for move-out?"

Already there is a mountain of proffered information, almost an endless number

of dimensions along which to cut it, and an unending procession of advisors on how to cut it. But one hesitates to espouse a given single approach. There are three reasons we feel one comprehensive model is warranted at this time:

(1) No present "storage box" accommodates all available information. One phenomenon repeatedly confirmed in the dissemination field is that when information is purveyed in overwhelming amounts which often are inconsistent if not contradictory, absorption of the information is cut off. No one likes to have thirst quenched by a fire hose. The approach to be suggested in this section will allow cataloguing and retrieving of existing information and presumably subsequent knowledge. After rather extensive use to this time, no emerging information on change has failed to fit conceptually within the model.

(2) A model linked to familiar theory is needed for flexible and inventive application. Though the model to be presented underwent logical clustering of information during its evolution, its development unavoidably converged with a familiar model of human behavior.

(3) A working model is needed which meets the criteria of adequacy. The following criteria encompass those proposed by Chin (1961) and extended by such writers as McGuire (1970), McClelland (1968), and Shepard (1965):

(a) The model, above all, should be practical.
(b) The parts of the model should be manipulable.
(c) Economy of use should be a primary consideration.
(d) Ease of communication is important.
(e) The model should be comprehensive.
(f) Synergism—the force of factors working together—is important to consider.
(g) The model should lend itself to intervening in phases.
(h) Differential investment in working with the components of the model should be possible.
(i) The model should call attention to how the change process influences the rest of the system.
(j) The model should be flexible and versatile enough to apply to different organizational systems.
(k) The model should provide a basis for a subsequent evaluation of the effectiveness of change.
(l) The model should recognize the humanness of the participants involved.

Whether the model to be discussed here meets all of those criteria will remain open to debate; however, its design has been steered by them.

Much of the work on change focuses on the generation of sound information and its effective communication. This holds true for the many sophisticated technology transfer systems within federal agencies (NSF, 1973). Only one-fourth of one percent of the federal R&D dollar is dedicated to utilization, that is, transfer efforts that go beyond dissemination.

It would be a great boon indeed to mankind if effective action could be counted on as the direct consequence of communication of sound solutions to measured problems. Someone said recently that anyone who believes that having a problem

pointed out to you, even backed by guidance on a solution that will evoke action to reduce that problem simply hasn't been married! The point was that in our daily lives we are richly blessed by "evaluators" and communicators of information on what we should do about those evaluations. The evaluation of the consequences of cigarette smoking, together with the solution to the problems discovered, may represent the best-disseminated information in the world. It is, of course, on the side of every pack of cigarettes. Yet the cigarette industry thrives. If the assumption we are talking about were valid, there would be no alcohol or drug abuse. Laws would not be broken. There would be no procrastination. Mental illness could be cured with advice. The puzzlement over why people who want to change and who know how to change cannot change represents a great human dilemma. It has been around a long time. Over 1,900 years ago, Saul of Tarsus, writing then as the apostle Paul (Romans 7:15) said, "For that which I do I allow not; for what I would do that do I not; but what I hate, that I do . . . But how to perform that which is good I find not."

Most of us can accept the reality of that dilemma at the individual level. But so often organizations are looked on as something ahuman. There are tables of organizations, functional statements, budget proposals, and systems designs. But are they? Brown (1973: 38) puts it this way: "Organization must be seen not as an abstract wall chart, but as a living reality, a structure of people with functions, capacities, interacting and tensing." Organization members " . . . have evolved as infinitely complex, distinct personalities, each with emotions, aspirations, intelligence, and incentives in unique combination" (1973: 10). Others (McGregor, 1960; Leavitt, 1965; Shepard, 1965; Marrow, 1972) have eloquently underscored that awareness.

The central characteristic of the model presented here is that it addresses the humans in organizations and social systems. It happens to espouse a behavioral model derived from learning theory, but any other concept of human performance probably would do well. The diverse backgrounds of evaluators from the social and behavioral sciences may very well lead them to adopt different conceptualizations of human performance. For instance, one of the commonly used techniques in organizational improvement is the Tavistock Group. Essentially it is a psychoanalytic model. A number of the approaches within the formal field of Organizational Development grow out of the Lewinian or Gestalt concepts.

If nothing further were stressed in terms of appropriate evaluation utilization, this would be enough; that is, assistance in appropriate utilization of evaluation findings addressing the human characteristics of persons involved would lead to significant gain in the field. This is particularly true in the human services area where so many evaluators have backgrounds of sophistication in addressing human characteristics.

In the form this particular model takes, there are three broad influencers to consider: (1) the motivation, drive, sensed *obligation* to "do something" about a matter; (2) availability of a selected course of action, an *idea* for achieving a solution; (3) consequences of implementing the idea for action. If the consequences are apt to bring displeasure, there will be *resistance* against choosing that particular

idea. If the anticipated consequences are pleasurable—in the broad sense—the perceived *yield* will increase the likelihood of that idea as being used to reduce the problem state.

It is as simple as that. We hold that this basic paradigm is constant in its effect whether viewed at the laboratory or societal levels. Clearly, complexity advances with the level.

Three other concepts have strong influencing effects on the basic paradigm:

(1) The *values* of the individual, organization, or society. This encompasses not only attitudes and beliefs of the performing group but characteristics facilitating or limiting performance as well. For example, there is a vast body of knowledge on characteristics of organizations that render them likely to adopt any needed change, without specific regard to an evaluation finding or its selected solution. This might be the counterpart of personal styles and self-concept at the individual level.

(2) The capacity or *ability* to perform according to a selected idea. Organizational change commonly is dependent upon availability of funds, talents, manpower, time, space, and so forth.

(3) Prevailing *circumstances* and *timing*. The circumstance of a cocktail party makes chit-chat more likely. New legislation often directly influences changes within social programs at the front echelon.

Recently when this concept was discussed with a leading social worker in the field of community organization, she responded, "But this is a clinical concept; we have to deal with quite different elements in the community." Findings from the field of persuasion advise that, if you use terms and concepts alien to the background of another, you are apt to lose her or him. That may be a reason no single working model of change will be acceptable to all evaluators. The jargon and derivation of this model perhaps leans toward psychology. McCullough (1974) reports that in community mental health Ph.D.'s in psychology appear approximately five times more frequently than any other specific background category. But evaluators come from such diversified backgrounds that even that represents only two out of five, and in community mental health at that! This might serve as an illustration of how one's own *values* (characteristics) limit the selection of an *idea* to match an *obligation*, in this case to help reduce suboptimum utilization of evaluation! But we would hope specialists with other backgrounds would translate the human approach to change into their own jargon and concepts.

In reviewing actual instances of change according to the human action, we will select other than clinical examples partly as an offer of assurance that this model by no means has to be limited to that level.

Analyses of Change by the Human Action Model

Obligation. Motivation for change is not, of course, always problem-focused. Renewal, growth, the desire for change itself, or creative expression perhaps accounts for as much or more change than does problem identification. Lippitt (1971) advised, in fact, that problem-oriented change is seldom as effective as

growth-oriented change. One might speculate that the reason for that might be found in the greater motivation, or obligation if you will, felt on the part of the growth-oriented innovator. But evaluation can enhance either source of motivation. Identification of fertile fields for invention as well as reinforcing confirmation of the effectiveness of positively motivated change seem to be essential contributions.

Not only should evaluation be seen as extending beyond problem identification; it may play a critical role in *reducing* what might otherwise be perceived as an obligation to change. As G. B. Shaw once said, "If it is not necessary to change then it is necessary not to change." A preoccupation here with processes of change does not imply that change is considered to be equated with goodness. Evaluation is an indispensable process in reaching that all-important decision on whether there is an obligation to change or an obligation not to change.

On Tuesday morning, October 16, 1962, the CIA presented an "evaluation" in the literal sense to the President of the United States. Photographs taken by U-2 aircraft had revealed areas of cleared foliage in Cuba. At first the clearings represented such a slight deviation from the base line photographs that the sense of obligation to take action was muted. But within hours the number of photographs taken would reach twenty-five miles if laid end-to-end! There no longer could be question of the threat to the life and dignity of the American people. The sense of obligation on the part of Congress and the people burgeoned after carefully planned visual presentation of evidence of the crisis through the news media (Kennedy, 1969).

More recently the Nation's unemployment rate jumped from 5.4% to 5.8% within one month. The wholesale index soared to a 46.8% annual increase. The Dow-Jones plunged 200 points for a twelve-year low of under 600. Prior to President Ford's message to the American people on inflation and recession, a national slogan was adopted by the Administration: "Inflation is our No. 1 enemy." With rapidly accelerating tempo, the news media carried stories on the gravity of the situation, especially with respect to inflation. In one day the Dow dived 28 points, conceivably a reflection of the effectiveness of the heightened awareness of the problem.

With more specific reference to a social program evaluation, an NIMH investigator reported his findings in late calendar 1973: Community mental health centers had not led to a reduction of public mental hospital residents as intended. He expressed disappointment over the inconspicous display of assumed obligation to take action. His perplexity perhaps was not unusual among evaluators who become concerned over the lack of utilization of their findings. But a more penetrating look may explain why.

His evaluation was a controlled investigation of the relationship between the advent of a mental health center in a catchment area and the reduction of state hospital resident rates for that same catchment. But he received data from only 16 states, and most of those represented rural catchment areas. There was reason for questioning the generalizability of his findings. Also, there had been six other contracted evaluations which yielded ambiguous conclusions but offering illumination on how exceedingly difficult it was to measure validly such a causal

relationship. One further in-house study had revealed a sizable difference between catchment areas with CMHC's and those without in terms of hospital resident rates. But that study did not control for pre-center rates.

On top of questions about the confidence in the data and conclusions themselves, there was the realization that all catchment areas had experienced a sharp reduction in hospital resident rates. From the standpoint of those who are expected to act on the evaluation findings, this problem loomed less large than myriad others demanding attention at the time.

This illustration also draws attention to the ethical dilemma of those involved both in producing evaluation findings and in utilizing the results. The evaluator felt conscience-bound to disseminate his findings broadly under a title well-planned to evoke alarm from those concerned with the CMHC program. His supervisor fully recognized his rights and even responsibility to make public the results of a tax-supported evaluation of a tax-supported program! But the supervisor also was concerned with clearing the report for publication because of the possibility of its being misleading. (The fact that admission rates in those catchment areas with CMHC's had been lowered was essentially lost in the report.) Outside pressure might well be evoked to place top priority on remedying this situation, not only at great cost but to the exclusion of other efforts considered to be of high priority. To withdraw resources from other priorities so that they might be reinvested in this pursuit would involve vast amounts of manpower and funds. The question was "Are the evaluation data and conclusions sufficiently cogent to warrant making a decision with such immense implications?" And should that decision be in effect turned over to possible sources that did not have responsibility for the full array of commitments of the CMHC program?

The supervisor took the risk of not clearing the report for publication in that form but did ask the evaluator to reconsider—not his data—but his conclusions and manner of expressing them. No whitewash occurred nor was it expected. The evaluator maintained his position on many points, and justifiably so. But others were re-expressed in words which, in one sense, would do a poorer job of increasing his sense of *obligation* but which also were less emotionally charged. The report, fine in most respects, was released and broad dissemination subsequently occurred.

Campbell (1974) has stated that any evaluators under his supervision would have full privilege of publishing their findings. And beyond doubt, the Freedom of Information Act eliminates any question about releasing evaluative data on federal programs. We also would hold that the evaluator has what amounts to a responsibility to present findings and conclusions as vividly as possible to decision-makers receiving the report. But it would seem to behoove the evaluator to proceed more circumspectly when it comes to amplifying the awareness of the *obligation* to act beyond those for whom the report is intended. In no way would this impair full presentation of data and objective interpretation of the findings. What we are saying is that, at the same time we are advocating that the evaluator take a role in stimulating motivation to take action on results, sensitive concern for the ethics involved must be maintained.

Decision-makers, too, must maintain the same concern. Who is to say that the

initial report in this example was not simply threatening to the evaluator's supervisor? Could not any supervisor judge the conclusions of an evaluation report invalid and assume justification in squelching them? Ochberg (1973) has suggested that, once an evaluation report is written, the time has passed when a decision-maker can take a position objecting to either its tone or its dissemination. That decision should be agreed upon before the findings are available, trusting that the evaluator will not "go beyond her or his data" for the sake of intensifying motivation for utilization.

Sometimes informal evaluative "findings" influence both the magnitude and direction of *obligation*. The D.C. Correctional Agency which had attained a commendable goal of 1% furlough violations could have amplified that finding to the point where it would have evoked invigorated support for the innovation. But from over 1,000 inmates who had been on furlough, one committed rape and another was apprehended with a sawed-off machine gun in his possession as he was boarding a Metroliner while on furlough. Needless to say, the sensed *obligation* on the part of the authorities and the citizenry amplified in the opposite direction.

Sometimes the "unintentional side effects" having little to do with attainment of the front stage goal of a program (Scrivens, 1974) can overshadow other motivations to respond according to major evaluation findings. Head Start continues not only because the soundness of the negative findings are in question but because the side benefits are so meaningful and valued.

Evaluators, very likely, will wish to move cautiously in stimulating motivation to act on the basis of their findings alone. But in concert with decision-makers who are in positions of integrating the complex array of vectors impinging on their decisions, the evaluator can be a significantly helpful guide and consultant.

The most choice practice in ensuring that optimum motivation to act will follow the presentation of an evaluation report may be sound design of the evaluation plan from the outset. Methodological soundness is, of course, the focus of the entire Handbook. But building into the evaluation design steps to ensure an aim toward a relevant target should be considered no less vital. Levine and Williams (1971) offer suggestions for such steps. They amount to questions that the evaluator both poses and answers before the final design and launching of the evaluation:

1. What will be the purpose of this evaluation: compliance control, budget allocation, program improvement, evaluation capability-building?
2. For whom is the evaluation being carried out, and who are the people and the programs they represent who will be involved with implementing any utilization of the evaluation?
3. How might alternative results affect the decision?
4. Who will make the final decision, specifically what person or office?
5. How will the availability of results match the decision timetable?
6. Will results be read and understood and will there be a possibility of misinterpretation?
7. Can an evaluation-based decision actually be implemented in the subject program?

8. Why do the decision-makers really want the evaluation results?
9. How credible can this evaluation be?
10. What is the program in question, and to what problem is it addressed?
11. What do we actually know about this program at this point?
12. What do we *think* of the program; do we have biases?
13. What possible alternative actions can we consider in terms of recommendations?
14. What additional knowledge would we like to have and can we get it?

At NIMH the Office of Program Development and Analysis, which administers the 1% contract evaluation program for the Institute, asks similar questions of each staff member who proposes an evaluation for consideration. The procedure is giving promise of sharply upturning the quality of evaluations over those once based on "Wouldn't it be interesting if we knew such and such."

If evaluators have dealt skillfully with what we term Obligation in this model, appropriate utilization of results already should be at a high level of probability. But there are further determinants at play.

Idea. Knowing whether action is necessary is important; but it is a truism that, unless an effective idea can be selected for solving the problem, appropriate utilization of the evaluation can hardly occur.

At the time of the Cuban missile crisis, greatest effort went into debating the selection of action. General LeMay urged a military attack on the missile and aircraft installations. At the other extreme, Adlai Stevenson pleaded for abandonment of Jupiter sites in Turkey and Guantanamo. The President favored a quarantine with blockade. Heated debates continued night and day. Whether the blockade was actually the correct selection remained a matter of breath-holding suspense to the very end.

To help solve the Nation's inflation crisis, debate was formally planned to allow a testing of the implications of alternative ideas. Would a gasoline tax work and would it be acceptable? Would a surtax on incomes above $15,000 per year work and would it be accepted? An extensive array of other solution ideas were aired for consideration before the final selection was proposed.

To meet the need for greater service from CMHC's in reducing state hospital resident populations an array of proposals were made, some by the evaluator himself. Rehabilitation might become a sixth required service of CMHC grantees. The required policies on continuity of care might be extended to encompass all patients from a catchment area admitted to a mental hospital. Innovative approaches developed and tested by certain centers toward reducing or eliminating hospital admissions might be featured in the collaborative grant-supported magazine *Innovations.* Further research and development projects on effective practices to work with chronically ill might be stimulated. A top priority work group on community care alternatives might be established.

Each idea proposed was carefully considered from the standpoint of capacity to implement them, negative consequences, probable payoff, timeliness, and so on. As discussions of the possible solutions continued, partly as a result of the evaluator's

gentle nudging, even the motivation to take action began to warm. Hope, feasibility, become stimulators of drive in themselves.

Some evaluators are urging strongly that the evaluation process formally encompass consideration of alternative decisions. The decision-theoretic approach (Guttentag, 1973) makes it explicit. Ciarlo (1974) specifically discusses decision alternatives as suggestions to users of reports. Though the number of trials of that method remain modest so far, there is early promise of exceedingly gratifying results.

There are three practices deemed advisable with respect to selecting ideas for solution:

1. Admit as large a pool of alternative proposals as can be accommodated initially.
2. Assess the suitability of proposals not only from the standpoint of the relevant determinants discussed in this model, but those of Glaser (1973: 436), known by the acronym CORRECT:
   a. *Credibility,* stemming from the soundness of evidence for its value or from its espousal by highly respected persons or institutions.
   b. *Observability,* or the opportunity for potential users to see a demonstration of the innovation or its results in operational practice.
   c. *Relevance* to coping with a persistent and sharply bothersome problem of concern to a large number of people (or to influential people).
   d. *Relative advantage* over existing practices (or yield, an incentive offer to change), that is, the conviction that the improvement will more than offset the considerable effort that may be involved in change.
   e. *Ease and understanding in installation* as contrasted to difficulty in putting it into operation or in transplanting it to different settings.
   f. *Compatibility* with potential users' previously established values, norms, procedures, and facilities.
   g. *Trialibility, divisibility, or reversibility,* which permits a pilot trial of the innovation one step at a time and does not call for an irreversible commitment by the system.
3. Persuasive communication should be planned for optimum effectiveness.

Conclusions from researches on communication indicate that the idea has a better chance of being accepted if: (1) the communicator identifies himself with his audience; (2) the presentation is pretested for readability, coherence, and understanding from the viewpoint of the audience for whom it is intended; (3) a factual report is made that people of prominence and influence agree, if indeed that is true; (4) positive reinforcement or benefits that can result are made clear, and any risks involved are surfaced and discussed; (5) logical and nonexaggerated emotional appeals are combined; (6) pictorial and other illustrative material are used where appropriate; (7) when objections are likely to arise they are taken account of at once; (8) the essential information is repeated, reiterated, and said again when practicable (Glaser, et al., 1966: Goldin, Margolin and Stotsky, 1969; Klein, 1968; Cohen, 1964).

Values. Decisions commonly are at least partly premade by individuals and organizations alike. Ideas proposed for adoption must match the range of considerable alternatives within the value system of those making decisions. This may serve as an example of what can happen: A member of a team of psychologists charged with serving a network of social agencies in Minnesota observed, during his testing, that many unmarried mothers were quite unfamiliar with contraceptive techniques. His solution was in the form of a rather nicely developed lecture and display of contraceptive devices. His demonstrations of the innovation were warmly accepted at Florence Crittendon and Lutheran Welfare homes, but then he tried it at Catholic Charities. His insensitivity to the values of the host agency led to what might be considered an abortion of his services there.

During the Cuban missile crisis, the values of the discussants of solutions were conspicuously reflected. Those who joined Le May and his proposal for attack were, for the most part, other military figures. Those siding with Stevenson's conciliatory position were primarily liberals. According to Robert Kennedy, the President and his close staff valued most the protection of lives, in both the United States and Cuba.

Solutions to the inflation crisis recognized the needs of industry and the political implications of a gasoline tax but also humanitarian concerns for the unemployed and those of low income.

In the case of evaluation findings about CMHC's and state hospitals, the values of the evaluator's supervisor quite likely played an unintentional role in the early resistance to dissemination of the findings. (This may be considered a fair statement because the senior author and the supervisor are the same person.) High-handed rule changes in the CMHC game at that late date were not seen as good form. The report as originally written conceivably could have been detrimental to the future of the community mental health movement. Indiscriminate emptying of state hospitals had never been accepted with high value. But planning for alleviation of the wretched conditions in communities faced by many discharged patients also was a high value, one to which the evaluator appealed in revising proposed solutions. Also appealed to was the value of the rights of an evaluator and the importance of utilization of such findings.

Characteristics of the organization and its members are also exceedingly important as determinants of change. The Organization Development field is almost totally dedicated to facilitating conditions that will allow an organization to become flexible and progressive. There are more references in the organizational change literature dealing with this element than with any other. The characteristics of the leader of the organization or of any of its components are critical. Five characteristics of the innovative leader drawn from researches are: She or he (1) advocates self-renewables of self and subordinates; (2) goal-oriented, not a stylist; (3) accepts risks; (4) rewards effectiveness; (5) and is an innovator herself or himself, as evidenced by past performance (Becker, 1970; Howard, 1967; Roberts and Larsen, 1971; Schmuck, 1968; Mackie and Christianson, 1967).

Fairweather (1974) has documented the critical importance of enthusiastic members of the organization who are willing to carry responsibility for seeing the

change through. Innovative types have been studied by a number of researchers, just as have the leaders. They are bright, usually more so than the average employee; enjoy rather high respect and status among the staff members; are "authentic," that is, are people who seem to be comfortable in presenting themselves as they really are; are deviants from the rest of their group despite the respect most of them enjoy; are not particularly buddy-buddy with others, but are nevertheless comfortable, nonhostile, and independent; are "cosmopolite" in that their interests extend far beyond the local facilities, and they seize opportunities to attend national meetings and to talk with persons with broader variety of experiences; are persons who have had positive experience in the past with change; are either younger or older than most of the other staff members; are really not too successful in the organization to the point where they have much to lose by risking change; are secure and assume that their usefulness to the organization does not depend upon their being excessively conforming or compliant (Coleman, Katz and Menzel, 1966; Katz, 1961; McClelland, 1968; Rogers, 1962; Rogers and Shoemaker, 1971).

From the sociological perspective, Hage and Aiken (1970) have dealt extensively with many other organizational attributes as they influence readiness for change, such as the diversification of disciplines, the affluence of the supporting community, and so forth.

Unless the evaluator is prepared to invest heavy commitments of time in promoting the health of the organization, the most fruitful address of Values may be from the standpoint of (1) selecting Ideas likely to be adopted, and (2) anticipating the likelihood that change of a specific magnitude can be brought about successfully.

Ability. Resources necessary to bring about change, such as manpower, funds, level of employee ability, and freedom from competing demands, represent the most overlooked consideration in the change literature. Yet, in an experiment conducted by Glaser and Ross (1971), resources proved to be the primary barrier to adopting a weekend treatment plan in community mental health centers.

In consideration of the appropriate plan for responding to the build-up of Russian arms in Cuba, the President called for precise data on required ships, aircraft, and troops. It was even ascertained that the cost of American lives would amount to 25,000 if military action had to be used as a backup to a failure of the blockade.

President Ford's presentation of solutions to the inflation and the recession threat were followed by a precise statement of the costs: a family of four with an income of $20,000 would pay an additional tax of 12¢ a day. A work program for the unemployed would cost $5 million. The duration of the expenses would be one year.

In reviewing ideas for greater benefits for chronic mental patients, Institute decision-makers were faced with dwindling abilities to alter requirements of CMHC grantees. The program was slated for termination at that point. A new research and development grant emphasis to further study community alternatives to hospitalization would require $250,000 a year of "new money." A writer could be sent to

programs in New York and Utah to prepare feature articles for *Innovations* magazine for $400 and an in-house task force on community alternatives could be established with ongoing operating funds. The evaluator could read his paper at an upcoming national meeting and submit it for publication with no funds other than those already committed.

In studying the utilization of the results of evaluation research projects, NIMH learned the inadvisability of funding innovative program trials the cost of which could never be met at the local level once federal funding terminated. Now all proposals for innovative program evaluations must estimate the basic cost of adopting the innovation if it does prove effective on evaluation.

Circumstances and Timing

More than human dignity will allow us to recognize, performance by both individuals and organizations is determined by the circumstances of the environment.

One of the best demonstrations of consummate skill in sensing appropriateness of timing and circumstances comes from history. In the early 1500s the priest, Martin Luther, had become concerned with the growing problem faced by poor people in purchasing indulgences, considered necessary at that time if one were to be cleansed of sins and thereby enter heaven. Instead of writing of his objections in a theoretical journal, he waited for the precise time to bring about change. As another priest, Tietzel, was moving through the local community selling indulgences, the resentment of the masses mounted. On the eve of All Saints Day it was the practice of the people in Germany to gather in the village squares to celebrate the driving-out of evil elements. At the height of the Halloween celebration, he marched to the church on the square in Wittenberg and nailed his 95 theses to the door. (A good change consultant would have recommended three which would have formed an acronym; but what did Luther know!) The move-out of his idea was launched rather more vigorously than he had anticipated. Another reformation was under way.

The Cuban missile crisis occurred on the heels of the cold war with Russia. Fears of communism remained great. The Bay of Pigs incident had been a recent stinging humiliation. The recollection in itself led to far more concerted planning on the missile crisis. The youthful spirited leadership thrived on challenge. If the buildup of installations had progressed more slowly, quite a different solution would have been chosen; namely, negotiations with Krushchev.

The advent of a new American president, confident and quite assured of congressional and citizen support, free from distracting stresses, almost surely influenced the direction of response to the inflation crisis. Political advisers urged delay of the implementation of action until after the forthcoming election out of their own sense of timing. Apparently, the rapidly mounting negative indicators of inflation and recession precluded such a consideration.

At the time the evaluation results on CMHCs in mental hospitals were reported, a multitude of demands for decisions on competing problems were pummeling the receivers of the report. Citizen backlash was mounting over what was seen as inappropriate return of some patients to inadequate community conditions. No

great pressure was on to increase the rate of emptying mental hospitals. But as time went on general stresses on the decision-makers were reduced, and new legislation supporting community mental health was initiated. With it came the opportunity for building in new emphases on rehabilitative services, as advocated by nonfederal bodies. Over the next few months, motivation to take action on the evaluator's findings mounted steadily.

The wise change consultant often will advise delaying the implementation of an idea until events occur which will increase the probability of adoption. Some common events having that effect include the arrival of a new leader, a new budget cycle, crises, new legislation, the availability of exciting and challenging practice techniques, mounting dissatisfaction with conditions, and even seasonal variations.

Resistances

We have been using a rating scale to measure readiness for a specific change in a number of organizations. An outstanding revelation provided by several hundred responses is that resistance receives the most extreme rating in the negative direction. The seriousness of this finding is that it is seldom so visible on the surface when dealing with people in the change situation. Perhaps the sanctions of employment induce people to comply without ready expression of their reactions to that event. Such resistance, like icebergs floating on the sea, may well explain why so many changes revert back to former patterns. And as a matter of opinion, it seems too bad to us that employees so commonly have to bear the brunt of unilateral decisions to change: it is hard for them; it is bad for the organizations in the long run.

The likelihood of dire consequences if the wrong action were selected represented tremendous resistance to almost all ideas expressed during the thirteen days of the Cuban missile crisis. Beyond realistic fears, important figures strongly resisted the idea of anything except an aggressive response to Russia and Cuba—as a matter of dignity. Robert Kennedy reported that facilitating the expression of resistance was one of the most important steps taken during that crisis. He said that, by contrast, almost no resistance-based argument occurred when the Bay of Pigs incident was being considered. He attributed that costly mistake to the absence of free expression of resistances. One of Kennedy's most disappointing observations was that certain high-level cabinet members would express their resistances in peer discussions, only to conceal them and take the side of the President during discussions in his presence. Fear of expressing resistance is quite surely a great disservice to a leader.

When plans were in preparation for the anti-inflation campaign, great pains were taken to ensure that representatives of many factions had a chance to express their opinions during the Economic Summit meetings. From the evidence available, considerable care was exercised in ensuring that as many objections as possible were accommodated in selecting actions to be taken. Beyond that, the very fact that so many had the opportunity to be involved in the planning must have helped. Even with all the sensitive attention given to probable resistances to any solution adopted, notable objections continued. That illustrates a point to keep in mind

about the change process: long after the move-out time, continual attention needs to be paid to resistances which may mount.

Resistances that seemed to arise in the face of evaluation results about the CMHC program and state mental hospitals were, it seems to us, quite understandable. To be confronted by one more problem at that point in time was not a welcome event in itself. To have an evaluator confront one with the assertion that a program to which there was great personal commitment had failed to achieve its objective was hardly "ego syntonic," particularly when there is other evidence to the contrary. The prospect of having possibly misleading information spread broadly was not inviting. The principle to learn from this is that, when an evaluator does feel she or he has negative data, the decision-maker might be asked to share the responsibility of making the interpretation. Of course, that runs the risk of unconscious underinterpretation. Fortunately, in the case at hand the evaluator was sufficiently patient and tactful to allow a smooth working-through of the initial resistances that were evoked.

It is often helpful for the change consultant to be able to anticipate typical sources of resistance. These commonly are among them:

Fear of economic loss.
Fears about personal security.
Fear of inability to learn readily the new skills required or to perform in a new role.
Fears about decreased personal convenience.
Fears about decreased job satisfaction.
Social fears (loss of status, separation from customary work associates).
Irritation with the manner of handling the change.
Cultural beliefs ("This will never work, it goes against what I have learned in the past, etc.").
Inertia.
Sense of present overcommitment.
Lack of interest.

There are numerous ways to address resistance. Perhaps the most important is to listen to its expression carefully to determine whether it is a front stage resistance that truly might call for a modification of plans. Discussion of anticipated problems among peers, with subsequent feedback in discussions with planners of the change, often helps. Trials of a new procedure may be advisable, with the understanding that an appraisal would be made collaboratively with the possibility of modification of the plan.

Persuasion may be used. Its success depends on the ability of the persuader to convince others that the rewards of the change counterbalance or outweigh the reasons for resistance.

Dispelling the fear that security is threatened might be carried out. This involves assuring a member of the organization that her or his position will not be eliminated in the process of change nor will the individual be called upon to perform new tasks that are beyond her or his capacity to master.

Developing a full understanding of the change is almost always a good idea. This includes why the change is needed, what is to be changed, how, by whom, when, what benefits can be expected, and what other outcomes can be anticipated. When there is a vacuum created by lack of understanding, it is filled by conjecture.

Often the change can be adroitly timed to coincide with growing feelings of dissatisfaction with the status quo. Speed often is important too; the longer the actual process of change takes, the greater the resistance.

The greater the extent of personal involvement in making decisions related to change, the less resistance there will be.

It is important to avoid implications of criticism. If those involved in the change process perceive it as criticism of what they have been doing, they will become resentful and defensive (Blum, Downing, 1964; Lippitt and Havelock, 1968; Mann and Neff, 1961; Watson and Glaser, 1965).

Yield

A significant reward that could be offered the American people for participating in anti-inflation measures was early leveling of inflation with subsequent benefits to each person. Even the wearing of WIN buttons was offered, deliberately or not, to provide the feeling of group acceptance and identification. Investment performance of industry was to be rewarded by tax benefits.

The putative failure of community mental health centers to reduce resident populations significantly faster than had occurred in catchment areas not served by centers was replaced by a consciousness of the challenge to do more for the chronically mentaly ill already in the community, as well as for those to follow. It became a positive exciting endeavor with the promise of intrinsic reward from seeing the growth of more appropriate community alternatives to hospitalization. Perhaps more could have been done, though it was hardly necessary. The advent of legislation for a new CMHC program provided a logical circumstance to address the evaluation findings directly. But the other ideas remained in force as well: dissemination of information about exemplary community programs for the chronically mentally ill, a special task force on community alternatives, and a somewhat extended research and development grant program on both mental hospital care and community alternatives. The improved state of affairs was, at the very least, in part the result of the evaluator's patient and persevering determination to ensure appropriate utilization of his evaluation results.

It would be difficult to think of any change experience at any level of organization in which the factors considered here have not played their roles as important influencers. Analysis in greater detail could be carried out for examples we have used, of course; but in reflecting on details not included here, we came to none that did not fit within the model of analysis.

The exercise also demonstrates the obvious; and that is, expertness in bringing about successful change does not require adherence to a prescribed schema; but the use of a guiding technique may well increase the frequency of successful change, simplify it, and reduce time and cost.

THE A VICTORY TECHNIQUE

There is a genuinely subjunctive mood underlying this description of the A VICTORY technique and outline. Appropriately seen, it is a vehicle to guide awareness and classification of the accumulating knowledge on planned change. Evaluation/change consultants may well design their own vehicles that would do as well or better; but as one way to get going, it represents a technique backed by as much diversified experience as any we know.

Before trying the A VICTORY technique in consultation practice, people commonly have asked, in essence, these three questions: (1) How much confidence can be placed in the usefulness of the A VICTORY technique? (2) Does A VICTORY call for a lock step approach to change? (3) Is it really necessary to address all the factors in planning for change?

As with other procedural checklists, A VICTORY sometimes has been looked on as a logical clustering of information at hand. One reviewer surmised that certain of the factors may have been chosen so that together they would spell a word! Actually, A VICTORY is a translation from a behavioral change model derived from learning theory. As such, its seven factors are considered to encompass the necessary and sufficient determinants of program attainment. For those who may be interested, the matching behavioral model has been expressed as follows:

$$B = E_s + T + S_c + (P + H_s) (D \times C) - I$$

Behavior,	B	= PA,	Program Attainment.
Capacity,	C	= A,	Ability, or resources required.
Self-expectancy,	E_s	= V,	Values that give purpose, perceptions, characteristics.
Pattern,	P	= I,	Idea for proposed action steps.
Stimulus conditions,	S_c	= C,	Circumstances which prevail at the time.
Timing,	T	= T,	Timing.
Drive,	D	= O,	Obligation, the felt need or motivation.
Inhibitors,	I	= R,	Resistances as they are relevant to the desired change.
Habit strength,	H_s	= Y,	Yield, or the rewards that the anticipated change may bring about.

The content under each of the factors appearing in the outline to follow is based upon distillations of the entire literature on knowledge utilization and organizational change as deemed to pertain to human services. The generation of A VICTORY also has been dependent upon a series of conferences and experimental studies over the past ten years supported largely through NIMH in-house resources, contracts, and collaborative grants. Extensive help has been provided by consultants working in the field of change outside the topical area of mental health. The A VICTORY technique, in its several developing stages, has been applied in technical assistance and in research consultation and administration within the services program at NIMH. It also has had continual use as an internal management approach within that program.

Currently further collaborative studies are under way to examine the effectiveness and feasibility of using the A VICTORY technique: American Institutes for Research (community mental health centers and hospitals); Center for Dialog (community change); Human Interaction Research Institute (mental hospital change); Program Evaluation Resource Center (utilization of evaluation); and the MITRE Corporation (mission-oriented research process). With respect to the payoff from applying the A VICTORY technique, data from the collaborative projects are not yet developed to the point where sound conclusions can be drawn. There are verbal reports that its use seems to help in consulation, but often as a back-of-the-mind orientation. Within the PERC study, Kiresuk's Readiness-for-Change Scale derived from A VICTORY appears to offer valid discrimination among social agencies in the Minneapolis area. Ciarlo at Denver General did not find that the scale discriminated between three CMHCs that adopted his evaluation system and three that did not, following common exposure. Among five components within NIMH considering adoption of a new program evaluation system, a fourteen-item semantic differential-type rating on A VICTORY variables did match other criteria of adoption. In other applications A VICTORY has highlighted the intensity of often unspoken resistances to change. At HIRI Glaser and Berger report that the A VICTORY assessment among change processes in mental hospitals seems to be matching their other more exhaustive assessments of those processes.

One conclusion that seems to be emerging from use of A VICTORY in consulting on change is that the final outcome of the change process results in a different state of affairs from that intended at the outset. Change mandated on the basis of authority, in contrast, generally seems to reflect a better fit between intention and outcome. From the standpoint of those in positions of program authority, this observation would speak against the use of planned change methods in utilizing evaluation results. On the other hand, one might propose that modifications in an original goal resulting from the participative approach and accommodation of other situations in the organizational milieu could lead to more effective utilization of evaluation in the long run.

There is one quantitative datum that may reflect the consequences of employing the A VICTORY technique: As it has been used in the consultation and management practices related to evaluative research in mental health services, the percentage of grant-funded projects which can report specific off-site utilization within one year after termination has grown from 11% in 1968 to 84% in 1974. This covers an investment of some $50 million. We do not suggest this has been a test of the A VICTORY technique by any means; numerous other factors have changed over those years, and the technique certainly has not been applied uniformly across all endeavors.

Perhaps the only conclusion we can draw at this point is that the A VICTORY technique seems to cause no harm and may at least offer the starting framework for planning the adoption of new policies or practices.

Does A VICTORY call for a lock step approach to change? As some people put it, "Would Michelangelo paint by numbers?" Though the factors in the A VICTORY outline give the impression of linear discreet steps, life does not work

like that, as everyone knows. Whatever model of organizational behavior may be used, it would be more accurately depicted as a Venn diagram. If the factors were to be represented by circles, most of them indeed would overlap reflecting their interaction, rotation of position, and expansion or contraction. Without the sensitivity and skill of the change consultant, employing A VICTORY would be like playing a 1912 Wurlitzer automatic orchestra: the clarinet, marimba, tambourines, drums, and cymbals may all be there and play on cue, but something akin to cacophony comes out. As Morgan (1972) said: "Managing change effectively often requires more than technique and strategy. It calls for a new kind of thinking about change—as an element in planning, as a factor in all decisionmaking, and as a pervading force in practically all other aspects of management."

Is it really necessary to address all the factors in planning for change? In the assessment phase, preparatory to setting the change process in motion, it probably is necessary to consider all the factors. In many instances this could be done with a few moments of reflection based on what one already knows or senses about the total situation. But when the adoption of a new policy or practice is going to involve a number of people or when other parts of the system are going to be affected, the consultant may wish to extend the assessment all the way to the use of a measuring instrument.

In the actual plan for change, even of major proportions, concentrated attention may be required for only one or two of the factors. Efficient planning calls for application of the "Pareto Principle." Zilfredo Pareto (1848-1923) was an Italian sociologist and economist living in Switzerland who discovered and applied the idea that, in most situations, a few factors influence the outcome, while a great many others prove largely irrelevant and can have little effect on the situation no matter what one does about them. Pareto's statistical analysis revealed that 80% of the results come from 20% of the action in most endeavors. The trick is in discerning which 20% to invest! There lies the payoff from the assessment phase of the A VICTORY technique.

Before going further in considering applying such a technique as A VICTORY in planning the utilization of evaluation results, we need to consider what is perhaps the most critical element in this whole matter: the feelings of people involved in the change process—ultimate beneficiaries and program personnel, persons with decision-making power, and the evaluator/change consultant's own feelings. Even when social program change is occurring at the national level, many of us have a vague sense that something is happening. There are few feelings worse than the powerlessness stemming from cues that change is afoot but without awareness of the facts, particularly when people are on the receiving end of decisions within closed systems. Accordingly, asking as many people as feasible to participate in structured planning for change sounds defensible. But it must be done with sensitivity. On one occasion we presented a proposal for planning change to a large number of staff employees in a facility. As it happened at that time, their supporting budget was being considered for drastic reduction, and they knew it. In that context the proposal for change was seen as part of a plot to weed out unpopular functions and perhaps persons. Their response was most negative. Openly confronting those people with a request to participate in planning for

change in that manner was not only insensitive but unkind under the circumstances. It is difficult to choose a path for appropriate participation: some people are made uneasy by lack of specification, but others are just as put off by overspecification smacking of manipulation. The only course to follow seems to be one of sensitive respect for the feelings and styles of consumers and employees alike. (The inadvisability of using a technique for manipulation hardly needs stressing here.)

As has been pointed out earlier, most decision-makers with sufficient power tend to be unconvinced that the more tedious, democratic, slow approach involved in planned change is worth it. They are too accustomed to seeing quick fidelity between their mandates and response from subordinates. To be sure, there are circumstances under which adoption of a solution by fiat makes much more sense than planned change. And, alas, it is still a matter of conjecture that participative change ultimately is more fruitful than mandated change, at least insofar as hard research results go. Further, decision-makers often have a multitude of pressures demanding action instead of contemplation. So at this level, too, the evaluator/ change consultant may have to perceive sensitively the feelings of people in power, keeping knowledge of change determinants in the back of his mind and demanding no commitment to a structured process. Still, effective help can be given without necessarily labeling the steps, as in working with an individual client or expressing love.

Again stressing Fairweather's (1974) primary conclusion that planned change is a consuming enterprise, we would urge change consultants to set their expectancies accordingly. Sometimes it simply will not be appropriate to invest sustained efforts in change; the process may give promise of occurring smoothly without guidance, time resources or role options may not be available, or even the desired change may not be that important. With respect to using a specific technique such as A VICTORY, it is understandable that many persons at the level of professional evaluator will develop their own unique approaches or even "wing it" as they go. For those persons we hope that A VICTORY will serve as a helpful reminder of factors influencing organizational change.

USE OF THE A VICTORY TECHNIQUE

The four steps in the use of the A VICTORY technique are: (1) Assessment, (2) Goal Definition, (3) Action, and (4) Follow-through.

(1) Assessment

For the purposes of this presentation, it will be assumed that the results of program evaluation are at hand. If the evaluation has been planned and conducted with an advanced eye on its ultimate utilization, the probability that the desired change will occur should be considerably higher than zero even at this point.

The assessment phase may be looked on as an evaluation in itself. However, in this case it is for the purpose of estimating the probability that the change will occur. It also has the purpose of guiding action plans toward enhancing the likelihood of change.

The qualitative assessment may be carried out by scanning the state of affairs as outlined below. The more affirmative the responses to the questions, the more

likely that the desired change will occur. Those factors under which there may be a predominance of negative responses would become the ones to be addressed by Action steps. In some instances a negative assessment of specific factors might call for a change in the Program Goal or the Idea to be used. We would underscore the importance of this consideration: any change model should, in our opinion, generally *accommodate* rather than *manipulate* the views of persons involved.

OBLIGATION—Felt need to do something about a problem.

Has evaluation of needs been carried out and interpreted soundly?

Are there informal clues indicating needs for change: mistakes, vague or conflicting goals, lack of communication, poor decision-making, complaints, rumors, low morale?

Have forecasts been made about new needs?

Have individual needs of staff or employees been considered, especially those that might represent secondary or backstage motivations? If multiple needs exist throughout the system, has a priority ranking been made?

Following the determination of needs, have steps been taken to amplify awareness of those needs among staff and employees?

IDEA—Information relevant to taking steps to solve the problem.

Has vigorous effort been made to explore all sources of information toward finding the most suitable action to meet the obligation: work experiences, group discussions, literature retrieval, special publications?

Does proposed information meet the correct criteria: credibility, observability, relevance, relative advantage, ease of understanding, compatibility, and timing?

Has special attention been given to methods of communicating the information to all relevant persons?

Have persons concerned been given an opportunity to challenge the selection of the information, to simplify it, to elaborate it?

VALUES—Pre-decisions, beliefs, manners of operating, and characteristics of the program organization.

Has the organizational climate been assessed—open communication rather than one-way, supportive administration, mutual support among colleagues, participation in decision making, high morale, adequate time for reflection and testing new ideas?

Are the organizational goals clear and written down?

Is the organizational structure characterized by decentralized and distributed power?

Is the organization large enough to accommodate the kind of change being considered?

Is the organization reasonably affluent, secure, and "in good" with its benefactors?

Is the community served by the facility a reasonably supportive and liberal one?

Are social and physical distances among persons involved sufficiently close to enhance innovation?

Are social relationships of staff so open as to render likely individual initiative of innovators?

Has the tenure of chief decision-makers been reasonably short?

Has the organization had a history of successful innovations?

Are staff members rewarded for performance rather than status?

Is the top man at the organization a self-renewing, goal-oriented type of person himself?

With respect to the persons who may be involved with the change, are they either younger or older than most? Is their economic status reasonably adequate? Are they people with a personal sense of security in the facility? Are they the sort who attend meetings and mix with other professionals beyond the facility in which they work? Are they bright, authentic, not afraid to be deviants from the total group? Has consideration been given to the danger that supporters of the change are motivated by their own dissidence, indifference to the organization, disaffection, or resentment?

ABILITY—Capacities to carry out the solution: staff, funds, space, sanctions.

Have the funds necessary to support the change been identified?

Have sources of the needed funds been identified?

Has a prediction been made regarding manpower required to carry out and sustain the change?

Will special orientation or training in the new patterns of action be necessary?

Has the need for additional facilities been determined—office space, meeting rooms, parking, etc.?

Has there been a review of the product-losses that would occur; that is, if resources have to be taken from another part of the system, have the consequences of that withdrawal been given consideration?

CIRCUMSTANCES—Prevailing factors pressing for or detracting from certain actions.

Have fixed organizational characteristics—openness, attitude of leadership, clarity of goals—been assessed from the standpoint of the probability that any change can take place? Have restrictions on the nature of the change been judged vis-à-vis the organizational values?

Have characteristics of the catchment area or region served been considered in relation to the proposed change?

Are there changing organizational situations that would bear upon the success of the change—new budget periods, change in leadership, new mission for the facility?

TIMING—Synchrony with other significant events.

Has the time for predicted major changes in the organizational milieu been estimated?

Has the possible advent of new community concerns, legislative interest, and economical circumstances in the community been assessed from the standpoint of timing?

Are there impending crises relative to the proposed change with which the initiation of change might be timed?

Has the phasing of events in the personal lives of staff and employees been considered—holidays, for instance?

Has continual sensing of staff readiness for change been employed?

RESISTANCES—Both frontstage and backstage concerns for loss if specific action is taken.

Have plans been made to sense reactions to the proposed change?

Has the advisability of the proposed change been reconsidered in the light of any rational resistances that have been detected?

Has there been a sensitive exploration of the irrational resistances of staff—fear of loss of status or job security, misunderstanding, etc.?

Has thought been given to those who might be affected by the change, such as beneficiaries of the program, even though their support is not necessary to bring about the change?

YIELD—Felt rewards, benefits to program participants and consumers alike.

Have reasons for expecting the change to pay off been communicated to persons concerned?

Have direct, tangible rewards been planned for persons instrumental to the change?

Have indirect rewards been considered, such as better working conditions, opportunity for professional advancement, and for self-actualization?

Has direct and personal support from the top of the organization been planned?

Another approach to assessment currently under examination is by means of a quantitative instrument. Kiresuk (PERC) and Glaser and Berger (HIRI) are studying the feasibility of scales to appraise the positions of persons involved in change on each of the A VICTORY variables. Whether these scales will meet the standards of reliability and validity across varying change situations remains to be seen. In the meantime, the use of brief questionnaires tailored for the specific change situation is proving helpful. Though the interpretations must be viewed with caution, they do assist in confirming impressions gained through the more informal scanning approach.

The questionnaire that follows was sent to approximately 100 persons in a division at NIMH. Consideration was being given to the adoption of a new operational evaluation system. The questionnaire took the form of differential ratings on dimensions pertaining to the A VICTORY factors. (Only one was written for Circumstances and Timing; the same item on Yield appeared twice in different form to estimate rather consistency.) Responses were not identified with individuals but were for program components of origin.

Total scores for each of the program components matched precisely the overall ratings of adoption by the five respective components. That rating was based upon continuing open discussions and actual response after move-out, or adoption, time. Responses were consistently on the positive side on such dimensions as Idea, Obligation, Values, and Yield insofar as the program benefits were concerned. They were consistently negative on the side of Ability, Circumstances and Timing, Resistances, and Yield in terms of personal benefits. The persons to be involved with the change were saying, in effect, that the new system was clear, that they had no intention about rebelling against any instructions to adopt the system, that it was the thing to do, and finally that the program would benefit from such adoption. But at the same time they were saying that it was a time-consuming endeavor to maintain, perhaps one for which the payoff was not commensurate with the time and energy demanded. That particular point in time was a poor one to initiate such a system because cutbacks in funds and staff appeared to be so eminent at that point. Perhaps for that reason the proposed evaluation system was perceived as being potentially threatening and even detrimental to maintaining program performance. There was little chance of gaining personal benefits from the proposed system. Subsequent discussions with personnel precisely confirmed these impressions, gross as the assessment had been.

In consequence, the change process was allowed until environmental circumstances became more sanguine, the system was redesigned to require far fewer resources, participative planning was followed, and director-level staff gave individual reinforcement to persons engaged in maintaining the system. Administratively, from the short view, addressing the views of personnel meant that implementation of the system fell months behind schedule. And its final form differed from the initial plan. But from the long view, the modified plan proved to be both more effective and more efficient than the initial one would have been by all indications.

The pattern of responses to this brief questionnaire has reappeared in quite different situations in other parts of the country. What seems to be emerging as a general phenomenon is that employees of organizations accept the responsibility to comply manifestly with directives. That may be an assumed agreement one makes when joining an organization. Perhaps this is why unilateral planning by authorities is a common pattern. But people can manifest compliance without really doing things much differently. These exercises with the participant responses are demonstrating to us that the slower and more tedious process of planning for change may yield a different outcome, one from which all concerned benefit more. This is what writers in the management field—Marrow (1972), McGregor (1960), Brown (1973)—have been telling us for some time!

These items were drawn together for the specific case we have just discussed; however, the reader may find the example more illuminating by making imaginary ratings at any point along the line from the standpoint of one's own personal view on A VICTORY at this point. (The capitalized factor labels in parenthesis are added here for clarification. They do not appear on rating forms.)

(2) Goal Definition

As stressed by McGuire, the task of defining meaningful goals is one of the most important in effective program development. Exactly the same should be said about the importance of a clear goal in planned change. Without performance of this task the subsequent evaluation of the success of the change effort becomes extremely difficult. This is not to say that the unintentional side benefits of program change are to be ignored, nor is it to pretend that goal-irrelevant motivators play a big part in change—such as visibility for the launch, as White has described. But few changes produce optimum benefits without continuing readadjustments in the early stages. Those adjustments—as with all program improvements—can be rendered most beneficial if they are based upon evaluation of progress toward a prescribed goal.

An additional reason for defining a clear goal to be attained by the change in policies or practices is that desirable consequences are more likely to occur. We like to refer to this phenomenon as "target tropism." If you establish a clear expectation, people will tend to fulfill it. The validity of this assumption may be more experiential than experimental, though.

The reason for delaying goal definition until after an assessment of the probability of change perhaps is obvious: If the views of persons involved in the realities of the situation are taken into consideration in shaping the goal, the expectation it represents surely should have a greater chance of fulfillment. That sequence also represents the position that the planner of change should aspire to accommodate reality insofar as possible rather than manipulate it. To be sure, some adjustment in the actions of some people and in some conditions virtually has to be assumed. The farther down in the bucket the ping pong ball to be moved is, the greater the shifting of the other ping pong balls. But here is little wisdom in taking on windmills like Don Quixote unless it is essential for the good of the cause!

Questionnaire

Clarity of Idea (Idea)

Very clear

Obscure
Unclear—but did not
"succeed" in confusing

Time Investment (Ability)

Approach calls for
negligible time
investment

Approach calls for
extravagant time
investment

Fit with My Style (Values)

I strongly prefer
a feel-as-you-go
approach

I do prefer defined
structure such as this
approach entails

Willingness (Resistance)

I would be most
reluctant to adopt
this approach

I feel comfortable
about adopting this
approach

Benefits (Yield)

I think I'll feel
personal benefits
from this approach

I will gain no personal
help from the approach

Appropriateness (Values)

Approach is just
what our situation
calls for

Approach is a poor
fit with our program

Perceived Responsibility (Obligation)

Adoption appears
to be optional

Adoption seems to
be necessary

Importance (Yield)

Approach such as this
is essential to good
program payoff

Nothing to be gained
from this endeavor

Soundness of Idea (Idea)

Seems invalid in basic concept and methods	Appears to be logical, based on solid material

Assessment (Resistance)

I anticipate no negative consequences to this approach	I see a number of negative consequences to this approach

Consequences (Yield)

Nothing to be gained by this approach	Approach will lead to greater program achievement

Felt Need (Obligation)

I feel strongly motivated to participate in this approach	I feel no need whatsoever to engage in this approach

Readiness of Implementation (Circumstances and Timing)

This is a poor time to adopt this approach	Things that are happening make it essential right now to adopt this approach

Required Skills (Ability)

Approach demands extensive orientation, practice, and skill	Approach seems simple to carry out

(3) Action

If the phases of the A VICTORY technique were to be followed in direct sequence, we now would be faced with taking action to shift conditions among critical factors to the extent necessary. But as is true in the individual helping relationship the assessment of the problem, the definition of the goal, and the action to improve determining conditions remain rather fluid and interchanging. The defined goal should remain intact for sufficiently long periods to lend itself to a measurement of whether things are proceeding as desired. A most important consideration in carrying out the action steps is the continual evaluation of how things are going. Change does not occur, of course, just at "move-out time," as

Fairweather terms it; rather, change progresses over time in the fashion of growth or root hairs of a plant. This process defies evaluation by most traditional methods. This may be another instance in which the decision-theoretic approach of Edwards (1965) and Guttentag (1973) would be of use, particularly in selecting specific plans for action.

The foregoing array of suggested actions could well evoke a response of weariness when confronted with what looks like an overwhelming burden, and most of us simply turn it off. But again we would like to emphasize that the list is cafeteria-like. Rarely would a change consultant find it necessary to employ the majority of the actions. Further, weariness is likely if the list is looked on as the result of someone's brainstorming session. Actually, the array represents a condensation of conclusions drawn from the body of literature and experiences on change. To be sure, many are based upon assertions derived out of authors' observations. But in those cases the conclusions will have been sufficiently frequent in their appearance in the literature to warrant.

OBLIGATION

Fight fire with fire, as it were; if true, indicate that a participative change at this time will preclude a coerced one later on.

If necessary, invoke the most common of all methods to stimulate motivation; namely, "normative sanction." The ultimate motivation for participating in change is to fulfill one's commitment to the job.

IDEA

Encourage participation in the selection of the action pattern, the solution, and the information about it. Encourage participants to challenge the information, to simplify it, to think of improvements.

Use available systems of retrieval, specialized journals, and digests.

Seek out expert consultants. If practicable, attend professional meetings and conferences in specific search of the needed information; take part in problem-solving exchange programs as they are developed.

Conduct discussion with key participants in change regarding treatment of the *information*—rendering it, prior to its communication to others, credible, observable, relevant to the *obligation* to change, manifestly superior in payoff to the present way of handling the problem, easily understood, and compatible with the agency's *value* systems.

Conduct a deliberate communication of the information or plan of action among all persons in groups concerned with the proposed change.

VALUES

Obtain consultation to help with objective review of the analysis already made of organizational values and characteristics, and also to help with feasible modifications.

Depending upon the change administrator's influence in the organization, in advance of specific attempts to bring about change, encourage top decision-makers to:

Advocate self-renewal of staff and employees.

Let it be known that experimenting persons have the right to make mistakes.

Create an atmosphere receptive to pilot experiments.

Encourage attendance at workshops, etc.

Arrange for rewards and recognition related to performance.

If there is top-level support for modifying the organization toward being more receptive to change in general, any of several techniques might be employed, usually through the assistance of a consultant:

Direct systemic alterations—bringing power systems (policy making, administration, socialization) into alignment with product systems (direct service and care to patients, community work).

Travistock group therapy—working through deeper interpersonal feelings about organizational social and working relationships.

Balancing the "managerial grid"—bringing about a *team* management system that is neither task-oriented (treating personnel as rented instruments) nor country club-oriented (treating personnel as though all stress were to be avoided).

Temporary systems —conducting a group session such as sensitivity training away from the usual work setting so that the usual barriers to close interpersonal relationships do not prevail; the purpose is to give staff self-understanding about their own roles in the organization.

Emerging needs monitoring—development of a standing group of personnel who carry the responsibility for continually advocating an orientation toward assessment of needs for change and stimulating their consideration.

In order to help adjust the fit of organizational values with a specific prospective change, the following might be employed:

Peer group discussion—participants in the change, without the presence of power figures from the organization, discuss their personal reactions to the change proposal and offer recommendations accordingly. (This approach also will be considered when dealing with *resistances* arising out of a clash between the *values* of the participants and requirements of the *information,* or action pattern; for instance, the values of professional mental health workers about new assignments of paraprofessional mental health workers within the organization.)

Mann systematic use of feedback—trial of the new approach followed by pre-arranged discussion sessions of relevant personnel about their experiences and appraisals of the trial vis-à-vis the organization.

Orientation sessions with benefactors and beneficiaries—early introduction to the planned change, when appropriate to pertinent representatives of the community, board, or other parts of the supra-system and with representatives of the client groups, including patients, their "significant others," and consultees.

Team piloting and specific change—early formation of key participants within the organization who will carry primary responsibility for bringing the change into actuality.

Legitimization of the change—arranging for the manifest endorsement and commitment of respected authorities.

ABILITY

Prepare specific budget for start-up costs and continuing costs.

Arrange inclusion of requests for funds in the organization's next periodic budget proposal.

Propose sources of immediate funds and discuss product-losses that would be involved, and how they might be covered. (If you use resources from A to start B, what happens to cover the losses of A?)

Explore grant mechanisms for start-up costs, using state and regional consultation.

Prepare manual or provide written references for participants if the information or pattern of action to be followed is sufficiently unfamiliar or complex.

Obtain an "action consultant" if available, a person thoroughly familiar with the *information* or action pattern who is also familiar with organizational problems and its employment.

Conduct a formal training program from the use of the *information*—conference, demonstration, study group, anticipatory rehearsal (dry run through the new practices followed by discussion).

Estimate specific facilities required and propose ways of arranging for them.

CIRCUMSTANCES

Review of earlier analysis—through group discussion or consultation, review of organizational characteristics in situations in a community conceivably influencing the proposed change.

Examine *circumstances* out of which the *information* grew—investigation, by visit if possible, of the attributes of the situation where a new action pattern

was developed and tested. (Rarely are these adequately described in communications about new service methods.)

Assess the interaction of all factors influencing the change—consideration of how all of the A VICTORY factors might be brought into interaction more conducive to fulfilling the desired change.

TIMING

Review *timing* of *circumstances*—anticipation of changes and events that might influence the process of change.
Coordinate staff readiness with timing of circumstances.

Prepare for mustering of resources and support at move-out time.

RESISTANCES

Appraise resistances deemed to be rational—final consideration of whether the change should be modified or even abandoned.

Decide on advisability of fait accompli approach—bringing about change quickly and without working through resistances if the change is imperative and indeed nonnegotiable; it may be preferable not to evoke expressions of resistances about which nothing can be done.

Employ rational persuasion—intensification and broadening of communication approaches.

Use selective individual counseling—personal discussions with individuals who seem to have unique problems in reaction to the change.

Resolve complex resistances through group dynamics—utilization of some of the same techniques suggested for changing organizational values, such as Tavistock Therapy, T-groups, discussion at retreats, etc.

Use listening as a deliberate approach—allowing persons to express their resistances through the rare experience of being listened to.

Use advisory groups—involvement of representatives of participating factions.

Approach the change implementation slowly—introduction of elements of the change a few at a time, beginning, if possible, with the least disturbing.

Settle on partial change, if necessary and if better than nothing.

YIELD

Provide information on adequacy of the proposed pattern of action as a solution to the problem, by:

Special presentations, especially by a person who has employed the pattern.

Demonstration of the pattern and its yield, if practicable.

Visit to site where pattern has been employed.

Reward participants with timely feedback, attention, and interest.

Provide and *carry out* plan for specifically deserved rewards—pay incentive, new titles, professional opportunities, group recognition.

(4) Follow-through

Under ideal conditions the evaluator/change consultant's "contract," in whatever form of understanding, would retain that person's presence throughout the duration of the change process. In reality, alas, this is seldom so. Outside consultants may be long gone on other pursuits by the time the follow-through phase arrives. Even the inside consultant may find that resources and sanctions for working with the change process wane over time. This is particularly unfortunate because an almost invariable phenomenon of change occurs, namely, regression back to practices it was intended to supplant. A critical function in nurturing change, according to Jenkins (1962) is to ensure that a new condition is stabilized. The resistant forces tend to push almost all adjustments back to the former conditions. It may be more accurate to describe follow-through as a phase that should continue without interruption from the move-out point. Early disappointments are apt to snowball into counterproductive pressures before innovations have a chance to give people the experience of the expected yield.

Evaluation becomes a key element in the follow-through stage. So many things happen to people in organizational life that even if a change has brought about a better state of conditions, awareness of that improvement may not be all that conspicuous. If an evaluation of the attainments of the program proves positive, and if assessment of the unintended side benefits turns out likewise, the dissemination of this information can serve as an important reinforcer to stablize the change.

The primary purpose of evaluation in the follow-through phase, of course, is to signal any further needs for modification of actions. Thus, the feedback cycle is realized. But the task does not end at that point. The essence of growth and renewal, as identified by Gardner (1064), is continual evaluation. Havelock (1970) stresses that the cycle must be repeated for continued organizational improvement and renewal, with an accompanying increment in the organization's capacity. Campbell (1969) says it another way: The first cycle in the administration of systematic change is much like an experiment, with smoother operations a greater payoff likely with subsequent cycles and refinements. At first blush, the prospect of such ongoing cycles brings a picture of staggering resources that must be consumed. But each cycle in practice should require a lesser investment of time and effort, allowing attention to other problems as they are identified by evaluations.

In this chapter we have held that: (1) evaluation provides great hope for ultimate beneficiaries of social programs; (2) to fulfill that hope, effective utilization of evaluation is essential and that the very field of evaluation may be dependent upon evidence of such payoff; (3) the destinies of evaluation results are at least to some extent predictable and the careers of those results can be enhanced; (4) evaluators should consider extending their role to change consultation; (5) there is a vast body

of information on change and models of conceptualization on which to base one's professional services; (6) utilization of evaluation may most effectively be achieved through the human approach to organizational change; and (7) the A VICTORY technique may at least represent a schema to consider in trying the evaluator change consultant role.

Finally, we must acknowledge that, if the A VICTORY technique is to be used in an attempt to increase the benefits from evaluation, one will be faced with a greater number of factors that must be addressed than in other approaches to change. But those factors are there whether or not the change consultant has invited them. If we do greet them, we can at least collaborate with them rather than having our evaluation results mastered by them.

Our final thought is about the great changes in history—how they could have been brought off so successfully without a change model to follow! Could it be that what we have described as the human action model, or the A VICTORY technique, is just an ordering of common sense? At the end of the Constitutional Convention, called in 1787 because the innovative solution to the problem of taxation-without-representation had struggled eleven years in adoption, Franklin walked to Washington's dais in Independence Hall where he had been presiding. Franklin sighed, "I didn't know until this day whether that carved sun-on-the-horizon on the back of your chair was rising or setting. Now I know it's rising." "Yes, Ben," said Washington, "it truly was A VICTORY."

REFERENCES

Attkisson, C. Clifford, et al., *A Working Model for Mental Health Program Evaluation.* Prepublication copy, November 1973.

Becker, Marshall H. Factors affecting diffusion of innovations among health professionals. *American Journal of Public Health,* 1970, 60 (2): 294-304.

Beigel. A. Evaluation on a shoestring. In Wm. A. Hargreaves et al. (eds.) *Resource Materials for Community Mental Health Program Evaluation.* San Francisco: NIMH, 1974.

Bennis. W. G. A new role for the behavioral sciences: Effecting organizational change. *Administrative Science Quarterly,* 1963, 8 (2): 125.

Blum, R. H. and J. J. Downing. Staff response to innovation in mental health service. *American Journal of Public Health.* 1964, 54: 1230-1240.

Brown, J. D. *The Human Nature of Organizations.* New York: Amacon, 1973. Pp. 10-38.

Buchanan, G. and J. Whaley. Federal level evaluation. *Evaluation,* 1972, 1 (1).

Campbell, A. and P. E. Converse. *The Human Meaning of Social Change.* New York: Russell Sage Foundation, 1972. P. 9.

Campbell, D. T. Experimentation revisted. *Evaluation,* 1973, 1 (3): 7-13.

———. Reforms as experiments. *American Psychologist,* 1969, 24: 409-429.

Chin, R. The utility of systems models and developmental models for practitioners. In W. G. Bennis, K. D. Benne, and R. Chin (eds.) *The Planning of Change.* 2d ed. New York: Holt, Rienhart & Winston, 1961. Pp. 297-312.

Ciarlo, J. Personal communication. August 1974.

Coheb, J. Factors of resistance to the resources of the behavioral sciences. *Journal of Legal Education,* 1959, 12: 67-70.

Coleman, J. S., E. Katz, and H. Mensel. *Medical Innovation: A Diffusion Study.* New York: Bobbs-Merrill, 1966.

Dahling, R. L. Shannon's information theory: The spread of an idea. In *Studies of Innovation and of Com munication to the Public. Studies in the Utilization of Behavioral Science.* Vol. 2. Stanford, Calif.: Institute for Communication Research. Stanford University, 1962. Pp. 117-140.

Davis, H. Innovation and change. In S. Feldman (ed.) *Administration in Mental Health.* New York: Charles C. Thomas, 1973.

Edwards, W. Tactical note on the relation between scientific and statistical hypotheses. *Psychological Bulletin,* 1965, 63(6): 400-402.

Fairweather, G. Experimental innovation defined. In H. H. Hornstein et al. (eds.) *Social Intervention: A Behavioral Science Approach.* New York: Free Press, 1971.

–––. Innovation: A necessary but cosufficient condition for change. *Innovations,* 1973, 1: 25-27.

Fairweather, G. W., D. H. Sanders, and L. G. Tornatzky. *Creating Change in Mental Health Organizations.* New York: Pergamon, 1974.

Gardner, J. W. *Self Renewal: The Individual and the Innovative Society.* New York: Harper & Row, 1964.

Glaser, E. Knowledge transfer and institutional change. *Professional Psychology,* November 1973, Pp. 434-444.

Glaser, E. M. et al. *Utilization of Applicable Research and Demonstration Results.* Final report to Vocational Rehabilitation Administration, U.S. Department of Health, Education, and Welfare, Project RD-1263-G. Washington, D.C., 1966.

Glaser, E. M. and H. L. Ross. *Increasing the Utilization of Applied Research Results.* Final report to the National Institution of Mental Health, Grant no. 5 R12 MH 09250-02. Los Angeles, Calif.: Human Interaction Research Institute, 1971.

Goldin, G. J., K. N. Margolin, and B. A. Stotsky. The utilization of rehabilitation research: Concepts, principles and research. *Northeastern Studies in Vocational Rehabilitation,* no. 6, 1969.

Guttentag, M. Subjectivity and its use in evaluation research. *Evaluation,* 1973, 1 (2): 60-65.

Hage, J. and M. Aiken. *Social Change in Complex Organizations.* New York: Random House, 1970.

Havelock, R.G. *A Guide to Innovation in Education.* Ann Arbor: Center for Research on the Utilization of Scientific Knowledge, Institute for Social Research, University of Michigan, 1970.

–––. *Planning for Innovation Through Dissemination and Utilization of Knowledge.* Ann Arbor: Center for Research on Utilization of Scientific Knowledge, Institute for Social Research, University of Michigan, 1969. Final report, Contract No. OEC-3-7-070038-2143, Office of Education, U.S. Department of Health, Education and Welfare.

Havelock, R. and M. Lingwood. *R & D Utilization and Functions: An Analytical Computation of Four Systems.* Ann Arbor: Institute for Social Research, University of Michigan, 1973.

Havelock, R. and E. Markowitz. *A National Problem-Solving System: Highway Safety Research and Decision-Makers.* Ann Arbor: University of Michigan, 1971.

Howard, E. How to be serious about innovating. *Nation's Schools,* April 1967, 79: 89-90, 130.

Jenkins, D. H. Force field analysis applied to a school situation. In W. G. Bennus, K. D. Benne, and R. Chin (eds.) *The Planning of Change: Readings in the Applied Behavioral Sciences.* New York: Holt, Rinehart & Winston, 1962. Pp. 238-244.

Katz, E. The social itinerary of technical change: Two studies on the diffusion of innovation. *Human Organization,* 1961, 20: 70-82.

Kennedy, R. F. *Thirteen Days.* New York: Norton, 1969.

Klein, H. D. *The Missouri Story, a Chronicle of Research Utilization and Program Planning.* Paper presented at the National Conference of Social Welfare, May 1968.

Leavitt, H. J. Applied organizational change in industry: Structural, technological and humanistic approaches. In J. G. March (ed.) *Handbook of Organizations.* Chicago: McNally, 1965.

Levine, R. A. and A. P. Williams Jr. *Making Evaluation Effective: A Guide.* Santa Monica, Calif.: Rand Corporation, 1971.

Lippitt, R. *Personal Communication.* Conference on change processes, Center for Research on the Utilization of Scientific Knowledge, 1971.

––– and R. Havelock. Needed research on research utilization. In *Research implications for educational diffusion.* East Lansing: Dept. of Education, Michigan State University, 1968.

Lynn, L. E., Jr. Notes from HEW. *Evaluation,* 1972, 1 (1): Pp. 24-28.

McClelland, W. A. The process of effecting change. Presidential address to the Division of Military Psychology, American Psychological Association, San Francisco, September 1968.

McCullough, P. *Training for evaluators–overview.* Supplemental material presented to the NIMH-sponsored conference on program evaluation in April 1974, Washington, D.C.

McGregor, D. *The Human Side of Enterprise.* New York: McGraw-Hill, 1960.

Mackie, R. R. and P. R. Christensen. *Translation and Application of Psychological Research.* Technical Report 716-1. Goleta, Calif.: Santa Barbara Research Park, Human Factors Research, Inc., 1967.

Maguire, L. M. *Observations and Analysis of the Literature on Change.* Philadelphia: Research for Better Schools, Inc., June 1970.

Mann, F. C. and F. W. Neff. *Managing Major Change in Organizations.* Ann Arbor, Mich.: Foundation for Research on Human Behavior, 1961.

Marrow, A. J. (ed.) *The Failure of Success.* New York: Amacon, 1972.

Menzel. H. A. Scientific communication: Five themes from social science research. *American Psychologist,* 1966, 21: 999-1004.

Morgan, J. S. *Managing Change.* New York: McGraw-Hill, 1972.

Mushkin, S. Evaluations: Use with caution. *Evaluation,* 1973, 1 (2): 31-35.

National Science Foundation. *Federal Technology Transfer.* Washington, D.C. 1973.

National Science Foundation. Knowledge into action: Improving the nation's use of the social sciences. Report of the Special Commission on the Social Sciences of the National Science Board. Report N S13 69-3. Washington, D.C.: U.S. Government Printing Office, 1969.

Ochberg, F. Personal communication. November 1973.

Richardson, E. R. Conversational contact. *Evaluation,* 1972, 1 (1).

Riecker, P. Prepublication document. 1974.

Roberts, A. O. H. and J. K. Larsen. *Effective Use of Mental Health Research Information.* Palo Alto, Calif.: American Institutes for Research, January 1971. Final report for National Institute of Mental Health, Grant no. 1 RO1 MH 15445.

Rogers, E. M. *Diffusion of Innovations.* New York: Free Press, 1962.

––– and F. F. Shoemaker. *Communication of Innovations: A Cross-cultural Approach.* New York: Free Press, 1971.

Sashkin, M., W. C. Morris, and L. Horst. A comparison of social and organizational change models. *Psychological Review,* 1973. 50 (6).

Schmuck, R. Social psychological factors in knowledge utilization. Pp. 143-173 in T. L. Eidell and J. M. Kitchel (eds.) *Knowledge Production and Utilization in Educational Administration.* Eugene: Center for the Advanced Study of Educational Administration, University of Oregon, 1968.

Scrivens, M. Personal communication. August 1974.

Shepard, H. A. Changing interpersonal and interagency relationships in organizations. In J. C. March (ed.) *Handbook of Organizations.* Chicago: McNally, 1965.

Suchman, E. A. *Evaluation Research.* New York: Russell Sage Foundation, 1962. P. 162.

Tiffany, Donald W. and M. Phyllis. A source of problems between social science knowledge and practice. *Journal of Human Publications,* 1971, 19 (2).

Watson, G. and E. M. Glaser. What we have learned about planning for change. *Management Review,* 1965, 54 (11): 43-46.

Weiss, C. *Evaluation Research.* Englewood Cliffs, N.J.: Prentice-Hall, 1972.

–––. Between the cup and the lip. *Evaluation,* 1973, 1 (2). (a)

–––. Where politics and evaluation research meet. *Evaluation,* 1973, 1 (3): 37-45. (b)

Windle, C. and E. M. Volkman. *A Working Model for Mental Health Program Evaluation.* Prepublication copy, November, 1973.

21

EVALUATION METHODOLOGY: A SELECTIVE BIBLIOGRAPHY

BARRY I. MILCAREK
and
ELMER L. STRUENING

Any suggestion as to relevant readings in so diversified an area as evaluative research must, of necessity, be selective in its focus. Contributions to the literature of this growing field are not only numerous but are also widely scattered over a variety of publications addressed to audiences of differing levels of interest and sophistication. Claims of closure or completeness, as such, are all but precluded for various guides to the literature, and writers are forced to choose between general and specific perspectives in recommending further readings.

In organizing the following readings, we have chosen to focus on what might best be regarded as general issues in the methodology of program evaluation. By so choosing we do not mean to lend credence to the notion that methodological issues are in any way separable from those of substance, or to suggest that method and technique are sufficient conditions for successful study. The aims of methodology are applied, not abstract, and only through the application of general rules for study to specific evaluative problems can we expect the youthful field of evaluation research to develop into a mature speciality within applied social science.

Our reference for selecting the following materials has been the value of evaluation-related discussion for integrating what now stands as little more than a sincere, multidisciplinary interest in objectively assessing the consequences of planned social action. Writings concerned with describing methodological resources, their limitations, and the modifications demanded by practical application have been given most serious attention. In this regard especially, we recommend the following sources to both the researcher and the student as a starting point, or general basis, for more specific readings.

For general treatment of methodological issues in program evaluation, see:

E. Herzog. *Some Guidelines for Evaluative Research.* Washington, D.C.: U.S. Department of Health, Education, and Welfare, 1959.

E. A. Suchman. *Evaluative Research: Principles and Practice in Public Service and Social Action Programs.* New York: Russell Sage Foundation, 1967.

C. H. Weiss. *Evaluation Research: Methods of Assessing Program Effectiveness.* Englewood Cliffs, N.J.: Prentice-Hall, 1972.

ISSUES IN CONCEPTUALIZATION

Among the most immediate and difficult problems confronting the evaluator are those involving conceptualization of program processes and outcomes. Compared to other phases of study the evaluator is here left without the advantage of commonly accepted procedural guidelines and is forced to rely on educated imagination and previous research experience.

The worth of such experience is, however, greatly reduced by what appears as general confusion among evaluators as to the nature of conceptualization and the role of concepts in evaluative study. Concepts are most usefully thought of as rules for subdividing subject matter in such a way as to facilitate the purposes of inquiry. Procedurally, conceptualization involves the grouping together of various processes and events on the basis of meaningful similarities or resemblances so that classes or categories can be used in propositions about the subject matter itself. The mark of sound conceptualization lies in the depth and consistency of such resemblances or similarities. When present, this depth and consistency allows for the discovery of new likenesses, enabling study to proceed through a process of progressive sharpening and differentiation. When not present we are left with what might be called forced or arbitrary classification. This, by contrast, usually does not afford new discoveries or enable a continuous progression of researchable propositions and intercorrelations. Arbitrary classification, in short, results in a prematurely rigid subdivision of subject matter on the basis of superficial or inconsistent similarities.

The way in which programs state their aims and objectives further compounds the already complex problems of concept formation in evaluative research. Ambiguity and lack of consensus regarding aims and objectives are characteristic of many, if not most, social programs. Even having solved the problems of multiciplicity, however, expected outcomes provide only a partial basis for concept formation. The evaluator must also consider the possibilities of unexpected, and unintended, outcomes and processes, more specifically, what they are likely to be. There is no way, of course, to ensure that such unanticipated effects will be imagined in time to make required pre-exposure measures. Here, as elsewhere in evaluative study, there is no substitute for a thorough knowledge of the program to be evaluated and others like it. Such familiarity may well serve to relieve our reliance on unaided imagination.

For further evaluation related discussion on methodological issues in concept formation, see:

E. F. Borgatta. "Research Problems in Evaluation of Health Service Demonstration," Milbank Memorial Fund Quarterly, 1966, 44 (4), part 2: 182-199.

G. G. Cain and R. G. Hollister. "The Methodology of Evaluating Social Action Programs," in P. H. Rossi and W. Williams (eds.) *Evaluating Social Action Programs: Theory, Practice, and Politics.* New York: Seminar Press, 1972.

J. S. Coleman. *Problems of Conceptualization in Studying Policy Impact.* New York: Social Science Research Council, 1971.

E. W. Deming. "The Logic of Evaluation," Chapter 4 in this volume.

H. H. Hyman and C. R. Wright. "Evaluating Social Action Programs," in F. G. Caro (ed.) *Readings in Evaluation Research.* New York: Russell Sage Foundation, 1971.

O. Klineberg. "The Problem of Evaluation Research," International Social Science Bulletin, 1966, 5 (2): 12-17.

L. S. Kogan and A. W. Shyne. "Tender-minded and Tough-minded Approaches in Evaluative Research," International Social Science Bulletin, 1966, 4 (2): 12-17.

P. F. Lazarsfeld. "Evidence and Inference in Social Research," Daedalus, 1958, 87 (4): 99-130.

J. Mann. "Evaluating Educational Programs," The Urban Review, 1969, 3 (4): 12-13.

M. Scriven. "The Methodology of Evaluation," in R. W. Tyler, R. M. Gagne, and M. Scriven (eds.), AERA Monograph Series on Curriculum Evaluation, no. 1. Chicago: Rand-McNally, 1967.

R. E. Stake. "The Countenance of Educational Evaluation," Teachers College Record, 1967, 68 (7): 523-540.

ISSUES IN MEASUREMENT

Sound conceptualization helps to assure that relevant measurement domains are comprehensively described. Measurement, in turn, concerns the operational definition of constructs and their specification as behavioral or outcome criteria. It is, essentially, a further step in the classification, or categorization, of subject matter.

For evaluative purposes measures are most useful when specified as descriptive indicators of program processes and probable effects. When fully and explicitly defined, they are likely to prove dependable. If not, interpretations based on them are open to criticism and less than likely to serve the final purposes of study. Accordingly, the research axiom is that no study can be better than the quality of measures on which it rests, the theory behind their selection, and the design that directs their manipulation. Measurement quality can be subdivided into three considerations: relevance, reliability, and validity.

The relevance of measures concerns their relationship to the constructs organizing study. Ideally, measurement involves a gradual development of indicators and indexes. Practical considerations of time and expense, however, generally restrict the opportunity for such gradual development in evaluative study. Instead, measures are selected on the basis of availability, raising questions about the strength of their relationship to the constructs the evaluator has in mind. Frequently, this relationship is weak and may well work against the overall quality of findings. At issue is the relevance of measures, and those that are most likely to

prove dependable for interpretation are characterized by strong and apparent affinity with the constructs being studied.

The quality of measures, and measures of change, depends as much on their stability as on their relevance to organizing constructs. Before relying on any rating or codification procedure, it is necessary to determine the extent to which results may arise from inconsistencies in classification rather than from differences in what is actually being measured. When ratings are involved, it must be shown that scores are being made consistently, both by different raters and by the same rater at different times. When tests of any kind are employed, internal consistencies and correlations between alternate forms must be demonstrated to achieve satisfactory levels. The higher such intercorrelations, the more reliable the measures are said to be. Satisfactory reliabilities are important for assurance that relationships are not, in fact, the accidental artifacts of random fluctuation in the codes, categories, and measures being used.

High reliabilities are a necessary, but not sufficient, condition for establishing the truth, or validity, of measures. In evaluating program-related outcomes, it is often an easier task to amass reliable evidence of change than it is to establish validity. There are, quite simply, no procedural guidelines upon which evaluators can rely. The only commonly accepted criteria we have derive, in the form of questions, from a thorough knowledge of the program to be evaluated, and others like it. Among the questions we must ask are the following: Do the contents of the measures adequately represent the domain under study? Have other obvious measures been overlooked? Do similar measures demonstrate a consistent pattern of intercorrelations? Are measures predictive of relevant behavioral or outcome criteria? Again, in assessing validity as with so much else in evaluation, we are left to rely on educated imagination and previous research experience.

For further treatment of methodological issues in measurement, see:

J. J. Bartke. "The Intraclass Correlation Coefficient as a Measure of Reliability," Psychological Reprints, 1966, 19: 3-11.

L. J. Cronbach "Validity," in C. W. Harris (ed.) Encyclopedia of Educational Research. 3rd ed. New York: MacMillan, 1960.

L. J. Cronbach and P. E. Meehl. "Construct Validity in Psychological Tests," Psychological Bulletin, 1955, 52: 281-303.

L. J. Cronbach and L. Furby. "How Should We Measure 'Change'—or Should We?" Psychological Bulletin, 1970, 74: 68-80. Errata. Psychological Bulletin, 1970, 74: 218.

J. Cohen. "A Coefficient of Agreement for Nominal Scales," Educational and Psychological Measurement, 1960, 20: 37-46.

———"Weighted Kappa: Nominal Scale Agreement with Provision for Scaled Disagreement or Partial Credit," Psychological Bulletin, 1968, 70: 213-220.

A. Etzioni and E. W. Lehman. "Some Dangers in 'Valid' Social Measurement," Annals of the American Academy of Political and Social Science, 1967, 373: 1-15.

J. L. Fleiss, J. Cohen and B. S. Everitt. "Large Sample Standard Errors of Kappa and Weighted Kappa," Psychological Bulletin, 1969, 72: 323-327.

J. L. Fleiss, R. L. Spitzer, J. Endicott and J. Cohen. "Quantification of Agreement in Multipel Psychiatric Diagnosis," Archives of General Psychiatry, 26, (1972) 168-171.

H. E. Freeman. "Strategy of Social Policy Research," Social Welfare Forum, 1963, 143-156.

A. Goldfarb, L. E. Moses and J. J. Downing. "Reliability of Newly Trained Raters in Community Case Finding," American Journal of Public Health, 1967, 57: 2149-2157.

N. Gronlund (ed.) Readings in Measurement and Evaluation. New York: MacMillan, 1968.

E. A. Haggard. Intraclass Correlation and the Analysis of Variance. New York: Dryden Press, 1958.

C. W. Harris (ed.) Problems in Measuring Change. Madison: University of Wisconsin Press, 1963.

H. H. Hyman, C. R. Wright, and T. K. Hopkins. Applications of Methods of Evaluation: Four Studies of The Encampment for Citizenship. Los Angeles: University of California Press, 1962.

P. Lerman. "Evaluative Studies of Institutions and Delinquents: Implications for Research and Social Policy," in F. G. Caro (ed.) Readings in Evaluation Research. New York: Russell Sage Foundation, 1971.

J. Loevinger. "Objective Tests as Instruments of Psychological Theory," Psychological Reprints, 1957, 3: 635-694.

P. F. Lazarsfeld and A. Barton. "Qualitative Measurement in the Social Sciences," in D. Lerner and H. D. Lasswell (eds.) The Policy Sciences. Stanford: Stanford University Press, 1951.

A. E. Maxwell and A. E. G. Pilliner. "Deriving Coefficients of Reliability and Agreement for Ratings," British Journal of Mathematical and Statistical Psychology, 1968, 21: 105-116.

K. MacCorquodale and P. Meehl. "On The Distinction Between Hypothetical Constructs and Intervening Variables," Psychological Review, 55: 95-107.

D. C. Miller. Handbook of Research Design and Social Measurement. New York: McKay, 1964.

J. C. Nunnally. Psychometric Theory. New York: McGraw-Hill, 1967.

——— "The Study of Change in Evaluation Research: Principles Concerning Measurement, Experimental Design, and Analysis," Chapter 6 in this volume.

——— and W. H. Wilson. "Method and Theory for Developing Measures in Evaluation Research," Chapter 9 in this volume.

——— and R. L. Durham. "Validity, Reliability, and Special Problems of Measurement in Evaluation Research," Chapter 10 in this volume.

E. Roget and I. D. Goldberg. "A Proposed Index for Measuring Agreement in Test-Retest Studies," Journal of Chronic Diseases, 1966, 19: 991-1006.

C. C. Sherwood. "Issues in Measuring Results of Action Programs," Welfare in Review, 1967, 5 (7): 13-18.

D. D. Sjogren. "Measurement Techniques in Evaluation," Review of Educational Research, 1970, 40 (2): 301-320.

ISSUES OF DESIGN

The importance of linking program processes with outcomes has, perhaps, resulted in more of an emphasis on issues of design in evaluation than in other areas of applied research. The most desirable design is that of controlled experimentation. Its desirability lies in its elegance and rigor in ruling out the influences of non-program-related factors in change. Its feasibility, however, is frequently limited by problems of control group selection, and its use is not common in evaluative study.

Methods for selecting comparable controls are often problematic in the practical context of evaluation research. Control groups can be selected from a target population by randomization or matching procedures. Frequency controls are used by selecting groups which are matched to each other in terms of their overall distribution of relevant characteristics. Where this is possible such matching is likely to prove highly sensitive, or precise, in discerning differential susceptibilities and effects. The use of frequency controls in evaluative study is curtailed, however, by inadequate knowledge of relevant factors and the high sacrifice of subjects it requires.

Precision controls are those where each individual in the experimental group is matched with a partner in the control group who shares relevant characteristics. This is the most precise procedure for determining the composition of control groups but unless the number of relevant factors is small, or the service population is homogenous in terms of these characteristics, the sacrifice of subjects may be so high as to make this procedure unfeasible.

A third, and more promising procedure, is that of self-matching. There are various ways in which a group or individual can be compared with itself at different times. A particular behavior or condition, for example, may be observed before and after a specific intervention in order to determine whether this type of intervention has any effect on it. Such comparisons may cumulate so that group comparisons are possible, but the groups will not be composed of entirely different individuals; rather, each individual will be represented in the experimental and in the control group. The basic assumption is that other relevant conditions have remained fairly stable, at least over a short period of time, while one or more crucial (or "test") factors are varied and effects observed. Self-matching procedures provide convincing support for interpretation of findings and may well prove of special interest to program evaluation.

Randomization is the most powerful procedure available to researchers for control group selection. Such controls are used by randomly assigning program applicants to treatment and nontreatment categories, thereby controlling for both known and unknown factors which are likely to influence susceptibilities and effects. Particularly with small, or highly specialized service programs, however, issues concerning the size of experimental and control groups, as well as the relationship between applicants and the general population, deserve immediate and careful consideration. Further, randomization may involve a withholding, or even denial, of services to certain applicants in need, resulting in serious ethical questions which may jeopardize further study.

Progress toward achieving adequate controls is best served by recognizing the difficulties inherent to establishing them. While much work needs yet to be done in identifying factors requiring control, program evaluators have available a variety of quasi-experimental and noncontrolled designs which promise an immediate, though modest, increase in the replicability of findings.

The general importance of quasi-experimental designs is the easy recognition they provide as to what either has, or has not, been controlled. This in turn, enables the evaluator to formulate findings with an appreciable amount of care and guards against the uncritical misinterpretation of results. Among those more readily applicable to the purposes of the program evaluation are the time-series, the multiple time-series, the nonequivalent control group, and the "patched-up" designs. While none of these provides the sort of blanket control achieved through randomization, they all have the very definite advantage of being practical when research conditions prohibit more rigorous experimentation.

Compared to experimental and quasi-experimental strategies, noncontrolled designs leave considerable room for differing interpretations as to what changes have occurred, and to what extent they are the consequences of program efforts. Nevertheless, single project before-and-after, after-only, and after-only with comparison group strategies provide us with more information than would be available without them. Given the difficulties of establishing adequate controls, or even substitutes, such strategies deserve careful consideration by program evaluators. Certain judgments can very well be made without the use of controls, and often the simple association of services and improvement is all the evidence required for continuing or increased financial support.

For further evaluation-related treatment of issues in research and data analytic designs, see:

D. T. Campbell. "Factors Relevant to the Validity of Experiments in Social Settings," Psychological Review, 1957, 54: 297-312.

D. T. Campbell. "Reforms as Experiments," Chapter 5 in this volume.

D. T. Campbell. "Considering the Case Against Experimental Evaluations of Social Innovations," Administrative Science Quarterly 1970, 15 (1): 110-113.

D. T. Campbell and J. C. Stanley. *Experimental and Quasi-Experimental Designs for Research.* Chicago: Rand-McNally, 1963.

W. G. Cochran, F. Mosteller, and J. W. Tukey. "Principles of Sampling," Journal of the American Statistical Association, 1954, 49.

A. L. Edwards. *Experimental Design in Psychological Research.* 3rd ed. New York: Holt, Rinehart and Winston, 1968.

G. W. Fairweather. *Methods for Experimental Social Innovation.* New York: Wiley, 1967.

J. M. Gottman, R. M. McFall, and J. T. Barnett. "Design and Analysis of Research Using Time Series," Psychological Bulletin, 1969, 72: 299-306.

B. G. Greenberg. "Evaluation of Social Programs," Pp. 155-175 in F. G. Caro (ed.) *Readings in Evaluation Research.* New York: Russell Sage Foundation, 1971.

S. Isaac and W. D. Michael. *Handbook of Research and Evaluation.* San Diego: Knapp, 1971.

L. Kish. "Some Statistical Problems in Research Design," American Sociological Review, 1959, 24: 328-338.

C. C. Sherwood, J. N. Morris, and S. Sherwood. "A Multivariate Nonrandomized Matching Technique for Studying the Impact of Social Interventions," Chapter 8 in this volume.

J. C. Stanley (ed.) *Improving Experimental Design and Statistical Analysis.* Chicago: Rand-McNally, 1967.

S. A. Stouffer. "Some Observations on Study Design," American Journal of Sociology, 1950, 55: 355-361.

R. Underhill. "Methods in the Evaluation of Programs for Poor Youth." Chicago: National Opinion Research Center, 1968.

B. J. Winer. *Statistical Principles in Experimental Design.* 2nd ed. New York: McGraw-Hill, 1971.

P. Wuebben. "Experimental Design, Measurement, and Human Subjects: A Neglected Problem of Control," Sociometry, 1968, 31: 89-101.

ISSUES OF INTERPRETATION

So much of the effort involved in program evaluation is aimed at resolving difficulties in conceptualization, measurement, design, and analysis that issues concerning the meaning and utility of findings often receive something less than the careful attention they deserve. Such issues are, nonetheless, among the most important in evaluative study, and it is poor research practice to assume that facts, in any way, speak for themselves.

Among the most difficult questions involved in interpretation are those concerning the reliability and validity of measures. Where significant conceptual criteria do not fully lend themselves to quantitative description or where convincing evidence of measurement stability has not been achieved, a candid discussion of deficiencies is required and interpretations must be appropriately qualified. Other important questions are those concerning the possibility of ceilings on change and those of interaction, or differential, effects.

Sound interpretation must afford convincing evidence of the extent to which program objectives either have, or have not, been achieved. Where analytic controls have been less than complete, problems in design should be described and the latitude for competing interpretations fully acknowledged. Implications uncovered in data analysis, involving extensions or relationships which tend to support or reject differing interpretations, should be fully reported. Generalizations must be tempered where conflicting or inconsistent information exists. The uncritical, or arbitrary, use of evidence must be avoided as should any tendencies toward an overly rigid statement of implications.

Such considerations are especially important when reporting small or unfavorable results. Programs may well be plagued with problems, but the meaning of unfavorable results is by no means an easily settled issue. Such results may merely imply that various strategies or techniques need improvement, and by no means

should they be used to judge the worth of ameliorative efforts. Recommendations concerning the sorts of improvements that can profitably be made are best offered as part of the interpretative process. Such recommendations should, of course, be made as specific as possible.

Apart from responsibilities involved in the comprehensive integration of findings, the evaluator is faced with an additional problem of enhancing their utility. Awareness of the complex nature of service programs alerts the researcher to the fact that no singular criterion of usefulness will suffice. Needs and expectations differ at the various levels of organizational hierarchy and can be expected to range from such general issues as whether or not to continue services to such practical questions as whether specific strategies and techniques require modification.

The notion of all-purpose research is, of course, poorly founded and, if pursued, all too likely to result in superficial findings of questionable integrity. Even the most broadly planned and generally designed study must be limited and cannot be expected to address itself to all possible needs and expectations. The use of summary analytic procedures, however, facilitates the number and types of questions that can be investigated in any single evaluation, an issue best settled in the formative phases of research. Through the use of multivariate procedures, for example, it is possible both to achieve a rigorous assessment of overall program effectiveness and to determine the relative effectiveness of component strategies. Where such summary determinations are employed, it is critical that they be interpreted in terms of their substantive implications, presented and explained in the style that most appropriately communicates both their meaning and their limitations to those most interested in them.

For further treatment of issues related to the interpretation and presentation of evaluative findings, see:

K. A. Archibald. "Alternative Orientations to Social Science Utilization," Social Science Information, 1970, 11 (2): 7-34.

S. H. Aronson and C. C. Sherwood. "Research versus Practioner: Problems in Social Action Research," Social Work, 1967, 12 (4): 89-96.

H. Becker. "Whose Side Are We On?" Social Problems, 1967, 14: 239-247.

G. G. Cain and H. H. Watts. "Problems in Making Inferences From the Coleman Report," in P. H. Rossi and W. Williams (eds.) Evaluating Social Programs: Theory, Practice, and Politics. New York: Seminar Press, 1972.

R. Cattel (ed.) Handbook of Multivariate Experimental Psychology. Chicago: Rand-McNally, 1966.

A. Cherns. "Social Research and Its Diffusion," in F. G. Caro (ed.) Readings in Evaluation Research. New York: Russell Sage Foundation, 1971.

J. Cohen, Statistical Power Analysis for the Social Sciences. New York: Academic Press, 1969.

H. Davis and S. Salasin. "The Utilization of Evaluations," Chapter 20 in this volume.

I. Deutscher. "Looking Backward: Case Studies in the Progress of Methodology in Sociological Research," American Sociologist, 1969, 4: 35-41.

A. Downs. "Some Thoughts on Giving People Economic Advice," in F. G. Caro (ed.) *Readings in Evaluation Research.* New York: Russell Sage Foundation, 1971.

M. Guttentag. "Subjectivity and its Use in Evaluation Research," Evaluation, 1973, 1 (2): 60-65.

S. J. Mushkin. "Evaluations: Use With Caution," Evaluation, 1973, 1 (2): 30-35.

W. F. Ogburn. "On Scientific Writing," American Journal of Sociology, 1947, 52: 383-388.

A. M. Rivilin. *Systematic Thinking in Social Action.* Washington: The Brooklings Institution, 1971.

P. H. Rossi. "Testing for Success and Failure in Social Action," in P. H. Rossi and R. G. Williams (eds.) *Evaluating Social Programs: Theory, Practice, and Politics.* New York: Seminar Press, 1972.

E. L. Struening and H. B. Peck. "The Role of Research in Evaluation," in R. G. Williams and H. D. Ozarin (eds.) *Community Mental Health: An International Perspective.* San Francisco: Jossey Bass, 1968.

R. Spitzer and J. Cohen. "Common Errors in Quantitative Psychiatric Research," International Journal of Psychiatric Research, 1968, 6 (2): 109-131.

D. A. Ward and G. G. Kassebaum. "On Biting the Hand that Feeds: Some Implications of Sociological Evaluations of Correctional Effectiveness," in C. H. Weiss (ed.) *Evaluating Action Programs: Readings in Social Action and Education.* Boston: Allyn and Bacon, 1972.

C. H. Weiss. "The Politicization of Evaluation Research," Journal of Social Issues, 1970, 26 (4): 57-68.

———. "The Politics of Impact Measurement," Policy Studies Journal, 1973, 1 (3): 79-83.

C. R. Wright and H. H. Hyman. "The Evaluators," in P. H. Hammond (ed.) *Sociologists At Work.* New York: Basic Books, 1964.

J. Zubin, "The Function of the Assessment Center in Community Mental Health," in L. M. Roberts, N. S. Greenfield and M. H. Miller (eds.) *Comprehensive Mental Health: The Challange of Evaluation.* Madison: University of Wisconsin Press, 1968.

ABOUT THE AUTHORS

ELMER L. STRUENING is currently Director of the Epidemiology of Mental Disorders Research Unit, Psychiatric Institute, New York State Department of Mental Hygiene, and Associate Professor, Columbia University. From 1965-1969 he was Director of Research, Lincoln Hospital Mental Health Services, Albert Einstein College of Medicine. His research interests include the methodology and application of social area analysis, the structure of attitudes, the social epidemiology of mental disorders, and the methodology of evaluation research.

MARCIA GUTTENTAG is President of the Division of Personality and Social Psychology of the American Psychological Association. A developmental social psychologist at the Harvard University Graduate School of Education, she was formerly Professor of Psychology at the Graduate Center, CUNY, and Director of the Harlem Research Center. She has served as evaluation consultant to UNESCO, the Office of Child Development, the National Institute of Mental Health, and other federal agencies. She was chairwoman of the Task Force on the Evaluation of Training in Community Mental Health, for the National Institute of Mental Health. She is co-author of the *Evaluation of Training* and many chapters and articles on evaluation, in addition to being a past president of the Society for the Psychological Study of Social Issues. She is currently engaged in a national evaluation study of women and mental health.

CAROL H. WEISS is Senior Research Associate at the Bureau of Applied Social Research of Columbia University. She is the author of *Evaluation Research: Methods of Assessing Program Effectiveness* (1972, Prentice-Hall) and *Evaluating Action Programs: Readings in Social Action and Education* (1972, Allyn & Bacon). She has done many books, professional papers, and policy reports in her fields of specialization, which include evaluation of government programs, processes, problems, design and measurement; utilization of social research in policymaking; characteristics of the research and the policy processes; and survey methods and validity of interviews. Previous to joining the staff at Columbia, she was Research Director of Associated Community Teams (ACT), Harlem.

DAVID TWAIN is Professor of Criminal Justice in the School of Criminal Justice, Rutgers University. He received his Ph.D. from the Pennsylvania State University and formerly taught in the doctoral program in clinical psychology at the City University of New York. He has previously been chief of the Center for Studies in Crime and Delinquency of the National Institute of Mental Health. He serves as a consultant to federal-, state-, and local-level institutions and agencies. His research and evaluation activities are in the service of program evolution. He is a Fellow of the Division of Community Psychology of the American Psychological Association.

W. EDWARDS DEMING is a consultant in statistical studies, the author of several books on statistical methods, and of 150 papers. He worked in Japan for more than a decade, beginning in 1950, and contributed to the revolution in the quality of most Japanese-manufactured products, causing the Cabinet of Japan to award to him in 1960 the Emperor's Medal of the Sacred Treasure. Japanese manufacturers have created in his honor the annual Deming Prize. He has lectured in many universities all over the world, and presently holds the position of Professor of Statistics at New York University.

DONALD T. CAMPBELL is Professor at Northwestern University. He has published extensively over the past twenty-five years in the fields of behavioral science, social psychology, experimental psychology and methodology, and clinical psychology, among others. Many of his works have become seminal to the disciplines. He is presently President of the American Psychological Association, and has previously been president of the Midwestern Psychological Association (1967) and of the Division of Personality and Social Psychology of the APA (1969). He was the recipient in 1970 of one of the Awards for Distinguished Scientific Contribution given by the APA.

JUM C. NUNNALLY is Professor of Psychology at Vanderbilt University. He received his Ph.D. at the University of Chicago, after which he worked with the American Institute for Research, performing studies of personality characteristics and abilities relating to successful performance of naval officers. He has also been on the faculty of the University of Illinois at the Institute of

Communications Research and the Department of Psychology, where his work involved studies of public attitudes and psychometric theory. His present research interests concern visual exploratory behavior and a variety of issues relating to human abilities, attitudes, and personality characteristics.

WARD EDWARDS is Director of the Social Science Research Institute, Professor of Psychology, and Professor of Industrial and Systems Engineering at the University of Southern California. He was previously associate director of the Highway Safety Research Institute and head of the Engineering Psychology Laboratory at the University of Michigan. He received his Ph.D. from Harvard University. He is a consultant to numerous American organizations, including the Panel on Earthquake Prediction of the National Research Council, the Office of Child Development of the Department of Health, Education and Welfare, and the RAND Corporation. He has published widely in professional journals including *The Journal of Experimental Psychology, the American Journal of Psychology,* and the *Psychological Review.*

KURT SNAPPER received his Ph.D. in psychology from the University of Michigan where his major field of research was psychological decision theory. He has authored several papers on decision theoretic approaches to evaluation research and social indicators. Currently he is Senior Research Scientist at the Social Research Group, George Washington University.

CLARENCE C. SHERWOOD is Professor of Sociology at the John Jay College of Criminal Justice of the City University of New York. He is also a research consultant to the Research and Training Center of the Rehabilitation Institute of the Tufts New England Medical Center. He is co-author (with Howard E. Freeman) of *Social Policy and Social Research* (1970, Prentice-Hall), and he recently co-authored (with John N. Morris) "Strategies for Research and Innovation," in *Long-Term Care: A Handbook for Researchers, Planners and Providers,* edited by S. Sherwood (1975, Spectrum). His major concerns include the development and implementation of methodologies for the evaluation of the impact of social interventions.

JOHN N. MORRIS is Assistant Director of Social Gerontological Research at the Hebrew Rehabilitation Center for Aged, Boston. He is co-author (with S. Sherwood, D. S. Greer and C. C. Sherwood) of *The Highland Heights Experiment* (1973, Government Printing Office) and has recently co-authored with Clarence Sherwood the article mentioned directly above. In these and other publications, he has dealt with measurement and other methodological issues relating to the evaluation of social interventions for elderly and handicapped populations.

SYLVIA SHERWOOD is Director of Social Gerontological Research at the Hebrew Rehabilitation Center for Aged, Boston. Her two major research efforts are a continuing study of the impact of medically oriented specialized housing on health and well-being; and an evaluation of the impact of a program of individualized home care services. She is a Fellow of the Gerontological Society and the American Sociological Association, and the editor and co-editor of *Research Planning and Action for the Elderly, Long-Term Care: A Handbook for Researchers, Planners and Providers,* and *The Highland Heights Experiment.* Her area of specialization is in methodological issues as well as substantive knowledge concerning the elderly.

WILLIAM H. WILSON received his Ph.D. from Vanderbilt University in 1973. Presently he is Assistant Professor at Middle Tennessee State University and a member of the American Psychological Association. His primary areas of research interests are in learning and motivation. Secondary areas of interest concern evaluation of attitudes in family planning and program evaluation in community mental health.

ROBERT L. DURHAM received his Ph.D. from Vanderbilt University in 1973. He is currently Assistant Professor of Psychology at the University of Colorado at Colorado Springs. He has recently been a consultant to Colorado School District 11 on research evaluation of innovative classroom techniques, their effects on student, teacher and parent reactions. His research interests currently are concerned with intrinsic motivation—specifically, the effects of information conflict on visual information-processing.

ABBOTT S. WEINSTEIN is presently Director of the Statistical and Clinical Information Systems of the Department of Mental Hygiene (Albany, New York). He was previously Director of the Biometrics Branch of St. Elizabeth's Hospital in Washington, D. C. He has served as a statistical consultant to the Judicial Conference of the District of Columbia Circuit and for

several research projects at Albany Medical College. He has published numerous professional articles in such journals as the *Journal of the American Statistical Association*, the *American Journal of Public Health*, and the *American Journal of Psychiatry*. He has served on several advisory committees and task forces for the U.S. Department of Health, Education and Welfare, and conducted seminars for and served as a consultant to the IBM Company.

STANLEY LEHMANN is Associate Professor of Psychology at New York University and Acting Director of the Community Research Program of the New York State Department of Mental Hygiene. He is also currently the Co-ordinator of the doctoral training program in community psychology at the university. His major interests lie in the area of community mental health, environmental factors in behavior, and reactions to stress. His most recent research has concerned the effects of crowding, the adaptation of mental patients to hospital environments and experimental studies of cognitive processing in schizophrenics.

M. SUSSER is Professor and Head of the Division of Epidemiology of Columbia University. He is the author of *Casual Thinking in the Health Sciences; Concepts and Strategies in Epidemiology* (1973, Oxford University Press) and *Community Psychiatry: Epidemiologic and Social Themes* (1968, Random House); and co-author (with W. Watson) of *Sociology in Medicine* (1971, 1962, Oxford University Press). He is author or editor of a series of reports under the blanket title of *Reports on the Mental Health Services in the City of Salford (England)*, from 1959 to 1965. He has authored or co-authored many scholarly and professional articles and monographs, both in the United States and abroad.

JOHN CASSEL is Professor and Chairman in the Department of Epidemiology, of the University of North Carolina (Chapel Hill). He previously served as chairman of the Epidemiology and Disease Control Study Section of the National Institute of Health and is a Fellow of the American Public Health Association. He has published extensively in professional journals, among them the *American Journal of Public Health*, the *Journal of Occupational Medicine*, the *New England Journal of Medicine*, and the *American Journal of Epidemiology*. His major present areas of research interest are the health consequences of rapid culture change, cardiovascular diseases, and health services research.

HERBERT EBER is presently President of the Psychological Resources Associates, of Atlanta, Georgia, and Assistant Professor of Experimental Psychiatry at the University of Alabama Medical School. He received his Ph.D. from the University of North Carolina with a major in clinical psychology. He is the author of several personality tests, "A personality test for persons of limited reading skills," and "IPAT Tests on Tape"; he has also authored a textbook, *Samples of Scientific Psychology*. He is co-author with Raymond Cattell of the 1963 revisions of the *16 Personality Factor Questionnaire*. His major areas of research concern are with personality testing and methodology.

JACOB COHEN is currently Professor of Psychology and Chairman of the Quantitative Psychology Area of New York University's Graduate Psychology Department. He previously worked extensively with the Veterans Administration, his research interests including practice and research in clinical psychology and later quantitative research methodology in the behavioral sciences. In addition to many articles and chapters in books, he has authored an introductory statistics text, and a handbook entitled *Statistical Power Analysis for the Behavioral Sciences* (1969, Academic Press). In collaboration with Patricia Cohen, he will be co-author in mid-1975 of a textbook/manual entitled *Multiple Regression/Correlational Analysis for the Behavioral Sciences* (Lawrence Erlbaum Associates.

ALBERT ERLEBACHER received his Ph.D. in psychology at the University of Wisconsin and he teaches at Northwestern University in the Department of Psychology. His area of interest is statistics and experimental design.

HOWARD R. DAVIS is Chief of the Mental Health Services Development branch of the National Institute of Mental Health. Among his primary professional interests is promoting the utilization of scientific knowledge in bringing about organizational change, a topic about which he has written extensively. Dr. Davis who holds B.A., MSW and Ph.D. degrees, taught, practised, and consulted in psychology before joining the NIMH Staff in 1963.

SUSAN E. SALASIN is Chief of the Research Diffusion and Utilization Section, Mental Health Services Development Branch of the National Institute of Mental Health. Among her profes-

sional responsibilities, she also serves as Editorial Director for *Evaluation* magazine, an experimental publication designed to further the adoption of program evaluation in human services organization. Ms. Salasin's primary professional interest is in program evaluation and knowledge utilization as a means of stimulating, facilitating, and guiding organizational change.

BARRY I. MILCAREK is a Ph.D. candidate in sociology at the Graduate School of the City University of New York. He has been active in community health organization efforts in East Harlem. He is presently Assistant Research Scientist in the Epidemiology of Mental Disorders Research Unit of the New York State Department of Mental Health.

AUTHOR INDEX